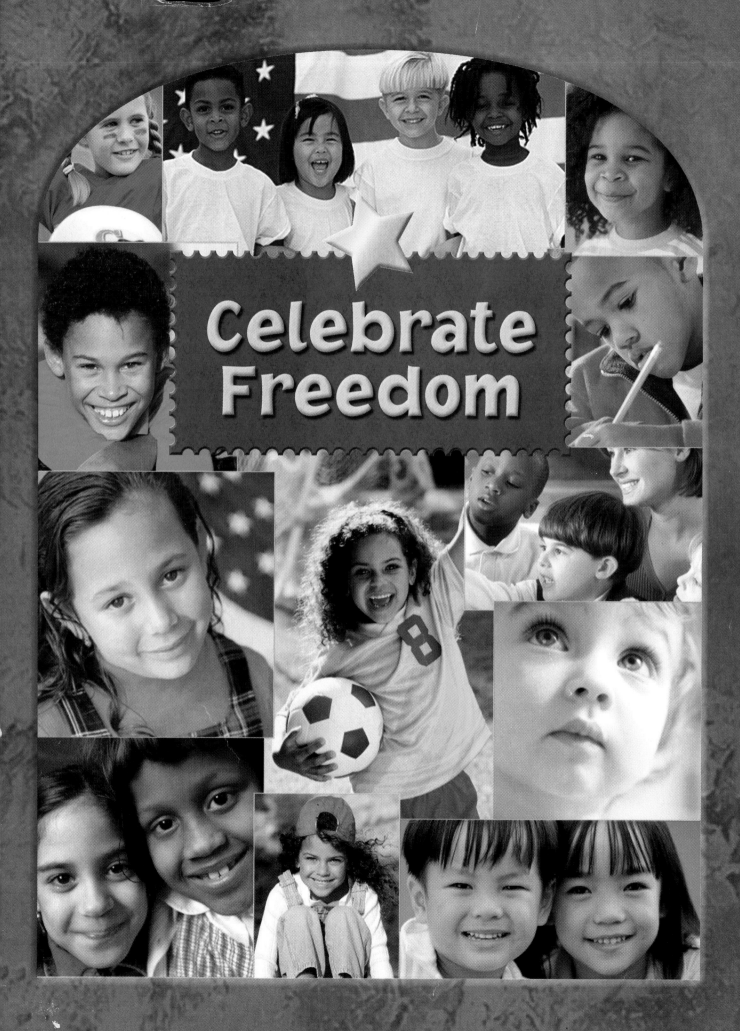

Celebrate Freedom

Celebrate Freedom

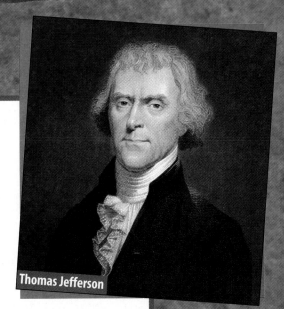
Thomas Jefferson

Our country's system of government is grounded in the Declaration of Independence, the Constitution of the United States, and the Bill of Rights. Each of these documents declares the rights and freedoms of every American citizen. They also lay out the functions and limits of a just form of government. Read excerpts from each document on these pages.

Declaration of Independence, 1776

We hold these truths to be self-evident, that all men are created equal, that they are endowed by their Creator with certain unalienable Rights, that among these are Life, Liberty and the pursuit of Happiness. That to secure these rights, Governments are instituted among Men, deriving their just powers from the consent of the governed. . . . It is the Right of the People to [change their government] . . . laying its foundation on such principles and organizing its powers in such form, as to them shall seem most likely to effect their Safety and Happiness.

- **What is the purpose of government, according to the Declaration of Independence?**
- **From whom does the government get its power?**

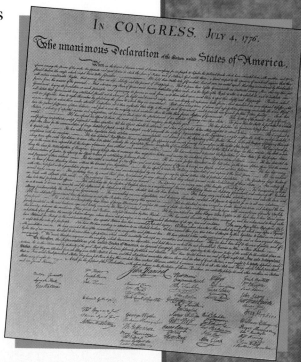

Constitution of the United States of America, 1789

We the People of the United States, in Order to form a more perfect Union, establish Justice, insure domestic Tranquility, provide for the common defense, promote the general Welfare, and secure the Blessings of Liberty to ourselves and our Posterity, do ordain and establish this CONSTITUTION for the United States of America.

- **What did the writers of the Constitution hope to achieve?**

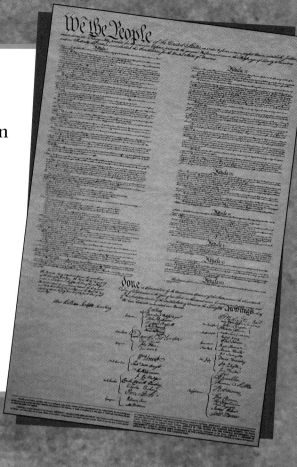

Bill of Rights, 1791

The first ten Amendments (additions) to the Constitution are called the Bill of Rights. They include:

- Freedom of religion
- Freedom of speech
- Freedom of the press
- The right to trial by a jury

- **Why do you think a trial by a jury is an important part of a democratic government?**

Celebrate Freedom

The Pursuit of Happiness

The Declaration of Independence says that all people have a right to pursue happiness. Each American pursues happiness in his or her own ways. Using pictures from magazines, the Internet, and other sources, make a collage poster showing ways you think Americans pursue the things that make them happy. Present your collage to the class.

Materials:
- Photographs from newspapers, magazines, advertisements
- Scissors
- Tape
- Markers
- Sheet of oak tag or construction paper

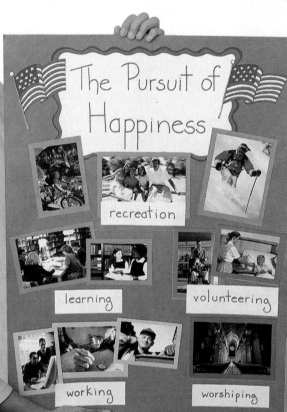

A Presidential Time Line

The Constitution establishes the three branches of our country's government. It also says that the President is the head of the executive branch of government. Research a President and create a time line of his term of office. List the key events that took place during the term. Include any important laws that were passed. Illustrate your time line with drawings or photos. Present your time line to the class.

Materials:
- Markers
- Pens
- Scissors
- Tape
- Sheet of oak tag

Celebrate Freedom

Classroom Newspaper

In our democracy the press plays a key role. It helps keep citizens informed so they can make important decisions about how our government should run, what it should be doing, and who should be elected. The first Congress thought this was so important that they made freedom of the press part of the very first amendment.

Gather in groups to create a class newspaper. Include important information about your class-room and your school. What sort of information do your fellow students need to be good classroom citizens? What school events or rules are important for students to know about? Perhaps each group can focus on different parts of the newspaper—news, sports, arts, or business. Write articles and stories. Illustrate your newspaper with photos, drawings, or cartoons. Share the newspaper with the class.

Materials:
- Paper
- Pen or pencil
- Markers
- Scissors and glue

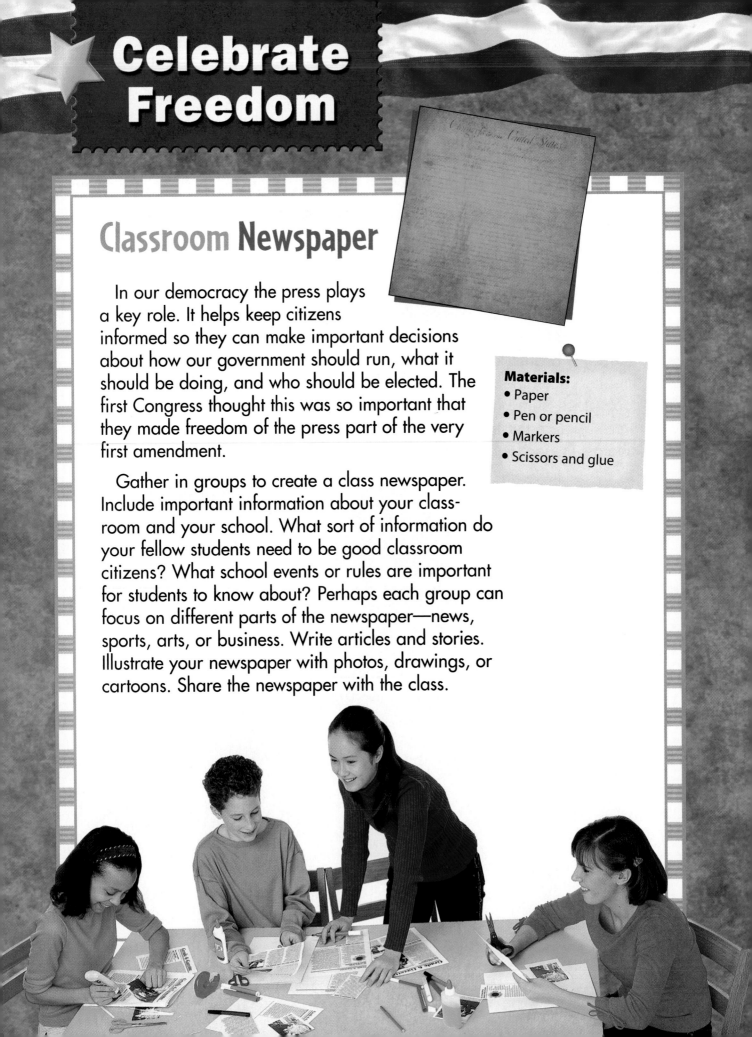

The Pledge of Allegiance

I pledge allegiance to the Flag of the United States of America, and to the Republic for which it stands, one Nation under God, indivisible, with liberty and justice for all.

The National Anthem

Oh, say, can you see, by the dawn's early light,
What so proudly we hailed at the twilight's last gleaming?
Whose broad stripes and bright stars, thro' the perilous fight,
O'er the ramparts we watched, were so gallantly streaming.
And the rockets' red glare, the bombs bursting in air,
Gave proof through the night that our flag was still there.
Oh, say, does that star-spangled banner yet wave
O'er the land of the free and the home of the brave?

A7

Fighting for Freedom

People around the world have struggled for freedom and equality. The courage of leaders to speak up for freedom inspires their fellow citizens and all freedom-loving people.

READING CHECK How have some leaders inspired people to fight for freedom?

Dr. Martin Luther King, Jr.

American civil rights leader

"Injustice anywhere is a threat to justice everywhere."

Dr. Martin Luther King, Jr., wrote this in a letter on April 16, 1963. King led a nonviolent movement against racial injustice in the United States.

Winston Churchill

Prime Minister of Great Britain

"We shall go on to the end. We shall fight in France, we shall fight on the seas and oceans, we shall fight with growing confidence and growing strength in the air, we shall defend our island, whatever the cost may be, we shall fight on the beaches, we shall fight on the landing grounds, we shall fight in the fields and in the streets, we shall fight in the hills; we shall never surrender."

Winston Churchill spoke these words of encouragement to the British people in 1940. The British were defending their country against Germany during World War II.

Nelson Mandela

First president of South Africa elected after the end of apartheid (separation of the races)

"We shall build a society in which all South Africans, both black and white, will be able to walk tall, without any fear in their hearts, assured of their inalienable right to human dignity—a rainbow nation at peace with itself and the world."

Nelson Mandela spoke these words at his inauguration as president of South Africa, May 9, 1994. Mandela was the leader of the country's anti-apartheid movement, dedicated to securing equal rights for all South Africans.

Aung San Suu Kyi

Leader of the democracy movement in Myanmar

"We think that the strength of our movement is really in the country itself. It is in the will of the people, and the great majority of people in Burma [Myanmar] want democracy."

Aung San Suu Kyi spoke these words in 1995. She follows the examples of Mohandas Gandhi and Dr. Martin Luther King, Jr., in urging nonviolent change.

Geography

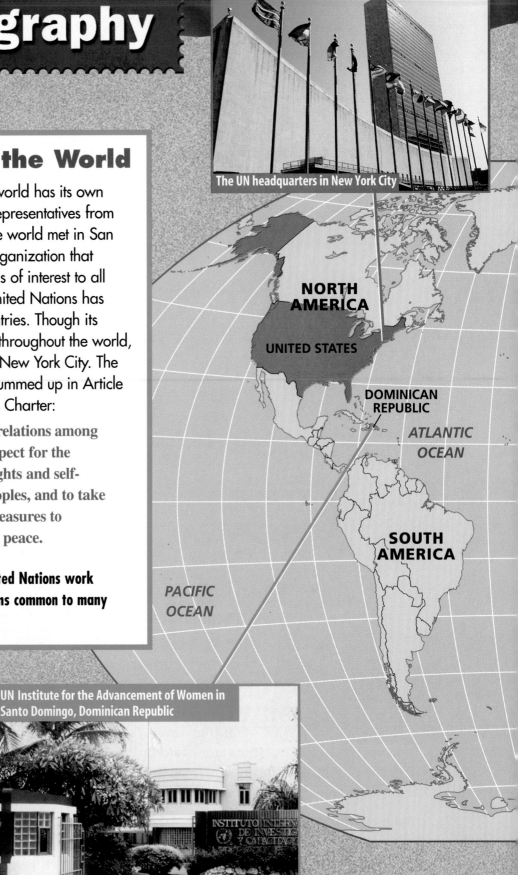

The UN headquarters in New York City

Nations of the World

Each country of the world has its own government. In 1945 representatives from 51 countries around the world met in San Francisco to form an organization that would address problems of interest to all countries. Today, the United Nations has over 185 member countries. Though its operations are located throughout the world, its headquarters are in New York City. The role of the UN is best summed up in Article 1 of the United Nations Charter:

> To develop friendly relations among nations based on respect for the principle of equal rights and self-determination of peoples, and to take other appropriate measures to strengthen universal peace.

 How does the United Nations work to address problems common to many countries?

NORTH AMERICA

UNITED STATES

DOMINICAN REPUBLIC

ATLANTIC OCEAN

SOUTH AMERICA

PACIFIC OCEAN

UN Institute for the Advancement of Women in Santo Domingo, Dominican Republic

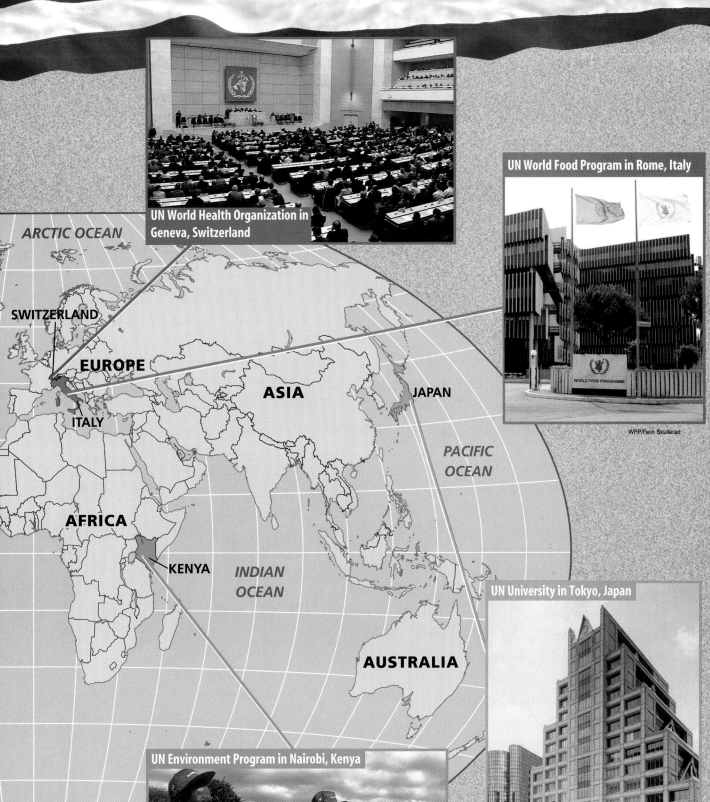

UN World Health Organization in Geneva, Switzerland

UN World Food Program in Rome, Italy

WFP/Rein Skullerad

ARCTIC OCEAN

SWITZERLAND

EUROPE

ITALY

ASIA

JAPAN

PACIFIC OCEAN

AFRICA

KENYA

INDIAN OCEAN

AUSTRALIA

ANTARCTICA

UN University in Tokyo, Japan

UN Environment Program in Nairobi, Kenya

Economics

Mexican petroleum production

United States wheat field

World Trade

Countries of the world depend on one another. Through trade, countries share the resources and products they have in exchange for the resources and products they need. No country can supply everything its citizens need or want. Food, fuel, clothing, medicine, technology, and transportation are all bought and sold around the world.

 Why do people in different countries trade?

Wool production in New Zealand

High-Tech automobile manufacturing in Japan

Government

South Africa's President Mbeki

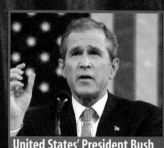
United States' President Bush

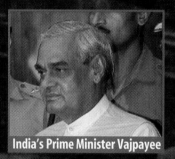
India's Prime Minister Vajpayee

Democracy in Action

Democracy means "government by the people." In a democracy, citizens elect their leaders by voting. Democracy takes many forms in countries around the world. Some democratic countries have parliaments that make laws and run the government. Others, such as the United States, have executive, legislative, and judicial branches of government.

READING CHECK What does *democracy* mean?

Australia's Parliament

Citizenship

Giving Aid

Floods, earthquakes, droughts, and storms destroy homes, crops, and water supplies each year. In 1999, for example, nearly one third of the world's population was affected by natural disasters. Many organizations come to the aid of countries suffering from natural disasters. Some, such as the International Red Cross, also train people and support public health programs.

 READING CHECK **What are some things that aid organizations do?**

El Salvador earthquake of 2001

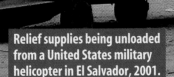

Relief supplies being unloaded from a United States military helicopter in El Salvador, 2001.

The Olympic Games

The modern Olympic Games encourage international understanding through athletics. The first Olympics were created by Ancient Greeks almost 3,000 years ago. At first, there was only one event, a 200-yard foot race. Winners were honored with wreaths of laurel, olive, and palm leaves. Today, more than 200 countries participate in the Summer and Winter Olympics. In addition, thousands of differently-abled athletes participate each year in the Special Olympics.

 READING CHECK **Who created the first Olympic Games?**

Special Olympics competitor

Olympic rowers

Opening Ceremony, 2000 Summer Olympics Sydney, Australia

Science, Technology, and Society

The International Space Station

The International Space Station orbits Earth because of international teamwork in technology. Sixteen nations are building the station in sections. When complete, the ISS will contain six laboratories in a structure the size of a football field. The first crew of three began living aboard the station in late 2000. The station orbits 220 miles above Earth and travels at 17,000 miles per hour!

READING CHECK How many countries are building the International Space Station?

Nations Building the International Space Station

Belgium	France	Netherlands	Sweden
Brazil	Germany	Norway	Switzerland
Canada	Italy	Russia	United Kingdom
Denmark	Japan	Spain	United States

Macmillan/McGraw-Hill

Our World

NATIONAL GEOGRAPHIC

BEING A GOOD CITIZEN

In this textbook you will meet special people and learn many important things. On the BIOGRAPHY pages and in the POINTS OF VIEW lessons, you will see eight important words that help define what it means to be a good citizen. These words are listed below. They help us understand how to be better citizens in our home, neighborhood, school, community, country, and world.

★**COURAGE**★
being brave in the face of difficulty

★**FREEDOM**★
making choices and holding beliefs of one's own

★**HONESTY**★
telling the truth

★**JUSTICE**★
working toward fair treatment for everyone

★**LEADERSHIP**★
showing good behavior worth following
through example

★**LOYALTY**★
showing support for people and one's country

★**RESPECT**★
treating others as you would like to be treated

★**RESPONSIBILITY**★
being worthy of trust

About the Cover: A reproduction of a nineteenth century compass and sundial sits in the foregound. In the background, the Great Wall of China snakes its way up a moutain ridge.

Macmillan/McGraw-Hill

Our World

James A. Banks

Richard G. Boehm

Kevin P. Colleary

Gloria Contreras

A. Lin Goodwin

Mary A. McFarland

Walter C. Parker

 NATIONAL GEOGRAPHIC

Mc Graw Hill **Macmillan McGraw-Hill**

New York

PROGRAM AUTHORS

Dr. James A. Banks
Russell F. Stark University Professor and Director of the Center for Multicultural Education
University of Washington
Seattle, Washington

Dr. Richard G. Boehm
Jesse H. Jones Distinguished Chair in Geographic Education and Director, The Gilbert M. Grosvenor Center for Geographic Education
Southwest Texas State University
San Marcos, Texas

Dr. Kevin P. Colleary
Curriculum and Teaching Department
Hunter College
City University of New York
New York, New York

Dr. Gloria Contreras
Professor of Education
University of North Texas
Denton, Texas

Dr. A. Lin Goodwin
Associate Professor of Education
Department of Curriculum and Teaching
Teachers College
Columbia University
New York, New York

Dr. Mary A. McFarland
Social Studies Education Consultant, K–12
St. Louis, Missouri

Dr. Walter C. Parker
Professor and Program Chair for Social Studies Education
University of Washington
Seattle, Washington

Washington, D.C.

HISTORIANS/SCHOLARS

Dr. Joyce Appleby
Professor of History
University of California, Los Angeles
Los Angeles, California

Dr. Alan Brinkley
Professor of American History
Columbia University
New York, New York

Dr. Nancy Cott
Stanley Woodward Professor of History and American Studies
Yale University
New Haven, Connecticut

Dr. James McPherson
George Henry Davis Professor of American History
Princeton University
Princeton, New Jersey

Dr. Donald A. Ritchie
Associate Historian of the United States Senate Historical Office
Washington, D.C.

PROGRAM CONSULTANTS

Betty Ruth Baker, M.Ed.
Assistant Professor of Curriculum and Instruction
Early Childhood Specialist
School of Education
Baylor University
Waco, Texas

Dr. Randolph B. Campbell
Regents' Professor of History
University of North Texas
Denton, Texas

Dr. Steven Cobb
Director, Center for Economic Education
Chair, Department of Economics
University of North Texas
Denton, Texas

Frank de Varona, Ed.S.
Visiting Associate Professor
Florida International University
Miami, Florida

Dr. John L. Esposito
Professor of Religion and International Affairs, and Director of the Center for Christian-Muslim Understanding
Georgetown University
Washington, D.C.

READING INSTRUCTION CONSULTANTS

M. Frankie Dugan, M.Ed.
Reading/Language Arts Consultant, K–6
Mansfield, Texas

Antonio A. Fierro
Program Director for the Texas Reading Initiative, Region 19
El Paso, Texas

Dr. William H. Rupley
Professor of Reading Education
Distinguished Research Fellow
Department of Teaching, Learning and Culture
College of Education
Texas A&M University
College Station, Texas

GRADE LEVEL CONSULTANTS

Karen L. Beattie
Assistant Principal
Pathways Elementary School
Ormond Beach, Florida

Eleita Brew
Sixth Grade Teacher
Thomas Tolbert Elementary School
Dallas, Texas

Mae Leech
Coordinator of Social Studies
Kansas City Public Schools
Kansas City, Kansas

Jane Palmer
K–12 Social Studies Curriculum Specialist
Seminole County Public Schools
Sanford, Florida

Patty Sullivan
Sixth Grade Teacher
Surfside Elementary School
Satellite Beach, Florida

Dr. Thomas S. Woodall
Instructional Supervisor for Social Science and Gifted Education
Loudoun County Public Schools
Leesburg, Virginia

David M. Wymer
Associate Director for Testing
Roanoke County Public Schools
Roanoke, Virginia

Lauri Zeller
Sixth Grade Teacher
Simpson Middle School
Phoenix, Arizona

CONTRIBUTING WRITERS

Dinah Zike
Comfort, Texas

Karen Edwards
New York, New York

Matt Goodman
Brooklyn, New York

Matt Kachur
Tuckahoe, New York

Dan Rosen
Charlotte, Vermont

Linda Scher
Raleigh, North Carolina

learning through listening

Students with print disabilities may be eligible to obtain an accessible, audio version of the pupil edition of this textbook. Please call Recording for the Blind & Dyslexic at 1-800-221-4792 for complete information.

Acknowledgments The publisher gratefully acknowledges permission to reprint the following copyrighted material:
From **Lost Civilizations: Sumer: Cities of Eden** by the editors of Time-Life Books. Copyright © 1993 Time-Life Books, Inc. Reprinted by permission.
From **Tropical Rainforests** by Arnold Newman. Text copyright 1990 Arnold Newman. Reprinted with permission of Facts On File, Inc., New York. From **The Iliad of Homer: The Wrath of Achilles**, translated by I.A. Richards. Translation copyright 1950 by W.W. Norton & Company, Inc., renewed 1978 by I.A. Richards. Reprinted with permission of W.W. Norton & Company, Inc. Excerpts from **Corpus of Early Arabic Sources for West African History.** Copyright © University of Ghana, International Academic Union, Cambridge University Press 1981. Reprinted with the permission of Cambridge University Press.

(continued on page R68)

Macmillan/McGraw-Hill

A Division of The **McGraw·Hill** *Companies*

Published by Macmillan/McGraw-Hill, of McGraw-Hill Education, a division of The McGraw-Hill Companies, Inc., Two Penn Plaza, New York, New York 10121.

Printed in the United States of America

ISBN 0-02-149268-9
3 4 5 6 7 8 9 027/043 06 05 04 03

Contents

FEATURES

Skills Lessons

Citizenship

Literature

Biographies

CHARTS, GRAPHS & DIAGRAMS

TIME LINES

NATIONAL
GEOGRAPHIC

Social Studies Handbook

The Social Studies Strands are a way of thinking about Social Studies, the study of the world and the people who live in it. The world is a big place and it helps to have a system for organizing your study of Social Studies. One way to think about Social Studies is to break it into parts, called strands. The pie chart on the next page shows the eight strands of Social Studies. Each strand teaches a different part of Social Studies. Studying all of the strands together helps you to better understand the world, past and present. And that understanding makes you a better citizen for tomorrow, the world of the future.

The Eight Strands of Social Studies

Economics
Wants and needs, goods and services. Basic human needs are met in a variety of ways.

Citizenship
Rights, responsibilities, pride, and hope. Our beliefs and principles help make up our national identity.

Culture
Holidays, traditions, and stories. We learn about ourselves and our families through the customs we share and celebrate.

Geography
Location, place, maps, and more. People and environments surround us and are ever changing.

Science, Technology, and Society
Inventions, computers, and ideas. Technology has changed how people live together in the world.

Social Studies Skills
Many special skills are needed to better understand the world around you.

History
Time and chronology, years and dates. Historical figures and ordinary people help shape our lives.

Government
People work to make the laws that influence our lives. People work with citizens to govern.

Thinking About Reading

Your social studies book traces the history of the world from ancient times to the present. In order to understand the information and ideas presented, it is important to read your book carefully. The strategies below describe several ways that can help you become a more effective social studies reader.

Preview ▶ **Ask** ▶ **Read** ▶ **Review**

How to Preview, Ask, Read, and Review:

1. **Preview the lesson.** Read the title, headings, and highlighted words. Look at the photographs, illustrations, and maps, and read their captions. Think about what you already know about the topic. Form a general idea of what the lesson is about.

2. **Ask yourself questions before you read and as you read.** For example, you might ask, "What will I learn about the Roman Empire?"

3. **Read and reread. Read carefully.** Figure out the main ideas, and pay attention to the details. When necessary, look up the meanings of unfamiliar words.

4. **Review what you have read by summarizing, either aloud or in writing.** Focus on the most important points. Make sure you have answers to the questions you raised.

Preview.
The title, the photograph, and its caption tell me this lesson will be about the economy of ancient Greece.

②

Ask yourself questions.
I can turn the title into a question: "What was the economy like in ancient Greece?"

③

Read and reread.
The main idea of each paragraph will help me focus my reading.

④

Review.
A good way to review is to write down the answers to my questions.

Economy of Ancient Greece

Sailing was an important part of life in Greece. Ancient Greek sailors traveled around the Mediterranean Sea to trade for grain. Greek merchants competed with traders from **Phoenicia** (fuh NEE shuh), in what is today Lebanon. Phoenician sailors were even more daring and traveled to ports as far away as the British Isles.

The most valuable Greek product was olive oil. Olive oil was important for cooking and flavoring food. It was also used as a lamp fuel and a body lotion. The profits from olive oil sales paid for the extra grain the ancient Greeks could not grow themselves.

Olive groves remain an important part of the economy of Greece.

H4

Use Visuals

When you use the **visuals** in this book, you can learn more from your reading. Visuals are the pictures, maps, charts, and graphs throughout your book. They provide useful information in a clear, easy-to-study form.

 Tip!

★ When looking at graphs, maps, or charts, read the legend or key to find out the meanings of special symbols.

★ Look for objects in the picture that might give additional information.

How To Use Visuals

Look closely at the visual. Then ask yourself the following questions:

- What does the picture, map, chart, or graph show?
- How does it help me understand what I have read?
- How does it add to the information I have read?
- What information does the caption or label provide?

Study the photograph below and answer the questions.

Farmers cultivate land almost to the cliffs of Cornwall.

Offshore rocks are a danger to boats.

Cornwall, in Britain, has a deeply indented coastline.

The caption tells us that the coastline is of Cornwall in Britain.

Study the photograph. Then copy the diagram on a separate sheet of paper. Think about the information that is given in the photograph and caption. Then complete the diagram.

Knights and their horses wore heavy armor into battle.

Visual Information

armor for a man and horse

Armor was worn for protection.

Visual Information   **Caption Information**

Practice Activities!

1. **Use Visuals** Find a photograph in your book. Tell what information the photograph and the caption provide.
2. **Create Visuals** Find another visual in your book. Use information from the visual to complete a diagram like the one above.

Context Clues

As you read a sentence or paragraph in your book, you may find a word or term that you don't know. One way to figure out the meaning of an unfamiliar word is by looking for **context clues**. Context clues are the words and sentences that are near the unfamiliar word. Using context clues will give you a better understanding of what you read.

Tip!

★ Have you heard this word before? How was it used?

★ Write down the context clues you used to find the meaning of the new word.

★ Use the new word in a sentence of your own to help you remember it.

How to Use Context Clues

Ask yourself the following questions:

- Are any parts of this word familiar?

- Are there other words, phrases, or sentences in the paragraph that can help me figure out the meaning of the word?

- What information do the other words, phrases, or sentences provide?

- Do the pictures give me any information about the word?

Read the paragraph below. What context clues would you use to identify the meaning of the word *domesticate*?

> Over time, farming provided a steadier food supply, especially since the big game animals in many areas were hunted out of existence. People no longer needed to travel great distances to gather food.
>
> People learned how to domesticate plants and animals. In addition to learning to plant seeds and care for plants such as wheat, barley, peas, and lentils to be useful to people, the first farmers also domesticated wild goats, pigs, cattle, and sheep. Domestication also means improving crops and animals. For example, farmers learned which wheat would yield the most grain, and planted it.

Context Clue:
provided a steadier food supply

Context Clue:
plant seeds and care for plants

Context Clue:
to be useful to people

Read the paragraph below about regions. Then copy and complete the diagram to find context clues for the word *regions*.

> Our world can be divided into many regions. The study of these regions is part of geography. Geography is the study of Earth, how it shapes people's lives and is shaped in turn by people's activities. Geography can help you learn how the conditions of a particular region have affected the people who live there. You can also learn how these people have altered their region to improve their lives.

Keep in Mind

For more help in reading social studies, keep these strategies in mind:

Reread.
Review each sentence carefully. Make sure you understand what you have read before going further.

Find the main idea.
As you read, think about the topic and the most important information in each paragraph or section.

Make prediction.
As you read, think about what might come next in your reading.

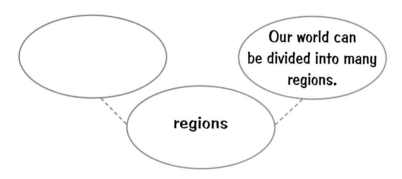

- What steps did you take to find the meaning of **regions**?

Practice Activities!

1. **Read** Find an unfamiliar word or term in your book. Explain to a partner how context clues helped you figure out its meaning.

2. **Write** Select a word from the glossary of your book. Write a short paragraph using the new word and two context clues.

WELCOME TO Our World

Human Systems:
Sydney's harbor is the busiest seaport in Australia, and the unique Sydney Opera House draws people from around the world.

Environment & Society:
In some parts of China, farmers have changed the natural landscape by building terraces along steep hillsides.

Physical Systems:
The Galápagos Islands off the coast of Ecuador have unique wildlife and vegetation partly because of their remote location.

Uses of Geography:
Trail maps help hikers to find the natural wonders of Banff National Park in Alberta, Canada.

Places and Regions:
The Cathedral of Notre Dame and artists along the Seine River are among the attractions that make Paris, France, special.

The World in Spatial Terms:
This aerial view of Cape Town, South Africa, shows how the port city is built around its harbor and sheltering mountains.

Mapping Earth

VOCABULARY

aerial photograph	Prime Meridian
globe	latitude
map	parallel
longitude	absolute location
meridian	

How Do We Acquire Geographic Information About Earth?

- **Aerial photographs** or photographs produced by satellites enable you to see patterns on Earth's surface. They also help identify patterns shown on maps.

- **Globes** also show Earth's surface. A globe is a round model that lets you see Earth's entire surface.

Looking at a globe is like looking at Earth from space.

- Since a globe shows the entire Earth, you can see all seven continents: Africa, Antarctica, Asia, Australia, Europe, North America, and South America. What continents can you see on the globe above?

- A globe also shows Earth's four oceans: the Atlantic, Arctic, Indian, and Pacific. Which oceans are shown in the globe?

- **Maps** are another way of representing the surface of Earth. These flat drawings of Earth usually show only a portion of the surface. How is the representation of Earth on the map on page H12 different from its representation on the globe?

How do you measure longitude and latitude?

- Globes and many maps include a system of lines to help locate places. They are measured in degrees.

- The lines running north-to-south are called **longitude** lines, or **meridians**. They measure distance east or west of the **Prime Meridian**, which is zero degrees. Look at the map on page H12. Which longitude runs through central Africa?

- Lines that measure how far north or south places are from the equator are called **latitude** lines, or **parallels**. Latitude lines run east-to-west. Near which parallel is the southern tip of Australia located?

- Latitude and longitude lines cross to form a global grid. This grid is used to locate places on Earth. This grid address is called its **absolute location**. The grid address of the city of Vitoria is 20°S, 40°W. On which continent is the city located?

Aerial photograph of the Colorado River in Utah.

The World: Continents and Oceans

Using Maps

VOCABULARY

cardinal directions

intermediate directions

relative location

scale

map symbol

map key

legend

locator

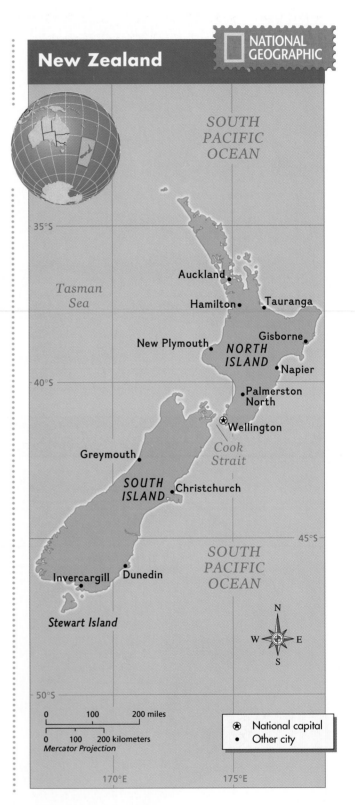

New Zealand

NATIONAL GEOGRAPHIC

What are cardinal directions?

- North, east, south, and west are the main directions, or **cardinal directions**. Suppose you are standing facing north. East will be on your right, west will be on your left, and south will be behind you. If you turned to face east, what cardinal direction would be behind you?

- Look at the compass rose on the map opposite. The cardinal directions are written as N, S, E, and W. In which direction is Auckland from Wellington?

What are intermediate directions?

- The points between the cardinal directions on the compass rose show **intermediate**, or in-between, **directions**.

- The intermediate directions are NE, SE, SW, and NW. What do you think SE stands for?

What is relative location?

- Intermediate directions help us describe **relative location**. Relative location describes one place in relation to another. For example, you say that Dunedin is southwest of Christchurch.

⊛ National capital
• Other city

What is a map scale?

- A map is always smaller than the actual area that it shows. To figure out real distance between places, most maps include a **scale**. The scale shows the relationship between distances on a map and actual distances.

- Map scales in this book include two measurements of distance. What are these two units of measurement?

How do you use map scales?

- You can use a map scale by measuring the distance with a ruler, or by marking the distance represented by the scale on a piece of paper and using that to measure distance on the map.

- To determine the distance between San Fernando and Arima, Trinidad, measure or copy the scale on Map A. One inch is 80 miles. Now measure the distance between the cities. You will see that it is about 40 miles.

- Different maps can show the same subject at different scales. Map A and Map B show Trinidad and Tobago. The islands look larger on Map B because this map has a larger scale than Map A. This larger scale allows more details to be shown. What is shown on Map B that is not shown on Map A?

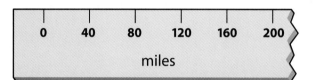

| 0 | 40 | 80 | 120 | 160 | 200 |

miles

Trinidad and Tobago: Map A

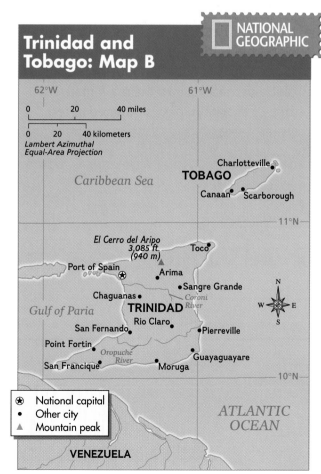

What does a map key tell us?

- Just as a map is a representation of a real place, **map symbols** are used to represent things in that place. A map symbol is anything on a map that stands for something else. On many maps a dot stands for a city. Other symbols can include a triangle to represent a mountain peak, or a red line to represent a road. What other symbols are found on maps?

- The same symbol can mean different things on different maps. The **map key**, or **legend**, tells you what each symbol stands for on that map. What does the triangle stand for on the map opposite? What does the black line represent on the map below?

How do locators help us?

- Maps use **locators** to tell us where in the world the subject of the main map is located. In this book, the locator is a small globe or map set into the main map. The area of the main map is outlined in red.

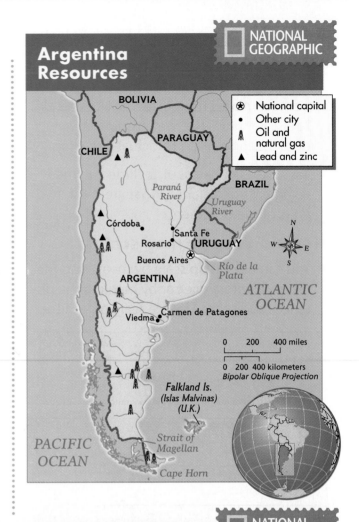

Argentina Resources

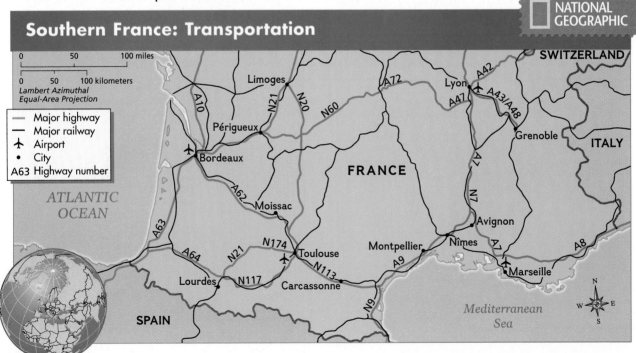

Southern France: Transportation

Using Maps to Find Geographic Information

What are different kinds of maps used for?

- Different types of maps show different things. In this section you will learn about four kinds of maps. When you start to study a map, first look at the title. It will tell you the subject area and the type of map it is. What does the map below show?

- A map may include areas that are not part of its subject area. In this book, such areas are shown in gray. What country or countries below are not in Southeast Asia?

What is a political map?

- A **political map** shows capital cities, states, countries, and other political information. Many use lines to indicate borders. They may also use colors to show different political areas.

- On the map below, what is the capital of Vietnam? How many countries are in Southeast Asia?

Southeast Asia: Political

Reviewing Geography Skills

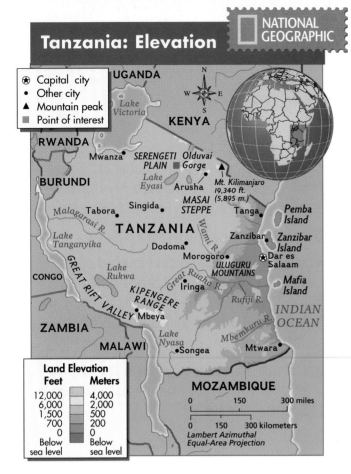

Tanzania: Elevation

NATIONAL GEOGRAPHIC

Land Elevation

Feet	Meters
12,000	4,000
6,000	2,000
1,500	500
700	200
0	0
Below sea level	Below sea level

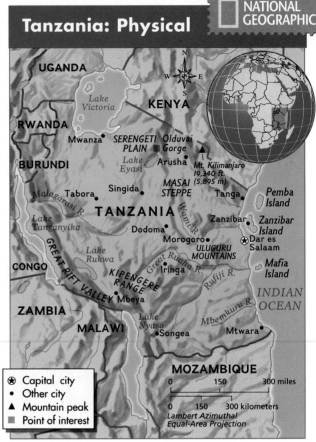

Tanzania: Physical

NATIONAL GEOGRAPHIC

What are some different types of physical maps?

- A **physical map** shows Earth's natural features such as landforms.

- One type of physical map is an **elevation map**. Elevation maps use color to show the height of land above sea level. In this book, elevation is measured in both feet and in meters.

- On the elevation map of Tanzania, what color represents the elevation of 0 to 700 feet? What areas of Tanzania have this elevation?

- Some physical maps use **relief**, or shading to show mountains, hilly areas, and changes in elevation. Areas with no shading are usually lowland areas with little elevation. Dark shading, or high relief, represents areas with sharp changes in elevation, such as mountains.

- On the physical map of Tanzania, which area has the light relief?

What is a historical map?

- A **historical map** shows information about the past or where past events took place. The map title tells the subject of the map and often includes the dates of the subject in the title.

- Look at the map of the United States on the opposite page. By what year did the United States gain California?

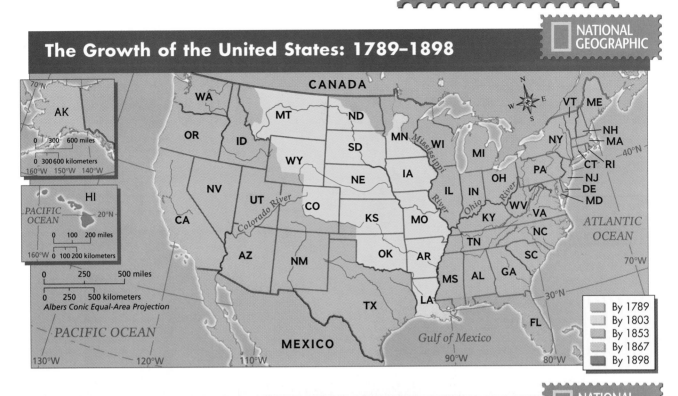

The Growth of the United States: 1789–1898

	By 1789
	By 1803
	By 1853
	By 1867
	By 1898

Russia: Vegetation

- Deciduous Forest
- Evergreen Forest
- Desert Vegetation
- Grassland
- High Mountain Vegetation
- Tundra

What is a distribution map?

- A **distribution map** shows how people, languages, religion, rainfall, or other information are spread out through an area. The map of Russia's vegetation is a distribution map.

- The map key on the distribution map above shows colors that represent different kinds of vegetation in Russia. What kind of vegetation covers the largest area of land?

H18

The World
and Its People

"The time has come," the Walrus said,
"to talk of many things:
of shoes—and ships—and sealing wax—
Of cabbages—and kings."

This poem was written over a hundred years ago. It could have been written about the study of history, the record of life from earliest times to today. History is about kings and queens, but it is also about ordinary people—what they ate and wore, and how they traveled.

World Regions

From earliest times people have been influenced not only by historic events, but also by the environments in which they have lived. Our world can be divided into many regions. The study of these regions is part of **geography**. Geography is the study of Earth, how it shapes people's lives, and how it is shaped in turn by people's activities. Geography can help you learn how the conditions of a particular region have affected the people who live there. You can also learn how these people have altered their region to improve their lives.

Geographers divide Earth into various kinds of regions. **Physical regions** are defined by Earth's natural environment. Any physical region contains features that set it apart from other areas. The largest land regions are the continents. Each continent can also be divided into smaller physical regions. Such a region may be identified by landforms such as plains or plateaus. For example, the Andes Mountains of South America form a smaller physical region.

Another way to organize regions is by **climate**. Climate is the pattern of weather in an area over a long period of time. The area of the North Pole, where the average temperature is –30 degrees Fahrenheit, forms one type of climate region. At the Equator, temperatures can reach 130 degrees Fahrenheit. It is hot year round, which makes a very different type of climate region.

READING CHECK ✓ How does the study of geography help us to understand the way people live?

World Cultures

Regions can also be based on **culture**. Culture is the way the people of a region live: their languages, beliefs, occupations, activities, and arts. A culture region can cross national borders as well as continents. For example, one cultural region includes North Africa and western Asia. Cultural regions may be divided into smaller regions. People within a large cultural region may have different traditions or practice different religions. For example, Europe forms a large cultural region based on its traditions and history. Yet, Europe also has many smaller cultural regions based on a variety of ethnic groups and languages. Many of these peoples and languages, though, are related!

Sometimes part of a culture region may continue traditional patterns, while the rest of the country changes. For example, most Hungarians wear clothes similar to those worn by people throughout the rest of Europe. Some Hungarian cowboys (right, bottom) however, continue to wear traditional costumes.

READING CHECK

What are some of the characteristics of a culture region?

DATAGRAPHIC

Identifying Languages and Culture Regions

Studying facts about language can tell us something about world cultures. Study the graphics on this page and answer the questions.

Most Commonly Spoken Languages of the World, 1996

Languages and Some Countries Where They Are Spoken	Number of Speakers
Mandarin Chinese •China, Taiwan, Malaysia	885,000,000
Spanish •Spain, Mexico, many countries in South America, the United States	332,000,000
English •United States, Britain, Canada, Australia, India, Liberia	322,000,000
Bengali •India, Bangladesh	189,000,000
Hindi •India, Nepal, Singapore	182,000,000
Portuguese •Portugal, Brazil, Cape Verde	170,000,000

Source: *Encyclopaedia Britannica Book of the Year* (1999)

NATIONAL GEOGRAPHIC

THE LANGUAGES OF INDIA

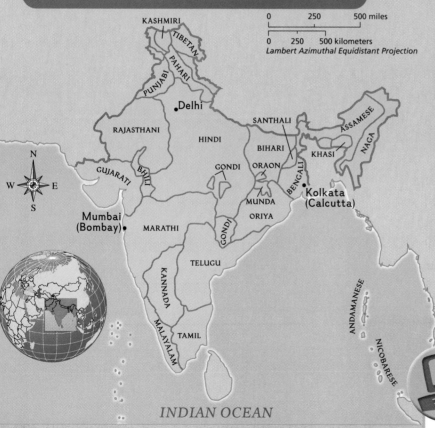

QUESTIONS:

1 In which countries do people speak more than one language?

2 The population of Great Britain today is about 59 million. Why do you think English is spoken by so many people outside of Great Britain?

3 Why might a country such as India have large groups of people who speak different languages?

To learn more, visit our Web site: **www.mhschool.com**

People and Culture

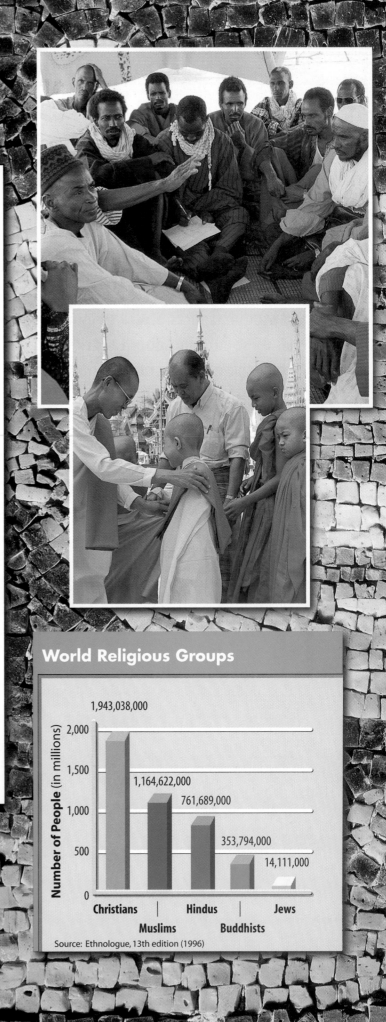

Probably the most important part of any culture is its **values**, the things that the people of that culture think are most important in life.

RELIGION

Many cultures base their values on their religious beliefs. Look at the graph of the world's largest religious groups. Almost all of Europe's 727 million people are Christians, for example. However, Christianity spread to other countries as Europeans settled in other regions. Many of Asia's religions have also spread to other regions.

GOVERNMENT

Political beliefs are also an important part of culture. In the United States, which is a democratic republic, citizens vote for leaders to represent them. Citizens in Canada and Mexico also vote for their leaders. However, other nations, such as Oman and Swaziland, have single leaders who consult with advisors and then make all decisions for their nations.

World Religious Groups

Number of People (in millions)

- Christians: 1,943,038,000
- Muslims: 1,164,622,000
- Hindus: 761,689,000
- Buddhists: 353,794,000
- Jews: 14,111,000

Source: Ethnologue, 13th edition (1996)

CUSTOMS

All cultures have distinctive **customs**, traditions, beliefs, and arts. Customs are ways of living that people practice regularly over time. Eating turkey at Thanksgiving is one custom in the United States. Some customs, such as east Asians eating with chopsticks, are practiced every day. Other customs may be observed only on special occasions, such as weddings.

READING CHECK How might people's values determine the way they live?

9

Culture and Change

No culture remains the same. Throughout history, cultures have changed because of wars or invasions. However, changes may come about peacefully as well. Sometimes a culture comes in contact with other cultures. Time passes and the customs or traditions are altered. When this happens, a new culture may develop and include characteristics of the other cultures.

Today, education often makes changes in a culture. Students studying in a foreign country learn new or different ideas or techniques. Living in a foreign country also helps students to see their world in a different way.

Modern transportation has changed almost every culture on Earth. Modern air travel has brought tourists and students to every corner of the planet. All cultures have adapted to this worldwide traveling trend. Immigration also changes cultures. Think of all the ethnic restaurants and music styles in the United States.

New inventions have a tremendous effect on cultures. Since the 1940s, many cultures have been changed because of the spread of movies and television throughout the United States and the world. Even isolated cultures can now see how people live and work in other cultures. This changes the way all cultures see the world.

READING CHECK What factors might make a culture change?

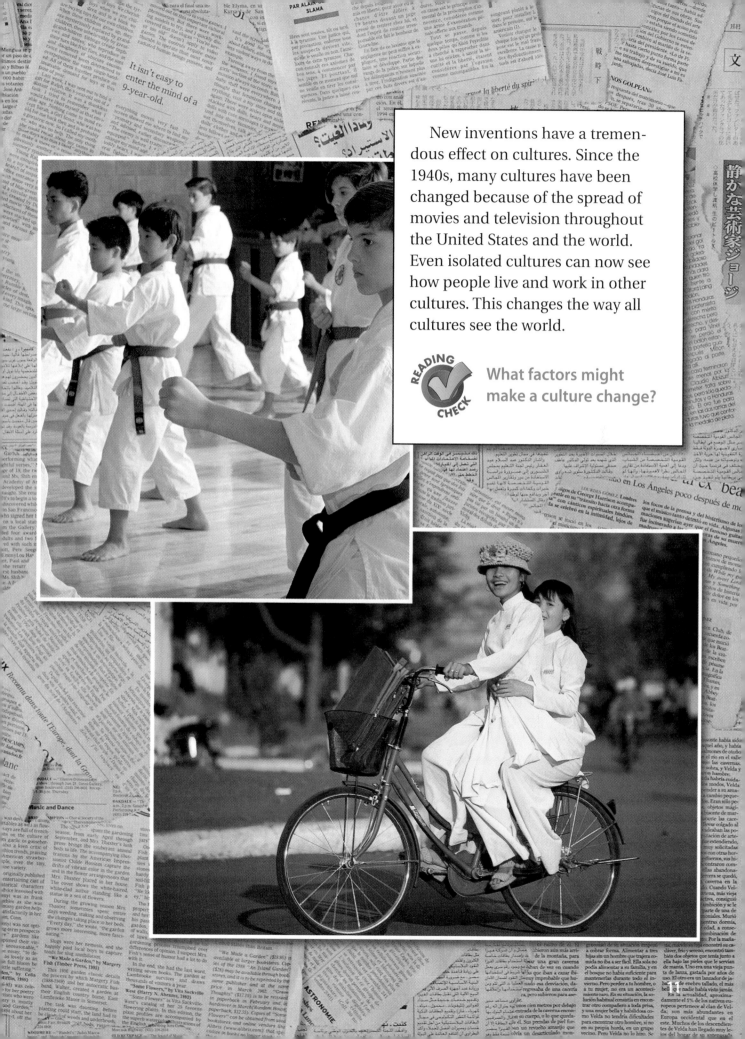

11

Taking Notes and Writing Outlines

Suppose you need to review for a test. You can make reviewing easier by writing notes and making an **outline** of your reading. An outline is a plan for organizing written information about a subject. Taking notes and outlining helps you to choose the most important facts and to organize them so you can review them quickly.

Prehistory

①

The period before writing is called prehistory. How do we know about life before there were written records? Scientists study weapons of ancient people. These tools can tell us how people hunted. We can learn how they prepared their food from their pottery and daily tools.

Sometimes, people left pictures or stone carvings behind. You may have heard of the famous cave paintings in Spain and France. We can see the kinds of animals that lived near the people of the time. We can also see how they hunted for their meat.

I. One way scientists learn about prehistoric people is to study their weapons and daily tools.
  A. Weapons tell us how people hunted.
  B. We learn how they prepared food from pottery and daily tools.

II. Art from prehistoric times also gives clues to the past.
  A. Pictures show us the animals of the time.
  B. Prehistoric art often tells us how people hunted.

LEARN THE SKILL

One way to organize your notes is to ask yourself questions such as the following.

1. **Identify the main idea or ideas.**
   In an outline, a Roman numeral goes before the main ideas in the reading. In this excerpt, the Roman numeral I goes before the first main idea, which is in the first paragraph. The Roman numeral II goes before the second main idea.

2. **Identify supporting facts.**
   A capital letter goes before important facts and ideas that support each main idea. The capital letters *A* and *B* go before details that support the main ideas of both paragraphs.

TRY THE SKILL

Now read the paragraph about a recent discovery in Turkey. Then answer the questions.

The Examiner

Recently, scientists in central Turkey made an exciting discovery. They found a complete Roman city, with houses, shops, libraries, and baths. That was the good news. The bad news is that a nearby dam will flood the site and bury the city under many feet of water.

1. What is the main idea of the paragraph?

2. How would you identify the main ideas in an outline?

3. How do you identify the details or examples that support the main ideas in the outline?

4. How does taking notes and writing an outline help you to better understand what you read?

EXTEND THE SKILL

Read the following paragraphs that continue the story of the discovery in Turkey. Suppose you have to use the information to make a more detailed outline for a longer report. Make a list of details you will research to add to your outline and research.

Among the exciting finds at the dam site in Turkey were many elegant mosaic floors. Scholars were delighted that the tiny pieces of colored stone forming pictures of everyday life were intact. In fact, the many magnificent examples of Roman mosaics in this Roman city were in almost perfect condition.

The new dam is badly needed because this part of Turkey suffers from frequent droughts. Work on the dam is almost completed and the water is beginning to rise behind the dam. With so little time left, scientists from all over the world are working quickly to save as much as they can of its treasures. Although the dam will flood the ancient Roman city, it focused the world's attention on the site and brought people together to save what they could.

● How can taking notes and making an outline help you to organize and understand information better?

Learning About the Past

How do we know about cultures that existed hundreds or even thousands of years ago? Historians, or people who study the past, use different kinds of **sources** to discover what they want to know. A source is anything that provides information or evidence.

Another way to learn about the past is to ask people who know about it. This valuable source is called **oral history**. It is history passed on by word of mouth. Oral history, or oral tradition, was how history was kept alive in cultures that had no system of writing.

Historians can also study **artifacts** (AHR tuh fakts), objects made by people in the past. An artifact might be all or part of an ancient Greek vase (opposite) or it could be something as ordinary as some bricks.

DIFFERENT KINDS OF SOURCES

Historians rely on **primary sources** for information about the past. A primary source is any artifact that was created at the time, such as this handwritten book by the painter Leonardo da Vinci (top). A primary source may also be a photograph, a song, or even a carved rock!

Information about the past is often found in a **secondary source**. This source was created later than that time in history. This textbook is one kind of secondary source.

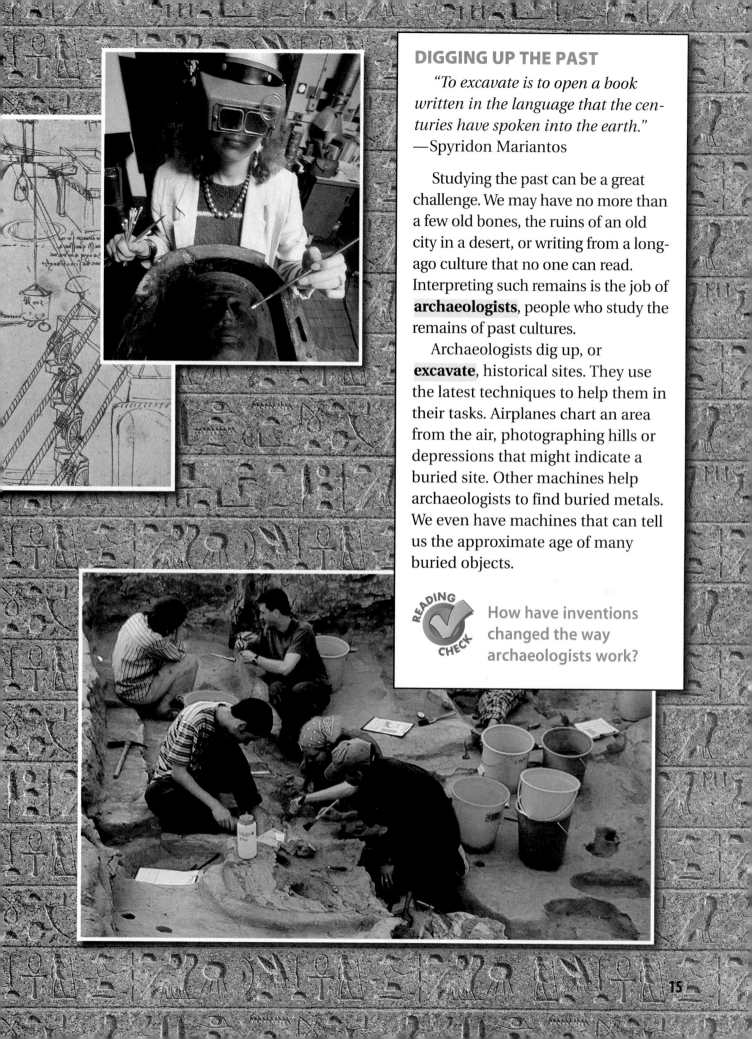

DIGGING UP THE PAST

"To excavate is to open a book written in the language that the centuries have spoken into the earth."
—Spyridon Mariantos

Studying the past can be a great challenge. We may have no more than a few old bones, the ruins of an old city in a desert, or writing from a long-ago culture that no one can read. Interpreting such remains is the job of **archaeologists**, people who study the remains of past cultures.

Archaeologists dig up, or **excavate**, historical sites. They use the latest techniques to help them in their tasks. Airplanes chart an area from the air, photographing hills or depressions that might indicate a buried site. Other machines help archaeologists to find buried metals. We even have machines that can tell us the approximate age of many buried objects.

READING CHECK How have inventions changed the way archaeologists work?

15

Ancient Cities

About 120 miles from Lima, Peru, there are six large mounds of packed earth. In 2001, archaeologists used a technique called carbon dating to determine the age of the mounds at a site called Caral. To their surprise, the mounds are the ruins of a city older than Egyptian ruins such as Hatshepsut's temple (right).

The city was built in 2627 B.C. just as Egyptian workers were putting the finishing touches on the Great Pyramid at Giza on the Nile. Clearly there were urban cultures in the Americas almost 1,500 years before historians had previously believed.

In this book, you will read about many ancient cities. Xian, in China, is over 3,000 years old. In recent years, archaeologists in Xian have been excavating an army of life-size clay soldiers (left). You will read more about this army in Chapter 5.

Teotihuacan (background) was once the largest city in the Americas. It disappeared about 1,200 years ago. Historians are still not sure who built the city or what happened to its population of over 100,000 people.

The ruins of ancient temples in Athens, Greece (above), were one of the earliest sites explored by archaeologists. These temples were built as a symbol of the glory of Athens.

Wherever they are found, the ruins of ancient cities have told us much about the way people lived thousands of years ago.

READING CHECK

What kinds of clues might historians find in the ruins of ancient cities?

Tracing Our Roots

Recently, scientists have been studying human **genes**. Genes are substances we are born with that pass human characteristics from parents to children. All genes contain DNA. Each person receives some DNA from the mother and some from the father. Another kind of DNA remains the same for females in a family through the generations (below). This fact has enabled scientists to trace family roots back to the distant past.

DNA has proven to be a useful tool in historical research, and it can even solve historical mysteries. For example, a young French prince died in 1795 (top). However, many dramatic stories said that he had not died, but had been smuggled to safety in another country. DNA tests made in 1999 proved that the boy who died in 1795 was, in fact, the son of the king of France.

In 1997, scientists made another astonishing discovery. The skeleton of a 9,000 year-old man (top) had been found in a cave near Cheddar, England. A local high school history class tested DNA to see if this "Cheddar Man" had any modern descendants. They compared the DNA of the cave man to the DNA of about 50 villagers, including their teacher.

Imagine how excited they were when they discovered that their teacher was related to the cave man! This means that the cave man was a direct ancestor of the teacher. Some of the cave man's DNA had been passed down from parent to child for over 9,000 years!

As science discovers new tests and as inventors create new machines, we will be able to learn more and more about the lives of the people who lived before us.

READING CHECK

Why is DNA useful in historical research?

Introduction REVIEW

VOCABULARY REVIEW

Number a sheet of paper from 1 to 5. Beside each number write the word or term from the list below that matches the definition.

culture	primary source
geography	values
oral history	

1. The study of Earth, how it is shaped by people, and how it shapes people's lives.
2. The way the people of a region live, including their languages and beliefs.
3. The things and ideas that the people of a culture think are most important.
4. History that is passed on by word of mouth.
5. A piece of writing or an artifact that was created at the time that an event took place.

TECHNOLOGY

For more resources to help you learn more about the people and places you studied in this section, visit www.mhschool.com and follow the links for Grade 6, Introduction.

SKILL REVIEW

In A.D. 1595, workers digging near Naples, Italy, found the ruins of an ancient Roman city. By the mid-1700s, treasure-hunters were digging out priceless statues and other art works from this site. These art works came from an ancient Roman city called Pompeii. In A.D. 79, Pompeii had been buried by a volcanic eruption. The ash preserved the city almost as it was on the day of the eruption.

In their search for treasure, early diggers destroyed much valuable evidence of how people lived in ancient Pompeii. It was not until the 1860s that people began to dig carefully and scientifically at Pompeii. Later, archaeological methods improved. Today, modern science helps us learn about what sorts of grains people ate and their health. Pompeii remains one of our best archaeological sources for information about Roman life.

6. **Study Skill** How do you organize an outline to show the main ideas and the facts and ideas that support the main idea?
7. **Study Skill** Write an outline of the passage above.
8. **Geography Skill** How can you tell if a map shows a physical region or a cultural region? Explain.
9. **Geography Skill** What makes up a cultural region? What is a climate region?
10. **Study Skill** What would a chart showing the world's five largest religious groups include? What could you learn from the chart about the world's cultures?

Activities

Language Arts

- Trace the roots of your family or guardians. Interview them to find out the place(s) of origin of their ancestors. Write a list of questions you plan to ask. Note any important information, such as the town(s) or region(s) in which they lived, the approximate years in which they lived, and important customs, such as the language(s) they spoke.

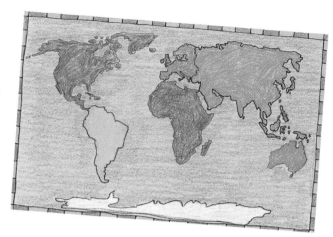

Make a Map of Family Roots

- Working in groups, trace a map of the world and cut and paste it across a large piece of oaktag.
- Write your name or create a symbol to place in each town or region where the ancestors lived.

- Research customs special to a region or country where an ancestor lived.
- Draw or cut out pictures of these customs and paste them onto the appropriate region or country on your map.
- Choose one person from your group to present the map to the class.

WRITING ACTIVITIES

Writing to Express *Write* a paragraph in which you express what custom or customs you enjoy most in your own culture. Write in a way that describes the custom to a person who may be unfamiliar with it.

Writing to Inform *Write* a paragraph in which you explain the importance of primary sources, secondary sources, and oral histories in uncovering information about the past.

Writing to Persuade Suppose you are an archaeologist who is writing an advertisement for someone to accompany you on an expedition. How would you write to persuade someone to join you?

LITERATURE

Secrets of the Ice Man

By Dorothy Hinshaw Patent
Art by Paul Wright

In 1991, two hikers in the Hauslabjoch [HOWS lahb yok] *Pass in the Austrian-Italian Alps discovered a body in the snow. They called the police. The world was stunned when Professor Konrad Spindler, an archaeologist, announced that the body was at least 4,000 years old.*

Professor Spindler's conclusion shocked the **forensic** scientists. Nothing like this had been found before. The oldest bodies previously discovered preserved in a glacier had been about 400 years old. . . . [P]eople had thought that nothing could survive longer than 1,000 years in the ice. But here was the body of a man as well as a collection of things he carried along to help him survive in the mountains. Not only were there a metal ax and some **flint** blades, but clothing made of animal hides and grass, wooden tool handles, and other items . . . .

Upon news of the sensational find, the international media went wild. The phones went crazy at the Institute, where new lines and fax machines were hastily added to meet the overwhelming demand.

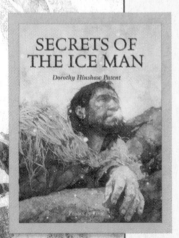

SECRETS OF
THE ICE MAN
Dorothy Hinshaw Patent

---

forensic: (fə ren′ sik) applying medical facts to legal problems
flint: (flint) a stone that makes sparks when struck against steel

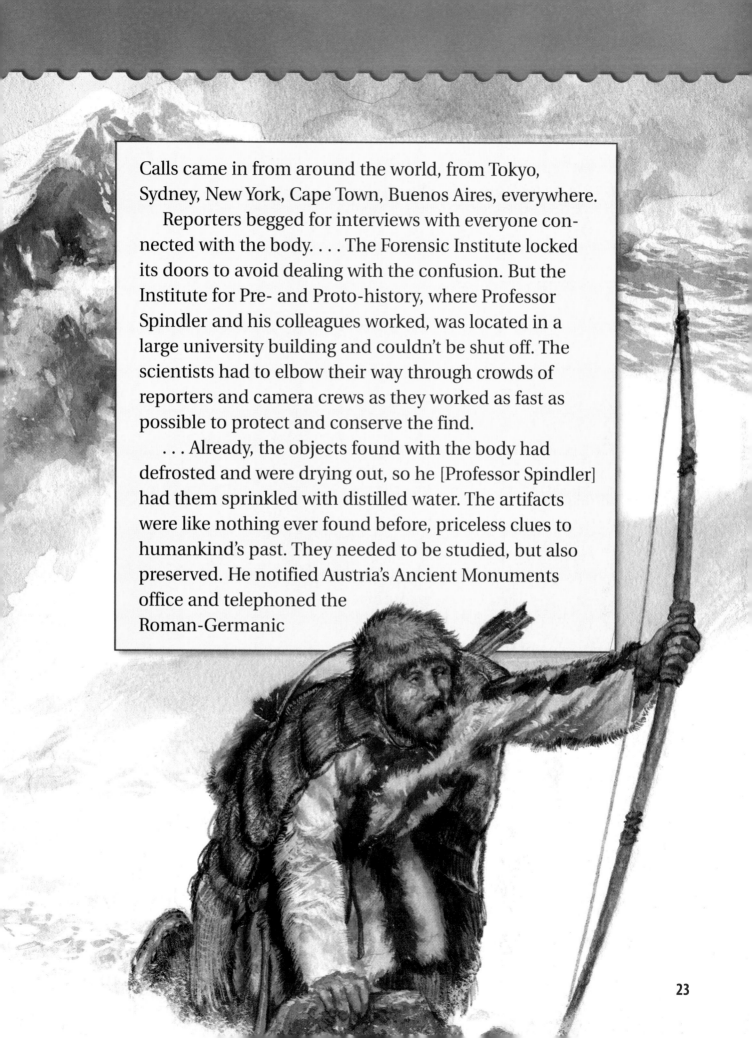

Calls came in from around the world, from Tokyo, Sydney, New York, Cape Town, Buenos Aires, everywhere.

Reporters begged for interviews with everyone connected with the body. . . . The Forensic Institute locked its doors to avoid dealing with the confusion. But the Institute for Pre- and Proto-history, where Professor Spindler and his colleagues worked, was located in a large university building and couldn't be shut off. The scientists had to elbow their way through crowds of reporters and camera crews as they worked as fast as possible to protect and conserve the find.

. . . Already, the objects found with the body had defrosted and were drying out, so he [Professor Spindler] had them sprinkled with distilled water. The artifacts were like nothing ever found before, priceless clues to humankind's past. They needed to be studied, but also preserved. He notified Austria's Ancient Monuments office and telephoned the Roman-Germanic

Central Museum in Mainz, Germany, where the world's greatest experts on preserving ancient artifacts worked.

But what to do about the body itself? It was beginning to thaw out, and Spindler and Henn had no experience with frozen mummies. Spindler tried to reach the Hermitage Museum in Russia, which had successfully dealt with mummies dug from the Siberian **permafrost**. But Russia was in turmoil—the Soviet Union was **disintegrating**, and he couldn't even get a phone call through.

The responsibility for preserving the body finally went to the Anatomical Institute in Innsbruck, where it was refrozen to a temperature of minus 6 degrees Celsius (21 degrees Fahrenheit), the mean annual temperature near the Hauslabjoch, where it had already spent several **millennia** . . .

Over the next few days, more bits and pieces of the Ice Man's equipment were collected. Some of the people who had visited the site before its importance was realized had taken bits of fur or other fragments with them. Fortunately, the archaeologists were able to interview everyone and retrieve these important items.

On October 2 and 3, 1991, a research crew helicoptered to the site. The scientists carefully surveyed the area and photographed it. They found more material, such as what looked like a mat of grass right under where the body had lain. By October 5, the weather had become so bad that the operation was suspended until the following summer.

---

permafrost: (pûr′ mə frôst) a layer of Earth that is permanently frozen
disintegrating: (dis in′ ti grāt ing) breaking up
millennia: (mi len′ ē ə) a period of 1,000 years

Beginning in July 1992, scientists began the final investigation of the site. A great deal of snow had accumulated since the previous October, but the scientists wanted to avoid using diesel-run equipment for fear of **contaminating** the find. So four men worked for more than three weeks shoveling away more than 600 tons of snow.

By August 10, enough snow had been removed so that the archaeologists could begin their work, even though ice still needed to be removed. Because it was hot and sunny, the scientists also had to battle with meltwater. During their work, they uncovered many small items, such as leaves and bits of charcoal. They also found the broken-off end of the Ice Man's bow and his cap, which was frozen in the ice beneath where his head had lain. On August 25, the researchers left, satisfied that they had found everything the Hauslabjoch had to offer them.

---

contaminating (kən tam′ ə nāt ing): making unclean, polluting

Write About It!

Based on details in this excerpt and the later discovery that the Ice Man was about 5,300 years old, write an announcement that the Forensic Institute might have released to the press.

Early History

TAKE A LOOK

How did early cultures develop?

Horses were tamed about 5,000 years ago. They were the most common form of transportation during peace and war until about 80 years ago.

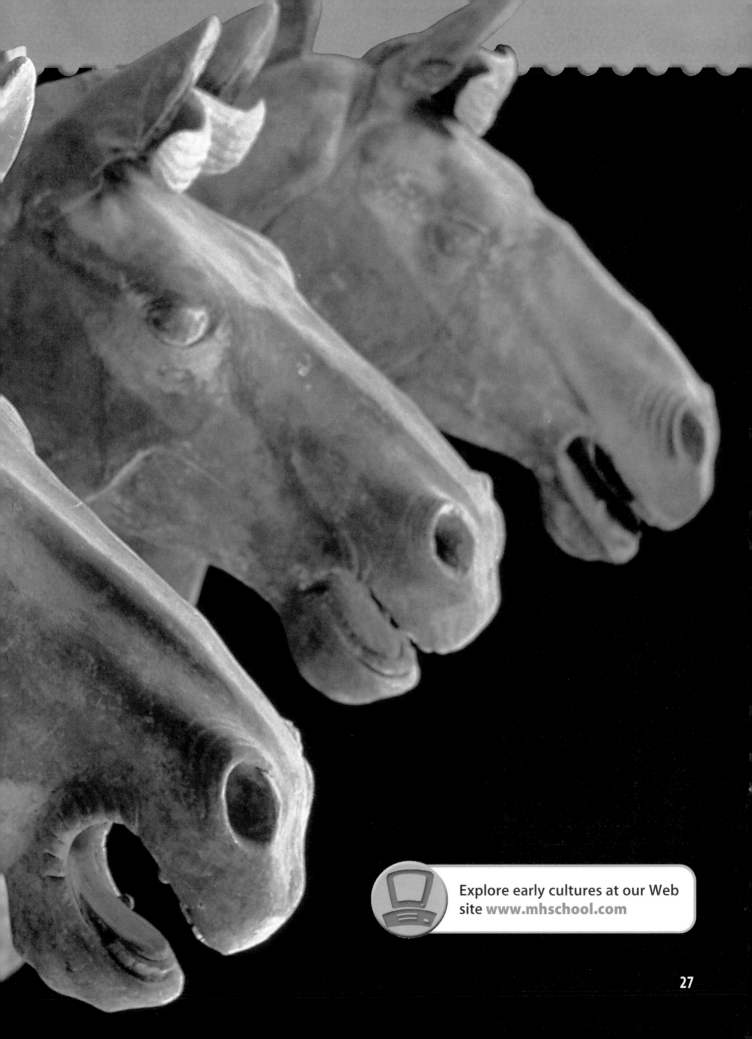

Explore early cultures at our Web site www.mhschool.com

The First Cultures

The world was a very different place 70,000 years ago. There were no cities, towns, or farms. Back then, people depended on their environment to survive. Their food, tools, and shelter were all made from things found in nature. For a long time, people moved from place to place following herds of animals. In time, however, some people began to stay in one place because they developed agriculture. Soon, people began to build the first towns.

EARLY PEOPLE

The earliest people live in Africa. They travel in small groups to hunt animals and gather plants for food. They also gather plants for use as medicine and they use fire. They have simple stone tools, which cause this period to be called the *Old Stone Age.*

PEOPLE AND TECHNOLOGY

About 12,000 years ago, ice covers most of the Northern Hemisphere. During this time, people make more complex tools from stones and animal bones.

THE AGRICULTURAL REVOLUTION

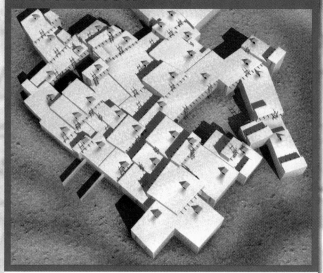

At the end of the last Ice Age, about 10,000 years ago, people in various parts of the world begin to farm. They improve plants for crops, and tame animals for milk and meat. The first towns develop.

Use your Foldable to record what you learn about the history and technology of our world's "First Cultures."

1. Fold a two-inch tab along the long side of a sheet of 8 ½" x 11" paper.
2. Fold the long side of the paper into thirds, forming three pockets.
3. Glue the ends of the pockets together and write the lesson titles on the pockets.
4. Record notes and information on cards and place them in the pockets.

Early People

How did early people survive?

VOCABULARY

Paleolithic Era
hunter-gatherers

READING STRATEGY

Copy the chart below. In the center circle write the main idea of the lesson. In the outer circles write supporting details.

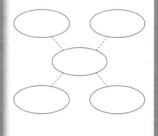

In the Pyrenees Mountains of France, cave paintings dating from around 10,000 B.C. show bison, deer, and horses.

BUILD BACKGROUND

Imagine life on Earth thousands of years ago. Thick sheets of ice covered the northern part of the world. Animals were huge and covered with long, wooly hair. The southern part of Earth was ice-free, but had heavy rainfalls. Small groups of people hunted the huge herds of animals that roamed across the land.

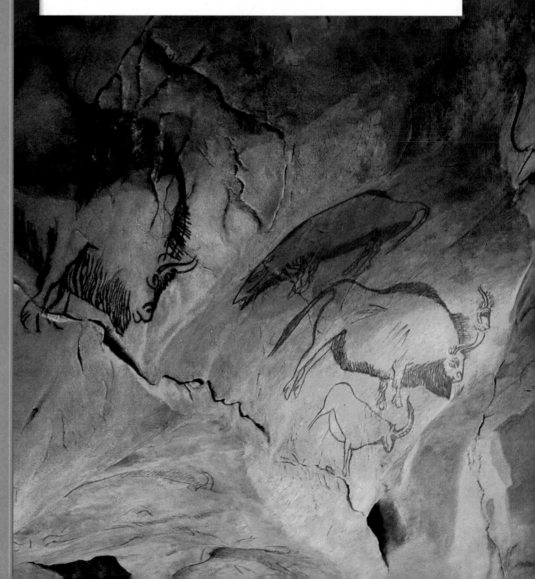

You Are Here
70,000 B.C. – 10,000 B.C.

PEOPLE OF THE OLD STONE AGE

What was the life of people long ago? Historians, archaeologists, and anthropologists have given many answers to this question, and they are still searching for clues. Anthropologists study the physical and cultural development of humans.

Many scientists believe that human life began in Africa over 2 million years ago and then spread throughout the rest of the world. This conclusion is based on human remains found by archaeologists in East Africa. They are the oldest of their kind ever found.

Stone Tools

At one site in the African country of **Tanzania**, a series of valleys cuts deeply through the surrounding plains. This is called the **Great Rift Valley**. Here are the dried lake bottoms from millions of years ago. In these ancient lakebeds, archaeologists have found remains that may be 2 million years old.

Among the remains are what may have been the first tools used by humans. Stones, like the one in the picture above, were shaped until they had an edge with a knifelike sharpness. They may not look like today's axes, but the sharp-edged stones could cut through the hides of animals and chop through wood. Stone tools were the most common tools until about 12,000 years ago. These simple tools are the first human technology. The period of time when people used simple stone

Archaeologists study artifacts to learn about the past.

tools is called the *Old Stone Age* or **Paleolithic** (pay lee uh LITH ik) **Era**. It lasted from about 70,000 years ago to about 12,000 years ago.

Remains of animal bones have been found with the stone tools. These bones suggest that early people hunted for survival. During the Old Stone Age, people also learned to make fire. Having fire meant people could cook their food. In colder climates fires helped people keep warm enough to survive through the long winters.

Why do you think people in the Old Stone Age used stone for tools?

31

MORE COMPLEX SKILLS

Until recently, the oldest carved-bone tools were about 25,000 years old. A recent discovery in South Africa, at a site called **Blombos Cave**, has moved this technology back to about 70,000 years ago. Archaeologists have found blades carved from animal bones. The blades were polished, probably with strips of leather. They were decorated with designs and stained with ocher, a yellowish powder. Archaeologists think the creators of these blades must have had a sense of beauty.

An Ancient Cave

Clues from another cave in South Africa have helped archaeologists create

a picture of life about 40,000 years ago. Find **Border Cave** on the map on this page. Border Cave was in the side of a cliff. It overlooked a grassy river valley dotted with buffalo-thorn trees and other shrubs. Herds of eland, a type of antelope, moved into the valley each year to graze. A group of hunters camped at Border Cave and hunted the eland.

Discoveries in Border Cave show that the hunters lined its cool floor with grass for bedding. They made campfires for cooking and for light at night.

Since the cave was high on the cliff, the hunters could keep watch over the animals' movements below. Small arrowhead-shaped stones found in the cave suggest that the people may have used bows and arrows to hunt.

Using the Environment

The people of Border Cave had other skills besides hunting. They knew a great deal about the plants around them. They knew which ones were useful as medicine

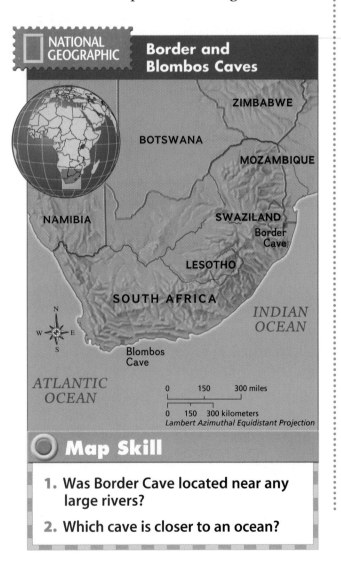

NATIONAL GEOGRAPHIC

Border and Blombos Caves

ZIMBABWE

BOTSWANA

MOZAMBIQUE

NAMIBIA

SWAZILAND

Border Cave

LESOTHO

SOUTH AFRICA

INDIAN OCEAN

N W E S

Blombos Cave

ATLANTIC OCEAN

0   150   300 miles
0   150   300 kilometers
Lambert Azimuthal Equidistant Projection

Map Skill

1. **Was Border Cave located near any large rivers?**

2. **Which cave is closer to an ocean?**

Admiring Beauty

Among the remains found in the Border Cave are the bones of a baby. Near the skeleton of the baby was a beautiful bead made from a seashell. Archaeologists who studied the bead drew conclusions about the Border Cave people. They think that the people cared deeply for the baby. Otherwise, why would they have bothered to bury it? Further, the bead found shows that the people admired beauty. The cave was 50 miles from the sea, the source of the seashell bead. Traveling that far for the shell would have required a real effort.

Scientists look for artifacts in Border Cave and Blombos Cave (above right). Border Cave paintings show animals such as herds of eland (bottom).

 READING CHECK How did the Border Cave people use their environment to survive?

or filled with dangerous poisons. Remains of ancient seeds and leaves show that the people who used the cave gathered wild plums, oranges, and starchy plants for food. Since these people met their needs by hunting animals and gathering plants, they are known as **hunter-gatherers**.

Some of the most important records of early humans are the paintings they drew in caves or on rocks. Some of the oldest known cave paintings were painted about 20,000 years ago in France and Spain. They may have been used in religious celebrations or to record events in a hunt.

❶ This painting from northern Europe shows a fishing scene.

❷ This painting from Utah shows herds of animals.

❸ This Australian painting shows a pignosed turtle.

❹ These hunters are from Algeria.

Diagram Skill

1. What clues do these paintings give about the way of life of the Old Stone Age?

2. What can you tell about the lives of Old Stone Age people from their art?

PUTTING IT TOGETHER

The Old Stone Age lasted from about 70,000 years ago to about 12,000 years ago. During this time, people used stone tools. They also hunted animals and gathered plants to eat. They lived in small groups in which older people were responsible for socialization. Socialization is the means by which people learn the rules of the group. People of the Old Stone Age developed a number of skills, including the use of plants for medicines. Some groups also showed great skill in painting. During the next 6,000 years, life began to change. People began to raise their own food and to make better tools. They also began to live in villages and towns.

This cave painting of a horse (above) dates from around 15,000 B.C. The bone needle (left) was found in Africa.

Review and Assess

1. Write one sentence for each vocabulary term.

   hunter-gatherers   Paleolithic Era

2. How long did the Old Stone Age last?

3. How did people live during the Old Stone Age?

4. What kinds of tools did the people of the Old Stone Age have?

5. How did archaeologists **draw the conclusion** that the people of Border Cave loved beauty?

Look at the map on page 32. Use the map scale to figure out how many miles Border Cave is from the Indian Ocean.

Suppose you are an archaeologist. **Write** an entry in your journal about a visit to Border Cave. Describe what you see and what conclusions you draw.

Using Map Projections

The world of people long ago was limited by what they could see with their own eyes. They could travel no farther than they could walk. Today we have aerial photographs, satellites, and other means of communicating information about our world. We represent this information on different types of maps. However, some maps are more accurate than others. Since Earth is a sphere, cartographers must stretch or cut parts of the globe to make them fit onto a flat map. This stretching and cutting causes **distortion** —errors that make the map less accurate.

When cartographers create a map of Earth's entire surface, they must use a **projection**. A projection is a way of showing parts of Earth on a flat map.

VOCABULARY
distortion
projection
equal-area projection
mercator projection
polar projection

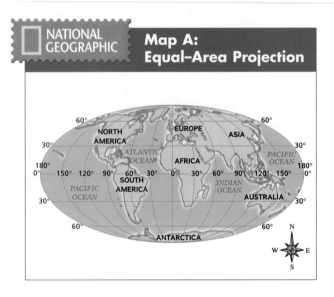

NATIONAL GEOGRAPHIC
Map A: Equal–Area Projection

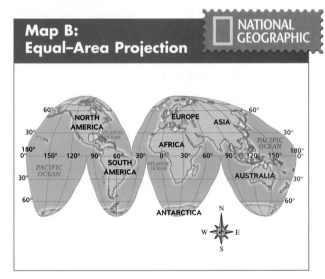

Map B: Equal–Area Projection
NATIONAL GEOGRAPHIC

LEARN THE SKILL

Follow these steps to learn about map projections.

1. **Identify the map projection.**
   In most regular atlases, the name of the map projection appears on the map.

2. **Find out how the map projection shows the size of lands and distances.**
   One of the most common types of map pro-

jection is the **equal-area projection**. Look at Map A. This map is useful for comparing sizes of land masses. However, it distorts the shapes of land. Distances between places at the edges of this map are also distorted.

Map B is also an equal-area projection. The shapes on Map B are more accurate than those on Map A. However, the cuts on this map make it difficult to tell the distances between places.

3. **Find out if the map distortion affects the area you need information about.**
Another kind of map, the **mercator projection**, is shown on Map C. Near the equator there is little distortion and sizes are accurate. As you move farther from the equator, sizes become more distorted.

4. **Determine whether the projection gives accurate information for limited areas.**
Some projections are accurate for the limited areas they show. One kind, **polar projections**, are used to show the area around the North Pole or the South Pole. Map D shows a polar projection of the North Pole. Sizes and shapes near the center are accurate. Near the edges, however, there is distortion.

TRY THE SKILL

Answer the following questions. Use the steps in Learn the Skill if you need help.

1. What kind of projection is useful for showing the sizes of landmasses?

2. Which map projection has little distortion near the equator?

3. Which projection gives correct information about sizes and distances in Greenland?

4. How does understanding map projections help us to obtain useful geographic information?

EXTEND THE SKILL

Choose one of the continents. Then look in atlases or other resources to find equal-area, mercator, and polar projections showing the continent. Study how the continent differs in each projection. Compare them to a globe. Then list the major ways in which the continent is shown differently on the projections.

● How does understanding map projections help us make better use of historical maps?

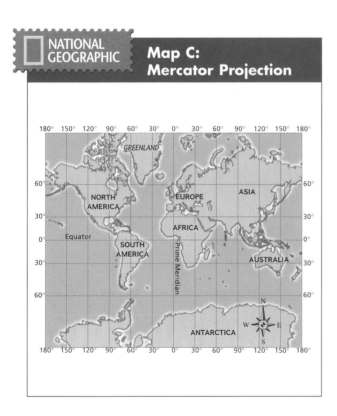

Map C:
Mercator Projection

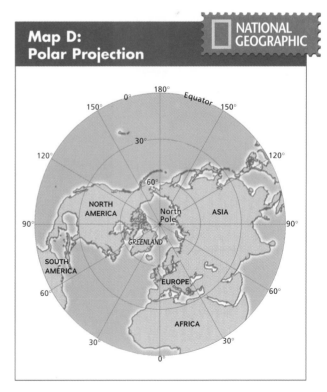

Map D:
Polar Projection

37

Stone Age Technology

What kind of technology was developed in the Paleolithic Era?

Lesson Outline
- Stone and Bone Tools
- Special Tools

READING STRATEGY

Copy this diagram. Then use it to compare modern technology in one circle with Stone Age technology in the other. Put shared technology in the middle.

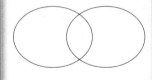

BUILD BACKGROUND

Think about the tools and items you use every day. You may have heard today's weather on the radio or ridden on a bus to school. Even your toothbrush is a type of tool.

Early people did not have such items. It took thousands of years for people to develop the tools we use today. However, each useful item, even a simple bone needle or a stone with a sharp edge, increased people's ability to survive.

STONE AND BONE TOOLS

As you read in Lesson 1, people of the Paleolithic Era had a toolbox of useful items. Think about what might have been in the toolbox of hunter-gatherers.

You may have thought of stone knives and axes, spears, and arrows with stone points. All of these were part of the **technology** of Stone Age people. Technology is the use of tools and skills to meet practical human needs. Until about 9,000 years ago, people had only wood, stone, or bone tools. These sharpened stones may not look like tools today. However, they were carefully crafted to make them into weapons or tools. Hunters shaped the stones by **flaking**, or chipping pieces off the edges. Also, although the tools were made of stone, the technology of producing them constantly changed.

READING CHECK How did flaking improve Stone Age tools?

Exploring TECHNOLOGY

Stone Tools

The hand axe was one of the first tools used by early people. These "axes" were really just rocks with sharp edges. Eventually, people found ways to make better stone tools for a variety of tasks.

Flaking Early people discovered that they could sharpen a rock by hitting it against another stone. Pieces of broken stone flaked off. After flaking, the stone had sharper edges than rock found in nature. The usual stone for flaking was flint, but obsidian and quartz were also used.

Advances Gradually, flaking techniques improved. Early people worked flint and other stones into flakes of different sizes and shapes that could be used for different purposes. Later, they sometimes baked the stone to make it harder.

How did flaking help early people to make better tools?

Cave art from the Sahara (far left) shows how people used bows to hunt. This stone tool (left) was made by a process called **flaking**.

SPECIAL TOOLS

Early people made tools for many purposes. There were spears and arrows with stone points for hunting as well as stone scrapers for cleaning hides. Other tools were made from parts of animals. For instance, bone needles could be made from deer antlers. Animal muscles were dried and used as thread.

Fire and Shelter

People also developed new skills to improve their lives. They used fire for warmth and for cooking. People also learned to build more permanent shelters from the materials in their environment. Archaeologists in Siberia have found a hut made of mammoth bones. In other places, they found huts made from tree branches.

Better Hunting Tools

Another invention was long-distance weapons such as the spear-thrower and the bow. It was safer to hunt wild animals from far away.

Chart Skill

1. On which continent were metal tools not used?

2. On which continent were simple stone tools used longest?

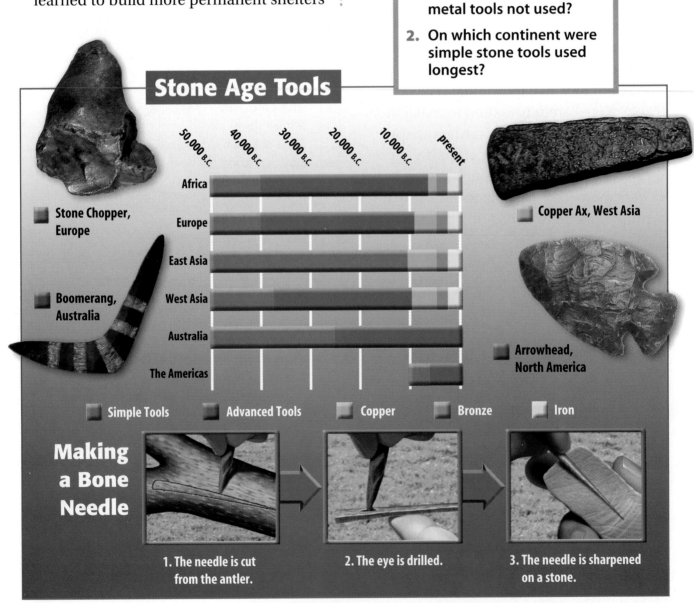

Stone Age Tools

50,000 B.C. | 40,000 B.C. | 30,000 B.C. | 20,000 B.C. | 10,000 B.C. | present

Africa
Europe
East Asia
West Asia
Australia
The Americas

Stone Chopper, Europe

Boomerang, Australia

Copper Ax, West Asia

Arrowhead, North America

Simple Tools | Advanced Tools | Copper | Bronze | Iron

Making a Bone Needle

1. The needle is cut from the antler.

2. The eye is drilled.

3. The needle is sharpened on a stone.

Over the course of many thousands of years, people also developed better stone tools. They began to notch the edges of stone tools, for example, and make them into different shapes. They also began to smooth and polish them. You can see some of these stone tools on the chart on page 40.

Beginning to Use Metals

In time, people discovered that they could use copper to make even stronger tools made of metal. Developing a more advanced technology allowed people to live more comfortably in their environments. In time, people began to use their technology not only to survive, but also to change the face of Earth.

What advances in technology did people in the Stone Age make over time?

This lamp from Lascaux Cave, France, was made about 37,000 years ago.

PUTTING IT TOGETHER

Human technology developed very slowly. In the beginning, people had only simple stone tools, but over thousands of years, they developed new and better tools. These tools helped early people adapt to a wide variety of environments. In the next lesson, you will read about another development that helped to shape the world of early humans.

Review and Assess

1. Write one sentence for each vocabulary word.

   flaking   technology

2. Why did Paleolithic people need bone needles?

3. How did technology change during the Paleolithic Era?

4. Explain why flaking was an important improvement in Stone Age **technology**.

5. What was an **effect** of people developing more advanced technology?

Suppose you are living in the Stone Age. Your group is looking for a new place to camp. Make a chart. List three features you would look for that might help you choose a new place to settle. Explain why these features are important.

Write a description that an archaeologist who had found a stone axe might make. It should include information about the people who made the axe.

41

Problem Solving

Early people solved many of their **problems** with technology. A problem is a question or issue that needs a solution.

For example, early people who hunted the wooly mammoth with its thick fur and thick skin had to figure out how to make long, very sharp stone tools.

LEARN THE SKILL

Follow these steps to solve a problem.

1. **Identify the problem.**
   Artun is a skilled hunter in a small band that just moved into a new area. The group is faced with a serious problem. To the east are vast marshes. The north has many animals, but another band of hunters chases away all strangers. In the south are high mountains. Artun's band wants to return to the west, but they left because there were few animals there to hunt.

2. **Gather information.**
   Artun sends a small group of scouts to see if there are animals in the mountains or if his band could cross a mountain pass. Another group is sent to watch the movements of the hunters to the north.

3. **Identify the options.**
   Artun tells his group what the scouts have learned. There are passes through the mountains, but they saw no animals and did not discover what is on the other side because the mountains are high. The scouts to the north have discovered a large river that the northern hunters never cross. No other people were seen across the river. The group can try to cross the mountains or the river or return to the west.

4. **List the possible consequences.**
   Each option, or choice, has a **consequence**, or result. The group does not know what they will find across the mountains. They know they will starve if they return to the west. The land across the river could have unfriendly people although none have been seen so far.

5. Choose a solution.

Artun's group decides to go north across the river, but to remain close to the river in case other hunters should appear.

6. Evaluate the solution.

The band settles into its new hunting grounds. No unfriendly people come near them. Based on this result, the band **evaluates**, or judges, the solution they chose. They decide they have found the best solution to their problem.

TRY THE SKILL

Suppose you are someone who lived during the Ice Age. Your region has been getting colder for years. Now, it is very cold and glaciers have appeared to the north. You and your band have to decide what to do if you are to survive.

Follow the steps on the previous page to solve this problem.

1. What is the problem facing you?

2. What information will help you solve the problem?

3. What are the possible options and consequences?

4. What is the best solution and why?

5. How might problem solving help you understand history better?

EXTEND THE SKILL

Understanding how to solve problems can also help you in your daily life. Think of a problem you have that involves the use of technology. Then use the problem-solving process to solve the problem.

● How can problem-solving skills help you in your daily life?

The Beginning of Agriculture

How did settling in villages change people's lives?

Lesson Outline
- The New Stone Age
- Catal Huyuk
- Crafts and Trades

VOCABULARY

migrate
Neolithic Era
agriculture
domesticate
surplus
specialize
civilization

READING STRATEGY

Make a chart like this one to compare and contrast. Write features about the life of hunter-gatherers in one column and features about the life of farmers in the other column.

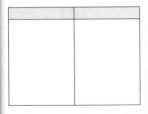

BUILD BACKGROUND

About 12,000 years ago, the Ice Age began to end. Earth became warmer, the glaciers shrank, and the level of the oceans began to rise. By the end of the Ice Age, Earth was a very different place from what it had been. In the Northern Hemisphere, the landscape had changed as glaciers melted. Coastlines changed as ocean waters rose.

People had **migrated** to most of the continents. To migrate means to move to a new place to live. In this lesson, you will read how people's lives changed.

40,000 B.C.	35,000 B.C.	30,000 B.C.	25,000 B.C.	20,000 B.C.	15,000 B.C.	10,000 B.C.	5000 B.C.	A.D. 1

You Are Here
10,000 B.C. – 4000 B.C.

THE NEW STONE AGE

As Earth's climate warmed, the number of plants and animals increased dramatically. This led to a change in the diets of some hunter-gatherers. They ate more wild grains and small animals. Many archaeologists think that some groups began to settle in areas with an abundance of natural resources.

The period of time when people began to settle permanently in one location is called the **Neolithic** (nee uh LITH ik) **Era**, or the New Stone Age. In this period, about 12,000 to 6,000 years ago, people still used stone tools, but new tools for specialized purposes were added.

The Rise of Agriculture

Agriculture began over a long period of time and in more than one place. Agriculture is the raising of crops and animals for human use. We do know it provided a way for people to live in large groups. However, people did not stop hunting all at once. At first, hunting was still easier than farming.

Over time, farming provided a steadier food supply, especially since the big game animals in many areas were hunted out of existence. People no longer needed to travel great distances to gather food.

People learned how to **domesticate** (duh MES tih kayt) plants and animals. To domesticate means "to train something to be useful to people." In addition to learning to plant seeds and care for plants such as wheat, barley, peas, and

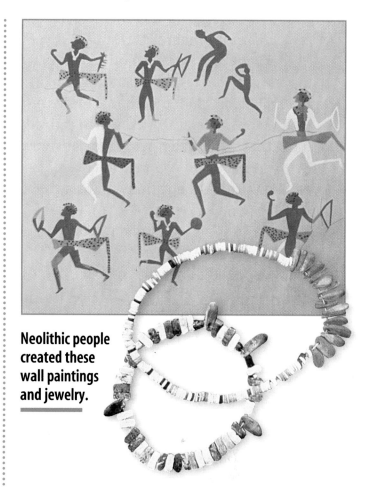

Neolithic people created these wall paintings and jewelry.

lentils, the first farmers also domesticated animals, such as wild goats, pigs, cattle, and sheep.

Domestication also means improving crops and animals. For example, farmers learned which wheat would yield the most grain, and planted it. They also bred wild sheep to produce sheep that had thicker layers of wool. Domesticated cattle provide more meat and milk than wild cattle do.

How did agriculture change the way people adapted to their environment?

45

CATAL HUYUK

Much of what we know about early agriculture comes from one of the world's first cities—**Catal Huyuk** (CHA tal HOO yuk). Today, it is a large mound on the banks of the Carsamba (chahr SHAHM bah) River in southern Turkey. This mound covers more than 32 acres, an area the size of 21 football fields. Underneath this ordinary-looking hill is Catal Huyuk, which thrived more than 8,500 years ago. Catal Huyuk is the largest ancient city ever uncovered by archaeologists. At one time, it was a city of 5,000 people.

Think of some ways that a 9,000-year-old city might be different from a city today. How would they be similar?

A City Without Streets

The houses in Catal Huyuk were sturdy. They had thick brick walls coated with white plaster. The flat roofs, though, were made of reeds placed on wooden beams. Houses were built against each other, perhaps to defend the city from attack. There were no streets in Catal Huyuk and no doors into the houses. People entered their homes through a hole in the roof, by climbing down ladders, as the Pueblo people of the American Southwest did.

Inside the House

From the outside, the houses of Catal Huyuk seemed plain. However, their interiors were often richly decorated. What may be the world's first wall paintings—of cattle, leopards, and plants—filled these rooms. This suggests that the people of Catal Huyuk valued their domestic crops and animals because they were important to the survival of people of the city.

Like many apartment buildings today, homes in Catal Huyuk were usually the

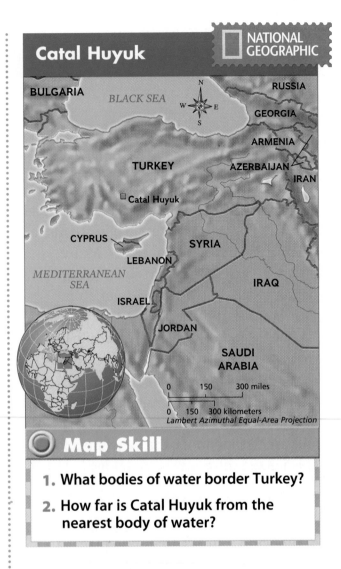

NATIONAL GEOGRAPHIC

Catal Huyuk

BULGARIA
BLACK SEA
RUSSIA
GEORGIA
ARMENIA
TURKEY
AZERBAIJAN
IRAN
Catal Huyuk
CYPRUS
SYRIA
LEBANON
MEDITERRANEAN SEA
IRAQ
ISRAEL
JORDAN
SAUDI ARABIA

0   150   300 miles
0   150   300 kilometers
Lambert Azimuthal Equal-Area Projection

Map Skill

1. **What bodies of water border Turkey?**
2. **How far is Catal Huyuk from the nearest body of water?**

same size and shape. Coming down from the roof, people entered a living room. Near the base of the ladder were a fireplace and an oven for heating and cooking. Raised platforms covered by reed mats were built into the walls. These platforms served as all-purpose sofas and beds. A tiny doorway led to the family's storage room. Large clay pots held wheat and barley.

Food Surpluses

People in Catal Huyuk depended on the grain stored in these clay pots. Agriculture created a food **surplus** that hunter-gatherers never had. A surplus is an extra supply of something. These extra crops in Catal Huyuk provided more food than a family needed throughout the year. In addition, cattle provided a steady supply of milk and meat.

The people who worked as farmers were able to provide food for all of the people of Catal Huyuk. There was also food left over for winter. However, farming for a whole community was a demanding job. It left farmers little time for other tasks.

Being able to create surpluses made it possible for some of the city's people to **specialize**, or do particular kinds of work. So, while some people farmed, other people made wheat into flour for bread. Still others specialized in making things such as tools, bricks, and pots. Since farmers could produce more food than their families needed, they could exchange their surplus food with workers who made other products.

The busy town grew until it had about 1,000 homes. Changes in community life sparked the growth of a complex new **civilization** (sihv uh luh ZAY shun) at Catal Huyuk. A civilization is a culture that has developed systems of specialization, religion, learning, and government. Many civilizations also developed cities.

How did the ability to produce surpluses affect the people of Catal Huyuk?

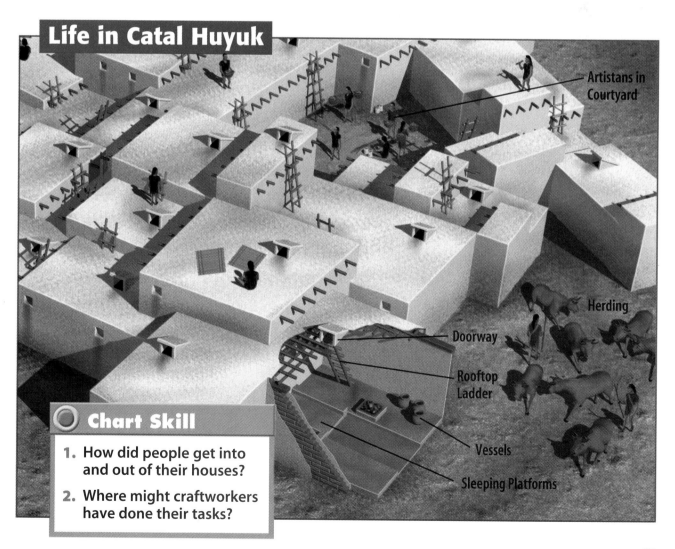

Life in Catal Huyuk

Artistans in Courtyard

Herding

Doorway

Rooftop Ladder

Vessels

Sleeping Platforms

◯ Chart Skill

1. **How did people get into and out of their houses?**

2. **Where might craftworkers have done their tasks?**

CRAFTS AND TRADES

Catal Huyuk was probably well known for its skilled craftworkers. These people developed the technology to make fine clay pots, woven cloth, and jewelry. These products were among the first of their kind in the world. By the age of 12, most children were already at work, learning from their mothers and fathers to make these products.

In time, the people of Catal Huyuk began to work with a new material: copper. Craftworkers made fires hot enough to soften pieces of copper ore. Then, they hammered the softened copper into the shapes of rings, beads, or pins.

The people of Catal Huyuk also made wool cloth. The wool from domestic sheep was separated and twisted into thread. Then the thread was woven into cloth on wooden looms.

An Active Trade

Catal Huyuk's crafts attracted people from other areas. In time, the city probably became an important center of trade, exchanging its products for the products of other cities or cultures.

One thing that people in Catal Huyuk had to trade was obsidian (ub SIHD ee un). Obsidian is a glassy, black rock used to make beautiful mirrors and razor-sharp knives. City residents probably traveled to a nearby volcano to gather the black stones. Craftworkers then made the obsidian into goods to trade.

Trade Grows and Spreads

Archaeologists have found the remains of goods and materials from other areas in Catal Huyuk. They believe, for example, that the people of Catal Huyuk probably traded obsidian knives and

Innovations in Agriculture

Date	c. 9,300 B.C.	c. 9,000 B.C.	c. 8,000 B.C.	c. 3,000 B.C.
Place	Dongting Lake, China	Zagros Mountains, Iraq	Chilca Canyon, Peru	Tehuacan Valley, Mexico
Innovation	Rice Farming	Domestication of Sheep	Sweet Potato	Maize

Chart Skill

1. Where and when did rice farming begin?
2. What crops began in the Americas?

arrowheads for wood from people who lived in oak forests miles away. The wood was needed for house-building. Red paint for temple decoration and copper ore for tools and jewelry were brought to the city from other regions. Pieces of Syrian pottery and even shells from the Red Sea have been found in Catal Huyuk. Archaeologists have found remains of the city's special obsidian goods in ancient settlements as far away as modern Syria.

READING CHECK Why did people come to trade in Catal Huyuk?

PUTTING IT TOGETHER

Agriculture made great changes in the way New Stone Age groups lived. The complex civilization of Catal Huyuk is a good example of these changes. However, there were more changes to come. Great civilizations began to grow up along other rivers. They left a record of their lives for us to read.

Artifacts from Catal Huyuk include this painting of a bull and a carved spoon and fork.

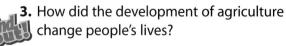

Review and Assess

1. Write one sentence for each vocabulary word.

   agriculture   **migrate**
   domesticate   **surplus**

2. During which period did people begin to settle in one place?

3. How did the development of agriculture change people's lives?

4. How did specialization affect the **culture** of Catal Huyuk?

5. **Compare** and **contrast** life in Catal Huyuk with life in Border Cave.

Based on what you have read in this lesson, make a product map of Catal Huyuk. Include a key for the items you include.

• •

Suppose you lived in Catal Huyuk thousands of years ago. **Write** a daily journal for one week of your life. Describe about what you do, what you eat, and how you earn a living.

Chapter 1 REVIEW

VOCABULARY REVIEW

Number a sheet of paper from 1 to 5. Beside each number write the word or term from the list below that matches the description.

domesticate   **surplus**

hunter-gatherers   **technology**

Paleolithic Era

1. A period of time when stone tools were commonly used

2. To train plants and animals to be useful to people

3. People who hunted animals and found plants to supply their needs

4. An extra supply of something, like food

5. The skills and tools we use to solve practical problems

CHAPTER COMPREHENSION

6. During the Paleolithic Era what covered most of the northern part of the world? How did people survive?

7. Where did archaeologists find what may have been the first tools used by humans?

8. What technological advances did people make in the New Stone Age?

9. How did the hunter-gatherers express themselves artistically?

10. What surplus items were made by people in Catal Huyuk?

11. Why did people travel to the city of Catal Huyuk?

12. **Write** a journal entry from the viewpoint of a craftworker in Catal Huyuk. Describe a workday and the goods or products you might make.

SKILL REVIEW

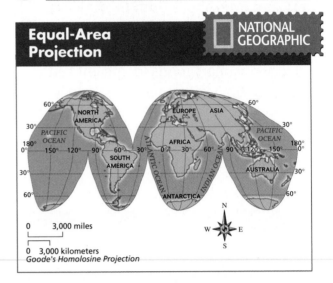

Goode's Homolosine Projection

13. **Geography Skill** What kind of map projection is shown above?

14. **Geography Skill** Why do flat maps of the world show distortion?

15. **Geography Skill** What are the advantages of the map above compared with the equal-area projection Map A on page 36?

16. **Geography Skill** On a mercator projection, where is the size of the land area most accurate, near the equator or far from the equator?

17. **Reading/Thinking Skill** What are the first two steps in solving a problem?

18. **Reading/Thinking Skill** Suppose that a person in the New Stone Age needed to solve the following problem: Our community needs food. What are the problem-solving steps to find a solution?

USING A TIME LINE

50,000 B.C.	40,000 B.C.	30,000 B.C.	20,000 B.C.	10,000 B.C.	A.D. 1

50,000 B.C.
Paleolithic Era; ice sheets cover Northern Hemisphere

40,000 B.C.
Early people inhabit Border Cave

30,000 B.C.
Rock paintings made in France and Spain

10,000 B.C.
Old Stone Age ends; New Stone Age begins

6500 B.C.
Catal Huyuk develops

4000 B.C.
New Stone Age ends

19. About how many years did the New Stone Age last?

20. Choose the event on the time line that you think shows a major turning point leading to the way we live today. Explain.

Writing **About Culture** Suppose you live in a small community of people in the Old Stone Age. Most of the time, your group follows herds of animals, but you have just found a large cave for the winter months. What would you do to make the cave livable?

Foldables

Use your Foldable to review what you have learned about early people and to compare and contrast their lifestyles and cultures. As you look at your notes in the pockets of your Foldable, mentally recall what you learned in each of the three lessons. Record any questions that you have on the back of your note cards. Discuss them with classmates or review the chapter to find answers.

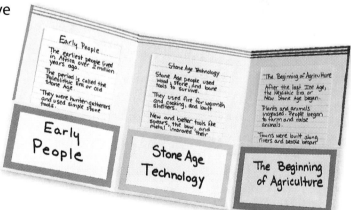

THE Big IDEAS ABOUT...

The Fertile Crescent

The first civilizations developed along rivers. Early agriculture depended on rivers for fertile soil and a plentiful supply of water. One early civilization appeared in a region called the Fertile Crescent, which was well-watered by the Tigris and Euphrates rivers. As people learned to work together to control the rivers, they built powerful cities. Read on to learn more about these first cities.

THE LAND BETWEEN THE RIVERS

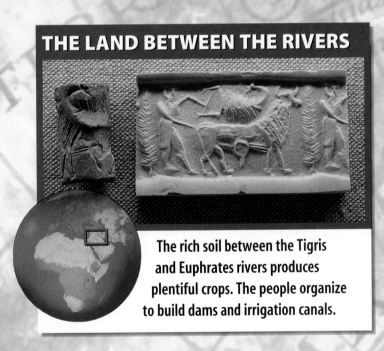

The rich soil between the Tigris and Euphrates rivers produces plentiful crops. The people organize to build dams and irrigation canals.

THE CITIES OF SUMER

The cities of the Fertile Crescent develop a complex civilization. Eventually, one city, Sumer, rules the entire region.

BABYLON AND ASSYRIA

Some cities of the Fertile Crescent form empires. The people of two empires, the Babylonians and the Assyrians, conquer large territories and develop a system of laws.

THE BIRTH OF JUDAISM

The western part of the Fertile Crescent is the birthplace of Judaism. The Jewish people have kept their heritage alive to this day.

Foldables

Make this Foldable study guide and use it to record what you learn about "The Fertile Crescent."

1. Fold a large sheet of paper in half like a hamburger.
2. Fold 1" tabs along the short sides of the hamburger.
3. Color these small tabs to represent the Tigris and Euphrates rivers. Label the tabs.
4. Draw lines dividing the inside of your Foldable into four horizontal sections. Label the four sections with lesson titles.

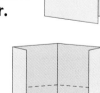

Geography of the Fertile Crescent

Find Out!

How did two great rivers affect life in the Fertile Crescent?

VOCABULARY

silt
drought
levee
irrigation
erosion

READING STRATEGY

In a chart like this one, write geographical features of Mesopotamia under "causes." Write how people adapted to them under "effects."

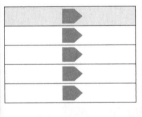

Lesson Outline
• The Land Between the Rivers
• Successful Farmers

BUILD BACKGROUND

"The flood ceased. . . .The landscape was as level as a flat roof. . . . Bowing low, I sat and wept. . . ."

This excerpt from an ancient story was written in a region of Western Asia called the **Fertile Crescent**. It was a lush green area through which two rivers, the **Tigris** (TI grihs) and the **Euphrates** (yoo FRAY teez), flowed. They made life possible in a dry region. However, the rivers also flooded the land.

THE LAND BETWEEN THE RIVERS

The ancient Greeks called the region between the Tigris and the Euphrates **Mesopotamia** (mes uh puh TAY mee uh). In Greek, Mesopotamia means "Land Between the Rivers."

Downhill to the Sea

Both the Tigris and Euphrates rivers begin in the Taurus Mountains of what is today Turkey. They continue to the plateau of present-day northern Iraq. In southern Iraq, the rivers flow across lower land to the Persian Gulf. The rivers deposit **silt** as they flow south, making the region a good place for farming. Silt is loose soil carried by water.

Farmers in southern Mesopotamia had to protect their fields from flooding each

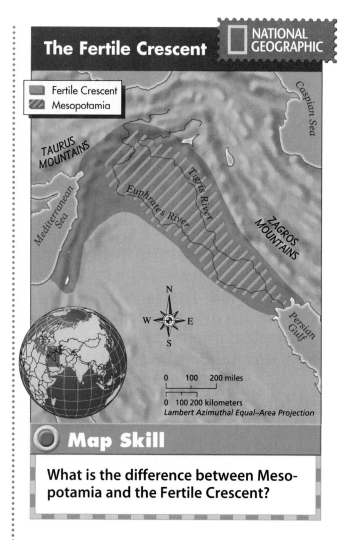

The Fertile Crescent — NATIONAL GEOGRAPHIC

Fertile Crescent
Mesopotamia

TAURUS MOUNTAINS
Caspian Sea
Mediterranean Sea
Euphrates River
Tigris River
ZAGROS MOUNTAINS
Persian Gulf

N W E S

0   100   200 miles
0 100 200 kilometers
Lambert Azimuthal Equal–Area Projection

Map Skill

What is the difference between Mesopotamia and the Fertile Crescent?

Exploring
TECHNOLOGY

Levees and Canals

The Tigris and Euphrates often burst into fields in fall, as the crops were about to be harvested. These floods destroyed crops, as well as lives and homes. Mesopotamian farmers found ways to control flooding.

Flood control To protect against floods, farmers built a system of **levees** (LEV eez) to keep the flood waters back. A levee is a wall that keeps a river within its banks.

Irrigation A system of canals to bring water to crops and fields is called **irrigation**. Mesopotamian farmers brought water from artificial lakes to irrigate their crops.

How did the Mesopotamians use technology to control their water supply?

Traditional boats continue to sail the Tigris and Euphrates rivers.

---

fall. During spring and summer, they needed water for their crops in the hot, dry climate. This region got only a few sprinkles of rain each year. **Droughts**, or long periods without rain, were a constant threat.

Northern Mesopotamia, in contrast, usually had enough rain to make some farming possible. Yet the earth of the northern plateau was mostly rocky and bad for farming.

READING CHECK

How were northern and southern Mesopotamia different?

SUCCESSFUL FARMERS

As you read in the lesson on Catal Huyuk, the first known agriculture began in western Asia about 8,500 years ago. The area's environment supported many wild plants, such as wheat and barley, which could be domesticated as crops. Animals, such as cattle, sheep, and pigs, were also found wild there.

Over time early Mesopotamian farmers learned how to grow many different crops. If you were able to go back in time, you would see fields of wheat and barley. These were the region's most important crops. You would also see gardens of beans, onions, lettuce, cucumbers, and herbs.

Ancient farmers also grew date palm, apple, and pomegranate trees. Because crops and trees need a lot of water, farmers often planted them along canal banks. There are few trees in the region today, but in ancient times large forests stretched from the Mediterranean Sea to the Persian Gulf.

Over time, people cut the trees for buildings or firewood. Tree roots hold soil in place, so much of the fertile soil dried up and blew away. The wearing away of soil by wind or water is called **erosion**. As a result, much of modern Mesopotamia is a desert due to erosion.

On the edges of farmland, you might have seen shepherds herding sheep and goats for their milk and wool. Ancient Mesopotamians also valued cattle. Cattle were work animals, and produced milk and meat. Herders guarded against wild animals. Lions were once common in this region, but today there are no lions in the Fertile Crescent. Why might this be true?

READING CHECK How did the Mesopotamians alter their region?

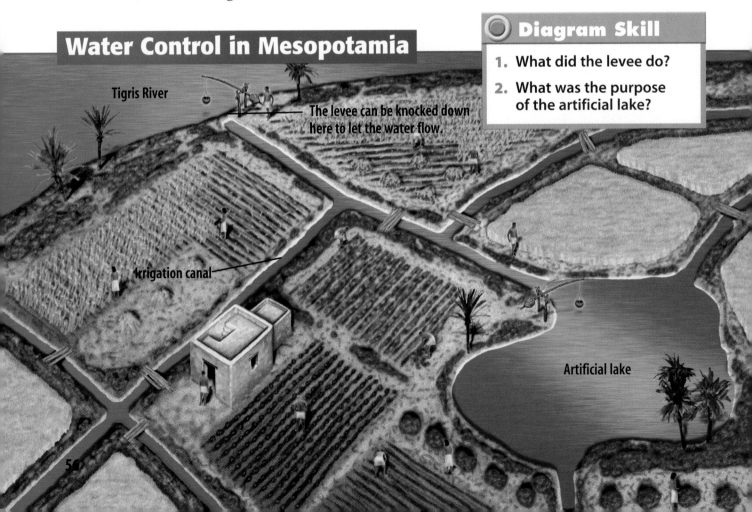

Water Control in Mesopotamia

Tigris River

The levee can be knocked down here to let the water flow.

Irrigation canal

Artificial lake

Diagram Skill

1. What did the levee do?

2. What was the purpose of the artificial lake?

PUTTING IT TOGETHER

Two great rivers, the Tigris and the Euphrates, influenced the environment of Mesopotamia. These rivers made it possible for farmers to raise surplus crops and to develop some of history's early cultures. Ancient Mesopotamians built irrigation canals.

In time, Mesopotamian farmers began producing more food than they could consume themselves. Not everyone had to be a farmer any more. Some people became soldiers, scholars, and leaders. Villages grew into cities as the Mesopotamians established a civilization. In the next lesson, you will learn about some of the accomplishments of this culture.

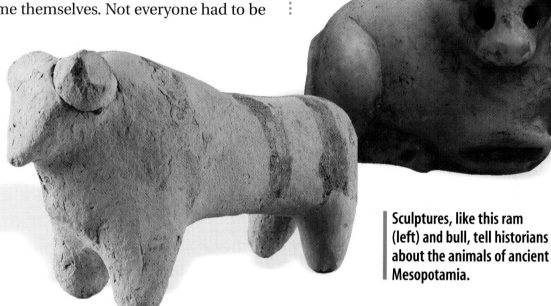

Sculptures, like this ram (left) and bull, tell historians about the animals of ancient Mesopotamia.

Review and Assess

1. Write one sentence for each vocabulary word.

   drought   erosion   irrigation

2. Where is Mesopotamia?

3. How did the Tigris and Euphrates rivers affect life in Mesopotamia?

4. How did Mesopotamian farmers alter their environment?

5. **Make a generalization** about the people of Mesopotamia. Give examples from the lesson to explain your generalization.

Look at the map on page 55. Write a tour guide entry for a journey from the Taurus Mountains to the Persian Gulf on either the Tigris or Euphrates river. Describe the scenery and the life you see along the river.

Suppose you are a farmer in ancient Mesopotamia. **Write** a speech persuading your village to build an irrigation canal.

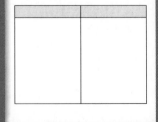
The Cities of Sumer

Find! out! *What kind of civilization did the Sumerians create?*

Lesson Outline

• Writing on Clay
• Sumer's City-States
• Daily Life in Sumer

BUILD BACKGROUND

"He had built the walls of the city, Uruk. Look at its brickwork! Nobody could build a better wall. It was made of copper and burnt brick, and was wide enough to walk upon."

Around 3000 B.C., a powerful king ruled Uruk. Uruk was one of about a dozen small cities in southern Mesopotamia, a region known as **Sumer** (SOO mur). Each city prized its independence. However, all Sumerians worshiped similar gods and had similar customs.

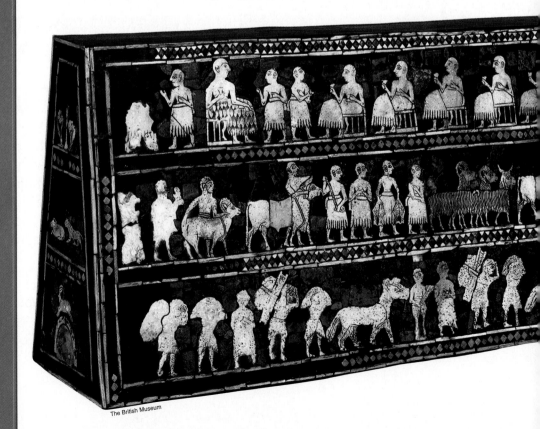

The British Museum

58

WRITING ON CLAY

The people of Sumer were great inventors. They made some of the world's first irrigation systems, wheeled vehicles, and sailboats. They developed the pottery wheel and ideas in science and math.

However, their most important invention was writing. Laws, letters, records, even riddles were written in a kind of writing we now call **cuneiform** (kyoo NEE uh form). Sumer's cuneiform writing system was one of the earliest writing systems in the world.

Cuneiform is made by scratching a wet clay tablet with a sharp reed pen. The oldest tablets date from about 3500 B.C. At this time, cuneiform was "picture writing." The symbols looked like the things they described. Over time, writers simplified the symbols to write them more quickly.

There were about 500 symbols used regularly in cuneiform! Cuneiform signs could represent ideas or sounds, as well as objects. For example, the sign for "arrow" called *ti* (TEE) looked like this . But *ti* can also mean "life", so the symbol could be used for that word, too. Look at the chart to see how cuneiform changed.

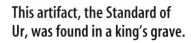

This artifact, the Standard of Ur, was found in a king's grave.

Sumer's Schools

Only a few boys, and almost no girls, went to school. First, the students learned to make clay tablets and "pens" from river reeds. Then, they practiced making the cuneiform letters. They also studied mathematics so that they could make accurate records. After years of studying, a student became a **scribe**, or an official writer. Trained scribes wrote everything. Scribes also recorded laws, legends, and songs.

READING CHECK Why was writing such an important development for the Sumerians?

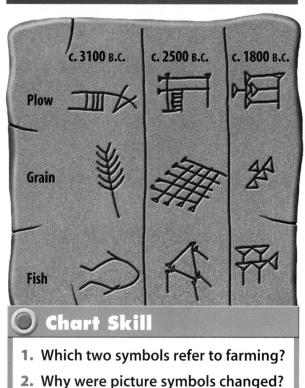

How Cuneiform Developed

	c. 3100 B.C.	c. 2500 B.C.	c. 1800 B.C.
Plow			
Grain			
Fish			

Chart Skill

1. Which two symbols refer to farming?
2. Why were picture symbols changed?

59

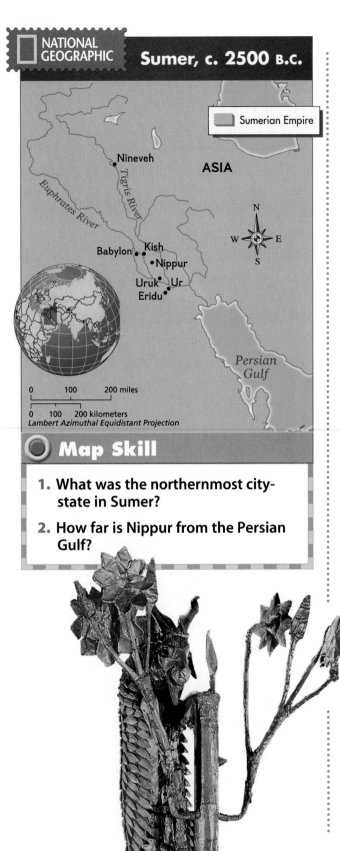

Sumer, c. 2500 B.C.

Sumerian Empire

Nineveh

ASIA

Tigris River

Euphrates River

Babylon Kish

• Nippur

Uruk • Ur

Eridu

Persian Gulf

N
W E
S

0   100   200 miles

0   100   200 kilometers
Lambert Azimuthal Equidistant Projection

Map Skill

1. **What was the northernmost city-state in Sumer?**

2. **How far is Nippur from the Persian Gulf?**

This jeweled ram in a golden bush was found in the tomb of a Sumerian princess in the 1920s.

SUMER'S CITY-STATES

You have read that cuneiform was developed around 3500 B.C. For the next thousand years, life in Sumer centered on its **city-states**. A city-state is a self-governing city that also governs nearby villages. The largest city-states were Ur, Uruk, and Eridu, all of which were near the Euphrates River. You can see these cities on the map on this page.

Walled Cities

City-states were often at war with each other. One of the main reasons they fought was to gain control of the precious waters of the Tigris and Euphrates rivers. Thick mud-brick walls protected each city-state. People entered and exited the city through large gates in these walls. People also gathered at these gates to buy fresh produce and other goods from nearby farms.

The king's palace could be seen from almost any point in the city. The king ruled the city-state from his palace, operated the courts and the army, and planned canals and other needed projects.

Sumerian Religion

At the center of most Sumerian cities was a tall, flattened pyramid made of mud-brick. This building was called a **ziggurat** (ZIHG oo rat). Each ziggurat had a temple on its flattened top.

Most historians believe that religion was the center of Sumerian life. The Sumerians practiced

polytheism, a belief in many gods and goddesses. They prayed to Ki for good harvests and to Enlil for rain. Each city and each family worshiped the gods that they believed protected them. The most famous goddess was Ishtar, the goddess of love and war. An important god was Enki, the god of water.

Through worship and giving gifts to the temples, Sumerians tried to please their gods and goddesses. One temple paid nearly 6,000 women and children to weave cloth for its goddess! This cloth covered the temple's statues and clothed temple workers. The priests and priestesses directed many workers in the temples. There were musicians, craftworkers, bakers, barbers, and scribes.

The City-States Unite

Enheduana (en hed WAHN uh) was a Sumerian priestess. She was also a scribe. About 4,000 years ago, she wrote a poem praising the gods and goddesses of Sumer. Her father was **Sargon**, a famous king of a city-state called Kish. In 2300 B.C. Sargon created the first great **empire** in history. An empire is a group of lands and people ruled by one government.

Sargon's empire began a new period in Mesopotamia's history. First, he united all the independent city-states of Sumer. Then, he extended his

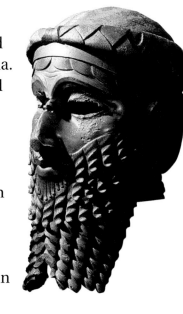

rule to the north and west, in modern Syria. His empire stretched over 900 miles–or about the distance from Los Angeles, California, to Portland, Oregon. Sargon built a new capital city called Akkad or Agada, although its location is not certain today. He ruled for about 56 years.

Because of cuneiform writing, Sargon was able to send messages and new laws across his kingdom. Cuneiform writing spread along trade routes across the Fertile Crescent. After Sargon's death, his empire broke up. The city-states regained their independence and went back to governing themselves.

READING CHECK How did Sargon use cuneiform to help rule his empire?

Sargon's (above) empire included many city-states, such as Ur, shown below in ruins today.

61

DAILY LIFE IN SUMER

From archaeological findings, we know that wealthy Sumerians lived in large, mud-brick houses with their servants and slaves. Slaves were usually prisoners of war from distant regions who were sold in Sumer's cities by slave merchants. Slaves wore a special haircut so they could be identified.

Sumerian Family Life

In poor families, everyone worked. Parents taught their crafts to their children, who worked from a young age. Their homes were small mud-walled huts with reed mats for sleeping. They used clay pots and baskets to store their few possessions.

These statues from Sumer show the clothing worn by men and women.

The head of both rich and poor Sumerian families was the father. Sons were taught to be future heads of their own homes. Daughters were taught to be obedient wives and mothers. Some wealthy girls became landowners and businesswomen, but they could never have the same rights as men. For example, a Sumerian woman, no matter how wealthy, could not divorce her husband. A man, however, had only to pay a fine to get a divorce.

Leisure Life in Sumer

Life was hard in Sumer, but there was time for fun. Many people enjoyed playing board games. Others enjoyed music and the great temple festivals. These festivals included parades, dancing, and feasts.

Sumerians were also storytellers. Their greatest legend told about a hero named **Gilgamesh** (GIHL guh mesh). He set out on a long journey to try to discover how humans could live forever. The legend also explains why the Sumerians honored him.

> *The great Gilgamesh was one who knew everything. He had seen all there was to see and done all there was to do . . . Gilgamesh was part god and part [man], and as strong as an ox. He was the strongest in the land, and the best fighter.*

In the legend, Gilgamesh had many adventures, but he never found the secret of living forever.

How did the lives of poor Sumerians compare to the lives of the wealthy?

The Wheel

Farmers in the Fertile Crescent may have been the first to use the wheel for work.

Speed and power Sumerian farmers had domesticated cattle and horses. The invention of the wheel made it possible to transport people and goods more quickly. A wheeled chariot pulled by horses could travel much faster than a human on foot. This gave the army an advantage. War chariots became a terrifying force in the Fertile Crescent.

Longer distances Before the invention of the wheel, most people traveled short distances over land. The invention of the wheel allowed people to move large loads and products for longer distances. This greatly improved trade.

How did the wheel improve farming and trade?

PUTTING IT TOGETHER

The ancient Sumerians were among the first to develop writing. Their cuneiform records have given historians valuable clues about the daily life of Sumer. These records include poetry, legends, and many of their laws. Because they left written records, the legacy of Mesopotamia has not been lost.

Among Sumer's many achievements were cuneiform writing and wheeled carts like this toy.

Review and Assess

1. Write one sentence for each vocabulary word or term.

   city-state   **polytheism**
   scribe   **empire**
   ziggurat

2. How did Sargon change life in Mesopotamia?

3. What were some features of Sumerian civilization?

4. How might the invention of the wheel have affected the **economy** of Sumer?

5. What was an **effect** of Sargon's decision to create an empire in Sumer?

Suppose you were a wheat merchant in Mesopotamia. Trace a map of the Fertile Crescent. Draw the route you would take from Sumer to reach the Mediterranean.

Write a postcard from a Sumerian city. Describe all the buildings and craft-workers you see during your visit.

Reading Time Lines

Archaeologists can tell us about the history of the Mesopotamians from remains, such as cuneiform records, which include dates of many kings and events.

One way to study these events is to use a **time line**. A time line is a diagram of events arranged in the order in which they took place. It gives dates and notes events.

VOCABULARY
time line
century
decade

Mesopotamia, 3900–1600 B.C.

c. 3500 B.C.
First cuneiform tablets

2750 B.C.
Gilgamesh rules Uruk

2100 B.C.
Sumerians reconquer Mesopotamia

4000 B.C.　　3500 B.C.　　3000 B.C.　　2500 B.C.　　2000 B.C.　　1500 B.C.

c. 3900 B.C.
The first Mesopotamian cities

c. 2900 B.C.
Sumerian civilization begins

2334 B.C.
Sargon begins his reign

c. 1600 B.C.
Hittites invade Mesopotamia

LEARN THE SKILL

Use the following steps to learn about time lines.

1. **Identify the time span.**
   The time line on this page begins in the year 3900 B.C. and ends at 1600 B.C.

2. **Identify the periods into which the time line is divided.**
   The time periods for this time line are 500 years each, or five centuries. A **century** is 100 years. A ten-year time period is a **decade**. Usually the periods of time on a time line are equal. A jagged break in a time line means that a number of years have been left out. The letter c stands for *circa*,

which is Latin for "about." Therefore, "c. 3900" means "about the year 3900."

3. **Identify the important events.**
   The events are: c. 3900 B.C. The first Mesopotamian cities; c. 3500 B.C. First cuneiform tablets; c. 2900 B.C. Sumerian civilization begins; and c. 1600 B.C. Hittites invade Mesopotamia.

4. **Identify the labels on the time line.**
   Notice the abbreviation B.C. The abbreviation B.C. stands for "before Christ." It identifies an event that took place before Christ, or before Jesus was born about 2,000 years ago. To read B.C. dates you need to remember that the higher the number, the earlier that year is in history.

The abbreviation A.D. means *anno Domini*, or "In the Year of the Lord" in Latin. A.D. is used for dates that occurred after the birth of Jesus. Sometimes the terms B.C.E. (before the common era) and C.E. (the common era) are used instead.

TRY THE SKILL

1. What is the time span covered in the time line below?

2. How many years are in each period in the time line below?

3. What labels are used on the time line?

EXTEND THE SKILL

Read the following paragraphs. Then, use the information to make a time line.

Sargon, the founder of the Akkadian Empire, reigned from about 2334 B.C. to 2278 B.C. After Sargon's death, his son Rimush defended his father's lands. He was assassinated after eight years. Then his brother, Manishtushu, ruled from about 2270 B.C. to 2255 B.C.

Manishtushu's son, Naram-Sin, ruled about 37 years. He was the first Mesopotamian king who claimed to be a god. Following Naram-Sin's death in 2218 B.C., the Akkadian Empire began to weaken.

● How can making a time line help you understand history?

This stone carving, called the "Stele of the Vultures," records a victory of a Sumerian king.

Mesopotamia, 2300–611 B.C.

1750 B.C.
Babylonian
empire begins

689 B.C.
Cities revolt
against Assyria

2400 B.C.   2000 B.C.   1600 B.C.   1200 B.C.   800 B.C.   400 B.C.

2300 B.C.
Sargon's
Sumerian
Empire begins

1400 B.C.
Assyrian Empire
begins

611 B.C.
Assyria's capital
is destroyed

Lesson 3

Babylon and Assyria

Find Out!

How were Assyria and Babylonia alike and different?

Lesson Outline
- Powerful New Kingdoms
- The Laws of Hammurabi
- A Common Heritage

VOCABULARY

code of law
aqueduct

PEOPLE

Hammurabi

READING STRATEGY

Copy this chart. Write data about Assyria in one circle and data about Babylonia in the other circle. Write common features in the center.

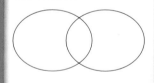

BUILD BACKGROUND

"The people . . . feared to engage in battle with me; they . . . fled like birds to the peaks of the lofty mountains. The terror of Ashur my Lord [king] overwhelmed them." These are the words of a king who ruled Mesopotamia in about 1150 B.C.

Ashur, later known as **Assyria**, was a large kingdom to the north of Sumer. To defend themselves, the people of Assyria developed a powerful army led into battle by their kings. By the early 1100s B.C., Assyria had conquered much of Mesopotamia.

POWERFUL NEW KINGDOMS

As you read, Sargon ruled Sumer for about 56 years. The empire he established united Mesopotamia and ruled it for about 100 years.

The Growth of Assyria

Some of the other city-states in Mesopotamia began to expand. One of them was about 400 miles north of Sumer. It was called Ashur, which was also the name of its chief god. "The Land of Ashur," or Assyria, had its own language and its own gods. However, it shared the traditions of Mesopotamia. For example, it used cuneiform and had conquered nearby cities. Most Assyrians lived in cities or were farmers, raising mainly barley and dairy cattle. Its largest cities were Ashur and **Nineveh**.

A King to the South

At around the same time, a powerful city-state in southern Mesopotamia, called Babylon, began to reunite the city-states of Sumer. Its king, **Hammurabi** (hah moo RAH bee), built dams across the Euphrates River. This gave him the power to control the river's water flow to cause floods or droughts downstream. City-states below Babylon had to cooperate with Hammurabi or face disaster. By 1750 B.C., Hammurabi controlled all of Mesopotamia including Ashur and Nin-

The Ishtar Gate was one of the main gates of Babylon.

eveh. Because his capital was Babylon, his empire was called **Babylonia**.

Silver, timber, copper, wine, and other trade goods from the Fertile Crescent and Turkey passed through Babylon. Soon Babylon became the wealthy and powerful capital of a great empire.

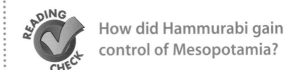

READING CHECK How did Hammurabi gain control of Mesopotamia?

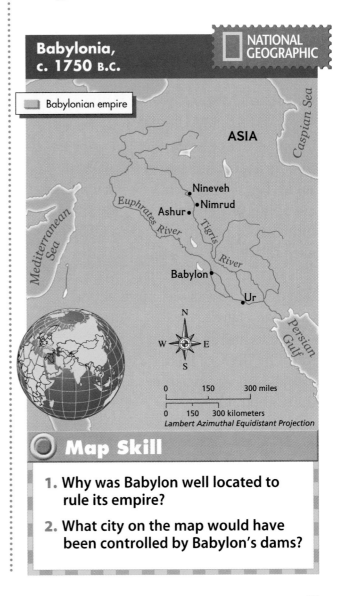

Babylonia, c. 1750 B.C.

NATIONAL GEOGRAPHIC

Babylonian empire

ASIA

Caspian Sea

Nineveh
Nimrud
Ashur
Euphrates River
Tigris River

Mediterranean Sea

Babylon

Ur

Persian Gulf

N W E S

| 0 | 150 | 300 miles |
| 0 | 150 | 300 kilometers |

Lambert Azimuthal Equidistant Projection

Map Skill

1. Why was Babylon well located to rule its empire?

2. What city on the map would have been controlled by Babylon's dams?

67

THE LAWS OF HAMMURABI

Hammurabi ruled Babylon, much as the Sumerian kings had ruled their cities. He ordered the building and repair of canals. He also acted as a judge, using traditional Sumerian laws to make his legal decisions.

We know about the laws of Hammurabi because of a discovery made in 1901. An archaeologist discovered a six-foot pillar with a picture of Hammurabi and 200 of his laws carved in cuneiform letters. Historians could now study the laws of Hammurabi, written 4,000 years earlier.

This **code of law** is called the Code of Hammurabi. A code of law is a written collection of the laws that apply to the people ruled by one government.

Words to Live By

Copies of Hammurabi's laws were found all over his empire. This means that he expected all citizens to obey them. Hammurabi's laws dealt with everything. There were laws for divorce, for workers' pay, for doctors' fees, and even for clumsy barbers! The code also tells us that Babylonia had slavery and that everyone was not equal under the code of laws.

The following excerpt is from the Code of Hammurabi. It tells you something about justice in Babylonia.

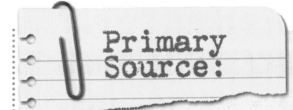

Primary Source:

excerpt from
the Code of Hammurabi
— about 1800 B.C.

[So] that the strong may not oppress the weak, to give justice to the orphan and the widow, I have inscribed my precious words. . . .

If a Freeman has put out the eye of another Freeman, they shall put out his eye.

If he breaks the bone of another Freeman, they shall break his bone.

If he puts out the eye of a Poor Man, or breaks the bone of a Poor Man, he shall pay 1 mina [17.5 ounces] of silver. If he puts out the eye of the Slave of another Freeman, . . . he shall pay half his price.

If any one be too lazy to keep his dam in proper condition . . . if then the dam break and all the fields be flooded; then shall he . . . be sold for money [as a slave], and the money shall replace the corn which he has . . . ruined.

What do Hammurabi's laws tell us about the values of Babylonian society?

Musée de Louvre

A Time of War

After the death of Hammurabi, the Babylonian Empire began to weaken. Ashur and Nineveh were among the first cities to break away. Assyria then began wars to conquer the Fertile Crescent.

Between 1400 and 600 B.C. Assyria fought many wars against Babylon and other city-states. By 600 B.C., the Assyrian Empire stretched from Egypt to the Persian Gulf and north into the area that is modern Turkey.

Assyria's armies were famous and feared because they had new ways of making war. They used special battering rams and towers on wheels to destroy the walls of enemy cities. The Assyrians were also among the first people to use fast, horse-drawn chariots for war. Warriors in chariots were both faster and more dangerous in battle.

Assyrian City Life

The Assyrians brought prisoners of war to their growing cities as slaves. These slaves worked farmlands or were put to work on building projects. Some prisoners managed to escape and return to their homes. Others started families and stayed in Assyria. They learned new skills and became Assyrian citizens. Assyrian men were famous as hunters, soldiers, and government leaders. Assyrian women had no legal rights. They stayed home and cared for their families.

 READING CHECK Why was Assyria able to conquer all of its neighbors so easily?

A war chariot leads Assyrian soldiers into battle in this stone carving from the royal palace in Nineveh.

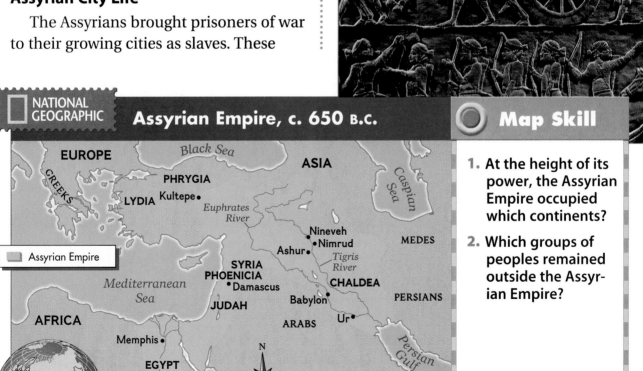

NATIONAL GEOGRAPHIC

Assyrian Empire, c. 650 B.C.

EUROPE
Black Sea
ASIA
PHRYGIA
GREEKS
LYDIA   Kultepe•
Euphrates River
Caspian Sea
•Nineveh
•Nimrud
Ashur•
MEDES
Tigris River
SYRIA
PHOENICIA
•Damascus
CHALDEA
☐ Assyrian Empire
Mediterranean Sea
JUDAH
Babylon•
PERSIANS
Ur•
AFRICA
ARABS
Memphis•
Persian Gulf
EGYPT
Nile River
Thebes•
Red Sea

N W E S

0   150   300 miles
0   150   300 kilometers
Lambert Azimuthal Equidistant Projection

Map Skill

1. At the height of its power, the Assyrian Empire occupied which continents?

2. Which groups of peoples remained outside the Assyrian Empire?

69

A COMMON HERITAGE

The rulers of Assyria deeply respected Babylon's culture. The Assyrians collected large libraries of Sumerian and Babylonian texts. Almost all of the knowledge we have of Babylon comes from records in Nineveh's royal library.

Nineveh was on the Tigris River, which made trade easy and provided water. One of Nineveh's rulers brought water from even farther away. He constructed a raised waterway called an **aqueduct**. It carried water from 30 miles away.

Nineveh Is Destroyed

In 689 B.C. the Assyrian king was threatened by a revolt in Babylon. He ordered the city to be destroyed. His soldiers looted Babylon's temples and burned its homes and palaces. They flooded Babylon with river water.

Babylon fought back. Finally, in 611 B.C. Babylon and its allies destroyed Nineveh. Assyria never recovered, but Babylon had one last period of glory.

READING CHECK Why and how was the Assyrian Empire defeated?

Aerial View of Babylon

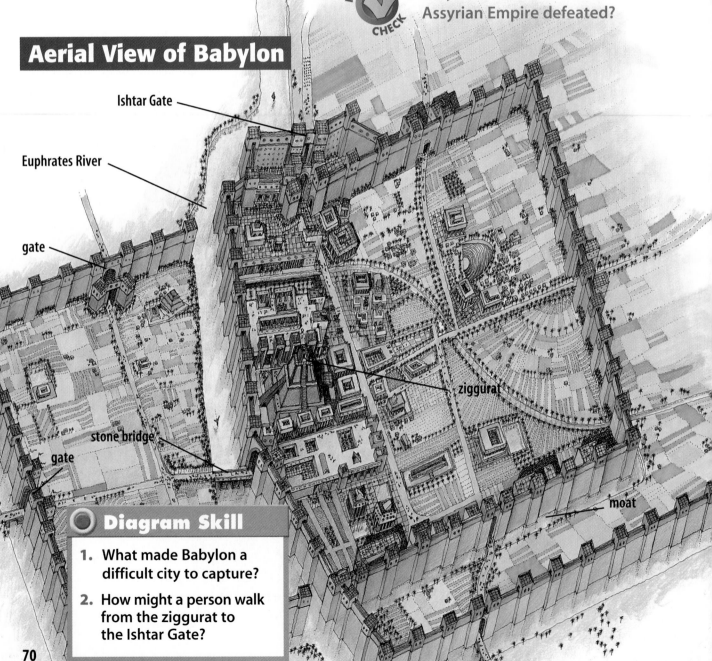

Ishtar Gate

Euphrates River

gate

stone bridge

gate

ziggurat

moat

◉ Diagram Skill

1. What made Babylon a difficult city to capture?

2. How might a person walk from the ziggurat to the Ishtar Gate?

HISTORY MYSTERY

Did the Hanging Gardens of Babylon exist?

The Hanging Gardens of Babylon were one of the Seven Wonders of the World. However, it is possible that they never existed. The Greek who included them in the list was repeating a legend about a Babylonian king. The king built the gardens to please a wife who missed her home in the mountains. The gardens are not mentioned in Babylonian records, and archaeologists have found no clues in the ruins of Babylon. Most historians today agree that the Hanging Gardens are probably a myth.

Why are the Hanging Gardens considered a myth today?

PUTTING IT TOGETHER

For over 1,000 years Babylon was at the center of Mesopotamian civilization. Under kings such as Hammurabi, its traditions built on the culture of Sumer to excel in literature and the arts. Even after they conquered Babylon, the Assyrians recognized that it was the most important city of Mesopotamia. The two cities shared gods and many traditions. After the defeat of Assyria, Babylon lost its power but continued as a rich and important city.

This elegant dagger might have been carried by a military officer.

Review and Assess

1. Write one sentence for each vocabulary term.

   aqueduct   code of law

2. Why did Hammurabi send copies of his law code all over his empire?

3. In what ways were Babylon and Assyria alike? How were they different?

Find Out!

4. How did the Assyrians bring water to their cities?

5. How did Hammurabi **solve the problem** of getting other city-states to cooperate with his plans?

Look at the map on page 69. Make a two-column chart. In one column, list the present-day countries that are located in the area of the Assyrian Empire. In the second column, list the cities that were inside the Assyrian Empire.

● ●

Write a letter for the king of Babylon to send to the rulers of other Mesopotamian cities. Try to convince the rulers to join Babylon in ending Assyria's rule.

The Birth of Judaism

Lesson Outline
- Abraham
- Moses Leads the Israelites
- The Kingdom of Israel

VOCABULARY

Judaism
covenant
prophet
Torah
monotheism
Ten Commandments
Diaspora

PEOPLE

Abraham
Moses
David
Solomon

READING STRATEGY

Copy this chart. Write **Judaism** in the center circle. Write details about this religion in the surrounding circles.

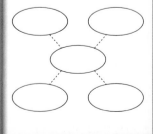

BUILD BACKGROUND

"And God spoke all these words, saying, I am the Lord thy God, who has brought you out of the land of Egypt, out of the house of bondage [slavery]. You shall have no other gods before me. You shall not make . . . any graven image [statues] . . .' "

In the late 1700s B.C., Jews began recording their beginnings. The early history of these people and their religion, known as **Judaism**, is found in the Hebrew Bible. The Hebrew Bible is considered sacred by Jews and Christians and is honored by Muslims.

You Are Here
1700 B.C. – 586 B.C.

ABRAHAM

According to the first book of the Hebrew Bible, the Jewish people are the descendants of a family that lived in the city-state of Ur. The Bible tells about a man named **Abraham**, and his wife Sarah:

The Lord said to Abraham: "Go forth from your native land and from your father's house to the land that I will show you. I will make of you a great nation, and I will bless you . . . ."

A Covenant with God

Abraham and Sarah set out. The travelers probably traveled on the trade routes that linked the major cities of the Fertile Crescent. Look at the map on this page to see their route. At last Abraham arrived in **Canaan**. The Bible says that God made the following **covenant**, or special agreement, with him.

I will establish My covenant with you, and I will make you exceedingly numerous. . . . I assign the land you sojourn [rest] in to you and your offspring to come. . . . I will be their God.

Jewish people consider this covenant to be the beginning of their history. Later, their descendants would become known as the people of Israel, or Israelites, after Abraham's grandson, Israel. They also came to be known as Jews.

Modern Israel (left) is part of ancient Canaan.

Migrating to Egypt

The Hebrew Bible says that there was a time of terrible hunger in Canaan. In about 1600 B.C. the people of Israel migrated to Egypt, where there was food.

The people of Israel were welcomed, but the Hebrew Bible says a new ruler "set taskmasters over [the people of Israel] to oppress them with forced labor." The people of Israel were enslaved.

READING CHECK What did God's covenant with Abraham provide?

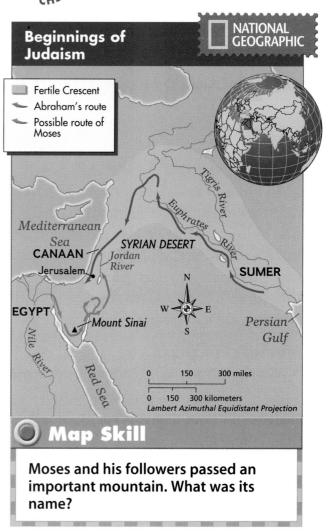

Beginnings of Judaism

NATIONAL GEOGRAPHIC

- Fertile Crescent
- Abraham's route
- Possible route of Moses

Mediterranean Sea
Tigris River
Euphrates River
SYRIAN DESERT
CANAAN
Jordan River
Jerusalem
SUMER
EGYPT
Mount Sinai
Nile River
Persian Gulf
Red Sea

0   150   300 miles
0   150   300 kilometers
Lambert Azimuthal Equidistant Projection

Map Skill

Moses and his followers passed an important mountain. What was its name?

73

These traditional foods and spices (right) remind Jews of the journey from Egypt which is shown above.

MOSES LEADS THE ISRAELITES

In time, a man named **Moses** rose to lead the Israelites. The Hebrew Bible tells that Moses was born to Israelite parents but was adopted as a baby by the pharaoh's daughter. Raised in the royal household of the pharaoh, Moses shared the wealth and power of ancient Egypt's rulers.

Moses as Prophet

One day, the Hebrew Bible says, Moses saw an Egyptian beating an enslaved Israelite. Furious at such cruelty, Moses killed the man and fled into the desert, to the land of Midian. Scholars think Midian was in present-day Saudi Arabia. Moses stayed there for many years, until God persuaded him to return to Egypt and lead his people out of slavery to Canaan.

At first Moses protested, saying, "Please, O Lord, I have never been a man of words. . . ." In the end, however, Moses obeyed God and made the long trek back to Egypt.

The Israelites now saw Moses as a **prophet**, or a person who speaks for God. He tried to convince the pharaoh to free the Israelites. Moses finally decided to lead them to safety.

The Torah

The Hebrew Bible tells how Moses led the Israelites out of Egypt. To this day Jews remember their escape to freedom during the holiday known as Passover.

Moses led the Israelites into the wilderness of eastern Egypt. There they wandered for 40 difficult years. Early in their journey the Israelites traveled to a mountain in the Sinai peninsula called **Mount Sinai**. Find Mount Sinai on the map on page 73. There, God gave Moses the first five books of the Hebrew Bible. They are called the **Torah** in Hebrew, from a word that means "to teach."

Some of the laws given to Moses are similar to laws that were common in Babylonia. Like the Code of Hammurabi, for example, the Torah had laws that forbade stealing and hurting others. In one very important way, however, the Torah was different. The God of the Israelites forbade them to worship any other gods. Belief in only one God is known as **monotheism** [mon oh THEE izm]. It set the Israelites apart from the other people in the Fertile Crescent and from most other ancient religions.

Among the laws that God gave Moses were the **Ten Commandments**. These commandments became the core of the Jewish religion and teachings.

READING CHECK How did Moses help the Jewish people?

Primary Source:

excerpt from
the Ten Commandments
— Exodus 20:1–4

1. *I the Lord am your God....You shall have no other gods besides Me.*

2. *You shall not make for yourself a sculptured image, or any likeness of what is in heaven above, or on the earth below....You shall not bow down to them or serve them.*

3. *You shall not swear falsely by the name of the Lord your God.*

4. *Remember the Sabbath [day of rest] and keep it holy.*

5. *Honor your father and your mother.*

6. *You shall not murder.*

7. *You shall not commit adultery.*

8. *You shall not steal.*

9. *You shall not bear false witness against your neighbor.*

10. *You shall not covet [desire]... anything that is your neighbor's.*

Which commandments require a person to tell the truth?

THE KINGDOM OF ISRAEL

After 40 years in the wilderness, the Israelites crossed the Jordan River into Canaan. Moses, however, was not with them. He had died just before they crossed the Jordan River.

The Nation of Israel

In Canaan, the Hebrews defeated several kings and established a nation of their own. They called their nation Israel. Israel became a powerful kingdom under the leadership of King **David**. David made the city of **Jerusalem** his capital in about 1000 B.C. Jerusalem became even more important to Israel when David's son **Solomon** built a great temple there. It was at the time of Solomon that priests and scribes began to write the Torah. As Solomon's capital, Jerusalem became a center of both religious and political life for the Jews. Jerusalem remains a center of religious and political life today.

The Babylonian Exile

After Solomon's death, in about 928 B.C., the kingdom of Israel split into two kingdoms. The northern kingdom kept the name **Israel**. It was conquered by the Assyrians in 721 B.C. The southern kingdom was called Judah. The name "Jew" comes from **Judah**. The southern kingdom survived until 586 B.C. In that year Babylonian armies destroyed Jerusalem and Solomon's temple. They also led many Jews away to Babylon. Scattering Jews away from their homeland is called the **Diaspora** (digh AS puh ruh).

Why are kings David and Solomon important in the history of Jerusalem?

PUTTING IT TOGETHER

From the Hebrew Bible we learn about the beginning of the world's first religion based on the belief in a single God. On the way out of slavery in Egypt, the Israelites stopped at Mount Sinai where Moses received a body of laws, the Ten Commandments. For many centuries, these laws have guided the lives not only of Jews but also of Christians and Muslims. The Jews were later forced out of their homeland and scattered to many lands, but they have continued to follow the practices of their faith. As you will read in later chapters, Christianity and Islam later adopted many of the ideas of Judaism.

The *menorah* is a candlestick used in Jewish worship and in temples. (left).

Review and Assess

1. Write one sentence for each vocabulary term.

covenant	**prophet**
Diaspora	**Ten Commandments**
monotheism	**Torah**

2. How did Moses change Judaism?

3. How does the Torah help to shape Judaism?

4. Why is the invention of writing in Mesopotamia important to Judaism?

5. **Compare** and **contrast** Judaism with Mesopotamian religions.

Activities

Look at the map on page 73. Copy the map, showing the probable route of Moses from Egypt to Canaan. Write the names of the modern countries the route crosses.

Choose an event from the lesson, such as the escape from Egypt. **Write** a news article about the event. Be sure to add an interesting headline.

Chapter 2 REVIEW

VOCABULARY REVIEW

Number a sheet of paper from 1 to 6. Beside each number write the word from the list below that best completes the sentence.

aqueduct	cuneiform
city-state	irrigation
covenant	polytheism

1. Farmers watered their crops by building ____ systems.
2. A ____ is a city that governs itself and also nearby villages.
3. Sumer's ____ writing system was one of the first in the world.
4. Nineveh's king built a (an) ____ that brought water from more than 30 miles away.
5. The Torah says that God made a special agreement, or ____, with Abraham.
6. ____ is the belief in many gods and goddesses.

CHAPTER COMPREHENSION

7. What two rivers run through the Fertile Crescent?
8. How did the farmers in Mesopotamia control flooding?
9. Why might scribes own tablets like the one to the right?
10. What was the Code of Hammurabi? What is an example of a law from that code?
11. With which empires were the sister cities of Nineveh and Babylon associated?
12. What nation did the Hebrews establish in Canaan?
13. **Write** a paragraph about how the invention of the wheel affected the people of Mesopotamia.

SKILL REVIEW

750 B.C.	700 B.C.	650 B.C.	600 B.C.	550 B.C.

721 B.C.	689 B.C.	611 B.C.	586 B.C.
Assyria conquers Israel	Southern cities revolt against Assyria	Babylon conquers Nineveh	Babylon conquers Jerusalem

14. **Study Skill** What is a time line?
15. **Study Skill** What are the time periods on this time line?
16. **Study Skill** What do the letters in the date 689 B.C. mean?
17. **Study Skill** In a time line, what does a jagged line mean?
18. **Study Skill** On this time line, how many years passed between the revolt of the southern cities and the destruction of Nineveh?

USING A TIME LINE

3500 B.C.	3000 B.C.	2500 B.C.	2000 B.C.	1500 B.C.	1000 B.C.	500 B.C.	A.D. 1

3500 B.C. Cuneiform writing invented in Mesopotamia

3000 B.C. Sumerians build first city-states

2300 B.C. Sargon creates a Sumerian empire

1750 B.C. Hammurabi creates the Babylonian Empire

1400 B.C. Assyrian Empire begins 800 years of fighting against Babylonia

1000 B.C. King David makes Jerusalem the capital of Israel

586 B.C. Babylonians destroy Jerusalem

19. Was the Babylonian Empire created before or after the empire created by Sargon? About how long before or after?

20. Which event on the time line refers to a most important advance in technology? Explain.

Activity

Writing **About Culture** Suppose you went on a journey to Babylon at the height of the Babylonian Empire. Write a letter home describing what you are doing and what you see in the city. What impresses you most?

Foldables

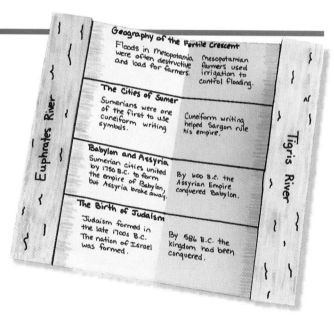

Use your Foldable to review what you have learned about the Fertile Crescent. As you look at the rivers on the inside of your Foldable, mentally recall major historic events that occurred in this region. Review what you learned about the people of this area and how they used their environment to provide for their basic needs—food, shelter, clothing, transportation, and the development of cities. Record any questions that you have. Discuss them with classmates or review the chapter to find answers.

The Nile River Valley

The people who lived along the fertile banks of the Nile River developed a great civilization. These ancient Egyptians built huge stone monuments and gigantic temples. They also created a system of writing and a culture that lasted for thousands of years.

THE GIFT OF THE NILE

On its way to the Mediterranean Sea, the Nile River carries rich soil to the lowlands of Egypt. This "gift of the Nile" makes the civilization of ancient Egypt possible.

THE KINGDOMS OF EGYPT

More than 5,000 years ago, a daring warrior united the two kingdoms, making Egypt the most powerful civilization of that time.

ANCIENT EGYPTIAN CULTURE

A little over 4,000 years ago, new rulers lead ancient Egypt to a time of prosperity and change. They expand the empire and its trade.

NUBIAN AND KUSHITE CIVILIZATIONS

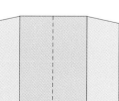

Nubia and Kush grow strong from trade with other regions of Africa. They adopt many aspects of Egyptian culture, and in time their kings rule Egypt.

Foldables

Make this Foldable study guide and use it to record what you learn about "The Nile Valley."

1. Fold a large sheet of paper into a shutterfold.
2. Draw a large map of the Nile River down the center of the front cover of your Foldable.
3. Divide the inside into four equal columns, and label them with the lesson titles.

The Gift of the Nile

Find! out!
How did the Nile River affect the life of the people of Egypt?

VOCABULARY

delta

Lesson Outline
• The Nile River
• High Water or Hunger

READING STRATEGY

Copy this chart. Write the main idea of this lesson in the center circle. In the outer circles, write how the Nile River helped the Egyptian people.

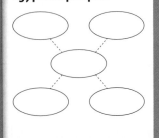

BUILD BACKGROUND

Each April, the people of **Egypt** waited nervously. The **Nile River**, which passed through their land, was at its lowest point. Soon the Nile would flood. When the waters rose, as they did every year, there could be rich crops.

A year of too little water meant hunger. A year of too much water meant disaster. The river is so important that the land of Egypt has been called "The Gift of the Nile."

THE NILE RIVER

About 2,000 years after farming began in Catal Huyuk, people settled along the Nile River valley in North Africa.

The Nile River flows through a desert. Fortunately, each year the Nile overflowed its banks. These floods helped ancient farmers turn the Nile Valley into a fertile agricultural area.

A Great River

The Nile is the world's longest river. It flows north over 4,000 miles from the mountains of East Africa. It passes through modern Uganda, Ethiopia, Sudan, and Egypt. Then the Nile empties into the Mediterranean Sea.

Much of East Africa has a rainy season from May until September. Heavy rainfall causes the river to rise, carrying silt as it flows north. When river waters reach Egypt, they slow and spill over their banks. Much of the silt is deposited where the Nile empties into the Mediterranean Sea. There the river divides into several branches, forming a vast, fan-shaped **delta**. A delta is very fertile, flat land made of silt dropped by a river as it drains into a larger body of water.

Northern Egypt is called **Lower Egypt** because it lies "lower," or downstream, on the river. **Upper Egypt** in the south is "upstream." In Upper Egypt, the Nile cuts through stone cliffs and desert sands. This landscape is very different from the fertile lowland of the delta.

READING CHECK What happened when the Nile flooded each year?

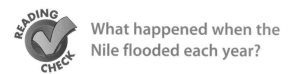

Both traditional and modern boats carry people and goods on the Nile today.

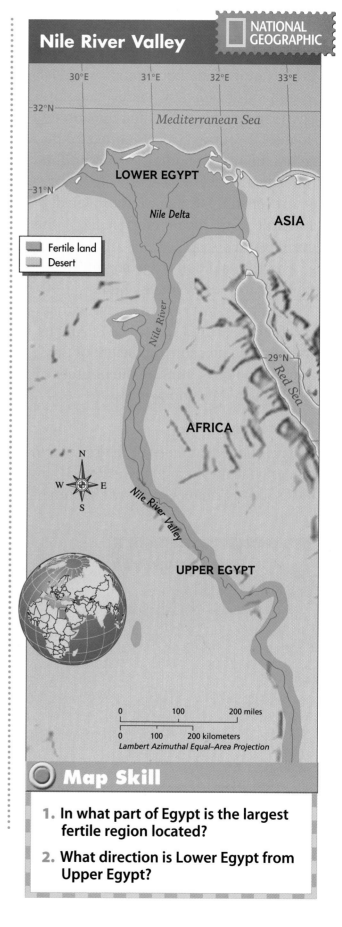

Nile River Valley

NATIONAL GEOGRAPHIC

Mediterranean Sea

LOWER EGYPT

Nile Delta

ASIA

Fertile land
Desert

Nile River

AFRICA

Red Sea

Nile River Valley

UPPER EGYPT

0   100   200 miles
0   100   200 kilometers
Lambert Azimuthal Equal–Area Projection

Map Skill

1. **In what part of Egypt is the largest fertile region located?**

2. **What direction is Lower Egypt from Upper Egypt?**

HIGH WATER OR HUNGER

Desert sand is unsuitable for agriculture. The silt-filled floodwaters were rich in minerals needed by plants. Therefore, Egyptian farmers welcomed the annual floods. Of course, farmers hoped for the *right* amount of flooding each year. Too much water meant villages were destroyed and farm animals drowned. Too little water meant crops failed. Either event was a disaster.

The annual floods were so important that the ancient Egyptians built a "Nilometer"—a special staircase with carefully measured steps. The Egyptians were able to measure the height of the annual flood by counting the number of steps covered by floodwaters.

Nile Farming

The flooded land began to dry in October, and farmers planted wheat and barley as well as smaller crops of cucumbers, lettuce, onions, and beans. Farmers also grew flax, a plant used to make linen, a kind of cloth. To water these newly planted crops, the Egyptians used irrigation as the people who lived in the Fertile Crescent did. They dug canals and used a device called a shadoof (shah DOOF) to lift water into their fields.

In March, crops were ready to be harvested. In good years, fields were filled with ripe vegetables and grains. Farming families had more food than they needed. This surplus was collected and taken to storehouses. As in Catal Huyuk, surpluses made specialization and community life possible.

Read this excerpt from an Egyptian song. What does the song tell you about Egyptians' feelings for the Nile?

◯ Diagram Skill

1. **How did water reach the farmers' fields?**

2. **What do you think was the purpose of the rock?**

Using a Shadoof

Ditch

Bucket for drawing water

Nile River

Pivots on frame

Rock counterweights the bucket

Ties

Mud

Dam

Frame

excerpt from "Hymn to the Nile"
— c. 2100 B.C.

Hail to you, O Nile!
Who shows itself over this land,
*   and comes*
To give life to Egypt!
Mysterious is your pouring forth
*   from darkness,*
On this day that we celebrate!

Water the orchards created by Ra,
*   to cause all the cattle to live,*
You give the earth [water] to
*   drink, eternal one!*
Path that descends from the sky . . .
*   you cause the workshops . . .*
*   to prosper!*

What did ancient Egyptians thank the Nile for doing?

The Nile River was the center of ancient Egyptian civilization. Egyptians used the river for irrigating their fields and for transportation. In addition, they depended on the annual floods to provide rich soil for their fields.

How did the Nile floods affect life for people in Egypt?

PUTTING IT TOGETHER

The Nile was the main route for people and goods to move from place to place. The 600-mile journey between Upper and Lower Egypt would take over a month to walk. In a reed boat it took only about half that time.

The British Museum

Review and Assess

1. Write a sentence for the vocabulary word.
   delta

2. What happened if the annual floods were too great or too small?

3. Why did life for the people of Egypt depend on the Nile?

4. What **technology** did Egyptian farmers use to get water from the Nile to their fields?

5. How did Egyptians **solve the problem** of irrigating crops during the dry seasons?

Activities

Draw a physical map of the Nile region. Color the areas of hills and mountains a different color from the areas of flat plains. Make the delta a third color.

• •

Write a journal entry for an ancient Egyptian farmer. Mention the floods and the tasks that the farmer would do.

Decision Making

When ancient people made **decisions**, or choices, making the wrong choice might be a disaster. Today, our lives are much different from those of people in ancient Egypt. Still, we also make important decisions. Should you talk on the phone with a friend, or help your younger brother with his homework?

When you choose, you are practicing **decision making**. Decision making is choosing from a number of **alternatives** to achieve your goal. An alternative is another way of doing something.

VOCABULARY

decision
decision making
alternative

LEARN THE SKILL

1. **Identify a goal.**
   Martin has a book report due next week. In order to finish the book, he'll have to spend all his free time reading. However, Martin also takes in-line skating lessons. In order to complete his book report, he might have to miss his skating class.

2. **Gather information.**
   Martin asks his skating instructor about the next class. Will something new be taught? Will there be a test? Martin also looks at his old book reports to see how he has been doing in reading this year.

3. **Identify the alternatives.**
   If Martin spends the weekend reading, he will be able to write a good book report. If he goes to skating class, he will get exercise and learn new skills.

4. **Predict the consequences of each alternative.**
   Every decision has consequences. If Martin reads his book, he will miss his in-line skating class. However, he may be able to make it up later. If Martin goes skating, he will not do as well on his book report. He may not be able to do it at all.

5. **Make the decision that best helps you to reach your goal. Check your decision with your parents, teacher, or other adult.**
   Martin's goal is to do well on his book report. He decides to read all weekend.

TRY THE SKILL

Jeannette is a sixth-grader at Martinez Elementary School. She must decide which after-school club she wants to join. Jeannette cares about Earth's future. She wants to make a difference in the world around her. On the other hand, she has always been interested in ancient Egypt and wants to travel to other countries. Which club will she join?

Look at the posters on this page. Then follow the steps to make your decision. Answer the questions below.

1. What is her goal?

2. What are the possible options and their consequences?

3. What is her best choice and why?

4. How can decision making help you in your daily life?

EXTEND THE SKILL

Go back to the lesson. Suppose that you are a member of a family of ancient Egyptian farmers. You want to make a trip to the delta region at the mouth of the Nile.

● Make a decision about the best time of year for your trip.

● Explain why you chose that time of year.

● How can understanding the process of making a decision help you to understand history better?

The Kingdoms of Egypt

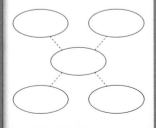

Find! Out!

What were the achievements of ancient Egypt during the Old Kingdom?

VOCABULARY

unification
pharaoh
Old Kingdom
mummification
pyramid
hieroglyphics
papyrus
economy

PEOPLE

Menes
Khufu
Jean Champollion

READING STRATEGY

Copy this chart. Write "Menes" in the center circle. Write the achievements of Menes in the other circles.

Lesson Outline

• Egypt Is United
• Egypt's Government and Religion
• The Glories of the Old Kingdom
• Deciphering Hieroglyphics

BUILD BACKGROUND

Sweating troops faced each other across the scorching desert. One army supported the king of Upper Egypt in the south. The king of Lower Egypt in the north led another army. Both kings were determined to unite their two lands. At the end of the battle, there would be only one king left. The two kingdoms were united in 3100 B.C., and Egypt became the largest empire of its time.

4000 B.C.	3500 B.C.	3000 B.C.	2500 B.C.	2000 B.C.	1500 B.C.	1000 B.C.	500 B.C.	A.D. 1

You Are Here
3100 B.C. – 2000 B.C.

EGYPT IS UNITED

The people along the Nile River had developed a thriving culture. Farmers grew surplus crops. Craftworkers had created new techniques for making tools, pottery, and jewelry. Trade along the river was increasing. Perhaps even more important, groups of communities had learned to cooperate.

The First Pharaoh

Life for the people in the villages was not peaceful, however. Ruins of walls around ancient towns and paintings of battles show that wars between villages were frequent.

Egyptian history changed when the forces led by **Menes** (MEE neez), king of Upper Egypt, swept north into the Nile River delta in about 3100 B.C. His army overthrew the king of Lower Egypt. To show his victory, Menes had a new crown made. Before this time, the king of Upper

Egypt wore a white crown and the king of Lower Egypt wore a red crown. The new crown was a combination of the two crowns. This double crown stood for the **unification** of Egypt. Unification is the joining of separate parts into one. The diagram on this page shows how the double crown of Egypt came about.

Menes became the first **pharaoh** (FAIR oh) of Egypt. The word *pharaoh* refers to the "great palace" in which the rulers of Egypt lived. Later it became the name given to all the rulers of Egypt. The time when Egypt's early pharaohs worked to build unity in the country is called the **Old Kingdom**. It lasted from about 2700 B.C. to about 2200 B.C.

 READING CHECK Why was the double crown an important symbol in ancient Egypt?

Diagram Skill

1. **What did the pharaoh's double crown represent?**
2. **What animal is used on the crown?**

The Double Crown of Egypt

Crown of Upper Egypt

Crown of Lower Egypt

Double Crown of Unified Egypt

89

EGYPT'S GOVERNMENT AND RELIGION

The early pharaohs concentrated on governing the kingdom and making sure it stayed prosperous. They accepted and, in many cases, expanded the customs of local governments, trade, and religion. Later pharaohs, however, became the center of Egyptian civilization. Their actions shaped life in all of Egypt.

A New Government

Menes made **Memphis**, located in Lower Egypt, his capital. From there, the pharaoh decided how Egypt's affairs should be run, from the highest to the lowest levels.

The pharaoh made local leaders serve the new government. These officials continued to perform former duties such as collecting taxes and serving as judges, but they also had new duties. One of these was to make sure flood waters were shared fairly among farmers through the use of canals and storage pools. They also had to report to the government in Memphis.

Religion in Ancient Egypt

Egypt's pharaohs had religious duties, as well as political power. One pharaoh, in describing his religious duties, said:

"The sun god made me the herdsman [shepherd] of his land, for he recognized that I would keep it in order for him . . . he entrusted me with what he protected."

Egyptian mythology is very complicated. Ancient Egyptians had many gods with a variety of responsibilities. For example, one god caused the annual flooding of the Nile. Another god gave potters and metalworkers their creative abilities. Egyptians believed that the pharaoh was the "beloved of Horus," the god who united the two Egypts. The most important goddess was Isis who was the mother of Horus. She protected people from sickness and harm.

The most important Egyptian god was Ra (RAH), the sun god. The Egyptians believed that Ra gave life to Earth, and the pharaoh, the child of Ra, gave life to Egypt and its people.

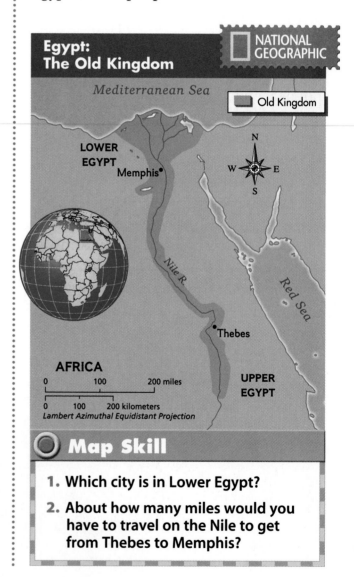

Egypt: The Old Kingdom

NATIONAL GEOGRAPHIC

Mediterranean Sea

Old Kingdom

LOWER EGYPT

Memphis

Nile R.

Red Sea

Thebes

AFRICA

0   100   200 miles

0   100   200 kilometers
Lambert Azimuthal Equidistant Projection

UPPER EGYPT

Map Skill

1. **Which city is in Lower Egypt?**

2. **About how many miles would you have to travel on the Nile to get from Thebes to Memphis?**

Preparing a Royal Mummy

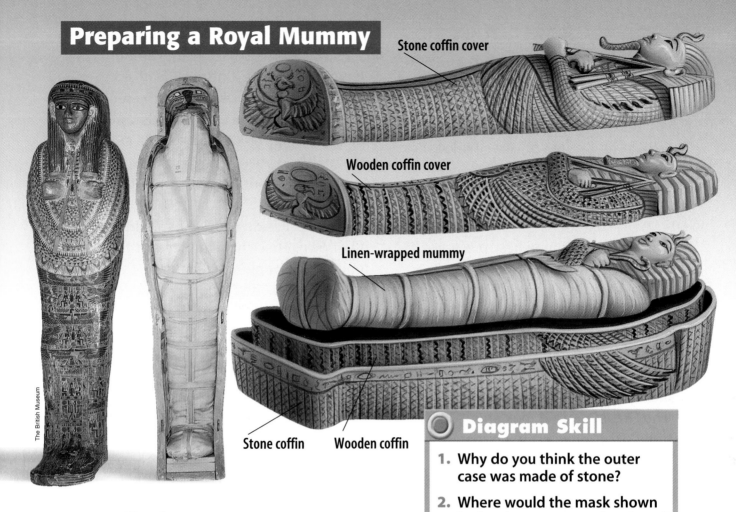

Stone coffin cover

Wooden coffin cover

Linen-wrapped mummy

Stone coffin

Wooden coffin

The British Museum

Diagram Skill

1. **Why do you think the outer case was made of stone?**

2. **Where would the mask shown in the chapter opener be placed?**

Mummification

Ancient Egyptians believed they would need their bodies in the afterlife. For this reason, they preserved the bodies of the dead with a process called **mummification**. Priests used spices and minerals to preserve the mummies, then wrapped them in strips of cloth. The mummies were enclosed in elaborate wooden or stone cases, like the ones in the diagram above.

At first, only the bodies of the pharaoh's family and important leaders were mummified. Later, a simpler process was used to preserve the bodies of ordinary Egyptians.

The Pyramids

Huge stone structures called **pyramids** were built as tombs, or burial places, for the pharaohs. Early rulers were buried in simple mud-brick tombs. The first pyramid was built for Pharaoh Zoser, who ruled around 2780 B.C. It was the work of Imhotep, who is the first architect to be known by name in history. The pyramid Zoser had built at Sakkara is the first large building to be made of stone.

Zoser's pyramid was unlike later ones. It did not have straight smooth sides. It was a stepped pyramid with several layers, each one smaller than the one beneath it.

READING CHECK

What role did the pharaoh play in Egypt's government and religion?

91

THE GLORIES OF THE OLD KINGDOM

The pyramids are important sources of information about ancient Egypt. They show the engineering skills of ancient Egyptians. In addition, many of them have records painted or carved on stones and walls. These explain the achievements of the rulers.

The Great Pyramid

The three largest and best-preserved pyramids are at Giza near Cairo. The largest of the three was the Great Pyramid of Pharaoh **Khufu** (KOO foo), built in about 2600 B.C. This mountain of stone was the Old Kingdom's most spectacular monument. Although it was a tomb for the pharaoh, it brought honor to all of Egypt.

The Great Pyramid took about 22 years to build. Historians estimate that as many as 100,000 people may have worked on it. The pyramids also used large amounts of Egypt's resources. Entire cliffs of stone were cut into blocks to make the monument. In some places, the landscape along the Nile changed as whole cliffs disappeared. Also, a large portion of the yearly taxes went to feed and clothe the workers.

Later rulers demanded pyramids of their own. These huge projects put a strain on Egypt's people and economy. The unity of Egypt weakened as local rulers began to resist the orders of the pharaohs.

Ancient Egyptian Writing

The Egyptians had developed a writing system even before Egypt was unified. Its system is called **hieroglyphics** (hi ruh GLIHF ihks). The system used

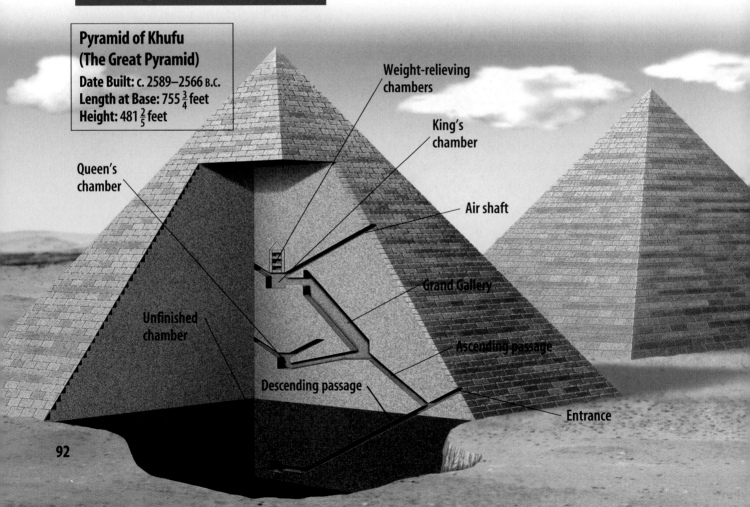

The Pyramids of Giza

**Pyramid of Khufu
(The Great Pyramid)**
Date Built: c. 2589–2566 B.C.
Length at Base: $755\frac{3}{4}$ feet
Height: $481\frac{2}{5}$ feet

Weight-relieving chambers

King's chamber

Queen's chamber

Air shaft

Grand Gallery

Unfinished chamber

Ascending passage

Descending passage

Entrance

about 800 picture-signs, or *hieroglyphs.* Each sign, or symbol, could stand for an object such as an eye, or a sound, such as that of the letter *i.*

Scribes

In Chapter 2, you learned that scribes are specially trained writers. Scribes traveled throughout Egypt keeping records, preparing letters, and contracts. Egyptians respected their scribes because it took many years of preparation to learn their skills.

Only boys could become scribes, and their training began when they were about ten years old. Boys spent hours practicing their writing over and over on broken pottery, which was their "scrap paper."

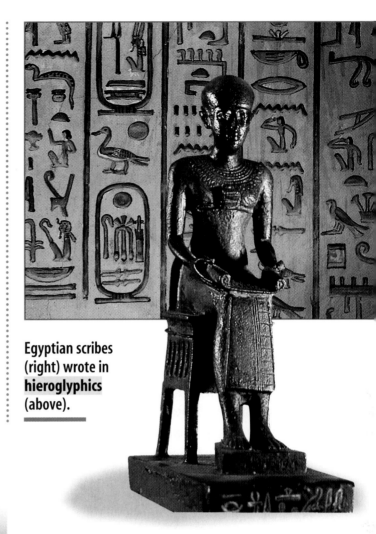

Egyptian scribes (right) wrote in **hieroglyphics** (above).

Diagram Skill

1. **Whose mummy was placed in the highest chamber?**

2. **How do you think the entrance corridor was closed to seal the tomb?**

Pyramid of Menkaure

Date Built: Unknown
    Menkaure reigned c. 2490–2472 B.C.
Length at Base: 356 $\frac{1}{2}$ feet
Height: 218 feet

Pyramid of Khafre

Date Built: c. 2558–2532 B.C.
Length at Base: 707 $\frac{3}{4}$ feet
Height: 471 feet

Once they learned hieroglyphics, young scribes wrote on **papyrus** (puh PIE rus). Papyrus is a reed plant that grows along the Nile. The reeds were pressed together to form a kind of paper. Notice how similar the words *papyrus* and *paper* are.

Scribes sharpened reeds to use as pens. They dipped the reeds into small disks of red or black ink. Then they wrote carefully on their rolls of papyrus.

Scribes had to be good at math as well as penmanship. They had to keep accurate records of taxes and of the pharaoh's goods.

How do you think writing helped the pharaoh keep control of his kingdom?

DECIPHERING HIEROGLYPHICS

Around 300 B.C. Egypt was conquered by Greeks. Gradually, Egyptians stopped using their hieroglyphic writing system. The meaning of the hieroglyphs was lost. The symbols on Egyptian walls and in tombs were a mystery to later people.

A Lost Language Recovered

In 1822, a French scholar named **Jean Champollion** (shahm pohl YON) figured out how to read hieroglyphs. A group of French soldiers had found a stone near the Egyptian city of Rosetta. The Rosetta Stone had the same passage carved in three kinds of writing—hieroglyphics, a late Egyptian form of writing called *demotic*, and Greek. Champollion could read Greek. He realized that the same message appeared in all three languages. Since he knew what the Greek text said, he was able to decode the meaning of the hieroglyphic writing as well.

The British Museum

Exploring ECONOMICS

Valuing Trade Goods

Ancient Egyptians paid taxes and made purchases using grain or other products. Using goods to make purchases or to pay fines is called *barter*. Barter can be a complicated way to buy and sell goods, especially for long-distance traders. Many cultures began to use gold, copper, or silver as a medium of exchange. A medium of exchange is usually a metal with a value that people will accept. In the beginning, traders paid for goods by weighing an agreed-upon amount of silver, gold, or other metal. In time, people began making metal objects of standard size and weight. These were the first coins. They came from Lydia, a kingdom in what is now Turkey.

Research a U.S. coin. Find out the metal it contains. Learn about its symbols. Share the information with your class.

Understanding the Economy

From studying hieroglyphic records, historians have learned about ancient Egypt's **economy**. An economy is the way a country manages its resources to produce goods and services. Scholars already knew that the economy of ancient Egypt was based on a surplus of crops. The hieroglyphic records told them how this economy worked.

The ancient Egyptians did not use money. Instead of tax money, the pharaoh took part of everything made in Egypt. Each year the pharaoh collected a large part of every farmer's crops as a tax, as well as a portion of products such as leather goods, linen cloth, and baskets.

The pharaoh's taxes also included days of work. For example, almost all Egyp-

PUTTING IT TOGETHER

The Old Kingdom laid the groundwork for a civilization that lasted more than 2,000 years. It had many accomplishments including a powerful, organized government and spectacular stone monuments. However, taxes for building huge structures such as the pyramids eventually grew too great. Anger against the rulers increased. In about 2000 B.C. leaders in Upper Egypt rebelled and brought the Old Kingdom to an end. They crowned their own pharaoh and built a new capital at Thebes. In the next lesson you will read how later pharaohs built one of the world's most powerful civilizations.

The Rosetta Stone (opposite) was found in 1799. The falcon on this necklace (above) was the symbol of the Egyptian god Horus.

tians worked on canals and government projects during the flood season. Farmers also had to serve in the army during wars.

Prisoners of war were brought back to Egypt as slaves. Some slaves worked in the government-owned gold mines. However, other slaves were trusted with high government positions.

READING CHECK How did understanding hieroglyphs help scholars learn about Egypt?

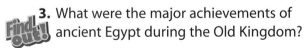

Review and Assess

1. Write one sentence for each vocabulary word.

    hieroglyphics   pharaoh
    mummification   pyramid
    papyrus

2. What part did Egyptian scribes play in government and trade?

3. What were the major achievements of ancient Egypt during the Old Kingdom?

4. What role did the pharaoh play in Egypt's religion?

5. How did Champollion **solve the problem** of deciphering ancient Egyptian writing?

Suppose you own an ancient Egyptian travel agency. Look at the map on page 90. Write a travel brochure describing a trip from Thebes to Memphis. Describe what you would see along the way.

· ·

Suppose you are in charge of a record-keeping office in Egypt. You are short of scribes. **Write** a help-wanted ad for a scribe. Include a description of the skills needed for the job.

Ancient Egyptian Culture

Find Out! *What made ancient Egypt's culture so rich?*

Lesson Outline

- Egypt's New Rulers
- Egypt Becomes an Empire
- Weakening of the Empire

VOCABULARY

expedition

PEOPLE

Ahmose I
Amenhotep I
Hatshepsut
Akhenaton
Ramses II

READING STRATEGY

Copy the chart below. Write details from the lesson in the outer circles. Write the main idea: "Egypt had a rich culture" in the center circle.

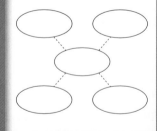

BUILD BACKGROUND

On November 26, 1922, three people peered through a hole into a newly excavated tomb in Egypt. The first to look was Howard Carter, the archaeologist. "Do you see anything?" his companions anxiously asked. "Yes," he whispered, "wonderful things!" The tomb of Tutankhamun, "King Tut," astonished the world with the extraordinary wealth and display of the artistic skills of ancient Egypt.

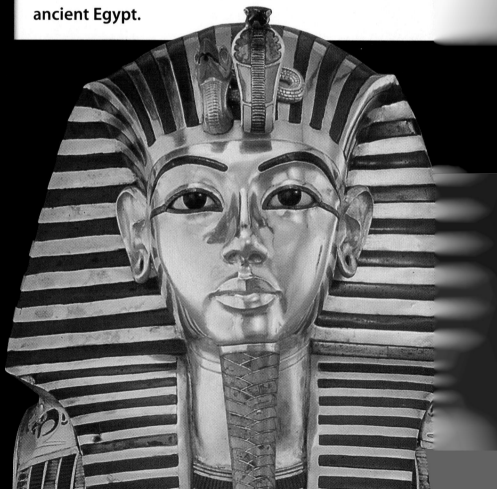

4000 B.C.	3500 B.C.	3000 B.C.	2500 B.C.	2000 B.C.	1500 B.C.	1000 B.C.	500 B.C.	A.D. 1

You Are Here
2100 B.C. – 1000 B.C.

EGYPT'S NEW RULERS

The Old Kingdom of Egypt came to an end around 2000 B.C. It was replaced by new rulers whose empire, called the Middle Kingdom, lasted until about 1700 B.C.

The Middle Kingdom was a time of change and prosperity. Many Egyptians gained rights that they had not had in the Old Kingdom. The pharaoh increased control over Egypt's government by replacing regional leaders with governors. These officials reported to the pharaoh and received instructions from him.

Expanding Contacts

The Middle Kingdom increased Egypt's contacts with other parts of the ancient world. To the south of Egypt was the wealthy kingdom of **Nubia**, which had important gold mines. Find Nubia on the map on page 98. Pharaohs of the Middle Kingdom conquered Nubia and used its wealth. In the same period, Egypt sent trade **expeditions** to Greece and to the Fertile Crescent. An expedition is a journey undertaken for a specific purpose.

As trade grew, people from Asia began to settle in the Nile delta region. Among the settlers were a people from the hills of western Asia called the Hyksos (HIK sohs).

The Hyksos Rule of Egypt

The Hyksos were skilled in warfare. In battles, they used horses and chariots, which were unknown to the Egyptians. They fought with bronze weapons and sturdy bows. The Hyksos conquered Lower Egypt around 1650 B.C. and ruled it for about 100 years.

The New Kingdom

In 1570 B.C., an Egyptian army led by Pharaoh **Ahmose I** (AH mohs) attacked Lower Egypt. He defeated the Hyksos, and a new period of Egyptian history began. It was called the New Kingdom. Ahmose I was determined that outsiders like the Hyksos would never again rule any part of Egypt. He and later pharaohs made Egypt the strongest military power in its part of the world.

 What events changed Egypt during the Middle and New Kingdoms?

The Egyptian army carried spears and cowhide shields.

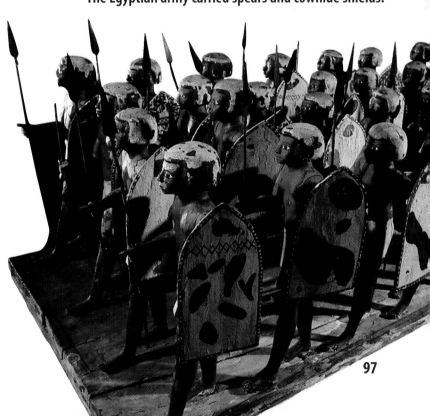

97

EGYPT BECOMES AN EMPIRE

During the New Kingdom, Egypt's armies conquered many nearby lands. This helped the pharaohs create an empire that stretched from **Kush** in the south to the Euphrates River in the north. Kush was a wealthy kingdom that con-

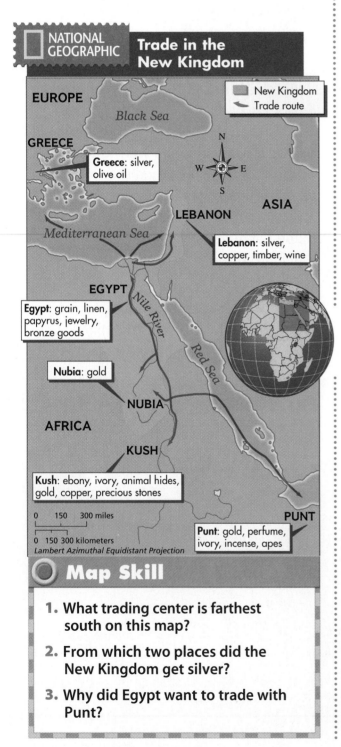

NATIONAL GEOGRAPHIC **Trade in the New Kingdom**

EUROPE

Black Sea

GREECE

Greece: silver, olive oil

Mediterranean Sea

LEBANON

ASIA

Lebanon: silver, copper, timber, wine

EGYPT

Nile River

Egypt: grain, linen, papyrus, jewelry, bronze goods

Red Sea

Nubia: gold

NUBIA

AFRICA

KUSH

Kush: ebony, ivory, animal hides, gold, copper, precious stones

0   150   300 miles
0   150 300 kilometers
Lambert Azimuthal Equidistant Projection

PUNT

Punt: gold, perfume, ivory, incense, apes

New Kingdom
Trade route

● Map Skill

1. **What trading center is farthest south on this map?**

2. **From which two places did the New Kingdom get silver?**

3. **Why did Egypt want to trade with Punt?**

An Egyptian expedition included soldiers and important officials.

trolled trade routes with other African kingdoms. Kush traded its gold, copper, and precious stones for ebony, leopard skins, and elephant ivory. When it conquered this huge region, Egypt gained a wide variety of resources and enriched its own economy.

The Empire at Its Peak

The empire reached its greatest glory under **Amenhotep I** (ahm un HOH tep), who became pharaoh in 1546 B.C. He made many allies and traded with people in Africa, Asia, and southern Europe. One of ancient Egypt's great builders, Amenhotep I is known for the temples he had constructed at Karnak and in Nubia.

Hatshepsut (hat SHEP soot), was one of Egypt's few female pharaohs. She is also known for her burial temple, Deir el-Bahri, which is one of the most beautiful buildings of ancient Egypt.

How did Amenhotep I strengthen Egypt?

BIOGRAPHY

Focus On: Responsibility

Hatshepsut is the first woman ruler known to history. She ruled as pharaoh in the 1400s B.C. after the death of her husband. Hatshepsut took her responsibilities as pharaoh seriously. She gave Egypt a long period of peace and wealth through trade. She also organized trading expeditions. One expedition went south to Punt, lasted two years, and brought back gold, ebony, incense, perfume, ivory, leopard skins, and even live monkeys for private zoos.

Hatshepsut was also a great builder. She added to the great temple complex at Karnak. She built her own funeral temple, which still stands in the Valley of the Kings. She also restored an old canal connecting the Nile to the Red Sea.

Hatshepsut was a wise and responsible ruler. Her reign was a period of Egyptian power and wealth.

Link to Today Think of a modern leader who is a responsible and wise ruler. Make a list of questions that you would like to ask this leader.

THE LIFE OF HATSHEPSUT	c. 1524 B.C Hatshepsut is born	c. 1511 B.C. Hatshepsut marries Thutmose II	1503 B.C. Hatshepsut becomes pharaoh	1482 B.C. Hatshepsut dies
1550	**1525**	**1500**	**1475**	**1450**
LIFE AROUND THE WORLD		1500 B.C. Metalworking begins in Peru	1500 B.C. Aryans invade Indus Valley	1400 B.C. Chinese begin using oracle bones to predict the future

WEAKENING OF THE EMPIRE

After Hatshepsut's death, the Egyptian Empire faced many challenges. Its legacy continued, influencing people in the ancient world. However, the unity and strength of the empire slowly weakened.

Akhenaton

Amenhotep IV became pharaoh in 1379 B.C. He angered Egypt's priests by forbidding the worship of Amon, the chief god supported by previous pharaohs. He closed the temples of Amon and destroyed the god's images. The pharaoh replaced Amon with Aton, god of the sun. He even renamed himself **Akhenaton**, (ahk uh NAH tuhn) in the god's honor. Akhenaton practiced

Akhenaton (left) and his wife Nefertiti wore clothes of fine linen. The statue of the hippopotamus (opposite) is decorated with lotus flowers.

monotheism, or the worship of only one god. He also encouraged a new style of art, in which people were represented realistically. However, Akhenaton was extremely unpopular. After his death, his religion, his new capital city, and even his name were forgotten. Led by their priests, the Egyptian people restored Amon and the worship of many gods.

Changes in the Empire

Akhenaton neglected his empire. Some conquered people regained their independence, and the empire was reduced in size. However, Egypt remained wealthy, as the treasures from the tomb of Tutankhamun show us. Tutankhamun became pharaoh shortly after Akhenaton's death, but he ruled for only a few years, and died at age 19.

The last strong pharaoh was **Ramses II**. He ruled for an incredible 67 years, from 1304 B.C. to 1237 B.C. He was a wise and powerful ruler, but the New Kingdom collapsed about 100 years after his death.

This empire was followed by many small kingdoms ruled by powerful priests or local princes.

Medicine, Mathematics, and Astronomy

Most Egyptian doctors were priests who learned their skills in temple schools. These schools taught a great wealth of medical knowledge. For example, Egyptian priest-doctors knew how to measure a person's heartbeat, or pulse.

Some Egyptian cures used ingredients that we still use today. For example, Egyptian doctors knew that moldy bread prevented infections. You may know that modern antibiotics, or germ-killing drugs, are often made from certain types of molds!

Egyptian Math and Science

Ancient Egypt weakened, but its ideas and skills spread to neighboring areas. Egyptian medicine, mathematics, and astronomy were famous around the ancient world.

Egyptian priests also knew a great deal about mathematics. They used their skills to solve practical problems, such as the mathematics needed to design and build the pyramids.

They also used their mathematics skills to study the stars. With this knowledge, they developed a calendar based on 12 months of 30 days each.

READING CHECK How did Egypt change at the end of the New Kingdom?

PUTTING IT TOGETHER

The New Kingdom was a period when Egypt prospered and expanded into a great empire. Splendid palaces and tombs were built. Egyptian science and medicine were well advanced. Religious arguments and weak pharaohs led to a breakup of the kingdom around 1000 B.C.

After the collapse of united Egypt, rival princes and powerful priests ruled small kingdoms. They were easy to conquer one by one. For the next 1,000 years, Egypt was ruled by invading Nubians, Persians, Greeks, and Romans.

Review and Assess

1. Write a sentence for the vocabulary word.
   expedition

2. What was the source of Nubia's wealth?

 3. What were some examples of the major achievements of ancient Egyptian culture?

4. What are some examples of ancient Egypt's scientific knowledge?

5. **Compare** and **contrast** the Middle Kingdom and the New Kingdom.

Look at the map on page 98. Write a plan for a trading expedition to collect products for the Egyptian market . List the products of Egypt you would trade to other countries. Your expedition should make at least three stops to trade before returning to Egypt.

Write a paragraph explaining why a particular pharaoh you have studied made important contributions to ancient Egypt. Support your opinion with reasons and examples from the pharaoh's life.

Nubia and Kush

What kind of civilization did ancient Nubia develop?

Lesson Outline
• The Land of Nubia
• Nubia and Kush Grow Wealthy
• Life in Kush

VOCABULARY

cataract
social pyramid

PEOPLE
Piye

READING STRATEGY

Copy this chart. Write about life in Kush in one column. Compare and contrast Egyptian society in the other column.

BUILD BACKGROUND

"In their customs, they [the people of Nubia] differ greatly from the rest of mankind . . . in the way they choose their kings . . . they find out the man who is the tallest of all the citizens, and of strength equal to his height, and appoint him to rule over them."

This description was written 2,500 years ago by a Greek historian named Herodotus. He was writing about people who lived along the southern banks of the Nile River. Thousands of years before Herodotus wrote, the land was known as Nubia and Kush.

King Aspalta (593–568 B.C.) (right) was one of the most powerful rulers of Kush.

4000 B.C.	3500 B.C.	3000 B.C.	2500 B.C.	2000 B.C.	1500 B.C.	1000 B.C.	500 B.C.	A.D. 1	A.D. 500

You Are Here
3000 B.C. – A.D. 350

THE LAND OF NUBIA

Nubia was located on the Nile River. Today, it would include parts of southern Egypt, Ethiopia, and the Sudan.

The Nile River is formed by the merging of two rivers in the southern part of ancient Nubia. The **Blue Nile** flows northeast out of Lake Tana and the **White Nile** flows north out of Lake Victoria. As you read in Lesson 1, the Nile River has stone cliffs. It also has **cataracts**, rocks, and waterfalls that make navigation along the river difficult. A cataract is a steep rapids in a river. There are six Nile cataracts in the land of Nubia. Boats sailing upriver could not go beyond the cataracts.

Nubia has a harsh desert climate where summer temperatures often are above 100 degrees Fahrenheit. In the winter, the temperature here can drop below freezing. Despite Nubia's harsh climate, the Nile provided water and good soil for people in this region.

Like ancient Egypt, Nubia had two regions. As you can see on the map, Lower Nubia was in the north and Upper Nubia was in the south. As in Lower Egypt, Lower Nubia had fertile farmland, although it was less fertile than that of ancient Egypt. Every year the Nile River flooded, leaving behind a layer of silt.

Upper Nubia had a rugged landscape with rocky cliffs and hills. These highlands were not well suited for farming. The people relied more on herding livestock, such as cattle, for their living. Upper Nubia was also rich in minerals. Archaeologists have discovered iron works there. Also much of the jewelry from the region was made of gold and copper from its mines.

 How was the land of Nubia similar to that of Egypt?

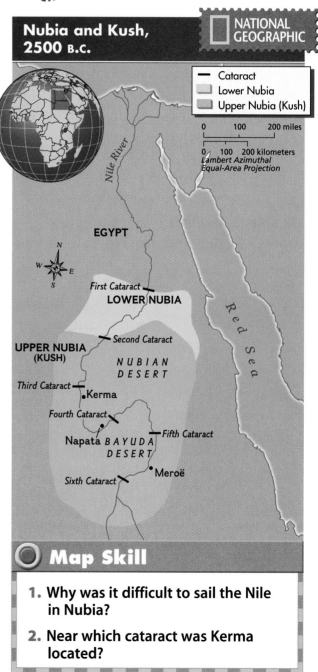

Nubia and Kush, 2500 B.C.

NATIONAL GEOGRAPHIC

Legend:
— Cataract
Lower Nubia
Upper Nubia (Kush)

0   100   200 miles
0   100   200 kilometers
Lambert Azimuthal Equal-Area Projection

EGYPT

Nile River

First Cataract
LOWER NUBIA

Second Cataract

UPPER NUBIA (KUSH)

NUBIAN DESERT

Red Sea

Third Cataract — Kerma

Fourth Cataract

Napata BAYUDA DESERT

Fifth Cataract

Sixth Cataract

Meroë

Map Skill

1. **Why was it difficult to sail the Nile in Nubia?**

2. **Near which cataract was Kerma located?**

103

NUBIA AND KUSH GROW WEALTHY

Archaeologists think that people first settled in Nubia about 10,000 years ago. The oldest artifacts from the area, pottery bowls and statues, date from 8000 B.C. That is 3,000 years earlier than any similar artifacts from Egypt. Early Nubians were probably hunter-gatherers, moving from place to place. Around 3800 B.C., they may have begun to keep herds of cows and goats. Some of the people in Lower Nubia also began to farm.

Like Egypt, Nubia developed cities, trade, a government run by kings, and complicated religious beliefs. Nubia grew wealthy from its gold, iron, and copper mines. For centuries Nubians were active traders, both with the Egyptians to the north and with other civilizations in Africa to the south.

Around 2000 B.C., during Egypt's Middle Kingdom, Egypt's pharaohs grew more powerful, and they began to expand Egypt's borders. They made northern Nubia part of the Egyptian Empire.

A New Kingdom

The Egyptians acquired the lands of Lower Nubia. However, they failed to conquer Upper Nubia because they could not defeat one of its kingdoms, called **Kush**.

The capital city of Kush was **Kerma**. Kerma was an important trading city where goods from Egypt and from other African cultures were traded. In the center of the city, archaeologists have found the ruins of a large building. It contained such trade goods as cloth, crafts, and ivory from southern Africa. The evidence indicates that this building was an important market.

The crafts and architecture of Nubia were influenced by Egypt.

Kush grew rich and powerful from its trade. Kush was also strong enough to defend itself from Egyptian armies for centuries. However, Kush was finally conquered by Egypt around 1525 B.C. For the next 550 years, Egypt ruled all of Nubia.

Blending Cultures

Egypt ruled Kush for more than 500 years and had a great influence on the Kushites. The people of Kush used Egyptian hieroglyphics as their written language. Egyptian pharaohs ordered the construction of temples for Egyptian gods. The chief Egyptian god, Amon, was also worshiped in Kush.

However, Egypt was not the only influence on Kush. Kush had trade contact with cultures all over Africa and western Asia. Archaeologists have found items that show the influence of these cultures on Kush.

The Rise of Kush

Around 1000 B.C. Egypt's rulers lost control of some lands. Kush drove the Egyptians out of their country. As Egypt continued to weaken, Kush grew stronger. Around 740 B.C., a king of Kush named **Piye** [PEE ay] invaded Egypt. First, he conquered the city of Memphis, and then

These Kushite ruins show a blend of influences from Kush, Egypt, and Greece.

all of Egypt. Piye became the ruler of Egypt and Nubia around 730 B.C.

The Kushite rule of Egypt lasted about 50 years. In the 670s B.C., the Assyrians from western Asia (the present country of Iraq) invaded Egypt. They defeated the Kushite rulers, who retreated to Nubia.

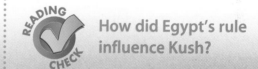

How did Egypt's rule influence Kush?

105

LIFE IN KUSH

Kush thrived for another 1,000 years, but Egypt remained a powerful influence. Twice the rulers of Kush moved their capital farther south, possibly to protect it from Egyptian attacks. By 300 B.C., the capital was **Meroë**, which had once been a Nubian city. As capital of Kush, Meroë was the center of a powerful kingdom for 600 years.

The ruins of the city show that it was large and had wide streets lined by buildings made of brick. At its center was a walled area called the Royal City, where there were temples and palaces.

Meroë was a rich city. It lay on a fertile plain east of the Nile where farmers grew barley and millet and raised cattle. Rain that fell during the rainy season was stored in huge reservoirs, or storage tanks. Meroë was also rich in minerals. Archaeologists have found furnaces for making iron from the ore mined in Kush. Some of these furnaces are nearly 2,500 years old.

Meroë Society

Differences in the ancient tombs at Meroë indicate that its society was much like that of ancient Egypt. At the top of its **social pyramid** was the king or queen. A social pyramid is a triangle-shaped chart that shows the rank of people in its society. The rulers of Kush were leaders of religion, the army, and government. After the rulers, priests and members of the army were next in order of importance. They were responsible for carrying out the orders of Kush's rulers. Below them were the merchants and farmers. At the bottom were enslaved people.

Women in Meroë had important responsibilities. For centuries the throne of Kush was passed to the daughter or son of the king's sister, not to the children of the king. Kush had a number of queens, and women who held important positions as priestesses, another important role in Kushite society.

 READING CHECK Summarize the social pyramid of Meroë.

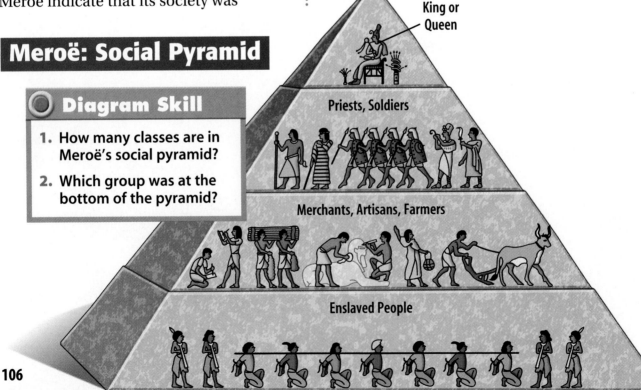

Meroë: Social Pyramid

Diagram Skill

1. How many classes are in Meroë's social pyramid?
2. Which group was at the bottom of the pyramid?

King or Queen

Priests, Soldiers

Merchants, Artisans, Farmers

Enslaved People

PUTTING IT TOGETHER

Nubia's history was closely tied to that of its powerful neighbor, Egypt. As a major trading power, the capital of Meroë was a link between Egypt and the rest of Africa. Kush adopted many Egyptian cultural features including hieroglyphics and religion. Kush was also heavily influenced by African culture. An elephant training area has been found in Meroë where African elephants were trained for battle.

Over the years, Kush began to lose power. By A.D. 350 the kingdom had been conquered by the empire of Aksum from nearby Ethiopia. It was the end of a civilization that was almost 3,000 years old.

The silver crown and pottery jar show the skill of Nubian artists.

Review and Assess

1. Write one sentence for each vocabulary word.

   cataract   social pyramid

2. Why did Kush move its capital to Meroë?

3. What were some characteristics of the Nubian civilization?

4. How did trade affect the lives of the people of ancient Nubia?

5. Why did Piye make the decision to invade Egypt?

Write a journal for a merchant traveling from southern Africa to Kush. In your journal, explain what trade goods you are bringing and how you will reach the city of Meroë. You should also talk about the Nubian goods you will try to buy.

Write a paragraph describing what you might see on a walk through Meroë.

Chapter 3 REVIEW

VOCABULARY REVIEW

Number a sheet of paper from 1 to 5. Beside each number write *T* if the statement is true or *F* if the statement is false. If the statement is false, rewrite the sentence using the underlined vocabulary word correctly.

1. A <u>cataract</u> is a rocky place with rapids in a river.
2. <u>Delta</u> was the name of a city in ancient Egypt.
3. The <u>hieroglyphics</u> took over 20 years to build.
4. Hatshepsut was a woman <u>pharaoh</u>.
5. The joining of separate parts into one is called <u>unification</u>.

CHAPTER COMPREHENSION

6. What happened every year to the Nile River?
7. What did the red and white crown worn by Pharaoh Menes symbolize?
8. Why was the first pyramid built?
9. On what was ancient Egypt's economy based?
10. How did Egypt become an empire?
11. Who was at the bottom of the social pyramid in ancient Kush?
12. Where was Kerma? What happened there?
13. Suppose you were one of the people who found the tomb of Tutankhamun. **Write** a letter to another archaeologist. Describe some artifacts you might have found. Explain what the artifacts tell you about the people who created the tomb.

 ## SKILL REVIEW

The British Museum

14. **Reading/Thinking Skill** King Piye of Kush had a goal. What was it? What decision did he make? What were the consequences of his decision?
15. **Reading/Thinking Skill** Suppose an ancient Egyptian student was trying to decide what to do with his or her life. What alternative could a boy consider that a girl could not?
16. **Reading/Thinking Skill** How did ancient Egyptians solve the problems of how to build the pyramids?
17. **Reading/Thinking Skill** How did the Rosetta Stone solve the problem of deciphering the Egyptian hieroglyphics?
18. **Study Skill** On the time line on the next page, add the following event in its correct place: Hyksos invade Lower Egypt, 1650 B.C.

USING A TIME LINE

3500 B.C.	3000 B.C.	2500 B.C.	2000 B.C.	1500 B.C.	1000 B.C.	500 B.C.	A.D. 1	500

3100 B.C.
Upper and Lower Egypt united

2700 B.C.
Old Kingdom begins

2600 B.C.
Work begins on the Great Pyramid

2100 B.C.
Middle Kingdom begins; Egypt conquers Lower Nubia

1550 B.C.
New Kingdom begins

1075 B.C.
New Kingdom ends

730 B.C.
King Piye of Kush rules Egypt and Nubia

A.D. 350
Kingdom of Kush Ends

19. How long after Upper and Lower Egypt were united did the Old Kingdom begin?

20. Choose the event on the time line that resulted in Egypt becoming the largest empire of its time.

Writing **About Culture** Suppose you lived in ancient Egypt in the time of Hatshepsut or Amenhotep. Write a long journal entry about a trading expedition you led. Include details of a city you visited, how you got there, and what goods you traded.

Foldables

Use your Foldable to review what you have learned about The Nile River. As you look at your map of the Nile River on the front of your Foldable, mentally recall what you now know about its importance to past civilizations—food, water for crops and homes, transportation, location of cities. Review your lesson notes under the tabs of your Foldable to check your memory and responses. Record any questions that you have. Discuss them with classmates or review the chapter to find answers.

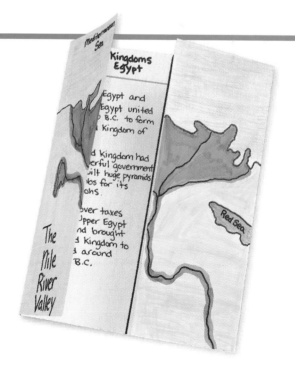

THE Big IDEAS ABOUT...

The Indus River Valley

A river valley civilization began in the Indian subcontinent about 8,000 years ago, around the same time Mesopotamia and ancient Egypt developed. Much of the heritage of modern India has its roots in this ancient culture. Two of the world's great spiritual traditions, Hinduism and Buddhism, also trace their beginnings to ancient India.

THE INDUS RIVER VALLEY

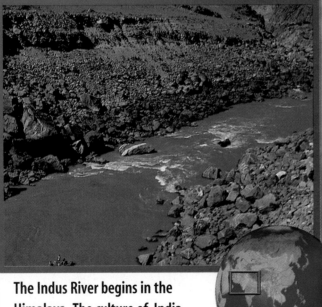

The Indus River begins in the Himalaya. The culture of India had its beginnings on the banks of this great river.

INDUS VALLEY CIVILIZATION

In 1921, archaeologists find the remains of a 4,500-year-old culture along the banks of the Indus River.

THE BIRTH OF HINDUISM

Hinduism blends Harappan religious beliefs with those of the Aryans who migrated to the subcontinent about 3,500 years ago.

THE BIRTH OF BUDDHISM

About 2,500 years ago Siddhartha Gautama set out to find answers to the world's problems. The answers he found are the beginning of Buddhism.

THE FIRST INDIAN EMPIRES

A powerful ruler creates a large empire in northern India around 300 B.C. His grandson, Asoka, spreads Buddhism.

Foldables

Make this Foldable study guide and use it to record what you learn about "The Indus Valley."

1. Fold a large sheet of paper into a shutterfold.

2. Fold the shutterfold in half and cut along the fold lines to form four tabs.

3. Draw or trace a map of India onto the front cover. Label the first tab with the titles of Lessons 1 and 2. Label the other tabs with the other three lesson titles.

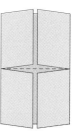

The Indus River Valley

Find Out!

How did the Indus River influence life in the river valley?

Lesson Outline
- Beginning in the High Mountains
- Indus Valley Agriculture

VOCABULARY

subcontinent

READING STRATEGY

Copy this chart. To compare and contrast, write features of the northern Indus River in one column. Write southern Indus River features in the other column.

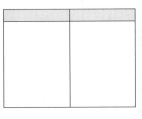

BUILD BACKGROUND

Suppose that you are standing on the edge of a great canyon. In places, this canyon is 3 miles deep. At the bottom you can just barely see a band of cocoa-brown water. This is the mighty **Indus River**. It begins in high, snow-covered mountains and flows southwest into the Arabian Sea. On its banks, one of the world's earliest civilizations came into being more than 8,000 years ago.

BEGINNING IN THE HIGH MOUNTAINS

A **subcontinent** is a large landmass that is geographically separated from the rest of a continent. The land of India is a subcontinent of Asia. Find it on the map.

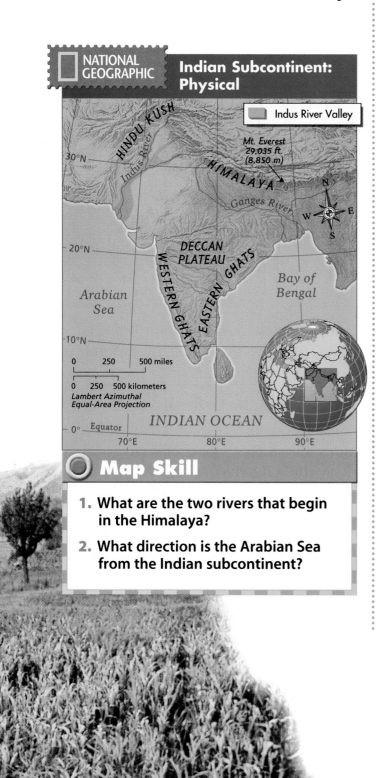

NATIONAL GEOGRAPHIC

Indian Subcontinent: Physical

Indus River Valley

HINDU KUSH

Indus River

30°N

Mt. Everest 29,035 ft. (8,850 m)

HIMALAYA

Ganges River

N W E S

20°N

DECCAN PLATEAU

WESTERN GHATS

EASTERN GHATS

Bay of Bengal

Arabian Sea

10°N

0   250   500 miles

0   250   500 kilometers
Lambert Azimuthal Equal-Area Projection

INDIAN OCEAN

0° Equator

70°E   80°E   90°E

Map Skill

1. **What are the two rivers that begin in the Himalaya?**

2. **What direction is the Arabian Sea from the Indian subcontinent?**

A towering mountain range separates the Indian subcontinent from the rest of Asia. These mountains are the **Himalaya** (hihm uh LAY uh). You have probably heard of their highest peak, Mount Everest. It stands 29,035 feet high. The Indus River begins as an icy stream high in the Himalaya.

The River's Gift

In the spring the Indus fills with melting mountain snow. It flows from the Himalaya south to the Arabian Sea, an 1,800-mile journey through what are today China, Pakistan, and India. The Indus flows swiftly through mountain passes, joined by other rivers before finally slowing down on the flat, dry **Indus Plain**.

During the spring flood season, the swollen river spills across the plain, spreading fertile silt. The Indus actually carries twice as much silt as the mighty Nile in Egypt. Like the Nile, the Indus branches into a huge delta before it reaches the Arabian Sea.

The people of the Indus River valley lived like the people of other river valley cultures in many ways. Like the people of Egypt, they counted on floods to bring rich silt to their fields. Like Mesopotamians, they built cities with temples and markets.

READING CHECK How is the Indus River like the Nile River?

The Indus River begins in the Himalaya Mountains.

INDUS VALLEY AGRICULTURE

Around 6000 B.C., people learned to farm the rich soil of the Indus Valley. This was some 1,000 years before the Egyptians began planting crops. Indus Valley farmers grew wheat, barley, beans, and sesame. Sesame seeds are used for flavor and to make oil. Indus farmers were also among the first to plant rice, bananas, black pepper, mustard, and cotton plants.

Crops grew quickly in the hot climate of the Indus Valley. Using irrigation canals, farmers were able to plant and harvest crops twice each year. Wheat and barley were planted in the fall and harvested just before melting snow caused spring floods. Then, farmers planted fields with cotton and sesame. Dirt walls

Some Indian farmers still use buffalo to pull plows or carts. For thousands of years, people in the Indus Valley have sold spices and other produce in busy markets.

protected these crops from the Indus floods. By the following fall, the second crops were ready for harvest.

Working with the Environment

Harvests were not guaranteed in the Indus River valley. Floodwalls did not always hold the river waters. When the walls collapsed, fields and entire villages could be flooded.

Wildlife in the valley could also bring problems. Tigers, jackals, and wild pigs threatened the lives of farmers. Deer and birds often ate farmers' crops. To have a successful harvest, Indus Valley farmers had to be alert to many dangers.

READING CHECK How many harvests could Indus Valley farmers expect each year?

PUTTING IT TOGETHER

The Indus River enabled farmers to irrigate and cultivate their fields, just as other rivers helped farmers in Egypt and Mesopotamia. Indus Valley farmers were able to plant several crops throughout the year. However, the river could also be cruel. Floodwaters could topple the earth walls and flood the countryside, ruining the farmers' fields. Around 3000 B.C. farming villages and towns had spread across the Indus Valley. The region was about to see great changes, with the birth of a rich and varied civilization.

Review and Assess

1. Write a sentence for the vocabulary word.
   subcontinent

2. Why is India called a subcontinent?

3. In what ways did the Indus River help the farmers of its river valley?

4. Why did Indus Valley farmers plant different crops at different times of the year?

5. **Make a generalization** about the importance of the Indus River to the people of the Indus River valley.

Trace the course of the Indus River on the map on page 113. Then write a travel guide for hikers who will follow the course of the river from its source to its mouth.

• •

Write a report about one of the crops grown in the Indus Valley. Include how the crop is grown and used past and present. Assemble your class's reports in a binder for your classroom library.

Using Latitude and Longitude

Over 2,000 years ago, Greek scientists developed a way to divide Earth into an imaginary **grid**, so all places could be exactly pinpointed. A grid is a set of intersecting lines. The Greeks based their system on two sets of lines called **latitude** and **longitude**. Lines of latitude run east and west. Lines of longitude run north and south.

VOCABULARY

grid	meridian
latitude	prime meridian
longitude	
parallel	global grid
degrees	

Lines of Latitude

NATIONAL GEOGRAPHIC

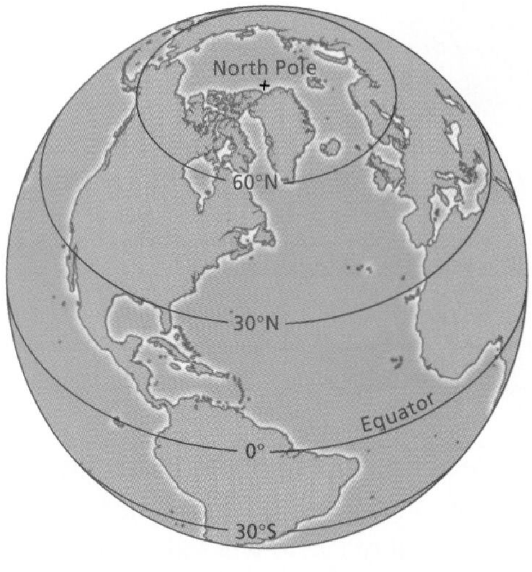

Lines of Longitude

NATIONAL GEOGRAPHIC

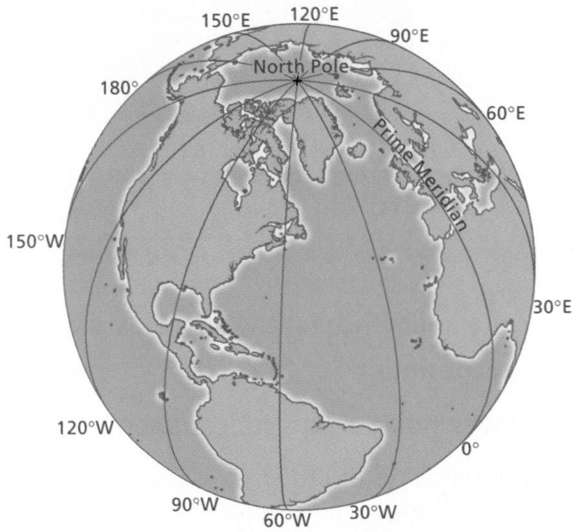

LEARN THE SKILL

Follow these steps to better understand latitude and longitude. Find the equator. This is the starting point for measuring how far north or south a place is from the equator.

1. **Identify the lines of latitude.**
   Lines of latitude are also called **parallels**.

Parallel lines are always the same distance apart and never meet. They measure distance in **degrees**. The symbol for degrees is °. Notice that latitude lines north of the equator are labeled "N," while lines south of the equator are labeled "S."

2. **Identify the lines of longitude.**
   Lines of longitude run north and south and

are also called **meridians**. Locate the **prime meridian** on the map, Lines of Longitude. The prime meridian is 0° longitude. Meridians measure distance east and west of the prime meridian, out to 180°, which runs through the Pacific Ocean. Meridians east of the prime meridian are labeled "E." Those west of the prime meridian are labeled "W."

3. **Study the grid.**
Lines of latitude and longitude cross to form a **global grid**. It can be used to locate any place on Earth.

TRY THE SKILL

Use the global grid map below to locate Cape Town, South Africa, and Los Angeles, California. Then answer the following questions.

1. Locate the city of Cape Town, South Africa. Which line of latitude is closest to this city?

2. Locate the city of Los Angeles, California. Which line of longitude is closest to this city?

3. Which city is near 20° E, 40° S?

4. When would it be helpful to use a global grid?

EXTEND THE SKILL

Suppose you are a pilot about to fly from St. Petersburg, Russia, to Oslo, Norway. You will plot your course using the global grid. About how many degrees of longitude is the whole trip? Along which parallel will you be flying?

● How might knowing about latitude and longitude be helpful to travelers?

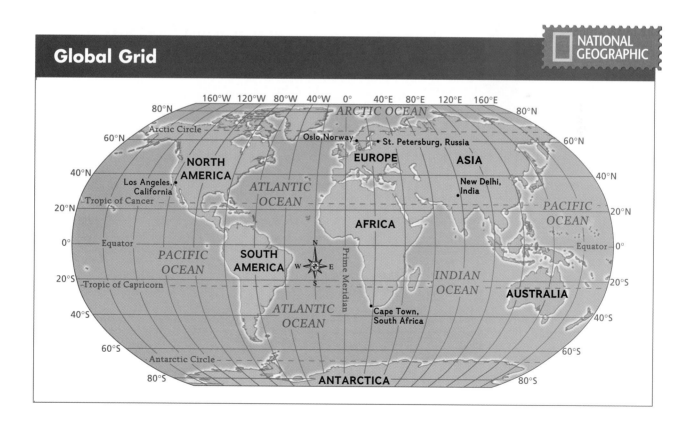

Global Grid

Lesson 2

Indus Valley Civilization

Find Out!

What do their cities tell us about the early people of the Indus River valley?

Lesson Outline

- Lost Cities of the Indus
- Harappan Culture
- The Aryans

VOCABULARY

citadel

READING STRATEGY

Copy this main idea chart. Write the main idea of this lesson in the center box and supporting details in the outer circles.

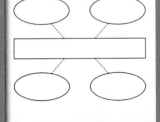

BUILD BACKGROUND

Beginning around 2500 B.C., the farming villages of the Indus Valley grew into huge cities. These cities had paved streets and city sewers. By 1600 B.C. this great civilization had vanished. It lay unknown beneath great piles of earth until 1921, when archaeologists found the remains of one of its cities. Who were the people of this civilization? What happened to them? Scientists are looking for answers to these questions today.

4000 B.C.	3500 B.C.	3000 B.C.	2500 B.C.	2000 B.C.	1500 B.C.	1000 B.C.	500 B.C.	A.D. 1

You Are Here
2500 B.C. – 1500 B.C.

LOST CITIES OF THE INDUS

The ruins of the city discovered by archaeologists in 1921 is called **Harappa** (huh RAH puh), after the name of a nearby town. Archaeologists don't know what the ancient people who lived in the city called themselves. Today, the entire Indus Valley civilization is called Harappan civilization. Find Harappa on the map. As you will read, this civilization lasted for about 1,000 years.

A year after Harappa was uncovered, archaeologists found a second ruined city. This city, about 400 miles to the south, was called **Mohenjo-Daro** (moh HEN joh DAH roh). *Mohenjo-Daro* means "Mound of the Dead" in Sanskrit, an ancient Indian language.

Mohenjo-Daro

Mohenjo-Daro was a large city. Historians think that as many as 40,000 people may have lived there. Streets crossed each other at right angles. Large avenues were paved with earthen bricks. Side streets were narrower and most of them were left unpaved.

Hundreds of one-room, brick houses lined the streets. Some apartment buildings were several stories high and had balconies and courtyards.

A **citadel** (SIT uh dul), or strong fortress, stood at the west end of Mohenjo-Daro. This citadel was surrounded by thick walls to protect it against enemies

Women climb steps in the ruins of Mohenjo-Daro (left)

and floodwaters. Beside the citadel stood a large grain storehouse, where the farmers of Mohenjo-Daro stored crops of barley and wheat. Also nearby was a pool-sized bath, which may have been used for religious ceremonies.

 In what ways were Indus Valley cities like modern cities?

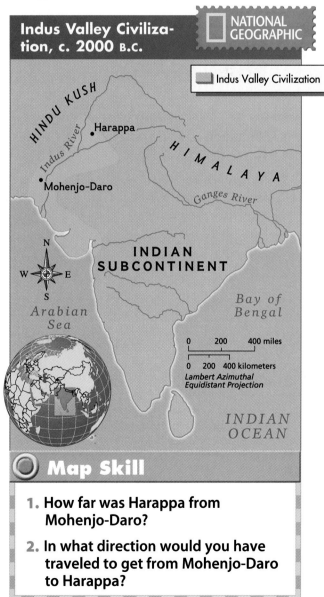

Indus Valley Civilization, c. 2000 B.C.

NATIONAL GEOGRAPHIC

Indus Valley Civilization

HINDU KUSH

Indus River

Harappa

HIMALAYA

Mohenjo-Daro

Ganges River

INDIAN SUBCONTINENT

N W E S

Arabian Sea

Bay of Bengal

0 200 400 miles
0 200 400 kilometers
Lambert Azimuthal Equidistant Projection

INDIAN OCEAN

Map Skill

1. **How far was Harappa from Mohenjo-Daro?**

2. **In what direction would you have traveled to get from Mohenjo-Daro to Harappa?**

119

HARAPPAN CULTURE

Archaeologists have studied the ruins of the Indus civilization, but they have had trouble learning how the Harappans lived. Scholars cannot read the symbols on Harappan artifacts yet. However, they have been able to make some conclusions about life in the Indus Valley. Many conclusions are based upon the remains found in Mohenjo-Daro.

Planned Cities

One of the most remarkable things about the ancient Indus Valley cities is their precise measurements. Harappan bricklayers used standard-sized bricks, unlike the irregular-sized bricks used in Mesopotamia. Harappans also pioneered ways to keep their city clean. Many houses had their own toilets, and the city had a sewer system complete with "manholes."

Projects like this need central planning by a strong government. Since the city of Harappa had almost the same layout as Mohenjo-Daro — even though the two were 400 miles apart — historians conclude that the Indus civilization must have had a strong central government.

Mohenjo-Daro

Apartment building

City gate

Diagram Skill

1. **What activities do you see in the picture?**

2. **Mohenjo-Daro had two large avenues. What was the one shown here used for?**

Wheat

Paved street

Bales of cotton

Specialized Skills

The ancient Harappans were skilled engineers and craftworkers. Archaeologists have uncovered artifacts in the ruins of the workshops that lined city streets. Jewelers made elegant jewelry with gold, conch shells, and gems. Skilled workers carved beautiful pictures into small squares of stone. These stone squares were probably used as seals to mark possessions. Potters decorated bowls, water jars, and other pottery containers with colorful paintings. Metalworkers used copper to make fish hooks and razors. They also made elegant bronze statues. Weavers in the Indus River valley may have been the first to make cotton fibers into cloth.

As in Egypt and the Fertile Crescent, such specialization required a surplus of food. Excess crops were collected and kept in large storehouses. Perhaps, as in ancient Egypt, government workers collected a part of farmers' crops as a tax. This stored grain may have been redistributed later, as payment to city workers or government employees.

What crafts did the Harappans develop?

Ancient Asian Trade Centers

Trade routes had connected India and Mesopotamia for a long time.

Merchants from Indus Valley cities gathered ivory, copper, and beads from surrounding areas. They sent these goods west to Mesopotamia, to trade for textiles, oil, and barley grain. In addition, Indian merchants wanted silver from cultures west of Mesopotamia.

It took many weeks to walk the length of these trade routes, so there had to be places along the route to stop and rest. Trading centers grew up along the route in places such as Dilmun (present-day Bahrain). Seals found in Iran indicate that Indus Valley traders may have lived in Mesopotamia to direct their businesses.

Activity

Draw a chart showing the trade goods an Indus Valley merchant might have sent to other centers. Then, list trade items the merchant might have brought from those centers.

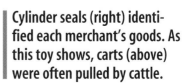

Cylinder seals (right) identified each merchant's goods. As this toy shows, carts (above) were often pulled by cattle.

121

THE ARYANS

The cities of the Indus Valley were abandoned around 1600 B.C. What happened? There are several theories.

The decline may have been due to a war or to a natural disaster, such as a flood or a lack of rainfall. A change in rainfall or lack of river water would have made farming very difficult.

Some archaeologists think that the Indus River changed course after a natural disaster such as an earthquake. An earthquake may have caused floods that destroyed the region's large cities; or it may have caused the course of the Indus River to change. Life went on in the Indus Valley, but the Harappan civilization never recovered.

Around 1500 B.C., life in the Indus Valley changed again. A new group began crossing the icy passes of the **Hindu Kush** mountains and moving east into the Indus Valley. These were Aryans (AYR ee unz), people from central Asia, who rode horses to herd cattle and sheep. Natural disasters or war may have caused them to migrate (MIGH grayt) south through the mountains. To migrate means to move from one place to another to live. The Aryan people migrated west into Europe and south into India. Follow their route into India on the map.

Aryan means "noble one" in Sanskrit. The Aryans brought the Sanskrit language to the Indus Valley and the rest of the subcontinent. They also brought new religious ideas, about which you will read in the next lesson.

READING CHECK How were the Aryans different from the people of the Indus?

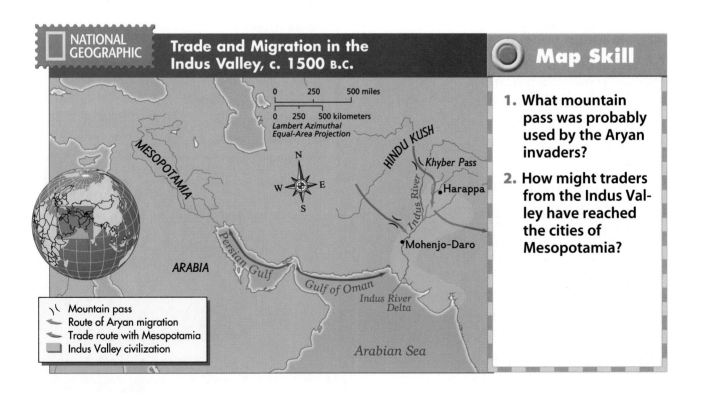

NATIONAL GEOGRAPHIC

Trade and Migration in the Indus Valley, c. 1500 B.C.

0   250   500 miles
0   250   500 kilometers
Lambert Azimuthal Equal-Area Projection

MESOPOTAMIA

HINDU KUSH

Khyber Pass

Indus River

Harappa

Mohenjo-Daro

ARABIA

Persian Gulf

Gulf of Oman

Indus River Delta

Arabian Sea

∧ Mountain pass
↤ Route of Aryan migration
↤ Trade route with Mesopotamia
▮ Indus Valley civilization

Map Skill

1. What mountain pass was probably used by the Aryan invaders?

2. How might traders from the Indus Valley have reached the cities of Mesopotamia?

Aryan invaders may have crossed the Himalaya through the Khyber Pass (above).

PUTTING IT TOGETHER

Harappan civilization was completely forgotten until scientists uncovered it in the 1920s. Even today, little is known about this civilization. However, the planning of these cities led historians to conclude that Harappan civilization had a strong central government and economy.

The Indus Valley civilization collapsed suddenly around 1600 B.C. About 100 years after this collapse, groups of herders called Aryans began to settle the Indus Valley. In time, their culture blended with that of the people of the Indus River valley to create a new culture.

Review and Assess

1. Write a sentence for the vocabulary word.
   citadel

2. How was the Aryan way of life different from that of the Harappan civilization?

 3. What was life like in the early Indus Valley cities?

4. How do you think the Harappans were able to make bricks that were exactly the same?

5. Make a **generalization** about the role trade played in the life of the people of the Indus River valley.

Draw a map of India and southwest Asia. Sketch some possible trade routes that Harappan merchants might have followed to reach Mesopotamia.

• •

Write a conclusion about the Indus Valley civilization. Include lesson details that support your conclusion.

The Birth of Hinduism

How has Hinduism helped to shape Indian culture?

Lesson Outline

• Ancient Writings
• The Hindu Way of Life
• Hinduism Today

VOCABULARY

Hinduism
Vedas
caste system
reincarnation
dharma

READING STRATEGY

Copy this word map. Write the main idea, "Hinduism" in the center circle. Use the outer blank circles to write supporting details about Hinduism.

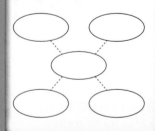

BUILD BACKGROUND

Hinduism, one of the world's oldest religions, began with the Aryan invaders of India. One of Hinduism's key ideas is the belief that all living things are connected. An ancient Aryan text has this verse:

"As the rivers flowing east and west
Merge [join] in the sea and become one with it,
Forgetting they were ever separate rivers,
So do all creatures lose their separateness
When they merge at last into pure Being."

Hindus worship at the Ganges River in India.

You Are Here
1500 B.C. – 500 B.C.

ANCIENT WRITINGS

Today, there are about 800 million Hindus. Like most religions, Hinduism is practiced in many different ways. Yet all Hindus share some basic beliefs. Hindus also share a history that stretches back to the ancient past of the Indian subcontinent.

When Aryans first came to the Indian subcontinent around 1500 B.C., they had little in common with the Harappans. The two people had different languages and cultures. Harappans had built great cities like Mohenjo-Daro. Aryan people lived in small villages, moving frequently to seek pastures for their herds.

Over time, the two groups began to learn from each other. Aryans became farmers and craft workers like their Harappan neighbors. The Harappans, in turn, learned ancient Aryan songs. At first, these songs, believed to be sacred, were passed down by oral tradition. Between 1000 and 300 B.C. the songs were written in books called the **Vedas** (VAY duz), or "Books of Knowledge."

The Vedas

The Vedas contain the basic beliefs of Hinduism. They offer an explanation of life, and they tell Hindus how they should live. The oldest Veda has more than 1,000 religious songs. It says that the world is controlled by many gods and goddesses, like the goddess in the song on this page.

 Why are the Vedas important to Hinduism?

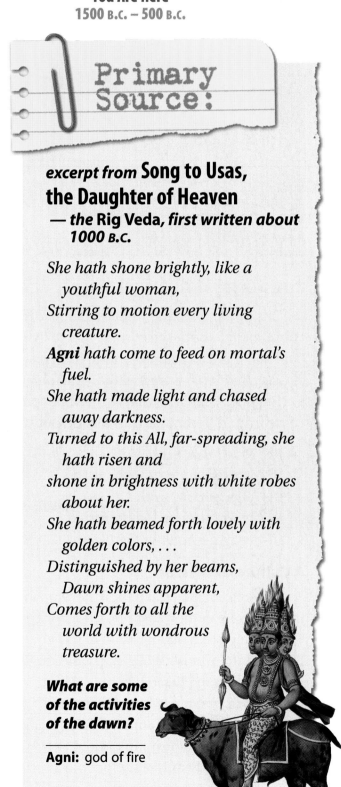

Primary Source:

excerpt from Song to Usas, the Daughter of Heaven
— **the Rig Veda, first written about 1000 B.C.**

She hath shone brightly, like a
  youthful woman,
Stirring to motion every living
  creature.
Agni hath come to feed on mortal's
  fuel.
She hath made light and chased
  away darkness.
Turned to this All, far-spreading, she
  hath risen and
shone in brightness with white robes
  about her.
She hath beamed forth lovely with
  golden colors, . . .
Distinguished by her beams,
  Dawn shines apparent,
Comes forth to all the
  world with wondrous
  treasure.

**What are some
of the activities
of the dawn?**

Agni: god of fire

125

Cows are often decorated (above)
for Hindu ceremonies (left).

THE HINDU WAY OF LIFE

This poem from the Vedas explains the Hindu belief about the correct way to live. One belief is that four different types, or classes, of people were created. The following poem explains that the first people came from different parts of a god's body.

The Priest was his mouth;
His arms became the Princes;
His [legs] produced the
Professionals and Merchants;
His feet gave birth to the [Servant].

A Culture of Classes

These four classes of people developed into India's complex **caste** (KAST) **system**. The caste system organizes all of India's Hindus into hundreds of groups and levels.

According to Hindu beliefs, each person is born into a caste, or level, and this cannot be changed. People of the priestly caste have the highest rank and respect. They must study and teach people about the Vedas. People of the servant caste are thought to be born to serve members of the other castes.

The Cycle of Life

According to the Vedas, people move in a continuing circle of birth, death, and rebirth. This cycle is called **reincarnation** (ree ihn kahr NAY shun). Each reincarnation is a punishment or a reward for the life one led before.

Hindus believe that rebirth is the only way to alter one's caste. Good deeds done in one's life are rewarded by birth into a higher caste in the next life. According to this belief, people born as servants, then, are paying for wrongs done in past lives. Members of the priest caste are being rewarded for good deeds they had done in a previous life.

Duty or Disorder

How do Hindus in each caste know how to behave? The Vedas also provide laws and duties, called **dharma** (DAHR muh). The dharma includes hundreds of rules that tell Hindus of each caste how to live.

For example, merchants are responsible for producing and selling goods and services honestly. Priests have to spend some of their time working to support their families. Part of the dharma of servants is to serve others cheerfully and without complaint.

The Vedas listed the jobs that could or could not be done by members of each caste. The Vedas also warned against breaking the rules of dharma, saying disorder would result. Following dharma kept Hindu society running smoothly. One of the sacred writings said:

> *If a person is engaged in doing his proper work, he reaches the highest end.*

People who married against the rules of their caste, or who did a job their caste was not permitted to do, were forced to live outside all castes. These "outcastes" were looked down upon by others and said to be "impure." Some Hindu priests performed a "cleansing" ceremony if they touched even the shadow of an outcaste.

Since the children of outcastes were also born outside the caste system, they too spent their lives as "untouchables." They usually lived in terrible poverty and were given only the worst kinds of jobs.

Many Paths, One Goal

Like other religions, Hinduism developed many different forms. Some Hindus believed dharma called them to perform special exercises, or to eat no meat, fish, or eggs. Other Hindus explored non-Hindu beliefs as they tried to understand the meaning and laws of life.

Hindu holy books are written in an ancient language called Sanskrit.

These different ideas did not upset Hindu priests. Unlike some other religions, Hinduism permits more than one god, and more than one way to truth. In one well-known Hindu book, the *Bhagavad Gita* (BUG uh vud GEE tah), the god Vishnu says:

> *Howsoever people approach me, even so do I accept them; for on all sides, whatever path they may choose is mine.*

What are some of the beliefs of Hinduism?

HINDUISM TODAY

Today, most Hindus live in the nations of India and Pakistan. The religion continues to influence the way people work, play, eat, and interact. Most modern Hindu families worship their favorite gods at home, at temples, and at special festivals. Some gods and goddesses, of course, are more popular than others. The god Vishnu, the Preserver, for example, is worshiped as "The One That Is the All." Shiva, "The God of Time and Destruction," is also widely honored. Other Hindus prefer the goddess Devi, "The Mother of All Creation."

Hinduism is an ancient religion with a deep respect for its traditions. Many Hindus still consider the Vedas the most holy books of their religion. Other books of adventure-filled stories, or epics, are also considered to be holy guides to living. Some of these stories have been made into popular feature films.

Hinduism has roots in the ancient past of India. Yet the religion has also changed over the years. One important change concerned the caste system. In 1950, the government of India ended the caste system and made it illegal to mistreat or to show disrespect for Hindu outcastes. Some Hindus still believe in the old rules, but in modern India, people from various castes mix at work or in crowded cities.

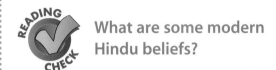 **What are some modern Hindu beliefs?**

Ganesh (left) is one of many Hindu gods. The god Vishnu (above) is generally shown with blue skin and holding his symbols.

PUTTING IT TOGETHER

Hinduism is one of the world's oldest religions. It came to India with the Aryans about 1500 B.C. Eventually, the songs and rules of Hinduism were written down in sacred books called the Vedas. The stories of the Vedas are told and retold in the Hindu regions today.

Today, Hinduism combines beliefs from different cultures and honors many gods and goddesses. The legacy of Hinduism continues to influence the arts, sciences, and society of millions of people in India, Pakistan, and other areas.

Colorful statues of gods are used in Hindu celebrations and festivals.

Review and Assess

1. Write one sentence for each vocabulary word or term.

   caste system   **reincarnation**
   Hinduism   **Vedas**

2. What is the importance of *dharma* to Hindus?

3. What Indian customs come from the teachings of Hinduism?

4. Some Hindus do not eat fish, meat, poultry, or eggs. How might this custom affect India's farm **economy**?

5. Why did the government of India **make the decision** to end the caste system?

On the Internet or in an encyclopedia, research places in India sacred to Hindus. You may wish to include the Ganges River, or sacred cities such as Benares. Then, make a map of India showing these sacred places.

....

Suppose a classmate's older sister has just returned from a year in India. **Write** a list of questions you would like to ask her about Hinduism and its effect on Indian life.

The Birth of Buddhism

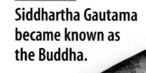

What were the teachings of the Buddha?

Lesson Outline
- The Life of Siddhartha Gautama
- Siddhartha's Search for Wisdom
- The Spread of Buddhism

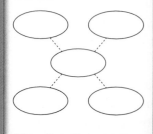
BUILD BACKGROUND

In a tiny kingdom of northern India, a queen is about to give birth. One night she has a dream that tells her that she will have a son. If he stays at home with his family, the prince will become a mighty ruler. If he leaves the palace, he will become a wise teacher. A boy is born, and the queen names him **Siddhartha Gautama** (sih DAHR tuh GOW tah muh). Her dream will come true in other ways as well.

Siddhartha Gautama became known as the Buddha.

4000 B.C.	3500 B.C.	3000 B.C.	2500 B.C.	2000 B.C.	1500 B.C.	1000 B.C.	500 B.C.	A.D. 1

You Are Here
563 B.C. – 100 B.C.

THE LIFE OF SIDDHARTHA GAUTAMA

Siddhartha Gautama was born around 563 B.C. in the small kingdom of **Kosala**. When the king heard his wife's dream, he decided he would make his son happy at home so he would become a mighty king.

A Prince's World

The king arranged for the prince to marry the woman of his dreams and he built magnificent gardens around the royal palace to surround Siddhartha with beauty. The king allowed nothing sad or ugly to enter his son's life.

One day, the prince was riding in the royal gardens. He saw an elderly man limping painfully. Siddhartha asked his servant what was wrong with the man. The servant answered that all people must grow old. The young prince said, "Shame on birth, since to everyone that is born, old age must come!"

Another time, Siddhartha met someone who was very ill, and learned that illness, too, was a part of life. On yet another day, the prince came upon a funeral procession. He learned that death ends every life.

The Prince's Choice

Then Siddhartha saw a man who seemed at peace with the world. This man was calm even while he was begging for his next meal. Siddhartha asked his servant about this man and learned that the man was a **monk**. A monk is a man who gives up all he owns and gives his life to his religion.

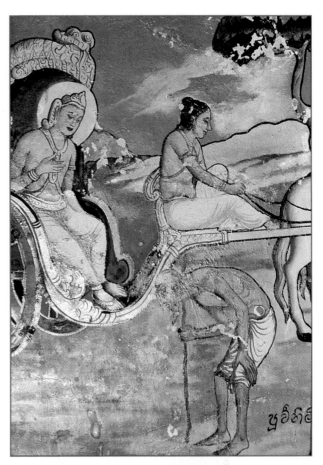

Prince Siddhartha sees old age for the first time in his father's gardens.

The prince was amazed that someone could be so at peace in a world filled with sorrow and suffering. Buddhist texts tell us that the prince made a difficult decision that day. He gave up all he had and became a monk. He said goodbye to his wife and newborn son, and he left the palace. His journey to find the meaning of life had begun.

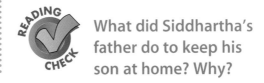

READING CHECK What did Siddhartha's father do to keep his son at home? Why?

131

SIDDHARTHA'S SEARCH FOR WISDOM

In his search for wisdom, Siddhartha spoke with Hindu priests, but he could not accept their answers. He traveled across northern India for six years, begging for food and seeking truth. He tried to focus his thoughts by refusing to eat, or fasting. He began to eat again when he nearly starved to death.

After much thought and searching, a great understanding came to the prince one day as he sat under a fig tree. Buddhist texts tell us that the wisdom he received that day made him the *Buddha*, or "Awakened One."

The Beliefs of Buddha

The Buddha used some Hindu ideas and changed others. Like Hindus, the

Buddha believed that all people went through a cycle of birth, death, and reincarnation, or rebirth. He also accepted the Hindu idea of **karma**. Karma is a force caused by a person's good and bad acts. Karma is said to affect future lives.

Unlike Hindus, however, the Buddha did not search for the one powerful force believed to connect all of life. He believed that the most important task in life was to reach peace by ending suffering. How did he reach these conclusions? How did he hope to put an end to suffering?

Buddhist monks (left) worship at shrines (above). Mani stones, carved with prayers (right), mark roads in Tibet. This Tibetan (far right) holds a Buddhist prayer wheel.

The Four Noble Truths

The Buddha decided that life is ruled by The **Four Noble Truths**. These are:

1. Life is filled with suffering.
2. Suffering is caused by people wanting more pleasure, more power, or a longer life.
3. Suffering can end if people stop wanting things.
4. People must follow eight basic laws if they are to stop wanting things.

The Eightfold Path

The Buddha explained these Four Noble Truths to his followers. He called his way to end suffering the **Eightfold Path**. The Eightfold Path is a set of instructions on the proper way to live. By following the Eightfold Path, the Buddha taught, people could end the suffering in their lives.

The laws of the Eightfold Path were neither too strict nor too easy. They represent a **Middle Way** of living. The Buddha compared the Middle Way to playing a stringed instrument. If the strings are too loose, they cannot make music. If they are too tight, they will break. Only the strings that are tightened perfectly will make beautiful sounds. Life works the same way, he said.

The Buddha Travels and Teaches

The Buddha continued to travel. He crossed India bringing his message to people of all castes. One day, he found himself back at his father's palace. The elderly king was shocked to see his handsome son as a humble monk. However, Buddhists believe, the king decided to follow the Buddha and his teachings. Later the Buddha's wife and son became followers as well.

There were thousands of Buddhists in northern India by the time the Buddha died at the age of 80, in 483 B.C. These Buddhists lived according to his Four Noble Truths and followed the teachings of the Eightfold Path. Like the Buddha, Buddhist monks gave up all they owned and depended on other Buddhist believers to give them food each day. They tried to live peacefully and to love all living things.

 READING CHECK

What were some of the ideas taught by the Buddha?

THE SPREAD OF BUDDHISM

Traveling monks introduced the Buddha's teachings to southern and eastern Asia. **Buddhism** spread to what are today China, Japan, Korea, Tibet, Sri Lanka, Thailand, Taiwan, Cambodia, Myanmar, Laos, and Vietnam.

The Buddha set his followers on the path to enlightenment. On this page, are some proverbs from the Buddha.

Different Schools

Different schools of Buddhism developed over the years. Some followers believed that the Buddha was a god. Others thought that he was a person who found a way to end suffering. Buddhists argued about how to live the Middle Way, and disagreed about how people reached truth and freedom from suffering. These differences continue among Buddhists today. Yet some basic teachings are shared by all Buddhists. These include honoring the Buddha's teachings and helping others to end suffering.

 READING CHECK How did Buddhism spread in its early years?

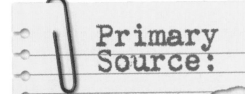 Primary Source:

excerpt from proverbs from **The Path**
— Buddhist text written around 100 B.C.

273. *Of paths the Eightfold is the best; of truths the Four Noble Truths are the best; of all states* **Detachment** *is the best . . . .*

276. *You yourself must make the effort. The [Buddha] can only point the way . . .*

277. **Transient** *are all . . . things; he who sees the truth of this becomes disgusted with this world of suffering. This is the path to purity.*

278. *Sorrowful are all . . . things; he who sees the truth of this becomes disgusted with this world of suffering. This is the path to purity.*

283. *Cut down the whole forest (of desires), not just a tree. From the forest arises fear. Cut down the forest and its brushwood, O monks, and be* **emancipated**.

What does this excerpt tell people to do if they want happiness?

detachment: freedom from wanting things
transient: temporary
emancipated: free

PUTTING IT TOGETHER

Buddhism is a religion that came into being when Siddhartha Gautama, a rich prince of northern India, sought a way to end suffering in the world. His beliefs came to be known as Buddhism, which spread first in northern India and then through southern and eastern Asia.

Differences among Buddhists developed after the Buddha's death, but all Buddhists share his basic teachings.

Statues express the spiritual peace of the Buddha. Prayer wheels (left) are believed to aid meditation.

Review and Assess

1. Write one sentence for each vocabulary term.

Eightfold Path	**karma**
Four Noble Truths	**monk**

2. Why did Siddhartha leave the life of a prince and become a monk?

3. What did the Buddha teach about the proper way to live?

4. How might Buddhism have changed the **culture** of the areas of India that accepted the Buddha's teaching?

5. **Compare** and **contrast** the life of Prince Siddhartha Gautama with his life as the Buddha.

Activities

Trace the map of Asia on page R12 in the Atlas at the back of this book. Color the countries in which Buddhism is an important religion (mentioned in the lesson) in red.

Write a list of questions you would ask a Buddhist if you were interviewing him or her for your school newspaper.

Indian Empires

Find out!

How did the Maurya and Gupta empires help shape Indian culture?

- The Mauryas Unify India
- The Gupta Empire

VOCABULARY

tribute
architecture

PEOPLE
Asoka
Chandragupta Maurya
Chandragupta I
Samudragupta
Chandragupta II
Kalidasa

READING STRATEGY

Use a Venn diagram to compare the Maurya and Gupta empires. Write features of one empire in each circle. Write features the two empires share in the central space.

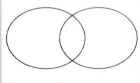

BUILD BACKGROUND

"All men are my children. As for my own children I desire that they may be provided with all the welfare and happiness of this world and of the next, so do I desire for all men as well."

These words were written by an Indian named **Asoka** (uh SOH kuh), who was an emperor of India from 265 to 238 B.C. Asoka had converted to the Buddhist religion and wanted to spread its beliefs throughout India. He was a ruler of the Maurya Empire, which lasted from 322 to 185 B.C. and had united almost all of the Indian subcontinent for the first time.

The Ajanta caves became a Buddhist shrine during the Gupta Empire.

1000 B.C.	750 B.C.	500 B.C.	250 B.C.	A.D. 1	A.D. 250	A.D. 500	A.D. 750	A.D. 1000

You Are Here
330 B.C. – A.D. 535

THE MAURYAS UNIFY INDIA

Around 330 B.C. there were many small kingdoms across India. It was at this time that the Greek general, Alexander the Great, conquered much of western India.

After Alexander's death, **Chandragupta Maurya** (chon druh GUP tuh MAWR yuh), a ruler in northern India, began to build his own empire around 300 B.C. He built an empire called the Maurya Empire that lasted 140 years. Its capital city was called Pataliputra.

The Maurya Empire

Chandragupta Maurya conquered a large part of northern India. However, ruling such a large area was an even greater challenge. Chandragupta appointed thousands of people to help him with this task. Tax collectors were sent across the empire to collect one fourth of farmers' crops and payments from herders and merchants. With the taxes, the Maurya rulers built thousands of miles of roads to connect the empire.

The Maurya rulers built a road connecting Pataliputra and the city of **Taxila**. This royal road survives to this day and is known as the Grand Trunk Road.

Asoka

Chandragupta's grandson, Asoka, ruled from 265 to 238 B.C. He extended the empire by conquering much of southern India. During the first years of his rule, Asoka was cruel, but he converted to Buddhism and turned away from violence.

Asoka introduced Buddhism to his empire and advocated tolerance for all faiths. Asoka spread Buddhism to neighboring lands as well. He ordered the building of thousands of *stupas*, or shrines, that contained remains of the Buddha.

READING CHECK What were the major achievements of the Maurya?

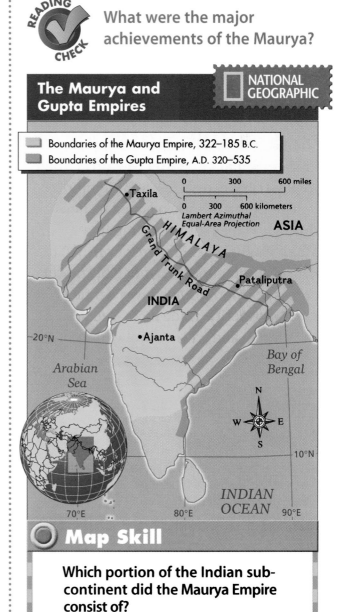

The Maurya and Gupta Empires

NATIONAL GEOGRAPHIC

Boundaries of the Maurya Empire, 322–185 B.C.
Boundaries of the Gupta Empire, A.D. 320–535

0   300   600 miles
0   300   600 kilometers
Lambert Azimuthal
Equal-Area Projection

Taxila
HIMALAYA
Grand Trunk Road
Pataliputra
ASIA
INDIA
20°N
Ajanta
Arabian Sea
Bay of Bengal
N W E S
10°N
INDIAN OCEAN
70°E   80°E   90°E

Map Skill

Which portion of the Indian subcontinent did the Maurya Empire consist of?

137

THE GUPTA EMPIRE

In A.D. 320 **Chandragupta I** founded the Gupta Empire in northeastern India. It is believed that Chandragupta chose his name to link his empire to the Maurya Empire. The Gupta Empire was not as large as the Maurya Empire, but it became a golden age for India. Not only did the empire bring peace and prosperity to India, it fostered the arts and learning, and was a time of great achievement. It lasted until A.D. 535.

The Expansion of the Empire

The Gupta Empire was expanded by **Samudragupta** (sah MOO druh GUP tuh), who ruled from 330 to 380. Instead of ruling directly over the lands he conquered, Samudragupta allowed the conquered kings to remain in power. He forced them to pay **tribute**, or taxes, to his empire.

The Gupta Empire reached its height during the reign of Samudragupta's son, **Chandragupta II**. Emperor from 380 to 415, Chandragupta expanded his power across northern India. It was a time of great prosperity. Trade increased across the empire and with distant countries

such as China as well. A lover of learning, Chandragupta II supported the arts and scholars at his court.

The Arts and Learning

One writer at the court of Chandragupta II was **Kalidasa** (kah lee DAH suh). A poet and playwright, Kalidasa wrote the play, *Shakuntala,* that is still performed throughout India today.

Among the achievements of the Gupta Empire are the paintings on the walls of caves near the city of Ajanta. They include lively scenes from Indian life and the life of the Buddha. The pictures illustrate all types of people, rich and poor, workers and beggars, and the animals and flowers of India.

Architecture and mathematics were also achievements of the Gupta Empire. Architecture is the art and science of designing buildings. Many of the beautiful old Gupta temples built more than 1,700 years ago still survive in northern India.

Mathematicians in the court of Chandragupta II invented zero and the way of writing numbers 1 to 9. Later, Arab mathematicians adopted the Indian system, and today we call the numbers used by Americans and many people around the world Arabic numerals.

These numerals and mathematics made it possible to make many kinds of complicated calculations. For instance, Indian astronomers determined the length of a year to be 365 days. They also were able to calculate that Earth is round, rotates on its own axis, and revolves around the sun.

Why is the Gupta Empire considered a "golden age" for India?

PUTTING IT TOGETHER

Two great empires ruled in India between 300 B.C. and A.D. 500. The Maurya Empire united most of India from 322 to 185 B.C. Under the emperor Asoka, Buddhism spread to much of India.

Under the next empire, the Gupta Empire, India experienced a great flowering of the arts, mathematics, and science. During this time, Indian mathematicians invented zero and the method of writing numbers that is used in many parts of the world today.

The Ajanta caves (opposite) are painted with colorful scenes of Indian life. Religion has been an important influence on Gupta art and architecture. This ancient temple (above) is one of many that are still standing .

End of the Gupta Empire

The Gupta Empire declined after the death of Chandragupta II. Around A.D. 450 weak rulers and the invasion of the Huns, a nomadic people from central Asia, led to the end of the empire. After 520, small kingdoms ruled northern India again.

Review and Assess

1. Write one sentence for each vocabulary word.

   architecture   tribute

2. Who was the founder of the Gupta Empire?

3. How did the Maurya and Gupta empires shape Indian culture?

4. Why was the invention of Arabic numerals significant?

5. What generalization can you make about the golden age of India?

Activities

The Indus and the Ganges are the two great rivers of northern India. The Indus River is 1,800 miles long; the Ganges is 1,560 miles long. Construct a bar graph that compares the length of these two great rivers.

Suppose you visit India at the time of the Gupta Empire. Write a diary entry about the arts and learning that you, as a traveler from another land to the court of Chandragupta II, observe in India.

Being a Good Citizen
Stepping Out for a Better Environment

In Bangladesh, average workers earn less than $1,600 a year. Many people have no jobs. Feeding a family takes effort and energy.

In spite of these challenges, a group of young people in Dhaka, the nation's capital, want students to be aware of the nation's environmental problems. They belong to a volunteer organization called STEP. The name stands for *Striving Towards Environmental Protection*.

"We must teach children about the need to protect our environment," says Afifa Raihana, STEP's president.

"We want to live in communities that are clean and green instead of gray and polluted."

She says, "Some of Bangladesh's most pressing problems today have to do with water quality, air pollution, and waste disposal. We want to live in communities that are clean and green instead of gray and polluted."

STEP has over 500 student-volunteers from high schools and colleges. Imran Junaid, age 17, visits fifth and sixth graders at schools in Dhaka and in nearby rural villages to talk about environmental and health issues.

"When we go to schools," he says, "we don't make long

"…we all have a part to play in protecting our environment."

speeches. We show videos or use charts or pictures to make our points."

One pressing problem that Junaid and others talk about is arsenic contamination. Arsenic, a poisonous metal, occurs naturally in ground water in some parts of Bangladesh. STEP works with the United Nations and other international organizations to make people more aware of the danger.

Children are more at risk than adults from polluted water. STEP volunteers talk to school groups about the importance of wells in making drinking water safe. Drinking water with arsenic can be deadly, but if arsenic poisoning is detected early, nutritious food and safe drinking water can prevent serious illness.

Junaid and other volunteers also do community service projects in Dhaka's poorest neighborhoods.

Junaid also says that "Bit by bit through our school talks and our community work, STEP is helping people understand that we all have a part to play in protecting our environment."

Dhaka

Be a Good Citizen

Making Connections

- **What are some environmental issues in your community?**

- **What could students in your community do to raise awareness of environmental or health issues?**

Talk About it!

- **How might Imran Junaid make a talk on drinking water interesting to sixth graders?**

Act On It

In the Community

Find out how water is made safe for drinking in your community. Ask a speaker from the water department to come to your class. Make a list of questions to ask before the speaker arrives.

In the Classroom

Make a list of environmental issues. Choose one to illustrate in a poster. Display your posters in your classroom.

VOCABULARY REVIEW

Number a sheet of paper from 1 to 5. Beside each number write the word or term from the list below that matches the description.

Buddhism	**monk**
caste system	**subcontinent**
Hinduism	

1. A man who gives up all for religion
2. A large landmass that is geographically separated from the rest of a continent
3. Indian religion based on the belief that all living things are connected
4. A religion founded by Siddhartha Gautama in India
5. The organization of Hindu peoples into four levels or classes

CHAPTER COMPREHENSION

6. How did the hot climate affect farming in the Indus Valley?
7. What is one theory about why the early cities of the Indus Valley were abandoned?
8. What was special about the city of Mohenjo-Daro? What do the similarities between it and the city of Harappa suggest about the ancient civilization of the Indus Valley?
9. What is dharma?
10. What does the Middle Way of living mean?
11. What were some of the accomplishments in mathematics and science during the Gupta Empire?
12. **Write** a short article for your school newspaper about Buddhism. Describe its main beliefs and practices.

● SKILL REVIEW

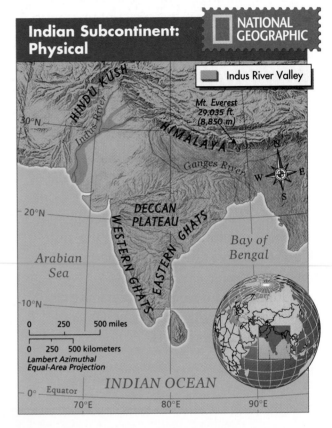

Indian Subcontinent: Physical

NATIONAL GEOGRAPHIC

Indus River Valley

13. **Geography Skill** In which direction do lines of latitude run? Of longitude?
14. **Geography Skill** What do lines of latitude measure? Lines of longitude?
15. **Geography Skill** What is the prime meridian?
16. **Geography Skill** On the map above, what line of longitude runs through the Indus Plain?
17. **Geography Skill** Locate the Bay of Bengal. Between what lines of latitude is it located?
18. **Geography Skill** About how many miles is the equator from the southernmost tip of India?

USING A TIME LINE

2500 B.C.	2000 B.C.	1500 B.C.	1000 B.C.	500 B.C.	A.D. 1	A.D. 500

2500 B.C.
Harappan civilization begins

1600 B.C.
Harappan civilization ends

1500 B.C.
Aryans migrate to Indus Valley

563 B.C.
Siddhartha Gautama is born

322 B.C.
Maurya Empire unites most of India

A.D. 320
Gupta Empire begins

19. About how long did the Harappan civilization last?

20. Choose the event on the time line that eventually led to the birth of a new religion.

Writing About Culture Suppose you are living in the Gupta Empire during the time of Chandragupta II. What sights would you suggest a visitor see? What information could you give the visitor to explain the importance of the sights?

Use your Foldable to review what you have learned about the Indus River Valley. As you look under the four tabs of your Foldable, mentally recall and sequence important events that occurred in this region during the period that saw the birth of Hinduism and Buddhism. Review your notes on the inside of your Foldable to check your responses. Record any questions that you have. Discuss them with classmates or review the chapter to find answers.

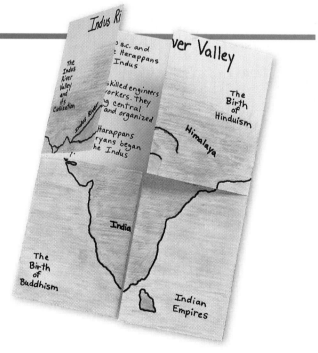

THE Big IDEAS ABOUT...

The Huang He Valley

From its beginning, over 6,000 years ago in the Huang He valley, Chinese culture influenced much of Asia. Over the centuries its culture has also influenced cultures in other parts of the world. In this chapter, you will learn about China's beginnings. It is a story of soldiers, scholars, emperors, and farmers. Read on to learn more about Chinese history and culture.

THE EARLY DYNASTIES OF CHINA

About 4,000 years ago people along the Huang River lay the foundations of Chinese government, society, and arts.

THE HUANG HE VALLEY

The river that is China's life is also called "China's Sorrow." This river that is vital to agriculture also floods.

144

THE FIRST CHINESE EMPIRE

A strong king unifies the kingdoms of China and creates China's first empire.

THE HAN

The Han rulers create a system of government based on Confucian ideas that lasts over 2,000 years.

Foldables

Make this Foldable study guide and use it to record what you learn about "The Huang He Valley."

1. Fold a large sheet of paper in half like a hamburger.

2. With the fold at top, sketch a map of China to cover the front. Then carefully cut along the southern boundary to make your Foldable the shape of China.

3. Label the countries and geographic features. Write the chapter title along the top of the Foldable.

Land of the Middle Kingdom

Find Out!

How have China's rivers contributed to Chinese civilization?

VOCABULARY

loess
famine
gorge
steppe

READING STRATEGY

Copy this compare and contrast chart. Write how the Huang He has helped China in one column and how it has harmed China in the other.

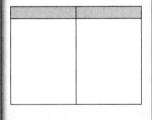

Lesson Outline

• Early Life on the Huang He
• Other Regions of China

BUILD BACKGROUND

For years, the Huang He, or "Yellow River" in English, has been called "China's Sorrow." The annual floods of the Huang He deposit rich yellow silt on the fields along its banks. However, those same floods can race across the land, destroying villages and towns and killing thousands. China's oldest civilization began as simple farming communities using the fertile soil along the banks of this river. This civilization spread to include other regions and groups of people.

EARLY LIFE ON THE HUANG HE

The towering Himalaya Mountains form the southern edge of a large high plain called the **Tibetan Plateau**. From these vast heights, the **Huang He** (HWAHNG HUH) begins its 3,000-mile trip downhill across northern China.

The Huang He flows through a region of hills made almost entirely of **loess** (LES). Loess is a dusty, yellow soil that is easily carried by the wind. During summer rains, huge amounts of loess wash into the Huang, making the water the muddy, yellow color that gives the river its name: *Huang* is the Chinese word for "yellow." *He* means "river".

The Huang He, or "Yellow River," flows for about 3,000 miles across northern China.

In low-lying areas, silt deposits raise the riverbed. When the Huang He floods the **North China Plain**, silt deposits also create rich farmlands. As early as 7,000 years ago, Huang He valley crops were being grown here.

The Huang He is also known as "China's Sorrow." In the past, river floods have killed thousands of people living along its banks. The floods have also caused **famines**, or widespread shortages of food. In addition, floods carry loess to the canals, where water systems become clogged. About 3,000 years ago, farmers began to build levees (LEV eez), or walls, to control the river's floods. In spite of levees, floods continue to affect China's people.

READING CHECK Why does the Huang He flood its banks?

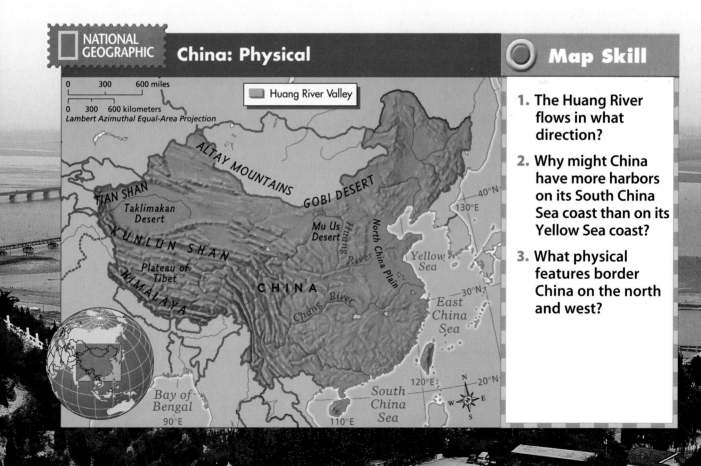

NATIONAL GEOGRAPHIC **China: Physical**

Map Skill

Huang River Valley

0   300   600 miles
0   300   600 kilometers
Lambert Azimuthal Equal-Area Projection

ALTAY MOUNTAINS
TIAN SHAN
Taklimakan Desert
KUNLUN SHAN
Plateau of Tibet
HIMALAYA
Bay of Bengal
GOBI DESERT
Mu Us Desert
Huang River
North China Plain
CHINA
Chang River
Yellow Sea
East China Sea
South China Sea
40°N
130°E
30°N
20°N
120°E
110°E
90°E

1. **The Huang River flows in what direction?**

2. **Why might China have more harbors on its South China Sea coast than on its Yellow Sea coast?**

3. **What physical features border China on the north and west?**

OTHER REGIONS OF CHINA

China has other geographical regions. In addition to rich river valleys such as the Huang He Valley, China has deserts, high mountain ranges, and vast plains. The Himalaya, Tibetan Plateau, and Tian Shan Mountains on the west have long formed barriers to transportation. So, too, has the Gobi Desert in northern China, which stretches over 1,000 miles from east to west.

The Chang River Valley

On the southern edge of the North China Plain is another great river of China, the **Chang Jiang**, or "Long River." The Chang, or Yangtze, is the world's third-longest river. The Chang Jiang begins on the Tibetan Plateau. It continues across central China for over 3,000 miles before it reaches the East China Sea. The Chang Jiang flows through several **gorges**, mountain passes with steep rocky sides, before reaching sea level.

The river can flood in summer, making silt-rich farmland along its banks. At the same time that farmers on the Huang River began growing grains, such as millet, farmers along the Chang Jiang were learning to cultivate rice. The Chang Valley remains a rich agricultural region producing about half of China's food crops. Today, China is working to construct a dam on the Chang Jiang in one of the world's largest construction projects. The purpose of this project, the Three Gorges Dam, is to control flooding and to save lives. The dam will cause some land areas to be submerged and people in rural areas to be relocated. In addition, valuable historical artifacts may be lost to rising waters.

People of China's northern **steppe** region (right) use horses to herd sheep and cattle. China's river valleys have terraced slopes for farming (above).

Northern Steppes

North of the Huang River Valley are huge, windswept **steppes** (STEPS). A steppe is a dry, treeless plain. China's steppe region is not suitable for growing crops. Instead, people in the steppes have herded sheep and cattle for food. In times of drought or famine, people such as the Mongols have attacked their more prosperous neighbors in the river valleys to the south.

 How have China's major geographical features affected its people?

PUTTING IT TOGETHER

Yellow loess, carried by the wind and deposited as silt by the Huang He, created a fertile area that was good for farming. Using levees, early people of the Huang Valley organized and learned to control the river and prosper by farming. The Chang Jiang also has a rich river valley and often floods.

Along rivers such as the Huang He and the Chang Jiang, people grew rice and millet. In the steppes of the north, other groups lived by herding animals. In times of drought or famine, these herding peoples would often attack their farming neighbors.

High mountains, huge deserts, and vast plains create tremendous barriers to transportation in China's northern and western regions. However, people in these areas have developed ways to survive.

Review and Assess

1. Write one sentence for each vocabulary word.

   gorge   loess   steppe

2. Why is the Huang He also called "China's Sorrow?"

3. How has China benefited from and been harmed by its main geographic features?

4. How did the Chinese try to control the dangerous flooding along the rivers of China?

5. What **effects** does flooding of the Huang He have on the land and people in the area?

Look at the map on page 147. Do research on the geographical features of the river valleys, North China Plain, and Tibetan Plateau. Make a three-column chart listing the features of each of these areas.

Suppose that you are a leader in a Chinese farming village. **Write** a speech telling the villagers why they should build levees before the next flood.

The First Dynasties of China

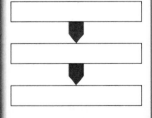
Lesson Outline
• The Shang Dynasty
• Shang Culture
• Inventions, Local Rule, and War
• A Man Named Confucius

VOCABULARY

dynasty
oracle bones
Mandate of Heaven
Warring States Period
Daoism

PEOPLE

Fu Hao
Wuwang
Duke of Zhou
Confucius
Lao Zi

READING STRATEGY

Make a chart like this one to show sequence of events. List the most important events in the lesson.

BUILD BACKGROUND

In 1899, a Chinese scholar was given a packet of animal bones covered with mysterious ancient writing. What did the writing mean? Archaeologists were sent to a site along the Huang He. They determined that a kingdom called Shang developed there at around 1700 B.C. A single family ruled the kingdom for a long time, so the government became known as the Shang **dynasty**. A dynasty is a line of rulers who belong to the same family. For 600 years the Shang dynasty shaped the lives of people living along the Huang He.

This bronze elephant shows the Shang style of combining natural shapes with elaborate decoration.

150

THE SHANG DYNASTY

The Shang dynasty ruled hundreds of towns along the Huang He. Shang kings also created new towns by giving land to their relatives, who oversaw the construction of the new towns. Each town was an important production center. Its farmers and workers supplied food, clothing, and other products for the Shang rulers. These towns also provided soldiers who were called upon to protect and expand the Shang kingdom. They were sent to war whenever they were needed. Prisoners taken in war were forced into slavery.

Near the end of the Shang dynasty's 600-year rule, the capital was destroyed by invaders. A new capital was built near the town that is today **Anyang** (AHN YAHNG). Archaeologists working at Anyang have uncovered many huts. Dug halfway into the ground, these "pit-houses"

served as homes and workshops for metal-workers, potters, and servants. Remains of what seem to be palaces lie at the city's center. Bronze cups, stone carvings, and magnificent chariots have been found in nearby royal tombs. Also found in the tombs were the remains of people, perhaps slaves, who were buried with the kings.

 **READING CHECK** Who ruled Shang towns and villages?

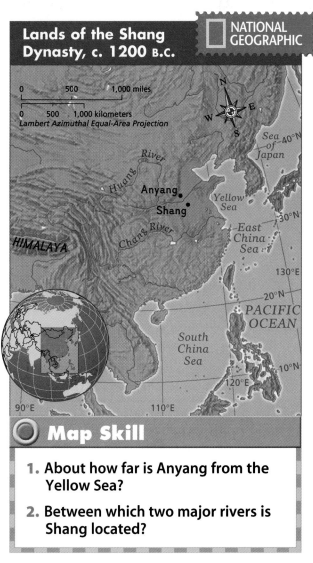

Lands of the Shang Dynasty, c. 1200 B.C.

NATIONAL GEOGRAPHIC

0   500   1,000 miles
0   500   1,000 kilometers
Lambert Azimuthal Equal-Area Projection

Map Skill

1. **About how far is Anyang from the Yellow Sea?**

2. **Between which two major rivers is Shang located?**

SHANG CULTURE

One royal tomb found at Anyang contained hundreds of bronze containers, ivory statues, and other valuable objects. Most Shang rulers are unknown. Because of records in the tomb, we know that it belonged to a woman named **Fu Hao** (FOO HOW), or "Lady Hao." Fu Hao was the wife of a king, Wu Ding. Records in her tomb tell us that she led troops to war and ruled her own town.

Bamboo and Bones: Shang Writing

A writing system had developed along parts of the Huang He even before the Shang dynasty. Like early cuneiform, the earliest Chinese signs looked like pictures of objects. By the time of the Shang dynasty, however, the characters had been simplified. Symbols could stand for objects or ideas. The chart on this page shows how China's writing system developed over time.

One ancient Chinese historian mentioned that Shang records were "written on bamboo and silk." Unfortunately, no bamboo tablets or silk cloth have survived from Shang times. Some writing, however, has been found on bronze pots and stone. More writing has been discovered on cattle and sheep bones like the one on this page. The bones were called **oracle** (AWR uh kul) **bones**. Shang priests heated the bones over a fire until they cracked. The pattern of cracks was thought to answer questions about the future. Shang rulers consulted oracle bones before making an important decision.

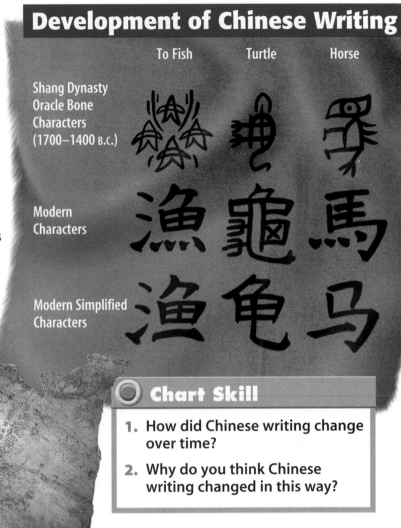

Development of Chinese Writing

	To Fish	Turtle	Horse
Shang Dynasty Oracle Bone Characters (1700–1400 B.C.)			
Modern Characters			
Modern Simplified Characters			

Chart Skill

1. **How did Chinese writing change over time?**

2. **Why do you think Chinese writing changed in this way?**

Shang Religious Beliefs

Shang Chinese believed that their ancestors lived in another world and controlled human life. If an oracle's prediction came true, they believed that it proved the king was being helped by his ancestors. This proved he was the right person to be king.

The people of the Shang dynasty also worshiped many different gods. They believed these gods controlled nature. The ancient people also believed that when they died, they would join their ancestors and the gods.

China's Classic Age

About 3,000 years ago, the Shang dynasty was conquered by western peoples led by a group called the Zhou (JOH). For many years, the Zhou state had been growing in western China. Sometimes, the Zhou and the Shang states were on friendly terms. At other times, the two states fought for power. Around 1100 B.C., the Zhou, under their king **Wuwang** (woo WAHNG), defeated the Shang army and established a new dynasty in the Huang Valley.

The Zhou dynasty has been called China's Classic Age because it was a time of great growth and creativity unequaled by any other time in Chinese history. The Five Classics, or the books that formed the basis of Chinese literary style, were written at this time. They were the *Book of Poetry* (or *Songs*), the *Book of History*, the *Spring and Autumn Annals*, the *Book of Changes*, and the *Book of Rituals*.

The Mandate of Heaven

The Zhou claimed they had the right to start a new dynasty because of the **Mandate of Heaven**. This idea is similar to the Shang belief that the king received help from his ancestors. The Mandate of Heaven says that governments may rule so long as they do so fairly, benefiting the people and performing the proper religious duties. The most important duty is to honor parents and ancestors. One writer said:

Now if a high noble or officer always acts in . . . evil ways, his family will surely come to ruin; if the prince of a country is like this, his state will surely come to ruin. The minister who does not try to correct such vices in the sovereign [ruler] shall be punished.

The Zhou claimed that the last Shang king had been an evil man. Therefore, the Mandate of Heaven had removed him and given power to Wuwang. Wuwang, however, died soon after his conquest of the Shang lands, leaving only an infant son. While this son was a child, Wuwang's brother, the **Duke of Zhou**, ruled for him.

The Duke of Zhou could easily have killed Wuwang's son and made himself king of China, but he did not. Instead, he defeated a rebellion led by the Shang heir and defended the kingdom against attacks from tribes in the east. The Duke of Zhou is remembered as a great Chinese hero and an example of good leadership.

READING CHECK **How did the Zhou explain their right to rule?**

Chinese objects such as this bronze vessel were used to make offerings to ancestors.

The Smithsonian Institution

153

Zhou throne. One king eventually won control, but the Zhou Empire was losing its hold on China. Local rulers began to fight among themselves.

Uses of Iron

During the Zhou dynasty important advances were made in the production of iron and iron products. New blast furnaces turned out a form of iron that was stronger and lasted much longer than previous forms. Iron was used to manufacture weapons such as daggers and swords, which were used in the constant wars along the borders of the Zhou kingdom. Zhou ironworkers also applied their skills to the production of other objects, including sculptures of animals.

Zhou ironworkers began to manufacture agricultural tools such as spades, knives, and sickles. These new iron tools soon replaced the wooden, stone, and bone tools that had been used for so long. With iron tools and irrigation, farming became easier and more productive. Larger crops enabled farmers to feed China's growing cities.

Horses and Chariots

Zhou people learned horseback riding from the herding people of the north and west. Messages could be carried quickly by someone riding a horse. Soldiers on horseback could travel more quickly and use bows and arrows more effectively. The Zhou developed chariots for battle. Zhou workers improved the harnesses used for chariot horses. Not until centuries later would Europeans improve on these harnesses invented by the Zhou.

INVENTIONS, LOCAL RULE, AND WAR

The Zhou dynasty was a time of great prosperity in China. Trade expanded as new roads and canals connected cities and swamps were drained. For the first time, merchants began to use metal coins instead of the sea shells used during the Shang dynasty. Zhou coins were widely accepted and increased Chinese trade.

The Zhou System of Rule

The Zhou system of government was much like that of the Shang dynasty. Smaller states in the kingdom were given to the king's friends and relatives to rule. However, each ruler was allowed to control little more than a fortified city. Zhou cities were surrounded by smaller towns whose people might not be friendly to Zhou rule.

The Warring States Period

For 200 years, the Zhou kept peace throughout their empire. There were wars fought against invaders from outside China and rebellions within, but the empire remained generally peaceful.

In 771 B.C., the Zhou king was killed by invaders. Two rival kings claimed the

The period of warfare continued for several hundred years. Because many local rulers went to war with each other, it is often called the **Warring States Period**, which lasted from about 475 B.C. to 221 B.C.

A Time of Changes

The Warring States Period was a very turbulent time, but it was also a time of cultural advances. Each local ruler tried to attract the best scholars and thinkers to help him rule his state wisely. Each thinker had his own idea about the best way to rule and to bring peace and unity to China. Because there were so many ideas, this period is also called the era of the "Hundred Schools" of philosophy.

China's most famous scholar lived during this time. His name was Kong Fu Zi, or, as he is known in English, **Confucius**. His teachings about government and family would change China forever.

Another famous Chinese thinker was **Lao Zi**. He was born in about 604 B.C. His teachings are the foundation of **Daoism**. *Dao* means "the way." Unlike Confucius, Lao Zi believed that nature should guide people in their lives. Lao Zi did not believe that worldly riches and high offices were important. Lao Zi's ideas had a great influence on Chinese thought, art, and medicine. During the time of the Hundred Schools, Daoist thinking gave an alternative way of dealing with the world.

READING CHECK **What caused the decline of the Zhou?**

Lao Zi rides a water buffalo (below). Animals from legends decorate this bronze water vessel (right). This jade dragon (opposite) was a good luck symbol.

155

A MAN NAMED CONFUCIUS

Confucius was born in about 551 B.C. in the small state of Lu, where many Zhou traditions had been preserved. Confucius traveled from state to state and advised many rulers. In his travels, he attracted students. After Confucius's death, these students wrote down many of his thoughts and ideas, as well as stories about his life. These writings are collected in a book called the *Analects*.

Confucius believed that society could be made fair and good. What do the *Analects* say about how people ought to behave?

Confucius did not start a religion. He saw himself as a teacher who gave knowledge of the past to people in the present. He studied the past and copied the example of such men as the Duke of Zhou.

Confucius and Education

Confucius believed that the key to happiness was a good education. Helping others was a natural result of a good education. Confucius taught that education develops *ren*, or "benevolence," which he thought was the most important quality in a person. "Benevolence" means always acting fairly towards others. Confucius believed that if everyone in the state,

Primary Source:

excerpt from the
"Analects of Confucius"
— written c. 500 B.C.

*Be dutiful at home, brotherly in public; be **discreet** and trustworthy . . .*

*The progress of the **virtuous** person is upwards; the progress of the selfish person is downwards.*

The virtuous person is modest in his speech, but [excellent] in his actions.

When a country is well governed, poverty and corruption are things to be ashamed of. When a country is poorly governed, riches and honor are things to be ashamed of.

When a prince's personal conduct is correct, his government is effective without the issuing of orders. If his personal conduct is not correct, he may issue orders, but they will not be followed.

What qualities did Confucius admire in a ruler and his people?

discreet: careful and sensible
virtuous: honorable

from the ruler down to the lowest officials, ruled with justice, then good government and prosperity would follow naturally.

 What did Confucius say would make a state run fairly?

PUTTING IT TOGETHER

The Shang won control of the Huang He delta in about 1700 B.C. Their dynasty expanded its kingdom along the river and founded new towns. The Shang developed new skills, including a system of writing.

The Zhou defeated the Shang in about 1100 B.C. The Zhou explained their takeover with a concept called the "Mandate of Heaven." Zhou rule lasted for about 200 years, and was followed by a period of warfare called the Warring States period. Confucius lived during this time. In the next lesson, you will read about how a strong ruler reunified all of China.

A grinning face decorates this bronze axe-head from the Shang period.

 **Review and Assess**

1. Write one sentence for each vocabulary term.

   dynasty   **oracle bones**
   Mandate of   **Warring States**
      Heaven   **Period**

2. What are oracle bones?

 3. How did the early dynasties shape the culture of China?

4. Why is the Zhou dynasty called China's Classic Age?

5. **Compare** the Shang system of government with that of the pharaohs' government in Egypt.

Activities

Make a chart of the Shang and Zhou dynasties. List the accomplishments of each dynasty in the appropriate column.

● ●

Write a paragraph comparing the Shang and Zhou dynasties of China.

157

Using Special Purpose Maps: Distribution Maps

The map below is a kind of special purpose map called a **distribution map**. Distribution maps show how something is spread out over an area. Some of the things distribution maps can feature include population, natural resources, language, climate, and products.

VOCABULARY

distribution map
population density

LEARN THE SKILL

Study the map on this page as you follow the steps to learn about distribution maps.

1. **Identify the title of the map.**
   The title of this map is "Qin China, A.D. 2: Population Distribution." It tells you that the map shows how the population was spread across China at this time.

2. **Study the map key.**
   The map is shaded in red, orange, yellow and green. The map key, or legend, identifies the **population density**, or the number of people who live per square mile or kilometer, represented by each color. Areas with many people per square mile are called high density areas. Areas with few people per square mile are called low density areas.

3. **Use the map key to interpret the color symbols on the map.**
   Refer to the map key as you examine the map. It shows that the most densely populated area was on the Huang River, east of Luoyang. Most areas of China are green, indicating that they had 0 to 29 people per square mile.

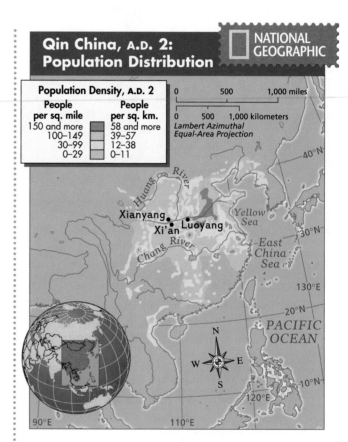

Qin China, A.D. 2: Population Distribution

NATIONAL GEOGRAPHIC

Population Density, A.D. 2

People per sq. mile	People per sq. km.
150 and more	58 and more
100–149	39–57
30–99	12–38
0–29	0–11

0   500   1,000 miles
0   500   1,000 kilometers
Lambert Azimuthal Equal-Area Projection

TRY THE SKILL

China today is much larger than it was 2,000 years ago. Use the population distribution map of China today to answer the following questions:

1. What does the title of the map tell you?

2. How many areas of population density does the map legend identify?

3. **Compare and contrast** China today to China long ago. What regions have a large population today but did not in A.D. 2?

4. How can distribution maps help you better understand history?

EXTEND THE SKILL

Often comparing different kinds of maps will give you information that will help you better understand a special purpose map such as a population distribution map. Compare the population map of modern China to the physical map of China on page 147. Then answer the questions below.

- On which landforms and near which physical features do people in high density areas live?

- What geographical features help explain why some areas of China have low population density?

- How can comparing distribution maps help you better understand the world today?

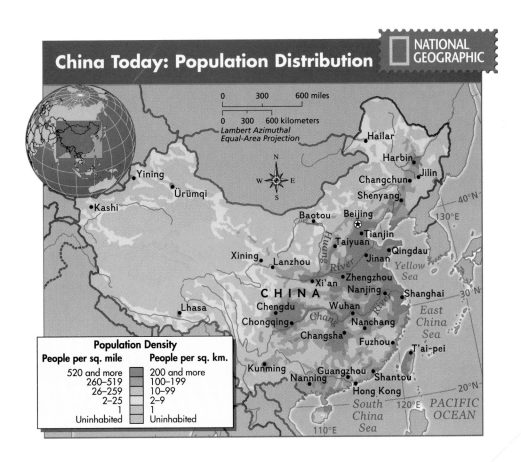

China Today: Population Distribution

Lesson 3

The First Chinese Empire

 **What did the Qin dynasty achieve?**

Lesson Outline
• A Chinese Empire
• Protecting a Growing Empire
• The Peasant Emperor

BUILD BACKGROUND

You have read how the Zhou kingdoms began to war among themselves. Over time, one small state, called **Qin** (chin), in northwestern China built up a strong army. In 246 B.C., a 13-year-old boy named Ying Zheng came to the throne of Qin. Within 25 years, this young king and his army had conquered the seven major states of northern China.

You Are Here
246 B.C. – 206 B.C.

A CHINESE EMPIRE

After his conquests, Ying Zheng declared himself China's emperor. An **emperor** is the supreme ruler of an empire, or group of states under one government. He celebrated his new power with a new name, **Shihuangdi** (SHEE hwahng dee), or "First Grand Emperor."

What made it possible for Shihuangdi and his armies to win power and to hold his empire together? Geography played a part. The original Qin region was protected by the **Qinling** (CHIN LING) **Mountains** on one side and by the Huang He on the other. From this central point, soldiers were able to protect and expand the empire.

Central Control

Shihuangdi also had new ideas about how a government should be run. These ideas were even more important than his armies in strengthening Qin's power. Shihuangdi divided the empire into 36 **provinces** (PRAHV in sez), or political divisions of land. He appointed a governor for each province, and he also let farmers own land. These moves weakened the power of local nobles.

By A.D. 1600, Chinese rulers had completed the Great Wall begun by Shihuangdi in 215 B.C.

Shihuangdi also forced many nobles to move to the capital city, **Xianyang** (shee AHN yang). Then, he took away their weapons so they could not challenge his rule or disrupt peaceful government.

 What steps did Shihuangdi take to ensure peace within his empire?

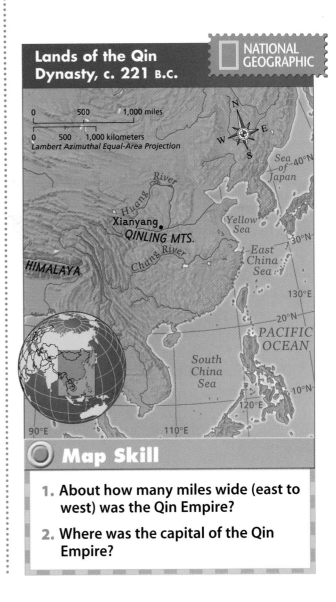

Lands of the Qin Dynasty, c. 221 B.C.

NATIONAL GEOGRAPHIC

0 500 1,000 miles
0 500 1,000 kilometers
Lambert Azimuthal Equal-Area Projection

Huang River
Xianyang
QINLING MTS.
Chang River
HIMALAYA
Sea of Japan
Yellow Sea
East China Sea
PACIFIC OCEAN
South China Sea
40°N
30°N
20°N
10°N
130°E
120°E
110°E
90°E

Map Skill

1. About how many miles wide (east to west) was the Qin Empire?

2. Where was the capital of the Qin Empire?

161

PROTECTING A GROWING EMPIRE

Shihuangdi tried to standardize many features of his empire. He set up a single system of writing which has greatly influenced the modern Chinese language. He ordered local rulers to use this writing system, to report to the capital, and to collect and record taxes. Shihuangdi ordered that roads should be made a standard size. He created a single system of money, and standardized common weights and measures.

Frequently throughout Chinese history, herding peoples from the northern steppes had raided the rich lands of China. Shihuangdi ordered protective walls to be built to block these invasions. Years later, similar walls were built across these same mountains and valleys, as later rulers tried to keep out northern invaders. These later walls made up the **Great Wall of China** that stands to this day.

The common people were the backbone of the Qin Empire. Their hard work as farmers, soldiers, and builders kept the empire strong. Life continued to center around the seasonal floods of the Huang He. Qin farmers grew wheat, rice, and other crops needed to feed the empire.

Toil and Taxes

Under Shihuangdi's leadership, reunified China grew stronger and richer. In time, however, the government began to make greater demands on its people. A larger portion of farmers' crops was taken as taxes. More farmers were forced to labor on public projects such as the highways and walls. This left less time and labor to grow crops needed to survive. Many people began to grumble about Shihuangdi's rule.

A Harsh Government

Shihuangdi used a philosophy of government called **legalism**. Legalism taught that actions that help the emperor and the state should be encouraged by a strict system of rewards and severe punishments.

Read the selection below from Sima Qian (soo MA CHAY en), a court historian who wrote about the Qin 100 years after the dynasty ended. In the selection, one of Shihuangdi's advisors tells how to be sure that no one can criticize the emperor's actions.

Primary Source:

excerpt from
Records of the Grand Historian
— *Sima Qian, c. 100 B.C.*

The prime minister Li Si said . . . "Scholars . . . judge each new [law] according to their own school of thought. . . . If this is not prohibited, the [emperor's] prestige will suffer. . . . I humbly propose that all historical records but those of Qin be burned. If anyone who is not a court scholar dares to keep [them], these should be **confiscated** *and burned. The only books which need not be destroyed are those dealing with medicine, [religion], and agriculture." The emperor [approved of] this proposal.*

Why did Li Si want to burn historical records?

_____

confiscated: seized by officials

Shihuangdi Fears for His Life

Shihuangdi made many enemies. Educated people were angered by his destruction of ancient books. Nobles were angry because the emperor took away their power and treated them cruelly. The common people were angry because the Qin taxed them heavily and forced them to work on building projects.

The Clay Army

One of the greatest building projects of the Qin Empire was the construction of a tomb for Shihuangdi. Construction began in 246 B.C. Thousands of Chinese worked to make the soldiers. The method they used is shown on page 164. Shihuangdi had 8,000 clay soldiers and horses placed in his tomb. Each soldier was a portrait of an actual person. When he died and was buried in 210 B.C., this "spirit army" was arranged to protect the dead emperor. Shihuangdi's burial place lies under a giant mound near the clay army. The tomb was forgotten until it was rediscovered accidentally in 1974.

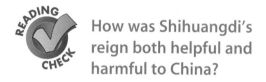

READING CHECK How was Shihuangdi's reign both helpful and harmful to China?

Archaeologists work to preserve bronze horses found in the emperor's tomb.

THE PEASANT EMPEROR

Shihuangdi's death was kept secret until his generals could make his second son, Hu Ha, the new Emperor of China. However, a rebellion against the dynasty broke out as soon as the Chinese people learned of the emperor's death. A general named **Hsiang Yü** and a peasant named **Liu Pang** led the rebellion. Hu Ha was unable to defeat the rebels and the Qin were overthrown about 200 B.C. Then Liu Pang defeated Hsiang Yü and established a new dynasty, the Han dynasty. Like his Zhou predecessors, Liu Pang used the "Mandate of Heaven" to justify his rule.

Making the Clay Army

Coils of clay are looped to make the body.

Clothing is molded in the clay.

Hands are made in molds.

The parts are assembled and painted.

The parts are baked in a kiln, a large oven.

Heads are molded separately.

⦿ Chart Skill

1. **What material was used to form the soldiers?**

2. **What parts were made separately?**

164

Shihuangdi's dynasty had ruled China for less than 20 years. However, this emperor left a mark on Chinese culture that lasts to this day. The Han adopted his administrative structure, system of weights and measures, and other improvements. The changes made by the first emperor marked China forever. In fact, the English name "China" comes from the Qin dynasty.

READING CHECK How did Shihuangdi change China?

PUTTING IT TOGETHER

By 221 B.C., the Qin had conquered all of China and created its first empire. Shihuangdi's reforms in transportation, money, and weights and measures helped to unify China.

Shihuangdi was a harsh ruler, and his reign was short. However, Shihuangdi left a lasting legacy, including having a centralized government and standardized systems of writing, money, and weights and measures.

Ancient Chinese believed Shihuangdi's clay soldiers (opposite) would guard his tomb. This bronze chariot and its horses (left) weigh over one ton.

Review and Assess

1. Write one sentence for each vocabulary word.

   emperor   legalism   province

2. Who was China's first emperor?

3. Identify ways in which the Qin dynasty changed China.

4. How would a standard system of money and measurement help trade?

5. **Compare** and **contrast** legalism and the ideas of Confucius.

Activities

Look at the map on page 161. Measure and write down the distance between Xianyang and the Yellow Sea.

. . . .

Suppose you were a scholar at the time of Shihuangdi. **Write** a letter expressing your opinion about the burning of ancient books and other acts of the emperor.

165

The Han Dynasty

How did Confucianism affect Han China?

Lesson Outline

- A New Kind of Government
- Han Science and Technology
- The Fall of the Han

VOCABULARY

Confucianism
bureaucracy
Grand School
seismograph

PEOPLE

Gao Zu
Wudi
Wang Mang

READING STRATEGY

Copy this cause and effect chart. In the left-hand column, list Confucian ideals. In the right-hand column, list actions Han rulers took to encourage each ideal.

BUILD BACKGROUND

When Liu Pang became Emperor of China in 206 B.C. he took the name **Gao Zu** (GOW ZOO). His family began the Han dynasty, which would rule China for over 400 years. This dynasty was so important in Chinese history that even today, the Chinese word for someone who is Chinese means "someone from Han."

Museum of Fine Arts, Boston

You Are Here
206 B.C. – A.D. 220

A NEW KIND OF GOVERNMENT

From the map on this page, you can see that the Han extended China's borders. Controlling this vast area was difficult.

The Han rulers decided to base government on **Confucianism**, or the teachings of Confucius, who had lived three centuries earlier. Han rulers gave government jobs to educated people, rather than to nobles. One of the emperors, **Wudi** (WOO DEE), who ruled China from 140 B.C. to 87 B.C., decided to expand the Chinese **bureaucracy**. A bureaucracy is an organization that runs the daily business of government.

The Grand School

Wudi created schools to prepare students for government service. These schools taught Chinese literature and Confucian ideas. Excellent students were sent to the best school in the empire, the **Grand School**. For one year, students learned Chinese history, proper behavior, poetry, and music. Teachers at the Grand School were China's most brilliant scholars. At the end of the year, students took a long test. If they passed, they earned jobs as government workers or teachers. They also won great respect in society for their education and skills.

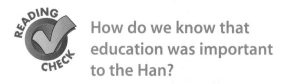

READING CHECK How do we know that education was important to the Han?

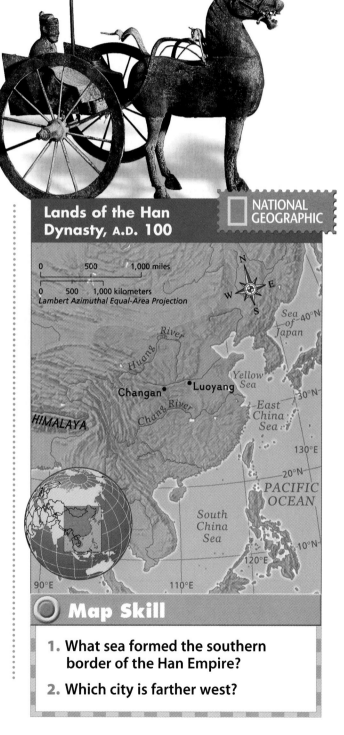

Han soldiers (opposite) carry silk banners. A Han official might have used a chariot like this one.

Lands of the Han Dynasty, A.D. 100

NATIONAL GEOGRAPHIC

0   500   1,000 miles
0   500   1,000 kilometers
Lambert Azimuthal Equal-Area Projection

Sea of Japan
Huang River
Yellow Sea
Changan
Luoyang
East China Sea
HIMALAYA
Chang River
40°N
30°N
130°E
20°N
PACIFIC OCEAN
South China Sea
10°N
120°E
90°E   110°E

Map Skill

1. **What sea formed the southern border of the Han Empire?**

2. **Which city is farther west?**

167

HAN SCIENCE AND TECHNOLOGY

Confucian emphasis on education increased knowledge and invention during the Han dynasty. Chinese scientists and mathematicians learned to predict eclipses of the sun. Doctors discovered new kinds of medicines, and poets wrote about the beauty of the land. In fact, during the Han dynasty, the Chinese language grew from 3,000 to 9,000 characters. In A.D. 100 scholars wrote the first Chinese dictionary.

The Han invented paper. Like Egyptian papyrus, paper provided a way to keep written records. The Han also built a silk-making industry. Silk is a very beautiful, light, and strong fabric. Chinese silk was traded as far as Europe. The Han also invented the wheelbarrow and produced beautiful vases and fine china.

One of the most remarkable Han inventions was the **seismograph** (SīZ muh graf) shown below. This machine detected earthquakes.

Inside a vase hung a long metal pendulum. When the ground shook even slightly, the pendulum swung toward the direction of the earthquake. The swinging pendulum hit a rod inside the vase. This rod would then knock a ball out of a dragon's mouth. The ball fell in the direction of the earthquake region. In this way, Han rulers almost immediately knew when and where earthquakes occurred. Thus they could send food and supplies to the damaged area without delay.

READING CHECK What were some Han inventions?

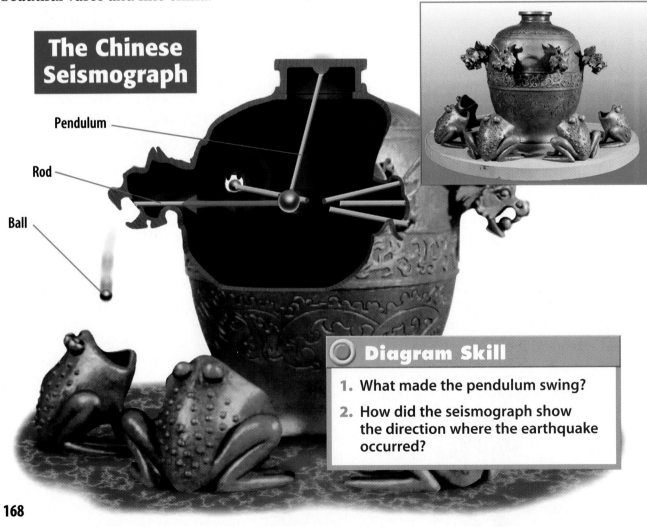

The Chinese Seismograph

Pendulum

Rod

Ball

◎ Diagram Skill

1. **What made the pendulum swing?**

2. **How did the seismograph show the direction where the earthquake occurred?**

Making "Rough-straw" Paper

Archaeologists say that paper was probably invented around 100 B.C. Study the graphics, then answer the questions.

STEPS USED IN MAKING CHINESE "ROUGH-STRAW" PAPER

1 Bamboo is husked and beaten.

2 Ground bamboo is soaked in lime mineral to soften.

3 Softened bamboo is steamed and boiled over an oven and rinsed. Process is repeated.

QUESTIONS:

1 What materials and equipment are used to make "rough-straw" paper? How long does the process take?

2 How long does the bamboo soak in the lime mixture?

5 Mixture is flattened into sheets, squeezed of excess water, and hung to dry.

4 Bamboo slush is mixed with ground birch leaves.

To learn more, visit our Web site: www.mhschool.com

Time Line from Raw Bamboo to Paper

DAY 1	DAY 1-4	DAY 4-49	DAY 49	DAY 56
Husk and beat the bamboo.	Soak bamboo in lime mixture.	Steam over an oven and rinse. Repeat.	Add birch leaves; flatten mixture and hang to dry.	Paper is ready for use.

THE FALL OF THE HAN

Under the Han dynasty, the emperor became all-powerful. He issued all laws and he was the final judge. He was also the chief priest at Chinese religious ceremonies. This situation worked well when the emperors were strong men and good leaders. When a weak man became emperor, the unity of the empire was weakened.

In A.D. 9, a man named **Wang Mang** seized the throne. Wang realized that the powerful nobles and landowners threatened his power. He tried to introduce changes, such as the abolition of slavery and economic reforms, to break the power of these landowners. Wang's reforms failed, and he lost support.

The Han dynasty overthrew him in A.D. 23, and Han power was restored. After Wang Mang's defeat, the Han capital was moved east from Changan to Luoyang.

The "later" Han dynasty had to compromise to stay in power. The powerful landlords became more independent, and the unity of the empire was much

This carving (right) shows weapons used by the Han. Silk production (below) helped the Han economy.

weaker than it had been under the first Han rulers 400 years earlier.

In spite of these difficulties, later Han rulers were able to re-establish the central bureaucracy. They even managed to extend the borders of the Chinese Empire.

The Han dynasty ruled until around A.D. 220. It finally collapsed because of military defeats and warfare among its leaders. China then split into three kingdoms.

 READING CHECK What caused the fall of the Han dynasty?

This bronze palace lamp is from the tomb of a Han princess.

PUTTING IT TOGETHER

The Han expanded China's borders, based their government on Confucian ideas, and founded a bureaucracy for which officials had to take an exam. Han inventions included paper, the wheelbarrow, and the seismograph. The Han also made great advances in crafts such as silk making and fine china.

The fall of the Han came about for many reasons. Later emperors withdrew from public life, leaving the government to be run by corrupt officials. The Han dynasty finally fell in A.D. 220.

Review and Assess

1. Write one sentence for each vocabulary word or term.

   **bureaucracy   Grand School
   Confucianism**

2. What is a seismograph?

3. How did Confucianism affect Han China?

4. What advances in **technology** were made during the Han dynasty?

5. What **effect** did the Han dynasty have on government in China?

Activities

The Han Empire ruled areas that are now parts of several modern countries. Use the maps on page 167 and on page R12 in the Atlas to list the countries.

 **Write** a paragraph that a newspaper reporter in Han China might write. Include your opinions about the ruler and your impressions of Han achievements.

VOCABULARY REVIEW

Number a sheet of paper from 1 to 5. Beside each number write the word or term that matches the definition.

bureaucracy   seismograph

Mandate of Heaven   steppe

province

1. A machine used to detect earthquakes
2. The belief that the emperor's right to rule is granted by the gods
3. A dry, treeless plain
4. A political division of China
5. An organization that runs the daily business of government

CHAPTER COMPREHENSION

6. What is the world's third-largest river? What did early Chinese farmers learn to grow in the river's valley?
7. What do oracle bones tell us about religion and writing during the Shang dynasty?
8. Why was the Zhou craftworker's ability to mold metal an important advance in technology?
9. What did Shihuangdi do to unify China?
10. What was the main idea of legalism? Which leader practiced it?
11. What contributions did the Han dynasty make to China's culture?
12. What is Confucianism? Which dynasty used the ideas of Confucianism and why?
13. **Write** a paragraph describing how an ancient Chinese invention or innovation has affected your life.

SKILL REVIEW

Chinese Dynasties

Dynasty	Original Location	Accomplishments
Shang 1700–1100 B.C.	Huang He Valley	• founded new towns • developed a writing system
Zhou 1100–221 B.C.	western China	• small states were united • time of prosperity and inventions
Qin 221–206 B.C.	northwest China	• created first empire • divided China into 36 provinces • standardized writing and units of measurement
Han 206 B.C.–A.D. 220	all of China	• expanded Chinese bureaucracy • established Grand School • emphasized education

14. **Study Skill** Which dynasty created the first Chinese empire?
15. **Study Skill** Why might the Han dynasty have had such a lasting influence on Chinese culture?
16. **Study Skill** What would you need to know to arrange the dynasties listed on the chart on a time line?
17. **Reading/Thinking Skill** What systems did the Chinese rulers develop to rule their lands?
18. **Reading/Thinking Skill** How did Chinese farmers solve the problem of the yearly flooding of the Huang He?

USING A TIME LINE

2000 B.C.	1500 B.C.	1000 B.C.	500 B.C.	A.D. 1	A.D. 500

1700 B.C.
Shang
dynasty
wins control
of Huang
He delta

1100 B.C.
Shang state
defeated;
Zhou
dynasty
begins

551 B.C.
Birth of
Confucius

221 B.C.
Shihuangdi
becomes
first
Emperor
of China

206 B.C.
Gao Zu
founds
Han
dynasty

A.D. 220
Han
dynasty
ends

19. How many years did the Shang dynasty rule China?

20. Which event on the time line was most helpful in unifying China? Explain your choice.

Writing About Culture Suppose you are a student in the Grand School during the Han dynasty. Write a letter to your parents or another adult explaining why the school is important for you and for China. Include details about ways in which the school will affect your behavior.

Foldables

As you look at China and the Huang He Valley on the front of your Foldable, see if you can answer the questions—what? when? where? and why? Review your notes inside the Foldable to check your responses. Record any questions that you have. Discuss them with classmates or review the chapter to find answers.

VOCABULARY REVIEW

Number a sheet of paper from 1 to 5. Beside each number write the word from the list below that best completes the sentence.

bureaucracy   subcontinent

city-state   technology

hieroglyphics

1. In Sumer, each ____ governed its own city and nearby villages.

2. The tools made by Stone Age peoples were the first examples of ____.

3. Egyptians used ____, or symbols, to keep written records.

4. The Han dynasty established a ____ to run the daily business of government.

5. India is a huge ____ that is part of Asia.

TECHNOLOGY

For resources to help you learn more about the people and places you studied in this unit, visit **www.mhschool.com** and follow the links for Grade 6, Unit 1.

SKILL REVIEW

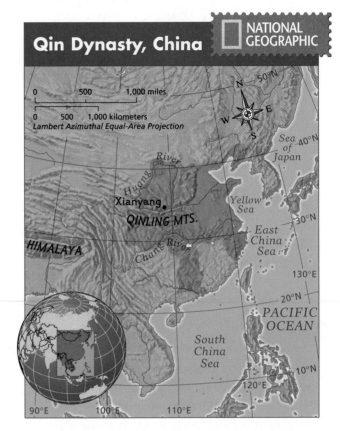

Qin Dynasty, China — NATIONAL GEOGRAPHIC

6. **Geography Skill** Which line of longitude is closest to the town of Xianyang? Between which lines of latitude is it located?

7. **Geography Skill** Why do equal-area projection and mercator projection maps have some distortion?

8. **Study Skill** Suppose a time line is divided into time periods of 500 years and has a time span of 2000 B.C. through A.D. 1000. What years will mark periods on the time line?

9. **Reading/Thinking Skill** What should you do to evaluate a solution to a problem?

10. **Reading/Thinking Skill** When making a decision, why is it important to predict the consequences of each option?

Read the passage and the questions that follow. Write the best answers to the questions on a piece of paper.

1 One of the most remarkable Han inventions was the seismograph. This machine detected earthquakes.

2 Inside a vase hung a long metal pendulum. When the ground shook even slightly, the pendulum swung toward the direction of the earthquake. The swinging pendulum hit a rod inside the vase. This rod would then knock a ball out of a dragon's mouth. The ball fell in the direction of the earthquake region. In this way, Han rulers . . . could send food and supplies to the damaged area without delay.

1 What caused a ball to fall out of a dragon's mouth in the seismograph?

A A rod inside the vase
B A swinging pendulum
C The shaking ground
D A larger ball in the vase

2 What problem did the invention of the seismograph solve for the Han?

F Preventing earthquakes from causing damage
G Responding quickly to areas damaged by earthquake
H Finding a practical use for the pendulum
J Measuring the size and strength of earthquakes

WRITING ACTIVITIES

Writing to Persuade Suppose you had lived in Catal Huyuk. *Write* what you would say to an outsider to persuade him or her to live in your city.

Writing to Inform Suppose that you are preparing an article for a children's magazine. *Write* an outline for information you would include on pharaohs and Egyptian religion to explain the purpose of the Egyptian pyramids.

Writing to Express Choose the topic of Hinduism, Buddhism, or Judaism. *Write* an essay that tells about the beliefs or ideas of the religion.

LITERATURE

THE FIRST FLUTE

Selections by Dorothy Sharp Carter
Art by Michael Jaroszko

The Maya of Central America had many folk tales. This tale tells how the most common Maya musical instrument, a flute called a chirimia, *was invented.*

During the glory of the Mayan civilization . . . there lived a **cacique** who had a . . . daughter, the Princess Nima-Cux, whom he loved dearly.

Not only was Nima-Cux beautiful, but she was possessed of talents. . . . Nima-Cux could sing like a bird . . .

As princesses should, Nima-Cux had everything she asked for. . . . No wonder Nima-Cux was happy.

[As] Nima-Cux neared her sixteenth birthday she became sad and **melancholy**. Nothing made her happy.

---

cacique (kə sēk′): Spanish for a tribal chief.
melancholy (mel′ ən kol ē): depressed; very sad.

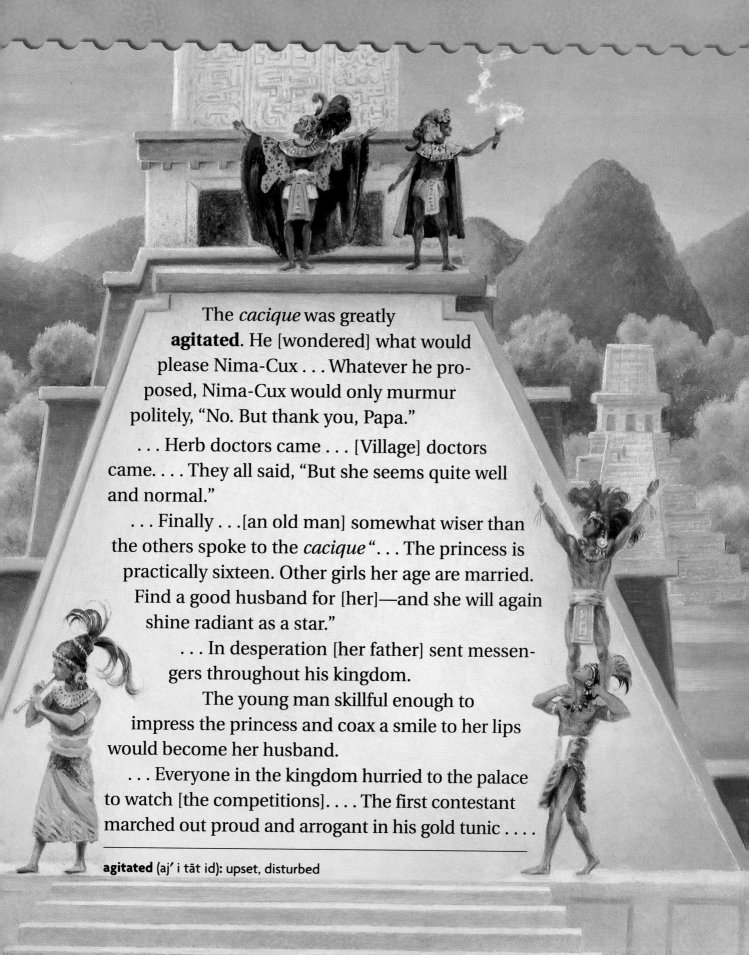

The *cacique* was greatly **agitated**. He [wondered] what would please Nima-Cux . . . Whatever he proposed, Nima-Cux would only murmur politely, "No. But thank you, Papa."

. . . Herb doctors came . . . [Village] doctors came. . . . They all said, "But she seems quite well and normal."

. . . Finally . . .[an old man] somewhat wiser than the others spoke to the *cacique* ". . . The princess is practically sixteen. Other girls her age are married. Find a good husband for [her]—and she will again shine radiant as a star."

. . . In desperation [her father] sent messengers throughout his kingdom.

The young man skillful enough to impress the princess and coax a smile to her lips would become her husband.

. . . Everyone in the kingdom hurried to the palace to watch [the competitions]. . . . The first contestant marched out proud and arrogant in his gold tunic . . . .

---

agitated (aj′ i tāt id): upset, disturbed

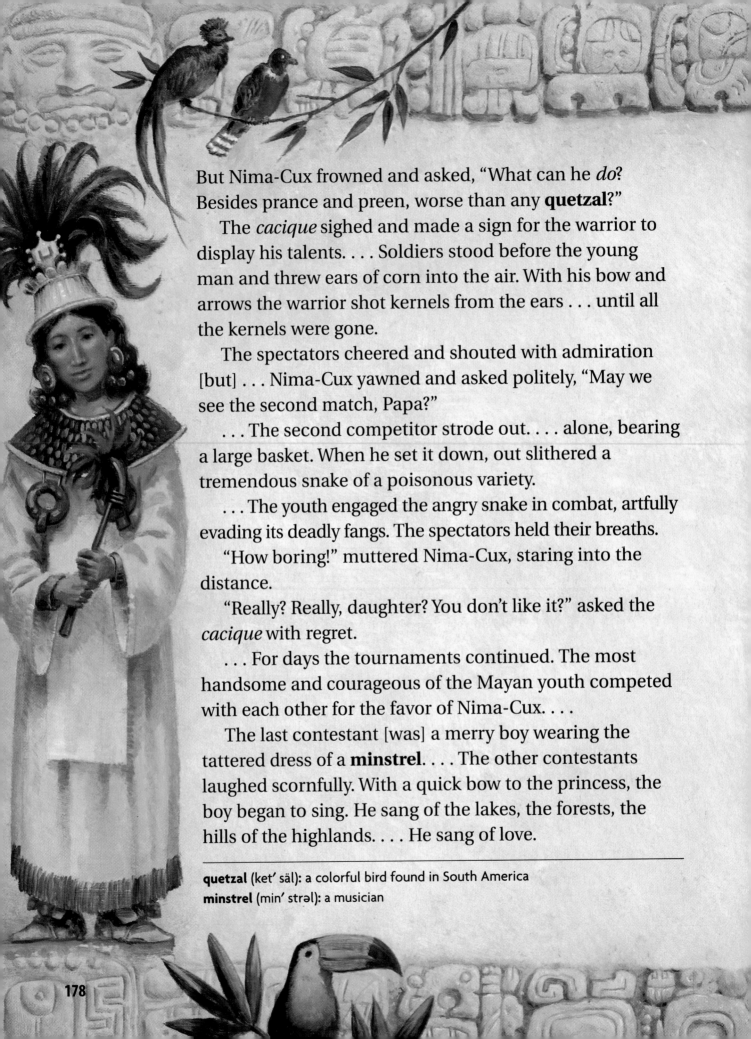

But Nima-Cux frowned and asked, "What can he *do*? Besides prance and preen, worse than any **quetzal**?"

The *cacique* sighed and made a sign for the warrior to display his talents. . . . Soldiers stood before the young man and threw ears of corn into the air. With his bow and arrows the warrior shot kernels from the ears . . . until all the kernels were gone.

The spectators cheered and shouted with admiration [but] . . . Nima-Cux yawned and asked politely, "May we see the second match, Papa?"

. . . The second competitor strode out. . . . alone, bearing a large basket. When he set it down, out slithered a tremendous snake of a poisonous variety.

. . . The youth engaged the angry snake in combat, artfully evading its deadly fangs. The spectators held their breaths.

"How boring!" muttered Nima-Cux, staring into the distance.

"Really? Really, daughter? You don't like it?" asked the *cacique* with regret.

. . . For days the tournaments continued. The most handsome and courageous of the Mayan youth competed with each other for the favor of Nima-Cux. . . .

The last contestant [was] a merry boy wearing the tattered dress of a **minstrel**. . . . The other contestants laughed scornfully. With a quick bow to the princess, the boy began to sing. He sang of the lakes, the forests, the hills of the highlands. . . . He sang of love.

quetzal (ket′ säl): a colorful bird found in South America
minstrel (min′ strəl): a musician

Not bad, not bad, nodded the *cacique.* . . . He glanced at his daughter. What astonishment! . . . She was smiling!

"I like him, Papa. We can sing together. I will marry him. Only first, he must learn the song of each bird of the forest. Then he can teach me."

The minstrel was happy to oblige. He had meant it when he sang of love. At once he disappeared into the jungle.

Day after day he practiced, imitating this bird, then that one. But Guatemala is home to . . . thousands of birds. The minstrel began to despair at his task.

The god of the forest, after listening for days to the young minstrel's efforts, took pity on him. He appeared before the minstrel.

"Perhaps I can help you," he offered.

Severing a small limb from a tree, the god removed the **pith** and cut a series of holes in the tube. And he instructed the young man . . . to blow into one end while moving his fingers over the holes.

With a **torrent** of thanks, the minstrel flew on his way, carrying the *chirimia,* or flute. . . . Nima-Cux . . . received the youth with joy. Enchanted she was with the flute and its **airs**. . . . The two were married and lived long and happily in the palace of the *cacique.*

---

pith (pith): the insides of a branch
torrent (tôr′ ənt): with overwhelming force
airs (ârz): melodies

Write About It!

Write about the folk tale. Use story clues to explain what the tale tells you about Maya life.

Unit 2

The Ancient World

TAKE A LOOK

What were the major achievements of the ancient "classic" ages?

The Romans built the victory arch (60 ft.) in the Forum to celebrate a victory. Gateway Arch (630 ft.) in St. Louis, the world's highest arch, honors American pioneers.

THE Big IDEAS ABOUT...

Ancient Greece

From a rocky peninsula in the Aegean Sea sprang a people who created a way of living that continues to inspire us to this day. Our own world owes a great debt to ancient Greek innovations in science, thought, and government. Their civilization spread around the shores of the Mediterranean Sea and was the basis for civilizations that followed. Read on to find out more about ancient Greece.

THE LAND OF GREECE

Greece is rocky without much land suitable for growing crops. Its mountainous terrain leads the Greeks to develop small city-states.

THE BIRTH OF GREEK CIVILIZATION

Greek culture is born out of the union of two very different peoples, powerful sea-going traders and invaders from the north. In time, these two peoples merge into one.

A GOLDEN AGE IN ATHENS

A powerful enemy threatens Greece. Athens defeats the invaders. This begins the golden age of Athenian culture.

ALEXANDER AND THE GREEK EMPIRE

King Philip of Macedon conquers the independent Greek city-states. After his father's death, Alexander builds a great empire.

Foldables

Make this Foldable study guide and use it to record what you learn about "Ancient Greece."

1. Fold a large sheet of paper into a shutterfold.
2. Illustrate the front to make it look like a Greek temple.
3. Draw four equal rows on the inside and label them with the lesson titles.

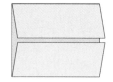

The Land of Greece

Find! out!

How did Greece's geography affect this ancient civilization?

Lesson Outline
- A Mountainous Region
- Economy of Ancient Greece

VOCABULARY

peninsula
harbor

READING STRATEGY

Copy this two-column chart. Then write the names of Greece's largest islands in one column. Write the largest peninsulas in the other column.

BUILD BACKGROUND

"The jewel in Earth's ring" is how one ancient poet described Greece. The ancient Greeks loved their land on the northeastern shores of the Mediterranean Sea. The geography of Greece was rugged and life was challenging. However, the cities of Greece produced one of the great civilizations of the ancient world.

The Mediterranean, the Aegean, and the Ionian seas surround the peninsula of Greece. Greek art used many designs from these seas (opposite).

A MOUNTAINOUS REGION

Ancient Greeks lived in south-eastern Europe and on more than 400 neighboring islands. The biggest of the islands is **Crete**. Crete is about one day's sail south of the Greek mainland. East of Crete lies **Rhodes**, an island near what is today Turkey.

Most of Greece consists of rugged mountains and hills, which cover about 90 percent of the land. Greece has little usable farmland, and traveling over land was difficult in ancient times.

The Greek Coast

Some of Greece's best farmlands lie on **Attica**, a **peninsula** that sticks out into the

Aegean Sea. A peninsula is an area of land nearly surrounded by water.

Attica also contains excellent **harbors** for ships and fishing boats. A harbor is a sheltered place along a coast.

The southern tip of the Greek mainland is a large peninsula, the **Peloponnesus** (pel uh puh NEE sus). Find it on the map. This large peninsula is a mountainous region ringed by a thin band of fertile land. Although the Peloponnesus does have several small rivers, most of these dry up in the summer.

READING CHECK How was Greece's geography different from that of other early civilizations?

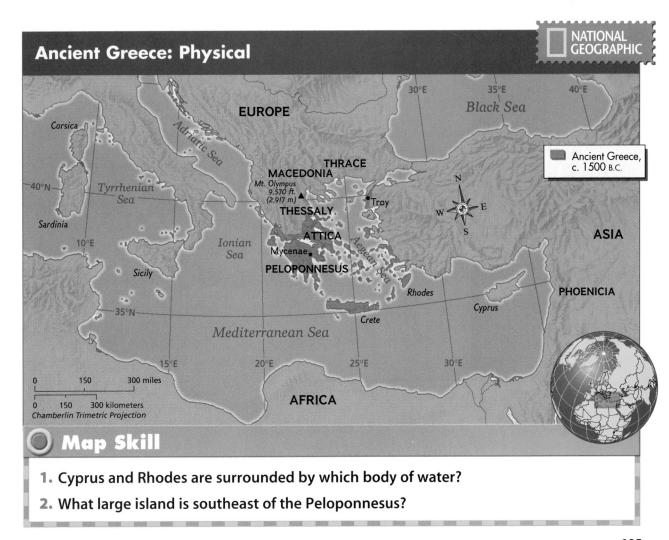

Ancient Greece: Physical

NATIONAL GEOGRAPHIC

EUROPE

Black Sea

Corsica

Adriatic Sea

THRACE

MACEDONIA

Mt. Olympus 9,570 ft. (2,917 m)

Troy

Ancient Greece, c. 1500 B.C.

40°N

Tyrrhenian Sea

THESSALY

N W E S

Sardinia

10°E

Ionian Sea

ATTICA

Mycenae

Aegean Sea

ASIA

Sicily

PELOPONNESUS

35°N

Rhodes

Cyprus

PHOENICIA

Crete

Mediterranean Sea

15°E   20°E   25°E   30°E

0   150   300 miles

0   150   300 kilometers
Chamberlin Trimetric Projection

AFRICA

Map Skill

1. **Cyprus and Rhodes are surrounded by which body of water?**

2. **What large island is southeast of the Peloponnesus?**

ECONOMY OF ANCIENT GREECE

The rocky soil of Greece is not as rich as the soils of the Nile or Indus River valleys, and the climate is particularly challenging for farmers. Summers are hot and dry, leaving fields dusty and lifeless. Winters can be windy and very rainy, so fields can become soggy from rain.

The ancient Greeks learned to live in this tough environment by raising crops and animals suited to the land. Barley and wheat were grown to make bread. Other food crops included grapes and olives, both of which grow well in rocky and hilly areas. Herds of sheep, goats, and cattle ate weeds and shrubs on Greece's many hills and mountainsides.

Trade and Competition

Sailing was an important part of life in Greece. Ancient Greek sailors traveled around the Mediterranean Sea to trade for grain. Greek merchants competed with traders from **Phoenicia** (fuh NEE shuh), in what is today Lebanon. Phoenician sailors were even more daring and traveled to ports as far away as the British Isles.

The most valuable Greek product was olive oil. Olive oil was important for cooking and flavoring food. It was also used as a lamp fuel and a body lotion. The profits from olive oil sales were used to purchase the extra grain the ancient Greeks could not grow themselves.

READING CHECK How did Greece's geography affect its development?

Greek farmers still cultivate olive trees today.

This ancient carving of a ram shows the importance sheep have long had in the Greek economy.

PUTTING IT TOGETHER

Without a major river to provide silt for fertile farmland, the ancient Greeks needed to find other ways to survive. They learned to grow specialized crops, such as olives and grapes. They also skillfully used the sea for travel and trade with other early cultures. In the lessons to come, you will learn how the Greeks built one of the ancient world's most powerful civilizations.

Review and Assess

1. Write a sentence for each vocabulary word.
   harbor   peninsula

2. Describe the land of the Greek peninsula.

3. How did Greece's mountainous terrain and long coastline affect ancient Greek life?

4. What part did the Mediterranean Sea play in the Greek **economy**?

5. If you think of the geography of Greece as a **cause**, how would you describe the **effect**?

Use the map on page 185 to plan a journey from Troy to Crete. List the bodies of water you would sail on and the land you would pass.

• •

You are a farmer in ancient Greece. **Write** a letter to your brother or sister who has moved to a Greek city. Explain the problems you have faced in raising this year's crop. Use the text of this lesson or a reference source for information.

The Birth of Greek Civilization

 How did civilization develop in Greece?

VOCABULARY

polis
acropolis
agora
commodity
citizen
monarchy
oligarchy
democracy
epic

PEOPLE

Homer

READING STRATEGY

Make a chart like this one. Write "Athens" in the center circle. In the other circles, write four characteristics of Athens.

Lesson Outline
- People of the Sea
- The City-States of Greece
- Sparta and Athens
- A Common Greek Culture

BUILD BACKGROUND

"The first person known to us by tradition as having established a navy is Minos. He made himself master of what is now called the Hellenic Sea (Mediterranean Sea). . . ."

Around 431 B.C. a Greek historian wrote about the beginnings of his country's history. Minos was the legendary founder of a powerful civilization on the island of Crete. However, the culture of Crete was only one of the influences on ancient Greece.

| This temple is in Athens, Greece.

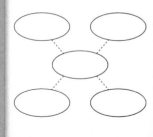

PEOPLE OF THE SEA

The arts and traditions of three cultures influenced the development of Greek civilization. These cultures are the Minoans, Mycenaeans, and Phoenicians.

The Minoans

About 100 years ago, Sir Arthur Evans and other archaeologists uncovered the ruins of an unknown civilization on the island of Crete. They named it **Minoa** after Minos, the king of Crete described by the Greek historian. From artifacts, archaeologists concluded that Minoa was a wealthy trading culture about 2,000 B.C. The Minoans exported pottery, metalwork, wine, and olive oil.

The Mycenaeans

Around 1600 B.C., people from the northeast had moved onto the Pelopon-nesus, settling at **Mycenae** (mi SEE nee). They traded metals from the Greek mainland for the beautiful Minoan exports. Around 1450 B.C., the Mycenaeans conquered Crete and took over Minoa's valuable trade. The Mycenaean civilization disappeared by 1100 B.C.

The Phoenicians

Phoenicia was a land in the eastern Mediterranean, in what is today Lebanon. Phoenicia founded colonies around the Mediterranean. A colony is an area under the control of another, usually distant, country. The Phoenicians developed the alphabet that is the basis of the alphabet we use today.

READING CHECK What cultures influenced Greek civilization?

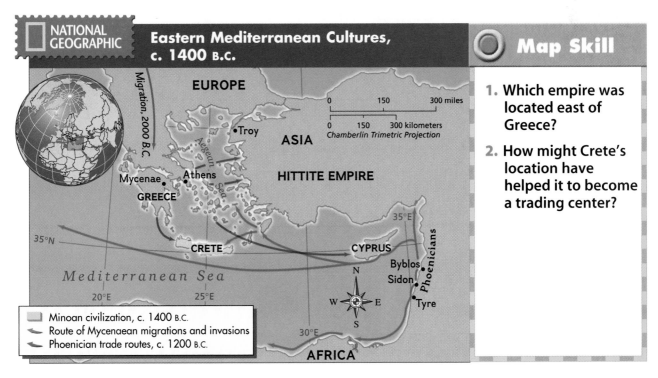

NATIONAL GEOGRAPHIC

Eastern Mediterranean Cultures, c. 1400 B.C.

Map Skill

1. Which empire was located east of Greece?

2. How might Crete's location have helped it to become a trading center?

Migration, 2000 B.C.

EUROPE

ASIA

Troy

Aegean Sea

HITTITE EMPIRE

Mycenae Athens
GREECE

35°N

CRETE

CYPRUS

35°E

Byblos
Sidon
Tyre

Phoenicians

Mediterranean Sea

20°E   25°E

30°E

AFRICA

0   150   300 miles
0   150   300 kilometers
Chamberlin Trimetric Projection

Minoan civilization, c. 1400 B.C.
Route of Mycenaean migrations and invasions
Phoenician trade routes, c. 1200 B.C.

189

THE CITY-STATES OF GREECE

By 700 B.C. Greek culture was shared across the peninsula. The small city-states shared a language and letters (chart below) but remained independent of each other. Each region usually had one city at its heart. The Greek word for this kind of city-state was **polis** (POH lihs).

Most city-states had a similar town plan. They were built around an **acropolis** (uh KROP uh lihs), a walled hill where people of the city could seek safety during an enemy attack. Farmers gathered at an open area near the acropolis to trade with each other and with local craftworkers. This open area, called an **agora** (AG ur uh), also served as a place for town meetings.

Most Greek cities were also busy ports. Wine and olive oil were exported and grain and metals were imported. Trade created wealth and connected the cities of the Greek world.

Exploring ECONOMICS

Ancient Greek Pottery

One of the most common artifacts of ancient Greek culture is pottery. Greek pottery was an important **commodity**, or traded product, in the ancient world. Pottery was used to store and protect foods such as wine or grain on long voyages. Pottery was also collected as a work of art. Several styles of pottery had emerged by 500 B.C., and each was special to a city or region. Thousands of pieces of Greek pottery have been found by archaeologists. Archaeologists trace these artifacts to understand Greek trade routes and trading partners.

Activity

What product would be typical of your community? What does this product tell about your region?

Development of the Modern Alphabet

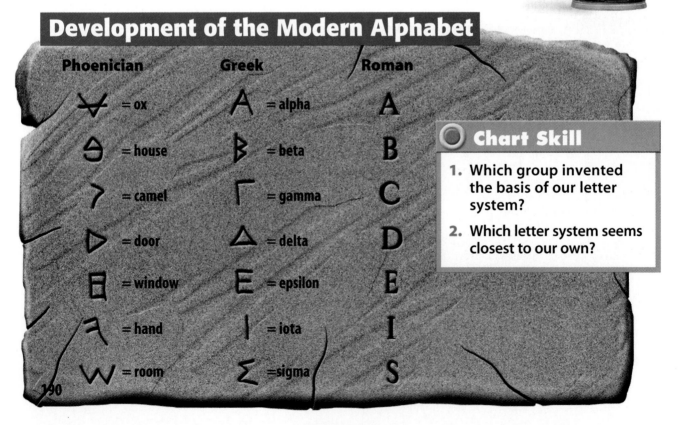

Phoenician		Greek		Roman
∀	= ox	A	= alpha	A
⊖	= house	B	= beta	B
↗	= camel	Γ	= gamma	C
▷	= door	△	= delta	D
目	= window	E	= epsilon	E
⇗	= hand	I	= iota	I
W	= room	Σ	=sigma	S

Chart Skill

1. Which group invented the basis of our letter system?

2. Which letter system seems closest to our own?

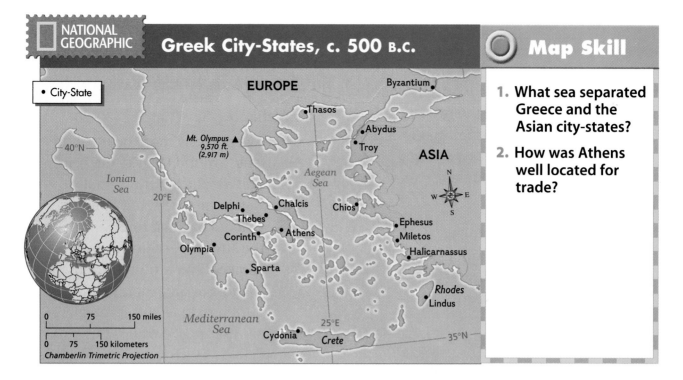

Developing Governments

The leaders of each Greek city-state had to be **citizens** of their polis. A citizen is a person who has rights and responsibilities in his or her country or community. In ancient Greece, only men could be citizens, and not even all men were granted this right. Women were not allowed to be citizens. In fact, women had few rights at all. Slavery was common throughout ancient Greece, and slaves could not be citizens either.

The kind of government varied from city to city. Some city-states had a single ruler. This type of government is called a **monarchy**. In other city-states, a small group of the richest and most powerful citizens controlled decision-making. This type of government is called an **oligarchy** (OL ih gahr kee).

How were the Greek city-states governed?

This carving shows Athena, the Greek goddess of wisdom.

SPARTA AND ATHENS

Sparta and **Athens** were the most famous Greek city-states. We know about these two city-states because many documents and artifacts from the two have been preserved. We know, for example, that daily life in these two powerful city-states was very different.

Sparta: City of Soldiers

In 700 B.C. Sparta controlled much of the southern Peloponnesus and was Greece's largest city-state. This polis controlled dozens of villages in its region. Sparta's central "city" was a cluster of villages about 30 miles inland from the Mediterranean Sea. Nearby, a small mountain formed Sparta's acropolis. At its base was the Spartan agora, where Sparta's leaders made the decisions that shaped life in this polis.

As in other ancient Greek city-states, farmers gathered at Sparta's agora to do business. Most Spartan farm workers, however, were *helots*. Helots could not leave the land they worked, and they had to pay half of their yearly crops to their Spartan conquerors as taxes. They were only a little better off than slaves.

Strengthening Sparta

There were many more helots than Spartans. Around 600 B.C. the helots revolted. The Spartans finally put down the revolt, but Sparta's leaders decided to make Sparta the strongest military power in Greece. This would prevent helots or any enemy from other city-states from conquering Sparta.

The Spartan people were determined to make their polis strong. At about age seven, boys and girls began training to defend their city. Although boys were taught to read and write, they spent much more time training to be soldiers. Girls also practiced running, throwing spears, and playing ball games. Spartan girls could not be soldiers, but they trained to be strong mothers of strong children. Duty to Sparta was considered more important than art or individual freedom.

Athens: City of the People

Athens lay on the peninsula of Attica, northeast of Sparta. Athenian life was very different from life in Sparta. Athenian girls did not practice sports. They stayed at home where they performed household tasks and learned to weave cloth from sheep's wool.

Most Athenian boys could not afford to attend school. They worked with their fathers as farmers, potters, or stoneworkers. Wealthy parents sent their sons to school to learn to read and write. After classes, these students went to a gymnasium to learn to wrestle or box.

Athenian Government

Most of Athens' early leaders belonged to rich and powerful families. The poorer Athenian citizens began to demand a

The Acropolis and Agora in Athens are shown above. Athenian women learned how to spin wool (right).

voice in their government. Eventually, the Athenian oligarchy was forced to share its power.

The new government of Athens was called a **democracy**. The word *democracy* combines two Greek words and means "rule by the people." In a democracy, every citizen is allowed to vote on government issues. There were large meetings to discuss and vote upon important decisions.

The beginnings of democracy marked an important moment in world history. Some historians, in fact, trace our own ideas of democracy to ancient Greece.

The Parthenon (far left) was a temple to Athena in Athens. Spartan women (left, center) trained to be strong mothers.

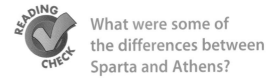

READING CHECK What were some of the differences between Sparta and Athens?

A COMMON GREEK CULTURE

All Greek city-states had much in common. For example, all city-states reserved several days each month to honor gods and goddesses.

The ancient Greeks were polytheistic. Most of their gods and goddesses were believed to live on **Mount Olympus** in northern Greece. The gods were honored by all Greeks, but each city had a particular god or goddess who was honored as that city's special protector. The people of Athens, for example, honored Athena, the goddess of wisdom.

All Greeks worshiped Zeus (ZOOS), the king of the Greek gods and goddesses. An important temple to Zeus was at Olympia. Every four years Greek athletes met at Olympia for the Olympic Games. These games were so honored that wars stopped during the Olympic contests.

A Greek Poet

The people of Greece enjoyed poems that described Greek history. One of the most famous ancient Greek poets was **Homer**. He probably lived between 800 and 700 B.C. Homer created two **epic** poems. An epic is a long poem that tells the story of a legendary hero or historical figure.

In the *Iliad*, Homer described a famous war between the Greek city-states and Troy, an enemy city in what is today Turkey. Homer also wrote the *Odyssey*, a poem that tells about one hero, Odysseus, and why it took so long for him to return to his home.

So now all who escaped death in battle or by shipwreck had got home safely except Odysseus, and he, although he was longing to return to his wife and country, was detained. . . . But as years went by, there came a time when the gods decided that he should go back . . .

 READING CHECK What cultural features did all Greeks share?

Homer (above) wrote about legendary events in Greek history. The ancient Greeks traveled by horse-drawn chariot (left).

PUTTING IT TOGETHER

Starting around 700 B.C., this shared Greek culture was carried across the Mediterranean by Greek colonies. Greek city-states soon surrounded the Mediterranean "like frogs around a pond," as one writer said in 500 B.C.

Greek city-states in western Asia faced a powerful Asian empire. This Persian Empire—centered in modern Iran—was the largest empire in the world. Wars with Persia would change Greece forever.

Greek art honored gods such as Apollo (right), the god of the sun, and illustrated scenes from daily life.

Review and Assess

1. Write one sentence for each vocabulary word.

   citizen   monarchy   oligarchy

2. What two epic poems did Homer write?

3.  What were some of the characteristics of the civilization of ancient Greece?

4. What was the main use of Greek pottery? What do we use for this purpose today?

5. **Make a decision** about which city you would prefer, Athens or Sparta. Support your decision with facts.

Activities

Look at the map on page 191. Make a list of Greek cities and the body of water each one faces.

Write a poem about someone you think is a hero. Share your poem with your classmates.

Using Historical Maps

VOCABULARY

historical map
map key

When the city-states of Greece went to war with Persia in 499 B.C., battles were fought around and in the Aegean Sea. This war for the control of Greece lasted for more than 20 years.

The **historical map** on this page traces some of the events and battles of the struggle between the mighty Persian Empire and the city-states of Greece. A historical map shows information about the past, such as when and where historical events took place.

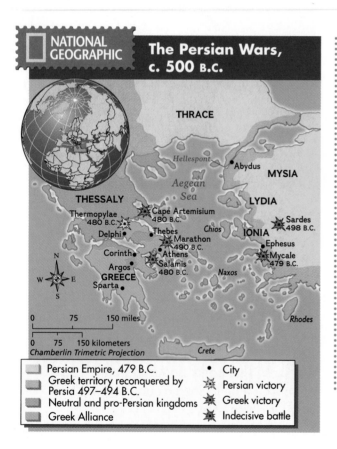

NATIONAL GEOGRAPHIC

The Persian Wars, c. 500 B.C.

THRACE

Hellespont • Abydus

MYSIA

Aegean Sea

THESSALY

LYDIA

Thermopylae 480 B.C.

Cape Artemisium 480 B.C.

Sardes 498 B.C.

Delphi •

Thebes •

Chios

IONIA

Marathon 490 B.C.

Ephesus

Corinth •

Athens •

Mycale 479 B.C.

Argos •

Salamis 480 B.C.

Naxos

GREECE

Sparta •

N W E S

0 75 150 miles

0 75 150 kilometers

Chamberlin Trimetric Projection

Rhodes

Crete

- Persian Empire, 479 B.C.
- Greek territory reconquered by Persia 497–494 B.C.
- Neutral and pro-Persian kingdoms
- Greek Alliance

• City
✳ Persian victory
✳ Greek victory
✳ Indecisive battle

LEARN THE SKILL

1. **Study the map title.**
   Look at the title of the map on this page. If the title tells you that the map shows places and events from the past, it is a historical map. The title of the map on this page is *The Persian Wars, c. 500 B.C.*

2. **Look for a date or date range.**
   Is there a date or date range given? The date for the map on this page is c. 500 B.C. and appears in the title.

3. **Look for symbols and the map key.**
   A **map key**, or legend, helps you understand the symbols appearing on the map. The map key explains that the symbols on this map show battles, cities, and the routes of armies.

TRY THE SKILL

Now try reading the map on this page. It shows Greek colonies around the Mediterranean Sea.

1. What is the map title?

2. What time period does this map show?

3. Is there a map key? What does it show?

4. What are some ways that historical maps can help you?

EXTEND THE SKILL

Use the maps on pages 196 and 197 and the chart below to make a time line. Show events that took place around the Mediterranean Sea in the 600s and 500s B.C.

Greek Colonies

Colony	Present-day location	Date founded
Miletus	Turkey	before 1400 B.C.
Cyprus	Eastern Mediterranean	before 1000 B.C.
Syracuse	Sicily, Italy	734 B.C.
Naucratis	Egypt	c. 650 B.C.
Cyrene	Libya	630 B.C.
Massilia	Marseille, France	600 B.C.

• How does using historical maps help you understand the past?

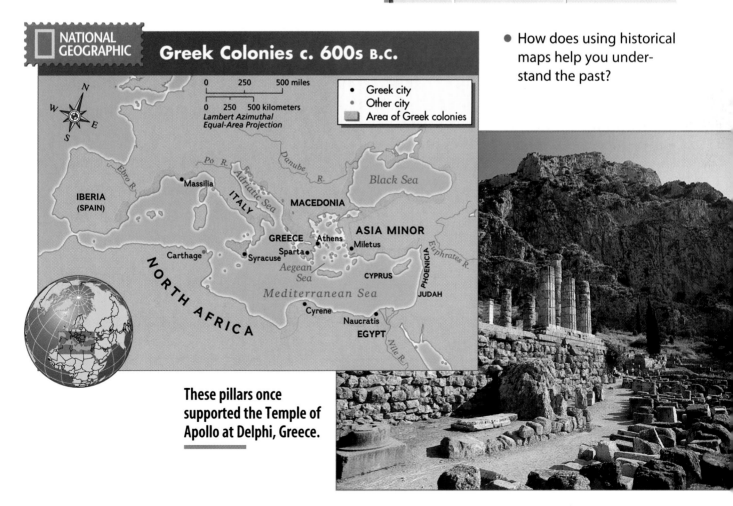

NATIONAL GEOGRAPHIC

Greek Colonies c. 600s B.C.

0   250   500 miles
0   250   500 kilometers
Lambert Azimuthal Equal-Area Projection

• Greek city
• Other city
▢ Area of Greek colonies

Po R.
Danube R.
Ebro R.
Adriatic Sea
Black Sea
IBERIA (SPAIN)
ITALY
MACEDONIA
ASIA MINOR
GREECE   Athens
Miletus
Carthage   Sparta
Syracuse
Aegean Sea
Euphrates R.
PHOENICIA
CYPRUS
JUDAH
NORTH AFRICA
Mediterranean Sea
Cyrene
Naucratis
EGYPT
Nile R.

These pillars once supported the Temple of Apollo at Delphi, Greece.

197

A Golden Age in Athens

What were the achievements of the Golden Age in Athens?

Lesson Outline
- Athens Rebuilds
- Government and Culture in Athens
- The Peloponnesian War
- A New Power—Macedonia

VOCABULARY

assembly
jury
philosophy
Peloponnesian War
phalanxes
orator

PEOPLE

Pericles
Socrates
Plato
Philip II

READING STRATEGY

Fill in a Main Idea Web with examples that show how Pericles changed Athens.

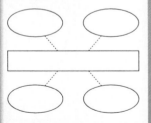

BUILD BACKGROUND

Greek soldiers waited nervously. Their enemy, the powerful Persian army, was coming from the east. The Persian force was so large, scouts had warned, that their arrows would darken the sky. A Spartan replied calmly, "Excellent! Then we can fight in the shade." The vast Persian Empire stretched from the Mediterranean to India. It certainly looked stronger than the scattered Greek city-states and colonies. Incredibly, the Greeks defeated the Persians and began the "Golden Age" of Greece.

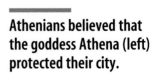

Athenians believed that the goddess Athena (left) protected their city.

700 B.C.	650 B.C.	600 B.C.	550 B.C.	500 B.C.	450 B.C.	400 B.C.	350 B.C.	300 B.C.

You Are Here
480 B.C. – 338 B.C.

ATHENS REBUILDS

Athenian life did not change after the victory over the Persians in the 470s B.C. Citizens still voted in their democracy. Athenians continued to gather at the agora and on the acropolis. Each summer, there was the festival to honor the goddess Athena. However, Athens changed as a city.

The large and powerful navy of Athens had helped to defeat the Persians. Athens now used its navy to become a leader in Greek affairs and to bring wealth through trade. Athens began a "golden age," a period of wealth and glory, such as Greece had not seen before.

The City of Athens

The Persians had focused much of their attack on Athens, and they had suc-ceeded in destroying a large part of the city. After the war, Athenians set about rebuilding their city on a grander scale.

The Acropolis, on its hill, boasted new buildings that displayed the city's increased wealth and power. At the heart of the Acropolis was a marble temple to Athena called the **Parthenon**. Its ruins still rise over Athens today. As you have read, every ancient Greek city had an acropolis; but when people today refer to "the Acropolis," they mean the hilltop in Athens. By about 460 B.C., Athens had become the leading city of Greece.

READING CHECK

How did Athens become the leading city in Greece during the Golden Age?

Diagram Skill

1. What building is at the top of the Acropolis?

2. What kinds of buildings surround the Agora?

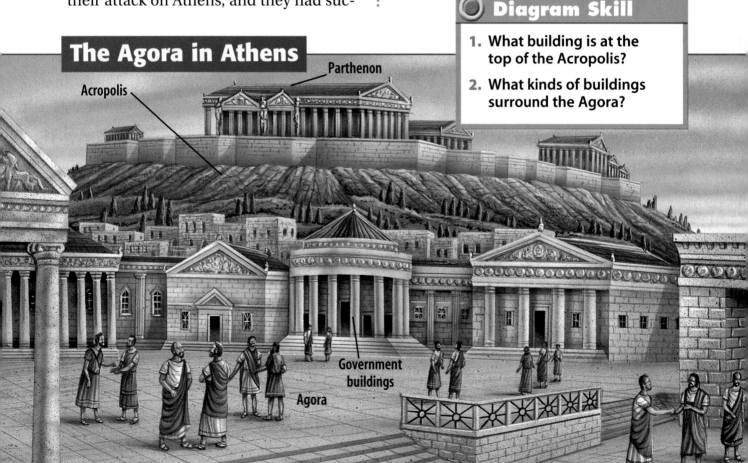

The Agora in Athens

Parthenon

Acropolis

Government buildings

Agora

GOVERNMENT AND CULTURE IN ATHENS

Athens was a democracy. An **assembly** of citizens voted on issues that concerned their city. An assembly is a lawmaking body of a government. Ancient Athens was one of the first governments to have an assembly where citizens could vote.

Pericles

Pericles (PER ih kleez) was the leader of Athens around 450 B.C. He saw to it that all citizens could take part in government. Any citizen, rich or poor, could serve in the assembly or sit on a **jury**. A jury is a group of citizens who hear evidence and make decisions in a court of law.

Pericles arranged for those who held office or served on a jury to be paid. This allowed farmers and other poor citizens to take part in their government. Read how Pericles described democracy.

Outdoor Greek theaters like this one were built into hillsides.

Primary Source:

excerpt from A Funeral Speech
— *by Pericles c. 430* B.C.

We do not copy our neighbors, but try to be an example. Our system favors the many instead of the few: this is why it is called a democracy. The laws give equal justice to all alike. . . . The freedom we enjoy extends also to ordinary life; we are not suspicious of one another, and we do not nag our neighbor if he chooses to go his own way. . . . But this freedom does not make us lawless. We are taught to respect. . . . the laws, and never to forget that we must protect the injured. . . . We are free to live exactly as we please . . . . An Athenian citizen does not neglect public affairs. . . . We consider a man who takes no interest in the state not as harmless, but as useless. . . . We do not see discussion as a stumbling block in the way of making a decision, but as a necessary beginning for acting wisely. . . .

What does Pericles say about a citizen who has no interest in government?

Philosophy

Ancient Athens also had special schools to teach **philosophy**, the search for wisdom and the right way to live. Students and teachers had discussions about good government and what it meant to be a good citizen.

In the middle 400s B.C., a teacher named **Socrates** (SAHK ruh teez), led discussions about ways to live. Socrates angered some people in Athens because he began to question their city's laws, customs, and even religion. In 399 B.C. Socrates was brought to trial for "urging Athens' young people to revolt." He was sentenced to death. His student, **Plato** (PLAY toh), wrote down Socrates' ideas. Plato later became a famous teacher.

Greek Drama

During the Golden Age, Greek writers invented a new theater form—the drama. In ancient Greece, dramas were plays that examined basic questions such as the choices of an individual, good and evil, and society. Ancient Greek writers, such as Sophocles (SAHF uh kleez) and Euripides (yoo RIP uh deez), pioneered forms such as tragedies in which the main characters died and comedies in which they did not.

READING CHECK What were some features of the Golden Age of Athens?

Ancient Greek Achievements

Achievements	Effects
Philosophy	Philosophy, or the "love of wisdom," was a way of asking questions about the world and people's place in it.
Theater	The first plays came from religious rituals. Soon, writers such as Aristophanes were using drama to make political points.
Architecture	The column came from Egypt, but Greek designs and styles have influenced architecture ever since.
Music	The idea of musical scales and harmony were influenced by the Greeks.
Sports	The Greeks held the first Olympics and came up with the idea of sports as peaceful competition.
Geometry	Besides its practical use, geometry was a way of showing that certain ideas could always be proven true. For example, the angles of a triangle will always add up to 180 degrees.

Chart Skill

1. **Which Greek achievement was influenced by Egypt?**

2. **How do Greek achievements affect your life?**

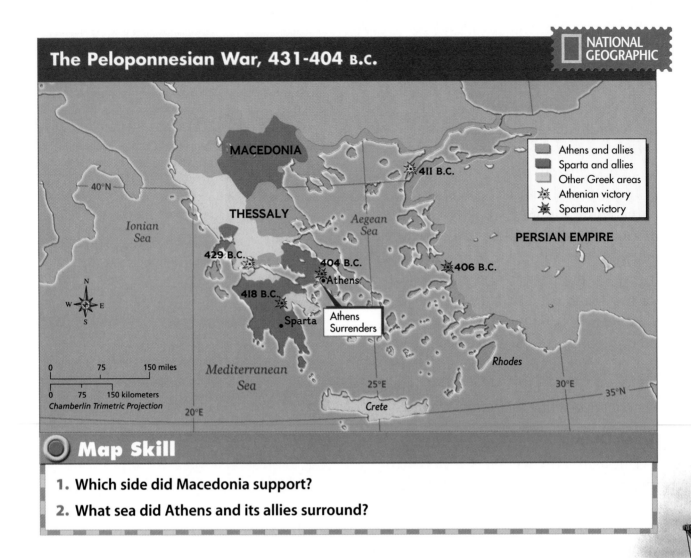

The Peloponnesian War, 431-404 B.C.

NATIONAL GEOGRAPHIC

MACEDONIA

411 B.C.

40°N

THESSALY

Ionian
Sea

Aegean
Sea

PERSIAN EMPIRE

429 B.C.

404 B.C.
Athens

406 B.C.

418 B.C.

Sparta

Athens
Surrenders

Rhodes

0   75   150 miles

0   75   150 kilometers
Chamberlin Trimetric Projection

Mediterranean
Sea

25°E

30°E

35°N

20°E

Crete

Legend:
- Athens and allies
- Sparta and allies
- Other Greek areas
- ✳ Athenian victory
- ✴ Spartan victory

Map Skill

1. **Which side did Macedonia support?**

2. **What sea did Athens and its allies surround?**

THE PELOPONNESIAN WAR

The Golden Age of Athens did not last long. Other Greek city-states were jealous and fearful of Athenian power. Sparta and its allies formed a union called the Peloponnesian League. The map on this page shows the allies of Athens and Sparta. In 431 B.C. the **Peloponnesian** (pel uh puh NEEZH un) **War** began to tear Greece apart.

Battles on Land and Sea

Sparta and its allies attacked Athens. Pericles knew that the Athenian army could not defeat the Spartans, so he ordered Athenians to move inside the city walls. The walls protected the city and its people, but Spartan soldiers destroyed the surrounding farmland.

The Spartans had hoped to starve the Athenians into surrender. However, the Athenian navy still controlled the Aegean Sea, and ship-loads of grain continued to reach Athens safely. The war settled into a long contest in which neither side could gain the upper hand. However, the continuing battles caused many people to lose their lives.

steering
oar

The War Ends

Neither Athens nor Sparta could gain an advantage. The powerful Athenian navy continued to control the Aegean Sea and won most of the battles at sea. However, the Spartan army won most of the battles on land.

Time was against Athens. As the war dragged on, a plague broke out inside the city. At least a third of the population died. Among the dead was Pericles. His death left Athens without a strong leader.

The city's leaders began to make mistakes. The Athenian navy was sent to attack a city on the island of Sicily. Many Athenian lives were lost in this battle, and the power of their navy was weakened. Sparta managed to cut off the grain sup-

ply from the Black Sea farms. The citizens of Athens faced starvation. Deserted by its allies and facing certain defeat, Athens surrendered in 404 B.C.

Sparta had won the wars at last. However, the victory did Sparta little good. At the beginning of the war, a Spartan leader had warned, "This day will be the beginning of great misfortunes to the Greeks." The fighting between city-states had dragged on for 27 years, and the Spartan ambassador's words had proven correct. The Golden Age of Greece had ended in disaster.

READING CHECK How did the Peloponnesian War end the Golden Age?

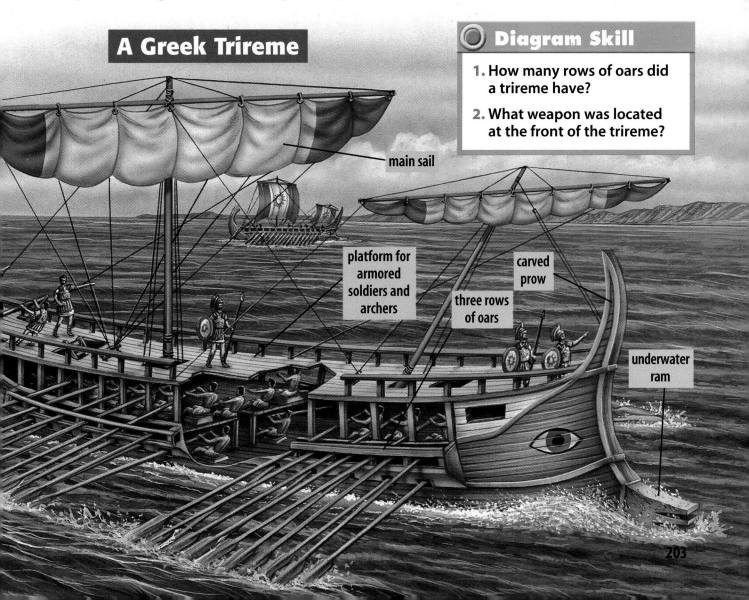

A Greek Trireme

main sail

platform for armored soldiers and archers

three rows of oars

carved prow

underwater ram

Diagram Skill

1. How many rows of oars did a trireme have?

2. What weapon was located at the front of the trireme?

A NEW POWER—MACEDONIA

The Peloponnesian War ruined Greece. Although Sparta had won the war, it could not control the region. In the next 50 years, several other city-states tried to conquer all of Greece. All of them failed. The destruction and chaos brought on by these continuing wars left Greece open to attack by a new invader.

Threat from Macedonia

The invader was **Macedonia**, a powerful kingdom to the north of Greece. The Macedonian king was **Philip II**. Philip never made a secret of his desire to conquer all of Greece. So determined was he to gain an empire that an Athenian orator said he would be willing to have, "an eye knocked out, gain his collarbone broken, his arm and leg maimed."

A Macedonian **phalanx** fights the troops of Persia's king.

To prepare for his conquest, Philip organized a powerful Macedonian army. He made some basic changes in the way armies of his day fought their battles. He armed his soldiers with 18-foot-long sharp spears and organized them into small units called **phalanxes** (FAY lanks uhz). Unlike previous military leaders, Philip depended more on cavalry, or soldiers mounted on horseback, than on foot soldiers.

Conquest and Defeat

While Philip was setting his plans for the conquest of Greece, only one Greek tried to alarm the people about the danger. This was an Athenian orator named Demosthenes (deh MAHS thuh neez). An **orator** is a person who is a skilled public speaker and his or her speeches are called orations. In a series of famous orations, Demosthenes begged the Greeks to unite against Philip. Only two city-states took his warning seriously.

In 338 B.C. Philip defeated the Greeks, who had fought bravely. Philip's 18-year-old son, Alexander, had led one of the cavalry charges against the Greeks. Philip was the new master of Greece, and the rule by the city-states had come to an end. However, he was not to rule for long.

READING CHECK

Why was Philip II able to conquer Greece?

HISTORY MYSTERY

Was there a place called Atlantis?

The Greek philosopher, Plato, was the first to describe the island civilization of Atlantis. Plato's Atlantis was an advanced civilization which had existed around 10,000 B.C. One day Atlantis simply disappeared.

How could an island just disappear? Plato does not say. Later legends say that Atlantis had either a massive volcanic eruption or an earthquake that caused the island to sink into the ocean.

Remains of Atlantis have never been found. Some scientists believe that Atlantis was a real island. Others say it is an imaginary place which Plato invented.

Why does Atlantis still interest people?

PUTTING IT TOGETHER

The century between 500 B.C. and 400 B.C. was a time of contrast for ancient Athens. Beginning with the close of the Persian War, Athens enjoyed a "Golden Age" of culture and creativity. During this time, Athenians improved their democracy, spread education, and glorified their city with beautiful new buildings.

The Peloponnesian War ended this Golden Age and wrecked Greece. The Macedonians from a kingdom north of Greece easily gained control of the peninsula. Two years later, the Macedonian king, Philip, was assassinated at his daughter's wedding. His son proclaimed himself king. In the next lesson, you will read about how the young Macedonian king spread the legacies of the Golden Age across his world. His name was Alexander the Great.

Review and Assess

1. Write a sentence for each vocabulary word.
   assembly   jury   philosophy

2. Why was Athens able to become the richest and most powerful Greek city?

3. What were the achievements of the Golden Age in Athens?

4. What duties did Pericles feel were important for a citizen?

5. How did the Athenians solve the problem of getting food after the Spartan army destroyed local farms?

Look at the map on page 202. Make a list of the geographical advantages and disadvantages of Athens and Sparta.

• •

Suppose you are a tourist in the Golden Age. Write a letter to a friend at home describing the city of Athens.

Points of View
Should Ancient Ruins
Be Reconstructed?

Historians study ruins to learn about ancient cultures. Some tourists, however, would prefer to see the buildings as they were. Should ancient ruins be reconstructed? Read and think about three different points of view, then answer the questions that follow.

NADIA LOKMA
Director of Conservation, Egyptian Museum, Cairo, Egypt
Excerpt from an Interview, 2001

66 Ruins should be preserved exactly as they are found. Ancient ruins bring us a message from the past. ...By analyzing how a part of a building was constructed and what materials it was made from, we can learn a great deal about the people who made it. If we try to reconstruct a building ...no one will know what is ancient. They will think it is all made up. 99

RUTH JACOBY
Lecturer, Hebrew University, Jerusalem, Israel
Excerpt from an Interview, 2001

66 The ideal way to preserve ancient ruins is to reconstruct where possible, but to make clear what has been reconstructed and what was actually found at the site. ...This helps people with little imagination or knowledge of a site to see what it looked like....If a tourist visits the ruins of an ancient Greek theater, we want them to know how it worked....You can't expect people who come for the first time ...to understand all this. 99

MOHAMMAD RAFIQUE MUGHAL
Former Director of Archaeology and Museums, Karachi, Pakistan.
Excerpt from Interview, 2001

❝Old is gold. Reconstruction is allowed only when we are going to use a building again in the same way that it was used in the past.... If a wall was built of stone, marble, or brick, it can be restored if exactly the same kind of material is used.... In most cases, we should keep the remains as we found them. We can use a diorama or computer-generated model to help people understand how the building looked before.❞

Thinking About the Points of View

1. What does Nadia Lokma believe is the best way to preserve ancient ruins?

2. In what ways does Ruth Jacoby disagree with Nadia Lokma? What reasons does she give for her point of view?

3. What rules does Mohammad Rafique Mughal give for reconstructing ancient ruins? Which of the other archaeologists is more likely to agree with him?

4. What other points of view might people have on this issue?

Building Citizenship

Courage
Find a monument to somebody courageous in your neighborhood or town. What did this person do that made people want to build a monument to him or her?

Write About It!

Bring a photograph or picture of a famous monument or building of the ancient world to class. Write a short speech telling how you feel about the way the building looks today.

Lesson 4

Alexander and the Greek Empire

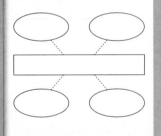

Find Out!

What influence did Alexander's conquests have on Greek culture?

Lesson Outline
• Alexander the Great
• The Greek Empire
• A New Culture Develops

VOCABULARY

Hellenism

PEOPLE
Alexander
Aristotle

READING STRATEGY

Use a main idea chart like this one to list the regions or countries conquered by Alexander the Great.

BUILD BACKGROUND

"Alexander was but twenty years old when his father was murdered, and he inherited a kingdom, surrounded by great dangers and hostile enemies."

This is how a Roman writer described the beginning of Alexander's rule. During the Macedonian conquest of Greece, 18-year-old **Alexander** had shown that he was already a bold general. As king and ruler, he showed that he was wise.

700 B.C.	650 B.C.	600 B.C.	550 B.C.	500 B.C.	450 B.C.	400 B.C.	350 B.C.	300 B.C.

You Are Here
331 B.C. – 323 B.C.

ALEXANDER THE GREAT

Aristotle (AR uh staht ul), one of the most famous philosophers of Athens, had been Alexander's private teacher. From him, Alexander learned to deeply respect Greek culture and traditions.

Alexander Marches East

Alexander was a brilliant military leader. His army never lost a battle. In 331 B.C. Alexander defeated the Persian king. Alexander then led his troops to the east, until they reached the Indus River valley, in 326 B.C. Here his soldiers had finally had enough. They forced their young leader to turn back toward Greece. The army reached Babylon where Alexander became ill. His soldiers lined up to say farewell as they filed past his sickbed. He died in 323 B.C.

Historians call this young king "Alexander the Great," because in a mere nine years he won control over the largest empire of his day.

READING CHECK **Why is Alexander called "Great"?**

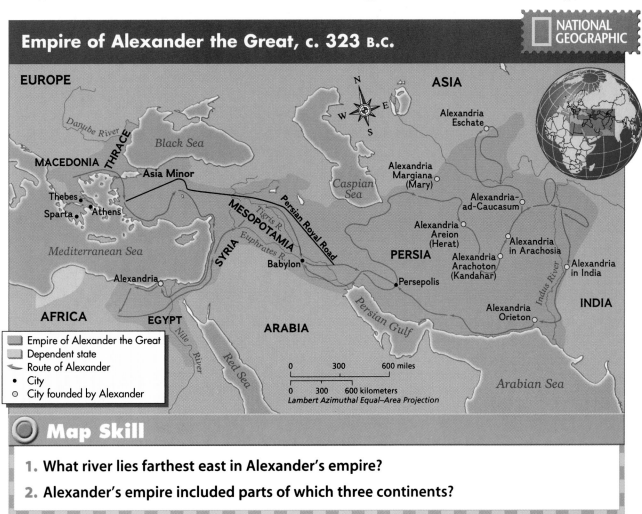

Empire of Alexander the Great, c. 323 B.C.

NATIONAL GEOGRAPHIC

EUROPE
ASIA
Danube River
Black Sea
THRACE
MACEDONIA
Asia Minor
Thebes
Sparta
Athens
Alexandria Eschate
Alexandria Margiana (Mary)
Caspian Sea
Alexandria-ad-Caucasum
Persian Royal Road
MESOPOTAMIA
Tigris R.
Euphrates R.
SYRIA
Mediterranean Sea
Babylon
Alexandria
Alexandria Areion (Herat)
PERSIA
Alexandria Arachoton (Kandahar)
Alexandria in Arachosia
Indus River
Alexandria in India
Persepolis
AFRICA
EGYPT
ARABIA
Persian Gulf
Alexandria Orieton
INDIA
Nile River
Red Sea
Arabian Sea

Empire of Alexander the Great
Dependent state
Route of Alexander
• City
○ City founded by Alexander

0   300   600 miles
0   300   600 kilometers
Lambert Azimuthal Equal–Area Projection

Map Skill

1. **What river lies farthest east in Alexander's empire?**

2. **Alexander's empire included parts of which three continents?**

THE GREEK EMPIRE

Alexander was only 33 years old when he died, but he had already conquered the largest territory in history. Moreover, his conquests changed the world he ruled. During his march through western Asia, Alexander founded dozens of new cities. The greatest of these proved to be a city in Egypt, on the western edge of the Nile Delta. The city was called **Alexandria** to honor its founder.

Alexandria quickly became one of the most important cities in the Greek empire. The city of Alexandria was an example of how Greek traditions and ideas were carried far beyond Greece.

Alexander

Alexandria

Alexandria boasted an agora, a theater, temples, a stadium, and a gymnasium. Its harbor was an important port for Mediterranean trade. Alexandria also had one of the first lighthouses in the world. This lighthouse was one of the Seven Wonders of the Ancient World. The fire burning at the top could be seen from many miles out at sea, to guide ships into its busy harbor.

The city, like Alexander's empire, was a mix of people and cultures. There were temples for Greek gods, as well as for Egyptian gods and goddesses such as Isis. The Greek and Macedonian

The Seven Wonders of the World

In the 200s B.C., a Greek travel writer created a list of seven structures that every traveler should see. They became known as "The Seven Wonders of the World."

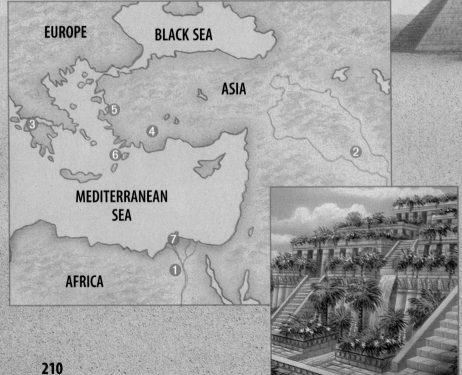

EUROPE

BLACK SEA

ASIA

MEDITERRANEAN SEA

AFRICA

❶ The Pyramids at Giza,
c. 2600–2500 B.C.

Begun by the Pharaoh Khufu, they are the oldest wonder and the only one still standing today.

❷ The Hanging Gardens of Babylon,
c. 605–562 B.C.

Thought to have been built by King Nebuchadnezzar for his homesick wife.

citizens of Alexandria came together in democratic assemblies. The Egyptians of Alexandria had courts of their own, and so did the city's Jews. Craftworkers made Greek-style pottery, and papermakers continued to practice their ancient craft.

The Great Library

The cultural center of Alexandria was the city's museum. Here, scholars were able to study the world and conduct research in the nearby library. Alexandria's library contained more than half a million papyrus rolls, and librarians were always looking for more. Inspectors searched all arriving ships for additional written works which they kept until copies could be made.

A Standard of Writing

Written Greek used a simple alphabet in which each letter matched a sound. This was an alphabet of thirty letters that the Greeks had adopted from the Phoenicians. This alphabet made it easier for people to learn to read and write. The great library helped to spread the use of Greek language, because it attracted scholars from across the vast empire.

READING CHECK In what ways was Alexandria a center of Greek culture?

Chart Skill

1. Where does the word *mausoleum* come from?

2. Which structure was useful to sailors?

3 Statue of Zeus at Olympia, c. 435 B.C.

The 40-foot high statue of the god Zeus sat at the temple at Olympia, site of the Olympic games.

6 Colossus of Rhodes, c. 280 B.C.

The Colossus, a huge bronze statue of the sun god Helios, watched over the city's harbor.

4 Mausoleum at Halicarnassus, c. 350 B.C.

Built by Queen Artemisia for her husband, Mausolus. Today, many buildings honoring the dead are called *mausoleums*.

5 Temple of Artemis at Ephesus, c. 325 B.C.

The enormous marble temple to the Greek goddess added to the fame of Ephesus.

7 Pharos of Alexandria, c. 280–200 B.C.

The Greek kings of Egypt had this giant marble lighthouse, or pharos, built to guide ships into Alexandria's harbor.

A NEW CULTURE DEVELOPS

Alexander's conquests helped to spread Greek culture throughout the lands of his empire. At the same time, Greek and Macedonian rulers were influenced by the traditions of the lands they conquered. Greek ideas blended with African and Asian traditions to produce an entirely new culture that we call **Hellenism**. Although Hellenism was primarily Greek, it also contained elements of many other cultures. Hellenistic philosophy, learning, science, and art spread to cultures as far away as the Indus River valley.

Both geometry and physics are products of Hellenism. In addition, one Hellenistic astronomer suggested that all the planets, including Earth, revolve around the sun. Another Hellenistic scientist made a fairly accurate estimate of Earth's size.

Hellenism encouraged realistic statues and paintings. The arts flourished throughout the Hellenistic world.

End of the Empire

Alexander had no child to inherit his empire. Also, after his death, no single leader was able to control such a vast territory. Alexander's generals carved up the empire, and by 300 B.C., there were many smaller kingdoms throughout the eastern Mediterranean region.

Meanwhile, in the western Mediterranean, two great cities were becoming powerful. The first was the Phoenician city of Carthage, in Africa. On the northern side of the Mediterranean, another city was starting to unite the Italian peninsula. This city was Rome, and it would eventually become the capital of the Mediterranean world.

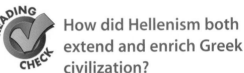

READING CHECK How did Hellenism both extend and enrich Greek civilization?

This statue and drinking horn are examples of Hellenism. They blend Asian, African, and Greek styles.

PUTTING IT TOGETHER

The blended culture of Hellenism was the foundation for many later civilizations, including Rome. Greek was widely spoken even in the Roman Empire, and it remained the language of scholars and educated people for hundreds of years. European culture was particularly influenced by Hellenism. Even in the United States, you will see Hellenistic influences in architecture, law, and political ideas. Legacies from ancient Greece influence our own ideas about education, philosophy, drama, art, and government.

This jewelry shows that Hellenistic artists combined technical skill, such as goldsmithing, with naturalistic decoration, like the leaves and berries on this crown (right).

Review and Assess

1. Write a sentence for the vocabulary word.
   Hellenism

2. Why was the library at Alexandria so famous?

3. How did Alexander the Great spread and change Greek culture?

4. How would the size of a large empire such as Alexander's affect its **economy**?

5. **Predict** how neighboring rulers might have reacted to Alexander's conquests.

Look at the map on page 209. Make a chart of continents, countries, and cities that were included in Alexander's empire.

. . . .

Write a description of the Great Library at Alexandria. Compare and contrast the ancient library with a large modern library.

VOCABULARY REVIEW

Number a sheet of paper from 1 to 5. Beside each number write the word or term from the list below that completes each sentence.

agora   peninsula

Hellenism   philosophy

oligarchy

1. An area of land nearly surrounded by water is a ____.

2. The farmers gathered at the ____ to trade with others.

3. The search for wisdom and the right way to live is called ____.

4. An ____ is a small group of rich, powerful citizens who control the decision-making in a government.

5. ____ is a culture with Greek ideas blended with African and Asian ideas.

CHAPTER COMPREHENSION

6. What made the terrain of Greece difficult for farmers?

7. What was the leading city-state in Greece in 450 B.C.? What made it strong?

8. Where was democracy established? Why did this democracy develop?

9. List five ancient Greek ideas or traditions that are still practiced today.

10. What lands, or parts of lands, did Alexander the Great conquer for Greece? What was Alexander's nationality?

11. What Phoenician invention did the Greeks improve?

12. **Write** a letter from the viewpoint of a farmer at the time of Pericles. Tell how you can participate in democracy.

SKILL REVIEW

The Peloponnesian War, 431–404 B.C.

NATIONAL GEOGRAPHIC

0   50   100 miles

0   50   100 kilometers
Chamberlin Trimetric Projection

Sparta and allies
Athens and allies
Other Greek areas

MACEDONIA

THESSALY

Aegean Sea

Ionian Sea

•Athens

Sparta •

Mediterranean Sea

13. **Geography Skill** What clues tell you this is a historical map?

14. **Geography Skill** What information is shown on this map?

15. **Geography Skill** During what period of time did the events on the map take place?

16. **Geography Skill** Did Athens or Sparta have allies with more land area?

17. **Reading/ Thinking Skill** Why might a community on the Aegean Sea make the decision to be an ally of Athens rather than Sparta?

18. **Reading/Thinking Skill** Why might it have been difficult for Sparta to communicate with its allies in Macedonia?

USING A TIME LINE

700 B.C.	650 B.C.	600 B.C.	550 B.C.	500 B.C.	450 B.C.	400 B.C.	350 B.C.

700 B.C. Rise of Greek city-states

600 B.C. Oligarchy rules Athens; Sparta's slaves revolt

499 B.C. Persian Wars begin

470 B.C. Athens's Golden Age begins

431 B.C. Peloponnesian War begins

404 B.C. End of Peloponnesian War

334 B.C. Conquests of Alexander begin

19. The Golden Age of Athens ended in 431 B.C. How long did it last?

20. Choose the event on the time line that expanded Greece's territories.

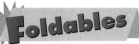

Activity

***Writing* About Culture** Suppose you traveled to the city of Alexandria by sea. What would you notice first as you approached the city? What places of learning and culture might you visit? What products might you see in the busy markets?

Foldables

Use your Foldable to review what you have learned about ancient Greece. As you look at the front of your Foldable, imagine walking through the building you have drawn, and mentally recall what you learned about the culture of ancient Greece. Discuss what the Golden Age of Greece was like politically, economically, and socially. Review your notes under the tabs to check your memory and responses. Record any questions that you have, and discuss them with classmates, or review the chapter to find answers.

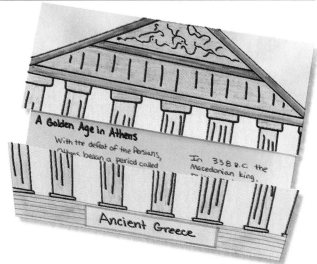

THE Big IDEAS ABOUT...

THE LAND OF ITALY

Italy is shaped like a boot extending into the Mediterranean Sea. Its farmers grow grapes and olives and raise sheep.

Ancient Rome

Rome was a small village in the rocky hills of Italy. In time, Rome would build a large and powerful empire and grow from a small town into one of the world's largest and most beautiful cities. More importantly, the great empire Rome founded would deeply influence the future of Europe's civilization.

THE ROMAN REPUBLIC

At first, the city of Rome is ruled by the rich. In time, a more equal system of government develops. It forms the basis of the American government today.

THE ROMAN EMPIRE

The Romans rule most of the land around the Mediterranean. To keep order, one man makes himself the ruler of the whole empire.

THE BIRTH OF CHRISTIANITY

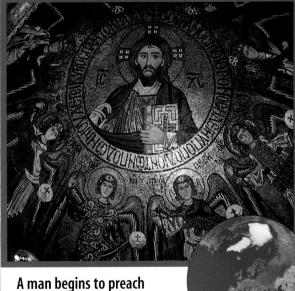

A man begins to preach in one of Rome's eastern provinces. The teachings of this man, Jesus of Nazareth, eventually become the religion of Rome.

ROME AND BYZANTIUM

To better defend Rome, the empire is split in two. The western empire is overrun, but the empire continues in the east.

Foldables

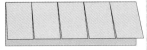

Use this Foldable study guide to record what you learn about "Ancient Rome."

1. Fold a sheet of paper like a hot dog, with one side 1" longer than the other.

2. Make four cuts on the short side to form five tabs.

3. Write the chapter title on the 1" tab, and the lesson titles on the short tabs.

4. Draw arches on each tab. Fold between each tab. Then fold down the center of each tab to make 10 sides. Bend the Foldable into a circle to resemble the Colosseum.

The Land of Italy

How did Italy's geography affect its development?

Lesson Outline

• Plains and Mountains
• The Founding of Rome

VOCABULARY

volcano

READING STRATEGY

Copy and complete the chart. Write the details that support the main idea "Rome's location had advantages."

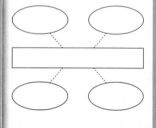

BUILD BACKGROUND

"The Greek cities are thought to have flourished [because of] . . . the beauty and strength of their sites. . . . [but] the Romans . . . have paved the roads, cut through hills, and filled up valleys, so that [goods] may be conveyed by [wagon] from the ports."

This description of Italy was written by a Greek writer named Strabo. In this description, he mentions several geographical features of Italy. He also mentions how the Romans used their technology to deal with the physical challenges they faced in Italy.

PLAINS AND MOUNTAINS

The Italian peninsula is part of the European continent. It juts out into the Mediterranean Sea like a boot. Find the "toe" of the boot on the map on this page. The island to the west of the toe is called **Sicily**. It was a popular destination for ancient Greek colonists because of its rich farmland. At the northern border of present-day Italy stand the craggy **Alps**. These mountains wall off Italy from the rest of Europe.

Another mountain range has had an even greater effect on life in Italy. The Apennine (AP uh nine) Mountains form a giant "backbone" down the Italian peninsula. Their towering height makes it difficult to travel across the peninsula. The Apennines also lack rich soil, so there is more sheep herding than farming done on the mountainsides.

Italy also has a number of fertile plains. One of the most important is in the Po River Valley. Another is **Latium** (LAY shee um), located on the west coast of central Italy. The **Tiber River** runs through the center of this plain. More than 2,000 years ago, a city located in Latium was the center of a vast empire. The name of this city was Rome.

What are the major mountains of Italy?

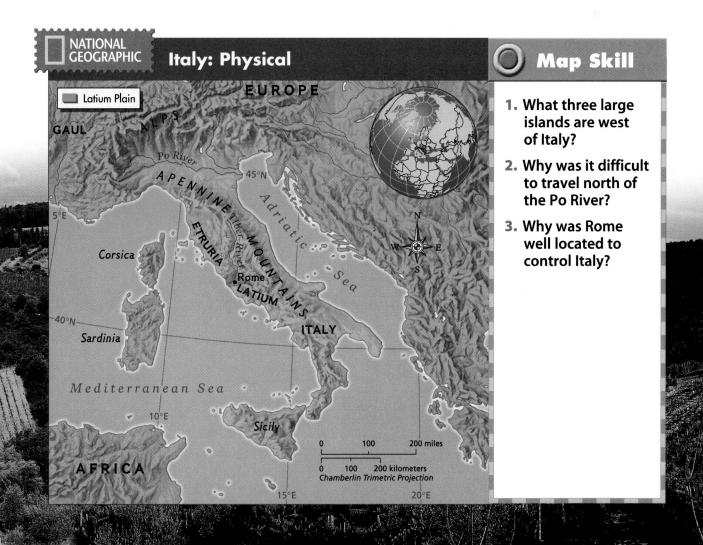

NATIONAL GEOGRAPHIC

Italy: Physical

Latium Plain

EUROPE
GAUL
ALPS
Po River
APENNINE
45°N
5°E
Corsica
ETRURIA
Tiber River
MOUNTAINS
Adriatic Sea
Rome
LATIUM
40°N
Sardinia
ITALY
Mediterranean Sea
10°E
Sicily
AFRICA
15°E
20°E

0   100   200 miles
0   100   200 kilometers
Chamberlin Trimetric Projection

N W E S

Map Skill

1. **What three large islands are west of Italy?**

2. **Why was it difficult to travel north of the Po River?**

3. **Why was Rome well located to control Italy?**

THE FOUNDING OF ROME

Rome is located on the Tiber River, on the northern edge of Latium. Today, Rome is the capital of the modern nation of Italy. However, Rome is a very old city. Archaeologists have found evidence of people in the area over 3,000 years ago.

There are many good reasons why Rome grew where it did. First, as Rome developed, it expanded across seven hills. These hills helped to protect the city from attack. Second, the Tiber River made a fine "highway" for travel between the mountains and the Mediterranean coast. Boats brought goods from faraway sea-ports, as well as news from communities upriver. Finally, the Latium plain is sur-rounded by inactive **volcanoes**. A volcano is an opening in the surface of the earth through which lava, gases, and ash are forced out. Frequent eruptions created a thin, but rich soil.

Mount Vesuvius, near Naples, Italy, has erupted often throughout history.

Prosperous Farms

The farmers of Latium grew wheat for bread. They also grew beans, cabbage, and lettuce, as well as fruits. They also raised grapes to make wine. Wine sold well in the marketplace. Most people drank watered-down wine at mealtimes. People poured wine into cuts and wounds to help them heal. In time, Italy's fine wines became a valued trade good.

The Etruscans

Before the founding of Rome, there were other civilizations in Italy. One group, the Etruscans, settled on the Etrurian plain northwest of the Tiber River. The land they settled was later named Tuscany, after them. Around 575 B.C., the Etruscan army conquered much of the Italian peninsula, including Rome. Etruscan kings continued to rule Rome for many years.

READING CHECK How did Rome's location help its trade?

PUTTING IT TOGETHER

Italy's landscape is marked by plains and mountains. The plains provide fertile farmland, while the mountains isolate the parts of Italy from one another, and from the rest of Europe. Rome is located on the fertile plain of Latium, on the Tiber River.

Eventually, Rome became a very important city. In the next lesson, you will learn how the Romans overthrew the Etruscans and went on to found a great civilization.

The Forum in Rome was a marketplace and a center of government.

Review and Assess

1. Write a sentence for this vocabulary word.
   volcano

2. Why did the people of Latium grow grapes?

3. What were the advantages and disadvantages of Italy's geography for settlers?

4. How did Latium's rich soil affect its **economy**?

5. Make a **generalization** about the land of Italy.

Look at the map on page 219. Using modeling clay, make a three-dimensional model of Italy. Be sure to indicate rivers and mountains.

Suppose you are walking along the Tiber River from its source to the Mediterranean. **Write** diary entries in which you describe the geography you see on your trip.

Lesson 2

The Roman Republic

Find Out! How did Rome become a republic?

Lesson Outline
• Early Rome
• Government of the Republic
• The Wars with Carthage
• Problems in Italy

VOCABULARY

plebeian
patrician
republic
representative
Senate
tribune
consul
Twelve Tables
Punic Wars

PEOPLE

Livy
Hannibal
Scipio Africanus

READING STRATEGY

Make a three-column chart like this one. Label the columns "Tribunes," "Senate," and "Consuls." Write the duties of each office in each column.

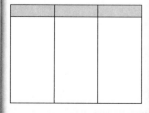

BUILD BACKGROUND

Polybius, an ancient writer, said that "three kinds of government . . . were all found united in . . . Rome. . . ." What he meant was that the Roman government had features of democracy, mixed with features of royal and noble governments. Over time, this Roman government had to be changed as Rome grew from a city-state into a large empire. In this lesson, you will see how Rome's government developed, and how it changed over time.

You Are Here
753 B.C. – 90 B.C.

EARLY ROME

According to legend, Rome was founded in 753 B.C. by twin brothers named Romulus and Remus. The legend says that Rome began as a walled city. However, archaeologists have found that Rome really started as a cluster of mud huts on the hills overlooking the Tiber River.

By 502 B.C. the Romans had driven out the Etruscan kings and set up a government in which more citizens had greater power. The Romans also improved their city by building a bridge across the Tiber. They drained the swamps and turned them into a marketplace called the Forum. Atop one of Rome's hills stood a great stone temple, while on the other hilltops of the city, wealthy citizens built fine brick homes.

Plebeians and Patricians

The division between rich and poor, and the powerful and not so powerful, affected the shape of the new Roman government. As in Greece, society in Rome was divided into two groups. Most Roman citizens were **plebeians** (plih BEE unz). Plebeians were farmers, tradespeople, and craftworkers. The second group, called the **patricians** (puh TRISH unz), was smaller. Patricians were members of Rome's noble families. They owned large farms and had plebeians work the land. At this time, Rome had few slaves, and Roman women could not participate in civic life.

Roman leaders (opposite) ordered bridges (above) to be built across the Tiber River.

Founding of the Republic

After the last king, Tarquinius, was overthrown, the patricians took power in Rome. Only patricians could belong to the ruling assembly or become government leaders. According to the Roman historian **Livy**, the plebeians rebelled against the patricians' rule in 494 B.C. They demanded changes in the government. The patricians, Livy wrote, were forced to accept the plebeians' demands. The new government was called a **republic**. *Republic* means "public thing" in Latin, the language of ancient Rome. In a republic, citizens choose their leaders. Rome's republic lasted for nearly 500 years.

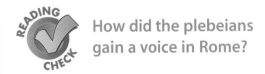

How did the plebeians gain a voice in Rome?

223

GOVERNMENT OF THE REPUBLIC

The citizens of Rome elected **representatives**, or people who acted for them, to run their government. Does this sound familiar? The government of the United States is also a republic. Citizens elect representatives to serve in Congress and state legislatures. However, in Rome not all the votes of the citizens were equal. In Rome the more power a man had, the more important his vote was.

The Branches of Rome's Republic

Three different government branches ran Rome's affairs. Each of these branches had decision-making powers that allowed it to have some control over the actions of the other branches.

The oldest and most powerful branch of the republic was the **Senate**. The Senate was controlled by Rome's patricians. The Roman Senate determined how Rome would act toward other governments. It also had control of all the money collected and spent by the republic.

The second branch of the government was a citizen assembly, elected by the plebeians. This assembly had less power than the Senate, but it elected the **tribunes** (trih BYOONZ). The tribunes were representatives of the plebeians and the leaders of the citizen assembly. They worked to protect the rights of the plebeians in the Roman government. These changes made the government more representative.

Rome's Early Years

753 B.C.
Legendary date of Rome's founding by Romulus and Remus

575 B.C.
Rome is unified into a city.

502 B.C.
Etruscan rule ends. Romans rule themselves.

Diagram Skill

1. How many years passed between Rome's founding and its self-government?

2. What event led to the founding of the Republic?

450 B.C.
The Twelve Tables

494 B.C.
Revolt of the plebeians. A republic is founded.

Consuls and Tribunes

The third branch of the government consisted of the **consuls**. Consuls served for one year as Rome's army commanders and most powerful judges. They were elected by the citizen assembly and could order anyone to be arrested. The consuls could also propose new laws for Rome. The assembly could veto, or forbid, any of the consuls' actions, and consuls could also veto each other. After 367 B.C., one of the consuls had to be a plebian.

After the revolt of the plebeians in 494 B.C., the citizen assembly elected tribunes. Early tribunes made sure plebeians got fair trials. They also brought plebeian complaints before the Senate and the consuls.

The Twelve Tables

For many years, only the patrician leaders knew Rome's laws. As a result, plebeians could not know what was and was not against the law. In court, plebeians could only hope that the patrician judges would give them a fair trial.

About 450 B.C., the plebeians protested this unfairness. The patricians agreed to write a collection of laws. These laws governed all aspects of Roman life, including marriage, trade, and warfare. They were written on twelve bronze tablets, or tables, and became known as the **Twelve Tables**. They were posted in the Forum, which was part market, part town square, and the place where citizens presented their cases before judges.

Why were the Twelve Tables important to the plebeians?

Primary Source:

excerpt from **the Twelve Tables** — *c. 450 B.C.*

If anyone summons a man before the magistrate [judge], he must go. . . .

One who has confessed a debt, or against whom judgment has been pronounced, shall have thirty days to pay it. After that seizure of his person is allowed.

Females should remain in guardianship even when they have become adults.

If one has broken a bone of a freeman with his hand or with a club, let him pay a penalty of three hundred coins. If he has broken the bone of a slave, let him pay one hundred and fifty coins. If one is guilty of insult, the penalty shall be twenty-five coins.

From this passage, what can you tell about people who lived in Rome?

The Punic Wars, 264-202 B.C.

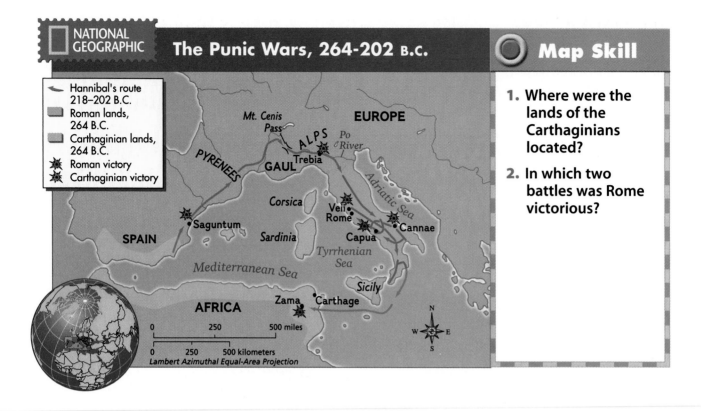

Hannibal's route 218–202 B.C.
Roman lands, 264 B.C.
Carthaginian lands, 264 B.C.
Roman victory
Carthaginian victory

Mt. Cenis Pass
EUROPE
ALPS
Po River
GAUL
Trebia
PYRENEES
Adriatic Sea
Corsica
Veii
Rome
Cannae
Saguntum
SPAIN
Sardinia
Capua
Tyrrhenian Sea
Mediterranean Sea
Sicily
Zama
Carthage
AFRICA

0   250   500 miles
0   250   500 kilometers
Lambert Azimuthal Equal-Area Projection

1. **Where were the lands of the Carthaginians located?**

2. **In which two battles was Rome victorious?**

THE WARS WITH CARTHAGE

During its early history, Rome was almost always at war. Sometimes, the Romans were defeated, as in 390 B.C., when an invading army almost destroyed the city. More often, the Romans were victorious. Roman territory expanded, until by 265 B.C., the Romans controlled the entire Italian peninsula.

In 264 B.C., Roman soldiers landed on the island of Sicily. Find Sicily on the map on this page. Their arrival sparked a series of conflicts with the powerful empire of **Carthage**. As you have read, Carthage was a Phoenician city in present-day Tunisia, on the north coast of Africa. Carthage controlled much of the land around the western Mediterranean, including Sicily. The Romans

called the war with Carthage the First **Punic War**. *Punic* comes from the Latin word for Phoenicia. In 241 B.C., after more than 20 years of bitter fighting, Carthage surrendered control of Sicily to Rome. The island then became Rome's first overseas province.

After its victory, Rome seized more of the lands controlled by Carthage. Many of the Carthaginian leaders wanted revenge. One of these leaders was a general named Hamilcar, who was the Carthaginian commander in Spain. Hamilcar made his son **Hannibal** swear to be Rome's enemy forever.

In 218 B.C., the Second Punic War began. Hannibal, who was 29 years old, was sent with a Carthaginian army to attack Rome.

Hannibal's Plan

Hannibal had a daring plan. Since Rome's navy controlled the waters around Italy, Hannibal's army would attack by land. Hannibal marched from Spain over the Alps to Rome with an army of about 90,000 men. He also had trained war elephants, which frightened the Romans. Hannibal faced 1,000 miles of enemy lands. He had to hold his troops together and feed them from the crops of the lands they crossed.

Hannibal actually succeeded, though thousands of his men died along the way. He won major battles in Italy and caused great destruction. However, he could not secure a victory for Carthage. He became stranded in Italy without supplies, and was forced to retreat to Africa by ship.

In Rome, a 25-year-old general, **Scipio Africanus** (SIHP ee oh af rik AN us), was elected consul. He led an army which defeated Hannibal near Carthage at the Battle of Zama in 202 B.C. The defeat of Carthage made Rome the most powerful nation in the Mediterranean region.

Contact with the Greeks

Rome had also increased its contact with Greek culture. Between 214 and 148 B.C., Rome conquered Greece. The Romans were very impressed with the art, science, and philosophy of the Greeks. Educated Romans learned to speak Greek, and the wealthy collected Greek art. Romans were so influenced by Greek culture that the Latin expression *victor victus*, or "the conqueror conquered" came into being.

READING CHECK   How did Rome build an empire?

Hannibal (below) invaded Italy with a large army that included war elephants.

PROBLEMS IN ITALY

Power brought problems. The patricians grew rich, but the common people grew poorer. Also, Rome's government was designed to govern a city, and could not adapt to running an empire.

Efforts at Reform

In the 120s B.C., two brothers, Tiberius and Gaius Gracchus, tried to reform Rome. They wanted to change Roman rule of conquered people, and to give land to the poor people of Rome. However, the brothers were killed by patricians who did not want to share power.

Rome's conquered territories felt they had no say in the government. In 90 B.C., Rome's Italian allies revolted. The Romans then gave Roman citizenship to people in conquered lands.

By the first century B.C., the government of Rome faced serious problems. Patricians and plebeians struggled for power. Slaves and conquered peoples revolted against Roman rule. Strong measures were needed to rule the new empire.

READING CHECK What problems did the Republic face?

The Gracchi (right) tried to reform Roman government. Soldiers and slaves (below) were forced to entertain Romans in large arenas.

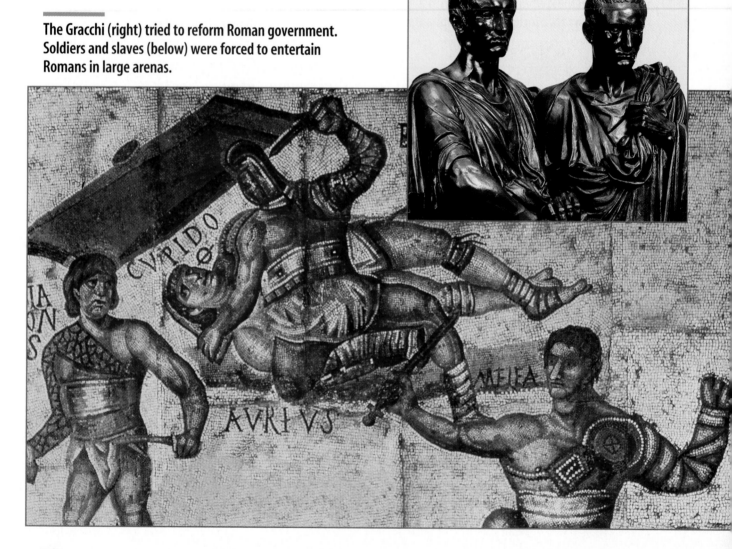

PUTTING IT TOGETHER

Rome was founded on seven hills overlooking the Tiber River. By 494 B.C., the Romans had founded a republic governed by the senate, the consuls, and the tribunes.

Rome expanded as a result of wars fought with its neighbors. However, the growing size of the land ruled by Rome led to problems in Italy. There were revolts and battles between powerful men for control of the government. The last years of the republic were a time of almost constant warfare.

In the next lesson, you will learn how the Romans changed their form of government so they could rule their new empire more efficiently.

The letters SPQR stand for *The Senate and the People of Rome*. A Roman official holds the symbol of his office.

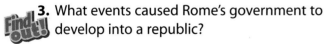

Review and Assess

1. Write one sentence for each vocabulary term.

consul	**Senate**
patrician	**tribune**
plebeian	**Twelve Tables**
Punic Wars	

2. According to legend, who founded Rome?

3. What events caused Rome's government to develop into a republic?

4. How did the plebeians exercise their rights of **citizenship**?

5. **Compare** and **contrast** the government of ancient Rome with the government of the United States.

Activities

Look at the map on page 226. Find the island of Sicily. Prepare for a debate in which you explain why Sicily is a battleground between Rome and Carthage. Explain why Rome and Carthage would want to control Sicily.

• •

Suppose you are a Roman senator. **Write** a speech to persuade the Senate to give rights to Rome's conquered peoples.

Making Generalizations

In the last lesson, you read about the Roman Republic and its growing problems with Carthage. So many events occurred at this time that it can be a difficult period to understand. You might see similarities that show how the wars caused changes in the way Rome was ruled. These similarities might help you to make a broad statement, or **generalization**, about the republic during its expansion. A generalization is a statement that shows common features shared by different things.

VOCABULARY

generalization

LEARN THE SKILL

Follow these steps to make a generalization about the expansion of Rome.

1. **Identify the topic.**
   You must decide about what you want to make a generalization. Here you want to make a generalization about the difficulties Rome experienced after it expanded.

2. **Gather examples.**
   Next, gather examples about your topic. In the last lesson, you learned about the political struggles for government control, attempts by the army to gain more power,

and demands by the conquered people and the poor to have a say in government.

3. **Examine the examples for similarities.**
   What is similar about the examples? What do they have in common? They all describe attacks on the government or demands for a share of government power.

4. **Make the generalization.**
   Use the common features to make a generalization about the expansion of Rome in the 100s B.C. This was a period of conflict as people struggled for power and control over the Roman Republic.

TRY THE SKILL

During the early republic, only patricians could become consuls or senators. However, only plebeians voted for the tribunes. Use this information to make a generalization about the government of the Roman Republic.

Think about what you have read in this lesson to help you make the generalization. Then answer the following questions.

1. Identify the topic about which you want to make a generalization.

2. What examples have you gathered?

3. What similarities do the examples share?

4. How can making generalizations help you to better understand what you learn?

EXTEND THE SKILL

Sometimes information comes from studying different types of sources. The map below shows the territory governed by Rome between the years 500 B.C. and 50 B.C. Study the map and its key. Compare it to the graph. Then make a generalization about Rome's population as Roman territory expanded.

● How does making generalizations help you to understand history?

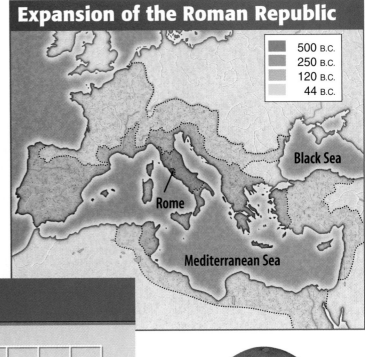

Expansion of the Roman Republic

500 B.C.
250 B.C.
120 B.C.
44 B.C.

Black Sea

Rome

Mediterranean Sea

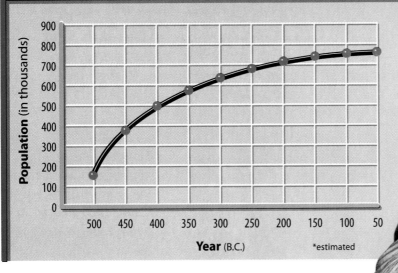

Population of the City of Rome*

Population (in thousands)

900
800
700
600
500
400
300
200
100
0

500 450 400 350 300 250 200 150 100 50

Year (B.C.)   *estimated

The Roman Empire

Find out!

How was the Roman Empire created?

Lesson Outline
• A Struggle for Leadership
• The Roman Empire Is Created
• Daily Life in Rome
• Rome's Great Projects

VOCABULARY

civil war
dictator
Pax Romana
gladiator
census

PEOPLE

Augustus
Julius Caesar
Pompey
Cleopatra

READING STRATEGY

On a main idea chart like this one, write examples of ways that Augustus improved Rome.

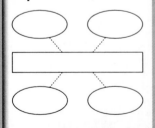

BUILD BACKGROUND

"In my nineteenth year. . . I raised an army with which I set free the state, which was oppressed. . . . I restored peace to the sea from pirates. . . . I extended the borders of all the provinces of the Roman people. . . ."

These words were written by **Augustus**, the first emperor of Rome. They tell of his deeds in restoring peace to Rome. In this lesson, you will learn how the Roman Republic was overthrown, how the empire was established, and what happened in the early years of the empire.

Augustus (left) was the nephew of Julius Caesar (opposite), who helped Cleopatra (coin, opposite) become sole ruler of Egypt.

500 B.C.	400 B.C.	300 B.C.	200 B.C.	100 B.C.	A.D. 1	A.D. 100	A.D. 200	A.D. 300	A.D. 400

You Are Here
100 B.C. – A.D. 79

A STRUGGLE FOR LEADERSHIP

As you read in the last lesson, Rome controlled much of the Mediterranean world by 100 B.C. However, the republic was having problems at home. Powerful generals and politicians struggled for power. They brought North African grain for the poor. They led troops against pirates and enemies of Rome. Then they used their fame and popularity to try to become the supreme ruler of Rome.

Julius Caesar

Julius Caesar (SEE zuhr) was born into a patrician family in 100 B.C. As a young man, he served in various offices, both in the government and in the army. He also made many enemies among the patricians who controlled Rome.

Caesar was ambitious. One writer described how Caesar looked at a statue of Alexander the Great and sighed that he had "as yet done nothing noteworthy...."

In 59 B.C. Caesar was elected Consul of Rome. The following year, he became the military governor of Roman **Gaul**, which today is part of France. In the next nine years, Caesar conquered the rest of Gaul extending Roman control to the English Channel. His victories gave him fame, riches, and the loyalty of a great army. He used these to make himself master of Rome.

The Senate worried about Caesar's growing power. They ordered him to return to Rome without his army. Instead, in 49 B.C., Caesar and his army crossed the Rubicon River, which separated Italy from Gaul. (Even today, the expression "crossing the Rubicon" means making a decision that can't be reversed).

Caesar's decision led to a **civil war**, or war between groups within one country. Caesar's main enemy was **Pompey**, another powerful general. Pompey's army was defeated and he fled to Egypt, where he was murdered.

Caesar sailed to Alexandria, Egypt, and joined forces with 21-year-old **Cleopatra** (klee uh PA truh), Egypt's queen. Caesar helped Cleopatra defeat her brother, who was also her rival for the throne. In return, she gave Caesar the money he needed to continue fighting for control of Rome.

In 45 B.C. Caesar returned in triumph to Rome and made himself **dictator**. A dictator is someone who rules with absolute power. Government under a dictator is called a dictatorship.

READING CHECK
How did Caesar become dictator?

233

THE ROMAN EMPIRE IS CREATED

Although Caesar's time as dictator was short, he made important changes in Roman life. Caesar gave land to his soldiers and free grain to poor citizens. He increased the number of people in the Senate. Also, he granted Roman citizenship to many people not born in Rome. Caesar ordered a new and more accurate calendar and named the month of his birth "July."

All these changes were too much for some senators. Others were frightened of Caesar's growing power and popularity. Some felt he was destroying the traditions of the Roman Republic. They thought he was planning to make himself king.

Tradition says that an oracle warned Caesar to "beware the Ides (ĪDZ) of March" (March 15). On March 15, 44 B.C., Caesar ignored the warning and arrived at the Senate without a bodyguard. There, he was stabbed to death by his enemies.

Julius Caesar was killed by Roman senators in 44 B.C.

Augustus Becomes Emperor

After Caesar's death, civil war broke out again. After 14 years of fighting, Julius Caesar's grand-nephew and adopted son Octavian defeated all his rivals. Though only 18 years old when the wars began, Octavian was able to defeat some of Rome's most experienced generals.

After his victory in 27 B.C., Octavian was acclaimed *imperator*, or "one who commands." Our word *emperor* comes from *imperator*. Octavian had the power to veto any law, rule all Roman provinces, and control the army.

As a sign of his new power, Octavian took the name Augustus, "honored one." The month of August is named after this powerful ruler and general. Augustus then set about reforming the government of Rome.

Pax Romana

Within a few years, Rome's troubles were ending. A period known as the **Pax Romana** had begun. *Pax Romana* is Latin for "Roman peace." Life throughout the Roman Empire changed during this period, which lasted about 200 years. Under Augustus, the government became more efficient. New roads, buildings, and water systems were built. Augustus also tried to create a single system of government and money throughout the empire.

Goods moved freely within his empire. In Rome people ate bread each day, thanks to shipments of North African wheat. Goods came in from all over the Mediterranean region. Romans could cook in pots made from Spanish copper. The wealthy could wear clothes made from Greek wool, Egyptian linen, or even Chinese silk.

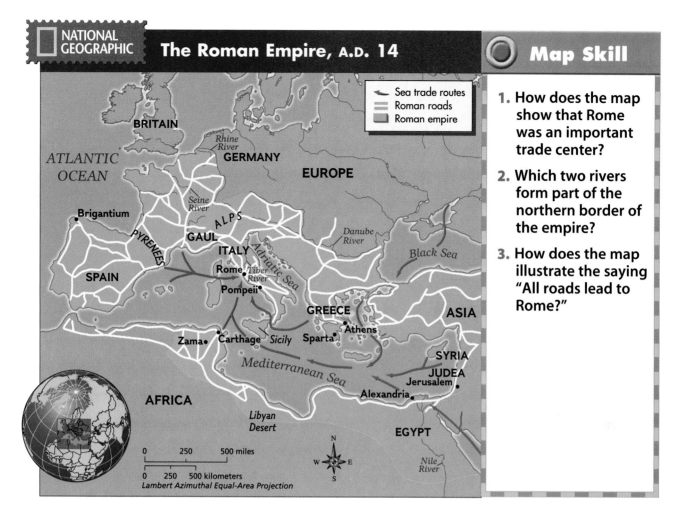

Sea trade routes
Roman roads
Roman empire

1. **How does the map show that Rome was an important trade center?**

2. **Which two rivers form part of the northern border of the empire?**

3. **How does the map illustrate the saying "All roads lead to Rome?"**

New Public Buildings

About one million people lived in the city of Rome. In the city's center, the Forum included large marble buildings. New theaters and public baths stood nearby. Aqueducts, raised waterways, brought streams of fresh water into the city.

Under Augustus, Romans enjoyed police and fire protection and received free bread. For their entertainment, **gladiators** were forced to fight in arenas. A gladiator is a slave or criminal condemned to death. One of Augustus' successors built an enormous stadium, the **Colosseum**, for these "games."

Controlling the Empire

The city of Rome was like a giant magnet. Everyone in the empire felt its pull in one way or another. Rome appointed governors to enforce the law and to act as judges. In addition, a **census**, or count, of people living in the empire, was taken every five years.

Running an empire is expensive. Rome taxed everyone to pay for its empire. Army units were posted far and wide to enforce Roman law, as well as to help build the empire's roads. Unlike the soldiers of the old Roman Republic, most soldiers of the Roman Empire were not citizens. They were paid to serve in the army full-time. For many poor men, the army offered the best chance to earn a decent living.

READING CHECK

How did the city of Rome change during the "Pax Romana?"

Ash covered Pompeii quickly, preserving the bodies of its citizens (above) and their homes (left).

DAILY LIFE IN ROME

Some later emperors were good rulers. Others were cruel men who wasted tax money and ignored their responsibilities. However, the Roman Empire continued to bring peace and prosperity to the Mediterranean region.

Pompeii, a Buried City

We know about life in the Roman Empire at this time because of a terrible disaster. In A.D. 79 Mount Vesuvius, a volcano in southern Italy, erupted and buried the city of **Pompeii** in ash. Because the disaster happened quickly, the people of Pompeii were caught by surprise at their daily tasks. Centuries later, archaeologists excavated the city. It provided a view of Roman life at the time of the eruption.

Pompeii was in many ways a typical Roman city of its time. It was laid out neatly in blocks, and contained many houses, of both the rich and the poor. It had public buildings, such as baths and theaters, built by wealthy citizens. Many houses and apartment buildings had shops on the ground floors, and there were small family workshops as well.

Many of the larger houses also had gardens. Even in the city, many people grew their own vegetables. Meals left half-eaten were preserved in ash. They included eggs, hazelnuts, and other familiar foods.

 READING CHECK What do the ruins of Pompeii tell us about ancient Rome?

Feeding Rome's Cities

The Roman Empire included many cities with over 100,000 residents each. Importing food from North Africa and Egypt, especially wheat for bread, to these cities was important. Study the graphics on this page and then answer the questions.

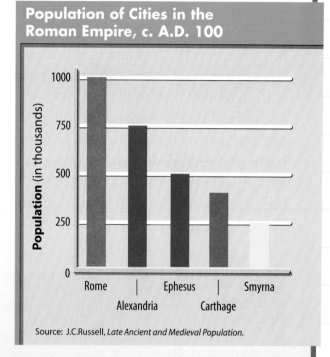

Population of Cities in the Roman Empire, c. A.D. 100

Population (in thousands)

1000
750
500
250
0

Rome | Alexandria | Ephesus | Carthage | Smyrna

Source: J.C.Russell, *Late Ancient and Medieval Population*.

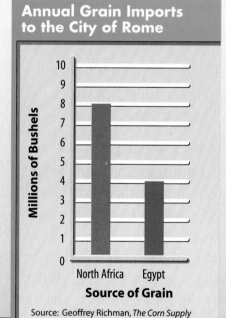

Annual Grain Imports to the City of Rome

Millions of Bushels

10
9
8
7
6
5
4
3
2
1
0

North Africa   Egypt

Source of Grain

Source: Geoffrey Richman, *The Corn Supply of Ancient Rome*

QUESTIONS:

1. How much grain in all was imported into the city of Rome each year?

2. Use the data from the graph on the left to predict how much grain would be imported to feed Rome, Alexandria, and Smyrna.

3. What does the organization of food delivery to these Roman cities tell you about the Roman Empire?

To learn more, visit our Web site: **www.mhschool.com**

237

ROME'S GREAT PROJECTS

Throughout the empire, Roman engineers built great aqueducts to bring fresh water to the cities. Engineers spanned rivers with stone bridges to speed the movement of soldiers and merchants. For cleanliness, engineers built public baths complete with heated floors.

To the Romans, baths were more than just a way to clean themselves. Roman baths also included libraries, museums, and art galleries. Romans went to the baths to discuss political affairs, business, or the latest gossip with their friends.

Arch and Concrete

The key to many of Rome's massive building projects was the use of the arch. Though the Egyptians and Greeks knew about arches, the Romans were the first to use them widely.

An arch can carry great weight because the center stone, called the keystone, presses down on the other stones. Increasing the weight on the arch locks the stones in more tightly. Because an arch holds many times its own weight, it is used for bridges and large buildings. The arch replaced the columns that had formerly held up large roofs—making a more open interior space.

Another innovation of Roman engineers was the use of concrete as a building material. To make concrete, the Romans mixed lime, volcanic ash, sand, and small stones with water. They used concrete to form walls of temples, bridges, and baths, many of which are still standing.

Rome's Heritage

Rome's legacy remains with us in many other ways as well. One Roman legacy is our political ideas. Also, many European languages, such as French and Spanish, are descendants of the Latin spoken in the Roman Empire. In the next lesson, you will learn about another important event that began in ancient Rome and has influenced our own world—the birth of a religion called Christianity.

What were some of Rome's contributions to architecture?

This Roman aqueduct still stands in Segovia, Spain.

PUTTING IT TOGETHER

In the first century B.C. there was a struggle for leadership in Rome. Julius Caesar, a powerful general, eventually made himself dictator of Rome. After Caesar's assassination, his grand-nephew Augustus became the first emperor of Rome. Augustus established the Pax Romana, a time of peace for the entire Mediterranean world.

Many of Rome's great works, such as roads and baths, were built during the Pax Romana. The Roman emperors also ensured peace, which helped build prosperity for the whole empire.

Review and Assess

1. Write a sentence for each vocabulary term.

   census   **gladiator**
   civil war   **Pax Romana**
   dictator

2. Who was Augustus?

3. What events led to the creation of the Roman Empire?

4. How did **technology** help Rome to manage its empire?

5. What technology did the Romans use to **solve the problem** of bringing water to their cities?

Look at the map on page 235. Suppose you are a Roman travel agent. Plan a trip from Rome to Athens. Try to complete the trip using only Roman roads.

· ·

Suppose you want to become the Roman emperor. **Write** a speech telling Romans what you will do for them after you become their ruler.

The Birth of Christianity

What are the teachings of Jesus?

VOCABULARY

New Testament
Messiah
Christianity
parable
apostle
crucifixion
bishop
pope

PEOPLE

Jesus
Peter
Paul
Constantine

READING STRATEGY

Copy and complete the chart. Write the sequence of events, from the birth of Jesus to the conversion of Constantine.

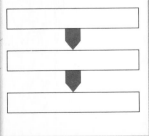

Lesson Outline

• The Life of Jesus
• Jesus' Message
• An Emperor Accepts Christianity

BUILD BACKGROUND

"There went out a decree from Caesar Augustus, that all the world should be taxed . . . And Joseph also went . . . [to] Bethlehem . . . to be taxed with Mary his . . . wife. . . . And she brought forth her firstborn son . . . and laid him in a manger [feedbox for an animal]; because there was no room for them in the inn."

These words tell of the birth of a child in a land called Judea. From these humble beginnings came a teacher whose ideas would influence people around the world.

400 B.C.	300 B.C.	200 B.C.	100 B.C.	A.D. 1	A.D. 100	A.D. 200	A.D. 300	A.D. 400

You Are Here
37 B.C. – A.D. 311

THE LIFE OF JESUS

The Roman Empire included modern-day Israel, which the Romans called **Judea**. When Augustus was emperor, a child was born in Judea. This young Jewish boy would grow into a man whose ideas would greatly affect the world. His name was **Jesus**.

The New Testament

The story of the life of Jesus is told in a collection of books called the **New Testament**, although little is said of his early years. The Hebrew Torah, which you read about in Chapter 2, came to be called the Old Testament by Christians. Together, the Old and New Testaments are called the Christian Bible. Its words are sacred to nearly 2 billion people today. Most of what we know about the life of Jesus is taken from the New Testament.

Rome had gained control of Judea in 37 B.C. Writers of Jesus' time tell us that the people of Judea disliked Roman rule. Many Jewish teachers roamed the land, warning people about the importance of living a just life.

Jesus the Teacher

Beginning at the age of 30, the New Testament says, Jesus spent much of his time as one of these teachers. The New Testament also says that many people came to hear him because they believed he could perform miracles.

Some people came to believe that Jesus was the **Messiah**. The Messiah,

according to Jewish belief, is a leader who would be sent by God to guide the Jewish people and to set up God's rule on Earth. The word *Messiah* in Greek is *Christos*. People who followed Jesus became known as Christians, and their religion became known as **Christianity**.

Why are Jesus' followers called Christians?

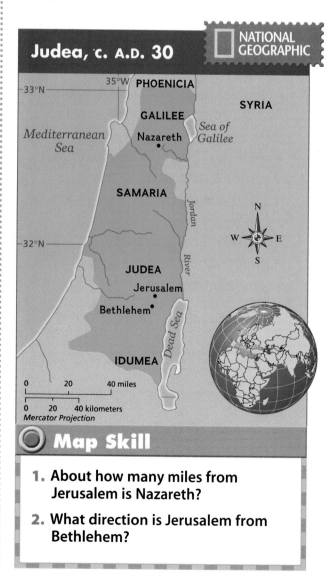

Judea, c. A.D. 30

NATIONAL GEOGRAPHIC

33°N   35°W   PHOENICIA

GALILEE   SYRIA

Mediterranean Sea   Nazareth   Sea of Galilee

SAMARIA

Jordan River

32°N

JUDEA

Jerusalem

Bethlehem   Dead Sea

IDUMEA

0   20   40 miles
0   20   40 kilometers
Mercator Projection

Map Skill

1. **About how many miles from Jerusalem is Nazareth?**

2. **What direction is Jerusalem from Bethlehem?**

JESUS' MESSAGE

Jesus' teachings as recorded in the New Testament often use **parables**, or simple stories that contain a message or truth. Some of these stories taught the value of seeking the right path in life. Others described the greatness of God's love for all people. Still others stressed the importance of loving all people.

Primary Source:

excerpt from
the Sermon on the Mount
— Matthew 22:37-40

"Jesus said unto him, You shall love the Lord your God with all your heart, and with all your soul, and with all your mind. This is the first and great commandment. And the second is like it, You shall love your neighbor as you love yourself. All the law and [the teachings of the prophets] depend on these two commandments."

commandment: law

What two things does Jesus tell his followers to do?

Jesus helped his followers understand his teachings.

The Apostles

Jesus' closest followers were called **apostles** (uh PAHS ulz). They were 12 men Jesus had chosen to help him in his teaching. The New Testament says that they came from many different ways of life. One, **Peter**, was a fisherman. Another, Levi, was a tax collector. The apostles had little in common, but they united as followers of Jesus and spread his teachings after his death.

The Death of Jesus

Jesus' growing popularity troubled some people. These people were afraid that Jesus wanted to be king of Judea. Such beliefs worried the Roman governor, who feared a revolt in Judea. When Jesus came to Jerusalem to celebrate the Passover festival, the Romans arrested him. The Roman governor sentenced him to die by **crucifixion** (kroo suh FIK shun). Crucifixion means "putting to death by hanging from a cross." The Romans commonly used crucifixion as a punishment for criminals.

The New Testament says that Jesus rose from the dead three days after his crucifixion. Then he rejoined the apostles and told them again of the coming kingdom of God. Afterwards, the New Testament says, Jesus rose to heaven. Today, Christians celebrate his renewed life on Easter Sunday.

Christian Churches Are Built

The New Testament says that early followers of Jesus carried his message to cities throughout the Roman Empire. They set up dozens of Christian churches. Soon these churches drew the attention of Roman leaders. Some Roman rulers punished Christians because they would not worship the emperor. Still, the new religion continued to grow and attract followers.

Paul Helps Spread Christianity

One man who helped to spread Christianity was not one of the first 12 apostles. Saul of Tarsus grew up in a big city in what is now Turkey. He was well educated in both Judaism and the Greek classics. At first he opposed Christianity, but later he became a Christian himself. He changed his name to **Paul** and spread Christianity through many cities.

The new churches included people from all nations and ranks in life. Paul reminded them that:

> *"There is no longer Jew or Greek . . . slave or free . . . male or female; for all of you are one in Christ Jesus. . . ."*

Early church historians wrote that the apostle Peter helped bring Christianity to Rome's crowded neighborhoods. Christians call Peter the first **bishop**, or regional church leader, of Rome. Later, Christians would give the bishop of Rome the title **pope** from the Latin word for "father."

READING CHECK What did Paul tell people about Christianity?

Jesus and his followers shared a meal on the night of his arrest.

AN EMPEROR ACCEPTS CHRISTIANITY

Several Roman emperors tried to stamp out the new faith, but Christianity continued to attract followers. By the end of the third century A.D. there were Christians throughout the Roman Empire. As much as ten percent of the empire's population may have been Christian.

Powerful Romans were also drawn to the message of love and hope. One of these was Helena, the mother of an army general named **Constantine**. He was fighting another general to become emperor. Constantine later said that he saw a cross in the sky with the words "in hoc signo vinces" ("in this sign, you will

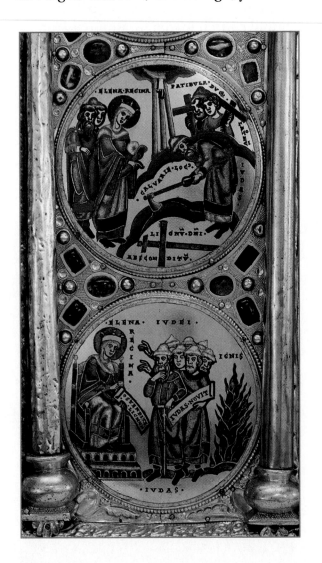

conquer") before an important battle in A.D. 311. He ordered the cross, the symbol of Christianity, to be placed on every soldier's shield. Constantine's army won the battle, and he gave credit to Christianity for his victory.

When he became emperor, Constantine ended the persecution of Christians. He made Christianity one of the official religions that Romans were permitted to follow. You will read about this historic turning point in the next lesson.

 READING CHECK How did Christianity come to be accepted in the Roman Empire?

Among the figures in early Christian art is Helena, the mother of Constantine. She is shown on the left in the circles.

Christians around the world worship in a variety of churches such as St. Peter's in Rome (left).

PUTTING IT TOGETHER

Christianity was founded in Judea about 2,000 years ago. Many people were attracted to the teachings of Jesus and came to believe that he was the Messiah. The Romans, afraid of Jesus' popularity, crucified him.

After Jesus' death, the early Christian church spread his message. One influential early Christian was Paul, who helped spread Christianity through the non-Jewish world.

As Christianity grew, bishops became local church leaders, and a pope was chosen to head the church. The emperor Constantine ended the persecution of Christians and made Christianity an official religion of the Roman Empire.

Review and Assess

1. Write a sentence for each vocabulary term.

apostle	New Testament
Christianity	parable
Messiah	pope

2. Why were Joseph and Mary traveling to Bethlehem?

3. What did Jesus tell his followers to do?

4. Why did Christianity spread throughout the Roman Empire?

5. What were the cause and effects of Constantine's interest in Christianity?

Activities

Write an itinerary, or trip plan, for a preaching journey for Paul. Start in Jerusalem and end in Athens.

• •

Suppose you are a reporter for a Roman newspaper. Write a news story about Christianity becoming an official Roman religion.

Lesson 5

Rome and Byzantium

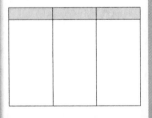

Why was the Roman Empire divided?

Lesson Outline
- Unrest and Invasion
- The Empire Divided
- The "New Rome"

VOCABULARY

persecution
Eastern Orthodox
 Christianity
Justinian Code

PEOPLE

Diocletian
Justinian
Theodora

READING STRATEGY

Complete a chart like this one. Write Diocletian, Constantine, and Justinian at the top of a column. Write three actions of each emperor.

BUILD BACKGROUND

"The decline of Rome was the natural . . . effect of immoderate [excessive] greatness. . . The story of its ruin is simple and obvious; . . . instead of [asking] why the Roman Empire was destroyed, we should rather be surprised that it had subsisted [lasted] so long."

British historian Edward Gibbon wrote these words nearly 300 years ago to explain *his* idea for the fall of Rome. Other writers before and since Gibbon have written their ideas about Rome's decline. In this lesson, we will explore some of the causes for the decline.

UNREST AND INVASION

The Pax Romana was a time of peace. Afterwards, Rome faced enemies on its borders. Germanic peoples were moving out of the forests of northern Europe to settle within the empire.

A Foreign Army

The empire began to rely on foreign soldiers to guard its borders. The empire grew weaker and poorer. Northern peoples began to spread across the Roman Empire, and the army was too weak to stop them.

These invaders destroyed cities and farms and stole from travelers. Trade declined. Western Roman cities built thick walls with gates that were kept locked at night. Wealthy country landowners made forts of their homes. The government could not collect taxes needed to pay for defending the empire.

Stone walls like these in Istanbul, Turkey (opposite), surrounded many Roman cities.

READING CHECK What threats faced the Roman Empire?

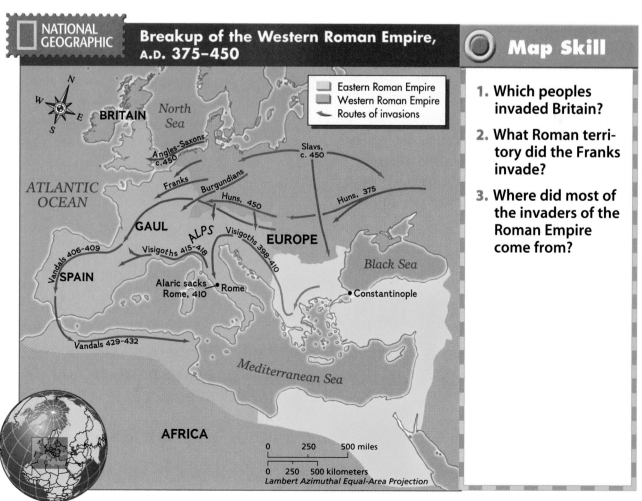

NATIONAL GEOGRAPHIC

Breakup of the Western Roman Empire, A.D. 375–450

Eastern Roman Empire
Western Roman Empire
Routes of invasions

BRITAIN
North Sea
Angles-Saxons c. 450
Slavs, c. 450
ATLANTIC OCEAN
Franks
Burgundians
Huns, 450
Huns, 375
GAUL
ALPS
Visigoths 415–418
Visigoths 398–410
EUROPE
Vandals 406–409
Black Sea
SPAIN
Alaric sacks Rome, 410
Rome
Constantinople
Vandals 429–432
Mediterranean Sea
AFRICA

0   250   500 miles
0   250   500 kilometers
Lambert Azimuthal Equal-Area Projection

Map Skill

1. **Which peoples invaded Britain?**

2. **What Roman territory did the Franks invade?**

3. **Where did most of the invaders of the Roman Empire come from?**

247

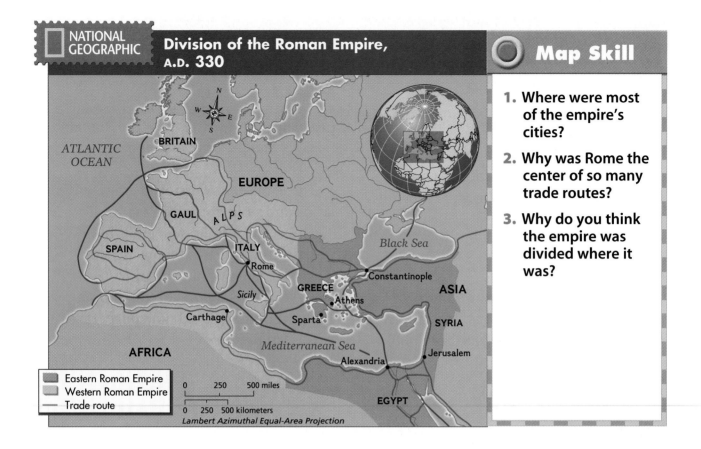

ATLANTIC OCEAN

BRITAIN

EUROPE

GAUL

ALPS

SPAIN

ITALY

Rome

Sicily

Carthage

GREECE

Athens

Sparta

Black Sea

Constantinople

ASIA

SYRIA

Jerusalem

AFRICA

Mediterranean Sea

Alexandria

EGYPT

Eastern Roman Empire
Western Roman Empire
Trade route

0   250   500 miles
0   250 500 kilometers
Lambert Azimuthal Equal-Area Projection

1. Where were most of the empire's cities?

2. Why was Rome the center of so many trade routes?

3. Why do you think the empire was divided where it was?

THE EMPIRE DIVIDED

In A.D. 284, an emperor named **Diocletian** (di uh KLEE shun) came to power. Diocletian was a strong general, but he was an even better ruler. He realized that the empire was simply too big to be ruled by one man. He divided the empire into two parts: an eastern and a western portion.

Diocletian himself took over the eastern half. This included the wealthy cities of Egypt, Greece, and western Asia. Assistants ruled the declining western half of the empire. He tried other reforms to slow the decline of the empire. He issued new coins to restore confidence and trade. He forced certain jobs, such as bakers and soldiers, on people because they were needed by the empire.

Diocletian saw Christians as a threat to his empire. They refused to worship the emperor as a god, so he thought they were working against the unity of Rome. He started one of the worst **persecutions** of Christians. A persecution is a policy of arresting, injuring, or even killing members of a religious, ethnic, or other minority group.

Diocletian's reforms created a major turning point in Roman history. Rome was no longer the most important city in the empire. Power had shifted from west to east.

Constantinople—a New Capital

Diocletian retired in 305. You read about Constantine's battle to become emperor and how he granted religious freedom to Christians. Constantine hoped to reunite the Roman Empire, but he soon realized that power and wealth were centered in the eastern half of the empire. He decided to abandon Rome for a new capital in the east.

In 330 Constantine moved his capital to a city named Byzantium (bih ZAN tee um), which was renamed **Constantinople** (kahn stan tuh NOH pul). Today the city is called Istanbul in Turkey.

Constantinople was located partly in Europe and partly in Asia, and was also on major trade routes. It was far from Rome and its traditions of government and religion. Moreover, Constantinople was easy to defend because it was built on a peninsula.

Constantine looted art treasures from other cities of the empire to make his capital brilliant. He ordered an elegant marble forum, public baths, and libraries. He also constructed aqueducts to bring fresh water into his city. The new capital was made as grand as Rome had once been.

Treatment of Christians

Constantine granted Christians freedom of worship. He also promoted Christian leaders to important positions and gave them land and money. He had many Christian churches built in Constantinople and throughout the empire.

Constantine was the first of many European leaders to see themselves as protectors of Christianity.

READING CHECK What were the advantages of Constantinople's location?

Constantine (above) chose Constantinople (below) as his capital in A.D. 330.

249

THE "NEW ROME"

While the eastern empire flourished, the western part of the empire grew weaker. From 376 to 476, Germanic invaders swept into the western empire. In 410 an army of invaders actually captured the city of Rome. In A.D. 476, another Germanic army seized Rome and removed the last emperor, who was a teenager. The thousand-year story of Rome's power had ended.

The Byzantine Empire

The eastern half of the Roman Empire lasted for another thousand years. It became known as the Byzantine Empire because its capital had been the Greek city of Byzantium.

Greek culture had a large role in Byzantine life. People spoke Greek rather than Latin. Byzantine art and building styles were influenced by Greek and western Asian styles. Greek philosophy and literature influenced Byzantine writers.

Diagram Skill

1. What was the highest point of the church?

2. How did the Roman arch influence the design of the church?

Hagia Sophia

dome

arch

enclosed walkway

gallery

entrance

Christianity in the Byzantine Empire

Byzantine Christianity was also influenced by Greek ideas. Western Christians regarded the pope in Rome as the only leader who could speak for the church. Eastern Christians differed about religious ideas and leadership of the church. They formed their own branch of Christianity called **Eastern Orthodox Christianity**.

A Great Byzantine Ruler

One of the greatest Byzantine emperors was **Justinian**, who ruled from 527 to 565. Justinian tried to unify the Byzantine Empire by allowing only certain types of Christian beliefs. He persecuted non-believers and non-Christians because he thought they were harmful to the unity of the empire. He also tried to recapture lands in Africa and Europe once held by Rome.

Rebuilding of Constantinople

Justinian wanted his capital to be a city of great beauty and splendor. The centerpiece of his new city was to be the magnificent Church of Hagia Sophia, which means "Holy Wisdom." For nearly a thousand years, this church was the world's largest building.

Justinian also built aqueducts, baths, schools, and hospitals. He imported dozens of statues from Rome and other cities of the empire to emphasize the new empire's connection with Rome's past. Justinian made Constantinople one of the great cities of the world.

The emperor Justinian (center) preserved Roman traditions and built Hagia Sophia (opposite).

The Justinian Code

Justinian believed that it was important to preserve Roman laws and traditions. He appointed a commission of legal experts. They produced a code of law called the **Justinian Code**. This code of law dealt with marriage, property rights, slavery, crime, and women's rights. The code was the basis of Byzantine law, and its principles are part of the laws of Western Europe and the United States.

Justinian depended on the advice and assistance of his wife, **Theodora**. You will read more about her in the biography on page 252. When Justinian died, he left a larger and stronger empire than he had found when he took power.

How did Justinian change the Byzantine Empire?

BIOGRAPHY

Focus On: Courage

Theodora was born in A.D. 502. She was the daughter of a circus performer and became an actress at a young age. She was 20 when she married Justinian, the future emperor.

In 527 Justinian and Theodora were crowned. Theodora helped Justinian with wise advice and strong support. She supported the rights of women, and she was famous for her charities, such as building hospitals and public kitchens.

Her courage once saved the empire. In 532, a revolt broke out in Constantinople. Their advisors told the rulers to flee the city. Theodora refused to leave. She said that it would be better to die as an empress than to run away.

Her courage inspired her husband and his advisors. Historians give her credit for saving their throne.

Link to Today

Think about a political leader today who is courageous. Compare and contrast this leader with Theodora.

THE LIFE OF THEODORA		502 Theodora is born.	527 Theodora and Justinian are crowned.	532 Revolt breaks out in Constantinople.	548 Theodora dies of cancer.
450	**475**	**500**	**525**	**550**	
LIFE AROUND THE WORLD	476 The city of Rome is conquered.	500 Ghana becomes the most important power in West Africa.	515 The Huns overthrow the Gupta Empire in India.	538 Buddhism reaches and influences Japan.	

Byzantine artists richly decorated this pin and book cover with jewels and gold.

PUTTING IT TOGETHER

German-speaking invaders from the north weakened the Western Roman Empire. To better govern Rome, Diocletian divided the empire into western and eastern empires. After Diocletian, Constantine made Christianity an official religion of the empire. He moved the capital to Constantinople. In A.D. 476 a Germanic invader seized Rome. This date marks the end of Rome's power. The Byzantine Empire continued Roman traditions. Justinian made a code of laws and strengthened the eastern half of the old Roman Empire.

Review and Assess

1. Write a sentence for each vocabulary term.
   Eastern Orthodox Christianity
   Justinian Code
   persecution

2. What challenges faced the Western Roman Empire?

3. Why did Diocletian divide the Roman Empire?

4. What economic reasons led to the choice of Constantinople as the new capital?

5. **Make a generalization** about the fall of the Roman Empire.

Look at the map on page 248. What city would you have chosen to be the new capital of the empire? Explain your choice in terms of its location.

• •

Suppose that you work for a Byzantine newspaper. **Write** an article after the death of the Empress Theodora. Include events from her life. Describe her influence on the Byzantine Empire.

VOCABULARY REVIEW

Number a sheet of paper from 1 to 5. Beside each number write the word from the list below that matches the statement.

census   representatives

Christianity   republic

plebeians

1. The religion of people who follow Jesus.
2. Roman citizens who worked as farmers, craftworkers, or traders.
3. People elected by the citizens to run the government.
4. A government in which people choose representatives to act for them.
5. The count of the number of people living in a place.

CHAPTER COMPREHENSION

6. How did the geography of Constantinople keep the city safe from attack?
7. What roles did the plebeians and the patricians have in the Roman Republic?
8. What power did the citizen assembly have over Rome's consuls?
9. Why did Hannibal attack Rome? How did this war end?
10. How did Julius Caesar help some Roman citizens? How did he change some traditions of the Roman Republic?
11. How did the Emperor Constantine change the official attitude of Rome to Christianity?
12. What was the Byzantine Empire? What form of Christianity flourished there?
13. **Write** a paragraph in which you compare the Twelve Tables to the Justinian Code.

SKILL REVIEW

14. **Reading/Thinking Skill** What is a generalization?
15. **Reading/Thinking Skill** Why is comparing examples necessary before making a generalization?
16. **Reading/Thinking Skill** Write a generalization you can make about how a small nation can overcome a large nation. Include three examples.
17. **Reading/Thinking Skill** How does the picture above support the following generalization: Roman builders were talented engineers and architects.
18. **Reading/Thinking Skill** What generalization can you make about the emperor Justinian?

USING A TIME LINE

| A.D. 1 | 100 | 200 | 300 | 400 | 500 | 600 | 700 | 800 | 1500 |

45 B.C.
Caesar
becomes
dictator
of Rome

27 B.C.
Pax Romana
begins under
Augustus

A.D. 284
Diocletian
divides
Roman
Empire

A.D. 330
Constantine
moves
capital to
Constantinople

A.D. 476
Western Roman
Empire ends

A.D. 1453
Byzantine
Empire ends

19. About how many years are there between the fall of the Western Empire and the end of the Byzantine Empire?

20. Which event on the time line marks the end of Rome's importance in the empire?

Writing **About Economics** A plebeian citizen of Rome paid taxes to the government. Write a paragraph explaining what services the citizen got for that tax money. Your paragraph should also explain what would have happened if the taxes had not been paid.

Foldables

Use your Foldable to review what you have learned about life in Ancient Rome. As you look at your standing Coliseum, mentally recall the events that led to the growth and eventual decline of the Roman Empire. Discuss ways in which the world is still influenced by this ancient civilization. Review your notes under the lesson titles on your Foldable to check your memory and responses. Record any questions that you have, and discuss them with classmates, or review the chapter to find answers.

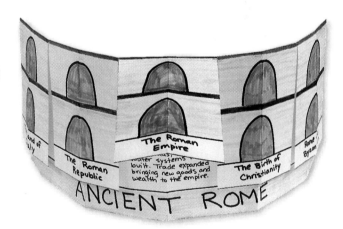

The Ancient Americas

Many scholars believe that people originally came to the Americas during the Ice Age. Some may have crossed a land bridge over what is now the Bering Strait. Others may have come across the glaciers between Europe and North America. While different cultures were emerging in Europe and Asia, the people of the Americas were developing their own unique societies.

THE LAND OF THE AMERICAS

North America has a great variety of regions. The people of the ancient Americas develop a diversity of lifestyles to deal with these different environments.

THE MAYA AND THE OLMEC

In the forests of what are now Mexico and Central America, two complex cultures appear. The Olmec and the Maya build vast stone cities, then vanish, leaving them to be swallowed by the forest.

ANCIENT NORTH AMERICAN CULTURES

In North America, the Anasazi and Hohokam learn to build thriving towns in the desert. Other peoples, in the eastern forests, leave mysterious mounds.

Foldables

Make this Foldable study guide and use it to record what you learn about the "Ancient Americas."

1. Fold a large sheet of paper into a shutterfold.

2. Sketch the shape of a pyramid from Ancient America on the inside, carefully cut along the top to give your Foldable the shape of the pyramid, and color the outside.

3. Label the three inner sections with the three lesson titles.

257

Lesson 1

Geography of North America

What are differences in the regions of North America?

Lesson Outline

• Continent of Contrasts
• North American Landscapes
• Adapting to Climate

VOCABULARY

land bridge
rain forest
tropical

READING STRATEGY

Copy this chart. In each box, describe the geography of a region of North America at the time of the first settlers. Start with the Canadian Shield and work down to Mexico and Central America.

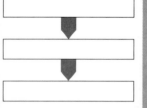

BUILD BACKGROUND

Some scientists believe that people crossed from Asia to North America about 30,000 years ago. More recent evidence indicates that some people may have migrated from Europe, Southeast Asia, and the Pacific islands, as well. Wherever they came from, archaeological evidence indicates that the new settlers spread slowly through the many regions that make up this continent.

258

CONTINENT OF CONTRASTS

During the Ice Age, glaciers contained so much frozen water that the level of the oceans dropped. This exposed a **land bridge**, or strip of land that connected two larger landmasses, such as Asia and Alaska. This land bridge is called Beringia because it crossed what is now the **Bering Strait**.

The first people to settle in North America may have come across this land bridge about 30,000 years ago. Others may have crossed the glaciers between Northern Europe and North America.

After the glaciers melted at the end of the Ice Age around 10,000 years ago, the level of Earth's oceans rose, covering the land bridge. People could not return to Asia or Europe. By then, people were moving south. They probably followed herds of animals, such as reindeer, or sailed in small boats along the coastlines.

The Ice Age Ends

Farther south, in what are today Texas, Arizona, and Mexico, the climate became hot and dry. To farm in these regions, people developed irrigation. Next, the migrants entered the year-round hot, humid climate of **Middle America**, the region that is present-day Southern Mexico and Central America.

READING CHECK How did Earth's climate change at the end of the Ice Age?

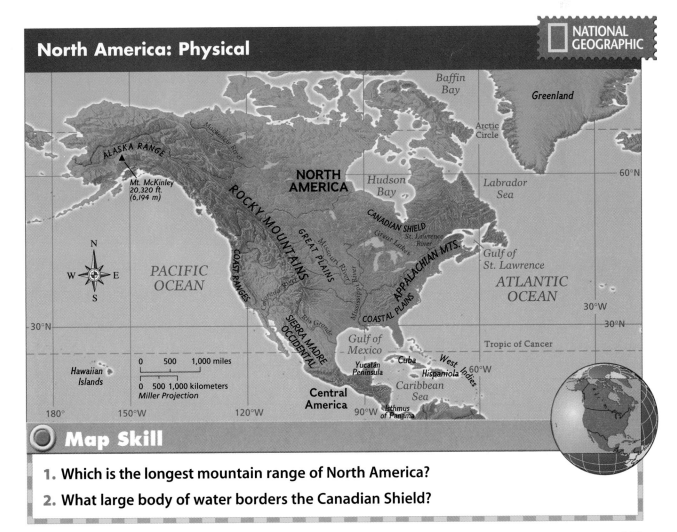

NATIONAL GEOGRAPHIC

North America: Physical

Baffin Bay

Greenland

Arctic Circle

60°N

ALASKA RANGE

Mt. McKinley
20,320 ft.
(6,194 m)

NORTH AMERICA

Hudson Bay

Labrador Sea

ROCKY MOUNTAINS

GREAT PLAINS

CANADIAN SHIELD

Great Lakes

St. Lawrence River

APPALACHIAN MTS.

Gulf of St. Lawrence

ATLANTIC OCEAN

30°W

Mackenzie River

Missouri River

COAST RANGES

PACIFIC OCEAN

N
W · E
S

Colorado River

Mississippi River

COASTAL PLAINS

30°N

30°N

SIERRA MADRE OCCIDENTAL

Rio Grande

Gulf of Mexico

Tropic of Cancer

Hawaiian Islands

0   500   1,000 miles
0   500 1,000 kilometers
Miller Projection

Yucatán Peninsula

Cuba

Hispaniola

West Indies

60°W

Caribbean Sea

Central America

Isthmus of Panama

180°   150°W   120°W   90°W

Map Skill

1. Which is the longest mountain range of North America?
2. What large body of water borders the Canadian Shield?

NORTH AMERICAN LANDSCAPES

Each region of the North American continent presented special advantages and disadvantages to the early settlers. People had to adjust their ways of life to survive in the many different regions of the continent.

The Far North

On the far north of our continent is an area called the Canadian Shield. This region of low hills and poor, thin soil is covered with ice and snow for much of the year (below, left). When the first settlers arrived in North America, this region was even less welcoming. Huge glaciers covered much of the area, and there were few plants, and even fewer animals in this environment.

After the glaciers finally melted about 10,000 years ago, great forests began to grow. Still, the northernmost part of this region, bordering on the Arctic Ocean, is windswept and snow-covered for much of the year.

The West Central Regions

Two mountain ranges run from north to south across North America, the high Rockies in the west, and the rolling Appalachians in the east. Between these mountain ranges lies a great Central Plain. The Central Plains are mostly flat or rolling land, with thick grasses (below, right) that supported huge herds of buffalo and deer. The people who settled in this region were hunters who followed the herds. Agriculture was difficult because the thick roots of the prairie grasses prevented digging to plant crops.

The land is drier in the southwestern part of what is today the United States. There is little rainfall and rivers can dry up for part of the year.

The East Central Region

Some groups settled in the eastern part of what are now Canada and the United States. This central region was an area of thick forests and broad rivers (below, left). Water and animals were plentiful in this part of North America. Most of these people became farmers and hunters. Some lived in villages of bark-covered huts. Hunters who moved about lived in tents made of animal skins. They used the rivers for transportation.

Middle America

The deserts of the American Southwest continue into northern Mexico. The central parts of Mexico are higher and drier than the coastal regions along the Pacific Ocean and the Gulf of Mexico. This central region of Mexico also has many active volcanoes.

Central America and the southern part of Mexico have thick **rain forests** (below, right). A rain forest receives more than 80 inches of rain each year. It has so many trees that very little sunlight can reach the floor of the forest.

Central America has a "spine" of mountains that runs down its center. Its narrow coasts run north and south on either side of the central mountains. The areas along the oceans have a **tropical** climate. Tropical refers to the area of Earth that is near the equator, where the climate is usually warm. However, the temperature in the mountains varies depending upon elevation. It may be tropical near sea level but very cool in the higher regions.

READING CHECK **What are some regions of North America?**

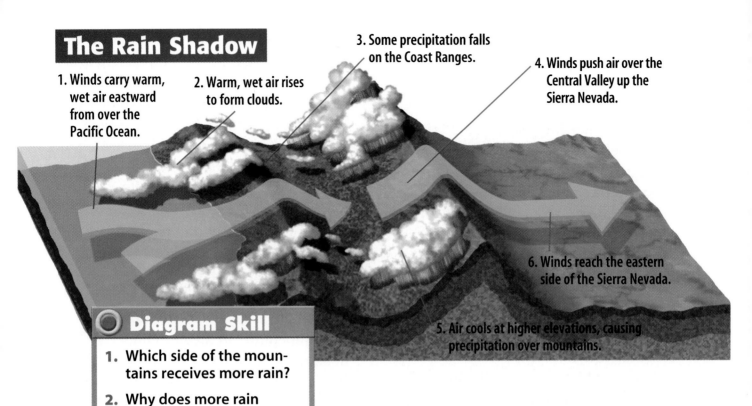

The Rain Shadow

1. Winds carry warm, wet air eastward from over the Pacific Ocean.

2. Warm, wet air rises to form clouds.

3. Some precipitation falls on the Coast Ranges.

4. Winds push air over the Central Valley up the Sierra Nevada.

6. Winds reach the eastern side of the Sierra Nevada.

5. Air cools at higher elevations, causing precipitation over mountains.

○ Diagram Skill

1. Which side of the mountains receives more rain?

2. Why does more rain fall on this side of the mountains?

ADAPTING TO CLIMATE

North America has many climate zones. As you have read, the northern regions are cold for much of the year.

The Rain Shadow

Most of North America has a temperate climate with four seasons. There are cold winters and hot summers. You may live in a region where the seasons change gradually, with colored leaves in the autumn and flowering bushes in the spring.

There is also a variety of climates in the center of North America because of the rain shadow caused by the mountains and the winds. Winds in North America generally blow west to east. When winds blow over water, they pick up moisture. So the winds coming off the Pacific Ocean carry heavy loads of moisture

inland. When these winds reach the mountains, they blow upward, where the air is colder. The moisture drops as rain or snow. As a result, the air reaching the eastern side of the Sierra Nevada is less moist. Death Valley, for example, receives less than 2 inches of rain a year.

Groups that settled in the central areas could farm small gardens and hunt for other food. Areas with good rainfall had forest products—logs, bark, and vines— to make houses, boats, and other needs.

The Tropics

As you have read, Central America and southern Mexico lie in the tropical zone. The groups that settled here had to clear away thick vegetation to make farms and villages. Although the climate is warm year round, farmers must also plan around seasonal, and often heavy, rains.

How do mountains affect the climate of North America?

262

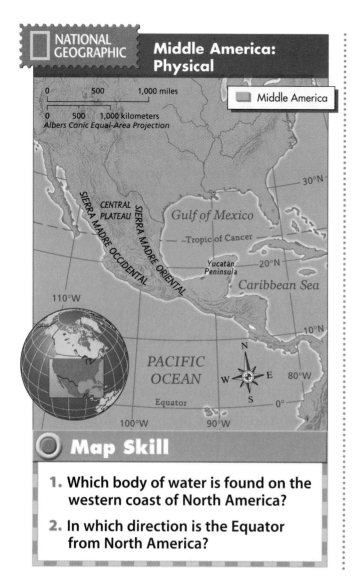

0   500   1,000 miles

0   500   1,000 kilometers
Albers Conic Equal-Area Projection

☐ Middle America

30°N

CENTRAL
PLATEAU

Gulf of Mexico

SIERRA MADRE OCCIDENTAL

SIERRA MADRE ORIENTAL

Tropic of Cancer

*Yucatán
Peninsula*

20°N

Caribbean Sea

110°W

10°N

PACIFIC
OCEAN

N
W   E
S

80°W

Equator

0°

100°W   90°W

◯ Map Skill

1. Which body of water is found on the western coast of North America?

2. In which direction is the Equator from North America?

PUTTING IT TOGETHER

As people moved south in the Americas, the weather changed, and so did the environment. Ice and freezing winters ended, and people found rich river valleys and wide plains. As the Ice Age ended, Earth's temperature rose. Plants and animals increased rapidly as a result. Groups began to settle where food was plentiful. Some developed farming. Others followed animal herds as hunter-gatherers.

The wide variety of North American climates and regions led to many different ways of life for the people who settled there thousands of years ago. In the following lessons, you will read about a few of these early North American peoples and their ways of life.

Review and Assess

1. Write a sentence for each vocabulary term.

**land bridge   tropical
rain forest**

2. How did early people enter North America?

3. How does the climate and the environment differ in North America's regions?

4. How did **geography** affect the way people lived in North America's regions?

5. What **generalization** can you make about the effect of climate on the life of early people in North America?

Find out!

Activities

Look at the map on page 259. Make a chart that describes each North American region. Your chart should include physical features, climate, vegetation, and the way of life of early people in each region.

Suppose you want to get people to cross Beringia and move to North America. **Write** a speech that will convince people to join you on the journey.

The Olmec and the Maya

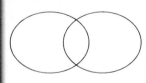
What did the Olmec and Maya achieve?

Lesson Outline
• The Olmec People
• The Maya
• Writing and Mathematics

BUILD BACKGROUND

Veracruz, a state in Mexico, has many tropical rain forests. For hundreds of years, these thick forests hid the ruins of one of the Americas' great civilizations. Huge pyramids and cities lay in the tangled vegetation.

About 150 years ago, a poor farmer was clearing fields when he came upon a carved stone head. His discovery led to other explorations. Soon the story of a rich culture began to emerge from its forest covering.

THE OLMEC PEOPLE

The Olmec (OHL mek) lived in the lush rain forest along the west coast of the Gulf of Mexico over 3,000 years ago. The name *Olmec* comes from a word meaning "people of the rubber country," because of the many rubber trees in the area. What the Olmec called themselves remains a mystery.

Olmec Agriculture

Archaeologists believe the Olmec flourished along the Gulf of Mexico from about 1200 B.C. to 400 B.C. This area is still almost entirely rain forest with broad rivers. The Olmec probably hunted and gathered, as earlier peoples in the region had done.

However, it was agriculture that allowed the Olmec to build their culture. They used a land-clearing method known as **slash and burn**. In this method, farmers clear, or slash, the dense jungle growth with stone axes. In the dry season, they burn the dead brush. Slash and burn is a quick way to clear new fields.

La Venta

By about 1000 B.C. the town of **La Venta** had become the major center of Olmec culture. The people who lived in La Venta did specialized work, such as farming, trading, and the carving of huge stone statues. The Olmec worshiped many gods, such as the gods of fire, rain, and sun. Archaeologists have found altars that were used in worshiping these gods. The Olmec also played ball games in open fields, possibly for religious purposes.

Around 400 B.C. Olmec civilization began to disappear. Historians do not know why the culture faded.

READING CHECK What do archaeologists know about the Olmec?

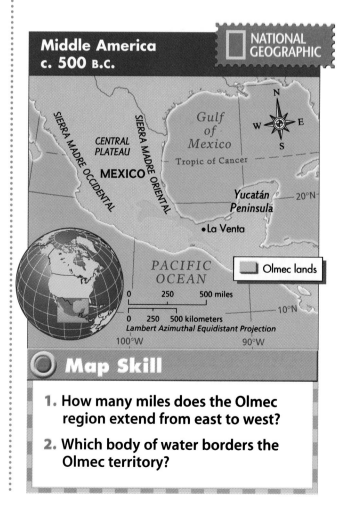

Middle America c. 500 B.C.

NATIONAL GEOGRAPHIC

SIERRA MADRE OCCIDENTAL
SIERRA MADRE ORIENTAL
CENTRAL PLATEAU
MEXICO
Gulf of Mexico
Tropic of Cancer
Yucatán Peninsula — 20°N
• La Venta
PACIFIC OCEAN
Olmec lands
0   250   500 miles
0   250   500 kilometers
Lambert Azimuthal Equidistant Projection
100°W   90°W
— 10°N

Map Skill

1. **How many miles does the Olmec region extend from east to west?**

2. **Which body of water borders the Olmec territory?**

The Olmec carved giant heads in stone and smaller statues from jade (above).

THE MAYA

The Maya (MAH yuh) developed a civilization in Middle America about 600 years after Olmec culture declined. Unlike the Olmec, the Maya created a written language. Most Maya books have been lost or destroyed so many details of their lives remain unknown. Stone pyramids and plazas, however, hint at a complex, thriving culture.

The Early Maya

The Maya lived in the southern part of Middle America as early as 1000 B.C. From the lowlands of the **Yucatán** (yoo kuh TAN) Peninsula in Mexico to the highlands of present-day Guatemala and Honduras, they developed a culture based on agriculture and hunting. They had contact with the Olmec and nearby groups.

Between about A.D. 250 and A.D. 900, the Maya built the richest civilization yet seen in the Americas. Historians call this period of Maya history its **Classic Period**. A classic period is a high point of cultural achievement for a civilization.

Maya Cities

One of the best preserved and most beautiful cities was **Palenqué** (pah lehn KAY) in Chiapas, Mexico. The largest was Tikal, which had about 40,000 people and about 50,000 in the countryside. Another center of classic Maya culture was **Copán** (ko PAHN), in what is

A Maya Temple

Diagram Skill

1. Where is the tomb chamber located?
2. Why do you think the altar is outside?

Decorated roof

Sculpture

Tomb chamber

Altar

today Honduras. Find Copán on the map. Among the impressive structures in the city is the ball court. Here a fierce ball game the Maya called *pokta-pok* (POHK tuh POHK) was played with a five-pound rubber ball. This game was part of Maya religion. Those who lost were sometimes killed, or **sacrificed**, to Maya gods. The Maya believed their gods would help them if they sacrificed something as important as a human life.

Between A.D. 600 and 800, Copán was home to about 20,000 people. Its buildings ranged from small plaster-and-thatch houses to huge stone pyramids and palaces that still stand today. Since

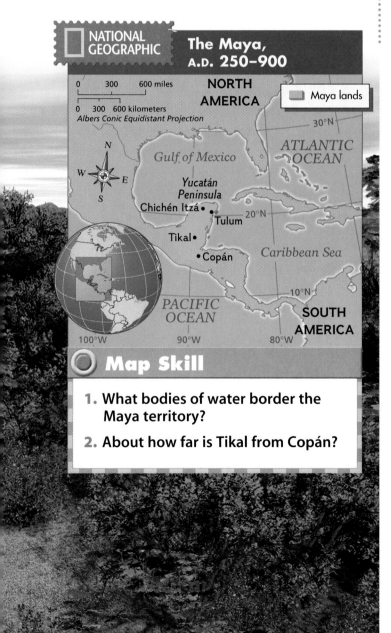

NATIONAL GEOGRAPHIC

The Maya, A.D. 250–900

0   300   600 miles
0   300   600 kilometers
Albers Conic Equidistant Projection

Maya lands

NORTH AMERICA

Gulf of Mexico

Yucatán Peninsula

Chichén Itzá•

•Tulum

Tikal•

•Copán

Caribbean Sea

ATLANTIC OCEAN

PACIFIC OCEAN

SOUTH AMERICA

30°N

20°N

10°N

100°W   90°W   80°W

◉ Map Skill

1. **What bodies of water border the Maya territory?**
2. **About how far is Tikal from Copán?**

the Maya did not have wheels or work animals, all the moving and lifting of the stone for pyramids was done by humans.

Agriculture

Maize (MAYZ), or corn, was the heart of Maya agriculture. Maize was first grown in Middle America in about 3000 B.C. The cob of this early maize was tiny, about the size of a shelled peanut.

Over the years, Middle American farmers improved their crops of maize. It was the most important part of the Maya diet. Yum Kax, the maize god, was an important figure in the Maya religion. The Maya performed special ceremonies for the planting and harvesting of maize.

The farmers of Copán also planted beans, squash, and peppers and avocado and papaya trees. They also grew cacao trees, which provided chocolate—the favorite drink of Maya rulers. Maya hunters killed animals, such as deer. Farmers and hunters sold many of their crops and products in city markets.

Many Gods

Religion was very important to the Maya. They worshiped hundreds of gods. For example, hunters, poets, and beekeepers each worshiped different gods. The king and other nobles led many of the religious ceremonies.

As part of their religion, the Maya closely studied the stars and planets. By studying the night sky, the Maya developed an accurate calendar. This allowed them to record the exact dates of events.

READING CHECK

How do we know that religion was important to the Maya?

WRITING AND MATHEMATICS

The Maya wrote with symbols, called **glyphs** (GLIFS), which they carved into the stones of Maya cities and towns. Some glyphs are pictures, like Chinese writing, and stand for objects. Others stand for sounds, as in our alphabet.

At Copán the Maya built a magnificent 72-step "hieroglyphic stairway," with over 2,200 glyphs. These symbols tell the story of Copán from its beginnings until A.D. 755, when the stairway was built. The stairway describes the heroic deeds and deaths of Maya leaders.

A Maya leader might order a tall, flat stone, called a **stela** (STEE luh), to be carved with glyphs. These stones were displayed in the city. A stela was often used to mark an important historical event.

An American explorer described his reactions to the accomplishments of the Maya.

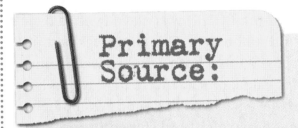

Primary Source:

excerpt from
Incidents of Travel in Central America, Chiapas, and Yucatán
— by John Lloyd Stephens, 1839

*The sight of this unexpected monument put at rest at once and forever, in our minds, all uncertainty in regard to the character of American **antiquities**, and gave us the assurance that the objects we were in search of were interesting, not only as the remains of an unknown people, but as works of art, proving, like newly discovered historical records, that the people who once occupied the Continent of America were [civilized].*

What did Stephens conclude about the ruins?

_____

antiquities: (an tik´ wi tēz) remains of cultures of ancient times

Maya Mathematics

The Maya also created a mathematical system. This system used glyphs to represent numbers. The Maya used the zero and had place value. This helped the Maya to make very exact calculations.

READING CHECK How do we know the Maya studied mathematics?

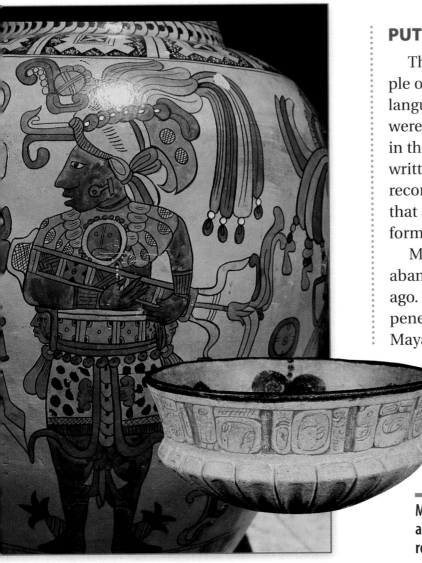

PUTTING IT TOGETHER

The Maya were probably the first people of Middle America to use a written language. While nearly all Maya books were lost or burned by Spanish explorers in the 1500s, the Maya also left behind a written record in stone. It is from these records, as well as from other artifacts, that archaeologists have been able to form a picture of Maya life.

Many of the great Maya cities were abandoned about one thousand years ago. Historians are not sure what happened. Some scientists believe that the Maya may have suffered crop failures. Others think that wars contributed to the decline of the civilization. Although they abandoned their cities, Maya people continued to live in the area.

Maya pottery makers used decorative **glyphs** and figures in their works. This **stela** (opposite) recorded events in Maya history.

Review and Assess

1. Write a sentence for each vocabulary term.

   glyph   **slash and burn**
   maize   **stela**
   sacrifice

2. In what part of North America were the Olmec and Maya cultures located?

3. What were the characteristics of the Olmec and Maya cultures?

4. In what way were the religions of the Olmec and the Maya similar?

5. **Make a generalization** about the cultural achievements of the Maya.

Compare the maps showing Olmec and Maya lands on pages 265 and 267. Make a list of statements about the two empires, such as *It had more cities* (Maya) or *It spread further north* (Olmec). Challenge your classmates to answer your list.

• •

Suppose you are a visitor to a Maya town. **Write** a description of the buildings you might see. Include details about jobs you see people doing.

269

Summarizing

Suppose that your friend is telling you about a trip she took with her family to Mexico. She tells you about the ruins she visited and about the crowds. Your friend takes only a few minutes to tell you the story. Yet you know that her trip lasted two weeks. What she told you was a **summary** of the event. A summary is a brief way of telling the main points of an event or an idea in your own words. Summarizing is a useful skill in remembering events in history.

The Maya played a fierce ball game called pokta-pok. *The game was more than just a sport: It was part of the Maya religion, and the losers were sometimes sacrificed to Maya gods. Two teams would try to move a five-pound rubber ball past a goal line. This was even harder than it sounds, since the players could not use their hands, and the ball could not touch the ground! No matter what the score was, a team would always automatically win by getting the ball through a 1-foot-wide stone hoop. Later cultures from this region, such as the Aztec played this game, as well.*

LEARN THE SKILL

Follow the steps to learn how to create a summary.

1. **Identify the topic.**
   Often, the topic is in the first sentence. In the paragraph above, the topic is in the first sentence, "The Maya played a fierce ball game called *pokta-pok.*"

2. **Choose supporting information.**
   Look for facts that support the topic. In the paragraph above, supporting information includes details about how the game was played, how points were scored, and what the consequences were for the losers.

3. **Organize information.**
   Choose only the facts that support the main idea. In the paragraph above, the last sentence, "Later cultures from this region, such as the Aztec, played this game, as well" is extra information that you do not have to include in your summary.

4. **Write the summary in your own words.**
   The summary should be brief. If possible,

state it in one sentence. Here is one possible summary of the paragraph: "The Maya played a sacred ball game called *pokta-pok*, which involved getting a rubber ball over a goal line or through a stone hoop."

TRY THE SKILL

Read the following paragraph. Then use it to answer the questions below. Next write a brief summary of paragraph

There is a common pattern to Maya cities. They were laid out around open courtyards. Tall pyramids and platforms surrounded each courtyard. On top of each pyramid was a small temple. The nearby platforms supported buildings with many rooms. These are often called palaces, although they were not used as palaces in the usual sense. Pyramids and platforms rose on a series of wide and beautifully carved steps. These stone buildings were covered with a white plaster that gleamed in the sunlight. The upper levels and interiors of the buildings were decorated with colorful carvings of gods and heroes. The arrangement of Maya cities indicates that religion was a central part of Maya life.

1. What is the topic?

2. What supporting information did you find?

3. What facts can you omit from the summary?

4. How can summarizing help you understand the information you read?

EXTEND THE SKILL

Knowing how to summarize is a skill you can often use in school and in your daily life. Suppose you want to enter a state history contest. The topic is "America's Vanishing Civilizations."

In the school library or on the Internet, read articles on the early American cultures you read about in this lesson. Take notes and then use them to write a brief summary of the topic.

● How did summarizing help you organize the information you gathered?

● What facts should be included in the summary?

● How can writing a summary help you better understand history?

Ancient North American Cultures

Find out!

How did the early Native Americans live?

VOCABULARY

pit houses
adobe
pueblo
kiva
dry farming
supernova
theory

READING STRATEGY

Complete a diagram like this one with features of the Anasazi/Hohokam and the Mound Builder cultures. List those they shared in the center.

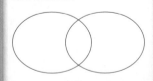

Lesson Outline

• The Hohokam
• The Anasazi
• The Mound Builders

BUILD BACKGROUND

"This portion of the country . . . has been enjoyed by my forefathers [ancestors] since the beginning of time. . . . The print of my ancestors' houses are everywhere to be seen in this portion."

Mishikinawaka, or Little Turtle, of the Miami people in the Ohio River valley spoke these words at a treaty signing in 1795. He was explaining that his people had lived in the Eastern Woodlands for a very long time. All across North America, Indian peoples had formed civilizations that had flourished long before Europeans arrived.

| 500 B.C. | 250 B.C. | A.D. 1 | A.D. 250 | A.D. 500 | A.D. 750 | A.D. 1000 | A.D. 1250 | A.D. 1500 | A.D. 1750 | A.D. 2000 |

You Are Here
300 B.C. – A.D. 1300

THE HOHOKAM

The Hohokam lived in what is now the Tucson Basin in Arizona. Their name comes from a Pima term that means "Those Who Have Vanished." Archaeologists believe that the Hohokam moved from Mexico to Arizona around 300 B.C. They set up communities along the Gila and Salt Rivers. About 600 years ago, the Hohokam way of life ended for reasons that remain unknown.

Farming the Desert

The Hohokam knew how to grow corn and cotton when they moved to Arizona. The challenge they faced in their new home was to figure out how to grow crops in the desert. They solved that problem by digging canals and irrigation ditches to bring water from the rivers to their fields.

Hohokam canals were lined with clay. This helped prevent evaporation of precious water in the scorching desert heat. The Hohokam also built dams to control the flow of water.

Building canals is a large undertaking and takes the cooperation of many people. From the number of canals the Hohokam built, we can conclude that they had a government that was able to organize people for such big projects.

The Hohokam eventually learned to grow other crops such as beans and squash. Armed with bows and arrows, Hohokam hunters also shot deer, rabbit, and other animals of the desert.

This earthenware pot shows typical Hohokam decoration.

Housing and Crafts

The Hohokam lived in villages in **pit houses**. The base was a pit dug 2 to 3 feet deep in the ground. Over this base the Hohokam put in posts and constructed a roof and walls made from mud, branches, and grass. These houses were cool in summer and warm in winter. Later, the Hohokam learned to make sturdier houses out of mud brick.

The Hohokam made pottery and jewelry. Archaeologists have found artifacts that show they traded with distant groups. Among these items were seashells from the Gulf of Mexico. The Hohokam also built ball courts similar to those found in Maya cities in Mexico.

How did the Hohokam use their environment to survive?

Some early Native Americans lived in the Sonora Desert of Arizona.

273

THE ANASAZI

The Anasazi were another group that came to the American Southwest about 2,000 years ago. By A.D. 900 the Anasazi had spread through what are now northeastern Arizona, southwestern Colorado, and northwestern New Mexico.

Archaeologists believe that there was regular contact between the Anasazi and the Hohokam. The early Anasazi built pit houses similar to those of the Hohokam. Eventually, they learned how to build houses out of **adobe** (uh DOH bee). Adobe is brick made from clay mixed with straw and left out in the hot desert sun to bake. Archaeologists believe that the Anasazi taught the Hohokam how to make adobe. When their population grew, the Anasazi built **pueblos**, or adobe houses. Pueblo is the Spanish word for town.

Between A.D. 1150 and 1200, the Anasazi left their pueblos on the valley floor. They began building huge apartment-like buildings on cliff sides. The largest is **Mesa Verde** in southwestern Colorado. There are more than 1,000 apartments in Mesa Verde. There are also 33 **kivas**, or pit structures used for religious ceremonies.

To reach the high structure of an Anasazi cliff dwelling, residents climbed ladders from the valley floor, where their farm fields were located. At night or when enemies attacked, they took shelter in their mountain homes and pulled up the ladders. Archaeologists believe as many as 5,000 people may have lived in the cliff dwelling at Mesa Verde.

Farming and Crafts

The Anasazi were expert farmers. They grew corn, squash, beans, and other crops, using irrigation. They also perfected **dry farming**, a technique for growing crops in an area with limited rainfall. In dry farming, no drop of scarce rainfall is wasted or allowed to run off. The soil is kept weed-free, and covered with clods of dirt or vegetable matter to keep the water from evaporating.

Like the Hohokam, the Anasazi also made pottery and baskets so tightly woven that they can hold water without leaking. The Anasazi traded for feathers

The Anasazi lived in cliff dwellings like Mesa Verde in Colorado.

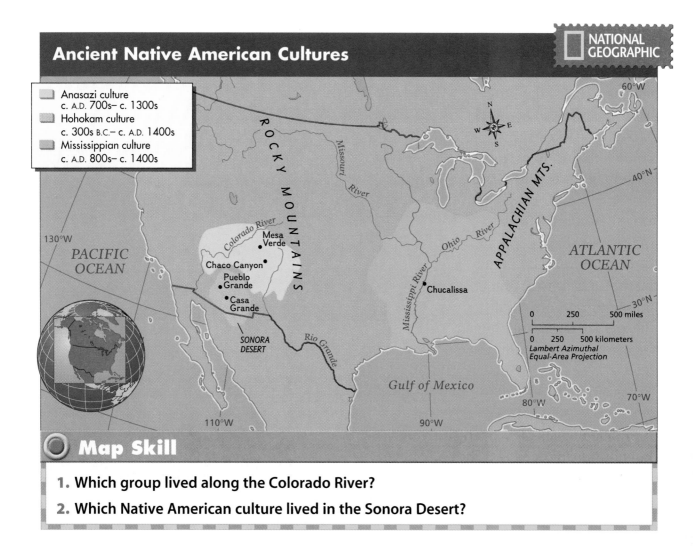

Anasazi culture
c. A.D. 700s– c. 1300s
Hohokam culture
c. 300s B.C.– c. A.D. 1400s
Mississippian culture
c. A.D. 800s– c. 1400s

ROCKY MOUNTAINS

APPALACHIAN MTS.

Missouri River

Ohio River

Mississippi River

Colorado River

Rio Grande

130°W

PACIFIC OCEAN

Mesa Verde
Chaco Canyon
Pueblo Grande
Casa Grande

SONORA DESERT

Chucalissa

ATLANTIC OCEAN

60°W

40°N

30°N

70°W

80°W

90°W

110°W

Gulf of Mexico

0   250   500 miles
0   250   500 kilometers
Lambert Azimuthal
Equal-Area Projection

Map Skill

1. Which group lived along the Colorado River?

2. Which Native American culture lived in the Sonora Desert?

with people in Mexico and for shells with people on the coast of the Gulf of Mexico.

Archaeologists have found evidence that the Anasazi knew astronomy. At Pueblo Bonito at Chaco Canyon, New Mexico, archaeologists found a painting of a **supernova**, or exploding star. Scientists know it lit up the night sky in 1054. Another nearby cave drawing is thought to show a solar calendar.

End of the Anasazi

Around 1300, the Anasazi left their homes. Archaeologists are not sure why. They do have several **theories**, though. A theory is an idea that has not yet been proved. Using the records provided by tree rings, we know that the time of the

Anasazi's disappearance was a time of drought in the American Southwest. Crop failure resulting from years of drought might have caused the Anasazi to move to a different place. Or they might have been defeated by more powerful enemies.

The fate of the Anasazi has remained a mystery. Experts believe that many of their traditions were taken up by the Hopi people and other Native American groups who live in the same area and survive to this day.

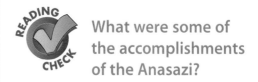

READING CHECK

What were some of the accomplishments of the Anasazi?

275

THE MOUND BUILDERS

In the late 1700s, European settlers crossed the Appalachians and traveled through the forests into the area that is now Ohio, Indiana, Illinois, and Michigan. They came across strange mounds of earth in different shapes. People weren't sure who had built the mounds or why. Some of the mounds are small hills of dirt. Others are huge. The Great Serpent Mound located near Cincinnati, Ohio, is more than 1,000 feet long.

Mound builders like this kneeling man (opposite) worked with metals (above) and built the Great Serpent Mound in Ohio.

Archaeologists have been studying the mounds for decades. They still have many questions about the mounds but no answers. However, they have learned that most of the mounds were used either for burial or as sites for religious ceremonies. In studying the mounds, archaeologists have learned about two ancient Indian civilizations.

The Adena

The Adena lived in the Ohio region beginning around 200 B.C. They had small farms, but the forests and streams were rich in game, fish, and edible plants. The Adena built round houses out of branches woven around wooden posts. These houses had thatched roofs. In the center of the earthen floor was a cooking fireplace. Archaeologists think that about 40–50 people lived in each house and that there were 4–5 houses in each Adena community.

The Adena buried their dead with their valued goods in pits or log tombs. As more people were buried from year to year, one large cone-shaped mound was formed.

The Hopewell

The Hopewell peoples lived between the Appalachian Mountains and the Mississippi River, and between the Great Lakes and the Gulf of Mexico. They were actually different groups of people who built mounds and traded with each other. Their name comes from a family named Hopewell who owned a farm where the first large mound was discovered in the 1800s.

Archaeologists believe the Hopewell lived in this part of the United States from around 200 B.C. to A.D. 500. The Hopewell farmed more than the Adena.

Hopewell mounds are different from Adena mounds. A single Hopewell mound might contain hundreds of graves. The Hopewell built their mounds in different shapes, such as octagons, squares or circles.

Archaeologists do not know what happened to the Hopewell. After A.D. 500, the Hopewell disappeared, and other Native American cultures settled in the region.

What were differences between the Adena and Hopewell cultures?

PUTTING IT TOGETHER

Native Americans civilizations thrived in what is now the United States over 2,000 years ago. In the Southwest the Hohokam and Anasazi farmed the desert. The Hohokam built canals, and the Anasazi developed techniques of dry farming. The two groups traded with each other and taught each other building techniques.

In the Eastern Woodlands between the Appalachian Mountains and Mississippi River, the Adena and Hopewell left behind earthen burial mounds of many sizes and shapes. Archaeologists are still learning about these early Native Americans.

Review and Assess

1. Write a sentence for each vocabulary word or term.

   adobe   **pueblo**
   dry farming

2. What evidence indicates that the Hohokam had contact with other civilizations?

3. How did the early Native American people live in the Southwest and the Eastern Woodlands?

4. What **technology** did the Hohokam develop to water their crops?

5. **Compare** and **contrast** the Hohokam and Anasazi cultures.

Make a two-column chart. In one column, list challenges facing the Anasazi. In the second column write solutions to the challenges developed by the Anasazi.

• •

Suppose you are a historian in Chaco Canyon and have found a new cave painting. **Write** a paragraph about your discovery.

VOCABULARY REVIEW

Number a sheet of paper from 1 to 5. Beside each number write the word or term from the list below that completes each sentence.

dry farming   **slash and burn**

glyph   **tropical**

pueblo

1. A fast way of clearing an area for farming is to ____.

2. The Anasazi once lived in the ____ at Chaco Canyon.

3. A ____ is a symbol that is the basis of the Maya writing system.

4. The climate of Earth near the equator is ____.

5. The Anasazi technique of ____ allowed them to grow maize in dry areas.

CHAPTER COMPREHENSION

6. In what two regions of the Americas can deserts be found?

7. What causes the rain that falls in the plains west of the Sierra Nevada?

8. What was La Venta? Where was it located?

9. What kind of specialized work did the Olmec develop?

10. What were some accomplishments of the Maya in their Classic Period?

11. How were the Hopewell and Adena civilizations alike? How were they different?

12. What is one theory about why the Anasazi civilization ended?

13. **Write** a paragraph in which you describe the way of life of the Hohokam civilization.

SKILL REVIEW

14. **Study Skill** What is a summary?

15. **Study Skill** Make a list of features of the mound in the picture above. Write a summary of your ideas.

16. **Study Skill** How would you summarize information about settlers in North America about 30,000 years ago?

17. **Reading/Thinking Skill** What generalization can you make about why we are not sure why civilizations like the Hopewell, Adena, and Anasazi civilizations ended?

18. **Study Skill** What does the jagged break on a time line mean? Why would such a break be included on a time line?

USING A TIME LINE

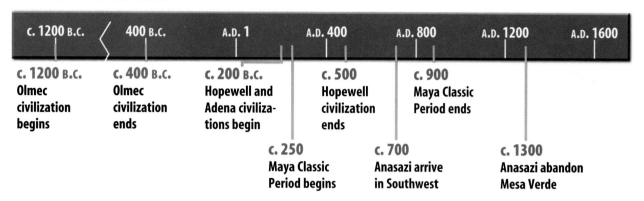

| c. 1200 B.C. | 400 B.C. | A.D. 1 | A.D. 400 | A.D. 800 | A.D. 1200 | A.D. 1600 |

c. 1200 B.C.
Olmec
civilization
begins

c. 400 B.C.
Olmec
civilization
ends

c. 200 B.C.
Hopewell and
Adena civiliza-
tions begin

c. 500
Hopewell
civilization
ends

c. 900
Maya Classic
Period ends

c. 250
Maya Classic
Period begins

c. 700
Anasazi arrive
in Southwest

c. 1300
Anasazi abandon
Mesa Verde

19. Did the Anasazi settle in the present-day southwestern United States before or after the end of the Maya civilization?

20. Which events on the time line tell about two great civilizations that flourished in present-day Mexico?

Writing **About Culture** Suppose that you lived in the Olmec center of La Venta. Write a journal entry about the way you live. Details should include information about the work you do, and some of the interesting features of the town.

Foldables

Use your Foldable to review what you have learned about the varied land and cultures of the Americas. As you look at the front of your Foldable, think of ways in which the ancient cultures influenced life in the Americas in the distant past, recent past, and modern times. Review your notes under the tabs of your Foldable to check your memory and responses. Record any questions that you have, and discuss them with classmates, or review the chapter to find answers.

The Arab World

From the deserts of Arabia came a new religion that influenced millions of people. Begun by a merchant who became a prophet, the religion of Islam united many Arab peoples. Islam also spurred its followers to create a civilization that developed legacies still shared by over a billion people today.

THE LAND OF ARABIA

The Arabian peninsula is a harsh desert. Since it is not suitable for farming, the Arab people trade goods across the vast deserts in caravans.

THE BIRTH OF ISLAM

In the Arabian trading city of Mecca, a new religion and way of life is born. Followers of this new religion, Islam, spread its teachings throughout the region.

THE ARAB EMPIRE

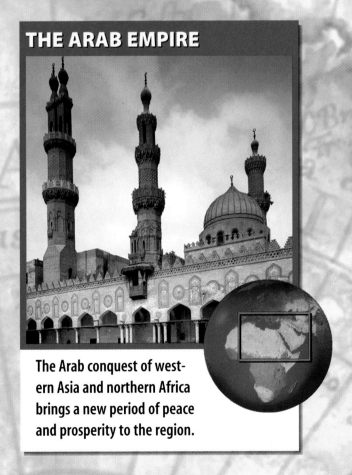

The Arab conquest of western Asia and northern Africa brings a new period of peace and prosperity to the region.

Foldables

Make this Foldable study guide and use it to record what you learn about "The Arab World."

1. Fold a large sheet of paper like a hot dog. Cut the hot dog in half along the fold line.

2. Tape the short ends of the two section halves together to make one long strip.

3. Fold the strip in half and then into thirds. Refold to make a six-tab accordion time line. Use two sections of this time line for each of the three lessons.

The Land of Arabia

Find! Out!

What challenges does the environment of Arabia present?

VOCABULARY

oasis
caravan

READING STRATEGY

Draw a chart like this one. Write "Arabia" at the top. Fill in the boxes with the names of the three regions of Arabia.

Lesson Outline

- The Arabian Peninsula
- The Arabian People

BUILD BACKGROUND

"Fiery blasts of air," "stirred-up dust." These are words that an ancient poet used to describe the heat in **Arabia**, a huge peninsula in southwestern Asia. Despite its harsh environment, people have lived in Arabia for thousands of years and built a flourishing civilization.

Sandy deserts cover much of the land of Arabia, where animals such as oryx (right) and lizards (opposite) live.

THE ARABIAN PENINSULA

The Arabian Peninsula is located between the **Persian Gulf** to the east and the **Arabian Sea** to the south. On the west, the **Red Sea** is a long, narrow body of water that almost completely separates Arabia from Africa.

Arabia has three major regions. The first region is the Jabal al Hijaz (JAB al al hih JAZ) mountains along Arabia's west coast. This is one of the few places in Arabia with enough rainfall to make agriculture possible. Its southern area may receive from 20 to 40 inches of rain a year.

The second region is the east coast. It, too, is fertile enough for farming. The third and largest region, the inner part of the peninsula, is mostly desert. About a quarter of Arabia gets little more than 4 inches of rain each year, and there are few rivers. The largest desert is the Rub' al Khali Desert, or the "Empty Quarter," in the southern part of the peninsula. All of Arabia's deserts have an oven-like heat in the summer. Some places have had no rain for 10 years or more.

Still, a few parts of the desert have enough water for people to grow crops. These places are called **oases** (oh AY seez). Oases are watered by underground streams. Some oases are even large enough to support large villages.

READING CHECK What makes Arabia a difficult place in which to live?

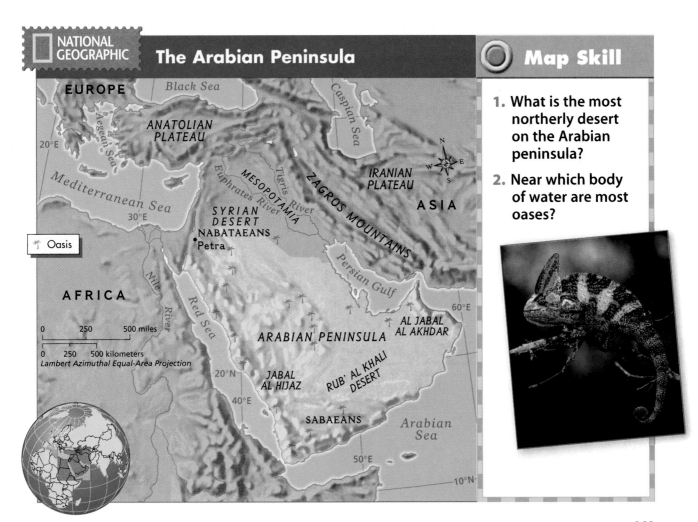

NATIONAL GEOGRAPHIC — The Arabian Peninsula

Map Skill

1. What is the most northerly desert on the Arabian peninsula?

2. Near which body of water are most oases?

EUROPE
Black Sea
Caspian Sea
ANATOLIAN PLATEAU
Aegean Sea
20°E
Mediterranean Sea
30°E
Euphrates River
Tigris River
MESOPOTAMIA
ZAGROS MOUNTAINS
IRANIAN PLATEAU
ASIA
SYRIAN DESERT
NABATAEANS
Petra
Oasis
Nile River
AFRICA
Red Sea
Persian Gulf
60°E
AL JABAL AL AKHDAR
ARABIAN PENINSULA
0   250   500 miles
0   250   500 kilometers
Lambert Azimuthal Equal-Area Projection
20°N
JABAL AL HIJAZ
RUB' AL KHALI DESERT
40°E
SABAEANS
Arabian Sea
50°E
10°N

THE ARABIAN PEOPLE

As you have read, people have lived in Arabia for a long time. The peninsula is named for the inhabitants. In fact, the Arab name of the peninsula, Jazirat al-'Arab, means "Island of the Arabs."

Fertile Regions of Arabia

Although most early Arabs lived in Arabia's few fertile areas, some lived in the southwestern area that is now the country of Yemen. As you read, this region receives enough rainfall to support agriculture.

Like most early people, the Arabs of the southwest, the Sabeans (suh BEE unz), herded sheep and goats and grew grapes and wheat. Irrigation canals built by farmers helped improve their harvests. As coastal towns developed, people began trading with the Egyptians.

Other Arab people, the Nabataeans (nab uh TEE unz), lived to the north, in what is today Jordan. Around 300 B.C. they built the city of **Petra** (PEH truh) in a place that had a large supply of water brought there by aqueducts.

Petra became an important stop on a trade route between the Mediterranean and the Red seas. Merchandise of Arabia and East Asia passed through Petra on the way to markets in the West. The

people of Petra grew rich from this trade. Petra remained a busy, rich city until about A.D. 100.

Camels and Caravans

The Arabs used camels for travel across the desert. Camels can carry heavy loads and go for days without water. Their milk provides liquid food and refreshment for desert travelers. Arab traders often traveled in **caravans**. A caravan is a group of people and animals that travel together. A camel caravan can proceed at a rate of about 3 miles per hour and can cover about 30 miles in a day.

Caravans traveled along well-known routes throughout the Arabian Peninsula. They traded with merchants in cities of the Fertile Crescent and in Egypt.

Bedouins and Herders

One of the groups of people who traded in Arabia was the Bedouins (BED uh wunz). The word *Bedouins* means "people of the desert." They lived mostly in the desert, traveling in caravans and sleeping in tents along the way.

Arabian caravans stopped at oases (right).

Mountain herders often moved about the deserts. Like most other herding people, they moved to new grazing lands at different times of the year. The difference in lifestyles between herders and farmers sometimes caused conflict.

 How did the people of Arabia make their living?

PUTTING IT TOGETHER

The Arabian Peninsula presented many challenges to the people who built civilizations there. While much of Arabia is desert, there are areas that receive enough rain to support agriculture. Towns and trade developed in fertile regions, at desert edges, and at oases. In this demanding environment, the people of Arabia would become unified under a new religion that you will read about in the next lesson.

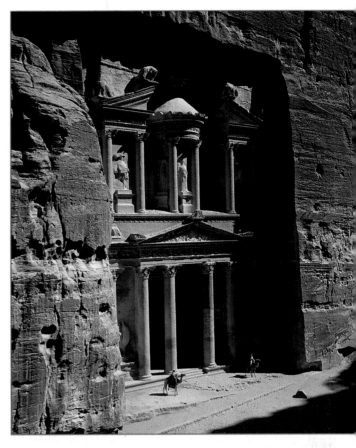

Ruins at Petra, such as this temple carved out of rock, show Mesopotamian, Arabian, and Roman influences.

Review and Assess

1. Write a sentence for each vocabulary word.

   caravan   oasis

2. Why are camels used in caravans in the desert?

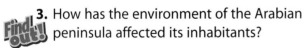 3. How has the environment of the Arabian peninsula affected its inhabitants?

4. Why would trade be important to the people of Arabia?

5. How did farmers of southwestern Arabia **solve the problem** of getting enough water for their crops?

Plan an itinerary for someone who wishes to travel to the southwestern tip of the Arabian Peninsula. Mention the landscape that the person would see and the approximate number of miles of the trip.

Write a letter to a friend explaining why your family moved to a city on the Red Sea from the Rub' al-Khali Desert.

The Birth of Islam

 What are the major beliefs of the religion of Islam?

VOCABULARY

Islam
Muslim
Kaaba
hijra
mosque
Quran
Five Pillars
hajj
pilgrimage

PEOPLE

Muhammad
Khadija

READING STRATEGY

On a chart like this one, write the supporting details for this main idea: "Five Pillars of Islam."

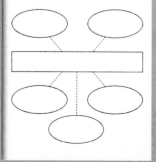

BUILD BACKGROUND

The sun is setting in a small town in the United States. A young man and his father hear a distant voice call out words that in English mean, "Allah is most great. I testify that there is no other God but Allah. I testify that Muhammad is the prophet of Allah. Come to prayer."

Allah is the Arabic word for God. Each man rolls out a small rug, kneels on it, and begins to pray. These men are among the millions of people throughout the world who practice the religion of Islam.

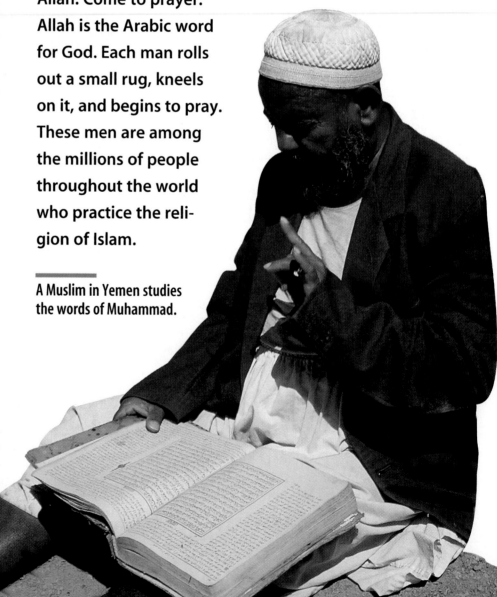

A Muslim in Yemen studies the words of Muhammad.

MUHAMMAD'S VISION

Before 800 B.C. the people of Western Arabia had developed a written language, Arabic. By A.D. 500 Arab traders had developed thriving trade routes.

Into this bustling civilization, **Muhammad** (moh HAH mahd) was born in the oasis city of **Mecca** in about A.D. 570. He was orphaned as a boy and was raised by an uncle who was a trader. While growing up, Muhammad mastered the skill of leading caravans. His skills came to the attention of a wealthy widow and merchant, **Khadija** (ka DEE jah). Working for her, Muhammad traveled to the Fertile Crescent to trade goods. When he returned from his journey, he and Khadija were married.

Muhammad had time to devote himself to thinking about religion. He was about 40 years old, according to Islamic tradition, when he went to a mountain cave to pray. There he had a vision. In the vision, the angel Gabriel appeared to him and said, "O, Muhammad, you are the prophet of Allah." As you learned in Chapter 2, a prophet is believed to speak for God. Muhammad's vision would lead to the creation of a new religion called **Islam** (iz LAHM). A person who believes in Islam is known as a **Muslim** (MUHZ luhm). Islam would mark a turning point in the history of Arabia.

Mecca and the Kaaba

The city of Mecca, lay on the main trading route through western Arabia.

The city also attracted other visitors. They came to pray at the **Kaaba** (KAH buh), Mecca's square-shaped temple. "Kaaba" is the Arabic word for "cube." The Kaaba housed a sacred black stone and honored the gods and goddesses worshiped by the people of Mecca.

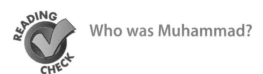 Who was Muhammad?

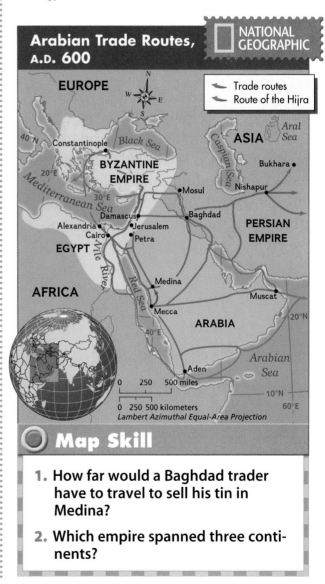

Arabian Trade Routes, A.D. 600

NATIONAL GEOGRAPHIC

Trade routes
Route of the Hijra

EUROPE · Constantinople · *Black Sea* · BYZANTINE EMPIRE · *Mediterranean Sea* · Mosul · Damascus · Baghdad · Alexandria · Jerusalem · Cairo · Petra · EGYPT · *Nile River* · *Red Sea* · Medina · AFRICA · Mecca · ARABIA · Aden · *Caspian Sea* · ASIA · *Aral Sea* · Bukhara · Nishapur · PERSIAN EMPIRE · Muscat · *Arabian Sea*

0 250 500 miles
0 250 500 kilometers
Lambert Azimuthal Equal-Area Projection

Map Skill

1. How far would a Baghdad trader have to travel to sell his tin in Medina?

2. Which empire spanned three continents?

THE RELIGION OF ISLAM

Muhammad was determined to persuade the people of Mecca to abandon their worship of many gods and goddesses. He set out to teach people in Mecca about Allah, and to worship only one God. Over the next three years, his group of followers slowly grew.

Opposition in Mecca

In spreading his beliefs, Muhammad aroused the anger of the leaders of Mecca. They were upset for many reasons. The main reason was that he criticized the Meccans' way of life and their belief in many gods. They also looked down on Muhammad because of his humble birth. The leaders of Mecca also feared that they would lose trade if pilgrimages to the Kaaba stopped.

Muhammad's Migration

In 622 Muhammad was forced to flee from Mecca. He settled in another oasis town, **Medina** (mee DEE nuh), over 200 miles north of Mecca. Muhammad's **hijra** (HIHJ ruh)—Arabic for "migration" —from Mecca to Medina marked a major turning point in Islamic history. The year of the hijra, 622, marks the starting point of the Islamic calendar.

In Medina, many people accepted Muhammad's teachings. There he organized a government and an army. In 630, with an army of 10,000, he entered Mecca in triumph.

After his victory, Muhammad destroyed the statues of the gods and goddesses in the Kaaba and proclaimed Mecca a Muslim city. The Grand **Mosque** in Mecca contains the Kaaba. A mosque is a building where Muslims worship.

Islam Grows

In 632, just before he died, Muhammad is said to have spoken to his followers at Mecca in these words: "[Muslim] believers are brothers of one another." By the time Muhammad died in 632, he had united most of Arabia.

The Quran: Sacred Book of Islam

After Muhammad's death, his teachings were written down by his followers in what became the holy book of Islam.

Muslims visit the Kaaba (below) in Mecca. These Muslim women have gathered to pray.

It is called the **Quran** (kuh RAN). The most important teaching in the Quran is that there is only one God in the universe—Allah. This belief in only one God makes Islam a monotheistic religion, like Judaism and Christianity. The Quran says that Allah is the God worshiped both by Christians and Jews.

We believe in God, and in that which has been sent down on Abraham . . . and that which was given to Moses and Jesus.

The Quran serves as a guide for living for Muslims, as the Torah does for Jews and the Bible does for Christians. Through its words, Muslims learn about Allah's teachings.

The Five Pillars of Islam

In the Quran are the five basic duties of all Muslims. The purpose of these duties, known as the **Five Pillars** of Islam, is to strengthen Muslims' ties to Allah and to other people. The first pillar is the belief in one God, Allah, and that Muhammad is Allah's prophet. The second pillar describes the prayers Muslims offer Allah five times each day. Wherever they are in the world, Muslims look toward Mecca, their holy city, as they pray. The third pillar speaks of giving to those in need. The fourth pillar instructs Muslims to fast during the holy month of Ramadan (rah muh DAHN). During Ramadan Muslims neither eat nor drink from sunrise to sunset. They spend time in worship. The final pillar instructs Muslims who can afford it to go on a **hajj**, or journey to visit Mecca, at least once in their lives. A journey for religious purposes is called a **pilgrimage**.

Here is part of the second chapter of the Quran. What do the words tell you about the nature of Islam?

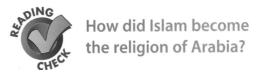

READING CHECK How did Islam become the religion of Arabia?

Primary Source:

excerpt from **The Quran,** *about* A.D. 650 — *Chapter two, Verse 286*

On no soul doth Allah place a burden greater than it can bear. It gets every good that it earns, and it suffers every ill that it earns. (Pray:) "Our Lord! Condemn us not if we forget or fall into error; our Lord! Lay not on us a burden like that which Thou didst lay on those before us; Our Lord! Lay not on us a burden greater than we have strength to bear. Blot out our sins, and grant us forgiveness. Have mercy on us. Thou art our Protector."

What does the prayer ask Allah for?

THE GROWTH OF ISLAM

In the 100 years after the death of Muhammad in 632, Islam spread and flourished. By 750 people living in lands from Spain to the Indus Valley in India had become Muslims.

The Islamic World Today

It is believed that there are over 1 billion Muslims in the world today. About 5 million live in the United States. The customs of Muslims often vary somewhat from one country to another. However, nearly all Muslims observe Ramadan, the month-long fast. Ramadan ends with a joyous feast. People wear new clothes to celebrate the beginning of the month following Ramadan.

There is no organized body of Muslim religious leaders, as there is in Christianity. Each community chooses its own clergy. Millions of Muslims from around the world make the pilgrimage to the holy city of Mecca every year, where they touch or kiss the black stone in the Kaaba. Muslims everywhere view the pilgrimage as one of the most important events in their lives.

Family Life

In Muhammad's teachings, women are equal to men. In Muslim practice, women's rights may be limited. In the home, however, women are often the dominant parent. Muslim women take the time to teach their children about the Quran. Muslim families have celebrations after sons or daughters have memorized large parts of the Quran. Some young people go on to study Islam and other subjects at Muslim schools and colleges.

READING CHECK What feature of Islam do most Muslims observe?

Muslims today continue traditional customs (right) and build new mosques, like this one in Spain.

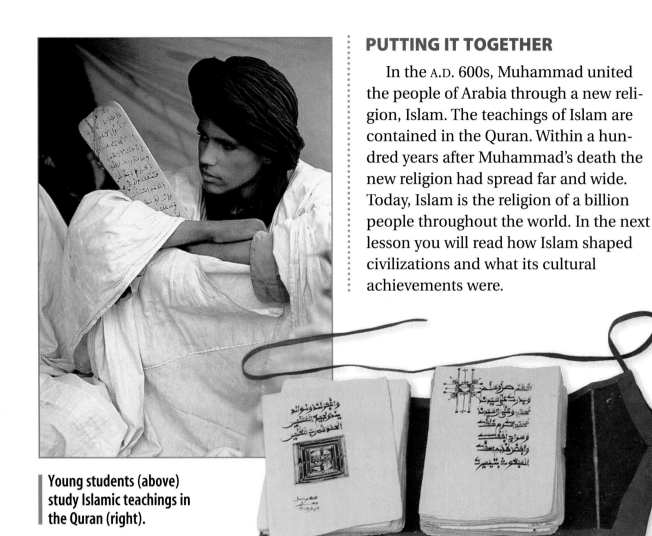

PUTTING IT TOGETHER

In the A.D. 600s, Muhammad united the people of Arabia through a new religion, Islam. The teachings of Islam are contained in the Quran. Within a hundred years after Muhammad's death the new religion had spread far and wide. Today, Islam is the religion of a billion people throughout the world. In the next lesson you will read how Islam shaped civilizations and what its cultural achievements were.

Young students (above) study Islamic teachings in the Quran (right).

Review and Assess

1. Write one sentence for each vocabulary word.

   hajj　　　　**pilgrimage**
   hijra　　　　**Quran**

2. What are the two holy cities of Islam?

3. What are the major beliefs of Islam?

4. What are some of the ways that Islam affected the cultures of its believers?

5. What decision did Muhammad make after the angel Gabriel appeared before him?

Prepare an itinerary that Muhammad might have followed when he was a young man leading caravans. Include not only the places he would have visited, but also the time required to get from place to place. Assume his caravan covered about 30 miles a day.

• •

You are a reporter in Mecca when Muhammad and his followers enter the city in 630. Write what you would say to describe the event.

Lesson 3

The Arab Empire

Who were the caliphs and what did they accomplish?

Lesson Outline
• Caliphs Govern the Empire
• Growth of the Muslim Empire
• Muslims Support New Ideas
• Art and Literature

VOCABULARY

caliph
caliphate
algebra
astrolabe
arabesque
calligraphy
minaret

PEOPLE
Rhazes
Avicenna

READING STRATEGY

On a chart like this one, write supporting details for this main idea: "The caliphate had scientists who made important contributions to medicine."

BUILD BACKGROUND

The story of *Aladdin and His Magic Lamp* is enjoyed by thousands of young people today. What most of them do not realize is that for hundreds of years it had also been a favorite of children in the Arabian lands where it originated. In this lesson you will learn what lands the Arabs conquered and about the contributions made by Muslim doctors, scientists, and artists.

Musicians and dancers entertain the Muslim ruler (above). Other Muslim artists created beautiful buildings like this one in Morocco (opposite).

CALIPHS GOVERN THE EMPIRE

In the A.D. 760s new leaders of the Muslim world came to power. By now, Islam was just over 100 years old. The new leaders were known as **caliphs** (KAY lihfs). *Caliph* means "successor." The caliphs were successors to the Prophet Muhammad. The lands ruled by the caliphs—Arabia, western Asia, northern Africa, and what is today Spain and Portugal—were called the **caliphate**.

The Caliphs

Caliphs were not only religious leaders but political and military leaders as well. One of their main goals was to expand Islam. To do this, the caliphs used well-trained armies. The soldiers believed that they had a holy mission to bring Islam to other lands. They believed that if they died in battle, they would be rewarded by entering paradise.

Religious Tolerance

In many places people welcomed the Muslim conquerors. Often, this was because they hated their own rulers and welcomed the chance to overthrow them. Not all of the people who were conquered became Muslims. In fact, they were permitted by their new rulers to continue to practice their own religions. However, the non-Muslims, such as Christians and Jews, had to pay higher taxes than the Muslims.

READING CHECK What did Arab leaders accomplish in the years after Muhammad's death?

293

GROWTH OF THE MUSLIM EMPIRE

As the map on this page shows, within 100 years of Muhammad's death, Islam had spread throughout Arabia and North Africa and into Asia and Europe.

The Empire Expands

With the aid of these new Muslims, the caliphs pushed south into Africa's interior. At about the same time, Muslim armies pushed into India. For many years, Muslims did not try to convert the Hindus to Islam, and the two peoples lived peacefully side-by-side.

In 711, Muslim forces crossed the Mediterranean into Spain and, advancing along old Roman roads, soon had most of Spain under their control.

Muslims established their capital in the city of **Cordoba**, in present-day Spain. Before long, Cordoba became a center of Muslim culture. Cordoba had half a million inhabitants, 300 public baths, and 3,000 mosques.

In 732 an Arab army crossed the Pyrenees and invaded France. Charles Martel, a Frankish war leader, defeated the Arab army at a battle near the city of Tours, about 150 miles southwest of Paris. Muslim rule in western Europe was limited to Spain, where it continued in power for the next six centuries.

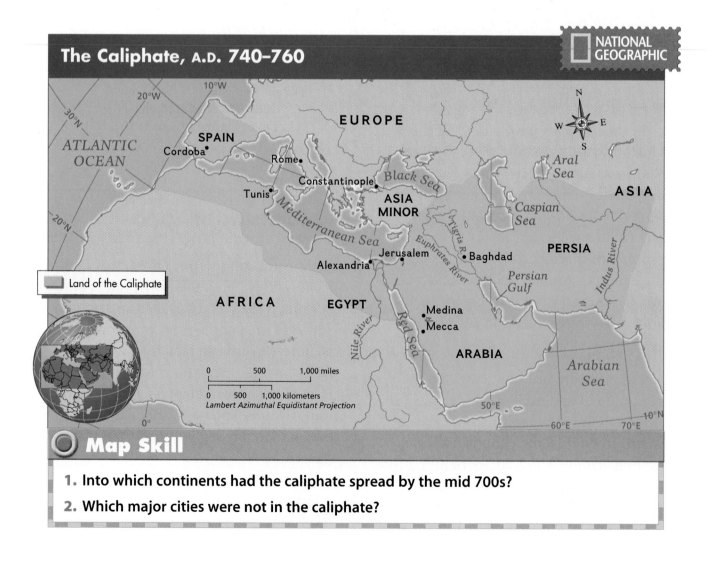

The Caliphate, A.D. 740–760

NATIONAL GEOGRAPHIC

Land of the Caliphate

Map Skill

1. **Into which continents had the caliphate spread by the mid 700s?**

2. **Which major cities were not in the caliphate?**

The Alhambra in Granada was a palace built by Spain's Muslim rulers.

Baghdad, Muslim Capital

In 762 al-Mansur, a Muslim ruler, decided to build a capital city on the Tigris River in what is today Iraq. From the late 700s until the 1200s Baghdad was the capital of the Muslim caliphate. Baghdad was one of the world's largest cities, with about a million residents. Established in the 760s, it quickly became the center of Muslims' greatest achievements in science, art, and architecture. The caliphs built a huge library there called the House of Wisdom.

From the center of Baghdad, four main roads branched out to all parts of the caliphate. Traders traveled over these roads to and from the farthest reaches of the caliphate and from non-Muslim lands as well.

As a result, Baghdad became an international city. Along the busy streets set up with small shops, or bazaars, shoppers could buy Arabian perfumes, Indian pepper, African ivory, Russian furs, and many other tempting goods. Some shops specialized in offering only certain products such as Chinese dishware or books.

 Why was Baghdad a good location for the capital of the caliphate?

Exploring TECHNOLOGY

Papermaking in Baghdad

In the year 751, Chinese war prisoners described the uses of paper, a Chinese invention, to the Muslims. Soon Baghdad craftworkers were making huge amounts of paper.

Government documents were written on paper and over 100 paper shops lined the Stationers' Market street in the capital. Handwritten cookbooks and storybooks, like *The Arabian Nights,* were sold. Knowledge of papermaking spread to Europe. The Muslim source of papermaking is remembered in the English word "ream," meaning 500 sheets of paper, from an Arab word meaning "a bundle."

How did knowledge of papermaking reach the Muslim caliphate?

بؤلن وانی توانند شد وأنرأ یسب شفا شمرد وبازلعمالخیر وسلخن توشه آخرت ازعلت کلا رأزار کونه شفای دهذکه معاودت صرن بندد وأن یحکم این مقذمات ازطب تبراینعلم ق

Physicians such as Avicenna (below left) were the leading doctors of the Middle Ages (left).

Advances in Medicine

Muslim doctors were responsible for many advances in the field of medicine. They were the first to diagnose and treat certain diseases such as measles and smallpox. They established the world's first school of pharmacy, where scientists discovered drugs, some of which are still in use today.

Doctors in the caliphate had to pass qualifying exams before they could practice medicine. Some of these doctors treated patients in Baghdad's large hospitals. Others managed the government's "moving hospitals." Doctors and nurses traveled to treat sick patients without charging them a fee. Such traveling teams carried beds, medicines, and other supplies by camel.

One of these outstanding medical scientists was Muhammad al-Razi (ahl RAY zee) who was known in Europe as **Rhazes** (RAY zeez). He published a huge medical encyclopedia to teach doctors how to treat many illnesses. Another medical pioneer was a Muslim doctor who lived in Persia. His name was Iben Sinah (IHB uhn SEE nuh), or **Avicenna** (av ih SEN uh) in Latin. Avicenna also wrote a large medical text. It was so valuable that it was used by medical students in Europe for 600 years. In it, he described how some diseases spread through air and water. He also wrote that stress could cause stomach problems and that cancer could be fought with surgery.

MUSLIMS SUPPORT NEW IDEAS

Muslims valued ideas, education, and learning. Muhammad was said to have declared, "He who travels in search of knowledge travels along Allah's path of Paradise." As a result, the caliphs encouraged scholars to preserve and translate works from all over the world. In Baghdad's library scholars translated ancient Greek, Roman, Indian, and Hebrew works into Arabic. Arab scholars read these books on history, science, law, and mathematics. Many of them went on to develop and improve these fields of study.

In addition, libraries for ordinary people were established. People in Baghdad could go to any one of 36 public libraries and read the great store of books there.

Avicenna was also a philosopher. He studied the works of the ancient Greek philosophers Plato and Aristotle, and his own ideas influenced thinkers about religion in later years in Europe.

New Knowledge of Math

Muslim scholars studied the works of ancient Greek mathematicians and made important advances in mathematics. To replace the awkward system of Roman numerals then in use, they adopted ideas about numbers from India. This system, known as Hindu-Arabic numerals, is the system we use today.

Muslim scholars also added to the branch of mathematics they called al-jabr (al JAH bur). In English this branch is called **algebra**.

Scientific Advances

There were many volumes on astronomy in Baghdad's House of Wisdom. Astronomy, the study of the stars and planets, is of great interest to Muslims because the Islamic calendar is based on the moon's movement. Stars helped people find their way while they were at sea. Muslims perfected an old Greek instrument, the **astrolabe** (AS truh layb), to find their position from the stars.

READING CHECK Which fields of learning did the Muslim leaders support?

Arabs used the **astrolabe** (right) to help them with their navigation. On this Arab map from 1150, north is at the bottom.

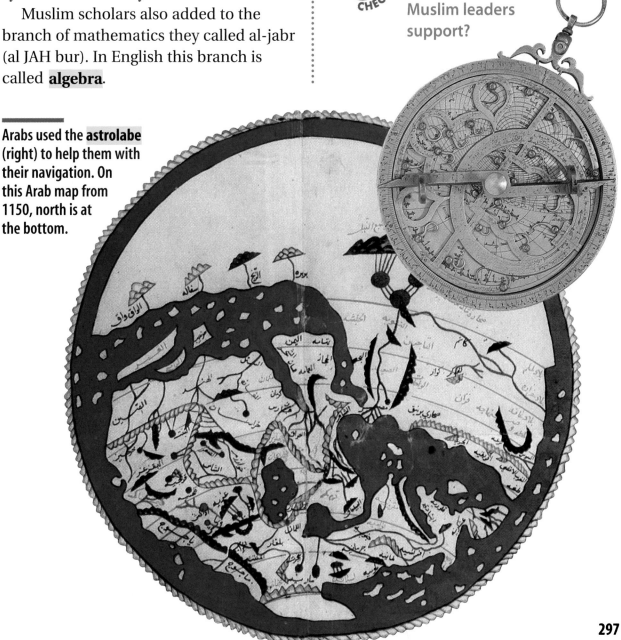

ART AND LITERATURE

Islam forbids people to make pictures showing human or animal forms. Instead, Muslim artists created works with beautiful abstract designs, many of them with **arabesques** (a ruh BESKS). Arabesques are flowing, lacy ornaments often intertwined with leafy forms and vines. Artists also made **calligraphy** (kuh LIHG ruh fee), or beautiful handwriting. Arabic calligraphy had a beautiful flowing style. Some Islamic cultures relaxed the rule and created miniature paintings of life in an Islamic society.

Muslim architects designed many beautiful mosques. These mosques have **minarets** (MIHN uh rets). Minarets are the tall slender towers with balconies, from which religious leaders called Muslims to prayer. Many such mosques are still standing.

Muslim Literature

Muslims regarded the Quran as the greatest work of literature because it revealed the word of God. Poetry was another well-loved form of literature among Muslims. Folk tales were also very popular. Favorite stories from Persia, India, and Arabia were collected into a book called *The Arabian Nights*. In it, a princess saves herself from death by telling her husband, the king, a different story each night for a thousand and one nights. Among the stories are exciting tales about Aladdin, Ali Baba and the 40 thieves, and Sinbad the Sailor.

READING CHECK What kinds of literature did the Arabs enjoy?

PUTTING IT TOGETHER

Under the leadership of caliphs based in the capital at Baghdad, Islam spread from Spain to India. With this expansion, Arabic as the language of Islam also spread. The rich heritage of Islam included the arts and sciences. In the centuries that followed, Europe would benefit from the contributions of Arabic thinkers, artists, and scientists during the great wave of creativity known as the Renaissance.

Colorful tiles often decorate the domes of mosques like this one in Isfahan, Iran. The bronze kettle (far left) shows Islamic decoration.

Review and Assess

1. Write one sentence for each vocabulary word.

   arabesque   caliph
   astrolabe   minaret

2. Which European country did the caliphate include?

3. What part did the caliphs play in the growth of Islam?

4. Why might some peoples have welcomed the Arab armies? What does this tell you about their attitude to the rulers the Arabs defeated?

5. What **generalization** can you make about the Muslim Empire?

Activities

Compare the map on page 294 to a modern map of the same region. Make a chart listing the names of modern countries that are included within the lands of the caliphate.

• •

Suppose it is the year A.D. 800. **Write** an ad to appear in the next issue of a travel magazine to get people to visit the city of Baghdad.

Chapter 9 REVIEW

VOCABULARY REVIEW

Each of the following statements contains an underlined vocabulary word. Number a sheet of paper from 1 to 5. Beside each number write T if the statement is true and F if the statement is false. If the statement is false, rewrite the sentence using the vocabulary word correctly.

1. A minaret is a Muslim place of worship.
2. The Quran is the most important book of Islam.
3. Islam is a religion founded in Arabia.
4. The Kaaba is a person from Arabia.
5. A caliph is a symbol used in algebra.

CHAPTER COMPREHENSION

6. What are the three main geographical regions of the Arabian Peninsula?
7. What was Muhammad's hijra? Why did it come about?
8. What is the most important teaching in the Quran?
9. What is the purpose of the Five Pillars of Islam?
10. What were the duties of a caliph?
11. What is Cordoba? What is its significance?
12. What important contributions were made by Muslims from about 700 to about 1200?
13. **Write** what you might have found for sale in the old city of Baghdad. Where did these items come from?

SKILL REVIEW

The Spread of Islam

Places controlled by Muslims	Date
Medina	622
Medina and Mecca	630
Arabia, North Africa, western Asia, Spain	c. 740

14. **Reading/Thinking Skill** From the chart above, what generalization can you make about the speed of Muslim conquests?
15. **Study Skill** How would you summarize the importance of the year 630 in Islamic history?
16. **Study Skill** How would you summarize the lifestyle of the Bedouin people?
17. **Geography Skill** What might a historical map of the Muslim Empire dated c. 740 show?
18. **Geography Skill** What does the map key on a historical map show?

USING A TIME LINE

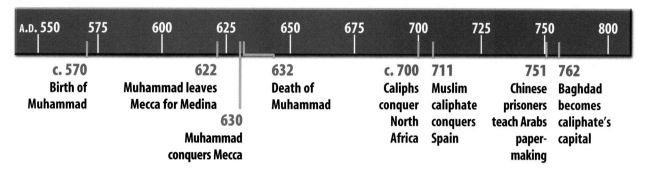

A.D. 550   575   600   625   650   675   700   725   750   800

c. 570
Birth of Muhammad

622
Muhammad leaves Mecca for Medina

630
Muhammad conquers Mecca

632
Death of Muhammad

c. 700
Caliphs conquer North Africa

711
Muslim caliphate conquers Spain

751
Chinese prisoners teach Arabs paper-making

762
Baghdad becomes caliphate's capital

19. How old was Muhammad when he left Mecca for Medina?

20. How can the time line help you understand that Islam spread very rapidly?

Writing **About Technology** Suppose you were a Muslim student in the 760s. You are writing a term paper about the advances in technology in Baghdad. What would you write about? Include specific examples such as particular medical treatments, types of literature, or architectural styles.

Use your Foldable time line to review what you have learned about the Arab World. As you look at the events and information sequenced on your Foldable time line, mentally picture what life might have been like in the Arab world during these ancient times. Use what you have already learned to recall events that were happening in other parts of the world at about the same time.

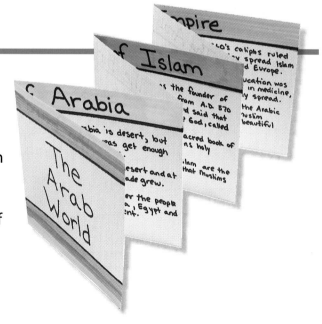

VOCABULARY REVIEW

Number a sheet of paper from 1 to 5. Beside each number write the word from the list below that best matches the statement.

Christianity	**pueblo**
Islam	**republic**
oligarchy	

1. A form of government in which the leaders are chosen by the people.

2. A religion in which people follow the teachings of Jesus.

3. A government that is run by a small group of powerful, rich citizens.

4. The religion practiced by Muslims.

5. A village of clay dwellings built by the Anasazi civilization.

SKILL REVIEW

6. **Reading/Thinking Skill** Why do you need several examples to support a generalization?

7. **Reading/Thinking Skill** What generalization can you make about how religions spread? What examples did you use?

8. **Study Skill** What can help you identify the most important information to include in a summary?

9. **Geography Skill** Why are the dates in the map title and map key important to interpreting the information on the map?

10. **Geography Skill** Was Spain part of the Muslim caliphate in the year 700?

 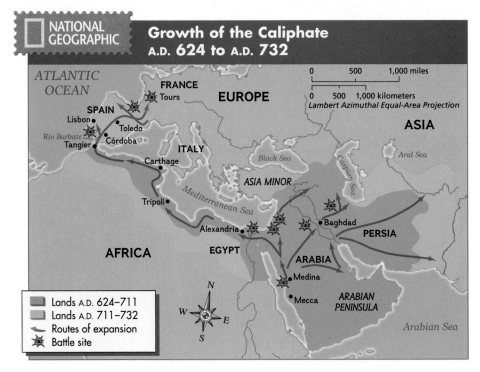

NATIONAL GEOGRAPHIC

Growth of the Caliphate
A.D. **624** to A.D. **732**

Lands A.D. 624–711
Lands A.D. 711–732
Routes of expansion
Battle site

TECHNOLOGY

For resources to help you learn more about the people and places you studied in this unit, visit **www.mhschool.com** and follow the links for Grade 6, Unit 2.

1   The Maya wrote with symbols, called glyphs, which they carved into the stones of Maya cities and towns. Some glyphs are pictures. . . . Others stand for sounds, as in our alphabet.

2   At Copán the Maya built a magnificent 72-step "hieroglyphic stairway," with over 2,200 glyphs. These symbols tell the story of Copán from its beginnings . . . [and] . . . heroic deeds . . . of Maya leaders.

3   Maya leaders also had tall flat stones, called stelae, carved with glyphs. These stones were put on display in the city. A stela was often used to mark an important . . . event. . . .

1   In this passage, the word *magnificent* is closest in meaning to—

A   priceless
B   grand
C   abundant
D   complicated

2   What generalizations can you make about Maya writing?

F   All Maya glyphs are pictures that stand for objects.
G   Maya glyphs mostly appear on stairways in cities.
H   Glyphs on stelae told fictional stories about common people.
J   The Maya often displayed their glyphs in public.

WRITING ACTIVITIES

Writing to Persuade Suppose you were a plebian and part of the citizens' assembly in Rome around 445 B.C. How would you convince a Roman senator that Rome's laws needed to be written down? *Write* a short dialogue between a plebeian and a patrician.

Writing to Inform Suppose that you are writing a letter from Baghdad to a friend telling about life in the city under the caliphs. Include information about Muslim practices in your letter.

Writing to Express *Write* a paragraph that imagines a day in the life of a young person living in the city of Copán.

SUNJATA

Retold by Nick Bartel
Art by Robert Van Nutt

Prince Sunjata was popular in Niani, one of Mali's small kingdoms. He and his mother, Sogolon, were exiled because the king's mother feared the people would prefer Sunjata as king to her son, Dankaran. Later Sumangaru conquers Niani and rules as a tyrant. This is the story of how Sunjata defeats Sumangaru in the Battle of Karina in A.D. 1235. Sunjata later united the 12 kingdoms of Mali to create the empire of Mali.

In Mali [wise men] whispered that the rightful heir would save them from their suffering under Sumangaru's rule. But where was the one who fled with his mother, brother, and sister many years before? Some of the elders secretly sent out search parties to find Sunjata.

Sunjata was now strong enough to fight enemies. At the age of eighteen he had **distinguished** himself in the army of the king of Mema and had a loyal following of young warriors.

---

distinguish (dis ting' gwish): to be deserving of special honor

The search party came to Sogolon and Sunjata. "Alas! We bring you sad news. Sumangaru, the powerful king of Sosso, has heaped death and destruction upon Mali. The king Dankaran, has fled and Mali is without a master. But the war is not finished yet. Warriors are waiting in the bush for a leader to return. Mali is saved because we have found you, Sunjata. The throne of your father awaits you. You are the **cyclone** that shall sweep the tyrant Sumangaru from the savanna forever."

Sogolon was overjoyed that her son was being called upon to greatness. She knew that the end of her mission in life **coincided** with the beginning of Sunjata's. That night the great woman who had nurtured Sunjata died.

With a small but well-trained cavalry . . . Sunjata set out to confront Sumangaru's forces. He wore a white turban and a long cape. He rode a magnificent horse at the head of his cavalry. The war drums sounded as they left Mema. The soldiers carried their lances and swords. A troupe of archers followed them. . . .

News of Sunjata's triumphal return to the savanna spread as if carried by the wind. Sons of Mali rallied to him and pledged their loyalty.

---

cyclone (sī′ klōn): tornado
coincide (kō in sīd′): to happen at the same time

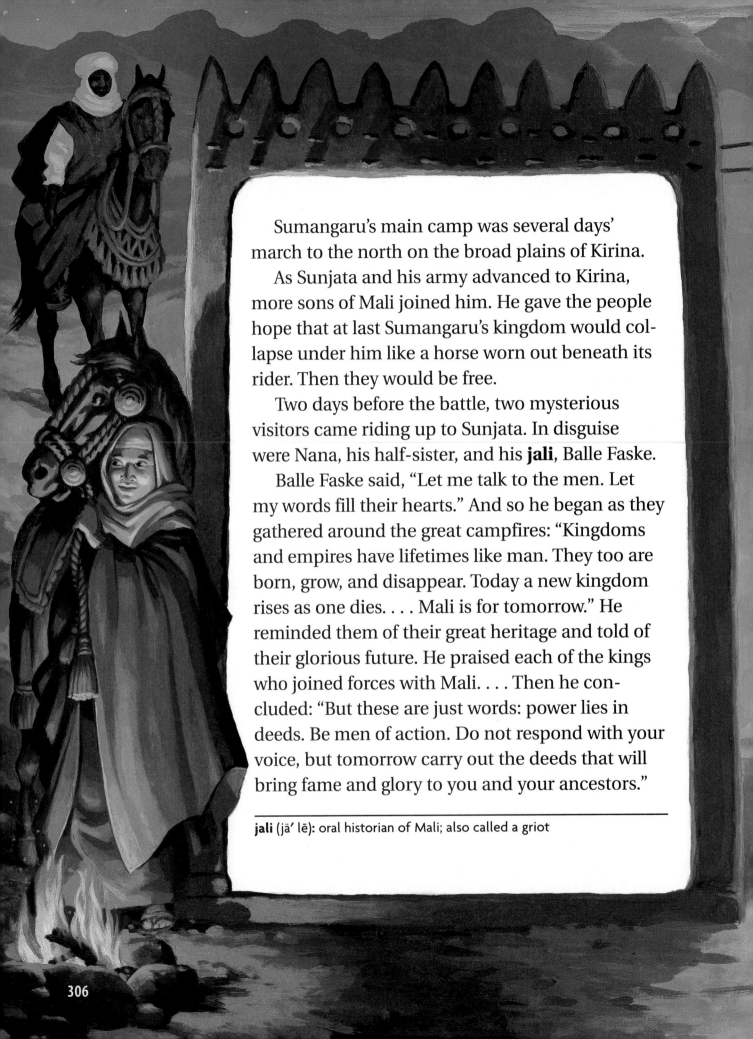

Sumangaru's main camp was several days' march to the north on the broad plains of Kirina.

As Sunjata and his army advanced to Kirina, more sons of Mali joined him. He gave the people hope that at last Sumangaru's kingdom would collapse under him like a horse worn out beneath its rider. Then they would be free.

Two days before the battle, two mysterious visitors came riding up to Sunjata. In disguise were Nana, his half-sister, and his **jali**, Balle Faske.

Balle Faske said, "Let me talk to the men. Let my words fill their hearts." And so he began as they gathered around the great campfires: "Kingdoms and empires have lifetimes like man. They too are born, grow, and disappear. Today a new kingdom rises as one dies. . . . Mali is for tomorrow." He reminded them of their great heritage and told of their glorious future. He praised each of the kings who joined forces with Mali. . . . Then he concluded: "But these are just words: power lies in deeds. Be men of action. Do not respond with your voice, but tomorrow carry out the deeds that will bring fame and glory to you and your ancestors."

---

jali (jä′ lē): oral historian of Mali; also called a griot

After Balle had inflamed their fighting spirit, each went to rest or to prepare for the morning's task without fear.

At first light the two great armies gathered facing each other across the plain. The drums sounded and the battle began. Sunjata's cavalry charged as his archers shot a **barrage** of arrows.

Sunjata's full army advanced. Swords clashed, hoof beats pounded, and war drums thundered. The battle was in full swing.

Sunjata saw Sumangaru at the **crest** of a hill. Raising his bow, Sunjata shot an arrow. . . . Immediately Sumangaru felt his powers leave him. Trembling, he let out a great cry. He looked up toward the sun. A great black bird flew over the battlefield and he understood. It was the bird of misfortune. "The bird of Kirina," he muttered. He turned his horse's head and took flight.

The forces of Sumangaru saw their king leave, and they fled in turn. It was a complete victory for Sunjata.

---

barrage (bə räj'): a great amount
crest (krest): the highest part

Write About it!

The story of Sunjata is told by a jali. Write a summary of what this oral historian said to describe Sunjata's victory.

Unit 3

New Forces in The World

TAKE A LOOK

What people and events laid the foundation for the modern world?

The Taj Mahal, an Indian ruler's tomb, took about 20 years to complete in 1650. New York's Empire State Building, five times as large, was built in 14 months!

Explore the world of A.D. 500 to 1500 at our Web site www.mhschool.com

THE Big IDEAS ABOUT...

African Civilizations

Africa is home to some of the oldest known civilizations. South of the Sahara Desert, wealthy rulers used their gold and other natural resources to build powerful empires. The fame of these trading kingdoms reached as far as Europe and the Middle East.

THE LAND OF AFRICA

From the Sahara Desert in the north to the rolling plains of the south, Africa has a wealth of natural beauty and resources.

THE KINGDOM OF AKSUM

The East African kingdom of Aksum develops south of Nubia and Kush, in modern Ethiopia. The inhabitants of Aksum grow wealthy from trade. They are also expert builders who carve giant churches from solid stone.

WEST AFRICAN EMPIRES

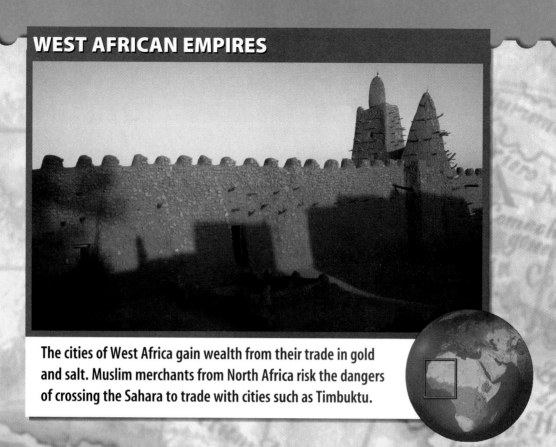

The cities of West Africa gain wealth from their trade in gold and salt. Muslim merchants from North Africa risk the dangers of crossing the Sahara to trade with cities such as Timbuktu.

EASTERN AFRICA

Great Zimbabwe and the coastal cities of eastern Africa grow wealthy from trade.

Foldables

Make this Foldable study guide and use it to record what you learn about "African Civilizations."

1. Fold a large sheet of paper into a shutterfold.
2. Fold the shutterfold in half and cut along the fold lines to form four tabs.
3. Draw or trace a map of Africa onto the front cover of your Foldable, and mark locations studied. Label the tabs with the four lesson titles.

311

African Geography

What is special about the geography of Africa?

Lesson Outline
- A Diverse Continent
- Landforms of Africa

VOCABULARY

Sahel
savanna
basin
hydroelectric
  power

READING STRATEGY

Copy the chart on a piece of paper. In the circles write supporting details for the main idea, "African Geography."

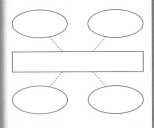

BUILD BACKGROUND

Africa is a large continent—larger than all of the United States and Europe combined. Within it are physical features of great size—very long rivers, large lakes, miles of deserts, vast grasslands, and huge thick forests. Here, too, are lands of intense heat and mountain peaks with year-round snow.

Zebra and other wildlife live on Africa's plains.

A DIVERSE CONTINENT

Africa is a continent of contrasts. The equator runs through central Africa, giving much of the continent a tropical climate. Africa has the largest desert in the world, the **Sahara**, as well as the Namib Desert and the Kalahari Desert.

South of the Sahara are the dry grasslands of the **Sahel** (SA hihl), an Arabic word meaning "shore." With little rain, parts of the Sahel are dry and dusty.

In West Africa and the Congo River basin are rain forests that receive from 60 to 100 inches of rain a year.

READING CHECK What are some of the varied physical features of Africa?

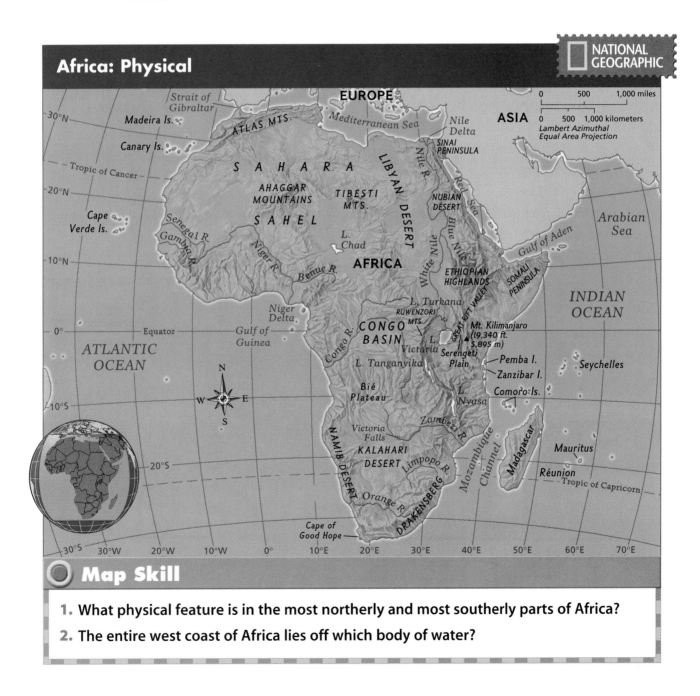

Africa: Physical

NATIONAL GEOGRAPHIC

Lambert Azimuthal Equal Area Projection

⬤ Map Skill

1. **What physical feature is in the most northerly and most southerly parts of Africa?**

2. **The entire west coast of Africa lies off which body of water?**

LANDFORMS OF AFRICA

Most of Africa is a large plateau. North and south of the rain forests are wide **savannas** (suh VAN uhz), grassy, tree-dotted plains. Many well-known African animals, such as lions, elephants, and giraffes, live in this region. The savannas have a dry season when savanna grasses turn brown, and the ground dries and cracks. When the rainy season starts, new grasses and leaves spring up.

Toward the edges of the continent there are mountain ranges, such as the Atlas Mountains in the northwest. The highest mountain in Africa is **Mount Kilimanjaro** in Tanzania. Although this mountain is close to the equator, snow lingers on its slopes year round.

In addition to plateaus, sub-Saharan Africa has huge **basins**. A basin is a large, bowl-shaped dip in the land into which rivers flow from surrounding highlands. Find the Congo Basin on the map on page 313.

The Great Rift Valley

In the eastern part of Africa is the **Great Rift Valley**. The word "rift" means a division or a gap. The Great Rift Valley is 3,000 miles long and divides eastern Africa from the western portion of the continent. This valley has high cliffs.

Over the years, rich soils have been washed down into the valley, where farmers grow corn, wheat, and other crops.

Rivers and Lakes

Many of Africa's large lakes are located in the Great Rift Valley. One of them, **Lake Tanganyika**, is the second deepest lake in the world. **Lake Victoria** is the world's second largest freshwater lake.

Africa has many major rivers. As you have read in Chapter 3, the Nile River in Egypt is the world's longest river. Other major African rivers include the **Congo River**, the **Zambezi River**, and the **Niger River**. The Congo and Zambezi rivers begin on Africa's central plateau. They fall over steep cliffs, forming rapids and steeply dropping falls. The Zambezi River, for example, tumbles 350 feet at **Victoria Falls** in Zimbabwe. These rapids and waterfalls prevent ships from sailing far

Victoria Falls (below) contrasts with the dry Serengeti Plain (bottom) east of Lake Victoria.

into Africa's interior. However, some of Africa's rivers provide excellent sources of **hydroelectric power**, or energy provided by falling water.

What are Africa's major landforms?

PUTTING IT TOGETHER

Africa's diverse physical features include large stretches of deserts, rain forests, savannas, long rivers, large, deep lakes, and mountains. They also include the Great Rift Valley, which divides the continent into eastern and western sections. In the next two lessons, you will learn about the different cultures that developed in this challenging environment.

Cheetahs (top) and elephants (left) are among the many animals that live in Africa's grassy plains.

Review and Assess

1. Write a sentence for each vocabulary term.
   basin
   hydroelectric power
   savanna

2. What is the world's largest desert?

3. What are some unusual features of the geography of Africa?

4. Why are ships unable to sail very far into the interior of Africa on many of the continent's rivers?

5. What feature of the Great Rift Valley led people to **make the decision** to use the land there for farming?

Look at the map on page 313. Prepare a display of five different physical features of the African landscape. Make drawings from photographs or use photographs you find in magazines or newspapers for your display.

. . . .

You have just completed a two-week tour of Africa. **Write** a letter to a friend in which you describe some of the things you enjoyed about the continent.

The Kingdom of Aksum

Find out!

What were some characteristics of the kingdom of Aksum?

Lesson Outline
• The Rise of Aksum
• Cultural and Economic Achievements

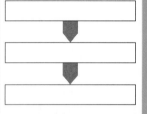
BUILD BACKGROUND

You read in Chapter 3 that the kingdom of Kush lasted until A.D. 350. By that time, another kingdom to the southeast, Aksum, had conquered Kush. Much like Kush, Aksum controlled trade in the region and became a powerful kingdom. Aksum's power in East Africa lasted for 800 years.

Parts of this church in Aksum, Ethiopia, were originally built in the 300s when Aksum converted to Christianity.

316

THE RISE OF AKSUM

Aksum developed south of Kush in the hills and mountains of what is now the nations of Eritrea and Ethiopia. When Aksum conquered Kush, it took over many of Kush's trade routes and made them even more successful. Aksum's chief city was **Adula** (AHD uh luh) near the Red Sea. Traders from Egypt, India, Arabia, and the Roman Empire came to the port to exchange such goods as ivory, cloth, rhinoceros horns, and gold. The variety of people who gathered in Adula produced a rich, diverse culture.

Christianity in Aksum

The traders who came to Aksum followed many religions. Around A.D. 300, the Aksum's people became Christians. Aksum, and its conqueror, Ethiopia, were among the first Christian countries in the world. Today nearly half the people of Ethiopia are Christians and follow Aksum's form of Christianity.

The Christians of Aksum formed their own branch of Christianity. They follow a leader called a **patriarch** (PAY tree ark). Many of their religious traditions and customs are different from those of other Christian churches.

The Rule of Ezana

The kingdom of Aksum reached its greatest power under King **Ezana** (ay ZAH nuh). Ezana ruled from A.D. 325 to A.D. 360. He expanded Aksum's power by conquering the part of the Arabian peninsula that is now Yemen. Ezana's success earned him the title, *negusa nagast*, which means "king of kings." Eventually, Aksum was invaded by Arabic peoples. By 900 the kingdom of Aksum was no more.

 **How did Aksum gain its wealth?**

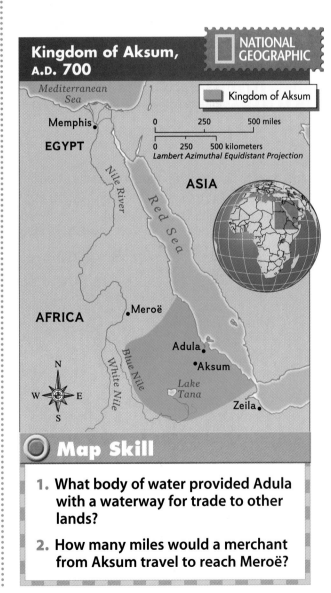

Kingdom of Aksum, A.D. 700

NATIONAL GEOGRAPHIC

Kingdom of Aksum

Map Skill

1. **What body of water provided Adula with a waterway for trade to other lands?**

2. **How many miles would a merchant from Aksum travel to reach Meroë?**

CULTURAL AND ECONOMIC ACHIEVEMENTS

Aksum became known for its distinct architecture, which used stone instead of mud bricks as earlier kingdoms in the area had done. The building stones were so perfectly fitted that Aksumites did not have to use mortar.

The kings of Aksum built monuments to celebrate their many military victories. Among them were huge stone stelae, or pillars. Some stelae, over 60 feet tall, are still standing.

Aksum was the first sub-Saharan kingdom to develop its own writing system. In addition, it was the first country south of the Sahara to mint its own coins. Many of these coins were printed with the saying, "May the country be satisfied."

Prosperous Trade Routes

Aksum was an influential trading center. Ships from the Roman Empire stopped at Aksum regularly. In fact, many Romans lived in Adula near the coast and in the capital city, also named Aksum.

The Romans were mainly interested in Aksum's gold, which Aksum obtained from southern mines. The Roman Empire needed the gold to make coins, so Roman ships often docked in Adula.

Aksum traders traveled to the mines just as regularly. They would load up with ox meat, salt, and iron and travel to the gold region. There, after lengthy bargaining about price, they exchanged their cargo for pea-sized nuggets of gold mined by the local people.

An Aksumite king had this church carved out of solid rock. The walls and columns of the church (right) are richly decorated with Christian symbols.

Aksum's Decline

Around A.D. 700, the Baghdad caliphate took control of the shipping on the Red Sea and Aksum lost its importance. Around A.D. 900 the last ruler of Aksum was overthrown by a group of local nobles called the Zagwe (ZAHG we).

The most powerful Zagwe ruler was a king named **Lalibela** (LAH lee be lah), who ruled from about 1185 to 1225. His kingdom, Ethiopia, had a capital city named Lalibela in his honor. Ethiopia continued Aksum's Christian tradition and created amazing architectural projects. Lalibela had 11 churches, each one carved from a single enormous block of stone.

READING CHECK
What were Aksum's major achievements?

PUTTING IT TOGETHER

The kingdom of Aksum was a major force in East Africa for about 800 years because of its strategic location. It was a rich trading center and was frequently visited by merchants from Rome and other Mediterranean lands. It was also one of the oldest Christian countries in the world. Among its outstanding cultural achievements are its unique architecture and its writing system. You will read about other powerful African kingdoms in the next lesson.

Coins of Aksum were stamped with images of its kings.

Review and Assess

1. Write a sentence for the vocabulary word.
   patriarch

2. Which king of Aksum brought the kingdom to its greatest power?

3. List three features of the kingdom of Aksum that made it special.

4. What technological achievement made the distinct architecture of Aksum possible?

5. What **generalization** can you make about the phrase "May the country be satisfied" which was on the coins minted in Aksum?

Activities

Look at the map on page 317. Which river runs along the western border of the kingdom of Aksum? To what lake does the river lead? Research the geographic features of the area where Aksum was located. Then create a table that lists the important features and facts about them.

Suppose you witnessed a trader at work in Adula bargaining with a Roman gold trader. **Write** a dialogue between the two traders. Describe the goods that will be exchanged.

Lesson 3

West African Empires

How did the empires of West Africa become powerful?

Lesson Outline
• Trade in Salt and Gold
• The Empire of Ghana
• The Wealth of Mali
• The Songhai Empire

VOCABULARY

supply
demand
griot

PEOPLE

Sunjata
Mansa Musa
Sunni Ali
Askia
  Muhammad

READING STRATEGY

Complete a cause-and-effect chart like this one with information from this lesson.

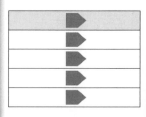

BUILD BACKGROUND

"Behind the king stand ten helpers holding shields and swords decorated with gold; . . . at the door of the pavilion are dogs guarding him. Round their necks they wear collars of gold and silver."

Around 1067 a Muslim writer named al-Bakri visited **Kumbi Saleh** (KOOM bee sah LEH), the capital of the Ghana Empire. He was amazed by the display of wealth in the royal palace, especially by the gold he saw. How did the king of Ghana gain this wealth?

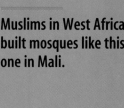

Muslims in West Africa built mosques like this one in Mali.

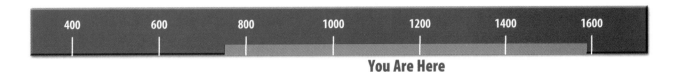
TRADE IN SALT AND GOLD

In the A.D. 700s Muslim traders from North Africa began to cross the Sahara and head for the lands to the south. Why did they undertake such a difficult journey? The answer: gold.

West Africa was rich in gold. In fact, before 1350 perhaps two-thirds of Europe's supply of gold came from West Africa. Even though the people of West Africa had gold, they did not have another important resource, salt. Salt was needed to preserve food in the hot climate of the region. Salt was plentiful along the North African coast of the Mediterranean Sea and in parts of the Sahara.

North African traders carried their salt in large bricks. When they traded with West Africans, they would cut the salt into smaller pieces. These would be weighed and, after much bargaining, the salt would be exchanged for gold.

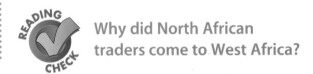 **Why did North African traders come to West Africa?**

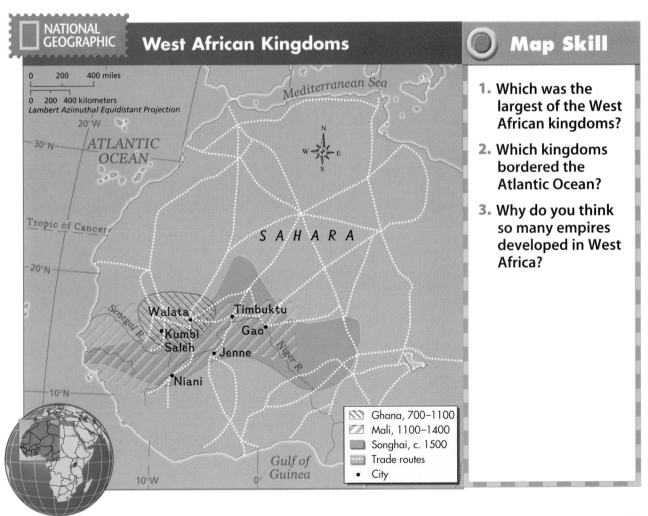

NATIONAL GEOGRAPHIC

West African Kingdoms

Map Skill

0   200   400 miles

0   200   400 kilometers
Lambert Azimuthal Equidistant Projection

20°W

30°N

ATLANTIC OCEAN

Tropic of Cancer

20°N

Mediterranean Sea

SAHARA

Senegal R.

Walata   Timbuktu
Kumbi   Gao
Saleh   Jenne

Niani

Niger R.

10°N

10°W   0°   Gulf of Guinea

⊠ Ghana, 700–1100
⊿ Mali, 1100–1400
▨ Songhai, c. 1500
▥ Trade routes
• City

1. **Which was the largest of the West African kingdoms?**

2. **Which kingdoms bordered the Atlantic Ocean?**

3. **Why do you think so many empires developed in West Africa?**

THE EMPIRE OF GHANA

By the 700s, the empire of Ghana was already a major power in Africa. Its ruler was called *ghana,* which meant "war chief" or "leader." The kings of Ghana grew wealthy because their kingdom was located along the major trade routes to and from North Africa. For many centuries West Africa was the major source of gold for the Mediterranean world. In fact, another title of the rulers of Ghana was "master of the gold." Ghana's wealth also brought power. The kings of Ghana commanded an army of 200,000 warriors, which helped them to control and rule surrounding territories.

The people of West Africa traded their gold for salt. Because salt was necessary to preserve food in the hot climate, its value often equaled that of gold. In fact, some cultures actually had coins made of salt.

North African traders had salt. They boiled seawater until it evaporated. The salt that remained was cut into large blocks for shipment to the lands to the south. It was exchanged for gold in the cities of Ghana.

North African salt traders (below) cut large salt blocks into smaller pieces. Traders in Ghana used spoons and weights to measure and weigh gold (left). They also traded cowrie shells.

The kings of Ghana controlled the gold-for-salt trade and set up its rules. Ghana's merchants were allowed to handle only gold dust. The king kept all the gold nuggets. Al-Bakri explained the reason for this practice.

All pieces of gold that are found in this empire belong to the king of Ghana, but he leaves to his people the gold-dust that everyone knows. Without this precaution gold would become so plentiful that it would practically lose its value.

The Source of Wealth

By keeping gold scarce, Ghana's kings followed a rule of economics called **supply** and **demand**. Supply is a quantity of a good, product, or resource that people are willing and able to sell. Demand is people's desire for and willingness to buy that particular item. According to the rules of supply and demand, items that are common have a low value, or price, because they are easy to find. On the other hand, items that are scarce have a high value because the demand for them is greater than the supply. By keeping the supply of gold scarce, Ghana's kings kept the demand for the metal, and therefore its price, high. If all of Ghana's gold were permitted into the marketplace, one visitor explained, "the people would [collect] gold until it lost its value."

The Importance of Trade

Over the years, caravans of salt arrived in Ghana. They departed regularly for the north with loads of gold. The profits of the salt-for-gold trade attracted many merchants to Ghana. By the 1000s, Muslim traders had settled in Ghana, and the

This West African brass weight was used with a scale to measure the weight of gold.

kings used Muslim advisors to help them run their empire. The kings adopted Islam, the faith of the Muslims. However, although the rulers converted to Islam, most of Ghana's people kept their traditional religions at that time.

The wealth of Ghana created envy among its neighbors. Rival kingdoms wanted to control the wealth of the gold trade. North African trading cultures realized that they could increase their profits if they controlled the source of the gold. About the middle of the 1000s these neighbors began to attack the kingdom of Ghana. Although they were unable to capture Ghana's capital, their attacks weakened the kingdom. By 1230 the kingdom of Ghana had disappeared.

What role did the king of Ghana play in the salt-for-gold trade?

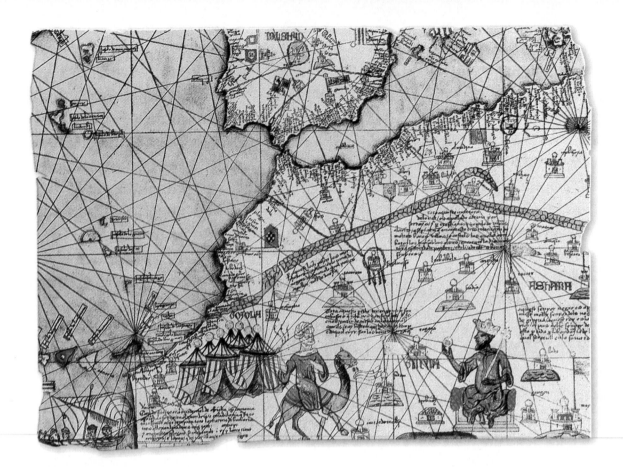

THE WEALTH OF MALI

About 1250 the new empire of **Mali** (MAH lee) arose. Mali became powerful because of a prince named **Sunjata** (sahn JAH tah). Legend says that the king of Ghana murdered every prince except Sunjata. The young prince was disabled, so the king of Ghana spared him. Sunjata surprised everybody by conquering his enemies, including Ghana, by the 1230s.

Sunjata won many battles, but he was also a talented ruler. He set up an organized system of government and spread his power over a wide region. In fact, some historians later compared him to Alexander the Great.

One of Sunjata's greatest achievements was to make the salt-for-gold trade even more profitable than it had been under Ghana. He set up a new capital at the city of Niani, which became the main center of commerce in West Africa.

West African trade routes are shown on this map from 1375. Mansa Musa is shown on the bottom right.

Another great city of the empire of Mali was **Timbuktu** (tim buk TOO). Timbuktu became a center of culture. It had large mosques and a famous university.

Like earlier rulers, Sunjata accepted Islam. He had mosques built and supported the efforts of Muslims to convert the people of his kingdom to Islam.

One of the greatest of these rulers was **Mansa Musa**. After Mansa Musa's death in 1337, the rulers of Mali grew weaker. They were unable to control the empire and its gold trade. Mali was replaced by an even stronger empire, the Songhai Empire.

In what ways was Sunjata like Alexander the Great?

BIOGRAPHY

Focus On: Respect

Mansa Musa was a grandson or grandnephew of King Sunjata. He extended the borders and the power of Mali to make it the most powerful African empire of its time. He is best known for the year-long pilgrimage he made to Mecca, in Arabia, in 1324. According to tradition, he traveled with 60,000 people in order to show respect for the holy places of Islam. In his parade were 500 servants—each servant carrying a solid gold cane. When Mansa Musa passed through Cairo, he gave away so much gold that the price of gold dropped and did not rise again for decades!

Mansa Musa also respected learning. He brought back Muslim scholars to make the city of Timbuktu into a great center of Muslim learning and religion. He helped to convert more of his empire's people to Islam and spread Islamic law and customs throughout Mali.

Link to Today Think of a modern ruler who shows respect for religions. Do some research on this leader and write a paragraph comparing the leader to Mansa Musa.

THE LIFE OF MANSA MUSA	**1312** Mansa Musa becomes ruler of Mali	**1324** Mansa Musa goes to Mecca	**1337** Mansa Musa dies		
	1300	**1320**	**1340**	**1360**	**1380**
LIFE AROUND THE WORLD	**1301** Osman founds Ottoman dynasty	**1325** Aztec found Tenochtitlán	**1348** Black Death sweeps over Europe	**1368** Ming dynasty rules China	

THE SONGHAI EMPIRE

While Mansa Musa was ruling Mali, the empire of **Songhai** (SOHNG hī) was gaining power. It had existed as a small state at the head of the Niger River since the 600s. Its capital was Gao.

Like Ghana and Mali, Songhai had some outstanding rulers who took control of the salt and gold trade. One of them was **Sunni Ali** (SOON ee ah LEE). By the time of his death in 1492, Sunni Ali had expanded Songhai to include Mali and parts of present-day Benin, Niger, and Nigeria. Sunni Ali had well-trained foot soldiers as well as cavalry, and he was a brilliant military leader. However, Songhai reached its greatest power under Sunni Ali's successor, **Askia** (AHS kee uh) **Muhammad**.

Among the important assistants to the Songhai kings were the nobles and **griots** (GREE ohz), people who tell stories and sing songs about historical events and important traditions. These stories and songs are repeated again and again so that people can learn about their past and their traditions. Songhai's kings also had scribes who wrote official documents in Arabic. Today what we know about Songhai and its people comes from these records and those of visitors.

Primary Source:

excerpt from

The Description of Africa
— by Leo Africanus, 1526

The houses of Timbuktu are huts made of clay.... In the center of the city is a temple built of stone and mortar... and in addition there is a large palace, constructed by the same architect, where the king lives. The shops of the **artisans**, *the merchants, and especially weavers of cotton cloth are very numerous. Fabrics are also imported from Europe to Timbuktu....*

The inhabitants are very rich, especially the strangers who have settled in the country; so much so that the current king has given two of his daughters in marriage to two brothers, both businessmen, on account of their wealth.

Why do you think the strangers of Timbuktu were especially rich?

artisan: craftsperson

Songhai Declines

The Songhai Empire was too large to rule effectively over a long period of time. In addition, the powerful Songhai armies did not have the modern weapons that countries in North Africa and Europe possessed. In 1591 the armies of Songhai were defeated by an army from Morocco armed with gunpowder and cannons.

How were Mali and Songhai alike and different?

National Museum of African Art

PUTTING IT TOGETHER

From about 700 to about 1500, three great empires flourished in West Africa. They were Ghana, Mali, and Songhai. The riches of these empires were based on trade with North Africa, which supplied salt in exchange for gold, which was plentiful in West Africa. Among the great rulers of the region were Sunjata and Mansa Musa of Mali, Sunni Ali and Askia Muhammad of Songhai. You will learn about another important African empire in the next lesson.

West African artists (opposite) include this present-day **griot** and the Songhai sculptors who made the head (opposite) and this statue of an archer (left).

Review and Assess

1. Write one sentence for each vocabulary word.

   demand
   griot
   supply

2. Which ruler made the kingdom of Mali most powerful?

3. How were the rulers of West Africa able to become so wealthy and powerful?

4. What economic reason made the salt traders cross the Sahara to West Africa?

5. **Make a generalization** about how Islam reached the people of the West African empires.

Look at the map on page 321. Then find and photocopy a map of modern-day West Africa. Draw the borders of one of the West African empires onto the photocopied modern map. Mark cities and trade routes. Add a map key to your new map.

• •

Suppose that you are a reporter for a newspaper in Mecca in 1324. **Write** an account of Mansa Musa's famous pilgrimage for your readers.

Lesson 4

Great Zimbabwe and the Coastal Cities

VOCABULARY

granary

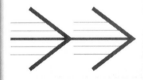

How did Zimbabwe and the coastal cities become rich?

READING STRATEGY

Fill in a cause-and-effect chart like this one. Write two causes for the effect: "Zimbabwe becomes powerful."

Lesson Outline
• City of Stone
• Wealth from Trade

BUILD BACKGROUND

To the southeast of the West African empires, two powerful civilizations were developing. One was the trading empire of the African east coast. The other is a great mystery. In the hilly region south of the Zambezi River was a powerful city surrounded by stone walls. The city had covered passages that led through sections within the walls. Even today historians know little about this community and the people who lived there.

CITY OF STONE

In the Shona language, *Zimbabwe* can mean either "houses of stone" or "honored houses." Archaeologists have found solid walls of stone, some of them standing as high as 32 feet. Within these walls are houses and a **granary**, a building for storing grain.

The builders of the city used large granite rocks from the area. Some rocks were larger than the homes people lived

The people of Great Zimbabwe used stones for homes (above), and a wall around their city (opposite).

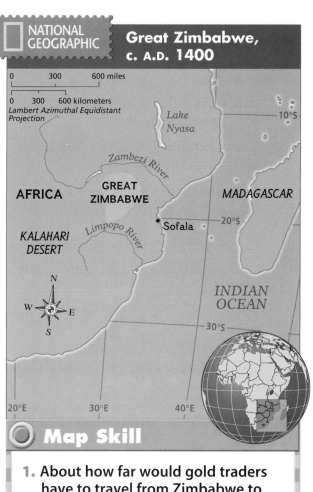

NATIONAL GEOGRAPHIC

Great Zimbabwe, c. A.D. 1400

0   300   600 miles
0   300   600 kilometers
Lambert Azimuthal Equidistant Projection

Lake Nyasa

Zambezi River

AFRICA

GREAT ZIMBABWE

MADAGASCAR

KALAHARI DESERT

Limpopo River

• Sofala

INDIAN OCEAN

10°S
20°S
30°S

20°E   30°E   40°E

N W E S

Map Skill

1. About how far would gold traders have to travel from Zimbabwe to the Indian Ocean?

2. What island is located off the coast of Africa in the Indian Ocean?

in. It is believed that workers heated sheets of the stone and then cracked them into pieces with straight edges. Then they cut the stones into brick-sized pieces. Workers stacked the granite bricks to form the high walls.

In fertile areas farmers raised crops. Great herds of cattle roamed the nearby savannas. Craftworkers made jugs and other containers from clay. By examining this pottery, archaeologists have determined that Great Zimbabwe developed between 1000 and 1400. However, we know very little about the life of the people who lived within those walls.

READING CHECK How have archaeologists determined the years when Great Zimbabwe developed?

329

WEALTH FROM TRADE

Great Zimbabwe was the largest of over 100 stone towns in southern Africa. Great Zimbabwe was located on a trade route that led from the gold-producing regions of southern Africa to the East African coast. Historians believe that the rulers of Great Zimbabwe gained much of their power by controlling the gold trade in the region.

Zimbabwe's Gold

Great Zimbabwe itself, according to archaeologists, sat on a rich gold mine, while some of southern Africa's richest gold fields were nearby. Archaeologists have found artifacts that show that wealthy families used some of the gold to buy luxuries from as far away as China.

However, most people used locally made goods. Gold wire was coiled into bracelets. The city's metalworkers also made iron hoes and axes for farmers. In the early 1400s, the period in which Great Zimbabwe thrived, about 20,000 people lived in the city in mud huts. Such a comparatively large population meant that farmers and herders had to work hard to provide food for the people of the walled city.

By the late 1400s the people of Great Zimbabwe had abandoned the city. Historians are not sure what caused this. Some scientists believe that residents left the city because too much cattle grazing had

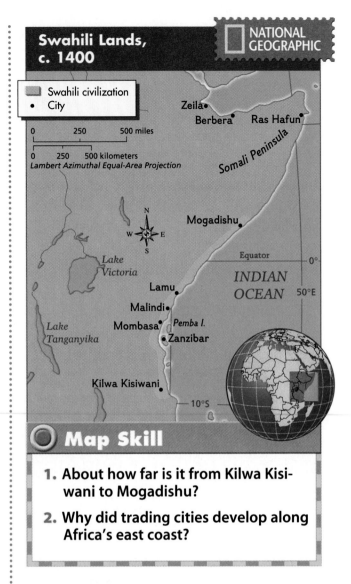

Swahili Lands, c. 1400

NATIONAL GEOGRAPHIC

- Swahili civilization
- • City

0   250   500 miles
0   250   500 kilometers
Lambert Azimuthal Equal-Area Projection

Zeila
Berbera   Ras Hafun
Somali Peninsula

Mogadishu

Lake Victoria

Equator   0°

INDIAN OCEAN   50°E

Lamu
Malindi
Lake Tanganyika   Mombasa   Pemba I.
Zanzibar

Kilwa Kisiwani

10°S

Map Skill

1. **About how far is it from Kilwa Kisiwani to Mogadishu?**

2. **Why did trading cities develop along Africa's east coast?**

worn out the land. Other scholars believe that there might have been a natural disaster such as a famine.

East Coast Trading Empire

Between 1000 and 1500 a trading civilization developed along Africa's east

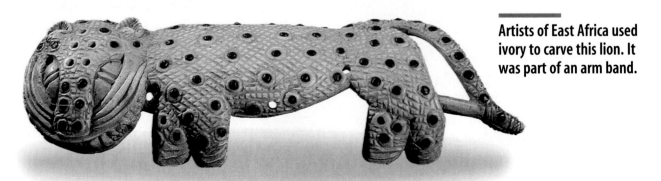

Artists of East Africa used ivory to carve this lion. It was part of an arm band.

coast. Many of the traders were Arab Muslims. Their civilization was called *Swahili*, which means "people of the shore" in Arabic.

Mogadishu (mohg uh DISH oo), in what is now Somalia, was one of the largest cities of the Swahili civilization. **Mombasa** (mom BAH suh), in what is now Kenya, and **Zanzibar**, in what is today Tanzania, were also important trading centers. The markets of these cities did a busy trade in products of Asia and Africa.

Africa's products from the interior of the continent included many goods, such as gold, leopard skins, and ivory. In the coastal cities, these goods were traded for metal tools, pottery, and cloth from Asia.

The Swahili civilization declined in the 1500s when Europeans began to reach their cities.

READING CHECK With whom did the coastal cities trade?

PUTTING IT TOGETHER

Great Zimbabwe developed in southern Africa beginning in 1000. The ruins of Great Zimbabwe include skillfully built stone walls and towers. Historians and archaeologists believe Great Zimbabwe thrived in the early 1400s when it controlled the gold trade in the region.

At the same time, the Swahili civilization was developing on Africa's east coast. Its cities were centers of the trade between Africa and Asia. Since many of the traders were Arab Muslims, the Swahili language had many Arab words and many Swahili people were Muslims.

Like many items from the eastern coastal cities, this ear ornament and horn are decorated with intricate designs.

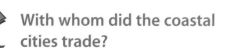

Review and Assess

1. Write a sentence for the vocabulary word.

   granary

2. In what part of Africa is Great Zimbabwe located?

3. **Find out!** What was the source of the wealth of Great Zimbabwe and the Swahili coastal cities?

4. Describe the technological process that was used to build the walls of Great Zimbabwe.

5. **Make a generalization** about the reasons for the growth of cities in Swahili culture.

Activities

Look at the map on page 329. Compare the area of Great Zimbabwe with a map of the modern nation of Zimbabwe. Create a chart with two columns. List the differences and similarities between the two places.

Imagine you are a trader visiting the city of Great Zimbabwe. **Write** an account of your visit to the city where you trade.

Chapter 10 REVIEW

VOCABULARY REVIEW

Number a sheet of paper from 1 to 5. Beside each number write the word that best completes each sentence.

demand   savanna

griot   supply

patriarch

1. ____ is the quantity of a good, product, or resource someone is able and willing to sell.

2. A ____ sings and tells stories that describe events in West African history.

3. Most of the well-known African animals live in the grassy plains of the ____.

4. People's desire for a good, product, or resource that they are willing and able to buy is ____.

5. The ____ was leader of Aksum's Christians.

CHAPTER COMPREHENSION

6. What landforms define North Africa?

7. What is the name of the first Christian country in Africa?

8. What activity linked Aksum with Rome?

9. What were some of the achievements of the Mali king Sunjata?

10. How did Mansa Musa influence religion in Mali?

11. What accounted for the defeat of the Songhai kingdom?

12. How did Great Zimbabwe become a great center of trade?

13. **Write** a paragraph describing how the kings of Ghana practiced the economic concept of supply and demand.

STUDY SKILLS

African Nations and Their Trading Partners		
Location	**Kingdoms or Cities**	**Trading Partners**
East Africa	Aksum	Rome, Egypt
West Africa	Ghana, Mali, Songhai	North Africans
Southern Africa	Great Zimbabwe	African Nations
East Africa	Zanzibar, Mogadishu, and Mombasa	Asia, Africa, Europe

14. **Reading/Thinking Skill** What problem did Rome try to solve by trading with Aksum?

15. **Reading/Thinking Skill** Give three examples that support the following generalization: Gold was the most important trade item in Africa from the 300s to the 1300s.

16. **Reading/Thinking Skill** What generalization can you make about how Muslim traders from North Africa influenced religion in West Africa?

17. **Reading/Thinking Skill** What problem with salt faced West Africans? How did they solve it?

18. **Study Skill** How would you summarize what archaeologists have learned from studying artifacts from Great Zimbabwe?

USING A TIME LINE

| 200 | 400 | 600 | 800 | 1000 | 1200 | 1400 | 1600 |

350
Aksum conquers Kush

c. 700
Ghana is a major power; Muslim traders begin regularly crossing the Sahara

c. 750
Kingdom of Aksum ends

c. 1000
Rise of Zimbabwe

c. 1230
Mali becomes a major power

1324
Mali king Mansa Musa makes a pilgrimage to Mecca

1591
Songhai is defeated by Morocco

19. Which event on the time line marks the beginning of Muslim influence in West Africa? Explain.

20. According to the time line, for about how many years did the West African empires last?

Activity

Writing **About Technology** If you were a visitor to Aksum or Great Zimbabwe, what questions would you ask about their stone buildings?

If you interviewed stoneworkers in both Aksum and Great Zimbabwe, what might they tell you about the stone buildings?

Foldables

Use your Foldable to review what you have learned about African civilizations. Look at the four lesson titles on the front of your Foldable, review the geographic locations marked on each tab, and try to recall three things you learned in each lesson. Review your notes under the tabs of your Foldable to check your memory and responses. Give yourself one point for each correct response. If you remember three things from each lesson, you will score 12 points and have a perfect score.

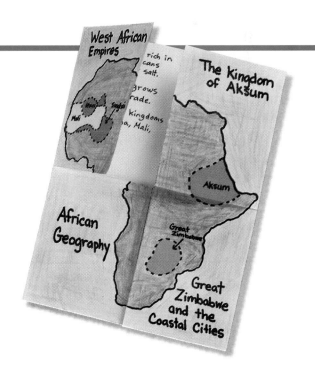

THE Big IDEAS ABOUT...

Europe in Transition

After the fall of the Roman Empire, Europe fell into a time of disorder. Slowly, peace and stability began to return to Europe. European merchants and scholars renewed their interest in other parts of the world. At this time, the culture of Greece and Rome inspired European artists and thinkers to reach new heights.

THE LAND OF EUROPE

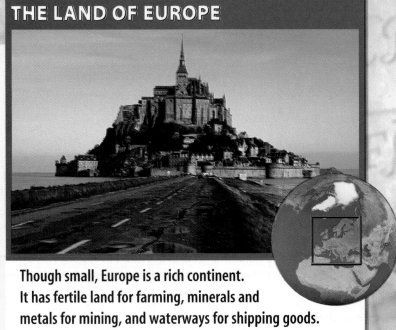

Though small, Europe is a rich continent. It has fertile land for farming, minerals and metals for mining, and waterways for shipping goods.

THE BIRTH OF THE MIDDLE AGES

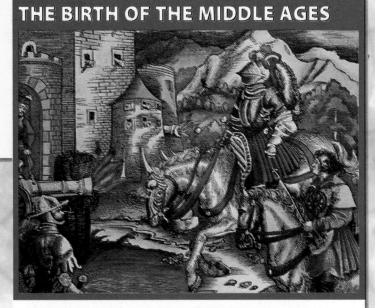

The peoples who invade Rome divide Europe among themselves. While small kingdoms struggle for power, new peoples from northern and eastern Europe and from Asia invade Europe.

CULTURE OF THE MIDDLE AGES

In time, the invasions end and Europe becomes more peaceful. Meanwhile, a unique culture begins to emerge in Europe.

THE RENAISSANCE

Europeans rediscover the art and ideas of the ancient Greek and Roman worlds.

THE REFORMATION

In Europe, Martin Luther posts a notice on the door of a church in Germany, beginning a call for reform.

Foldables

Make this Foldable study guide and use it to record what you learn about "Europe in Transition."

1. Fold a large piece of paper in half like a hot dog.

2. Fold into thirds and then cut one side along the folds to form three tabs. Label the tabs "The Middle Ages," "The Renaissance," and "The Reformation."

3. Collapse your Foldable like an accordion to make a booklet. Write the chapter title on the outside front cover.

Lesson 1

The Geography of Europe

 Find! out!

How have Europe's physical features affected its people?

Lesson Outline
- The Peninsula of Europe
- Rivers, Forests, and Plains

VOCABULARY

temperate
fjord
navigable
deforestation

READING STRATEGY

Copy the main idea web for Europe's geography. Write the main idea in the center box. Write details in the outside circles.

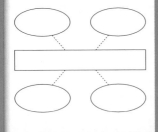

BUILD BACKGROUND

In the first century A.D. a Roman writer named Tacitus described northern Europe's waterways: "The northern parts of the country are [surrounded] by the sea. . . . The Rhine rises from . . . the Alps and afterwards turns slightly westward to flow into the North Sea. The Danube . . . [empties] into the Black Sea." Even 2,000 years ago, European life was influenced by the waterways of Europe.

Some of Europe's oldest cities are built on its rivers, such as the Rhine River.

THE PENINSULA OF EUROPE

After Australia, Europe is the world's smallest continent. Europe and Asia together, however, make up the world's largest landmass, called **Eurasia**. Find the Ural (YUR uhl) and Caucasus (KAW kuh sus) mountains on the map. These mountains are considered the border between Europe and Asia.

Europe is surrounded by the Atlantic Ocean, the Mediterranean Sea, the **North Sea**, and the **Baltic Sea**.

The climate of Europe is mainly **temperate**, or mild, because winds bring warm air from currents in the Atlantic Ocean. Even areas near the Arctic Circle can be fairly warm. Extreme temperatures are found mostly on the border with Asia and high in the Alps in the center of the continent.

READING CHECK ✓ **What makes Europe's climate temperate?**

Europe: Physical

NATIONAL GEOGRAPHIC

Map Skill

1. **Which mountains separate the Italian peninsula from the rest of Europe?**

2. **What are the largest islands off the coast of Europe?**

RIVERS, FORESTS, AND PLAINS

Waterways are an important part of Europe's geography. Its long, jagged coastline creates natural harbors for boats. The Scandinavian peninsula in northern Europe has narrow inlets called **fjords** (FYORDZ), where the sea surges in between cliffs.

Fish are especially plentiful in the North Atlantic, where fishing has been an important industry since Europe's earliest history. Europe's rivers are also important to the economy. Traders can transport goods on Europe's many **navigable** (NAV ih guh bul) rivers, such as the Rhine, the Elbe, and the Danube. Navigable waterways are deep enough to be traveled by boat. For over 2,000 years, Europeans have been using the water from their rivers to turn waterwheels for grinding wheat.

Some of Europe's oldest and largest cities developed along its rivers. One such city is Paris, France, on the **Seine River**. Another is London, England, on the **Thames River**. Europeans have created additional waterways by building canals.

Clearing the Forests

Europe has many natural resources, such as forests and minerals. Two thousand years ago, most of Europe was covered by dense forests. After about A.D. 1100, however, Europeans began to clear forests to make room for farms and cities. The process of clearing forests is called **deforestation**. Although many of Europe's forests have been cut down, parts of Europe, especially in the north, still have thick forests, such as the Black Forest of Germany.

After forests were cleared, Europeans were able to grow crops such as wheat. In southern Europe where it is warm,

European waterways include this **fjord** in Norway (left) and the canals in Amsterdam (below).

Winter snows gave farmers in Switzerland's Alps (above) time for crafts, such as carving wooden cuckoo clocks (right).

oranges, olives, grapes, and other fruits are grown. The most fertile farmland in Europe is found in a region called the **North European Plain**. Find this region on the map on page 337.

What are some benefits of Europe's rivers?

PUTTING IT TOGETHER

Although it is relatively small in area, Europe has a variety of geographic features, including plains, waterways, and deep harbors.

Europe has several high mountain chains that have hindered land transportation in the past. The **Pyrenees**, the **Alps**, and the Carpathian mountains have helped to separate European regions, adding to the development of distinctive cultural regions.

The warm currents of the Atlantic Ocean, along with natural resources such as forests, minerals, and fertile soil, all make Europe a rich continent.

Review and Assess

1. Write a sentence for each vocabulary word.

   deforestation   navigable
   fjord   temperate

2. How do Europe's many waterways help its trade? In what other ways is the sea a valuable resource?

3. Why are plains and waterways important features of the geography of Europe?

4. How have geographical features of Europe affected the **economy** of the continent?

5. Make a **generalization** about the effect of ocean currents on Europe's climate.

Look at the map on page 337. Create a map of Europe that shows its major rivers and seas.

● ●

Suppose you are flying over Europe in an airplane. **Write** a description of what you see from your plane window.

Lesson 2

Birth of the Middle Ages

Find out!

What was life like for people in the Middle Ages?

VOCABULARY

Middle Ages
feudalism
fief
vassal
serf
manor
chivalry
Magna Carta

PEOPLE

Charlemagne
William the Conqueror
Eleanor of Aquitaine
King John

READING STRATEGY

Use a chart like the one below to write the sequence of events of this lesson.

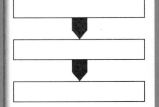

BUILD BACKGROUND

"Woe to thee, Rome, that thou art crushed and trodden down by so many peoples; who has been seized by a northern king, and thy folk slaughtered and thy strength brought to nothing." This is how a monk recounted the collapse of Roman rule and the beginning of a period in European history known as the **Middle Ages.** It occurred between A.D. 500 and the 1400s.

This painting shows the royal palace in Paris in the 1400s.

A NEW EMPIRE

As you read in Chapter 7, the western Roman Empire was invaded by peoples from northern Europe. The Franks established themselves in Gaul—or France, as it is known today.

The Visigoths settled in Spain, but in 711, the Muslims defeated them and established a Muslim state. From Spain, the Muslims tried to conquer the rest of Europe. However, in 732, Charles Martel, a Frankish war leader, defeated a Muslim army at Tours, in present-day France.

Charles Martel came from one of the many small kingdoms in western Europe. The greatest leader of the Franks was Charles Martel's grandson. He is known as "Charles the Great," or **Charlemagne**.

Charlemagne conquered kingdoms in the southwestern part of what is now France, and lands in Italy and Germany. He also spread Roman Christianity throughout Europe.

READING CHECK What is the importance of the Battle of Tours?

NATIONAL GEOGRAPHIC

Europe, A.D. 700

- 20°W
- 10°W
- 60°N
- North Sea
- 50°N
- ANGLO-SAXON KINGDOMS
- SLAVIC KINGDOMS
- English Channel
- FRANKISH KINGDOMS
- ATLANTIC OCEAN
- BRITTANY
- Seine R.
- Danube River
- Tours
- Bordeaux
- Lyon
- ALPS
- LOMBARD KINGDOMS
- Rhône River
- Oviedo
- Toulouse
- Ravenna
- PYRENEES
- 40°N
- VISIGOTHIC KINGDOM
- Zaragoza
- Corsica
- Rome
- Adriatic Sea
- Constantinople
- Lisbon
- Córdoba
- Valencia
- Sardinia
- Naples
- Seville
- Balearic Islands
- 0°
- 10°E
- BYZANTINE EMPIRE
- Sicily
- Mediterranean Sea
- 20°E
- 0 — 250 — 500 miles
- 0 — 250 — 500 kilometers
- Lambert Azimuthal Equal-Area Projection

Map Skill

1. What kingdoms bordered the Frankish kingdoms in the east?

2. What separated the Franks from the Anglo-Saxon kingdom?

Charlemagne

EMPERORS AND INVADERS

Charlemagne's greatest achievement came in 800, when he arrived with his army in Rome. The leader of the Roman Church, Pope Leo III, placed a golden crown on Charlemagne's head and declared him emperor. For a while, it appeared to western Europeans that the old Roman Empire had risen again.

At his court at **Aachen** (AH khun), in present-day Germany, Charlemagne set up a school. He put Alcuin (AL kwin), a learned man from England, in charge of it. Although the emperor never learned to read, one scholar said, "how rare it is to find a man who takes the trouble to know these things!"

After Charlemagne's death in 814, his empire was passed on to his only surviving son, Louis. After Louis's death, his sons divided the Frankish kingdom into three parts. Europe was again thrown into disorder.

At this time, tribes from the east, such as the Magyars, began invading Europe. Sea raiders from the north and Muslim pirates on the Mediterranean upset the whole continent. These northern raiders were called Vikings. They came from the Norse culture in what is now Denmark, Norway, and Sweden. Though most Northmen, or Norsemen, were peaceful farmers, the Vikings plundered villages and churches and terrified all of Europe. Later, a group of Norse called Normans settled in present-day England and Ireland. Another Norse group, called the Rus, conquered Russia. The Vikings were also great explorers who settled Iceland and Greenland, and even established colonies in North America.

National Portrait Gallery, London

The Invasion of England

In 911, Charlemagne's grandson gave a Viking chief named Rollo the land around

the mouth of the Seine River. These Normans adopted Christianity, the French language, and many Frankish customs. Their region later came to be called **Normandy**. Today, it is part of northwestern France.

In 1066, William, Duke of Normandy, crossed the English Channel with about 5,000 knights. At Hastings he defeated Harold, the Saxon king of England, and made himself king. Because of this victory, he became known as **William the Conqueror**.

William established a strong government in England, and also brought many elements of French culture to the island. The new kingdom was a blend of Norman and Saxon. Even the language we speak today, English, is a mixture of the old French the Normans spoke and the middle English the Saxons spoke.

How did Europe change after the death of Charlemagne?

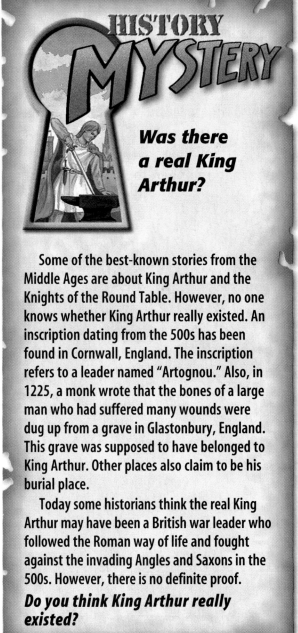

HISTORY MYSTERY

Was there a real King Arthur?

Some of the best-known stories from the Middle Ages are about King Arthur and the Knights of the Round Table. However, no one knows whether King Arthur really existed. An inscription dating from the 500s has been found in Cornwall, England. The inscription refers to a leader named "Artognou." Also, in 1225, a monk wrote that the bones of a large man who had suffered many wounds were dug up from a grave in Glastonbury, England. This grave was supposed to have belonged to King Arthur. Other places also claim to be his burial place.

Today some historians think the real King Arthur may have been a British war leader who followed the Roman way of life and fought against the invading Angles and Saxons in the 500s. However, there is no definite proof.

Do you think King Arthur really existed?

343

FEUDALISM

Around 800, a system of government called **feudalism** (FEW duh liz m) developed as a way to keep the peace in Europe. To help control their lands, most kings divided them into **fiefs** (FEEFS). A fief is land a king or other powerful landowner would give to nobles. In return these nobles swore to give the king their loyalty, support in a war, and promised to keep the peace. These nobles who took an oath of loyalty to their lords were called **vassals**.

Serfs and Manors

When a noble received a fief, he also received the peasants who worked the land. These peasants were called **serfs**. Serfs lived in villages around a fortified house that belonged to the fief's owner, or lord. A settlement like this was called a **manor**. A manor would also probably have a church. Serfs were not slaves, but they were not permitted to leave the manor without their lord's permission. They also had to pay taxes in crops and by working for their lord.

A Hard Life

For most, life was hard in the early Middle Ages. Peasants grew barely enough food. War and disease were common, and most people died at an early age.

In time, conditions began to improve. Around A.D. 1000, great changes in European life began. Farmers started to use improved methods of farming, which allowed them to produce more food. Towns and trade began to revive. Much trade was for short distances. A farmer, for example, brought extra crops to market. However, people also began to travel

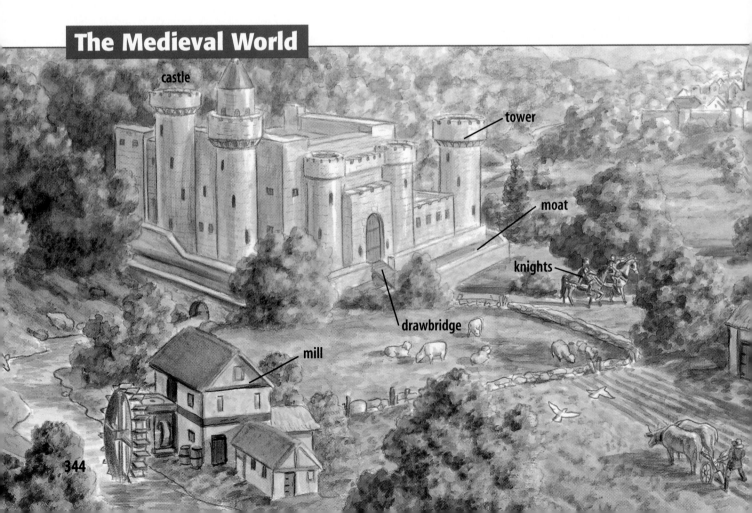

The Medieval World

castle

tower

moat

knights

drawbridge

mill

longer distances to towns with skilled craft-workers, such as weavers or goldsmiths. Sometimes, nobles founded a town in order to collect taxes on its trade.

Towns also gave commoners hope for the future. By moving to a town, serfs could escape harsh life on the manors. One saying was "town air makes you free." In some places, a serf was free if he or she remained in a town for a year and a day. Peasants also built new settlements in cleared forests or settled near monks who wanted to live away from the busy medieval world.

The Code of Knighthood

Nobles in the Middle Ages saw them-selves as "those who fight." In the feudal system, nobles agreed to fight for a king or a powerful landowner in return for land. The English word for these soldiers is *knight*. Knights usually fought from horseback in armor.

Religion influenced the growing idea of **chivalry**. Chivalry is the code of con-duct that knights believed they should follow. In addition to fighting, knights were supposed to know music and poetry and to have good manners. A knight was also supposed to be a good Christian and defend the Church.

One person who helped make the idea of chivalry popular was **Eleanor of Aquitaine**. She was the wife of a French king and, later, of an English king. In the 1140s, Eleanor spread the ideas of chivalry among French knights.

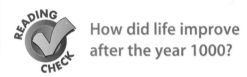

How did life improve after the year 1000?

Diagram Skill

1. **What kinds of tasks did people who lived on a manor do?**

2. **Why might the mill be located near the stream?**

city

city wall

village church

manor house

merchant

THE MAGNA CARTA

Just as vassals had duties towards their kings, kings had to respect their vassals. In 1215, **King John** of England was forced by his vassals to sign an important document. It was the **Magna Carta**, which means "Great Charter" in Latin. It stated that the king could not violate the rights of free men and women by setting unfair taxes or making unfair demands of goods or labor. King John had demanded more taxes to pay for his wars. He also claimed the power to imprison people without a trial. The Magna Carta, part of which you can read below, established legal rights enjoyed by English people and Americans.

Why did King John sign the Magna Carta?

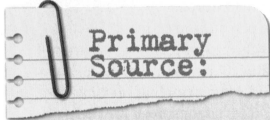

excerpt from The Magna Carta
— *Runnymede, England, 1215*

"John, by the grace of God, King of England . . .TO ALL FREE MEN OF OUR KINGDOM we have. . .granted . . .all the liberties written out below

Ordinary lawsuits shall not follow the royal court around, but shall be held in a fixed place.

There shall be standard measures of wine, ale, and corn. . . throughout the kingdom.

No free man shall be seized or imprisoned. . . except by the lawful judgement of his equals . . .

. . .no official shall place a man on trial . . . without producing credible [reliable] *witnesses to the truth of it.*

To no one will we sell, to no one deny or delay . . . justice.

What were some of the promises made by King John in the Magna Carta?

Knights and their horses wore heavy armor into battle.

PUTTING IT TOGETHER

The western Roman Empire was overrun by invaders, but much of Rome's legacy remained: its language, culture, and religion. Life in the early Middle Ages was hard. Agriculture was poor and war and disease were common. Most people did not live past 40 years of age. However, things began to improve slowly. Agriculture improved and trade revived.

In 800 a powerful ruler, Charlemagne, founded a new empire in Western Europe and helped to spread Roman Christianity. After his death, the Frankish kingdom eventually became the two kingdoms of France and Germany. When the Normans defeated the Saxons in 1066, England became a blend of the two cultures. Out of this blend of cultures came the English language. Later, the Magna Carta was a first step toward limiting the power of a ruler by law.

Review and Assess

1. Write a sentence for each vocabulary term.
   feudalism   **serf**
   Magna Carta   **vassal**

2. What promises did lords and vassals make to each other?

3. What was European life like during the Middle Ages?

4. How did the change in European life around 1000 affect the **economy** of Europe?

5. **Compare** and **contrast** the feudal life in Europe with life in Europe during the Roman Empire.

Compare the map of Europe on page 341 to the European physical and political maps on pages R14 and R15. Make a map of the Frankish kingdoms. Label rivers, mountains, and present-day countries.

● ●

Suppose you are a serf living in Europe in the early Middle Ages. **Write** a journal entry describing your daily life.

347

Using Maps at Different Scales

Mapmakers have to decide what to show on a map. They can show a particular city, such as London, or they can show a larger area, such as all of Britain. Mapmakers do this by using a **scale**. A map scale is a unit of measure, such as an inch, used to represent a distance on Earth.

VOCABULARY

scale

small-scale map

large-scale map

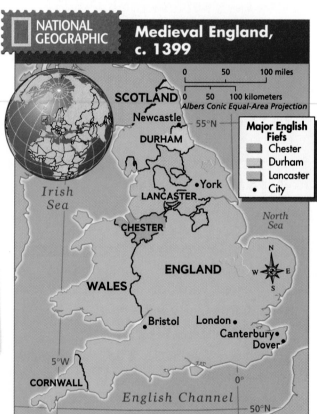

NATIONAL GEOGRAPHIC

Medieval England, c. 1399

0   50   100 miles
0   50   100 kilometers
Albers Conic Equal-Area Projection

SCOTLAND

Newcastle

55°N

DURHAM

Irish Sea

York

LANCASTER

North Sea

CHESTER

ENGLAND

WALES

N W E S

Bristol   London

Canterbury
Dover

5°W

CORNWALL

0°

English Channel

50°N

Major English Fiefs
- Chester
- Durham
- Lancaster
- City

LEARN THE SKILL

1. **Study the map scale.**
   Look at the scale measure of the map. It shows miles and kilometers.

2. **Does the map show a large area?**
   Real distances on Earth do not change, but mapmakers can use a **small-scale map** to show a great distance per unit of measure —say, 200 miles for each inch on the map.

A small-scale map like the one above gives a "big picture," but less detail.

3. **Does the map show a lot of detail?**
   If the map shows many details, the scale uses a smaller unit of measure, such as 20 miles per inch. This is a **large-scale map**. Large-scale maps, such as the one on page 349, show smaller areas.

TRY THE SKILL

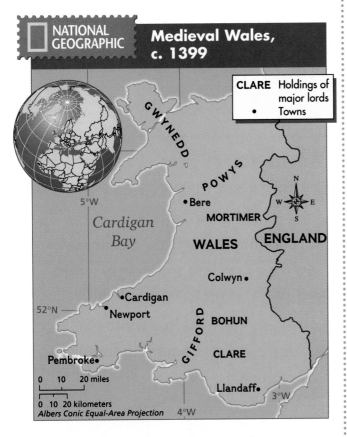

NATIONAL GEOGRAPHIC **Medieval Wales, c. 1399**

CLARE Holdings of major lords
• Towns

GWYNEDD

POWYS

5°W

• Bere

MORTIMER

Cardigan Bay

WALES   ENGLAND

Colwyn •

52°N   • Cardigan
• Newport

GIFFORD   BOHUN

CLARE

Pembroke •

Llandaff •

0 10 20 miles

0 10 20 kilometers
Albers Conic Equal-Area Projection   4°W   3°W

Look at the maps of Britain on these pages. Both maps show Wales. Notice that both maps are the same size, and that they both show towns and counties. The maps differ, however, in their scale.

1. Which map shows a larger area and broader overview?

2. Which map shows a smaller area and more detail?

3. How many miles per inch does the small-scale map show? What about the large-scale map?

EXTEND THE SKILL

Try your hand at making a large-scale map of your school or neighborhood. What approximate distance in the real world will your map illustrate? Be sure to include an appropriate map scale.

- What is the area of your map? Does the title accurately reflect the information in the map?

- Have you provided a map scale, so that readers will understand what area is covered?

- How can using maps at different scales improve your understanding of history?

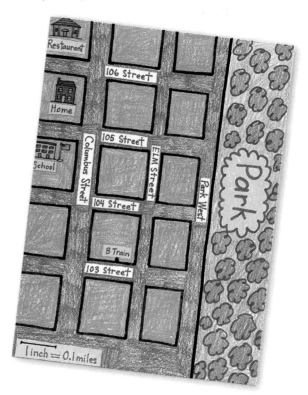

Lesson 3

The Middle Ages and the Church

Find out!

What events changed life in the Middle Ages?

Lesson Outline
- The Roman Church
- A Time of Change

VOCABULARY

monastery
nun
saint
Crusades
Reconquista
cathedral
Gothic
plague

PEOPLE

Hildegard of
  Bingen
Urban II

READING STRATEGY

Use a chart like the one below to write the cause and an effect for events in this lesson.

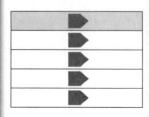

BUILD BACKGROUND

A monk named Radolphus Glaber wrote these words shortly after A.D. 1000: "So [in] the . . . thousandth year . . . throughout the world . . . churches were rebuilt. . . . So it was as though the very world had shaken herself and cast off her old age, and [was] clothing herself everywhere in a white garment of churches." Europe was beginning to build a unique medieval culture.

THE ROMAN CHURCH

The Roman Catholic Church was involved in all aspects of medieval life. Few people could read, so the writings of monks are valuable records of life in Europe after the Roman Empire. Time was measured by prayers that were said at specific hours.

Monasteries

Large amounts of land belonged to Church leaders and **monasteries**. Monasteries were communities where monks lived and dedicated their lives to God.

An Italian monk named Benedict wrote the first plan for monasteries in the A.D. 500s. Monks had to obey the head monk, who was called the abbot. Here are some of Benedict's rules:

No one, without permission of the abbot, shall . . . give, or receive, or keep as his own, anything whatever: neither book nor tablets, nor pen: nothing at all . . . All things are to be common to all.

Monasteries were churches, farms, homes, and schools all rolled into one. Most monks spent much of the day in prayer. They also farmed, studied, and made wine, medicines, and craft goods.

Monasteries served as centers of learning in the Middle Ages. Most monasteries had a scriptorium, or a room for making books. Since no printing presses existed, all books were carefully copied by hand. Monks wrote books of prayer and poetry. They also copied old Greek and Roman texts. These beautifully decorated books are called manuscripts. Some had such value that they were chained to desks.

Women in the Church

Women in the Middle Ages also shared in religious life. Those who chose to serve God by becoming **nuns** lived in special communities called convents. There were also many female **saints** noted for helping the poor. A saint is a person believed to be holy. An example of a medieval religious woman was the German **Hildegard of Bingen**, who lived from 1098 to 1179. She wrote books, composed religious music, and founded a community where nuns lived and worked.

READING CHECK What served as centers for learning in the Middle Ages?

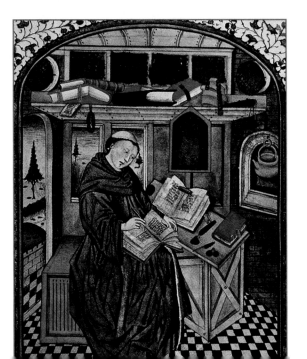

Colorful windows decorated churches, such as Notre Dame in Paris, France (left). Many monks copied and illustrated religious books (right).

A TIME OF CHANGE

In 1095, Pope **Urban II** called for a war to capture Jerusalem and nearby lands where Jesus had lived. Seljuk Turks, who were Muslims, had captured this region, which Christians called the "Holy Land." The series of wars to take the Holy Land was later called the **Crusades**.

The armies of the First Crusade defeated the Muslims and held the Holy Land for about 100 years. Later, the Muslims took back their lost lands. Seven more Crusades followed, but Muslims held on to the Holy Land.

The Crusades changed Europe. Europeans came into renewed contact with the Middle East and the Byzantine Empire. They began to want trade goods from the East, such as silks and spices. The Crusades also inspired attacks on non-Muslims. This resulted in the persecution of the Jews of Europe and Eastern Orthodox Christians.

War in Spain

Christians struggled to drive the Muslims out of Spain, as well. As you read, Spain had been captured by Muslim armies in the early 700s. The **Reconquista** (ray kohn-KEES tuh) was a long war fought by Christian armies to recapture Spain. It began in 718, but it did not end until 1492. During this long contact with the Arab world, Spain was deeply influenced by Islamic culture.

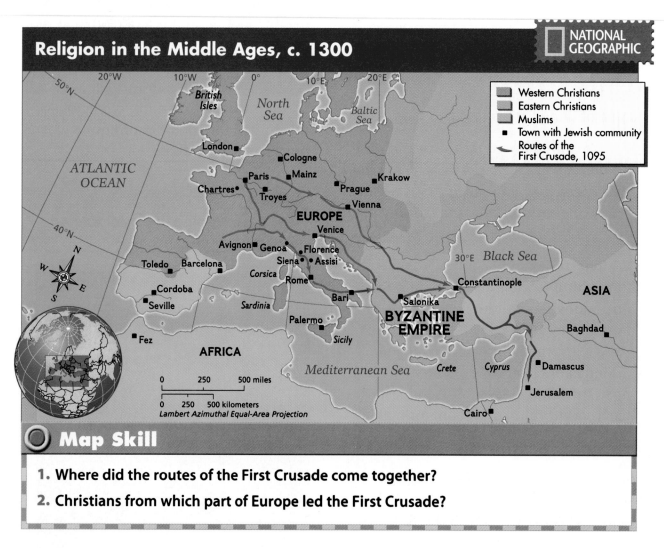

Religion in the Middle Ages, c. 1300

NATIONAL GEOGRAPHIC

Legend:
- Western Christians
- Eastern Christians
- Muslims
- Town with Jewish community
- Routes of the First Crusade, 1095

0   250   500 miles
0   250   500 kilometers
Lambert Azimuthal Equal-Area Projection

Map Skill

1. Where did the routes of the First Crusade come together?
2. Christians from which part of Europe led the First Crusade?

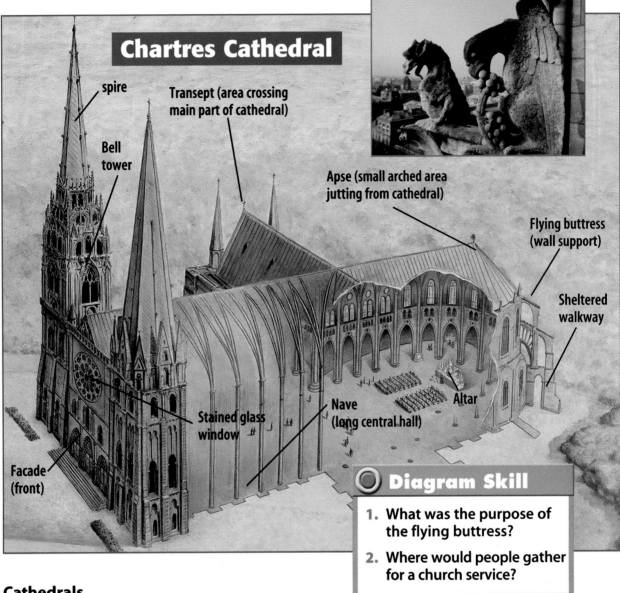

Chartres Cathedral

spire

Bell tower

Transept (area crossing main part of cathedral)

Apse (small arched area jutting from cathedral)

Flying buttress (wall support)

Sheltered walkway

Stained glass window

Nave (long central hall)

Altar

Facade (front)

Diagram Skill

1. What was the purpose of the flying buttress?

2. Where would people gather for a church service?

Cathedrals

After 1100, Europeans began to build **cathedrals**, or large Christian churches. About 1140, a French churchman named Suger (SOO jay) had an idea. By using a series of arches, buildings could be made higher and could have many windows. The style that developed with pointed arches, soaring spaces, and buttresses for support is called the **Gothic** style. **Chartres** is one of the most famous Gothic cathedrals.

Black Death

Siena, Italy, was one of Europe's bustling cities. Trade flourished and the people of Siena had been building a great cathedral since the 1100s. Its construction was halted in 1348, when a **plague** struck Western Europe. A plague is a terrible disease that spreads quickly. It is caused by bacteria spread by rats and fleas.

This plague, later called the Black Death, wiped out one third of the western European population during the next 130 years. At that time no one knew what caused the sickness.

READING CHECK

How did church architecture change in the Middle Ages?

DATAGRAPHIC

Bubonic Plague

The bubonic plague was the most frightening disease of the Middle Ages. Fleas spread the disease from rats to humans. Ninety percent of the people who caught the bubonic plague died. Look at the graph and primary source on this page and answer the questions below.

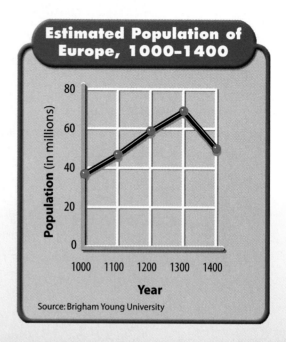

Estimated Population of Europe, 1000–1400

Population (in millions) vs. Year

Source: Brigham Young University

Primary Source:

excerpt from **The Muqaddimah: An Introduction to History** —*by Ibn Khaldun*

In the middle of the [fourteenth] century, civilization both in the East and the West was visited by a destructive plague, which devastated nations and caused populations to vanish. It swallowed up many of the good things of civilization and wiped them out. It overtook the dynasties . . . . It lessened their power and curtailed their influence. . . . Settlements and mansions became empty, dynasties and tribes grew weak. The entire inhabited world changed.

QUESTIONS:

1. In the period between 1300 and 1400, what was the drop in Europe's estimated population?

2. What percentage of Europe's population was this?

3. What effect, according to Ibn Khaldun, did the rapid decrease in population have on governments?

To learn more, visit our Web site: **www.mhschool.com**

PUTTING IT TOGETHER

Around the year 1000, Europe began to recover from the collapse of Roman power. Great buildings, such as cathedrals, were built in the new Gothic style.

Pope Urban II encouraged Christian knights to go to the Holy Land in the Middle East and conquer the lands where Jesus had lived. These Crusades introduced Europeans to the learning and wealth of the western Asian world. Demand for trade goods from these areas revived trade throughout Europe. However, contact with the rest of the world helped spread a disease that killed more than one-third of Europe's population. It would take many years before Europe would fully recover.

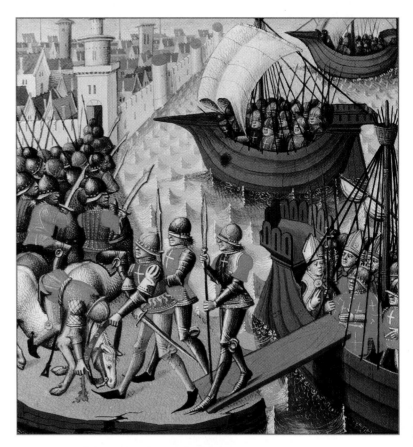

Crusaders leave their boats near a walled city in the Holy Land.

Review and Assess

1. Write a sentence for each vocabulary word.

   cathedral   Gothic
   Crusades   Reconquista

2. How did monasteries protect learning?

3. List three events that changed life in the Middle Ages.

4. For Pope Urban II, what was the main purpose of the Crusades?

5. Make a **generalization** about the effects of the Crusades on Europe.

Activities

Copy the map on page 352. Write other routes to the Holy Land that the Crusaders might have used.

• •

Suppose you are a visitor to Chartres, France, in the Middle Ages. **Write** a letter to friends at home describing the new cathedral.

The Renaissance

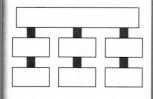
Find Out!

How did the Renaissance change life in Europe?

Lesson Outline
- Roots of the Renaissance
- Renaissance Writers and Painters
- The Renaissance Spreads

VOCABULARY

Renaissance
humanism
patron
perspective

PEOPLE

Lorenzo Medici
Petrarch
Christine de Pisan
Niccolo
  Machiavelli
Leonardo da
  Vinci
Michelangelo
William
  Shakespeare
Miguel de
  Cervantes

READING STRATEGY

Copy the chart. Write "Renaissance" in the top box. Name artists and writers in the other boxes.

BUILD BACKGROUND

"I used to marvel [be surprised] . . . that so many . . . arts and sciences from the . . . antique past could [have been] almost wholly lost."

In 1436, an Italian philosopher wrote that he saw a revival of interest in ancient Roman and Greek learning in his city. This renewed interest is called the **Renaissance**, a French word meaning "rebirth." The Renaissance was a time of great creativity in arts and sciences. It began in Italy and within a century had spread to the rest of Europe.

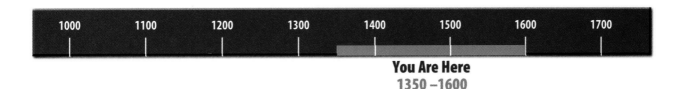
ROOTS OF THE RENAISSANCE

People of the Renaissance were usually very religious, but during this time, people also developed a powerful interest in **humanism** (HYOO muh niz um). Humanism is the concern for human interests and values.

Florence

The Renaissance began in a city in northern Italy called **Florence**. Traders from Florence brought spices and silks to Europe from Asia and Africa. Florence also had many workshops that made high quality woolen cloth and other goods. By

The dome of the cathedral of Florence, Italy, rises above the city, an important center of the Renaissance.

1400 Florence was one of the richest cities in Europe. One of the wealthiest families in Florence was the Medici (MED ih chee). It gained wealth through banking and trade. The most famous member of the family was **Lorenzo Medici**. He came to power in 1469.

Some people thought Lorenzo was a tyrant, but one citizen said, "If Florence was to have a tyrant, she could never have a better or more delightful one."

Lorenzo was a **patron**, or supporter, of the arts. Scholars and artists flocked to Florence, where "Lorenzo the Magnificent" supported their work.

Why did the Renaissance start in Italy?

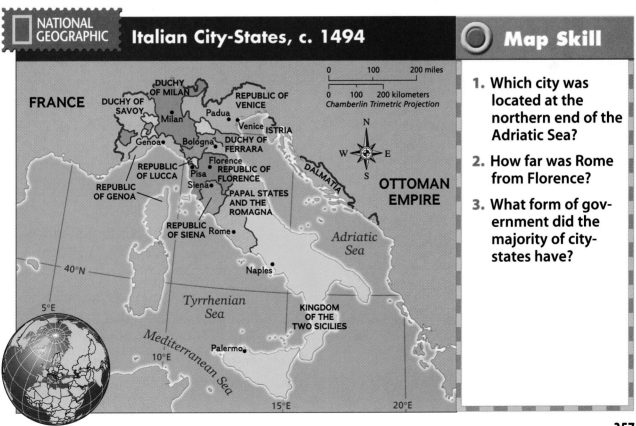

NATIONAL GEOGRAPHIC **Italian City-States, c. 1494**

Map Skill

1. **Which city was located at the northern end of the Adriatic Sea?**

2. **How far was Rome from Florence?**

3. **What form of government did the majority of city-states have?**

RENAISSANCE WRITERS AND PAINTERS

During the 1300s, humanists began to search the Italian countryside for artifacts from ancient Greece and Rome. They found examples of classical cultures such as manuscripts, coins, and statues to study.

Arab scholars in Baghdad had preserved and developed Greek, Roman, and Indian scientific knowledge. As a result of the Crusades, trade between Europe, Asia, and Africa grew, spreading new products and knowledge.

A New Kind of Writer

Beginning in the 1200s, writers began to write in their own languages for local readers. One of these was **Petrarch** (PEH trahrk), an Italian poet who lived from 1304 to 1374. He loved to read, and he decided that the works of classical Greek and Roman writers were better than the works written later.

Petrarch wrote in Italian, but translations made him the most famous poet in Europe. He wrote about his love of reading and literature in these words:

> *"There is no lighter burden, nor more agreeable, than a pen. As there is none among earthly delights more noble than literature, so there was none more lasting, none gentler or more faithful...."*

Another Renaissance writer, **Christine de Pisan**, was born in Venice in 1364 but spent most of her life in France. Most women writers of the Renaissance wrote about personal subjects, such as family or friendship. Christine de Pisan wrote poems, histories, and political commentaries.

Niccolo Machiavelli

The Florentine **Niccolo Machiavelli** (NIHK oh loh mah kee ah VEL lee), who lived from 1469 to 1527, wrote many books about government. His most famous book, *The Prince*, gives advice to rulers on how to run their governments efficiently.

Artists of the Renaissance

Renaissance painters in Italy and the Netherlands also studied ancient Greek and Roman artifacts. One of the skills they learned was a drawing technique called **perspective**. This technique seems to create three dimensions on the flat surface of a painting. Perspective made Renaissance paintings seem more realistic than paintings of the Middle Ages.

Renaissance painters also changed the subjects of their art. In addition to painting religious themes, Renaissance artists began to paint more worldly subjects. Inspired by Roman and Greek models, their subject matter often came from ancient myths and legends.

One of the most famous Renaissance artists was named **Leonardo da Vinci** (lee uh NAHR doh duh VIHN chee), who lived from 1452 to 1519. Leonardo was so talented that Lorenzo Medici invited him to set up his studio in the Medici garden. The young painter often followed people around Florence and then went back to his studio to paint them from memory.

Leonardo was a very talented painter, but painting was only one of his interests. He also studied engineering, music, and the natural world around him. He sketched his ideas, such as an armored cart, human muscles, and even a helicopter, in hundreds of notebooks.

Another famous Renaissance artist was **Michelangelo** (MY kuhl an jel oh) who lived from 1475 to 1564. He, too, used classical and ancient ideas in his paintings, sculptures, and architecture.

His famous paintings on the ceiling of the Sistine Chapel in Rome show scenes from the Bible. His sculpture, *David*, shows us the Biblical hero as a Greek or Roman warrior might have appeared.

 READING CHECK **How did art change during the Renaissance?**

Renaissance developments in art included the use of **perspective** (below) and sculptures of the human form such as Michelangelo's *David* (right).

Erasmus (below) was painted by Hans Holbein. Other Renaissance paintings were by El Greco (below left), and Jan Van Eyck (left).

Metropolitan Museum of Art

THE RENAISSANCE SPREADS

In the late 1400s ideas from the Italian Renaissance began to move into northern Europe. People from present day France, England, Germany, and the Netherlands came to Italy to study or for business. They carried Renaissance ideas back to the countries where they lived.

Two of these men were Erasmus (1466–1536) from the Netherlands and the Englishman, Thomas More (1478–1535). Interestingly, these men were friends as well as fellow humanists. In fact, Erasmus wrote his most famous book, making fun of greedy merchants and conceited leaders, while he was a guest at Thomas More's house.

The most famous writer of the Northern Renaissance was an Englishman named **William Shakespeare**. Born in 1564, he was an actor, a poet, and a playwright. Many consider Shakespeare to be the greatest playwright of all time. The plays of Shakespeare show a deep understanding of human thoughts and feelings. By the time he died in 1616, Shakespeare had written 37 plays and 154 poems.

Art in the North

Painting also flourished in the north, especially in the Netherlands and Germany. The Flemish artist Jan Van Eyck (ĪK) (1395–1441) was one of the first to use the new technique of painting with oil on canvas. Van Eyck's oil paintings have a more natural, glowing quality than the egg tempera on wood that other artists of the time were using.

Other northern artists included the German Albrecht Dürer (1471–1528) and Hans Holbein the Younger (1497–1543).

Dürer is known for his self-portraits and his study of nature. Holbein was a portrait artist. Both artists carved woodcuts that illustrated the first printed books.

The Renaissance in Spain

Throughout the Renaissance, Spain enjoyed prosperity, but its art did not change that much. Still, Spain was home to one of the Renaissance's great artists, a Greek painter named Domenikos Theotokopoulos (doh MEN ee kohs thay oh toh KOH poo lahs), who lived from 1541 to 1614. Known as El Greco, or "the Greek," Theotokopoulos was known for painting in flowing colors.

Renaissance Spain was also home to one of the world's great writers, **Miguel de Cervantes** (mee GEL dee sair VAHN tais), who lived from 1547 to 1616. He wrote *Don Quixote*, a novel that made fun of old-fashioned nobles.

Impact of the Renaissance

The Renaissance marks a turning point in the history of Europe. The growth of banking and trade spread luxury goods all over Europe and enabled merchants to gain vast fortunes. By studying ideas such as those of Machiavelli, kings began to turn their kingdoms into nations.

In addition to artistic advances, there were scientific discoveries. The telescope and the microscope helped scientists to study the world around them. Other inventions such as eyeglasses and portable clocks made daily life easier.

Gunpowder had been made since the Middle Ages. During the Renaissance, better techniques of metalworking made the first practical guns possible. Guns ended the age of knights because a common soldier with a gun was no longer at the mercy of the mounted knight.

Most important was the impact of the Renaissance on thought. Human society and the matters of trade, government, and business were seen as important and worthy of study. It was also during this time that "Greensleeves" and other songs about feelings became popular.

READING CHECK What changes did the Renaissance bring to Europe?

Exploring ECONOMICS

The Growth of Banking

Many of the practices of modern banking began in Italian cities during the Renaissance. The revival of trade required a better system of borrowing and lending large sums of money. The Medici family, for example, had grown rich on the woolen trade in Florence, and they invested their profits by making loans to other merchants. In many ways, the Medici family was like a modern international bank. They had a headquarters in Florence, but they also had branch offices in most Italian cities and in most of the important trading cities of Europe. Merchants could deposit funds in one Medici bank and withdraw the same amount in another city. The Medici family charged a percentage of the money as their profit.

Do research to learn how a bank transfers money today. Explain your findings to your class.

GREENSLEEVES

Traditional English Song, c. 1580

PUTTING IT TOGETHER

The Renaissance began in Italy around 1400 and changed the way Europe thought. There was a new interest in the art and writings of ancient Rome and Greece. Authority shifted away from the Church, and more interest was shown in studying human society and human beings. Beginning in Florence, wealthy patrons supported artists and scholars. People began to think and live in new ways as the ideas of the Renaissance spread. Artists began to use perspective and other techniques to make their paintings and sculptures more realistic. Writers began to write about new themes and to suggest ways to improve human life. The world of the Middle Ages had become a human-centered world of exploration and discovery.

William Shakespeare (right) wrote many plays. His play, *Henry V,* (above) portrays events from English history.

Review and Assess

1. Write a sentence for each vocabulary word.

   humanism   **perspective**
   patron   **Renaissance**

2. Who was Lorenzo Medici?

3. What changes did the Renaissance bring to Europe?

4. How did the Renaissance contribute to new developments in **technology** and science?

5. **Summarize** changes the Renaissance brought to painting and sculpture.

Look at the map on page 357. Write a speech for a citizen of Florence. Explain why Florence has the best location in Italy for trade and the arts.

• •

Suppose you are an English merchant visiting Florence in the 1400s. **Write** a letter home describing what you find there.

Points of View

Should We Have a World Language?

The world seems to be getting smaller, but people speak about 6,500 languages. Some languages have fewer than a thousand speakers, and others are spoken by hundreds of millions of people. Some people want a "world language," a language everyone can speak. Read and think about three different points of view, then answer the questions that follow.

YOSHITAKA ARAI

Business worker, Tokyo, Japan
excerpt from an Interview, 2001

❝For ordinary conversations, we don't need a world language.... For business, scientific, or technical matters, we do need a common language, but it should not be English. If we have a common language, we should create a new one that everyone has to learn. ...If a new language is created, and we use it as a common language, then everybody is equal.❞

MAXINE LIPSON

Research Associate, Faculty of Modern Languages
University of Bologna, Bologna, Italy
excerpt from an Interview, 2001

❝A common second language is a good idea.... This world language should not, however, take the place of the native language. Language is the way people express themselves.... It reflects how people see the world.... When we learn other languages, we learn about other cultures. All languages should be protected, because it shows that we respect [different] cultures...❞

TANIUSKA HASLAM

Teacher of English, St. George Academy
Matagalpa, Nicaragua
excerpt from an Interview, 2001

66 We are already starting to create a world language. . . . In Nicaragua. . . . we speak Spanish but many business people, doctors, scientists, and other professionals also learn English. . . Spanish and English are constantly borrowing words from each other. We are starting to create a common language for North and South America. . . . Then in the future [we] will borrow words from languages spoken in Africa, Asia, and Europe and we will move closer to having a world language. 99

Thinking About the Points of View

1. Yoshitaka Arai had to learn English to do his job at a Japanese company. How do you think this might have influenced his opinion on this question?

2. For many years Taniuska Haslam has taught English to Spanish-speaking students in Nicaragua. What reasons might she have for her point of view?

3. Maxine Lipson studies how languages are formed and how words affect the way we think. How might her studies have affected her opinion?

4. What other points of view might people have on this issue?

Building Citizenship

Respect

How does learning someone else's language show respect for his or her culture? What are the advantages of learning other languages?

Write About It!

Make a list of the advantages and disadvantages of having a world language. If you think a world language is needed, decide what this language might be. Then write a newspaper editorial stating your opinion.

The Reformation

How did the Reformation change Europe?

VOCABULARY

95 Theses
indulgence
Reformation
Protestant
Anglican Church

PEOPLE

Martin Luther
Leo X
Henry VIII
Johannes
 Gutenberg
Elizabeth I
Ignatius of Loyola

READING STRATEGY

Make a chart like this one. Write "Protestant Leaders" in the center circle. Write the name of one Protestant leader in each of the outer circles.

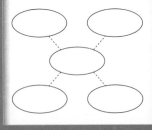

BUILD BACKGROUND

Martin Luther, a German monk, had driven in the last nail. The paper hung loosely from the cathedral door. It was October 31, 1517, and Luther had listed **95 Theses**, or arguments for reform in the Church in Rome. Luther did not plan to begin a new church. He simply wanted to reform the Roman Catholic Church. Nevertheless, he began a movement that resulted in a permanent split in the Church.

PROBLEMS IN THE CHURCH

In the previous lesson, you learned about the Renaissance. Renaissance thinkers questioned the traditions of medieval life. Many also felt that the Church in Rome had lost its spiritual direction. Other writers supported the Church. They thought that many artists and scientists of the Renaissance had moved too far from religion. Their argument grew more heated around 1500.

The Dutch writer Erasmus was one of the chief critics of the Church. He and others questioned many Church practices, such as the selling of Church jobs. They also felt that many Church leaders were more interested in worldly matters than in religion.

Martin Luther was especially upset by the sale of **indulgences**. An indulgence is a pardon, or forgiveness of sins, and is sold by the Church. In 1517, Pope **Leo X** needed money to complete construction of Saint Peter's Church in Rome. He decided to sell indulgences in Germany to raise the money he needed.

Luther's protest against these indulgences started a movement called the **Reformation**. The Reformation was a movement to reform the Church in Europe. It led eventually to a new division in Christianity.

Martin Luther (right) objected to the sale of indulgences by Pope Leo X (below).

What caused the Reformation in Europe?

367

Henry VIII

THE CALL TO REFORM

Luther wrote in German. Most people in Germany did not speak the Latin of Church leaders, so Luther's use of German won him the support of the German-speaking common people.

In 1520, Pope Leo X ordered Luther's writings to be burned. Many Germans sided with Luther and left the Church. They were called **Protestants** because they protested against the Church of Rome. Western Christians were divided into Protestants and Roman Catholics.

Not all Protestants agreed with Luther. Protestant leaders, such as John Calvin in Switzerland, founded their own churches. All Protestant groups were united in refusing to follow the Pope.

Henry VIII Breaks with Rome

Henry VIII became king of England in 1509. He supported the Pope, but he faced a difficult problem. He had no son to inherit his kingdom and his wife could not have any more children. Henry wanted to divorce the queen, but the Pope refused.

The king took over the English church and called it the **Anglican Church**. He seized church lands and wealth and cut England's ties to the Pope.

How did Protestant ideas spread across Europe?

Exploring
TECHNOLOGY

The Printing Press

During the Middle Ages, people wrote entire books by hand. It could take a year to produce even a small book. In 1455, a man named **Johannes Gutenberg** changed the way books were produced in Europe. Gutenberg invented movable type. Instead of having to carve an entire page of a book, printers could reuse letters to form new words page by page. Gutenberg also invented a printing press that made books quickly and cheaply. His press could produce 300 pages a day. Printed books spread ideas all over Europe and were cheap enough for almost all readers.

How did the printing press help to spread new ideas?

BIOGRAPHY

Focus On: Leadership

Elizabeth I of England was the daughter of Henry VIII and his second wife, Anne Boleyn. When Elizabeth became queen in 1558, religious differences and foreign enemies threatened England. With courage and intelligence, she led her people through difficult times. Elizabeth chose to make England a Protestant nation, but she also eased religious tensions. Elizabeth feared a long and expensive war. One of her greatest moments was when she led her people in the quick victory over the Spanish Armada in 1588.

Elizabeth was interested in overseas explorations. Her leadership encouraged English voyages of discovery and began the creation of Britain's overseas empire.

Elizabeth was also interested in literature and the arts. In particular, the plays of Shakespeare are associated with what became known as the Elizabethan Age.

Link to Today As a female leader, Elizabeth I faced challenges to her power. Choose a modern female leader. Write a paragraph comparing Elizabeth's career with the career of the modern female leader.

THE LIFE OF ELIZABETH	**1533** Elizabeth is born in Greenwich Palace, England	**1558** Elizabeth becomes Queen of England	**1588** Spanish Armada is defeated by the English	**1603** Elizabeth dies

1450	**1500**	**1550**	**1600**	**1650**

LIFE AROUND THE WORLD	**1521** The Spanish overthrow the Aztec Empire	**1591** The Songhai Empire in West Africa ends	**1603** Tokugawa Ieyasu becomes Shogun in Japan

THE COUNTER-REFORMATION

Protestant churches attracted many followers, but many others in Europe remained loyal to the Church of Rome. Nevertheless, the Roman Church realized the need for reform. From 1545 to 1563, a Church council met in the city of Trent in Italy. As a result, church finances were reformed, and parts of church services were held in local languages.

The Jesuits

One important Catholic leader at this time was **Ignatius of Loyola**. He grew up in his father's castle in Loyola, Spain. He later became a soldier for Spain and was injured in a war. After he recovered, he decided to become a "soldier for Christ," or priest. In 1540, Ignatius founded a religious order called the Society of Jesus, or the Jesuits. The Jesuits became very powerful and spread Roman Catholic teachings to Asia and Latin America.

Leaders of the Roman Catholic Church met at the Council of Trent (below) on issues of reform.

Europe Divided

In 1529, war broke out between Germany's Catholic and Protestant rulers. Finally in 1555, a treaty allowed each territory to follow the religion of its ruler.

The map on this page shows the religious divisions in Europe at this time. These religious divisions led to continuing conflict. Western Europe would never again be united under one Church. The power of the Church was weakened and the power of local rulers increased.

READING CHECK How did the Reformation change Europe?

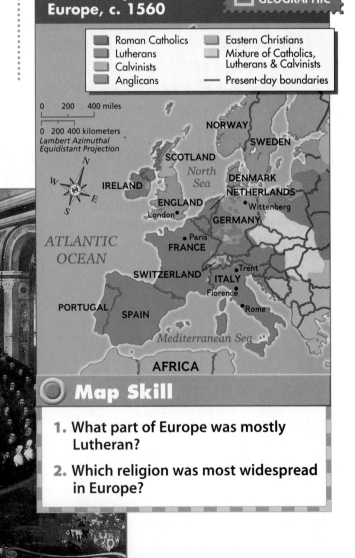

Christianity in Western Europe, c. 1560

NATIONAL GEOGRAPHIC

- Roman Catholics
- Lutherans
- Calvinists
- Anglicans
- Eastern Christians
- Mixture of Catholics, Lutherans & Calvinists
- — Present-day boundaries

0   200   400 miles
0 200 400 kilometers
Lambert Azimuthal Equidistant Projection

NORWAY
SWEDEN
SCOTLAND
North Sea
DENMARK
IRELAND
NETHERLANDS
ENGLAND
Wittenberg
London
GERMANY
ATLANTIC OCEAN
Paris
FRANCE
SWITZERLAND
Trent
ITALY
Florence
PORTUGAL
SPAIN
Rome
Mediterranean Sea
AFRICA

Map Skill

1. **What part of Europe was mostly Lutheran?**

2. **Which religion was most widespread in Europe?**

PUTTING IT TOGETHER

The Reformation began with the 95 Theses of Martin Luther. Many who believed the Church had become corrupt began to talk about breaking from Rome. Soon, Europe was divided between Catholic and Protestant Churches. The Church then launched the Counter Reformation to reform the Church and win back people who had left.

This weakening of the Church and the growth of powerful kings was the beginning of the modern nation-state. The kings of England and France were among the first to build strong governments to help them rule.

Ignatius Loyola presented Pope Paul III with a book of the Jesuit order (above). Many copies of the Bible (right) were produced by Gutenberg after 1454.

Review and Assess

1. Write a sentence for each vocabulary term.

   95 Theses   **indulgence**
   Anglican Church   **Reformation**

2. Who was Ignatius Loyola?

3. What political effect did the Reformation have on Europe?

4. Look at the map on page 370. In general, are Protestant countries in the north or in the south of Europe?

5. Write a **summary** of Henry VIII's break with Rome.

Activities

Look at the map on page 370. Make a two-column chart. Write the name of each country on the map in one column. Write the religion of the country in the other column.

Suppose that you are the editor of an English newspaper in 1588. **Write** about the defeat of the Spanish Armada. State your support for the leadership of Queen Elizabeth during the crisis.

VOCABULARY REVIEW

Number a sheet of paper from 1 to 5. Beside each number write the word from the list below that matches the description.

indulgence	**Reformation**
Magna Carta	**serf**
patron	

1. A wealthy person who supports artists and writers

2. A pardon of sins sold by the Church

3. An English document stating that the king would respect certain rights

4. A commoner who was required by law to stay and work on a fief.

5. The movement in the 1500s that caused a division of the Roman Church in Europe

CHAPTER COMPREHENSION

6. Why does most of Europe have a temperate climate?

7. What were some results of the rule of Charlemagne?

8. How were land and society organized under feudalism?

9. What was similar about the Crusades and the Reconquista? Where did each occur?

10. What was chivalry? What were two important ideas of chivalry?

11. What was the Renaissance? When and where did it begin?

12. What did Martin Luther do that changed the Roman Catholic Church?

13. **Write** a paragraph describing some of the events that occurred in England during the reign of Elizabeth I.

SKILL REVIEW

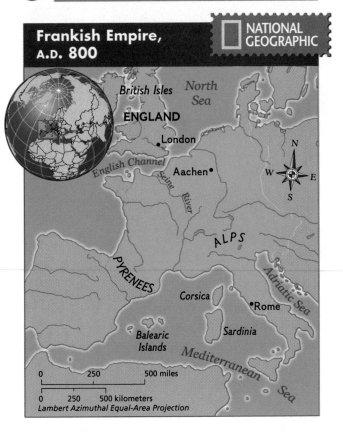

Frankish Empire, A.D. 800

NATIONAL GEOGRAPHIC

North Sea
British Isles
ENGLAND
London
English Channel
Aachen
Seine River
ALPS
PYRENEES
Corsica
Rome
Adriatic Sea
Balearic Islands
Sardinia
Mediterranean Sea

0   250   500 miles
0   250   500 kilometers
Lambert Azimuthal Equal-Area Projection

14. **Geography Skill** What does scale mean? What is the scale of the map on this page?

15. **Geography Skill** What does a large-scale map show? A small-scale map?

16. **Geography Skill** What kind of map is shown above? About how many miles is it from Aachen to Rome?

17. **Reading/Thinking Skill** What generalization could you make about life in the Middle Ages around A.D. 1000?

18. **Study Skill** How would you summarize the importance of the invention of the printing press?

USING A TIME LINE

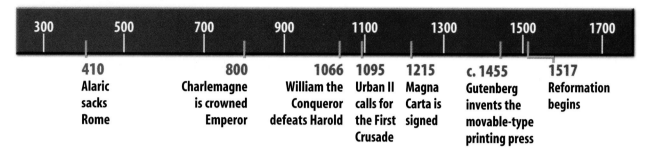

| 300 | 500 | 700 | 900 | 1100 | 1300 | 1500 | 1700 |

410
Alaric
sacks
Rome

800
Charlemagne
is crowned
Emperor

1066
William the
Conqueror
defeats Harold

1095
Urban II
calls for
the First
Crusade

1215
Magna
Carta is
signed

c. 1455
Gutenberg
invents the
movable-type
printing press

1517
Reformation
begins

19. Which event on the time line led to increased contact between people of Europe and the Muslim world?

20. Did the invention of the printing press happen before or after the Reformation began? How long before or after?

Writing **About Culture** Suppose that you lived in Florence during the Renaissance and took a friend on an art tour. Write a description of an art tour of Florence. Name some artists and some works of art that you might see. Explain the term *perspective*.

Foldables

Use your Foldable time line with tabs to review what you have learned about Europe in Transition before and during the Middle Ages, the Renaissance, and the Reformation. As you look at the three periods listed on the front of your Foldable, mentally review what occurred during each, and explain how it affected the life and culture of the people. Look at your notes on the inside of your Foldable to check your memory and responses. Record any questions that you have, and discuss them with classmates, or review the chapter to find answers.

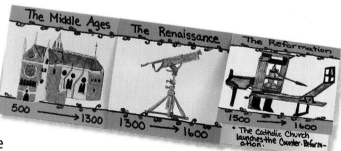

THE **Big** IDEAS ABOUT...

New Empires in Asia

Between A.D. 1000 and 1650 several Asian civilizations expanded their influence. Countries became united and some developed into empires.

THE GEOGRAPHY OF ASIA

The largest continent in the world is a land of high mountains, deserts, and fertile plains.

THE OTTOMAN EMPIRE

A new Islamic power develops in the Middle East in 1301.

CHINA'S GREAT DYNASTIES

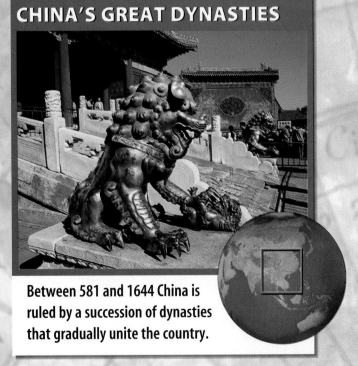

Between 581 and 1644 China is ruled by a succession of dynasties that gradually unite the country.

THE MUGHAL EMPIRE

Beginning in the early 1500s, India is ruled by the Mughal dynasty which enriches the country economically and culturally.

FEUDAL JAPAN

From 1590 until the late 1800s, Japan is organized as a feudal society.

SOUTHEAST ASIAN KINGDOMS

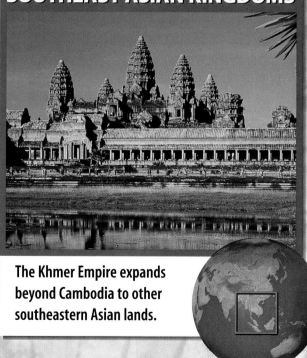

The Khmer Empire expands beyond Cambodia to other southeastern Asian lands.

Foldables

Make this Foldable study guide and use it to record what you learn about "New Empires in Asia."

1. Stack four sheets of paper together, leaving a 1" tab between each sheet.

2. Roll the bottom of the four sheets up to make seven tabs the same size. Fold and staple.

3. Write the title of the chapter on the top tab, and the lesson titles on the first six of the small equal-sized tabs. Use the bottom tab for Vocabulary.

Geography of Asia

How do mountains and winds affect Asia?

Lesson Outline
• The Asian Continent
• A Continent of Contrasts

READING STRATEGY

Copy this chart. Use it to explain the causes and effects of Asia's climate.

BUILD BACKGROUND

"The summer sun, who robbed the pleasant nights, and plundered [stole] all the water of the rivers, and burned the earth, and scorched the forest trees, is now in hiding; and the autumn clouds, spread thick across the sky to track him down, hunt for the criminal with lightning flashes."

Indian poet Amaru, writing in Sanskrit, described India's yearly change of seasons over 1,000 years ago. This change is a big event for many people across Asia. Many, in fact, depend on it for their lives.

THE ASIAN CONTINENT

Asia is the world's largest continent. It stretches from the Caucasus Mountains in the west to China, Japan, and the Philippine Islands in the east.

The **Himalaya** (him uh LAY uh) and neighboring mountains make up the heart of Asia. Many of the world's highest peaks are here, including the world's tallest—Mount Everest at 29,035 feet. The Himalaya, which means "abode of snow" in Sanskrit, forms the southern border of the vast Tibetan Plateau. This plateau is a high mountain plain where many of the continent's powerful rivers begin.

Asia also has many island nations. One of them, Japan, is an **archipelago** (ahr kuh PEL uh goh), or island chain, off the coast of Asia. As the map shows, the Philippines are another archipelago.

READING CHECK Where do many of Asia's most powerful rivers begin?

Asia: Physical

NATIONAL GEOGRAPHIC

- Winter monsoons
- Summer monsoons

0 400 800 miles
0 400 800 kilometers
Two-Point Equidistant Projection

Map Skill

What mountain ranges border the Gobi Desert to the east and northeast?

A CONTINENT OF CONTRASTS

The Himalaya and neighboring mountain ranges form a 1,500-mile wall that divides India and Nepal from Tibet and China. Many of its peaks are over 25,000 feet high. This barrier makes travel through the region difficult.

The Himalaya affects the climate of much of Asia. It blocks clouds that blow north from the Indian Ocean. This causes heavy rainfall on the ocean-facing sides of the mountains and small amounts on their northern sides. Even less rain falls in

the Gobi (GOH bee), a desert in northern China and Mongolia.

Seasonal Rains

Farmers need rain for their crops. However, most of South Asia's rain falls during only one season. The rest of the year remains dry. Rain clouds are brought to the region by seasonal winds called **monsoons**.

In India the months of November through May remain dry and, in May, intensely hot. During these months dry winter monsoons blow across South Asia from the northeast. From about June through October, however, moisture-bearing monsoons from the southeast and southwest sweep across the continent. These are the summer monsoons. Farmers welcome the monsoons' heavy sheets of rain that water their rice, sorghum, millet, and chickpeas, among other crops. However, if too much monsoon rain falls, it may lead to flooding and a loss of life and property. In 1887 monsoon rains caused the Huang He to flood and kill about a million people.

Facts About Asia

Total Land Area	16,992,000 sq. miles 44,009,00 sq. km
Highest Mountain	Mt Everest, Nepal 29,035 feet (8,850m)
Longest River	Chang River, China 3,915 miles (6,300 km)
Largest City	Tokyo, Japan Population 8,112,000
Current Population Percent of World Population	3,389,000,000 61%

Chart Skill

1. **About how many miles high is Mount Everest?**

2. **Which continent has the largest population?**

How do monsoons affect the climate of Asia?

READING CHECK

PUTTING IT TOGETHER

Asia is the world's largest continent, with a variety of climates, landforms, peoples, and histories. The Himalaya, the tallest mountains in the world, and other mountain ranges affect the climate of Asia. They block clouds blowing north from the Indian Ocean. As a result, large amounts of rain fall to the south of the mountains, while little falls to the north. Monsoons also affect Asia's climate. Farmers depend on the rains the monsoon winds bring, but the monsoon rains can be severe and cause flooding and destruction.

India's rain forests (above) receive heavy rainfall, while the Himalaya blocks rainfall in the Gobi Desert (left).

Review and Assess

1. Write a sentence for each vocabulary word.

   archipelago   monsoon

2. How is Japan different geographically from China and Korea?

3. What effect do the mountains of Asia have on the continent?

4. How does the rainy monsoon season affect the agricultural **economy** of South Asia?

5. What **generalization** can you make about how the geography of Asia affects the lives of the people who live there?

Look at the map on page 377. Identify five major rivers in Asia. Use an encyclopedia or other geographical reference source to create a table on which you list the rivers and some important facts about each, such as their lengths and the countries through which they flow.

Suppose that you were a newspaper reporter in China covering the 1887 flood. **Write** a short newspaper article in which you describe the rains and the destruction they caused.

379

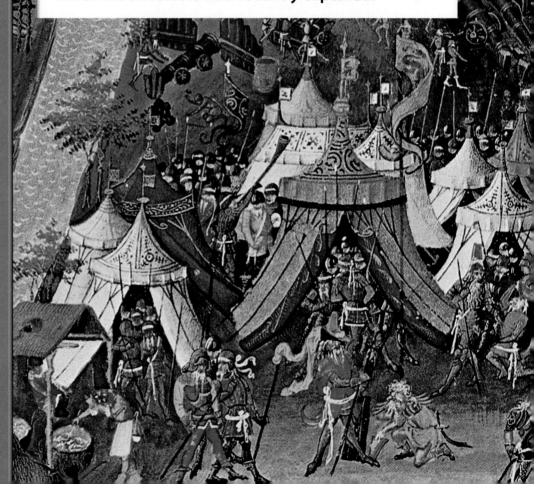

The Ottoman Empire

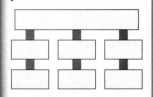
What was life like in the Ottoman Empire?

VOCABULARY

sultan
grand mufti

PEOPLE

Osman
Suleyman
Sinan

READING STRATEGY

Copy the chart below. Write this main idea: "Under Suleyman, the Ottoman Empire reached its peak." Write details from the lesson that support this main idea.

Lesson Outline

• A New Empire Begins
• Inside the Ottoman Empire
• The Empire Declines

BUILD BACKGROUND

"In Baghdad I am the shah [king], in Byzantine realms the caesar, and in Egypt the sultan; who sends his fleets to the seas of Europe, North Africa, and India."

This is how the ruler of one of the world's biggest empires described himself in the early 1500s. His capital was the city of Constantinople, which his ancestors had recently captured.

A NEW EMPIRE BEGINS

As you read earlier, the Byzantine Empire was the eastern half of the old Roman Empire. Although it ruled land in Europe, most of the empire lay in **Anatolia**, in what is today Turkey. Its capital was Constantinople, the city that Constantine made the Roman capital around A.D. 330. Many trade routes passed through this city, and it became wealthy and powerful. However, Constantinople was also in the path of many invaders. By the 1400s, it had become a small and weakened city-state.

In the 1300s, a group of people called Turks had become powerful in Central Asia. They were skilled in warfare, and they wanted Constantinople.

Osman the Conqueror

In 1301, various Turkish warriors united under a leader named **Osman** (OHZ mahn). Calling themselves "Osmanlis" they defeated the Byzantine armies and moved into Anatolia. In the next 150 years the "Osmanlis" became known as Ottomans, and their empire surrounded Constantinople.

Muhammad II

Muhammad II used cannons from Europe to conquer Constantinople in 1453 (left).

The Conquest of Constantinople

Constantinople was on a peninsula, which meant it was protected on three sides by the sea. In addition, it had the strongest walls in Europe. There were moats and ditches outside these walls. Even if an army could cross these ditches, it would have to break through massive stone walls to get inside the city. Defenders could shoot arrows and pour flaming oil from the tops of these walls.

In 1453, the Ottoman ruler was named Muhammad II. Although he was only 22 years old, he was determined to capture Constantinople. To do this, he used the newest and largest cannons in Europe. These cannons hurled half-ton cannonballs more than a mile against the walls of the city.

In the early hours of May 29, 1453, the Ottomans broke through the walls of Constantinople. Before the morning was over, Constantinople had fallen to the Ottomans.

The Byzantine Empire was no more. However, the new Ottoman Empire would be a force in Europe for the next four centuries.

 READING CHECK

Why were the Ottomans able to conquer Constantinople?

381

INSIDE THE OTTOMAN EMPIRE

Constantinople became the capital of the Ottoman Empire in 1453 and remained its capital and most important city until 1918. Today the city of Constantinople is called **Istanbul**, a Greek word meaning "in the city." It is still the largest city in Turkey.

During the 500 years of Ottoman rule, a **sultan**, or emperor, governed the empire. When he died, control of the empire passed to his oldest or favorite son. There were often power struggles before a new sultan won the throne.

The Ottomans were Muslims, and the Ottoman Empire was governed according to Islamic law, which is based on the Quran. A religious leader called a **grand mufti** interpreted the laws of Islam and applied them to life in the empire.

Suleyman the Magnificent

The Ottoman Empire reached its greatest power between 1520 and 1566 under a sultan named **Suleyman** (SOO lay mahn).

Suleyman's empire sprawled across three continents. It included North Africa, Palestine, Arabia, and Europe as far north as Hungary and Austria. Suleyman's armies were feared in Europe. His court was so rich and elegant that he was nicknamed Suleyman the Magnificent.

Trade and Ethnic Diversity

The ancient Romans used to boast "All roads lead to Rome." Similarly, Suleyman could have boasted that all routes in the Ottoman Empire led to Constantinople. Coffee flowed into the city's coffeehouses from southern Arabia. Ships from Egypt brought rice and gold. Butter, cheese, grain, and wheat, which helped feed the Ottoman army, were shipped across the Black Sea from present-day Ukraine, along with Russian furs.

Constantinople was a city of many religions and minorities. Ottoman rulers were tolerant of these differences. When the Jews were driven out of Spain in 1492, the sultan invited them to live in

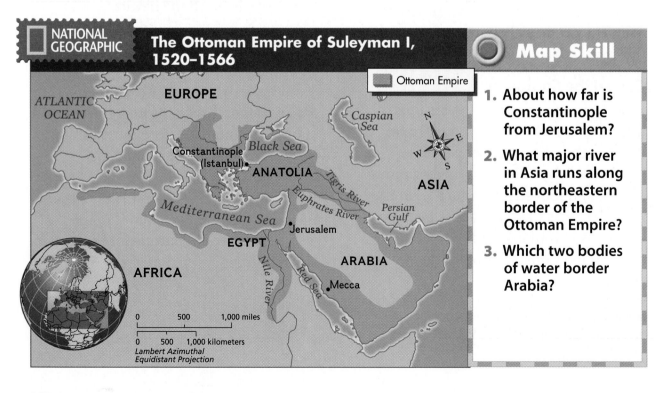

NATIONAL GEOGRAPHIC

The Ottoman Empire of Suleyman I, 1520–1566

Map Skill

Ottoman Empire

ATLANTIC OCEAN

EUROPE

Caspian Sea

Constantinople (Istanbul)

Black Sea

ANATOLIA

ASIA

Tigris River

Euphrates River

Persian Gulf

Mediterranean Sea

Jerusalem

EGYPT

ARABIA

Nile River

Red Sea

AFRICA

Mecca

0   500   1,000 miles

0   500   1,000 kilometers
Lambert Azimuthal
Equidistant Projection

1. **About how far is Constantinople from Jerusalem?**

2. **What major river in Asia runs along the northeastern border of the Ottoman Empire?**

3. **Which two bodies of water border Arabia?**

Suleyman's army marches into Europe.

became Suleyman's chief architect. He designed dozens of libraries, hospitals, and colleges. Sinan also built buildings for Suleyman's wife, Hurrem Sultan. Among these buildings were a school for orphans and a soup kitchen for the poor. Sinan's greatest achievement was the mosque he designed for Suleyman. The "Mosque of Suleyman," as it is called, still stands in the center of Istanbul. Renaissance architects were much influenced by his work.

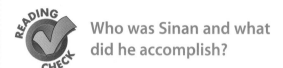 Who was Sinan and what did he accomplish?

his capital. Constantinople was also home to Greeks and Italians, who controlled the city's trade. Jews, Christians, and other non-Muslims paid higher taxes, but they were allowed to worship openly.

Enslaved people in the Ottoman Empire could gain positions of great power. For example, almost all of Suleyman's assistants, military commanders, and closest advisers were enslaved.

Every year government officials visited villages and towns throughout the empire. They selected non-Muslim boys who were at least 8 years old. These boys were sent to Constantinople to serve as slaves at the palace. Here the boys studied Islam and learned many jobs. Some became craftworkers, surgeons, or architects.

Sinan

One of these boys was **Sinan** (suh NAHN), the son of an Anatolian stoneworker. After years of training, he

Exploring ECONOMICS

Tulipmania

In the 1630s some Dutch merchants began to *speculate*. Speculate means to invest money in hopes of making a large profit quickly. The merchants almost ruined the Dutch economy, and they were speculating in tulips!

Tulips had come to the Netherlands from the Ottoman Empire and quickly became popular. Merchants began competing fiercely for the finest bulbs. Some speculators risked everything, paying as much as 50,000 dollars for a single tulip bulb. Prices shot up overnight.

Then tulips became more common. Prices dropped, and thousands of investors lost everything. The Dutch government stepped in to end "tulipmania."

Prepare a speech for your class. Explain why people pay more for rare or unusual items.

383

THE EMPIRE DECLINES

Suleyman lived in a palace called the Topkapi. It was a series of small palaces set in beautiful gardens and surrounded by a high wall. In many ways, it was the heart of the Ottoman Empire. In the vast outer courtyard of the palace merchants blended with thousands of guards, weavers, armor makers, horse tenders, and gardeners.

An inner courtyard had a beautiful walled-off garden and palace. The sultan lived and worked within these walls, along with his grand mufti, advisers, court musicians, painters, and poets.

After Suleyman's death in 1566, the power of the Ottoman Empire gradually weakened. Later sultans lost control of much of the empire's lands. By the 1800s,

Ottoman architects built Constantinople's Blue Mosque with its colorful, tiled interior.

the Ottoman Empire was so weak that it began to be called "the sick man of Europe." It ended in the early 1900s.

 Why did people begin to call the Ottoman Empire "the sick man of Europe" in the 1800s?

PUTTING IT TOGETHER

In the 1300s, a group of people called Turks emerged from Central Asia. Turkish warriors under a leader named Osman began to attack the weakened Byzantine Empire. In 1453, they finally conquered the Byzantines and established the Ottoman Empire. Over the next 400 years, the Ottoman Empire was a major power. The empire flourished under a ruler named Suleyman the Magnificent.

This elaborately decorated helmet is from the time of Suleyman.

Topkapi Sarayi Muzesi

Review and Assess

1. Write a sentence for each vocabulary term.
   grand mufti   sultan

2. Who was Osman and why was he an important figure in the history of the Ottoman Empire?

3. List at least two characteristics of life in the Ottoman Empire.

4. What geographic feature of Constantinople made it difficult to capture the city?

5. What fact about the Ottoman Empire supports the **generalization** that in order for an empire or a nation to flourish, it must be led by strong leaders?

Activities

Look at the map on page 382. Plan a tour across the territories of the Ottoman Empire. Use a modern map of the same region to list the countries that you would visit on your tour.

Write a travel brochure that describes the Topkapi Palace. Your brochure may include illustrations from your research and should list the outstanding features of the palace, as well as the treasures that are housed in it.

Lesson 3

China's Great Dynasties

What were the accomplishments of China's middle dynasties?

Lesson Outline
• The Tang Dynasty
• The Song Dynasty
• The Rise of the Ming
• Ming Accomplishments

VOCABULARY

Grand Canal
porcelain
Silk Road

PEOPLE

Wu Hou
Genghis Khan
Kublai Khan
Marco Polo
Zheng He

READING STRATEGY

Copy the main idea chart. Write details that support the main idea: "Kublai Khan was a powerful ruler."

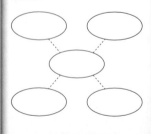

BUILD BACKGROUND

"The [Mongols] never remain fixed, but as the winter approaches remove to the plains of a warmer region, to find sufficient pasture. . . . Their huts or tents are formed of rods covered with felt, exactly round. . . . They live entirely upon flesh and milk."

A European named Marco Polo wrote this description in the 1200s. In this lesson, you will learn about how the Mongols influenced China.

THE TANG DYNASTY

After the fall of the Han dynasty in A.D. 220, which you read about in Chapter 5, China went through a period of unrest during which it was divided into several smaller kingdoms. A new dynasty reunited China in A.D. 578, but its rule was short-lived. The next dynasty, the Tang dynasty (618–907), expanded China's size and wealth. It was another golden age for China.

Under the Tang, China's borders reached as far west as Afghanistan and as far south as Vietnam and into Tibet. It also ended the invasions from the people of the northern steppes.

China became culturally diverse with Indians and western Asians living in China. Trade across Central Asia thrived. The arts also flourished. Many of China's stone Buddhas were carved at the time of the Tang. Poetry and philosophy flowered as well.

The government of China was stabilized and centralized. Agriculture production increased. Large government projects were undertaken, such as rebuilding the Great Wall. The **Grand Canal**, which connected the Huang and Chang rivers, had been built by a previous dynasty. The Tang repaired this canal and added to its length.

Buddhism in China developed a new form called Chan Buddhism, which emphasizes the relationship between a teacher and a pupil. Trade connections

The Tang dynasty of China was famous for pottery, such as this horse (opposite) and temple guardian.

helped to introduce Chan Buddhism into Japan, where it became known as Zen.

The Tang dynasty produced the only woman in Chinese history to take the title of emperor. She was **Wu Hou**. Later Tang rulers were less skilled. Arabs defeated Chinese armies on the western borders, and the people of the northern steppes invaded China again. In 907 the last Tang emperor was murdered, and China split into small kingdoms again.

READING CHECK

What were the achievements of the Tang dynasty?

387

THE SONG DYNASTY

The Song dynasty reunited China in 960, but the Song Empire was never as strong as the Tang had been. In spite of its weakness, Song China was a period of cultural and economic development. Chinese painting reached new heights under the Song dynasty. Artists produced elegant landscapes with tall mountains and rushing streams. Other painters focused on a single flower or tree branch. Painters stopped using bright colors and many sketched in black ink only.

Traditional Chinese society also developed during this period. These traditions survived even after the collapse of the Song dynasty.

Song China

Song China developed gunpowder and explosive weapons, as well as the abacus for counting. The use of currency, which had developed under the Tang, was expanded under the Song. Increasingly, cash replaced barter in payment for debt and in trade.

The government bureaucracy remained the surest way to advance in Chinese society, but Song prosperity encouraged mobility. People moved from farms to cities, and many merchant families prospered.

Port cities such as **Guangzhou** (GWAHNG JOO), or Canton, were centers of Chinese trade with other countries. China's bustling cities produced paintings, compasses, printed books, and a type of fine pottery called **porcelain**. The Chinese also designed and built the largest ships in the world.

The Song Dynasty Is Defeated

Invaders from the north took advantage of Song weakness. Invading forces defeated the Song in 1127. The Song were driven south, where they were able to keep control of central and southern China until 1279.

Song dynasty achievements included landscape paintings on silk (left) and the abacus (below) for quick mathematical calculations.

The Yüan Dynasty

The Mongols were a nomadic herding group from what is now Mongolia. In 1206, a Mongol leader named **Genghis Khan** (CHING gihs KAHN), a military and political genius, united the Mongol communities. He used fear of the powerful Mongol cavalry to force his enemies to surrender. By the time Genghis Khan died in 1227, he controlled most of northern China.

Kublai Khan

In 1252, Genghis Khan's grandson, **Kublai Khan** (KOO blī KAHN), invaded southern China. After 27 years, all of China surrendered to the Mongols, who established the Yüan dynasty.

Kublai Khan placed Mongols in charge of China's government bureaucracy. He also improved Chinese paper money that he made into a nationwide system of cur-

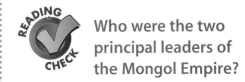

Genghis Khan

rency. His paper money was widely accepted. Eight pounds of coins could be replaced by one paper note. Kublai Khan supported Confucianism, and he left Chinese local leaders in power.

Kublai Khan directed the expansion of the Grand Canal to connect the new capital city, **Beijing** (BAY JING), with cities over 1,000 miles to the south. Kublai Khan had his army patrol the **Silk Road**, the ancient trade route connecting Asia with Europe. It was along the Silk Road that an Italian named **Marco Polo** made his way to China. When Polo's adventures were written down, Europeans were astonished by his tales of the riches of China.

READING CHECK Who were the two principal leaders of the Mongol Empire?

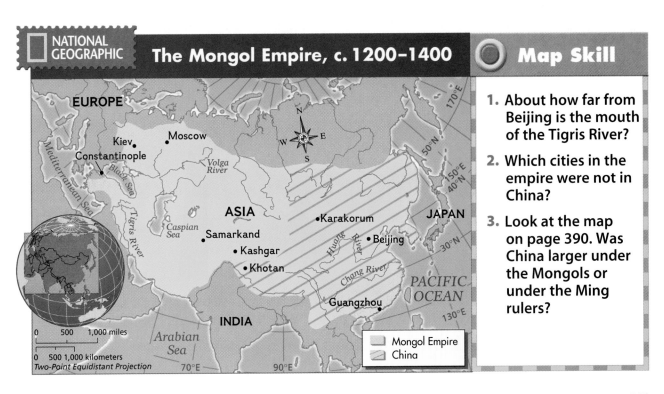

NATIONAL GEOGRAPHIC

The Mongol Empire, c. 1200–1400

Map Skill

EUROPE

Kiev
Moscow
Constantinople
Volga River
Black Sea
Mediterranean Sea
Tigris River
Caspian Sea
ASIA
Samarkand
Kashgar
Khotan
Karakorum
JAPAN
Beijing
Huang River
Chang River
Guangzhou
PACIFIC OCEAN
INDIA
Arabian Sea

0 500 1,000 miles
0 500 1,000 kilometers
Two-Point Equidistant Projection
70°E   90°E   130°E   170°E   50°N   40°N   30°N   150°E

Mongol Empire
China

1. **About how far from Beijing is the mouth of the Tigris River?**

2. **Which cities in the empire were not in China?**

3. **Look at the map on page 390. Was China larger under the Mongols or under the Ming rulers?**

THE RISE OF THE MING

After Kublai Khan's death in 1294, Mongol control over China began to weaken. Floods along the Huang He, famine, and disease added to the country's distress. In 1368, the Mongol rulers were driven out by rebel Chinese forces. They were replaced by the Ming dynasty, which would bring prosperity to China.

The Voyages of Zheng He

In 1405, the Ming admiral **Zheng He** (CHENG HO) was sent on the first of seven voyages of exploration. Zheng He's fleet was enormous. He had over 60 ships, the largest of which was about 400 feet long. His ships carried about 28,000 soldiers and sailors. Cannon, war rockets, and crossbows made his fleet a powerful force.

Zheng He, a Muslim, stopped in Arabia to make the pilgrimage to Mecca. Later his fleet reached East Africa. He brought back many rare and wonderful things, such as animals from Africa and spices from India.

The Forbidden City

The Ming ruled from a walled area of palaces and temples in Beijing called the **Forbidden City**. Common people and foreigners were forbidden to enter this walled area without special permission. Between 1417 and 1420, nearly one million people worked on the 1,000 palaces, libraries, temples, and gardens.

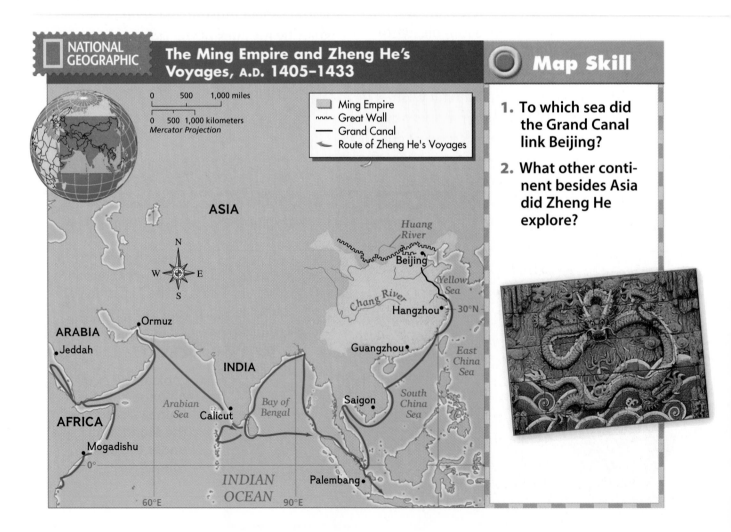

NATIONAL GEOGRAPHIC

The Ming Empire and Zheng He's Voyages, A.D. 1405–1433

0 500 1,000 miles
0 500 1,000 kilometers
Mercator Projection

- Ming Empire
- ~~~ Great Wall
- —— Grand Canal
- ← Route of Zheng He's Voyages

ASIA

Huang River
Beijing
Yellow Sea
Hangzhou
30°N
Chang River
Guangzhou
East China Sea
Saigon
South China Sea
ARABIA
Ormuz
Jeddah
INDIA
Arabian Sea
Calicut
Bay of Bengal
AFRICA
Mogadishu
0°
Palembang
INDIAN OCEAN
60°E   90°E

Map Skill

1. To which sea did the Grand Canal link Beijing?

2. What other continent besides Asia did Zheng He explore?

The Forbidden City in Beijing was decorated with mythic designs (above left).

Turning Inward

Zheng He's voyages had made China a great sea power. Sixteen nations were so impressed by Zheng's fleet that they sent tribute to the Chinese government. European merchants were eager to obtain more porcelain, silks, and other Chinese luxuries.

The emperor who sponsored Zheng He's voyages died in 1424. After his death, a group of Confucian scholars took power in the Forbidden City. These scholars thought China should look inward, not outward. The Chinese government took over China's trade. These officials closed China to foreigners and carefully regulated trade to prevent foreign influence from reaching the Chinese people.

The Ming Decline

Later Ming emperors worried about Mongol invaders. They strengthened and extended the Great Wall, begun by Shihuangdi almost 2,000 years earlier.

The Great Wall was expensive. The Ming abandoned shipbuilding and lost interest in voyages of exploration. China's attention was turned inward for the next few centuries.

By 1600 the Ming dynasty had become weak and corrupt. Taxes were raised to finance the luxurious life of the emperor's court. Several bad harvests caused millions to starve. Rebellions and riots undermined the Ming government.

 READING CHECK

What was the purpose of the voyages of Zheng He?

MING ACCOMPLISHMENTS

Crafts flourished under the Ming. Before the Chinese closed themselves off from the rest of the world, traders came to China from Europe, Africa, and the Middle East for the luxury wares that Ming workshops produced. One of China's most famous exports was porcelain. Thousands of porcelain workshops produced blue-and-white dishes that became world-famous. The secret of producing this special porcelain was closely guarded.

The Ming government also controlled the silk workshops. In those shops, women and children worked to produce valuable silk cloth. Many of these luxury products went to the Ming rulers in the Forbidden City. Others were transported along the Silk Road or shipped to Europe from ports such as Guangzhou. European merchants were eager to trade for the products of China's luxury workshops. One European visitor described the eating customs he saw while in Ming China:

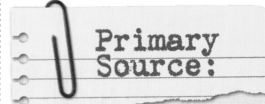

Primary Source:

excerpt from A Spanish Diplomat Visits China, 1575

The principal food of all Chinese is rice, for although they have wheat and sell bread kneaded therefrom, yet they do not eat it save as if it were a fruit. Their chief bread [grain] is cooked rice.... They eat seated at tables, but they do not use table-cloths or napkins; for they do not touch with their fingers anything that they are going to eat, but they pick up everything with two long [little] sticks....

What surprised the writer about the way the Chinese ate?

Ming craftworkers created elegant silk robes and beautiful porcelain (below).

Fogg Art Museum, Harvard University

Agriculture is Favored

In spite of its busy ports and booming workshops, China did not become a nation of large industries. The whole idea of trade offended the Confucian scholars who ruled the Ming court. They felt that merchants profited from "foreigners and robbery." The Chinese economy also favored agriculture. The Ming tax system rewarded farmers and punished merchants.

The Ming dynasty was overthrown in 1644 by the Manchu, a people from eastern China. The new dynasty, the Qing, would rule China until 1911.

Why did the Ming dynasty shut China off from foreigners?

PUTTING IT TOGETHER

From the 600s to the 1100s, China developed paper currency, cannons, advanced compasses, and powerful ships. During the 1200s Mongol invaders conquered China and built a vast empire.

In 1368 the Ming dynasty ended Mongol rule. Chinese ships sailed as far as Africa, increasing China's prestige. Later Ming rulers ended Chinese contact with the outside world.

This jeweled crown is from the Ming period.

Review and Assess

1. Write a sentence for each vocabulary term.

   **Grand Canal   Silk Road
   porcelain**

2. What was the Forbidden City?

3. What were some achievements of the Tang, Song, Yüan, and Ming dynasties?

4. What technologies were invented in China between 700 and 1600?

5. What **generalization** can you make about Ming China?

Use an encyclopedia and other references to learn more about the Silk Road. Then photocopy a map of Asia and draw the route of the Silk Road in color.

Suppose you live in a port visited by Zheng He's fleet. **Write** a journal entry about your experience.

The Mughal Empire

Find out! How did Mughal rule affect India?

Lesson Outline
- The Mughals Conquer India
- Akbar and His Empire
- Mughal India

VOCABULARY

shah

PEOPLE
Tamerlane
Babur
Akbar
Shah Jahan
Mumtaz Mahal

READING STRATEGY

Copy the chart. Label one column "Akbar" and the other "Shah Jahan." List the major achievements of each ruler in his column.

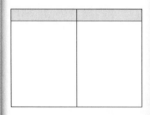

BUILD BACKGROUND

A terrifying army swept out of the deserts north of India. They were led by Timur-leng, sometimes called **Tamerlane**, a warlord who delighted in war and loot. The armies of the Muslim rulers of India were defeated easily. Their capital at Delhi was destroyed so completely that "for two months, not a bird moved in the city."

At this dark moment in Indian history, a new leader arose. He would create India's greatest empire, the Mughal Empire.

Taj Mahal

800	900	1000	1100	1200	1300	1400	1500	1600	1700	1800

You Are Here
1526 – 1700

THE MUGHALS CONQUER INDIA

The Hindu rulers of India were challenged by the rise of Islam. By A.D. 1200, most of the Indus plain had come under Muslim control. The new Islamic rulers, called sultans, ruled from **Delhi**, a city in northern India.

The Delhi Sultans

Hindus had to pay a special tax, which cost ordinary workers as much as a month's wages. Moreover, Hindus were forbidden to build temples. These rules caused anger and resistance among the conquered Hindu population.

The Delhi sultans were defeated by Tamerlane in 1398, and their empire broke up into many semi-independent kingdoms. From one of these kingdoms, in what is now Uzbekistan, came a man named **Babur** (BAH boor). Babur claimed to be descended from Genghis Khan and Tamerlane.

Babur led his followers, called the Mughals, into the Indus Valley in 1526. Within three years the Mughals controlled much of northern India. Babur had created the Mughal Empire.

Mughal India

Babur wrote long letters and journals about his daily life. We know that he was a strong and wise ruler. Sadly, his son, Humayun, was a weak and foolish ruler who lost most of Babur's empire.

In fact, Humayun and his family were driven into hiding to escape their enemies. During that time a son was born.

They named the infant **Akbar**, an Arabic word meaning "great." Akbar was an appropriate name for this child because he grew up to become the greatest ruler of Mughal India.

READING CHECK How do you think Babur changed the way India was ruled?

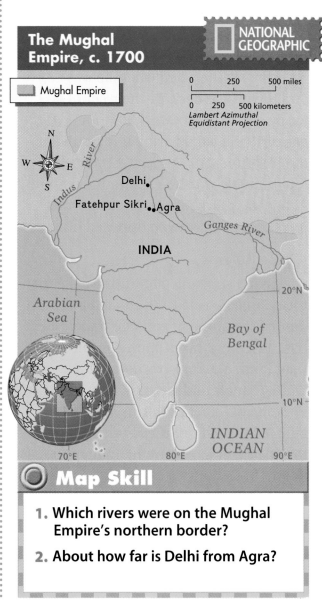

The Mughal Empire, c. 1700

NATIONAL GEOGRAPHIC

Mughal Empire

0 250 500 miles
0 250 500 kilometers
Lambert Azimuthal Equidistant Projection

Indus River
Delhi
Fatehpur Sikri
Agra
Ganges River
INDIA
Arabian Sea
Bay of Bengal
20°N
10°N
INDIAN OCEAN
70°E 80°E 90°E

Map Skill

1. **Which rivers were on the Mughal Empire's northern border?**

2. **About how far is Delhi from Agra?**

AKBAR AND HIS EMPIRE

Akbar's father died when he was 13, and the prince became the ruler of a weak and war-torn Mughal Empire. At the age of 19, he led an army into battle for the first time. For the next 43 years, he fought many wars to expand the empire. Akbar was a brilliant general who was merciless to those who opposed him.

A Wise Ruler

Akbar also worked to improve life for the people he ruled. He created a central money system to encourage trade. He based farmers' taxes on the fertility of their land. Akbar also ordered the digging of new canals and wells.

Some of Akbar's reforms greatly affected the lives of the Hindus, who formed the majority of the Indian population. In fact, his tolerance of all religions created a remarkable period of unity and power.

A Time of Tolerance

Akbar married the daughter of an important Hindu leader. The young emperor then brought his wife's father and other Hindus to his capital city of Agra. For the first time, Hindus became top officials in a Muslim-led government.

In 1579 the emperor ended the tax that former Muslim rulers had forced all non-Muslims to pay. Akbar also allowed Hindus to build temples again. The emperor wanted Hindus to be treated fairly under Mughal law.

Akbar himself had a strong interest in other religions. His palace had a separate building where Muslims, Hindus, Christians, Jews, and leaders of other religions could meet and explain their beliefs. It is said that Akbar would pace back and forth on walkways over the hall, listening to the discussions below him. He would even toss out occasional questions that sparked heated debates.

Akbar and the Arts

In addition to listening to debates, Akbar learned from books in his library. The library included special translations of Hindu, Persian, Arabic, and Greek classics. Since he could not read, Akbar had someone read to him every day. His extraordinary memory helped him to remember what he heard.

Akbar also loved the beauty of arts and crafts. He spent great sums to bring Asia's best painters, poets, musicians, and craftworkers to his palace. During the day he often visited the palace's 100 workshops, where experts made carpets, curtains, weapons, jewelry, and paintings, among other things. It was not uncommon to see the emperor himself hammering iron, shaving camel hair, or discussing painting. At night musicians played for him, and sometimes he joined in by playing the drums.

A New Capital

Akbar did not want to live in the old Muslim capital of Delhi. He moved his court to Agra. Later, he built a second and even more spectacular capital city at **Fatehpur Sikri**. The source of water for the new city dried up, and his capital returned to Agra in 1586. Today, Fatehpur Sikri is a perfectly preserved museum of Mughal art and architecture.

When Akbar died in 1605 at the age of 63, his empire was one of the wealthiest and most powerful in the world at that time. Akbar's grandson, **Shah Jahan**

(SHAH juh HAHN), ruled the Mughal Empire from 1628 to 1658. **Shah** is a Persian word that means "emperor." Shah Jahan's name meant "Emperor of the World." He was well named. Visitors called him "the Great Mughal" because of the brilliance of his court.

READING CHECK In what ways did Akbar improve conditions for the Hindus under his rule?

Among the many beautifully crafted Mughal items were jeweled pendants (left) and paintings on ivory (below).

397

MUGHAL INDIA

Shah Jahan was a powerful ruler who expanded the Mughal Empire, but he is more famous as a patron of craftworkers and artists. He ordered a Peacock Throne made from solid gold and covered with jewels. It cost twice as much as the palace of Akbar in which Shah Jahan sat!

The Taj Mahal

Shah Jahan had a favorite wife named **Mumtaz Mahal** (mum TAHZ mah HAHL), or "Chosen One of the Palace." Mumtaz Mahal died during childbirth in 1631. The grief-stricken emperor ordered a spectacular tomb for her in Agra. No expense was spared. It took more than 20 years to complete, but the Taj Mahal remains one of the most beautiful buildings in the world.

The white marble dome of the Taj Mahal soars nearly 200 feet above the ground. Sentences from the Quran are carved elegantly over each gateway. They describe the Muslim paradise. In this way the Taj Mahal honors Mumtaz Mahal and her husband, and also the beliefs of Islam.

Indian Trade Thrives

One reason Shah Jahan could afford to spend so much on his projects was the booming Indian trade. India's cotton fabric clothed people in Asia, Africa, and even Europe. Merchants from Portugal, England, and the Netherlands came to trade for Indian spices and silks. Such trade made the Mughal Empire rich.

Shah Jahan (left) built the Taj Mahal in memory of his wife, Mumtaz Mahal (far left). Visitors from Europe were treated to the luxury of the Mughal Empire (below).

The Decline of the Mughals

What the Europeans did not realize was that Shah Jahan was to be the last of the great Mughal rulers. Even as he lay dying, he saw his sons battling for control of his empire. The son who succeeded Jahan restored the tax paid by Hindus and destroyed Hindu temples. Many of the Mughals' Hindu subjects rebelled. Over time, the Mughal Empire was reduced to the area around Delhi. The weakness of the declining empire allowed Europeans to begin their takeover of India.

 Why did Shah Jahan build the Taj Mahal?

PUTTING IT TOGETHER

In 1200, the Delhi sultans were attacked by Tamerlane, and their empire broke up into smaller Muslim and Hindu kingdoms. In the 1500s, a Muslim from the north, Babur, established an empire in India that became known as the

Many Mughal carpets have a patterned border, trees, and flowers.

Mughal Empire. Babur's grandson, Akbar, strengthened and expanded the empire. Akbar was a wise and tolerant ruler who freed Hindus from the taxes placed on them by the Delhi sultans. Akbar's grandson, Shah Jahan, was known as the Great Mughal because of his luxurious life and elegant palaces and monuments, including the Taj Mahal.

Review and Assess

1. Write one sentence for the vocabulary word.

   shah

2. How did Akbar improve the lives of his Hindu subjects?

3. What were some features of Mughal rule in India?

4. How did Akbar's rule help promote good **citizenship** among his people?

5. Why did Akbar make the **decision** to create a central money system?

Compare the map on page 395 to a map of south Asia today. Make a list of modern nations with land that was once part of the Mughal Empire.

Suppose you were a Hindu living in Babur's empire. **Write** a letter to Babur respectfully protesting the restrictions and special laws against Hindus.

399

Feudal Japan

 **What was life like in feudal Japan?**

Lesson Outline
• The Land of Japan
• Emperor, Shogun, and Daimyo
• Life in the Shogunate

VOCABULARY

Shinto
daimyo
samurai
shogun

PEOPLE

Minamoto
  Yoritomo
Tokugawa Ieyasu
Lady Murasaki
  Shikibu

READING STRATEGY

Copy the chart below. Write: "Japanese Feudal Society" in the top box. Under it, write the groups of Japanese society in order of importance.

BUILD BACKGROUND

"Nothing is so important in a warrior as loyalty," wrote a Japanese soldier in the 1400s. His words describe a way of life for many Japanese for about 700 years.

 Feudal Japanese soldiers wore elaborate and colorful armor.

THE LAND OF JAPAN

As you have read, Japan is made up of a group of islands off the coast of mainland Asia. The four main islands of Japan form a 1,300-mile-long chain. These islands are very mountainous, with little land suitable for farming and few mineral resources.

The Japanese originally came to Japan from mainland Asia thousands of years ago. Its location close to the Korean Peninsula had great influence on Japan. From earliest times, Chinese and Korean ideas flowed from the Asian continent into the Japanese islands.

By the A.D. 500s, Japan had absorbed many elements of Chinese and Korean civilization, such as rice growing, Buddhism, Confucianism, the Chinese writing system, Chinese art, and the system of government.

The Japanese blended these ideas into its own developed culture. One important part of that culture was their religion, **Shinto** (SHIN toh), which means "the way of the gods." According to Shinto belief, everything in nature, including crops like rice, has a spirit of its own. To insure good harvests, Japanese farmers offered prayers before both planting and harvesting. Shintoists also believe Japan's emperor is descended from their sun goddess.

READING CHECK What is Shinto?

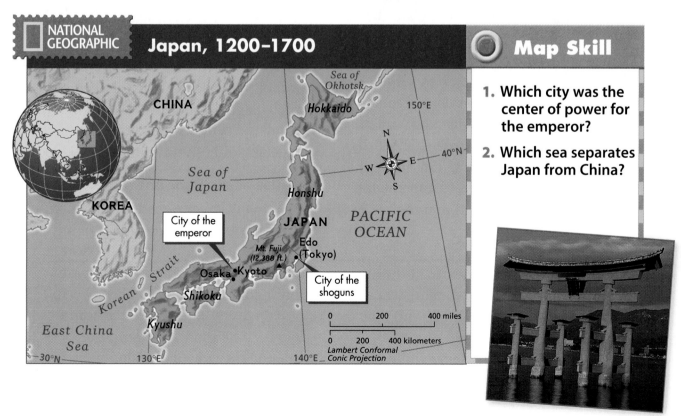

NATIONAL GEOGRAPHIC

Japan, 1200–1700

Map Skill

1. **Which city was the center of power for the emperor?**

2. **Which sea separates Japan from China?**

Sea of Okhotsk

CHINA

Hokkaido

150°E

40°N

Sea of Japan

Honshu

KOREA

City of the emperor

JAPAN

PACIFIC OCEAN

Mt. Fuji
(12,388 ft.)

Edo
(Tokyo)

Osaka • Kyoto

City of the shoguns

Shikoku

Kyushu

0   200   400 miles

0   200   400 kilometers
Lambert Conformal
Conic Projection

East China Sea

30°N

130°E

140°E

Korean Strait

401

EMPEROR, SHOGUN, AND DAIMYO

The emperor was the ruler of Japan and held a special place in Japanese society. However, Japan also had several very powerful families who fought for control.

Daimyos and Shoguns

Each family was headed by a **daimyo** (Dī mee yoh), who controlled large areas of land. In fact, life in Japan was very much like life in Europe under the feudal system. Lords controlled the land, which was worked by peasant farmers. The lords had soldiers called **samurai** (SA moo rī), who fought for the lord and protected his land. The samurai believed that their most important duty was to be loyal.

Although lords held great power in their regions, they were vassals of the **shogun** (SHOH guhn), or military leader of Japan. The shogun, his lords, and their samurai formed the upper part of the social pyramid of Japan. Below this ruling class were the farmers, craftworkers, and

Japan's feudal rulers enjoyed performances of traditional drama.

merchants. They were non-noble and had to show absolute obedience and respect to those above them in the social pyramid. Whenever a lord and his samurai passed through a village, for example, servants ran ahead calling for everyone in the village to fall face down on the ground as a symbol of their respect. Those who did not do so might be killed.

The Rise of the Shogun

Originally, the government of Japan had resembled the government of imperial China. In 1192, the Japanese system of government changed. The emperor appointed the first shogun, a powerful daimyo named **Minamoto Yoritomo** (yawr ee TOH moh). The emperor remained the spiritual leader of Japan, but the shogun became the actual ruler.

Tokugawa Ieyasu

The shogun was head of a military government, the shogunate, which lasted over 250 years. By 1467, the power of the shogun had weakened and a civil war allowed local daimyo to gain power. In 1590 Toyotomi Hideyoshi defeated the local daimyo and established a strong central government. Hideyoshi took the weapons away from everyone but the samurai. He also ordered a census of Japan and forbade people to change their jobs without permission.

Tokugawa Ieyasu (toh koo GAH wah ee yeh YAH soo) became shogun in 1603. He began the Tokugawa Shogunate. Under the Tokugawa family, Japan became unified and remained at peace for over 200 years.

Tokugawa Rule

The Tokugawa remained the unchallenged masters of Japan. They reorganized the entire structure of Japanese society. Daimyo supervised local government in Japan, especially tax collecting, and daimyo who opposed the shogun lost their lands.

All daimyo and samurai were required to live in **Edo** (ED oh), which is called Tokyo today.

Samurai wore elaborate armor (right) in the period of Tokugawa Ieyasu (far right).

Here Tokugawa could keep his eye on them. The daimyo could return to their own lands every two years, but their wives and families remained in Edo to insure the daimyo's return.

READING CHECK What was the shogunate?

Japanese drama (left), sometimes performed with masks (opposite), became popular under the shogunate.

LIFE IN THE SHOGUNATE

The Tokugawa shoguns invented elaborate rules. Daimyo had to give expensive gifts to the shoguns and wear expensive costumes at court. These rules were designed to force daimyo to spend so much money that they would not be able to afford a war against the shogun.

Two Capitals

The Tokugawa shoguns ruled from Edo. However, the emperor continued to live in Japan's old capital at **Kyoto** (KYOH toh). The shoguns built a 300-mile road to connect the two capitals. This road was crowded with servants of the shogun carrying messages to and from the emperor. Merchants as well as lords also used this road.

Edo grew rapidly. More than 200 lords and their families had to move into large homes along with thousands of their servants. At the same time, the children of farmers were coming to the city to seek work as servants or laborers.

The wealth in the city also encouraged new forms of art and entertainment. Actors performed a new kind of popular theater called kabuki (kuh BOO kih). Popular plots involved love, samurai adventures, and the conflict between duty and freedom.

Bookmakers created new books and reprinted classics such as *The Tale of Genji* (GEN JEE) by **Lady Murasaki Shikibu**. The main character, Genji, was a prince who searched for happiness. Written around A.D. 1000, this is considered to be the world's first novel.

The Japanese tea ceremony, *chado*, also developed at this time, as did print-making and flower arranging.

Japan Closes to Foreigners

The Portuguese arrived in the 1500s, which led to an increase in Japan's foreign trade. In 1635, Shogun Tokugawa Iemitsu decided to end foreign influence in Japan. He ordered,

> *Japanese ships are forbidden to leave for foreign countries. . . . No Japanese is permitted to go abroad. If there is anyone who attempts to do so secretly, he must be executed.*

Japan remained closed to the rest of the world for over 200 years.

 READING CHECK What were some cultural developments during the Tokugawa period?

PUTTING IT TOGETHER

Japan is a chain of islands over 1,300 miles in length. Japan is mountainous, and much of its land is poorly suited to rice farming.

At the top of the Japanese social pyramid were the rulers and the great lords and their soldiers. At the bottom were the majority of the population, artisans, merchants, and farmers.

Japan under the shogun was generally peaceful and prosperous. Many new cultural forms were developed, including new types of theater and the tea ceremony. In 1635 the shogun decided to end foreign influence in Japan. Travel to and from Japan was forbidden for over 200 years.

Review and Assess

1. Write a sentence for each vocabulary word.

   daimyo   **Shinto**
   samurai   **shogun**

2. What is Lady Murasaki Shikibu best known for doing?

3. Describe life in Japan under the Tokugawa Shogunate.

4. How did Japan's geographic location affect its history?

5. Make a **generalization** about the samurai under the shogunate.

Use the map on page 401 to identify the four main islands of Japan. Then consult an encyclopedia and an atlas to help create a table. List the names of the islands and important facts about each, such as size, population, cities, and geographic landmarks.

• •

Write a *haiku*, which is a traditional Japanese poem. It has three lines and 17 syllables. The first line has five syllables. The remaining 12 syllables are in the next two lines. A haiku describes how the writer feels about something in nature. Share your poem with your class.

Using Software

In the last lesson, you learned about the history and culture of feudal Japan. Suppose you wanted to learn more about the life of a samurai, the Japanese tea ceremony, or see a map of Japan in the 1600s.

You can go to the library, search the Internet, or use a **software** program. Software is a set of instructions that tells a computer what to do. You can use software to perform simple or complex tasks on a computer. For instance, software can direct the computer to display an article on Japanese martial arts or to play Japanese flute music. It can help you to make a map of Japan or to build a three-dimensional model of a Japanese house.

VOCABULARY

software

icon

menu

LEARN THE SKILL

To use software, it can help to follow the steps below:

1. **Decide whether this software will help you.**
   Be sure to choose the right software. If you are writing a report on the tea ceremony, a program that draws maps would not be useful. A word processing program would help more.

2. **Start the program.**
   To start most software programs, use your mouse to click on the program's **icon** on the computer screen. An icon is a symbol that stands for something else. Or, you can select the program from a **menu** in the computer. A menu is a list of choices.

3. **Look for menu choices.**
   Most software will give you a menu. For instance, the "file" selection in many programs will help you open a file to begin a new job, to print your work, and to save your work. If you have questions, use the "help" feature and follow the instructions.

4. **Experiment.**
   Don't be afraid to experiment with software. Many programs have an "undo" feature that lets you take back a mistake.

5. **Perform the task.**
   Once you feel confident, you can begin to work. Be sure to save your work.

TRY THE SKILL

Your teacher will give you an assignment. Use the software on your classroom computer, a computer in the library, or your computer at home to perform this task.

1. What software did you choose to do this job?

2. Did you click on a computer icon or choose a program from the menu?

3. How did you learn to use these features?

4. How can software help you with your schoolwork?

EXTEND THE SKILL

People use software every day for a variety of tasks. Even the textbook you are reading was designed using software. In the future, computers will be used for more and more tasks.

Choose a topic about Japan. Use a software program to create a project on your topic.

● What topic did you choose?

● What software did you choose to do the job?

● Why is knowing how to use software important?

Japanese tea ceremony
Project by Anita Cruz

Lesson **6**

Southeast Asian Kingdoms

VOCABULARY

complex

PEOPLE

Jayavarman II
Suryavarman II

READING STRATEGY

Make a chart like this one. In one circle write features of Angkor Wat. Write features of Angkor Thom in the other circle. Write features the two temples share in the intersection of the two circles.

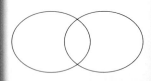

Find Out!

What cultures influenced the Khmer kingdom?

Lesson Outline
• A Great River Kingdom
• A Brilliant Capital

BUILD BACKGROUND

"The great stone temple walls enclose an area larger than two of Europe's countries. . . . At the center, five towers shaped like the buds of water lilies rise into the air. On the first day of spring, visitors standing at the temple's west gate see the sun rise directly over the highest tower."

This temple is called **Angkor Wat** (ANG kawr WAHT). Today it is a tourist attraction in Cambodia. Some 700 years ago, however, it was the center of a great kingdom in Southeast Asia.

A GREAT RIVER KINGDOM

About 2,000 years ago merchants from India visited ports on the peninsula of Southeast Asia. Some stopped at the mouth of the **Mekong** (MAY KAHNG) River. They brought Indian traditions of Hinduism and Buddhism to Southeast Asia. Chinese merchants and diplomats also came to the peninsula. As a result, Indian and Chinese traditions blended.

The Khmer Kingdom

The Mekong River provides water and silt to farmers of Southeast Asia. During the monsoon rains, the Mekong floods. There is so much rainwater that part of the river flows backward into **Tonle Sap** (tahn LAY SAP) or "Great Lake." Locate the Mekong River on the map.

A kingdom rose along the shores of the Mekong River about 1,200 years ago. This was called the Khmer (kuh MER) kingdom. It began in what is now Cambodia. For centuries, Khmer farmers along the Mekong River and Tonle Sap grew large crops of rice.

Like many farmers in ancient Egypt and medieval Europe, Khmer farmers often worked land they did not own. The land was owned by religious groups or government officials.

Much of the food surplus went to the Khmer king. The Khmer believed that their leader was a living god. One Khmer king, **Jayavarman II** (jah yah VAHR mahn), ruled in the 800s. He claimed to be a human form of the Hindu god Shiva.

Kings judged disputes and led their troops in war. In addition, kings built reservoirs, canals, and roads. Reservoirs held monsoon waters for use throughout the year. Canals brought water to the fields.

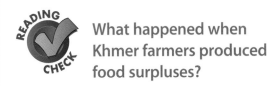 **What happened when Khmer farmers produced food surpluses?**

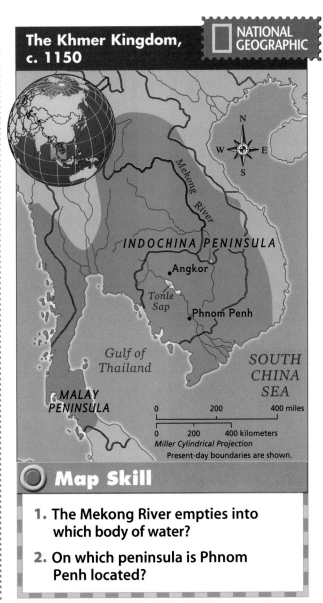

The Khmer Kingdom, c. 1150

NATIONAL GEOGRAPHIC

INDOCHINA PENINSULA

Mekong River

Angkor

Tonle Sap

Phnom Penh

Gulf of Thailand

MALAY PENINSULA

SOUTH CHINA SEA

0   200   400 miles
0   200   400 kilometers
Miller Cylindrical Projection
Present-day boundaries are shown.

Map Skill

1. The Mekong River empties into which body of water?

2. On which peninsula is Phnom Penh located?

409

A BRILLIANT CAPITAL

Between 800 and 1200, Khmer armies expanded the borders of the kingdom into present-day Vietnam, Laos, and Thailand. This expansion made the kingdom rich. In the early 1100s the Khmer king was **Suryavarman II** (sur yuh VAHR mun). He used a large part of his wealth to build a temple **complex**, or group of different buildings, in his capital city at **Angkor**, on the north shore of Tonle Sap. Angkor means "holy city" in the Khmer language.

Angkor Wat, one of the world's great architectural creations, covers about a square mile. It is dedicated to the Hindu god Vishnu. On the walls are carved Hindu stories of the world's creation and death. It was also used as an astronomical observatory.

Another Temple Complex

One of the boys who watched Angkor Wat being built was the Khmer king's great-grandson, the future Jayavarman VII. When he became king in 1181, Jayavarman VII set out to create an even grander temple complex than Angkor Wat. He built Angkor Thom (ANG kawr TAWM). In 1296, a Chinese diplomat visited the temple. He wrote this description:

> The . . . walls are approximately 2.5 miles in circumference. They have five gateways and each gate is a double one. On the outer side of the wall is a great moat [a water-filled trench]. On either side of the moat's bridges are 54 stone gods like "stone generals"; they are gigantic and terrible to look at.

Buddhism had replaced Hinduism as the main religion of Cambodia by the reign of Jayavarman VII. Because the king was a Buddhist, the new temple honored Buddhist, rather than Hindu, beliefs. In the center of the complex stood a huge temple with dozens of carved stone heads. The heads are said to resemble Jayavarman VII himself.

Angkor Thom includes delicately carved towers up to 75 feet high. Rows of stone figures (opposite) line the paths of the Angkor Thom temple complex.

The End of the Empire

The great building projects of Angkor Wat and Angkor Thom exhausted Khmer resources. So did the constant wars that Khmer kings waged against neighboring kingdoms. Their strongest enemies were kingdoms in what are today Vietnam and Thailand. Jayavarman VII won control over both kingdoms, but they broke free of Khmer rule after his death. In the 1430s, Thai soldiers captured and looted Angkor itself. The city was abandoned shortly thereafter.

Khmer rulers moved their capital to a site farther south on the Mekong. Later the kingdom would become known as Kampuja. The capital, **Phnom Penh** (puh NOM PEN), remains Cambodia's capital city today.

Which religion did the temple at Angkor Thom honor?

PUTTING IT TOGETHER

The Khmer kingdom of Southeast Asia emerged along the Mekong River in what is today the country of Cambodia. The kingdom was located along major shipping routes between India and China. Indian and Chinese traditions became part of Khmer life.

Khmer kings were considered to be living gods who deserved great power and respect. At its height, the Khmer kingdom won control over much of the Indochinese peninsula. In the 1100s and 1200s, Khmer kings ordered the construction of great buildings and temples at Angkor.

Review and Assess

1. Write one sentence for the vocabulary word.
   complex

2. What happened as a result of the building of the grand temples at Angkor?

3. What cultures affected Khmer society? Why did these cultural effects occur?

4. Along what geographic feature did the Khmer kingdom develop?

5. Why did Jayavarman VII **make the decision** to build a new temple at Angkor Thom?

Photocopy the map on page 409. Use an encyclopedia or atlas to learn the names of the modern countries on the southeast Asian peninsula. Write the names of the countries and their capitals on your map.

• •

Research and **write** a short report on the current condition of the temples at Angkor in Cambodia. List the problems the ruins face and what conservationists are doing to preserve them.

411

VOCABULARY REVIEW

Number a sheet of paper from 1 to 5. Decide whether the underlined vocabulary word makes the sentence true or false. If the statement is true, write T. If the statement is false, write F, and then write the word that makes the statement true.

archipelago	**Silk Road**
shah	**sultan**
shogun	

1. The ruler of the Ottoman Empire was the <u>shah</u>.
2. One <u>Silk Road</u> is an island chain off the coast of Asia.
3. A <u>shogun</u> was the military dictator in Japan.
4. <u>Sultan</u> is a Persian word meaning "emperor."
5. The <u>archipelago</u> was a trading route connecting China with Europe.

CHAPTER COMPREHENSION

6. What is a monsoon?
7. What lands were included in the Ottoman Empire under the ruler Suleyman?
8. Who was Kublai Khan?
9. What did the Khmer believe about their king?
10. What was the Forbidden City?
11. What did Akbar do to strengthen the Mughal Empire in India?
12. What is the main belief in the Shinto religion? How has that belief influenced Japanese culture?
13. **Write** a paragraph in which you describe the class system of Tokugawa Japan.

SKILL REVIEW

14. **Study Skill** What is software?
15. **Study Skill** What is an icon? How does an icon help you to use software?
16. **Study Skill** What kind of program would help you find the map displayed on the computer in the picture above?
17. **Reading/Thinking Skill** What problem was Tokugawa Iemitsu trying to solve when he decided that no Japanese were allowed to go to foreign countries?
18. **Reading/Thinking Skill** Use the example of the Mughal emperor Akbar to support this generalization: "Effective rulers make their people feel that they are being treated fairly."

USING A TIME LINE

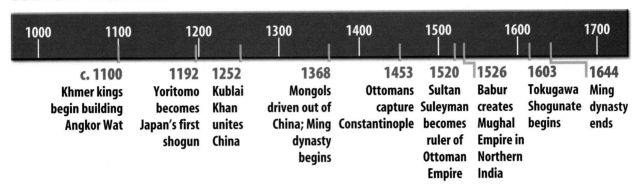

| 1000 | 1100 | 1200 | 1300 | 1400 | 1500 | 1600 | 1700 |

c. 1100
Khmer kings begin building Angkor Wat

1192
Yoritomo becomes Japan's first shogun

1252
Kublai Khan unites China

1368
Mongols driven out of China; Ming dynasty begins

1453
Ottomans capture Constantinople

1520
Sultan Suleyman becomes ruler of Ottoman Empire

1526
Babur creates Mughal Empire in Northern India

1603
Tokugawa Shogunate begins

1644
Ming dynasty ends

19. How long did the Ming dynasty last?

20. Which date on the time line marks the time when the Ottoman Empire was at its height?

Activity

***Writing* About Culture** Suppose you are a tourist guide at the Taj Mahal. What historical details would you tell tourists? What features of the building would you point out? Are there other nearby places you would suggest that people visit?

Foldables

Use your Foldable to review what you have learned about the many New Empires in Asia. As you look at the front of your Foldable, review the geography of the continent of Asia. Mentally recall what you learned about each of the empires studied, and try to sequence the key events that contributed to their rise or decline. Look at your notes on the inside of your Foldable to check your memory and responses. Record any questions that you have, and discuss them with classmates, or review the chapter to find answers.

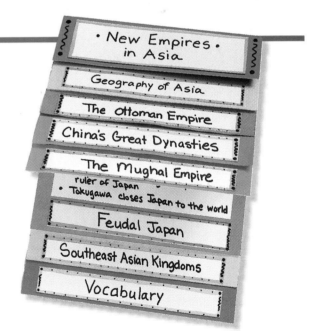

- New Empires in Asia
- Geography of Asia
- The Ottoman Empire
- China's Great Dynasties
- The Mughal Empire
  - ruler of Japan
  - Tokugawa closes Japan to the world
- Feudal Japan
- Southeast Asian Kingdoms
- Vocabulary

THE Big IDEAS ABOUT...

New Empires in the Americas

The people of what are now Mexico and Peru developed powerful empires. They also became skilled farmers who traded across a wide area, built large cities, and learned much about the heavens and the world of numbers.

GEOGRAPHY OF SOUTH AMERICA

South America stretches for about 4,500 miles from north to south. The Andes Mountains run parallel to the west coast of the continent. The Andes and the Amazon River are important elements in the physical make-up of South America.

The Aztec build a great city in the middle of a lake and gain control of the entire Valley of Mexico. Conquered peoples are put to work helping to make the Aztec Empire rich.

THE INCA

In the rugged Andes Mountains of South America the Inca build one of the richest and most powerful civilizations of the Americas.

Foldables

Make this Foldable study guide and use it to record what you learn about "New Empires in the Americas."

1. Fold a large sheet of paper like a hot dog, with one side 1" longer than the other.
2. Fold the hot dog in half. Cut along the fold line through one thickness of paper to form two tabs.
3. Write the chapter title on the long tab. Label the short tabs "The Aztec" and "The Inca" and draw a map of Middle and South America on the front of your Foldable.

Geography of South America

Find! out!

What are the main geographic features of South America?

Lesson Outline
- The Land of South America
- South American Landforms
- South America's Climate

VOCABULARY

isthmus
timberline
pampas
gaucho
El Niño

READING STRATEGY

Write "South America" in the center circle. Write regions of South America in the outer circles.

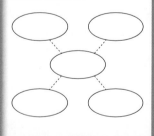

Snowy peaks of the Andes rise above the high plains where llamas graze.

BUILD BACKGROUND

"Here the river escapes from the cold plateau by tearing its way through gigantic mountains of granite. . . great snow peaks looming above the clouds more than two miles overhead; it has also. . . orchids and tree ferns. . . one is drawn irresistibly onwards by [endless] surprise."

This description of South America's mountains was written by Hiram Bingham, an American archaeologist and explorer in the early 1900s. He was one of many travelers who was deeply moved by the variety and beauty of South American geography.

THE LAND OF SOUTH AMERICA

South America is a continent of great contrast. It has nearly every kind of landform. The world's largest tropical rain forest and the Amazon River, the largest river in the world, are in South America. The continent also includes Angel Falls in Venezuela, the world's highest waterfall, and the Atacama Desert, one of the world's driest regions.

Find 20° S latitude on the map. The Atacama Desert stretches from there about 600 miles south along the Andean coast. This desert receives less than half an inch of rain a year. All of these landscapes have shaped the way people live in South America.

A Narrow Bridge

The large glaciers of the Ice Age did not cover the land of South America as they did much of North America. However, the melting glaciers did cause the level of Earth's oceans to rise. Along the coast of Central America, rising waters covered the low-lying seashores, leaving only an **isthmus** (IHS mus) between the continents. An isthmus is a narrow strip of land that connects two larger landmasses. Find the Isthmus of Panama on the map.

READING CHECK How was the isthmus formed between North and South America?

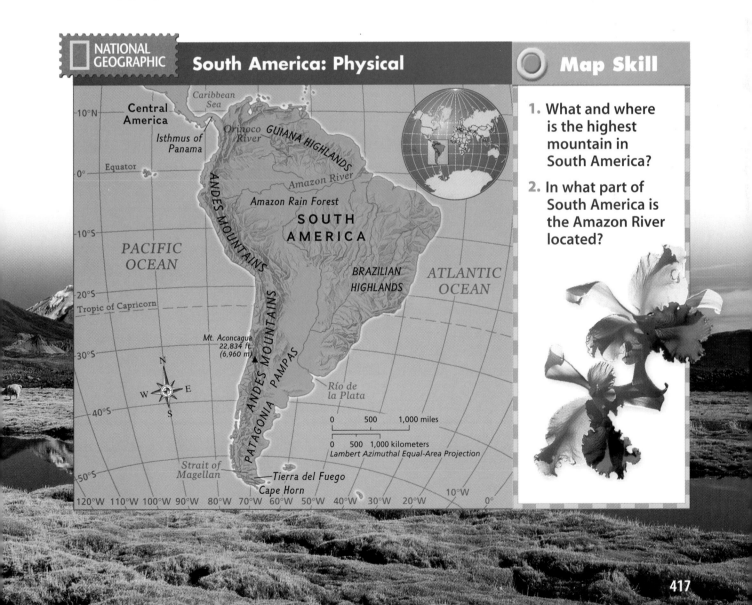

NATIONAL GEOGRAPHIC

South America: Physical

Map Skill

1. **What and where is the highest mountain in South America?**

2. **In what part of South America is the Amazon River located?**

Central America

Caribbean Sea

Isthmus of Panama

Orinoco River

GUIANA HIGHLANDS

Equator

ANDES MOUNTAINS

Amazon River

Amazon Rain Forest

SOUTH AMERICA

BRAZILIAN HIGHLANDS

PACIFIC OCEAN

ATLANTIC OCEAN

Tropic of Capricorn

Mt. Aconcagua 22,834 ft. (6,960 m)

ANDES MOUNTAINS

PAMPAS

PATAGONIA

Río de la Plata

Strait of Magellan

Tierra del Fuego

Cape Horn

0   500   1,000 miles

0   500   1,000 kilometers

Lambert Azimuthal Equal-Area Projection

-10°N   0°   -10°S   -20°S   -30°S   -40°S   -50°S

120°W 110°W 100°W 90°W 80°W 70°W 60°W 50°W 40°W 30°W 20°W 10°W 0°

SOUTH AMERICAN LANDFORMS

The **Andes Mountains** run like a spine down the western coast of South America. These mountains are the world's longest mountain range, stretching about 4,500 miles from north to south. The only higher mountains on land are in the Himalaya of Asia.

The Andes have shaped the lives of South Americans for centuries. Their high altitudes affect rainfall, wind patterns, and plant life. Few animals can survive above the **timberline**, an imaginary line on a mountain above which trees cannot grow.

Because of their length and height, the Andes have affected life and transportation as well. You will read more about this when you read about the civilizations of South America.

Life in the Mountains

At higher altitudes, oxygen becomes more scarce. Decreased oxygen makes movement and activity more difficult.

In spite of this challenge, humans have adapted to life in the Andes Mountains. In fact, one of South America's most advanced early civilizations developed in the highlands of the Andes.

A lack of water is another challenge to human life in the Andes. Early peoples of this region learned to build irrigation systems and developed effective ways of fertilizing the soil. They found ways to farm crops such as maize, peppers, and potatoes on the slopes of the Andes.

Travel in the Andes region presented special challenges as well. To travel any distance, people had to climb steep mountains or descend into deep valleys. The people of the Andes region developed rope bridges, like the modern suspension bridge, to make travel easier across this mountainous region.

People and llamas cross rope bridges in the Andes.

The Amazon Region

The **Amazon River** in Peru and Brazil is the largest river in the world. It drains nearly 3 million square miles of land, and it carries almost one-fifth of all the fresh water on Earth.

Ocean-going ships can sail upstream on the Amazon as far as Peru. For many years, the Amazon was the only way to get into central Brazil. The thick rain forest of the Amazon region prevented land travel until highways were built in the 1960s and 1970s.

These rain forests cover nearly a third of the land of South America. They are a home for many rare kinds of birds and animals. They also provide valuable products such as timber. Recently, farmers and loggers have been cutting down the rain forest. This logging is a concern to many people around the world.

Trees take in carbon dioxide and give off oxygen. The Amazon rain forest produces much of the oxygen we need to breathe. As the trees are cut down, less oxygen is produced. Also, the rare animals and birds have nowhere to live. There is a growing movement to save the remaining Amazon rain forest.

Vast Grasslands

Another region of South America is a region of sweeping **pampas**, or grasslands, located in the central and southern part of the continent. The pampas look much like the Great Plains of the United States. Like the Great Plains, the pampas are used for raising cattle and horses. There are even South American cowhands called **gauchos** (GOW choz).

READING CHECK What are the differences in South America's regions?

Rain forests of the Amazon region often extend to the shoreline (below). These cowboys work in Brazil (right).

419

SOUTH AMERICA'S CLIMATE

The equator crosses the northern region of South America. This means that much of the continent is tropical or sub-tropical. Since most of South America is south of the Equator, its seasons are reversed from ours. Summer is from December to March and winter is from June to September.

Wind Patterns

In the Southern Hemisphere, winds tend to blow from west to east. However, they also move northward toward the equator. When these winds come off the ocean, they tend to drop large amounts of rain—as much as 80 inches a year—on the regions they blow across.

Ocean currents also affect climate in South America. The most famous current is called **El Niño** (ell NEE´ nyo). This current carries warm water north along much

of the west coast of South America. In some years, El Niño moves farther north and affects climate all over the world.

The 1990s were a period when El Niño moved north. The southern United States had unusually warm winters. There were droughts in other regions. Scientists are still studying El Niño. They hope to predict its movements more accurately.

A Variety of Climates

As you have read, there is a wide variety of climates in South America. The Amazon Region is wet and hot. The Andes region is cold and dry. Although most areas have plenty of rain, some of the driest places on Earth are in northern Chile. One region has not had rain in over 14 years. Each of South America's climate regions affects how people live.

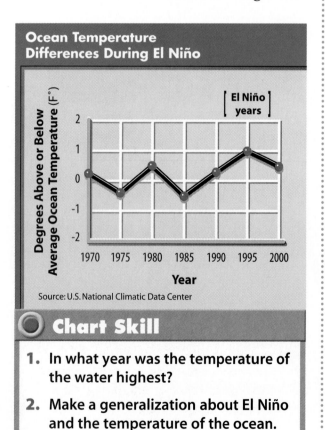

Ocean Temperature Differences During El Niño

Degrees Above or Below Average Ocean Temperature (F°)

El Niño years

Year

Source: U.S. National Climatic Data Center

Chart Skill

1. **In what year was the temperature of the water highest?**

2. **Make a generalization about El Niño and the temperature of the ocean.**

READING CHECK

How does El Niño affect the world's climate?

PUTTING IT TOGETHER

The melting glaciers raised ocean levels and created the Isthmus of Panama, which connects North America and South America. The Andes Mountains are the world's longest mountain range. Their height makes their region cold and dry.

The Amazon is the world's largest river. It flows through a huge region of tropical rain forests into the Atlantic Ocean.

The pampas are in southern South America. They are an area of vast grasslands like the North American prairies.

The climate of South America includes plenty of rainfall. An ocean current called El Niño changes its course and affects climate around the world.

Snow-capped peaks and deep fjords are found along the coast of Chile. Toucans (right) live in South America's humid rain forests.

Review and Assess

1. Write a sentence for each vocabulary term.

   El Niño   **isthmus**
   gaucho   **timberline**

2. Why is the Amazon rain forest important for life on Earth?

3. What are the main features of South American geography?

Find! Out!

4. What effect do you think the Andes Mountains and the Amazon rain forest might have on trade in South America?

5. **Make a generalization** about the effect of El Niño on the world's climate.

Make a map of South America. Do some research to make a product map for the continent. Make a map key to illustrate and label each product.

. . . .

Suppose you are on a ship sailing up the Amazon River from east to west. **Write** a journal entry telling about what you see on your journey. You may want to do some research to add interesting details to your journal.

The Aztec

How did the Aztec build their empire?

Lesson Outline
- The Aztec Come to Mexico
- Aztec Power Grows
- Aztec Culture

VOCABULARY

chinampas
sacrifice
codex

READING STRATEGY

On a chart like this one write "The Aztec" in the center circle. Write supporting details about the Aztec in the outer circles.

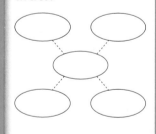

BUILD BACKGROUND

"The great city has many broad streets . . . half of each is hard earthlike pavement, and the other half is by water, so that the people leave in their canoes or barks, which are of wood hollowed out . . . . The residents go for a stroll, some in canoes and others along the land, and keep up conversations."

This is how a Spanish soldier in 1519 described the beautiful capital of the Aztec Empire. In this lesson, you will read more about this empire.

THE AZTEC COME TO MEXICO

According to legend, the Aztec, who called themselves *Mexica*, searched for years for a place to settle. In the 1100s they came to the **Valley of Mexico**. This high valley surrounded by mountains has several lakes. Around 1325 the Aztec arrived on the shores of **Lake Texcoco** (tay SKOH koh).

The Aztec Capital

On an island in the lake, Aztec historians say, they received a sign. An eagle landed on a cactus and began to eat a snake. The wanderers built their city on that island, and named it **Tenochtitlán** (te noch tee TLAHN), which means "place of the prickly pear cactus" in the Aztec language, Nahuatl (NAH wah tul).

Tenochtitlán began as a group of reed huts surrounding a temple. The land was poor, so the Aztec copied the system of agriculture used by neighboring peoples. They dug canals through the marshland. They used the dirt to make small islands, known as **chinampas** (chin AHM pahz). Chinampas were held in place by wooden stakes and the roots of willow trees. Some chinampas actually floated and could be moved from one place to another.

A Floating City

Most Aztec were farmers, but skilled stoneworkers built the stone buildings

that gradually replaced the reed huts. They also built bridges that connected the island to the shore of the lake.

Most Aztec lived in one-room stone or mud houses, but Aztec rulers lived in grand palaces with luxurious gardens. A Spanish soldier described one of these palaces: "I walked until I was tired and never saw the whole of it."

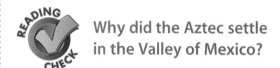

READING CHECK Why did the Aztec settle in the Valley of Mexico?

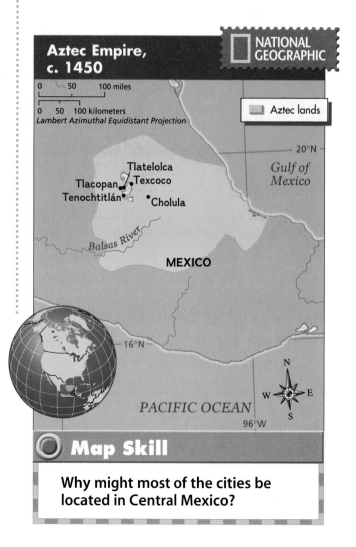

Aztec Empire, c. 1450

NATIONAL GEOGRAPHIC

0   50   100 miles
0   50   100 kilometers
Lambert Azimuthal Equidistant Projection

Aztec lands

Tlatelolco
Tlacopan • Texcoco
Tenochtitlán •
• Cholula

Balsas River

MEXICO

20°N

Gulf of Mexico

16°N

PACIFIC OCEAN

96°W

N E
W S

Map Skill

Why might most of the cities be located in Central Mexico?

This map of the Aztec capital (left) shows the city's broad streets and waterways.

AZTEC POWER GROWS

When the Aztec first came to the Valley of Mexico, they had to pay tribute, or taxes, to the rulers of nearby cities. This tribute was usually a part of their crops, which people carried by boat and on foot from Tenochtitlán to the other cities.

Forming Friendships

Before long, Tenochtitlán was collecting tribute of its own. The Aztec had become one of the most powerful groups in the Valley of Mexico. In 1428 the Aztec joined forces with two other cities, Texcoco and Tlacopan (tlahk oh PAHN). Soon the Aztec and their partners gained control of the entire Valley of Mexico.

By 1450 Aztec power had spread beyond the mountains surrounding the Valley of Mexico. Under the leadership of the ruler Ahuitzotl (ah WEE soht ul), the Aztec armies conquered areas west to the Pacific Ocean and south to what is today Guatemala.

One Aztec poet wrote proudly about the soldiers who died in battle, "There is nothing like death in war." Prisoners were given as a **sacrifice** to honor the Aztec god of the sun, Huitzilopochtli (weet si loh POHCH tlee). A sacrifice is a gift or offering made to a god. The Aztec believed that the sun god lived on human blood, and he needed to eat each day.

The tribute the conquered cities paid brought great wealth to the Aztec. Each year brought a tribute of more than one million loads of food to the Aztec capital. Tenochtitlán grew until it had a population of about 150,000 people. Later a Spanish visitor described the Aztec capital.

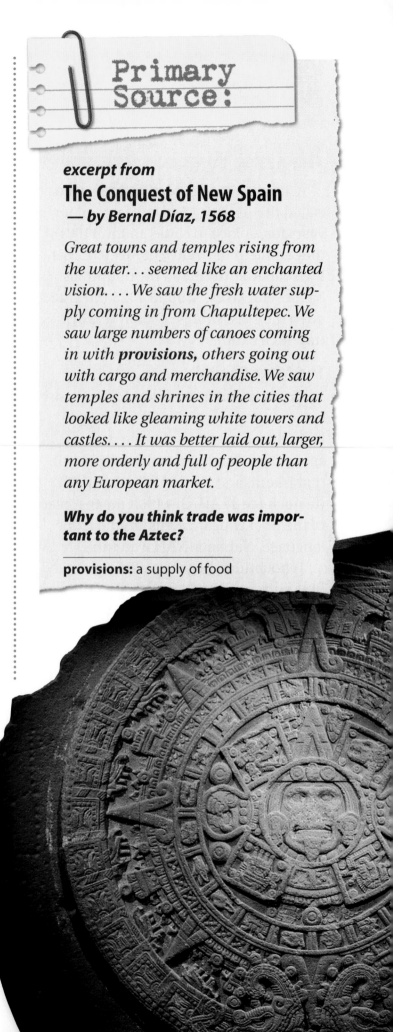

Primary Source:

excerpt from

The Conquest of New Spain
— *by Bernal Díaz, 1568*

*Great towns and temples rising from the water. . . seemed like an enchanted vision. . . . We saw the fresh water supply coming in from Chapultepec. We saw large numbers of canoes coming in with **provisions,** others going out with cargo and merchandise. We saw temples and shrines in the cities that looked like gleaming white towers and castles. . . . It was better laid out, larger, more orderly and full of people than any European market.*

Why do you think trade was important to the Aztec?

provisions: a supply of food

Ruling the Empire

The Aztec social pyramid had several levels. At the top was the emperor, who held great political and religious power. He was the richest person in Tenochtitlán and the leader of the Aztec army. The emperor was worshiped by the Aztec people, who believed he had godlike powers. The emperor even had a special color—turquoise. The emperor was the only one who was allowed to wear clothing of this color.

Below the emperor were nobles and government workers. Nobles ran the Aztec Empire. They collected tribute, supervised temple construction, and saw that streets were cleaned. Nobles also planned and led wars.

Most of the population formed family groups called *calpulli* (kahl POOL lee). *Calpulli* means "groups of houses" in Nahuatl. In Tenochtitlán there were 20 calpulli. Each had its own leaders for its part of the city. Each also had its own temple, school, and farmland. Members worked as farmers, merchants, craftworkers, and soldiers.

Near the base of Aztec society were landless farmers. They were among the poorest members of society, since they owned no land and had to work for others.

However, there was another group beneath the landless farmers. The lowest group were the enslaved people. Only about 2 percent of the people in Tenochtitlán were enslaved. Most of these were captured outside Aztec lands and brought to the capital by merchants. Enslaved people had no freedom and had to do whatever work their owners told them to do. However, people enslaved by the Aztec had one advantage: the children born to these people were free and could make their own choices about their lives.

READING CHECK How did the Aztec become wealthy and powerful?

Aztec artifacts include this enormous calendar stone (left) and a mosaic serpent (below) to be worn on the chest.

425

AZTEC CULTURE

At its peak around 1500, the city of Tenochtitlán was a busy center of trade and learning. Aztec doctors could choose from over 1,000 medicines, including plants to heal wounds, reduce fevers, and cure stomach aches. Aztec astronomers built on the knowledge of the Maya to predict eclipses and to study the movements of planets. Craftworkers created beautiful feather headdresses, gold and copper jewelry, ceramic jars, and cloth.

Temple of the Sun

From birth until death, from morning until night, religion played a central role in Aztec life. The temple district was the center of religious life in Tenochtitlán. Here stood temples to different gods, homes and schools for priests, and ball courts. Rising as high as an eight-story building was the Great Temple. The Aztec built this temple to honor Huitzilopochtli, their sun god, and Tlaloc (TLAH lohk), their rain god. At the top, on the temple platform, priests sacrificed thousands of war prisoners every year.

Aztec Records

Priests calculated the Aztec calendar so that they could predict future events. Others kept records, using the Aztec system of writing. Colorful pictures and symbols were drawn on a long folded sheet

This codex (far right) shows Aztec gods. A statue of the god of flowers and song is at right.

of paper. Each of these folded sheets was called a **codex** (KOH deks). A codex told about the history, religion, government, and science of the Aztec. Unfortunately, few of these works remain because the Spanish destroyed most Aztec records in the 1500s.

The Aztec also had a strong oral tradition. People memorized poems, songs, and speeches. Poems were often recited on special occasions, accompanied by drums and flutes. This is one Aztec poem:

> *An emerald fell to the ground,*
> *and a flower was born; this is your*
> *song!*
> *Whenever you sing your songs here*
> *in Mexico*
> *the sun shines eternally [forever].*

Why were priests so powerful in the Aztec culture?

PUTTING IT TOGETHER

The Aztec built one of the most powerful empires in the Americas. Efficient government and farming techniques helped the empire to grow and to run smoothly. However, constant warfare made many enemies. In 1521, these enemies would join the Spanish to defeat the Aztec.

Food such as maize, Aztec crafts, and even the Nahuatl language are all part of Mexican culture today. Moreover, you can still see the Aztec symbol of the eagle and the snake in the center of the Mexican flag.

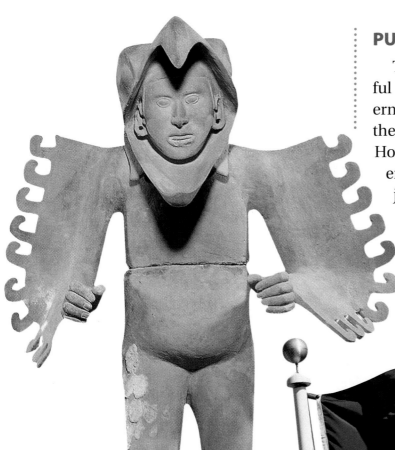

Aztec symbols, such as this eagle warrior (left), remain part of Mexico's heritage. The Aztec eagle symbol is on its flag (above).

Review and Assess

1. Write a sentence for each vocabulary word.

   **chinampas   sacrifice
   codex**

2. Where did the Aztec finally settle?

3. How were the Aztec able to build a powerful empire? Find Out!

4. How did the wars of conquest affect the Aztec **economy**?

5. **Make a generalization** about why the Aztec were feared by their neighbors.

Activities

Look at the map on page 423. Write a paragraph explaining why the Aztec capital was especially well located.

• •

Suppose that you are one of the Spanish soldiers who came to Tenochtitlán. **Write** a letter to a friend back in Spain describing the Aztec capital.

Drawing Conclusions

There are many parts of Aztec life that we don't understand because so much Aztec writing was destroyed by the Spanish. Therefore, when archaeologists find an Aztec artifact, they must draw a **conclusion** about its purpose or its use. Whenever you reach an opinion after looking at evidence, you draw a conclusion.

VOCABULARY
conclusion

LEARN THE SKILL

Follow these steps to draw a conclusion.

1. **Gather Information.**
   In 1978, workers digging a ditch in Mexico City found a large, round stone disk. It showed a carving of an Aztec goddess.

2. **Identify the subject.**
   The subject is an Aztec carving. Archaeologists look for details that may give clues to the statue's identity. They decided that the statue was a carving of an Aztec goddess, the sister of the Aztec god of war.

3. **Look for connections between the pieces of information.**
   Workers had been digging up Aztec artifacts here for years. Historical records showed that the most important Aztec temple was located in the area. Other records indicated that a stone carving similar to this one was part of the stairway of the temple.

4. **Draw a conclusion.**
   Archaeologists drew the conclusion that this was the statue from the stairway of the Great Temple. They realized that they could dig near the site to find other parts of the Great Temple.

TRY THE SKILL

Now try reading this passage on the Aztec religion. Follow the steps and draw a conclusion from the information in the text.

> *The Aztec believed that their sacrifices were necessary for the continuation of the world. Sacrifices made the sun rise. For some festivals, thousands of prisoners were killed on the altar of the sun god. These prisoners were usually taken in wars with other states. Often, the Aztec would launch wars in order to gain the large numbers of prisoners to sacrifice.*

1. What is the subject of the information in the passage?

2. What connection is there between the pieces of information?

3. What conclusion can you draw about Aztec relations with their neighbors from the information in this article?

4. How can drawing conclusions help you to make sense out of the different pieces of information?

EXTEND THE SKILL

You draw conclusions every day. For example, you see an ad for a new CD by your favorite band. You draw the conclusion that you will probably like the CD. Or, you may read about an event in the newspaper and reach a conclusion from the information that is given to you.

Think of a newspaper or television news story that you have learned about recently.

Do some research to find out more information about the event.

Write a brief outline of the event. Include the subject of the event. List the important information you have found. State the conclusion you drew from the information.

- What was the subject of the event you chose?

- What information did you use to draw a conclusion?

- How does drawing conclusions help you to understand events in history?

Lesson 3

The Inca Empire

What were some of the achievements of the Inca?

Lesson Outline
• Empire in the Andes
• Sweat of the Sun
• Farming the Andes

VOCABULARY

terrace
quipu

PEOPLE
Pachakuti Inca

READING STRATEGY

Copy the word map. Write "Inca" in the center circle. Write four features of Inca culture in the outer circles.

BUILD BACKGROUND

"I am rich in silver
I am rich in gold."

These words come from an Inca poem. They celebrate the wealth of the Inca civilization, which developed in the Andes Mountains of South America. In these mountains the Inca mined the large amounts of metal and minerals that made their empire rich. They also built cities and followed traditions that made their culture rich as well.

430

EMPIRE IN THE ANDES

At the same time the Aztec were conquering Mexico, another great American empire was growing in the Andes Mountains of South America. This group took its name from their ruler, the Inca. Their empire stretched from what is today Ecuador to central Chile.

At its peak the Inca Empire ruled about 12 million people. Like the Aztec, the Inca worshiped the sun, depended on maize, and organized a strong army.

From Village to Empire

The Inca began around 1200 in **Cuzco** (KOOS koh), a small village in a fertile valley in what is today Peru. A drought reduced their farmland, so the Inca took over their neighbors' land. During the 1300s the Inca ruled most of the valley and received tribute from other groups.

In 1438 a ruler called **Pachakuti** (pah chah KOO tee) **Inca** extended the Inca borders west to the Pacific Ocean and south to **Lake Titicaca** high in the central Andes. The Inca army won victories easily. In fact, the Inca seemed to enjoy war. The word *Quechua* (KECH oo uh), in the Inca language, means both "to fight" and "to enjoy oneself."

Pachakuti was called "Sapa Inca," or "Supreme Inca." He set about organizing the conquered lands into provinces. He appointed local governors. He forced defeated people to move, and gave their land to loyal people. He also demanded labor from the people.

Pachakuti spread the Inca religion throughout his empire. This religion centered on a god called Viracocha. Although conquered people had to worship Viracocha, they were permitted to worship their own gods, as well.

READING CHECK How did the Supreme Inca organize his vast empire?

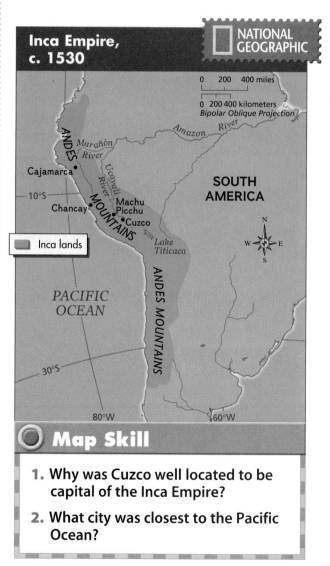

Inca Empire, c. 1530

NATIONAL GEOGRAPHIC

0 200 400 miles
0 200 400 kilometers
Bipolar Oblique Projection

Amazon River
Marañón River
Cajamarca
ANDES
Ucayali River
10°S
Chancay
Machu Picchu
Cuzco
MOUNTAINS
SOUTH AMERICA
Lake Titicaca
☐ Inca lands
PACIFIC OCEAN
ANDES MOUNTAINS
30°S
80°W
60°W
N W E S

Map Skill

1. **Why was Cuzco well located to be capital of the Inca Empire?**

2. **What city was closest to the Pacific Ocean?**

This thin metal head of a god shows the Inca skill as goldsmiths.

SWEAT OF THE SUN

The Inca worked rich gold mines. They called this metal "sweat of the sun" and used it to decorate temples to their sun god. His temple in Cuzco had a huge golden sculpture of him decorated with precious stones. There was even a golden "garden" with golden flowers and birds.

The Inca Capital

Cuzco served as the center of government, religion, and trade. The temples and government buildings at the center of Cuzco were constructed of stone blocks. These blocks fit together so well that it is impossible to put a knife between them. They also can withstand earthquakes.

Beyond the main plaza were the palaces of the emperor and wealthy nobles. The song on page 433 tells how the Inca felt about Cuzco and their land. The nobles wore special headbands and earrings. One of the Spanish soldiers to visit the city was impressed by Inca wealth and skill. He wrote the following description in the 1500s:

> *The interior of the temple [of the Sun] was . . . a mine of gold. On the western wall was . . . [the sun god] . . . engraved on a massive plate of gold of enormous [size], thickly powdered with emeralds and precious stones. . . . the morning sun fell directly upon it at its rising, lighting up the whole apartment . . .*

READING CHECK Why were the Spanish visitors impressed by Cuzco?

The Inca created walls (below) made from huge stones as well as this small detailed statue (left) made of gold.

El Condor Pasa

Music noted by Daniel Alomias Robles

Quechua (Inca Language)

Yau kuntur llaqtay orgopy tiyaq
Maymantam gawamuhuakchianqui,
  kuntur kuntur
Apayllahuay llaqtanchikman, was-
  inchikman chay chiri orgupy.
Kutiytam munany kuntur kuntur.

(chorus)
Kuzco llaqtapyn plazachallampyn
  suyaykamullaway,
Machupicchupy Huaynapicchupy
  purikunanchiqpaq.

Spanish

Oh majestuoso Cóndor de los
  andes, llevame, a mi hogar,
  en los Andes,
Oh Cóndor.
Quiero volver a mi tierra querida y
  vivir con mis hermanos Incas,
que es lo que man añoro,
Oh Cóndor.

(chorus)
Espérame en Cuzco, en la plaza
  principal,
para que vayamos a pasearnos
  Machupicchu y Huayna picchu.

English

Oh majestic Condor owner of the
  skies, take me home, up into the
  Andes
Oh mighty Condor.
I want to go back to my native place
  to live with my Inca brothers,
that's what I miss the most,
Oh mighty condor.

(chorus)
Wait for me in Cuzco, in the main
  plaza,
so we can take a walk in Machu
  Picchu and Huayna Picchu.

FARMING THE ANDES

Outside Cuzco, workers and farmers lived in small mud huts with high windows. Also outside the city were many government storage buildings. Some contained food, such as maize, dried fruit, or salt. Others contained neat piles of beautiful wool and cotton cloth. There was even a building just to hold the feathers of hummingbirds, which were used as decoration for clothing.

Inca Farmers

Every year the Inca emperor, followed by a group of nobles, traveled to a field outside Cuzco and dug up the ground with a plow made of pure gold. This ceremony signaled the importance of agriculture to Inca society.

Inca farmers grew potatoes, maize, and peppers. They adapted their farming methods to the geography of different parts of the empire. On hills, they built **terraces**, level platforms of earth that climbed each hill like a staircase. In rocky areas, they dug huge pits 20 feet deep. Farmers placed dead fish in the pits to

The Inca built **terraces** on hillsides to hold rainwater for their crops.

Exploring TECHNOLOGY

Speaking With Thread

The Inca had no written language. Yet they were able to run a vast empire and send orders to governors in distant regions.

The Inca used special cords called **quipus** (KEE pooz). A quipu was about 2 feet long and had threads of different colors hanging from it. For example, white threads stood for silver, yellow stood for gold, and red stood for war. By tying knots in the strings in a particular order, the Inca could record trade items, battles, or births and deaths in a village. The quipus were carried to Cuzco by swift Inca runners so the central government would know of conditions throughout their empire.

How did the quipu help the Inca to run their large empire?

enrich the soil. Inca farmers also brought water to dry fields through a system of canals and aqueducts. One stone aqueduct brought water over 500 miles.

Farming was done by human labor because of the lack of draft animals to pull or carry heavy loads. However, the Inca raised animals for other tasks. They used llamas as pack animals to carry lighter items. Another type of llama had wool so fine that only nobles were allowed to wear clothing made from it. The Inca also hunted deer.

At its peak, the Inca Empire held about 12 million people. Because of its well-organized government, it was able to feed and clothe all of these people.

A Lost City

The Inca built a vast network of highways over 19,000 miles in length. One road climbed high into the Andes and ended at a city called **Machu Picchu** (MAHCH oo PEEK choo). This town was forgotten until an American explorer named Hiram Bingham came across it in 1911.

No one is sure why Machu Picchu was built or why it was abandoned. Machu Picchu is just one of many Inca mysteries. Although Spanish conquerors destroyed many Inca treasures in the 1500s, those remaining can give us a sense of the brilliant culture created by the "Children of the Sun."

How do we know that the Inca were brilliant engineers?

PUTTING IT TOGETHER

The Inca built a huge empire in the Andes Mountains of South America. Their capital, Cuzco, began as a farming village. As their power grew, Cuzco became a city of palaces and temples which were decorated with gold and silver.

Inca farmers used terracing and fertilizer to increase the crops their land produced. Inca engineers built large aqueducts and a network of roads that connected the large empire.

The Inca Empire controlled much of western South America until it was conquered by the Spanish in 1532. However, the Inca legacy remains. Millions of people still speak the Inca language, and many of the songs and poems of the Inca are still recited today.

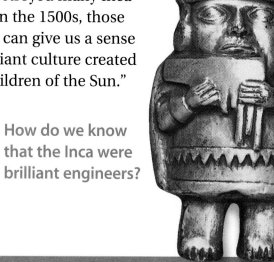

This Inca figure made of gold shows a musician in traditional dress and with pipes.

Review and Assess

1. Write a sentence for each vocabulary word.

   quipu   **terrace**

2. How did the Inca adapt agriculture to their region?

3. What were some major accomplishments of the Inca Empire?

4. How was the **economy** of the Inca Empire organized?

5. The city of Machu Picchu was forgotten until 1911. What **conclusion** can you draw about the city from this fact?

Look at the map of the Inca Empire on page 431. Compare it to the political map of South America in the Atlas on page R10. Make a list of the countries with land that was part of the Inca empire.

• •

Suppose that you are with Hiram Bingham in 1911. **Write** a letter to a friend describing Machu Picchu.

VOCABULARY REVIEW

Number a sheet of paper from 1 to 5. Beside each number write the word that best matches the statement.

codex   **isthmus**   **terrace**

El Niño   **quipu**

1. A folded sheet on which the Aztec writing system of pictures and symbols appears.

2. Knotted and colored cords that allowed the Inca to keep records.

3. A narrow strip of land that connects two larger landmasses.

4. Level earth platform on a hillside.

5. The current that carries warm water northward along much of the western coast of South America.

CHAPTER COMPREHENSION

6. What landform runs like a spine down the western coast of South America?

7. About how much of the land in South America is rain forest?

8. What were the *chinampas*?

9. Why did Tenochtitlán join two other cities to form an alliance in 1428?

10. What were some of the accomplishments of the Aztec in the field of science?

11. What was remarkable about the Inca network of roads?

12. How far did the Inca Empire extend under the ruler Pachakuti in 1438?

13. **Write** a paragraph describing how and why the Inca farmed on terraces.

SKILL REVIEW

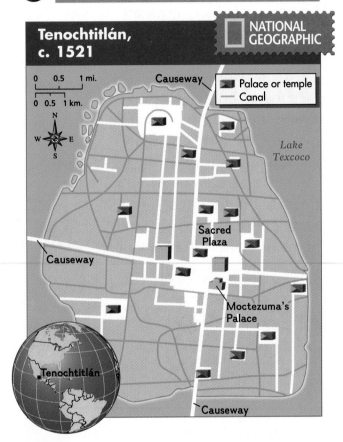

Tenochtitlán, c. 1521

NATIONAL GEOGRAPHIC

0 0.5 1 mi.
0 0.5 1 km.

Causeway

■ Palace or temple
— Canal

Lake Texcoco

Sacred Plaza

Causeway

Moctezuma's Palace

Tenochtitlán

Causeway

14. **Reading/Thinking Skill** What does "draw a conclusion" mean?

15. **Reading/Thinking Skills** Look at the map above. What conclusion can you draw about the building skills of the Aztec?

16. **Reading/Thinking Skills** Think about the Aztec and Inca empires. Both empires were conquered by Spanish soldiers. What conclusion can you draw about why Spain might have wanted to conquer these empires?

17. **Geography Skill** Is the map above a large-scale map or a small-scale map? How do you know?

18. **Study Skill** What software would you use to find general information about the Inca?

USING A TIME LINE

| 1100 | 1150 | 1200 | 1250 | 1300 | 1350 | 1400 | 1450 | 1500 | 1550 |

1100
Aztec settle
in Valley of
Mexico

1200
Inca settle
in Cuzco

c. 1325
Aztec settle
around Lake
Texcoco

1428
Aztec control
Valley of
Mexico

c. 1450
Aztec conquer
peoples of
Middle America

1532
Cuzco conquered
by the Spanish

19. Which event on the time line marks the beginning of the powerful period of the Aztec Empire? Explain.

20. During what centuries did the Inca control Cuzco? How many years was that?

Activity

Writing About Economics Suppose you are an environmentalist who wants to save the Amazon rain forest by preventing logging. Make a list of facts and arguments. Use your list to write a speech to present to those who want to cut down the trees of the Amazon basin.

Foldables

Use your Foldable to review what you have learned about the rise and fall of great civilizations—Aztec and Inca—in the Americas. As you look at the map on the front of your Foldable, review the geography of Middle and South America. Test yourself to see what you recall about the Aztec and Inca civilizations. Look at your notes under the tabs of your Foldable to check your memory and responses. Record any questions that you have, and discuss them with classmates, or review the chapter to find answers.

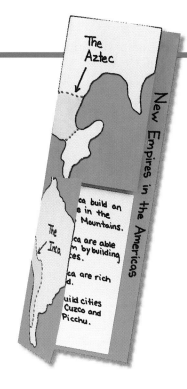

Unit 3 REVIEW

VOCABULARY REVIEW

Number a sheet of paper from 1 to 5. Beside each number write the word from the list below that best completes each description.

Reformation   **sultan**

sacrifice   **terrace**

shogun

1. A gift or offering made to a god.

2. A military ruler in feudal Japan.

3. A movement in the 1500s that resulted in a split in the Christian church.

4. A level platform of earth on a hill.

5. The title of the ruler of the Ottoman Empire.

TECHNOLOGY

For resources to help you learn more about the people and places you studied in this unit, visit **www.mhschool.com** and follow the links for Grade 6, Unit 3.

SKILL REVIEW

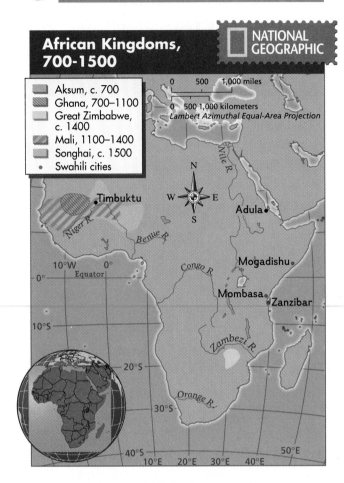

African Kingdoms, 700-1500

- Aksum, c. 700
- Ghana, 700–1100
- Great Zimbabwe, c. 1400
- Mali, 1100–1400
- Songhai, c. 1500
- Swahili cities

6. **Geography Skill** Is the map above a large-scale map or a small-scale map?

7. **Geography Skill** How does the map help you understand African history?

8. **Study Skill** What should you consider when you buy software?

9. **Reading/Thinking Skill** Think about the following facts:

   - Aksum had gold mines.

   - Rome needed gold to mint its coins.

   - Aksum traded with Rome.

   Draw a conclusion from these facts.

10. **Reading/Thinking Skill** What conclusion can you draw about the Ottoman Empire from the fact that Muslims, Jews, and Christians worshiped freely there?

1   Constantinople was on a peninsula. . . . it had the strongest walls in Europe. There were moats and ditches outside these walls. . . . Defenders could shoot arrows and pour flaming oil from the tops of these walls.

2   In 1453, the Ottoman ruler was named Muhammad II. . . . he was determined to capture Constantinople. . . . he used the newest and largest cannons in Europe. These cannons hurled half-ton cannonballs more than a mile. . .

3   In the early hours of May 29, 1453, the Ottomans broke through the walls. . . . Before the morning was over, Constantinople had fallen. . . .

1   After the Ottomans broke through the walls of Constantinople, they gained control of the city in—

   A   one week
   B   a few days
   C   one hour
   D   a few hours

2   From this article you can conclude that—

   F   Constantinople could resist any outside attack.
   G   the Ottoman victory surprised the people of Constantinople.
   H   Muhammad was a kind and just ruler of the Ottomans.
   J   cannonballs had never before been used in battle.

WRITING ACTIVITIES

Writing to Persuade Suppose you are the owner of a hotel in Africa's savannah. You organize photographic safaris to a big-game preserve. *Write* an advertisement in which you persuade people to take a vacation at your hotel.

Writing to Inform Suppose that you are a writer for a children's magazine. You have been asked to *write* an article about Angkor Wat and Angkor Thom. Be sure to include interesting details in your article.

Writing to Express Suppose you are writing a fictional story set in Machu Picchu at the time of the Inca. *Write* a description of the setting of the story. Describe the buildings and the city's location. You may wish to do some research to provide interesting details for your description.

439

LITERATURE

KARATE-DŌ
My Way of Life
Gichin Funakoshi

Losing a Topknot

Selections by Gichin Funakoshi
Illustrated by S. Saelig Gallagher

Gichin Funakoshi, "the father of modern karate," was a schoolteacher from the island of Okinawa. In this excerpt from his autobiography, **KARATE-DŌ, MY WAY OF LIFE,** *Funakoshi describes how the modernizing of Japan changed his life. One of the traditional symbols of the samurai, the Japanese warrior, was the topknot, a way of wearing their hair. When Japan began to modernize after 1868, the government forbade this hairstyle. The author's father did not approve of this change.*

The Meiji Restoration and I were born in the same year, 1868. The former saw the light of day in the shogun's former capital of Edo, which came to be known as Tokyo. I was born in the district of Yamakawa-chō in the royal Okinawan capital of Shuri. If anyone were to take the trouble to consult official records, he would learn that I was born in the third year of Meiji (1870), but the true facts are that my birth occurred in the first year of the reign and that I had to falsify my official record so as to be allowed to sit for entrance examinations to a Tokyo medical school. . . . Having thus altered the date of my birth, I sat for the examinations and passed them, but still

I did not enter the Tokyo medical school. The cause, which seemed very reasonable then, would seem rather less so now, I imagine.

Among the many reforms instituted by the young Meiji government during the first twenty years of its life was the **abolition** of the topknot, a masculine hairstyle that had been a traditional part of Japanese life for much longer than anyone could possibly remember. In Okinawa, in particular, the topknot was considered a symbol not simply of maturity. . . . but of manhood itself. As the **edict** banning the **revered** topknot was nationwide, there was opposition to it throughout the country, but nowhere, I think, were the lines of battle so fiercely drawn as in Okinawa. . . .

My family had for generations been attached to a lower-ranking official, and the whole clan was unanimously and **adamantly** opposed to the cutting of the topknot. Such an act was utterly **abhorrent** to every member of my family, although I myself did not feel strongly one way or the other. The outcome was I bowed to family pressure, for the school refused to accept students who persisted in the traditional style, and thus the whole future course of my life was influenced by so slight a matter as a bushy topknot. . . .

---

abolition (ab ə lish′ ən) ending, forbidding
edict (ē′ dikt) official order
revered (rə vîrd′) honored, respected
adamantly (ad′ ə mənt lē) fiercely, strongly
abhorrent (əb hôr′ ənt) hated, repulsive

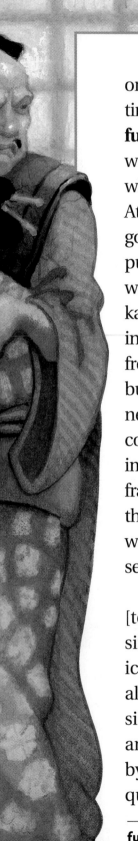

[Many years prior to this] I became close friends with one of my primary school classmates. This too was destined to alter the course of my life (and in a far more **fundamental** way than the topknot), for my classmate was the son of Yasutune Azato, a most amazing man who was one of Okinawa's experts in the art of karate. . . . At that time the practice of karate was banned by the government, so sessions had to take place in secret, and pupils were strictly forbidden by their teachers to discuss with anyone the fact that they were learning the art. . . . karate practice could then be held only at night and only in secret. Azato's house was situated quite a distance from that of my grandparents, where I was still living, but once my enthusiasm for the art began to take hold I never found that nighttime walk too long. It was after a couple of years' practice that I realized my health had improved tremendously, and that I was no longer the frail child I had been. I enjoyed karate but—more than that—I felt deeply indebted to the art for my increased well-being, and it was around this time that I began to seriously consider making Karate-Dō my way of life.

However, the thought did not enter my mind that [teaching karate] might also become a profession and since the thorny topknot controversy had put a medical career beyond my reach, I now began to consider alternatives. As I had been taught the Chinese classics from early childhood by both my grandfather and Azato, I decided to make use of that knowledge by becoming a schoolteacher. Accordingly I took the qualifying examinations and was granted a position

---

fundamental (fun də men′ təl) basic

as assistant instructor at a primary school. My first experience in taking charge of a classroom occurred in 1888, when I was twenty-one years old.

But the topknot still **obtruded**, for before I could be permitted to enter upon my duties as a teacher I was required to get rid of it. This seemed to me entirely reasonable. Japan was then in a state of great **ferment**; tremendous changes were occurring everywhere, along every facet of life. I felt that I, as a teacher, had an obligation to help our younger generation, which would one day forge the destiny of our nation, to bridge the wide gaps that yawned between the old Japan and the new. I could hardly object to the official edict that our traditional topknot had now become a relic of the past. Nevertheless, I trembled when I thought about what the older members of my family would say. . . .

My father could hardly believe his eyes. "What have you done to yourself?" he cried angrily. "You, the son of a samurai!" My mother, even angrier than he, refused to speak to me. . . . and fled to her parents' home. I imagine all this hullaboo must strike the youth of today as almost inconceivably ridiculous.

---

obtruded (əb trüd′ əd) forced itself upon another
ferment (fər′ ment) excitement

Write About It!

Write an essay explaining why you think a hairstyle was such an important symbol to the author's family and to the people who wanted to modernize Japan.

The World Expands and Changes

TAKE A LOOK

How did revolutions and new ideas shape our world?

Ships of the 1600s carried about 100 people and traveled about 5 miles an hour. Modern liners carry thousands of people at speeds of 30 miles an hour.

444

Explore the beginnings of the
modern world at our Web site
www.mhschool.com

Technology and Expansion

Beginning about 1400, new ideas and new discoveries changed the way Europeans looked at the world. Using new inventions, scientists made discoveries about Earth and its place in the universe. European explorers set sail for many parts of the world. As a result, countries built colonies in lands that were new to them.

REVOLUTION IN SCIENCE AND THOUGHT

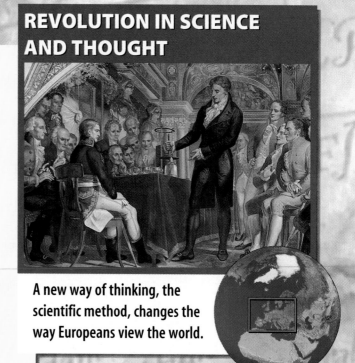

A new way of thinking, the scientific method, changes the way Europeans view the world.

AN AGE OF EXPLORATION

Explorers from Europe search for new ways to reach the rich markets of Asia. They explore the lands of North and South America and start colonies.

CONQUERING THE AMERICAS

The rich empires of the Aztec and the Inca fall to Spanish conquerors. Spain becomes wealthy and powerful.

SLAVERY IN THE AMERICAS

European colonists in the Americas need workers for their farms and mines. The colonists turn to Africa to get the workers they need.

EUROPEANS IN THE PACIFIC

Europeans explore the islands of the Pacific Ocean. An English sea captain, James Cook, lands in Australia, and the British later colonize the continent.

Foldables

Make this Foldable study guide and use it to record what you learn about "Technology and Expansion."

1. Fold a large sheet of paper in half like a hot dog, leaving a 1" tab.

2. Make four cuts on the short side forming five tabs.

3. Write the chapter title on the 1" tab and the lesson titles on the five tabs.

A Revolution in Science and Thought

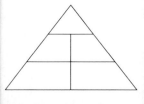

What changes in thought helped create the modern world?

Lesson Outline

• Understanding the Solar System
• The Telescope and Space
• Laws of the Universe
• Advances in Science

BUILD BACKGROUND

According to a legend, one day in the 1600s, an apple fell onto the head of an Englishman who was sitting under a tree. That apple was part of a revolution in thinking that led to the development of modern science.

The man was the brilliant scientist and mathematician, Isaac Newton. He was one of several scientists and thinkers of his time who were searching to understand the universe.

UNDERSTANDING THE SOLAR SYSTEM

During the Middle Ages, most people believed that Earth was the center of the universe. The Christian Church supported this **geocentric** (jee oh SEN trihk) theory. In some ways it made sense. After all, the sun seemed to move across the sky each day.

Around 1400 Italian philosophers began to reread the writings of Greek and Roman scholars. These philosophers began to use ancient ideas to challenge accepted ways of thinking.

Copernicus

Some of these new ideas came from a Polish scientist named **Nicolaus Copernicus** (1473–1543). He suggested the idea that Earth was not the center of the universe. His theory was **heliocentric**, (hee lee oh SEN trihk), or sun-centered. He believed that Earth and all the other planets moved in orbits, or paths, around the sun.

Copernicus caused a lot of excitement with this theory. People began to wonder if their whole view of Earth, and its people, was wrong.

Studying the stars (opposite) became a popular hobby for kings and nobles in the 1600s after Copernicus (above) showed that Earth revolves around the sun (right).

Copernicus spent many nights studying the sky. He also spent much time doing mathematical calculations. He believed that mathematics was an important part of astronomy. Astronomy is the science that deals with the sun, moon, stars, and planets.

Galileo

Galileo Galilei was an Italian born in 1564. He was interested in mathematics. He wondered if heavy objects fell faster than lighter objects. Aristotle, of ancient Greece, had said they did. However, Galileo *watched* falling hailstones hit the ground at the same time no matter what their size. He decided that Aristotle was wrong. A new age was born where ideas would be tested by experiments.

READING CHECK What did Copernicus's studies lead him to believe about Earth and the sun?

THE TELESCOPE AND SPACE

Astronomy was aided by a new invention called the **telescope**, an instrument that made distant things seem close. The same invention had also helped Galileo in his scientific studies.

Studying the Moon and the Stars

Galileo was a teacher. He was not paid much, but he had time to pursue his own studies. He improved the original Dutch telescope and sold his design to the navy of Venice. Galileo's invention made him rich, and he was able to spend more time studying the night sky.

One night Galileo looked at the moon through his improved telescope. Ancient Greeks believed the moon had a smooth surface. This is what Galileo expected to see. He was surprised to see that the

moon was "rough and uneven, covered everywhere . . . with huge mountains and deep valleys."

Galileo set about studying the night sky carefully. He realized that the universe was more complicated than people had thought. With his telescopes he could see many more stars than people could see with their eyes alone. He also discovered that the planet Jupiter had several moons in orbit around it. His most dramatic discovery was that Earth was spinning and was circling in an orbit around the sun.

Galileo's discoveries convinced him that Copernicus's heliocentric view was correct. He expected others to be as excited as he was about his discoveries. They could check his ideas by looking through the telescope themselves. Galileo was in for a surprise when his findings were published in 1613.

Galileo worked and studied in his home in Florence, Italy.

The Telescope

Galileo's telescope was a metal tube, about as long as your arm, with two lenses.

The First Telescope A Dutch eyeglass maker named Hans Lippershey found that distant objects seemed closer if he looked at them through two curved lenses. He created the first telescope in 1608 for military leaders to study advancing armies or ships. Galileo was the first to use a telescope to study the stars.

Telescopes Today Telescopes were constantly improved. Different kinds of lenses were used. Some reflected light through mirrors to create a better image. Today, telescopes are housed in huge buildings, with reflectors 1,000 feet across. Telescopes in outer space study distant stars that cannot be seen from Earth's surface.

Why was the telescope such an important invention?

The Church and Heliocentrism

Galileo was famous, so his writings came to the attention of Roman Catholic Church leaders. They told Galileo that the heliocentric idea went against the teachings of the Church. If Galileo did not stop writing, he would be arrested, tried by a Church court, and could possibly be put to death.

Galileo's books were **banned**, which meant that they could not be printed or sold. He was not allowed to leave his home, but he did continue his studies. In 1633, he was arrested and brought to Rome for trial. Galileo was told to abandon his heliocentric theory or face life in prison.

Galileo gave up his heliocentric idea, but it was a difficult choice. He knew that his discoveries were correct, but he was a sincerely religious man. He wrote:

I have two sources of comfort—first, that in my writings there cannot be found the faintest shadow of disobedience towards the Holy Church; and second, the truth of my own conscience, which only I and God in Heaven thoroughly know.

READING CHECK Why did the Church punish Galileo?

Galileo's telescope (left) allowed him to chart the moon's surface (above).

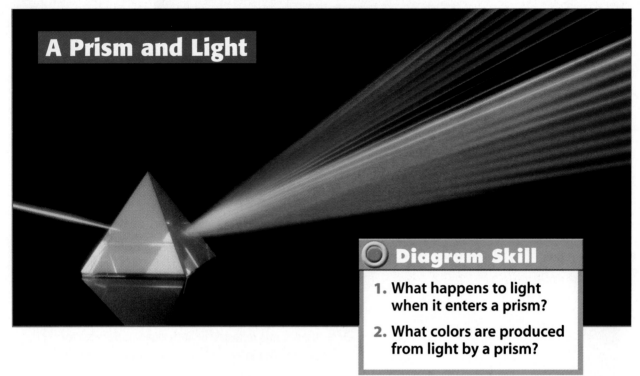

A Prism and Light

Diagram Skill

1. **What happens to light when it enters a prism?**

2. **What colors are produced from light by a prism?**

LAWS OF THE UNIVERSE

In 1642, the same year that Galileo died, Isaac Newton was born in the English countryside. Newton became one of the world's giants in science. In fact, he built on Galileo's scientific legacy.

Gravity

The story of Newton being hit on the head by an apple is now thought to be a myth. True or false, it illustrates the law of **gravity**, the force that pulls things toward Earth. Newton calculated that the same force that pulls a falling apple toward Earth also pulls at the moon. Newton also explained why the moon did not crash into Earth. Newton's study of gravity helped scientists in the late 1600s to understand better how a heliocentric universe worked.

Had Newton developed the law of gravity and nothing else, he would still have been an important scientist. However, Newton made many other discoveries as well. He developed an entirely new area of mathematics, called calculus.

Newton also developed the theory of motion, which is an important part of developing a space program.

In addition, Newton studied color and light. He used a prism, an instrument that bends and separates light, to show that it is made up of many bands of color. His work led to the modern invention, the spectroscope.

Newton realized that his studies of light could improve the telescope. He developed a telescope that used mirrors to reflect the light from stars.

Newton was a remarkably modest man. He said of himself,

> *I seem to have been only like a boy playing on the seashore. . . . now and then finding a prettier shell. . . . while the great ocean of truth lay undiscovered around me.*

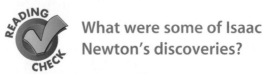

What were some of Isaac Newton's discoveries?

BIOGRAPHY

Focus On: Responsibility

Isaac Newton was 83 years old when he republished his great book, *Principia Mathematica* ("Mathematical Principles") in 1725. He had published the original book nearly 40 years earlier, but copies were rare and too expensive for students of mathematics. Also, Newton felt he should explain some of his ideas more completely.

This sense of responsibility was typical. While at England's Cambridge University, he risked his job and his freedom to protest the king's choice of an unqualified teacher.

Newton felt responsibility to himself as well. The German mathematician, Gottfried Leibniz, claimed the invention of calculus, giving no credit to Newton, who demanded his share of credit. Devoted to new ideas, Newton is often called "The Father of the Enlightenment."

Link to Today

Think about inventions or technology today. What responsibility does an inventor or company have when they sell a product?

THE LIFE OF ISAAC NEWTON	1642 Isaac Newton is born	1668 Newton builds a telescope	1687 Newton publishes his most famous book	1727 Isaac Newton dies

1630	1650	1670	1690	1710	1730

LIFE AROUND THE WORLD	1632 Mughal Emperor Shah Jahan begins the Taj Mahal	1644 Manchus found China's Qing dynasty	1673 The French explorers Jacques Marquette and Louis Jolliet explore the upper Mississippi River	1724 Dahomey becomes the leading power in West Africa

ADVANCES IN SCIENCE

René Descartes was born in France in 1596. He developed the **scientific method**, a way of testing ideas to determine if they are true. Descartes believed traditional European thinking, called deductive reasoning, was backwards. Deductive reasoning begins with a theory and then looks for reasons that prove the theory.

Descartes developed a way of thinking called inductive reasoning. He believed in looking at facts first. He used the facts to form a general principle, or theory. Then he tested his theory by looking at additional facts.

Medicine and Chemistry

Inductive reasoning became the basis of scientific discoveries. In England in 1628, William Harvey discovered that the heart pumps blood through the body. In France, around 1777, Antoine Lavoisier developed the idea of chemical elements, simple sub-

stances such as oxygen, iron, or gold that cannot be broken down into anything else.

In America, Benjamin Franklin conducted experiments that proved that lightning was electricity. He invented a device called the lightning rod to protect buildings during lightning storms.

The Enlightenment

European thinkers also began to look for universal laws they believed controlled government and society. This period, mainly through the 1700s, is called the **Enlightenment**. "To enlighten" means to give or receive wisdom.

In Europe, some rulers used Enlightenment ideas. Catherine the Great, Empress of Russia from 1762 to 1796, supported Enlightenment ideas. So did Frederick the Great, a German king from 1740 to 1786.

The Enlightenment had a strong impact on the 13 English colonies. For example, the Declaration of Independence was influenced by Enlightenment ideas. In 1787, the founders of the new nation, the United States, used ideas of Enlightenment thinkers, such as **John Locke**.

Lavoisier's wife, Marie (below), worked with her husband in his laboratory. Descartes, second from left (above), advises the Queen of Sweden.

John Locke

John Locke examined the relationship between people and government. Before Locke, most people in Europe believed that it was their duty to serve their rulers. They thought that God chose kings and wanted people to obey them. This was called the *divine right of kings.*

Locke argued that, instead, a contract, or agreement, between rulers and their people is the basis of government. A good ruler has the *consent of the governed.* If a ruler does not serve the people, they have the right to overthrow him. Locke's ideas started an age of political change.

John Locke

How did Enlightenment ideas affect the United States?

PUTTING IT TOGETHER

Historians call the 1600s and 1700s, the Enlightenment, or the "Age of Reason." European scientists and philosophers used reason to evaluate facts as they searched for the laws of science, government, and law. The development of inductive reasoning led to the birth of modern science and government.

Thinkers such as Descartes and Locke used reason to reach new conclusions about the world. The political ideas of John Locke influenced the leaders of the new republic, the United States of America and appeared in the Constitution they wrote for their new government.

Review and Assess

1. Write a sentence for each vocabulary word or term.

    geocentric   **scientific method**
    gravity   **telescope**
    heliocentric

2. Why did Galileo believe the heliocentric view of the universe was correct?

3. How did changes in science and thought lead to the development of the modern world?

4. How did the Enlightenment change ideas about **government**?

5. **Summarize** the work of Descartes and Locke.

Make a chart of the Enlightenment. On your chart, list the names of people you read about in this lesson. Write the dates of their lives, the country where they lived, and the reason that they are considered important.

Read the preamble (first paragraph) of the United States Constitution. **Write** a paragraph showing how it contains ideas of Enlightenment thinkers.

An Age of Exploration

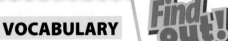
How did European explorers connect distant parts of the world?

VOCABULARY

caravel

strait

Northwest
  Passage

PEOPLE

Prince Henry

Bartolomeu Dias

Vasco da Gama

Christopher
  Columbus

Amerigo Vespucci

Ferdinand
  Magellan

Jacques Cartier

Henry Hudson

Lesson Outline

• Europeans Journey Eastward

• Explorers Sail the World

• Other Europeans Explore

BUILD BACKGROUND

"We were eating biscuits that were no longer biscuits but crumbs full of. . . [insects]. We also often ate sawdust."

In 1519, a Portuguese sea captain set off with five Spanish ships and 230 men on the first voyage around the world. The little ships sailed for months without seeing land. They ran out of food and many sailors died. Only one of the ships crept back into a Spanish harbor and just 18 of its crew were still alive. But they had proven Earth is round.

READING STRATEGY

Copy the chart. Label the three columns: "Explorer," "Country for which he sailed," and "Where did he land?" Complete the chart.

EUROPEANS JOURNEY EASTWARD

You have read how Marco Polo visited China in the late 1200s. His trip took 20 years, and he risked death on the Silk Road of Central Asia. He brought back silks and spices that sold for great profits in Europe. Europeans could charge high prices for Asian goods, but few were willing to risk Polo's journey even for such high profits.

A Prince's School for Navigators

In the late 1400s Europeans began to think about new ways to reach Asia. **Prince Henry** of Portugal (1394 to 1460) devoted his wealth and his life to finding a sea route to the riches of Africa and Asia.

The prince built a school where the most skillful sailors, mapmakers, and shipbuilders could work. These experts improved the compass and the astrolabe and updated maps.

The experts also developed a new kind of ship called a **caravel** (KA ruh vel). Caravels combined the broad bodies of European ships and the three-sided sails of Arab boats. Earlier European ships had to sail with the wind. The new caravel could sail in almost any direction.

Sailing Around Africa

In 1469, Portuguese sailors reached the coast of western Africa. A Portuguese navigator named **Bartolomeu Dias** (bahr tu lu MAY oo DEE ush) sailed around the southern tip of Africa, the Cape of Good Hope, in 1488. Dias had discovered a sea route from Europe to Asia.

Nine years later, another Portuguese, **Vasco da Gama**, reached India, the first European to sail so far east. Da Gama returned to India with warships in 1502, to conquer rich port cities for Portugal. This began a period of European rule in India that lasted more than 400 years.

READING CHECK Why were Europeans eager to reach Asia?

Experts under Prince Henry (below) improved the astrolabe.

457

EXPLORERS SAIL THE WORLD

Portugal's success encouraged its neighbor, Spain, to look for a sea route to Asia. In 1492, Spain was ready to send out an explorer of its own.

Columbus's Atlantic Adventure

An Italian seaman, **Christopher Columbus**, asked Spain's rulers to finance his plan to reach Asia by sailing west. No one realized that two large continents lay between Europe and Asia. Columbus set sail in August 1492 and came ashore three months later at an island that he called San Salvador. Columbus was convinced that he had landed in Asia.

He claimed the lands he sighted for Spain. He also traded with the people he saw, whom he called "Indians" because he believed he was in the Indies in Asia. In his journal he wrote:

> *I presented them with some red caps and strings of glass beads. . . . they came swimming to the boats. . . . bringing parrots, balls of cotton thread, javelins [spears], and many other things. . . . They. . . . gave what they had with the utmost good will.*

Sadly, the good will was not to last. Spain's rulers hoped that the lands Columbus had visited were rich in gold, so they sponsored other explorers to sail to the west.

Two New Continents

Columbus never admitted that he had sailed to a new continent. He continued to think he had discovered a new route to Asia. However, some later explorers realized his mistake.

Amerigo Vespucci (uh MAYR ih goh vehs PYOO chih) was an Italian explorer. Between 1497 and 1507, Vespucci made six voyages to explore the coast of South America. He understood that this was not Asia, and he wrote about the new continents in his journals, which were published widely in Europe. A German mapmaker included Vespucci's two conti-

The German mapmaker Martin Waldseemüller first showed the Americas as two continents in 1507 (below). Columbus (right) continued to insist he had reached Asia.

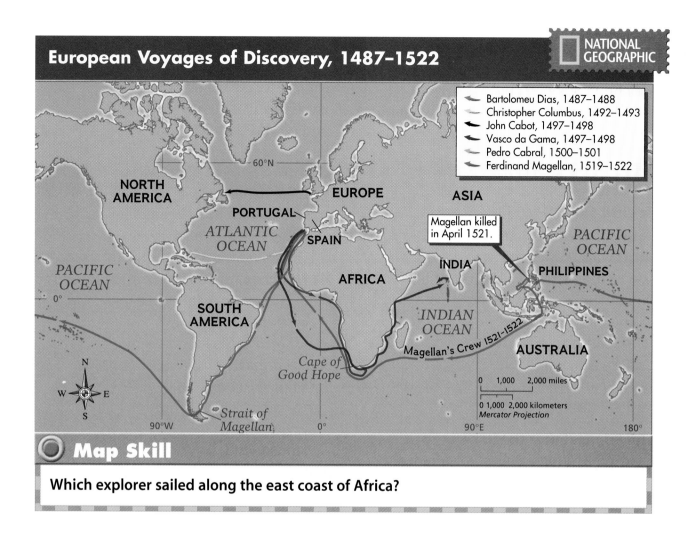

European Voyages of Discovery, 1487–1522

NATIONAL GEOGRAPHIC

Bartolomeu Dias, 1487–1488
Christopher Columbus, 1492–1493
John Cabot, 1497–1498
Vasco da Gama, 1497–1498
Pedro Cabral, 1500–1501
Ferdinand Magellan, 1519–1522

NORTH AMERICA
EUROPE
ASIA
PORTUGAL
ATLANTIC OCEAN
SPAIN
Magellan killed in April 1521.
PACIFIC OCEAN
PACIFIC OCEAN
INDIA
PHILIPPINES
AFRICA
SOUTH AMERICA
INDIAN OCEAN
Magellan's Crew 1521–1522
AUSTRALIA
Cape of Good Hope

0   1,000   2,000 miles
0 1,000 2,000 kilometers
Mercator Projection

Strait of Magellan
90°W
0°
90°E
180°
60°N
0°

Map Skill

Which explorer sailed along the east coast of Africa?

nents on a map in 1507. It was this map-maker who called the continents America in honor of Amerigo Vespucci.

Magellan's Voyage

You read about another historic voyage at the beginning of this lesson. A Portuguese seaman, **Ferdinand Magellan**, proposed to sail around the tip of South America to reach Asia. No one had ever tried to sail around the world before.

Magellan's ships struggled through the rough waters of a **strait** at the tip of South America. A strait is a narrow channel, or body of water, between two larger bodies of water. This strait is now called the **Strait of Magellan** in his honor. Three of Magellan's five ships reached the calm

waters of an ocean he called the Pacific, or "peaceful," Ocean.

As you read, the voyage across the Pacific Ocean was anything but peaceful. In the Philippines, Magellan was killed in a battle with local people. Finally, in 1522, his crew returned to Spain. The voyage had taken three years, but one small ship had completed the first journey around the world.

When the cargo, or freight, of the ship was sold, the profits covered the costs of the voyage and the cost of the four ships that were lost.

What was the importance of Magellan's voyage?

459

OTHER EUROPEANS EXPLORE

The rulers of other European countries were interested in the riches of Asia. The voyages they sponsored did not produce the wealth that Spain and Portugal had found, but they did establish colonies for settlers from Europe.

English Explorers

England's explorers hoped to find a **Northwest Passage**—a water route—to the wealth of Asia. In 1497, an Italian named John Cabot was hired by the king of England to find this passage. Although Cabot failed to find the passage, he did explore Newfoundland, Labrador, and Nova Scotia. He claimed these lands for England.

The French Enter the Race

In 1524, the French hired an Italian sailor named Giovanni de Verrazano (ver ray ZAH noh) to find the Northwest Passage. Verrazano failed, but he was the first European to sail into the harbor of present-day New York.

In 1534, a French explorer named **Jacques Cartier** (kahr TYAY) continued Verrazano's explorations. He sailed up the St. Lawrence River in Canada. It was not the Northwest Passage, but it gave France a claim in North America.

Henry Hudson and the Dutch

The most important Dutch explorer wasn't Dutch at all. His name was **Henry Hudson** and he was English. However, he was hired by Dutch merchants to find the Northwest Passage to Asia.

He failed to find a water route to Asia, but he discovered a broad river that still bears his name. In 1609 he sailed up the Hudson River to what is today Albany, New York. There he realized that he had failed to find the Northwest Passage.

Hudson did not give up. Two years later, he explored Hudson Bay in northern Canada for the English. He insisted that the bay must have a western outlet. Fearing they would never see their homes again, his crew mutinied and set Hudson, his son John, and seven crew members adrift in a small boat. They were never heard from again.

The Benefits of Exploration

Better ships and navigation instruments, together with human courage, added greatly to Europe's knowledge of the world in the late 1400s and the 1500s. As ships explored new sea routes, regions

France's Jacques Cartier (left) explored eastern Canada. Henry Hudson (above) asked Native Americans about the Northwest Passage.

Prince Henry the Navigator of Portugal began an age of exploration when he supported the search for new routes to Africa and Asia. Two Portuguese explorers, Bartolomeu Dias and Vasco da Gama opened up a route from Portugal to India. Spain sent Christopher Columbus across the Atlantic Ocean to the Americas. Ferdinand Magellan's expedition was the first to sail completely around the world.

Other nations, such as England, France, and the Netherlands, also joined in the search for routes to Asia. Their explorers tried to find a Northwest Passage across North America to the Pacific Ocean, but they failed to do so.

became more closely linked through trade and communication. Such links led to further exploration and conquest.

What was the Northwest Passage?

Review and Assess

1. Write a sentence for each vocabulary term.

   caravel   **strait**
   Northwest Passage

2. What were Prince Henry the Navigator's contributions to exploration?

3. How did European explorers bring distant parts of the world into contact?

4. What new technological innovations helped European sailors explore the world?

5. **Compare** and **contrast** Spanish exploration with French.

Trace or draw the map on page 459. There is a Northwest Passage, but only modern steel ships can use it. Draw the route of this passage on your map.

Suppose that you are a crew member on a European expedition of the 1500s. **Write** an entry in your diary explaining what you see and experience as your ship sights land in the Americas.

Using Maps to Compare

VOCABULARY

relief

In this chapter you used historical maps to find information. Elsewhere in the textbook you studied maps that communicate other kinds of information. For example, you used physical maps to identify natural features of areas. Such maps have **relief**, or shading, to show sharp differences in elevation. However, sometimes you need information that cannot be obtained from one map alone. You need to compare the same area on different kinds of maps.

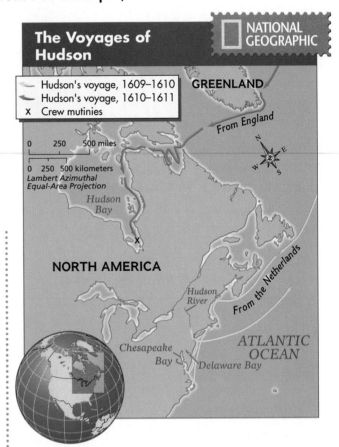

The Voyages of Hudson

NATIONAL GEOGRAPHIC

— Hudson's voyage, 1609–1610
— Hudson's voyage, 1610–1611
x   Crew mutinies

GREENLAND

From England

0   250   500 miles

0   250   500 kilometers
*Lambert Azimuthal
Equal-Area Projection*

*Hudson
Bay*

X

NORTH AMERICA

*Hudson
River*

From the Netherlands

*Chesapeake
Bay*

ATLANTIC
OCEAN

Delaware Bay

LEARN THE SKILL

Follow these steps to compare maps.

1. **Identify what types of information you need.**
   You want to know where Henry Hudson was when he disappeared, as well as the modern-day names of the waterways he traveled. A historical map will show where Hudson traveled but it may not give you the present-day information you seek.

2. **Identify the types of maps you have.**
   The map on this page shows the routes of Henry Hudson's voyages. The map on page 463 is a physical map of North America.

3. **Identify areas you need to study.**
   The historical map shows you that Henry Hudson's crew mutineed in an area of what is now called Hudson Bay. You need to study the same area on the physical map to find its present-day name.

4. **Use landmarks to compare the maps.**
   The physical map shows that Hudson sailed westward along the southern coast of Baffin Island, then south into Hudson Bay. The bay in the southern portion of Hudson Bay is today called James Bay.

TRY THE SKILL

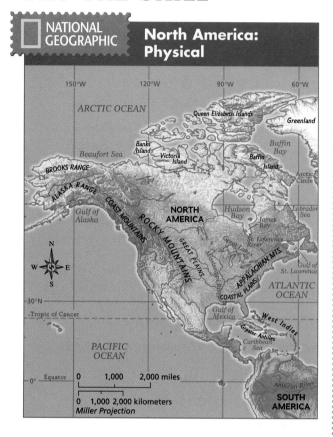

North America: Physical

By comparing the historical and physical maps on pages 462, 463, and R11 you can learn the modern names of many natural features that Henry Hudson saw on his first voyage. Use the steps to help you compare the maps.

1. What information do you need?

2. How will the types of maps on these pages help you find the information you need?

3. Which areas on the maps will you compare?

4. Which landmarks will you look at?

5. Why do people often need more than one map to obtain information?

EXTEND THE SKILL

Suppose you want to find which groups of Native Americans lived in New York State when Hudson arrived. Research the information. Then decide which kinds of maps would be most useful in locating this information. Draw the two maps you need. Include labels, a map key, and any other useful information.

● How can comparing and contrasting maps help you to learn more about the geography and history of the United States?

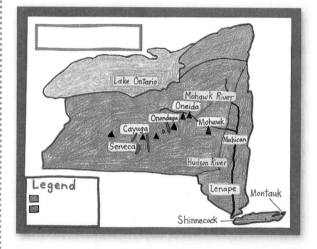

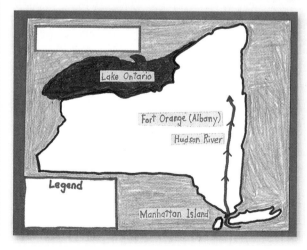

463

Conquering the Americas

How did European colonizers change life for people in the Americas?

Lesson Outline
- Dividing the Americas
- The Spanish Conquests
- Life in a Spanish Colony
- Other Europeans in the Americas

VOCABULARY

Line of Demarcation
conquistador
Creole
mestizo
hacienda
missionary
patroon

PEOPLE

Pedro Cabral
Hernando Cortés
Moctezuma
Atahualpa
Francisco Pizarro

BUILD BACKGROUND

On April 22, 1500, a ship appeared off the shores of eastern Brazil. The Tupikinim Indians watched as a group of Portuguese explorers came ashore. Gifts were exchanged—a Portuguese hat for a Tupikinim headdress. Within a few years, Portugal had conquered thousands of Tupikinim. About 20 years later Cortés (below) entered Mexico peacefully before conquering the Aztec.

READING STRATEGY

Complete this chart. Write details to support the main idea of the lesson: "The Spanish Build an Empire in the Americas."

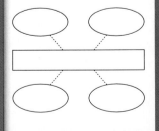

You Are Here
1493 – 1700

DIVIDING THE AMERICAS

In 1493, Columbus brought more than 1,000 people to the island he called **Hispaniola** (his puhn YOH luh).

In 1494, Portugal and Spain agreed on an imaginary line, called the **Line of Demarcation**, dividing the world in half. All territory west of the line was Spanish. Territory to the east was Portugal's.

Portugal claimed Brazil because of an explorer named **Pedro Cabral** (PE droh kah BRAHL). He had set sail for India in 1500, but a storm blew his ships to what is now Brazil.

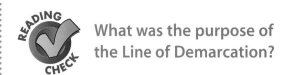

READING CHECK What was the purpose of the Line of Demarcation?

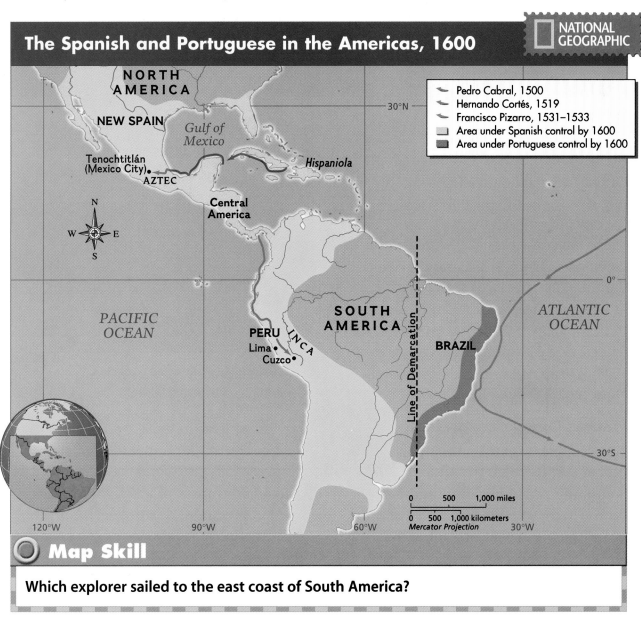

The Spanish and Portuguese in the Americas, 1600

NATIONAL GEOGRAPHIC

- Pedro Cabral, 1500
- Hernando Cortés, 1519
- Francisco Pizarro, 1531–1533
- Area under Spanish control by 1600
- Area under Portuguese control by 1600

Map Skill

Which explorer sailed to the east coast of South America?

465

THE SPANISH CONQUESTS

After Columbus's voyages, Spain began sending expeditions to the Americas. The men who led the expeditions were called **conquistadors** (kon KEES tuh dawrz), or conquerors, because they seized the lands and riches of Native Americans.

Cortés's Victory over the Aztec

In 1519, the conquistador **Hernando Cortés** (er NAHN doh kor TES) and an army of 500 men arrived in the area that is now Mexico. Cortés had heard stories of the rich and powerful Aztec Empire in Mexico.

Scouts of the Aztec emperor, **Moctezuma** (mahk tuh ZOO muh), reported Cortés's movements to their ruler. The Spanish headed for Tenochtitlán, the Aztec capital.

Moctezuma was dazzled by the Spanish, with their horses and guns, which he had never seen before. Believing that they might be gods, he welcomed them into the city and offered them gifts.

His welcome eventually proved the downfall of Moctezuma and the Aztec Empire. The Spaniards kidnapped Moctezuma. He was later killed in a riot. With the help of Indians who hated the Aztecs, Cortés captured the capital in 1521. Within a few years, Spain was in control of the Aztec Empire and its riches.

Pizarro's Conquest of the Inca

As you have read, another powerful Indian empire ruled the Andes region of South America. A civil war for the Inca throne had just ended in 1532. The winner of the Inca civil war, **Atahualpa** (ah tah WAHL pah), was the new ruler of the Inca Empire. However, his reign would be a very short one.

Cortés (above) defeated the Aztec army and conquered Mexico.

A conquistador named **Francisco Pizarro** (fran SEES koh pee SAHR roh) had heard rumors of a rich Indian kingdom in the Andes. Pizarro set out to conquer the Inca Empire.

Pizarro captured Atahualpa in a surprise attack. He murdered the Inca ruler, and many bloody battles followed.

New Spain stretched from southern Central America north into what is now the southwestern United States. The Spanish destroyed the Aztec city of Tenochtitlán and built their capital, **Mexico City**, on its ruins.

The colony of Peru—the name of a country today—included most of South America except Brazil, the Northeast, and the southern tip. Peru's capital was the coastal city of **Lima**, built by Pizarro in 1535. Gold, silver, and other goods poured into Spain, making it the richest European country of its day.

 How did the Spanish conquer the Inca Empire?

Despite its bravery, the Inca Empire fell to the Spanish by 1535.

The Spanish in Control

By the 1540s, Spain claimed land extending from what is today Kansas to the tip of South America. This enormous region was divided into two colonies, called **New Spain** and **Peru**.

Atahualpa (right) was the Inca ruler. The Spanish melted down many Inca treasures, like these (below), for their gold.

467

LIFE IN A SPANISH COLONY

The city of Lima is an example of life in the Americas under Spanish rule. Lima had Spanish-style churches and a university. At the center of the city were homes for Peru's most important citizens. At first, these were Spaniards who came to Lima to govern the colony. They usually returned to Spain after their term in office.

People of Spanish descent who were born in the Americas were known as **Creoles** (KREE ohlz). There were also the children of marriages between Creoles and Indians throughout the Spanish colonies. Known as **mestizos** (mehs TEE zohs), they worked at jobs from laborers to lawyers, but they rarely had important jobs in the government. At the lowest level of society were the Indians and enslaved Africans.

Indians in New Spain

Few of the Indians lived in the cities. Instead, the Spanish used Indians to work the rich gold and silver mines of Mexico and Peru. In the mines, Indians worked in darkness, with candles tied to their fingers. They had to haul loads as heavy as 300 pounds at a time. There were frequent accidents on what was sometimes a 60-story climb from the mine pits to the mine entrance.

Life on the Haciendas

Other Indians were forced to work on the **haciendas** (ah see EN dahs) owned by Spaniards or the Catholic Church. *Hacienda* is Spanish for a large area of land used for agriculture. Indian families lived and worked on haciendas raising wheat, grapes, cattle, and other products that were sold in colonial cities. Indians were unpaid or worked for low wages, so the hacienda owners made large profits from their lands.

Spanish colonists rebuilt cities such as Cuzco (below) and started ranches called **haciendas** (right).

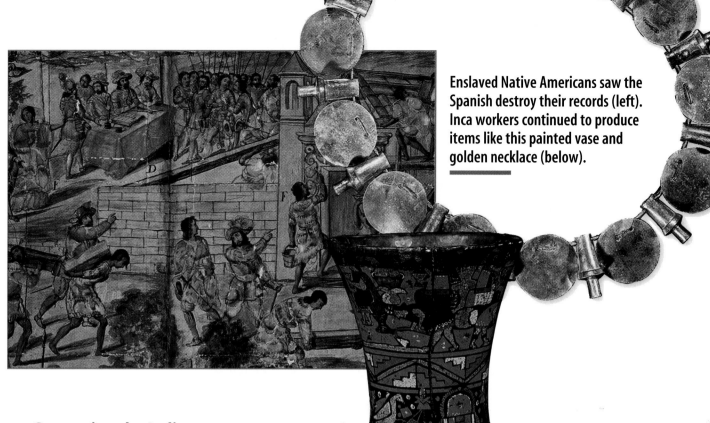

Enslaved Native Americans saw the Spanish destroy their records (left). Inca workers continued to produce items like this painted vase and golden necklace (below).

Converting the Indians

Many Spaniards came to the Americas to get rich. However, others came to convert Indians to Christianity. Those who teach their religion to others with different religious beliefs are called **missionaries**. The Spanish government gave these missionaries land grants where they set up missions. The mission had a church and a school where the Indians were taught about the Catholic religion.

The missionaries' goal was to make the Indians become Roman Catholics. Some missionaries, at times, used force to convert the Indians. They also made Indians support life at the mission. Some Indians learned European farming methods while others trained to be carpenters, blacksmiths, or other craftworkers. Some Indians learned to read and write Spanish.

Decline of Indian Workers

From their first contacts with Europeans, Indians caught European diseases such as smallpox and measles. Because they had lived for centuries without contact with Europe, the Indians had no immunity, or resistance, to these diseases. They began to die in great numbers. In fact, disease was the major cause of death among the Native American population after Europeans arrived.

In the 50 years after the Spanish conquest, New Spain's Indian population fell from an estimated 25 million to under 3 million. In Peru the population decreased from about 9 million to under 2 million.

You will read more about how Indians were treated in the next lesson. You will also read about what hacienda and mine owners did to replace the declining numbers of Native American workers.

What work did Indians do in Spanish colonies?

t' Fort nieuw Amsterdam op de Manhatans

Collection of the New York Historical Society, Detail

Dutch settlers in New Amsterdam brought items such as this tile (right) from their homeland.

OTHER EUROPEANS IN THE AMERICAS

Through the 1500s, the Spanish and Portuguese were the only European powers to settle colonies in the Americas. In the early 1600s, the Dutch, the French, and the English began to establish colonies as well.

The Dutch Colonies

The Dutch established settlements in the Hudson River valley of what is now New York beginning in the early 1600s. The colony was called New Netherland. It included Manhattan Island, now part of New York City, which they bought from the Native Americans in 1624.

The Dutch also gave large land grants to landowners they called patroons. The patroon was required to bring at least 50 Dutch settlers to work the land. In return, the patroon was given complete control over the lives of the people on his estate. The plan was never very popular with the settlers, and few Dutch settlers agreed to work for these patroons.

New Netherland became New York in 1664 when the English navy sailed to New Netherland, and it surrendered.

The French in the Americas

France also established a colony, called New France. It was what is now eastern Canada. Many French settlers were fur traders. They bought furs from the local Indians and sold the furs to dealers in Europe for large sums of money.

New France never had many settlers. By 1660, only about 3,000 Europeans lived in the colony. This number grew slowly when the French government encouraged new settlers to set up farms.

The English Colonies

The first permanent English colony was started in 1607 at Jamestown in what is now Virginia. Within 100 years there were over 300,000 settlers in 13 colonies along the east coast of North America. At the same time thousands of Native Americans lost their homelands.

In the northern and middle colonies, most settlers had small farms. In the south, many farms were large, and were worked by enslaved Africans who grew crops for sale.

The 13 English colonies were part of the British Empire until 1776. In that year, they revolted. In 1783 they became an independent country called the United States of America.

 Which countries established colonies in North America?

PUTTING IT TOGETHER

Within a few years of Columbus's voyages, Spain and Portugal had grown rich from their American colonies. Conquistadors conquered the Aztec and Inca empires. By 1540 Spanish colonies stretched from present-day Kansas to the tip of South America.

France, the Netherlands, and England also established colonies. The Dutch colony on Manhattan was a center of trade. France claimed part of Canada, but few settlers went there. England established a string of colonies along the east coast of North America.

Early English colonists built houses like the ones they had left in England.

Review and Assess

1. Write a sentence for each vocabulary word or term.

   conquistador   **Line of Demarcation**
   Creole   **missionary**
   hacienda

2. Why did Dutch settlers not want to work for a patroon?

3. What effect did the coming of the Spanish and Portuguese have on the lives of the Indians?

4. Why did New France have few settlers?

5. **Draw a conclusion** about why European nations wanted to establish colonies in the Americas.

 Activities

Look at the map on page 465. Which part of the continent of South America was not a Spanish colony? Look in an encyclopedia to learn more about this region. Create a table in which you list its major geographical features.

Write a letter that a Spanish soldier might have written to his wife in Spain shortly after his arrival in Lima, Peru. Include details that describe the way of life in the colony.

Slavery in the Americas

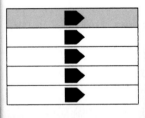 Why did slavery develop in the Americas?

Lesson Outline
• Enslaved Indians
• The African Slave Trade
• Slavery in the British Colonies

VOCABULARY

Middle Passage
triangular trade
cotton gin

PEOPLE

Olaudah Equiano
Bartolomé de las Casas

READING STRATEGY

Copy this cause and effect chart. Write two effects of the cause: "European settlers needed labor for their large farms."

▶	
▶	
▶	
▶	
▶	

BUILD BACKGROUND

"When I looked around the ship . . . and saw . . . black people of every description chained together . . . I no longer doubted my fate; and, quite overpowered with horror and anguish, I fell motionless on the deck and fainted."

That is how **Olaudah Equiano** (AHL uh duh ih kwee AH noh) described the experience of a slave ship in his autobiography. Recently, some historians have questioned his claim. In either case, Equiano describes the experience of thousands of Africans who were taken across the Atlantic Ocean and sold into slavery.

ENSLAVED INDIANS

The Spanish and Portuguese were eager for wealth from their American colonies. They realized that their plantations and mines needed many workers, and the few Europeans weren't willing to do the work. They began to enslave the American Indians to fill their labor needs.

Indians as Slaves

The Portuguese were the first Europeans in the Americas to use Indians as slave laborers. The Portuguese raided the villages of the Tupinamba Indians and put the people to work on sugar plantations along the northeast coast of Brazil.

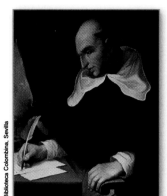

Biblioteca Colombina, Sevilla

Bartolomé de las Casas

In the Caribbean islands, the Spanish enslaved the Indians who had greeted Columbus on his first voyage. Among these were the Arawak. The Spanish also used enslaved Indians on the haciendas as you read in the last lesson.

Many Spanish masters treated their enslaved Indians badly. A Spanish priest named **Bartolomé de las Casas** protested strongly against this harsh treatment. The king of Spain agreed and ordered an end to Indian slavery. At the same time, diseases introduced by Europeans had killed thousands of Indians. There were not enough left to provide the labor the Spanish needed. The Europeans had to look elsewhere for workers.

READING CHECK Why did the Europeans stop enslaving Indians?

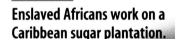

Enslaved Africans work on a Caribbean sugar plantation.

473

THE AFRICAN SLAVE TRADE

As you have read, the Portuguese explored the west coast of Africa in the late 1400s. They profited from their trade with Africans. Then, about 1530, the Portuguese began to capture Africans and send them to Brazil. During the next 70 years, the Portuguese sent thousands of enslaved Africans to the Americas.

Other Nations in the Slave Trade

By the mid-1500s, the trade in enslaved Africans had risen to 27,000 a year, and in the following century the number rose to 70,000 a year. The Netherlands, England, Denmark, Spain, and France began to bring captive Africans into their colonies as well. By the mid-1800s more than 10 million Africans had been shipped to the Americas. About 38 percent went to Brazil, 27 percent to the Caribbean islands, and 6 percent to the 13 colonies. The rest went to other colonies.

The Middle Passage

Most enslaved Africans were kidnapped in West Africa and in the interior of the continent by African and Arab traders. These kidnapped people were then brought to West African ports, where they were loaded on ships sailing to the Americas.

The voyage across the Atlantic was called the **Middle Passage**. It was the middle part of a journey from Africa to a new life in the Americas. The three-month passage was a living nightmare for the enslaved Africans. They were chained below decks in crowded spaces so low that they couldn't stand upright. They were fed spoiled food and unclean water. Some Africans jumped overboard rather than endure these conditions. Many died before reaching land.

Once ashore, the Africans were sold and quickly put to work. Olaudah Equiano, whom you read about earlier in this lesson, claimed he was kidnapped as an 11-year-old and sold to work on a Virginia plantation.

This painting (left) by a British eyewitness shows the terrible conditions on a slave ship (model, below) during the Middle Passage.

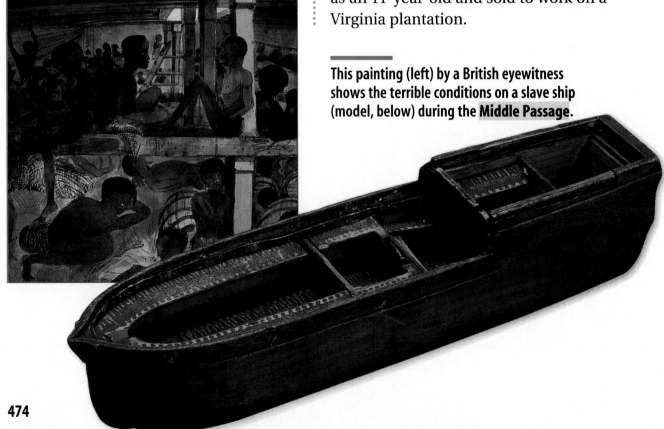

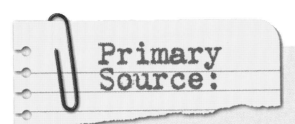
excerpt from **The Life of Olaudah Equiano**
— written by himself, 1789

*"We were conducted immediately to the merchant's yard, where we were all **pent up** together, like so many sheep. . . . We were not many days in the merchant's **custody**, before we were sold after the usual manner. . . . On a signal given (as the beat of a drum) buyers rush at once into the yard where the slaves are confined, and make a choice of the parcel they like best. . . . In this manner, . . . are relations and friends separated, most of them never to see each other again. I remember in the vessel in which I was brought over . . . there were several brothers who, in the sale, were sold in different lots; and it was very moving . . . to see and hear their cries in parting."*

What did Equiano think was worst about the sales?

pent up: locked up; penned up
custody: care; possession

Profiting from Slavery

Plantation owners depended on enslaved workers for their profits. Enslaved people cleared forests for planting. They prepared the soil and kept fields clear of weeds. On a sugar plantation at harvest time, they cut sugar cane all day in the hot sun. They carried the stalks to plantation mills, where they were crushed. The cane juice was boiled to produce sugar crystals. Then the workers filled barrel after barrel with sugar.

The Results of Slave Labor

Sugar became a very valuable overseas trade item, and the profits were enormous. Some sugar was shipped across the Atlantic to Europe. Later, sugar also went to New England, where it was converted into rum. These products were then shipped to Africa, where they were exchanged for more enslaved Africans for colonial plantations. This trade between Africa, New England, and the Caribbean formed a triangle, so it is called the **triangular trade**.

Some plantations in the British colonies produced indigo, tobacco, rice, or cotton. The owners made large profits from the crops raised by enslaved Africans. Plantation owners bought European luxuries with their profits. They also bought more captives and expanded the size of their plantations, creating both wealth and sorrow in the Americas.

READING CHECK What made slavery so profitable?

SLAVERY IN THE BRITISH COLONIES

Africans came to Britain's North American colonies when a Dutch ship arrived in Jamestown, Virginia, in 1619. Later, slavery became common in every British colony. It was widespread in the southern colonies, where enslaved Africans produced crops of tobacco, cotton, and indigo. These crops brought good prices and high profits.

British colonies to the north also allowed slavery. In fact, in the late 1700s New York City had more slaves than any British settlement other than Charleston, South Carolina.

In southern colonies, plantation owners depended on the special skills of enslaved workers. In the 1690s, for example, enslaved Africans brought their knowledge of rice cultivation with them to South Carolina. Soon rice became a leading crop in that colony. The slave population of the southern colonies grew. By 1708, the slaves of South Carolina formed a majority of its population.

Cotton Becomes King

Cotton was another southern plantation crop, but cotton required hours of hand labor to separate seeds from the cotton fibers. This meant that cotton was not a profitable crop.

In 1793, a New Englander named Eli Whitney invented the **cotton gin**, a machine that separated cotton fibers from their seeds. With a cotton gin, a worker could clean up to 50 times as much cotton as he or she could by hand. Suddenly cotton became a very profitable crop. Plantation owners rushed to plant new cotton crops. Almost immediately,

Cotton plantations made huge profits after the invention of the **cotton gin** (right).

cotton became a leading export of the United States.

Cotton was so profitable that it caused slavery to spread quickly in the South. By 1860, there were almost 4 million enslaved people in the United States. European countries had ended slavery in their countries and colonies in the first half of the 1800s. However, slavery in the United States did not end until the North won the Civil War in 1865.

Why did the number of enslaved workers rise in the American South?

PUTTING IT TOGETHER

European colonies in the Americas needed large numbers of workers for their farms and mines. At first, they put Indians to work as slaves, but many Indians died from European diseases. Thousands of enslaved Africans were brought to the Americas under terrible conditions to work colonial mines and plantations.

Enslaved workers produced profitable crops, such as sugar cane and cotton. Planters imported more enslaved Africans and expanded the size of their plantations to increase their profits. Slavery ended by law in most European colonies by 1850. However, slavery in the United States ended only in 1865 after the Civil War.

Review and Assess

1. Write a sentence for each vocabulary term.

   cotton gin   **triangular trade**
   Middle Passage

2. Why did sugar and cotton plantations require many workers?

3. Why did the Europeans use enslaved Africans to work mines and plantations in American colonies?

4. What effect did slavery have on the **economy** of European colonies?

5. What **conclusion** can you **draw** about Olaudah Equiano's attitude to slavery?

Activities

Review the information about the triangular trade on page 475. Draw a map of the lands surrounding the Atlantic Ocean. On your map, draw the three legs of the triangular trade. Draw pictures or write what was carried by ships on each stage of the triangular trade.

Write an editorial for a newspaper in a British colony. Express your opinion about the growth of the slave trade.

Lesson 5

Europeans in the Pacific

VOCABULARY

penal colony

PEOPLE

James Cook
Kamehameha
Liliuokalani
Elizabeth Veale

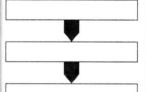

READING STRATEGY

Make a sequence-of-events chart like this one. Write events in the lesson in chronological order on your chart.

Find Out!

Why did foreigners settle Hawaii and Australia?

Lesson Outline
• Islands in the Pacific
• The Europeans Arrive
• Settlement of Australia

BUILD BACKGROUND

"We all went ashore where we were met by some hundreds of the inhabitants whose faces . . . gave evident signs that we were not unwelcome guests. . . . The first who [approached] us . . . gave us a green bough [branch] the token of peace."

James Banks, a young scientist who sailed with British explorer **James Cook** in 1768, described the people of one Pacific island in this excerpt. In this lesson, you will learn more about Cook's voyages and the lands he saw.

478

ISLANDS IN THE PACIFIC

The friendly people the English explorer described were Polynesians (pah luh NEE zhun), people who had settled many of the Pacific islands thousands of years earlier. The Polynesians were expert sailors and navigators, who sailed across the Pacific Ocean guided only by the stars. On page 480, you will find a rowing song from the island of Tahiti.

The Pacific islands are separated by many miles of ocean, but Polynesians spoke similar languages and followed similar customs. Many had a class structure similar to that of feudal Europe.

Hawaii

The Hawaiian Islands, now the state of **Hawaii**, were settled by Polynesians around A.D. 300 to 600. Until the late 1700s, the islands were ruled by local nobles who were often at war with each other. In 1796, King **Kamehameha** (KA meh a meh a) began to unite the Hawaiian Islands under his rule.

In the early 1800s, whaling ships and ships trading with China began to stop at the Hawaiian Islands. The foreign sailors brought new diseases and many of the native Hawaiians died.

Americans came to the islands in the mid-1800s, some as missionaries, and others to plant cash crops such as pineapples and sugar. A group of American plantation owners overthrew the last Hawaiian ruler,

---

Kamehameha (right) unified the Hawaiian Islands.

Colonization in the Pacific

Island or Territory	Colonized by
Guam (1565)	Spain
Tahiti (1768)	France
New Zealand (1769)	Great Britain
Fiji (1874)	Great Britain
New Guinea (1884)	Germany and Great Britain
Samoa (1899)	Germany

Chart Skill

1. **Which European country had the most colonies?**

2. **Which island was colonized by two countries?**

Queen **Liliuokalani** (li lee yew oh kah LAH nee), in 1893 because she tried to reduce their power.

Many of the other islands of the Pacific had a similar history. They became colonies of European nations and their traditional way of life declined as European settlers took control of the islands.

READING CHECK

What did many of the Pacific islands have in common?

479

Hoe Ana

Tahitian Folk Song
Collected and Transcribed by Kathy B. Sorensen

Tahitian: Ho-e a-na, ho-e a-na, ho-e na te va-ka te va-ka nei.

Hae-re mai na, hae-re mai na, hae-re mai e i-ne ma - e.____

Paddle, paddle, paddle the canoe
Paddle, paddle, paddle the canoe
Come back, come back, come back to everyone
Come back, come back, come back to everyone

480

THE EUROPEANS ARRIVE

The Spanish, the Portuguese, and the Dutch were the first Europeans to explore the Pacific region. Dutch explorers landed in Australia in the early 1600s, but they did not realize it was a continent. They did nothing about their discovery.

On other expeditions to the Pacific region, European explorers landed at many of the islands. The Europeans traded with the Polynesians and claimed some of the islands as colonies. By the late 1700s Great Britain, Spain, France, and the Netherlands had claimed many of the Pacific islands.

Captain James Cook

The most famous Pacific explorer was an Englishman named James Cook.

In 1768, the British government selected Cook to lead an expedition to the Pacific to explore the region.

Cook's first voyage was a scientific expedition in which he discovered many unknown plants and animals. It also made the first complete map of New Zealand and claimed Australia for Britain. The first British colony in Australia was called **New South Wales**.

Cook tried to make friends with the native people he met on this voyage. Some later European explorers had conflicts with local peoples which sometimes led to violence.

 **READING CHECK** What did James Cook's expedition accomplish?

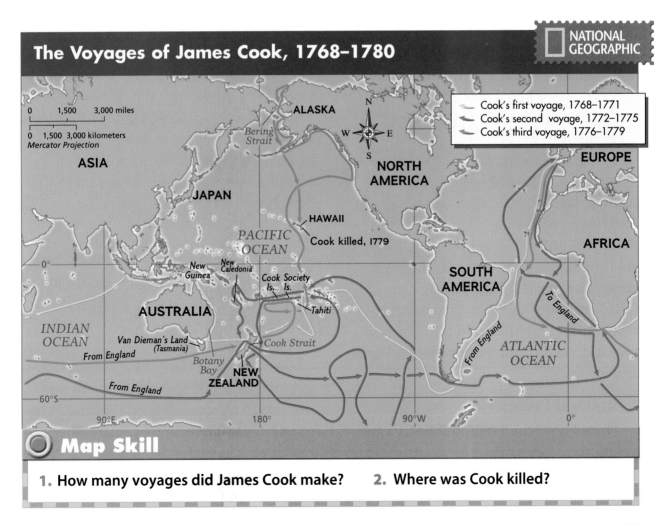

The Voyages of James Cook, 1768–1780

NATIONAL GEOGRAPHIC

0   1,500   3,000 miles
0   1,500   3,000 kilometers
Mercator Projection

- Cook's first voyage, 1768–1771
- Cook's second voyage, 1772–1775
- Cook's third voyage, 1776–1779

ASIA

JAPAN

ALASKA

Bering Strait

NORTH AMERICA

EUROPE

HAWAII
Cook killed, 1779

PACIFIC OCEAN

AFRICA

New Guinea

New Caledonia

Cook Society Is. Is.

SOUTH AMERICA

To England

AUSTRALIA

Tahiti

INDIAN OCEAN

Van Dieman's Land (Tasmania)

Cook Strait

From England

ATLANTIC OCEAN

From England

Botany Bay

NEW ZEALAND

From England

ASIA

60°S

90°E   180°   90°W   0°

Map Skill

1. **How many voyages did James Cook make?** 2. **Where was Cook killed?**

481

SETTLEMENT OF AUSTRALIA

Captain Cook met only a few people when he landed at Australia. However, hunter-gatherers had lived on the continent for about 40,000 years.

Aboriginal People

These people are today called aboriginal (ab oh RIJ uh nuhl) people, which means the first people to live in a place. Australia's aboriginal people gathered wild plants and hunted with stone weapons.

The simple technology of the aboriginal people contrasted with their rich culture and elaborate spiritual beliefs. They believed that land was a gift from their gods and could not be owned. The aboriginal people believed the land was created by "great spirits" during a period called "dreamtime." They also believed that spirits created "dream trails" across the land, connecting places that had food and water.

Australia as Penal Colony

Throughout the 1700s, the British government had used some North American colonies as **penal colonies**, a colony

English settlers in Australia cut down trees and laid out farms and cities.

where criminals are sent as punishment. Many of these criminals had been sentenced for their political beliefs or for minor crimes.

After American independence, Britain needed a new penal colony. Prisoners were first sent to Australia in 1788. Prisoners worked side by side with guards to survive. They had few tools to build houses. Droughts and unfamiliar soil conditions ruined crops. Often these first British settlers faced starvation.

New Settlers

By the 1790s, however, the colony was a success. The promise of land and a fresh start attracted free settlers. Many later settlers used convicts to provide the labor for their farms.

The success of the colony owed much to its women. **Elizabeth Veale**, who was married to a successful sheep owner, was often left in charge of their estate. She managed so well that wool production became an important industry in Australia.

Clash with Aboriginal People

To raise sheep, colonists needed large amounts of land, but the aboriginal people also needed large spaces for their hunter-gatherer way of life. As a result, British colonists clashed with the aboriginal people. Many aboriginal people were killed, and forced to stop hunting and gathering. Even after Australia became an independent country in 1901, the aboriginal people found it difficult to continue their traditional way of life. Today the Australian government is trying to find ways to right the injustices done to them.

 Why was the colony of Australia a success?

PUTTING IT TOGETHER

The Pacific islands were first settled by Polynesians, a great sailing people. Their sailing skills helped them to spread their culture across the Pacific over thousands of years.

The aboriginal people arrived in Australia about 40,000 years ago. They led a simple hunter-gatherer life with rich spiritual beliefs.

Europeans arrived in the Pacific in the 1500s. The voyages of James Cook established a British claim to the continent of Australia. During the 1800s, Britain and other European countries claimed various Pacific islands as colonies.

The Australian government is trying to help the remaining aboriginal people by building schools and clinics.

Review and Assess

1. Write a sentence for the vocabulary term.
   penal colony

2. Who was King Kamehameha?

3. How did Australia and Hawaii become settled by Europeans?

4. What effect did sheep raising have on the **economy** of Australia?

5. **Make a generalization** about the Australian aborigines' belief about the land.

Look at the map of Oceania on page R17 in the Atlas. Think about a Polynesian voyage across these huge spaces of water. Make a list of items Polynesians would need to take along for such a journey.

• •

Suppose you are a scientist accompanying James Cook. Do some research on the animals of Australia. **Write** a journal entry telling about an animal that Europeans had never seen before.

VOCABULARY REVIEW

Beside each number write the word or term from the list below that best completes the sentence.

conquistador   Northwest Passage

Line of   scientific method
  Demarcation

Middle Passage

1. European explorers tried to find the ____, a water route through North America to Asia.

2. The ____ is a method of analyzing ideas to determine if they are true.

3. Spain and Portugal divided land in the Americas between themselves by establishing the ____.

4. The ____ was the ocean voyage to the Americas made by captured Africans.

5. A ____ was a Spanish conqueror of the Americas.

CHAPTER COMPREHENSION

6. Why is Isaac Newton important?

7. What effect did the growth of science have on law, philosophy, and government?

8. Why was Prince Henry called "Henry the Navigator?"

9. What Native American empires did the Spanish conquer in the Americas?

10. What happened to the Native Americans in New Spain and Brazil?

11. Who are the native peoples of Australia?

12. Why did England want to found a colony in Australia?

13. **Write** a paragraph in which you describe a voyage of a ship in the triangular trade. Begin at a Caribbean island. List what is carried in each step of the voyage.

STUDY SKILLS

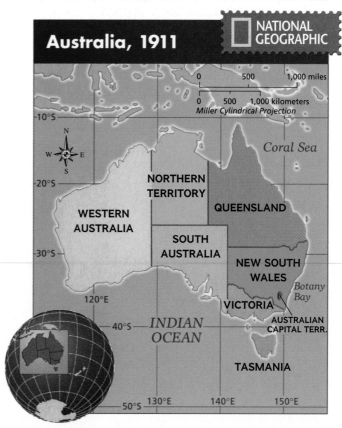

Australia, 1911 — NATIONAL GEOGRAPHIC

14. **Geography Skill** What is a political map? Why is the map above a political map?

15. **Geography Skill** How could you use maps to find the name of a modern Australian city founded by convicts?

16. **Reading/Thinking Skill** What conclusion can you draw about the effect of foreign settlement in Hawaii?

17. **Reading/Thinking Skill** Use the example of the aboriginal people to make a generalization about European attitudes to native peoples' claims to their land.

18. **Study Skill** How would you summarize the effect of scientific developments on the history of Europe?

USING A TIME LINE

1450	1500	1550	1600	1650	1700	1750	1800	1850

1497
Vasco da Gama sails to India

c. 1530
Portuguese begin slave trade in Brazil

c. 1540
Spain controls New Spain and Peru

1619
Enslaved Africans are brought to Jamestown

1642
Galileo dies; Isaac Newton is born

1788
Britain establishes penal colony in Australia

c. 1850
10 million enslaved Africans had been sent to the Americas

19. Which event on the time line marks the beginning of the enslavement of Africans in the Americas?

20. Explain the meaning of this date on the time line: "c. 1540: Spain controls New Spain and Peru."

Writing About History Suppose that you were writing a newspaper article about Descartes's idea of inductive reasoning. Explain the importance of this new method of reasoning to your readers. Also discuss how it differs from deductive reasoning.

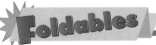

Use your Foldable to review what you have learned about technology and expansion. As you look at the five lesson titles on the front of your Foldable, mentally review how and why advances in technology led to expansion. Look at your notes under the tabs of your Foldable to check your memory and responses. Record any questions that you have, and discuss them with classmates, or review the chapter to find answers.

THE Big IDEAS ABOUT...

Revolutions and Expansion

In 1789 a revolution in France ended the rule of the French king and nobles. It was the first of a chain of revolutions that altered the governments and economies of many nations. Some of these revolutions, such as the ones that gained independence for the American colonies, were violent. Others, such as the revolution in manufacturing, were gradual. However, all of them changed the way people lived.

THE FRENCH REVOLUTION

The French people overthrow their king and establish a republic. Napoleon Bonaparte plunges Europe into war.

INDEPENDENCE IN THE AMERICAS

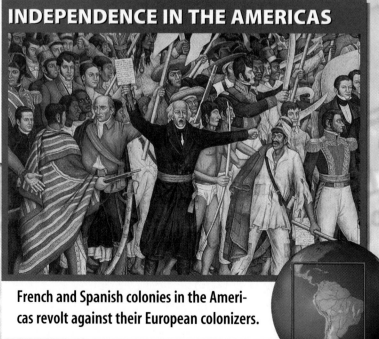

French and Spanish colonies in the Americas revolt against their European colonizers.

THE INDUSTRIAL REVOLUTION

In the late 1700s a new way of manufacturing begins in Britain. The 1800s, an age of invention, see changes in the way products are made and how people live around the world.

IMPERIALISM

Europeans found colonies in Asia and Africa. Colonial raw materials supply European factories and colonies provide markets for Europe.

THE BIRTH OF MODERN JAPAN

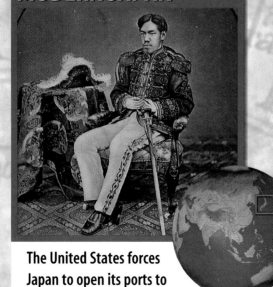

The United States forces Japan to open its ports to trade. Japan transforms itself quickly from a closed feudal island to a nation that is a world power.

Foldables

Make this Foldable study guide and use it to record what you learn about "Revolutions and Expansion."

1. Fold a large sheet of paper lengthwise into thirds.
2. Fold the thirds in half to form sixths.
3. Open the folded paper to see six rows.
4. Label five tabs with lesson titles, and label the sixth tab "Vocabulary of Revolution and Expansion."

The French Revolution

Find out! What were the causes of the French Revolution?

Lesson Outline
• The Kingdom of France
• The Revolution Turns Violent
• The Empire

VOCABULARY

absolute monarch
revolution
estate
aristocracy
peasant
Bastille
Declaration of the Rights of Man
Napoleonic Code

PEOPLE
Louis XVI
Marie Antoinette
Robespierre
Napoleon Bonaparte

READING STRATEGY

Copy this chart. In the center circle, write "French Revolution." In the outer circles write its causes.

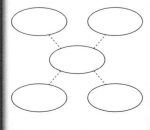

BUILD BACKGROUND

"To arms, to arms, you brave!
Take out the avenging sword!
March on, march on—all hearts resolved (determined)
On liberty or death!"

These words are part of the national anthem of France. The words were written in 1792 by a man who wanted the people of France to fight for their liberty against their king and foreign invaders. These words capture the ideals of the French Revolution, an event that changed Europe.

THE KINGDOM OF FRANCE

In 1789, **King Louis XVI** of France was an **absolute monarch**, a king who held all political power in his country. All laws began "Louis, by the Grace of God, King of France," a phrase that stated the king's divine right to rule. You read about this belief in divine right in Chapter 14.

Across Europe, other divine-right monarchs headed a system of nobles and church leaders that had not changed much since the Middle Ages. While most people worked the land, a few powerful nobles controlled the government, the military, and the church in each country.

By 1789 the unfairness of this system angered the common people of France so much that it would lead to a **revolution**, a sudden or great change. This revolution not only would change the government of France, it would change life in Europe forever.

Three Estates

As the chart shows, the people of France were divided into three **estates**, or social classes. The Catholic clergy, France's religious leaders, made up the First Estate. The First Estate owned nearly 15 percent of France's land and paid no regular taxes.

The Second Estate included the **aristocracy** (ar uh STOHK ruh see), members of France's noble families. The nobles owned about 25 percent of France's land, but paid no taxes.

The French Revolution began with the storming of the royal fortress in Paris in 1789 (left).

The rest of the French population, nearly 98 percent of the French people, belonged to the Third Estate. This group included **peasants**, or poor farm workers, craftworkers, and other laborers. Merchants, lawyers, and city-dwellers were also in the Third Estate. A few members of the Third Estate were rich. However, all members of the Third Estate had two things in common: they paid taxes and they had no voice in government.

 READING CHECK Who were the members of each of France's three estates?

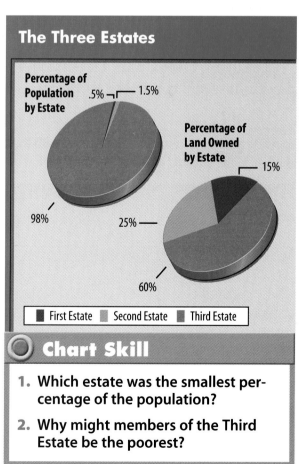

The Three Estates

Percentage of Population by Estate

.5% ¬ 1.5%

98%

Percentage of Land Owned by Estate

15%

25% ——

60%

■ First Estate ■ Second Estate ■ Third Estate

Chart Skill

1. **Which estate was the smallest percentage of the population?**

2. **Why might members of the Third Estate be the poorest?**

489

THE REVOLUTION TURNS VIOLENT

The French Government had spent huge sums to help the Americans win their independence. The costs of this war were one reason the French government had run out of money by 1789.

The king tried to tax the nobles, but they demanded a meeting of the Estates General, an assembly of representatives from the three estates. Louis XVI agreed to open the first meeting of the Estates General at his splendid palace at **Versailles** (vair SI) in May of 1789.

The Third Estate represented the largest number of people, but it had only one vote, like the other two estates. Members of the Third Estate demanded a vote to match their numbers. The king refused, so the members of the Third Estate formed a new national congress, called the National Assembly.

Resistance Becomes Revolution

On July 14, 1789, a rumor swept Paris that troops were coming to arrest the National Assembly. The people of Paris marched to the **Bastille** (bas TEEL), a royal fortress in the center of the city. They hoped to seize weapons to defend the National Assembly. A cannon was fired into the crowd. In the fighting that followed, 98 people were killed, but the citizens captured the Bastille. The anniversary of Bastille Day is still celebrated in France every July 14.

The Monarchy Is Overthrown

In August of 1789, the National Assembly adopted a document called the **Declaration of the Rights of Man**. It proclaimed that all men were "born and remain free and equal in rights." Soon shouts of "Liberty! Equality! Fraternity [brotherhood]!" echoed across France.

A new democratic spirit seized France. The king remained head of the government, but real power belonged to the National Assembly. In 1791, the king had to swear to support the Assembly.

Louis XVI and Marie Antoinette (right) lived with their children in the splendid palace of Versailles (below).

Worried, **Queen Marie Antoinette** (muh REE an twuh NET) organized an escape for the royal family, but the attempt failed. It was the end of the monarchy in France.

Revolution Turns to Terror

France became a republic in 1792, but the change did not come smoothly. The new leader of the French republic was named **Maximilien Robespierre** (MAX ih mihl yen ROHBZ pee air). He waged a war against the enemies of the Revolution. Although aristocrats were Robespierre's first targets, anyone could be arrested, tried and executed for "crimes" against the republic.

Robespierre's chief weapon of execution was a machine, called a guillotine (GEE oh teen), with a sharp steel blade that dropped to cut off people's heads. In January 1793, the king was executed by guillotine in a public square. Queen Marie Antoinette's execution followed in October. Thousands of people died during this "Reign of Terror", which did not end until Robespierre himself was guillotined in 1794.

Napoleon Comes to Power

A series of governments followed the Reign of Terror. Ambitious and greedy men struggled for power, but France was exhausted. Most people were worse off than they had been in 1789. The French began to wish for a strong leader who would put an end to the chaos.

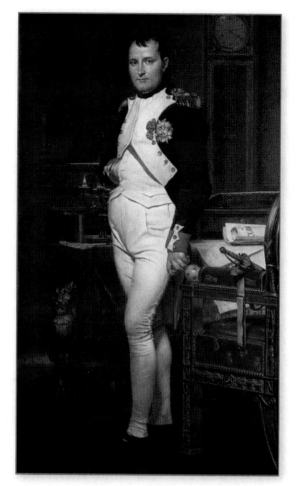

The guillotine (below) executed thousands of victims during the Reign of Terror. Napoleon (above) seized power in France in 1799.

In 1799, a 26-year-old general named **Napoleon Bonaparte** (nuh POH lee un BOH nuh pahrt) seized power. He maintained all the appearances of the republic, but Bonaparte was really the dictator of France. Ironically, the French Revolution had created an absolute ruler more powerful than Louis XVI.

READING CHECK

Why did the French people turn to Napoleon?

491

THE EMPIRE

In 1804, France became an empire. Napoleon staged a splendid coronation and invited the Pope. After the coronation, Napoleon began to conquer and reorganize other nations.

Completing the Revolution

In some ways, Napoleon continued the reforms of the French Revolution. His laws guaranteed equal justice to all citizens and supported freedom of religion. He also redrew the map of France, creating an efficient system of regions that is still in use today.

Napoleon also made taxes equal for all citizens throughout his empire, and he ended serfdom. However, he believed that his most important reform was the **Napoleonic Code**. This set of laws was so well organized that it is still the basis of the legal system of France and many other European countries.

The Napoleonic Code guaranteed religious freedom and gave every adult male the right to vote. However, the new laws actually limited the freedoms of speech and the press that the National Assembly had guaranteed. Napoleon also did not allow women to vote or even to own property.

Waterloo

Napoleon expanded his empire by defeating the Netherlands, Belgium, Germany, Italy, Spain, and Portugal. However, he was defeated in 1814 and exiled. He escaped, and, in 1815, his armies fought the combined armies of his enemies near a Belgian village called Waterloo. It was a total defeat for Napoleon. He was forced to leave France, and his empire came to an end.

READING CHECK What changes did Napoleon bring to France?

The Pope attended the splendid coronation of Napoleon in 1804.

were also changed. The ideas of liberty and representative government had spread to Germany and Italy. The French Revolution and the reign of Napoleon had ended the age of absolute monarchy.

Napoleon lost his throne after the Battle of Waterloo, but the French still award the medal (left) he created in 1802 to reward excellence.

PUTTING IT TOGETHER

Napoleon's defeat did not mean the end of the ideals of the French Revolution. France emerged from the defeat of 1815 as a stronger and better-organized country. In addition, many of the countries that had been conquered by France

Review and Assess

1. Write a sentence for each vocabulary word or term.

   absolute monarch   **Napoleonic Code**
   aristocracy   **revolution**
   estate

2. Why did Louis XVI call the Estates General?

3. Why did the people of France revolt against their royal rulers?

4. How did the French Revolution change the **government** of France?

5. Make a **generalization** about France after the Revolution.

Activities

Make a two-column chart. In one chart, write features of France before the Revolution. In the other column, write how that feature was changed by the Revolution.

• •

Suppose that you were a reporter covering the French Revolution. **Write** a list of questions you would ask Robespierre about his policies. Then, write the answers you think he would have given.

Reading and Thinking Skills

Frame of Reference

To understand the variety of opinions about the French Revolution, you need to understand **frame of reference**. A frame of reference is what a person uses in reaching a point of view. Frame of reference includes culture, economic background, geography, and experience. The speaker's age can also determine frame of reference.

VOCABULARY
frame of reference

"The [French] Assembly ... acts ... with as little decency as liberty. They act like the comedians of a fair ... they act amidst the ... cries of a mixed mob of ferocious men, and of women lost to shame. ...This assembly which overthrows kings and kingdoms....They have a power... to destroy, but none to construct ..."

-Edmund Burke

"The cause of the French people is that of all Europe, or rather of the whole world; but the governments are by no means favorable to it. It is important that we should never lose sight of this distinction [difference]. We must not confuse the peoples with their governments; especially not the English people with its government."

-Thomas Paine

LEARN THE SKILL

Follow the steps below to learn about frame of reference.

1. **Research the backgrounds of both speakers.**
   To understand a speaker's frame of reference, you must know about the speaker's life. Edmund Burke was a member of the English parliament, and a politician.

   Thomas Paine, on the other hand, was a citizen of the new American republic. Paine was living in Paris in 1789.

2. **Identify the points of view.**
   Identify the feelings of the speaker. Thomas Paine felt that the French Revolution was connected to the American cause. Edmund Burke thought that the French assembly was destroying the orderly world he knew.

3. **Compare the speaker's background and his or her view of the event.**
   As a supporter of the English king, Burke would disapprove the overthrow of a monarchy. Paine, a strong supporter of the American Revolution, would back uprisings against kings.

TRY THE SKILL

Now read another passage and answer the questions that follow.

> Olympe de Gouge (OH lamp duh goozh) was a French writer at the time of the French Revolution. A supporter of equal rights for women, she said
>
> *Male and female citizens, being equal in the eyes of the law, must be equally admitted to all honors, positions, and public employment, according to their capacity [ability] and without other distinctions besides those of their virtues and their talents.*

1. What is the writer's background?

2. What is her point of view about the rights of citizens in France?

3. How does knowing her frame of reference help you to evaluate her statement?

4. How does knowing a speaker's frame of reference help you understand the opinions you read in history?

EXTEND THE SKILL

Many newspapers, magazines, and television stations interview people about current events, such as sporting events or elections. Choose a recent event and find two interviews about it. Try to identify the speaker's frame of reference.

- What experiences or events in their lives might affect their frame of reference?

- How can determining frame of reference help you understand what you read and hear in the media?

Independence in the Americas

How did countries in the Americas win their freedom?

VOCABULARY

Latin America
decree

PEOPLE

Simón Bolívar

Toussaint
  L'Ouverture

Miguel Hidalgo

José María
  Morelos

Agustín de
  Iturbide

José de San
  Martín

READING STRATEGY

Make a sequence of events chart like this one. In the boxes, write the events in the order that led to freedom in Latin America.

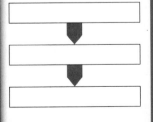

BUILD BACKGROUND

"[The Spanish] have violated the sacred rights of nations. They have broken the most solemn agreements and treaties. In fact, they have committed every manner of crime . . . ."

Those words were written by **Simón Bolívar** (see MOHN boh LEE vahr) to the people of Venezuela in 1813. Bolívar was one of the leaders of the rebellion against Spanish colonial rule.

THE COLONIES REVOLT

The revolutions in the United States and France excited people in colonies of the Americas. They began to consider seeking their freedom, too.

European colonial rulers were often dishonest. Taxes were high and trade with other countries was often forbidden. Most important, colonial people had no voice in their own government.

In 1800, most European colonies were in **Latin America**. Latin America is a cultural region south of the United States that has been strongly influenced by Spain, Portugal, and France.

Haiti

Revolution against a colonial ruler first broke out on the island of Hispaniola. In the French colony of Saint Domingue, enslaved Africans worked on coffee and sugar plantations. News of the French Revolution electrified them.

In 1791, an army of 100,000 slaves drove out the plantation owners. This slave army was led by **Toussaint L'Ouverture** (too SAN loo ver TYUR), a former slave. L'Ouverture forced the French to abolish slavery and took control of the colony's government in 1796.

In 1802, Napoleon sent an army to reestablish French rule in the colony. Toussaint defeated the French, but he was captured. Nevertheless, the colonists established the independent country of Haiti in 1804.

 Why did colonial people resent European rule?

Simón Bolívar (left) leads his troops into battle.

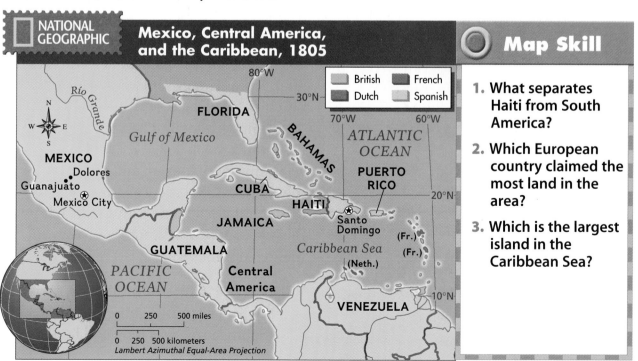

NATIONAL GEOGRAPHIC

Mexico, Central America, and the Caribbean, 1805

British   French
Dutch   Spanish

80°W
30°N
FLORIDA
70°W   60°W
Río Grande
Gulf of Mexico
BAHAMAS
ATLANTIC OCEAN
MEXICO
Dolores
Guanajuato
Mexico City
CUBA
PUERTO RICO
HAITI
Santo Domingo
JAMAICA
20°N
(Fr.)
GUATEMALA
Caribbean Sea
(Fr.)
(Neth.)
PACIFIC OCEAN
Central America
10°N
VENEZUELA
0   250   500 miles
0   250   500 kilometers
Lambert Azimuthal Equal-Area Projection

Map Skill

1. **What separates Haiti from South America?**

2. **Which European country claimed the most land in the area?**

3. **Which is the largest island in the Caribbean Sea?**

Mexican artist José Orozco's mural shows Miguel Hidalgo's *Call of Dolores*.

REVOLUTION IN MEXICO

Mexico was the richest of all the Spanish colonies in the Americas. However, more than half of its wealth was sent to Spain every year, leaving most Mexicans very poor.

The Call of Dolores

In 1810, a poor Mexican priest named **Miguel Hidalgo** (mee GEL ee DAHL goh) told the people in his small church in the town of Dolores that it was time for Mexicans to improve their own lives. His speech, known as *The Call of Dolores*, inspired his listeners. Hidalgo demanded equality for all people, including the Native Americans and mestizos, the people of mixed European and Mexican ancestry. Hidalgo also opposed slavery, which gained him support from Mexicans of African descent.

A crowd, armed mostly with clubs or pitchforks, marched out of Dolores. As they marched, they were joined by thousands of others. A well-armed Spanish army stopped them on the road to Mexico City, and Hidalgo was captured and executed.

Another priest, **José María Morelos** (ho SAY mah REE ah moh RAY lohs) carried on the struggle. In 1813 he called the first national congress and declared Mexico independent from Spain. However, in 1815 Morelos, too, was executed by the Spanish.

Independence at Last

In 1821, the cause of the Mexican revolution was taken up again by **Agustín de Iturbide** (ee toor BEE day). He was an officer in the Spanish army that had fought Hidalgo and Morelos.

Iturbide, a skilled military leader, was able to defeat the Spanish. Eleven years after Father Hidalgo first rang the bell of his church in Dolores, Mexico was free.

Iturbide turned out be more ambitious than patriotic. In 1822 he declared himself Emperor of Mexico and dismissed the Congress. Mexico was free from Spain, but it would be a long time before the Mexican people were given a say in their government.

Independence in South America

The struggle to free Latin America from Spanish rule was long and hard.

It was not until 1830 that the Spanish-speaking countries of Latin America were free of Spanish rule.

José de San Martín

Napoleon Bonaparte invaded Spain in 1808 and replaced the king with his own brother. This change of government in Spain encouraged the people of Latin America to revolt against Napoleon's Spanish government.

Freedom came first in the south. In 1816 the people of Argentina drove the Spanish forces out of their country. An Argentine general named **José de San Martín** (ho SAY day sahn mahr TEEN) led this fight for freedom. San Martín had been a Spanish officer, and he used his skills to win Argentina's independence.

Another Spanish army was in Chile, which is separated from Argentina by the tall peaks of the Andes Mountains. Spanish leaders in Chile believed that the Andes were like a wall protecting them from San Martín's army.

José de San Martín freed
Argentina and Chile.

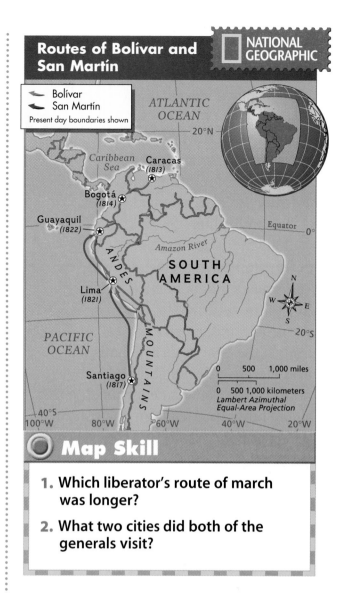

Routes of Bolívar and San Martín

NATIONAL GEOGRAPHIC

Bolívar
San Martín
Present day boundaries shown

ATLANTIC OCEAN

Caribbean Sea

Caracas (1813)

Bogotá (1814)

Guayaquil (1822)

Amazon River

SOUTH AMERICA

Equator

Lima (1821)

PACIFIC OCEAN

ANDES

Santiago (1817)

MOUNTAINS

0   500   1,000 miles
0   500 1,000 kilometers
Lambert Azimuthal
Equal-Area Projection

Map Skill

1. **Which liberator's route of march was longer?**

2. **What two cities did both of the generals visit?**

San Martín knew what the Spanish leaders thought, so he trained his army to do the impossible—to cross the Andes. In one of military history's great successes, he led his army across the snow- and ice-covered peaks. He surprised and defeated the more powerful Spanish forces and freed Chile.

The grateful people of Chile offered to make San Martín their president. He refused in favor of Bernardo O'Higgins, a Chilean general who had helped San Martín.

READING CHECK

How was San Martín able to defeat the Spanish?

BOLÍVAR AND INDEPENDENCE

In the northern part of South America, Simón Bolívar started the war for independence in 1810. By 1813 he had driven the Spanish out of Venezuela. A year later, a Spanish army returned and defeated Bolívar, who had to flee for his life.

Bolívar did not let this defeat stop the fight for Venezuela's independence. In 1817 he returned to Venezuela and led an army against the Spanish. The Spanish troops were defeated, but Bolívar was not finished. He was determined to free all of South America from Spanish rule.

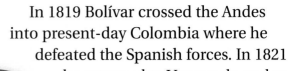

Bolívar met San Martín in Ecuador in 1822 (below). Both generals fought troops of Spain's king, Ferdinand VII (above).

In 1819 Bolívar crossed the Andes into present-day Colombia where he defeated the Spanish forces. In 1821 he returned to Venezuela and won another victory against Spanish forces.

The Generals Meet

The only part of Latin America still held by the Spanish in 1821 was the present-day countries of Peru and Bolivia. San Martín attacked the Spanish from the south while Bolívar captured the city of Guyaquil. In Guyaquil, which is now in Ecuador, the two generals met to decide how to free Peru.

What happened at this historic meeting in 1822 remains a mystery. No one knows what the generals discussed. After the meeting, San Martín left Peru and resigned from the army. He lived the rest of his life in France.

Bolívar went on to win freedom for Peru. Despite his great victories, he was a very unhappy man when he died in 1830. Spanish rule had ended, but the people of Latin America were not free. They had exchanged Spanish rule for dictators from their own countries. Freedom was still many years away for the people of Latin America.

READING CHECK Why was Bolívar unhappy after South America was freed from Spanish rule?

BIOGRAPHY

Focus On: Honesty

Simón Bolívar has been called the "George Washington of South America." Like Washington, Bolívar led a war for independence and was his country's first president. Also like Washington, Bolívar was famous for his honesty.

Bolívar had a dream—a "United States of South America." Bolívar wanted Spain's former colonies to unite as the 13 English colonies in North America had. He never saw his United States of South America. His honest opinions about other leaders made him unpopular.

Today, Bolívar is seen as a great leader and an honest man. His idea of a South American union may also be reconsidered.

Link to Today

Think of a political leader today who has led his or her country to independence and is known for his or her honesty. How did this leader free the country? Write a paragraph describing how this leader is like and unlike Bolívar.

THE LIFE OF SIMÓN BOLÍVAR	1783 Bolívar is born in Caracas, Venezuela			1821 Bolívar frees Venezuela	1825 Bolivia is named after Bolívar	1830 Bolívar dies
	1780	**1790**	**1800**	**1810** **1820**	**1830**	**1840**
LIFE AROUND THE WORLD		1788 First British convict-settlers arrive in Australia		1804 Napoleon makes himself Emperor of the French	1822 Liberia is founded as a home for freed U.S. slaves	1834 Slavery is abolished in the British Empire

INDEPENDENCE FOR BRAZIL

Brazil was a Portuguese colony. Napoleon conquered Portugal as well as Spain, but Brazil became independent without a war.

The Colony Becomes a Country

In 1807 the French invaded Portugal. The king, John VI, and many Portuguese nobles set sail for Brazil. The king settled in Rio de Janeiro, Brazil's largest city.

King John was popular in Brazil. He opened Brazilian ports to all countries. He built a royal library, a military academy, a law school, and a medical school in Brazil. Finally he issued a **decree**, or royal command, making Brazil a part of Portugal rather than a colony.

Napoleon was defeated in 1815, but the Portuguese king remained in Brazil until 1821. When the king finally returned to Portugal, he left his son, Pedro, in charge of Brazil.

A New Nation

Trouble soon broke out between Portugal and Brazil. Portuguese leaders wanted Brazil to be a colony again, not a part of Portugal. Laws were passed to end many of the improvements the king had made in Brazil.

People in Brazil wanted Pedro to declare independence from Portugal. In 1822, Pedro called an assembly and declared independence. He called himself Emperor Pedro I of Brazil.

Unlike the rest of Latin America, Brazil did not fight a war for independence.

Brazil's largest city, Rio de Janeiro, in the 1800s (above) and today (right).

However, Brazil had other problems. Emperor Pedro I was a harsh ruler, and he made many enemies. In 1831, the emperor was forced to give up his throne and leave Brazil. His 5-year-old son became Pedro II.

The Last Emperor

Emperor Pedro II was a much wiser ruler than his father. He ruled Brazil for 50 years and helped it grow into a strong nation.

Brazil was a rich agricultural country with coffee and cotton as its two leading exports. Both crops were grown on large plantations with enslaved Africans. Pedro II wanted to end slavery, but the plantation owners were the most powerful group in Brazil. The emperor managed to free groups of slaves gradually until slavery was finally ended in 1888.

The end of slavery also marked the end of the emperor's rule. The slave

Emperor Pedro II (left) lost his throne in 1889 when Brazil became a republic.

owners rebelled and forced him to leave Brazil, but they could not restore slavery.

How was Brazil's struggle for independence different from the struggle in Mexico?

PUTTING IT TOGETHER

The French and American revolutions encouraged Latin America's fight for independence. In 1791, Toussaint L'Ouverture and an army of slaves freed Haiti from French rule.

In 1810, Father Miguel Hidalgo began Mexico's struggle for independence. Agustin de Iturbide finally defeated the Spanish, and in 1821 Mexico became an independent nation.

José San Martín and Simón Bolívar drove the Spanish out of their South American colonies by 1830. However, dictators seized power and the people of Latin American were still not free.

Brazil won independence without a war. The son of Portugal's king declared independence in 1822. Pedro II was a wise ruler, but he was overthrown when he freed the last of Brazil's slaves.

Review and Assess

1. Write a sentence for each vocabulary term.
   decree
   Latin America

2. Who led the fight for independence in Haiti?

3. What methods did countries in Latin America use to win their freedom?

4. How did Spanish colonial rulers affect the **economy** of the colonies?

5. Describe the different **frames of reference** for Simón Bolívar and Pedro II of Brazil.

The Andes Mountains crossed by San Martín's army are the second-highest mountain range in the world. The tallest peak in the Andes is Mount Aconcagua in Argentina. Research and create a table showing the height of the five tallest peaks in the Andes Mountains.

Write a short biography of one of the leaders in this lesson. Include some details of this person's life, and explain why he is an important Latin American historical figure.

The Industrial Revolution

READING STRATEGY

Make a chart like this one. In the columns write the benefits and drawbacks of the Industrial Revolution.

How did the Industrial Revolution change Europe?

Lesson Outline

• Industrialism Begins in Britain
• New Inventions
• New Social Classes
• The Labor Movement

BUILD BACKGROUND

The people lived and worked in "a town of machinery and tall chimneys, out of which . . . serpents [snakes] of smoke trailed themselves for ever and ever . . . . It had a black canal in it, and a river that ran purple with ill-smelling dye . . . ."

This is how one industrial town looked to British author Charles Dickens. The new industries were darkening the skies over English cities, but they were also changing the way people lived.

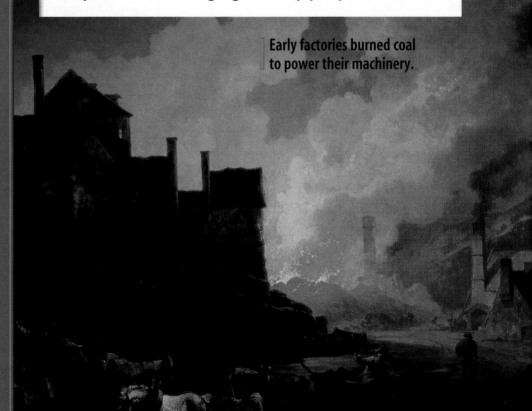

Early factories burned coal to power their machinery.

INDUSTRIALISM BEGINS IN BRITAIN

Throughout the 1700s, a revolution was taking place in England. The **Industrial Revolution** changed the way goods were made. Instead of being made by hand, goods were produced by machines powered by water and steam.

The Industrial Revolution started in Britain for several reasons. The country's population doubled in the 1700s, providing labor for factories and markets for products. Britain also had a rich supply of raw materials, especially coal and iron. Britain also had many merchants who knew how to run businesses.

New Inventions and Industries

By the middle 1700s, the growing population created a demand for **textiles**, or cloth. New machines were invented to spin and weave cloth. The first machines were powered by running water. They were housed in large buildings called **factories**, located near swift streams.

The steam engine, invented by **James Watt** in 1769, used coal for fuel and provided a steady source of power. With the invention of the steam engine, factories could be built almost anywhere although most were built near coal mines.

The new factories used large quantities of coal. Fortunately, coal was plentiful in Britain. The new industries also needed iron to make machines. Britain also had plenty of iron ore. Within a few years, Britain's iron output went up 400 percent.

 READING CHECK Why did the Industrial Revolution begin in Britain?

Major Industrial Inventions

Steam Engine
James Watt, 1769
Powers machinery more efficiently than water power.

Power Loom
Edmund Cartwright, 1785
Weaves cheaper textiles more quickly.

Locomotive
Richard Trevithick, 1804
Uses steam power to transport goods and passengers.

Blast Furnace
Henry Bessemer, 1855
Produces better, stronger, less expensive steel.

Chart Skill

1. Which invention changed how machines were powered?

2. Which inventions needed to be housed in factories?

NEW INVENTIONS

The Industrial Revolution started with textiles, but quickly spread to the manufacture of entirely new products. None created as much interest or was as important as the steam locomotive and the iron rails on which it ran.

The Iron Horse

The first passenger railroad in Britain opened in 1825. In 1829, a locomotive named the *Rocket* ran at the astounding speed of 16 miles per hour.

Within 15 years, more than 1,000 miles of track crisscrossed Europe. By 1870, the railroad had cut the travel time from London, England, to Edinburgh, Scotland, a distance of 370 miles, from 4 days to 12 hours. In 1888 the railroad, now nicknamed the "iron horse," linked Europe from Calais, France, in the west all the way to Constantinople, Turkey. Passengers and goods could now reach distant places faster than ever before.

Steam-Powered Ships

The steam engine was also used to power ships. In 1807, **Robert Fulton**, an American, built the first successful steamboat. People hooted at the vessel, calling it "Fulton's Folly." However, it proved useful by running from New York City to Albany, New York, a distance of about 150 miles, on its first voyage. Before long, steamships were carrying passengers and cargo on the rivers of the world. The first steamship crossed the Atlantic Ocean in 1838.

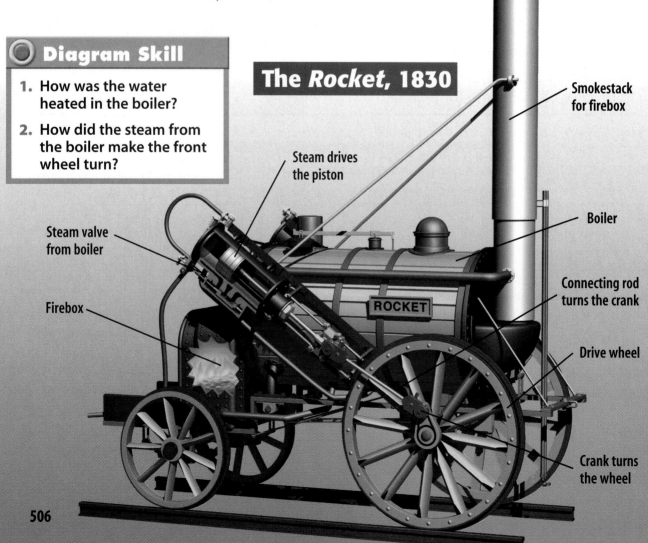

Diagram Skill

1. **How was the water heated in the boiler?**

2. **How did the steam from the boiler make the front wheel turn?**

The *Rocket*, 1830

Steam drives the piston

Smokestack for firebox

Steam valve from boiler

Boiler

Firebox

ROCKET

Connecting rod turns the crank

Drive wheel

Crank turns the wheel

McCormick's reaper enabled farmers to harvest larger crop yields. Before the reaper, farmers had cut their crops by hand with a scythe, a tool like the one below.

New Machines for Farmers

During these same years, there were many changes in agriculture. Farmers learned to rotate, or change, crops to produce more of each crop from the same field. They also used new fertilizers to increase their crop yields.

The new factories paid higher wages to workers than a farmer could. Many young people moved to the cities to look for work in the new industries. Farmers needed help if they were to care for their larger harvests.

New machines were developed to take the place of farm workers. **Cyrus McCormick**, an American, improved the horse drawn reaper, a machine that uses sharp blades to cut and harvest grain. A farmer could cut, or reap, 2 or 3 acres of wheat in one day. With the new reaper, the same farmer could increase the harvest to 12 acres a day.

Another American, **John Deere**, developed a better plow. The old wooden plows were unable to break up roots of grasses in new fields in the Great Plains of the United States. Deere took a steel saw and bent it across a log. His new steel plow cut through the roots easily.

All of these changes made farm products cheaper and more plentiful. Farms increased in size to take advantage of the new machines. Farmers began to run their farms as businesses, making farming more profitable.

READING CHECK

How did the Industrial Revolution change transportation and agriculture?

NEW SOCIAL CLASSES

The changes in industry also created changes in society. The king and the nobles had been at the top of the old social pyramid. Everyone else had been beneath them. The Industrial Revolution created a new social pyramid. A large and wealthy **middle class** of business people like merchants, lawyers, factory owners, and bankers grew rich from the new industries. Their wealth gave them power in politics and in setting standards for society.

More important than middle class wealth were middle class values. The power of the new industrialists led to political and social reforms, such as the rights of the individual, support for hard work and education, and a strong belief in the progress of society in general. These middle class values led to the political and social reforms of the 1800s.

The Working Class

The largest group in industrialized society was the **working class**. In the early years of the Industrial Revolution, most members of the working class were farm workers who came to cities for better-paying jobs. Many new workers left Ireland where harsh British policy made a crop failure even worse.

As people came to work in the new factories, the industrial centers expanded quickly. Most cities were not equipped to handle the new workers. They lived in crowded, poorly built houses without running water. Sewage ran freely along trenches in the streets. Black smoke from coal-burning factories filled the air. One writer described this life:

> *You went down one step from a foul area into the cellar in which a family of human beings lived. It was very dark inside. The window-panes, many of them were broken and stuffed with rags. . . . the smell was so fetid [bad] as almost to knock the two men down.*

READING CHECK How did the Industrial Revolution create a new social pyramid?

Life for the **working class** in large cities (left) was different from life for the **middle class** owners of factories and mills (below).

DATAGRAPHIC

In the Factory

Thousands of women went to work in factories during the 1800s, but they were not treated the same as male employees. Study the table and the text. Then answer the questions.

Employees in a Silk Factory

Job	Weekly Wages	Number
MALES		
Overseers and clerks	15s-32s	26
Mechanics and engine drivers	17s-25s	6
Carpenters and blacksmiths	14s-21s	3
Lodgekeeper	15s	1
Loom attendants	14s-15s	16
Mill machinery attendants	10s-15s	18
Spindle cleaners, messengers, sweepers	5s-12s	5
Watchmen, Coachmen, and van driver	5s-10s	1
Winders	2s-4s	38
Total Males	**114**	
FEMALES		
Gauze examiners	10s-11s	4
Overseers	9s-10s	4
Warpers	7s-10s	16
Twisters	7s-10s	9
Wasters	6s-9s	4
Weavers	5s-8s	589
Plugwinders	6s-7s	2
Drawers and doublers	4s-6s	83
Winders	2s-4s	188
Total Females	**899**	

Source: Under Control: Life in a Nineteenth-Century Silk Factory, Cambridge University Press

s=shillings   1 shilling in 1833 = $3.92 in 2001 U.S. dollars

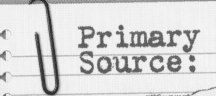

Primary Source:

excerpt from **Hannah Goode**
— *Factory Inquiry Commission Great Britain, 1833*

"I work at Mr. Wilson's mill. I think the youngest child is about 7. I daresay there are 20 under 9 years. . . . We never stop to take our meals, except at dinner. William Crookes is over-looker in our room. . . . he beats the little children if they do not do their work right. . . . If [the little children] are catched asleep they get the strap. They are always very tired at night. . . ."

QUESTIONS:

1. At about what age did children begin working in factories?
2. Were factory overseers mostly male, or mostly female?
3. How did women's wages compare to men's wages?

To learn more, visit our Web site:
www.mhschool.com

THE LABOR MOVEMENT

Conditions in factories led many workers to organize **unions**. A union is a group of workers who join together to demand improved working conditions. They wanted safer factories and higher wages.

Unions had few ways of forcing a factory owner to meet their demands. In a **strike**, union members left their jobs until their demands were satisfied. At times strikes led to violence. Sometimes striking workers lost their jobs because owners fired them.

Karl Marx

Demand for Basic Changes

Some workers believed that limits on work hours and improvement in wages and working conditions were not enough. They wanted changes in the economic system itself. Many followed the ideas of a German thinker who lived in England. His name was **Karl Marx**.

Marx told working people to revolt against the existing system. "Workers of the world, unite," he wrote. "You have nothing to lose but your chains."

Marx believed that the world was entering a new economic period. Workers would seize control of the economic system and the government. Later he wrote that there would be no social classes and government would fade away.

Many people became interested in his ideas, which became known as **socialism**. They supported an economic and political system based on public or government ownership of all resources and industries. Much later, Russia, China, and other countries claimed that their governments were based on Marxism.

READING CHECK ✓ **What changes did Karl Marx call for?**

Both male and female factory workers went on **strike** to improve wages or working conditions.

A Consumer Society

The first department stores were built in the mid-1800s. They sold the products of the factories of the Industrial Revolution. Department stores were—and are—a sign of a consumer society. A consumer society is one in which people are able to buy more than just the basic necessities of life.

Before the Industrial Revolution, only the rich were able to have more than they needed. As the middle class grew during the Industrial Revolution, many people had more money and they could spend it freely. Soon the first department stores opened, and were filled with manufactured goods such as furniture, bed linens, toys, and dishes, never before available to so many people.

Activity

Design a poster for a department store of the 1800s. Your poster should make shopping seem attractive to consumers.

PUTTING IT TOGETHER

The Industrial Revolution was a change in the way things were made. Machines using water and steam power produced goods that had formerly been made by hand. Beginning with the textile industry in England in the 1700s, the Industrial Revolution soon spread to transportation, farming, and other industries in European countries and the United States. It brought people to work in factories and led to the rapid growth of cities.

The middle class grew in importance, while the working class often went to work in dangerous conditions. Workers formed unions to improve conditions.

Review and Assess

1. Write a sentence for each vocabulary word or term.

factory	**socialism**
Industrial Revolution	**strike**
middle class	

2. What is a union?

3. What changes in Europe were caused by the Industrial Revolution?

4. Name three inventions that used the new **technology** of steam power.

5. **Draw a conclusion** about the Industrial Revolution. Was it good for society in Europe in the 1800s?

Activities

Research and draw a resource map of England. Show the location of coal and iron deposits. Label the important rivers. Locate the large industrial cities of the 1800s on your map.

Suppose that you are a worker in a factory during the early years of the Industrial Revolution. **Write** a speech persuading workers of the benefits of a labor union.

Being a Good Citizen
Saving Sight in Ghana

Before going to college, many British teenagers like to take a break. Jenny Mcloughlin, of Brighton, England, decided to spend part of her "gap year" as it is called in England, doing volunteer work in Ghana, which is located in Africa. "I wanted a break from education, but I didn't want a wasted year out," she says.

In February 2001, a British charity called Raleigh International sent Mcloughlin to Ghana for ten weeks. She helped a Ghanaian medical team called Sight Savers.

"It's amazing that you can make such a difference...."

"About 100 of us flew to Accra, the capital of Ghana, where we learned about the work that Sight Savers does. This group goes to rural villages in Ghana to find and treat people with eye diseases. In rural areas many eye diseases are not treated because they are not detected early enough. One common eye disease is cataracts. A cataract is a thick coating that forms over the lens of the eye."

When the volunteers arrived in Accra, they were divided into smaller groups. Mcloughlin's group joined three local Sight Saver nurses in Dunkwa in central Ghana. "We traveled by bus with them to different villages in central Ghana. At each village, the team offered the people in the community a chance

"I didn't want a wasted year out."

to have their eyes tested. Before we started. . . .We also learned some basic phrases in Twi, the language most people spoke. We learned phrases like 'Can you cover your right eye?'"

Mcloughlin and the other volunteers reported the results of the screenings to the nurses who used special optical equipment to test for cataracts or other serious eye diseases. "Most people who had cataracts were elderly," said Mcloughlin, "but some were young children."

After the screenings, everyone returned to a hospital in Dunkwa. Doctors operated on the patients to remove cataracts. "We assisted the doctors by passing them scalpels and threads for sewing up the cuts."

Mcloughlin is now training to become a nurse. She hopes to volunteer in Ghana again after completing her degree. "People get their sight back," she says. "It's amazing that you can make such a difference to someone's life."

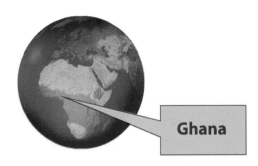

Ghana

Be a Good Citizen

Making Connections

- **What are some ways volunteers help doctors and nurses in the United States?**

- **How might teenagers in your community volunteer to help with health programs?**

Talk About It!

- **Jenny says that her experience helped her "focus her ideas and hopes for the future." What do you think she means by this?**

- **What do you think the Ghanaians might have found most challenging in working with volunteers?**

Act on It

In the Community

Use a telephone directory or other source to make a list of volunteer organizations in your community. Beside each organization's name, write the services it provides. You may want to ask some of these organizations to send you materials about their work.

In the Classroom

Ask your teacher to invite a representative of a local hospital or health care center to speak to your class. Prepare questions in advance.

The Age of Imperialism

How did European empires affect the people of Africa and Asia?

Find Out!

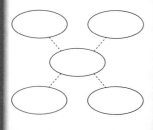

VOCABULARY

imperialism
nationalism
sphere of influence
sepoy
Boxer

READING STRATEGY

Write "Reasons for Imperialism" in the center circle. Write the reasons in the outer circles.

Lesson Outline

• The Rush for Colonies
• European Expansion
• The "Scramble for Africa"

BUILD BACKGROUND

"This magnificent African cake."

This is how Belgium's King Leopold described the region of the Congo River in Africa. Leopold and other Europeans devoured this "cake" in the 1880s. Asia was also the scene of European expansion in the 1800s. As European nations developed their industries, they expanded their power to create colonial empires.

THE RUSH FOR COLONIES

As you have read, European countries had been building colonial empires for many years. England, for example, first entered India in the mid-1600s. After 1850, however, the European industrial powers rushed to extend their colonial empires. One country's control of the government and economy of another country or region is known as **imperialism**. The period from 1850 to 1914 is often called the "Age of Imperialism."

Reasons for Imperialism

There were several reasons why European countries were interested in acquiring overseas colonies in the second half of the 1800s. Many countries were becoming more industrialized, and they needed raw materials such as rubber, oil, and minerals for their factories.

Their factories produced quantities of goods that soon filled markets at home. New markets for these products had to be found. In addition, there was increasing European demand for African and Asian crops such as sugar, bananas, rice, and coffee. European countries wished to control the supply of these products and to make money at the same time.

Another reason for imperialism among European countries was **nationalism**. Nationalism is a form of national pride. However, nationalism in some countries led to a feeling that the country was superior to other countries. These countries

European rulers (opposite) created vast colonial empires like the British Empire of Queen Victoria (above).

began to build colonial empires because they believed that ruling lands overseas showed their superiority.

It also seemed to many Europeans that Asian and African cultures were inferior because they did not have railroads and factories. Improved technology, particularly weapons, helped these European countries to take over large areas of Africa and Asia.

READING CHECK How did the Industrial Revolution lead to a search for colonies?

515

EUROPEAN EXPANSION

Asia, with its millions of people and its valuable raw materials, was a target for European powers that wanted to expand. By 1900, almost every Asian country was controlled by foreign powers.

India—"The Jewel in the Crown"

The British called India, their most valuable colony, the "jewel in the crown." India supplied Britain with tea, coffee, cotton, and other agricultural products. India's 300 million people were sold British manufactured goods, especially cheap textiles. In fact, Britain prohibited Indians from producing their own textiles so that they would not compete with British exports.

British rulers did bring some benefits to India. Travel and communication were improved when the British built railroads and roads and installed telegraph and telephone lines. Britain also established schools and colleges for Indians.

The Dutch and the French in Asia

The Dutch controlled a chain of southeast Asian islands they called the **Dutch East Indies**. These islands are now the country of Indonesia. The Dutch owned large plantations that grew products for export. The islands were one of the richest colonies, but the Indonesians did not share in this wealth.

France had colonies in **Indochina**, a peninsula in Southeast Asia that includes present-day Vietnam, Laos, and Cambodia. Like the Dutch, the French formed plantations that grew crops for export. The French also built roads, railroads, telegraph and telephone systems, schools, and hospitals. Young men were educated in France to be doctors, engineers, and architects in their native lands.

The French (right) established their rule in Vietnam, and the British ruled India (above).

Imperialism and China

Throughout the 1800s, China had grown weaker. Europeans took advantage of this weakness by seizing regions of China. Each region was called a **sphere of influence**, an area where a European country had economic privileges including the exclusive right to control factories, mines, and railways.

Europeans did not control the Chinese government in Beijing, but they ruled in their spheres of influence. They forbade Chinese people to enter European parts of Chinese cities without permission. Europeans accused of crimes were tried in European courts rather than in Chinese courts. Furthermore, European business people forced the Chinese government to give them favorable treatment.

Resentment by Asia's People

The Asian people were not happy about the European control of their lives and their countries. They also resented new practices that went against traditional beliefs. Hatred of foreigners throughout Asia built up over the years. From time to time this hatred erupted into violence. For example, in 1857 a group of Indian soldiers, known as **sepoys**, staged a rebellion against British rule of India. In 1900 in China, a group known as **Boxers** tried to drive foreigners out of China by attacking the foreign section of the city of Beijing.

What were the benefits and drawbacks of British rule in India?

Foreign merchants in Canton (now Guangzhou) (above) ignored the laws of China. **Sepoy** rebels tried to end British rule of India (below).

THE "SCRAMBLE FOR AFRICA"

After 1880, European powers rushed to claim colonies in Africa. This became known as the "scramble for Africa." By 1900, only Liberia and Ethiopia remained independent nations.

Europeans often placed people of different groups, sometimes traditional enemies, into the same colony. These people spoke different languages and had different cultures.

In many colonies Africans had to grow cash crops. Others were forced to work in mines, on rubber plantations, or build roads. Africans also were taxed heavily.

Large-scale wars for independence took place in the early 1900s in Portuguese Angola and German East Africa. However, most African lands did not gain their freedom until the 1960s.

 READING CHECK How did the creation of European colonies change Africa?

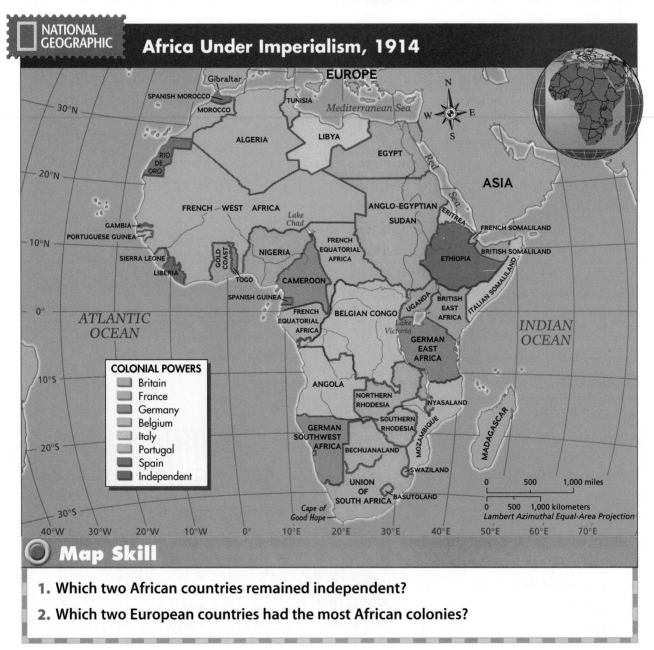

NATIONAL GEOGRAPHIC

Africa Under Imperialism, 1914

COLONIAL POWERS
- Britain
- France
- Germany
- Belgium
- Italy
- Portugal
- Spain
- Independent

0   500   1,000 miles
0   500   1,000 kilometers
Lambert Azimuthal Equal-Area Projection

Map Skill

1. **Which two African countries remained independent?**

2. **Which two European countries had the most African colonies?**

518

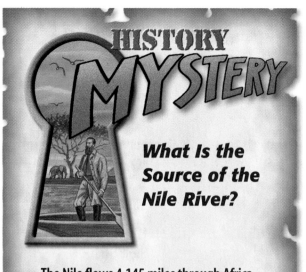

HISTORY MYSTERY

What Is the Source of the Nile River?

The Nile flows 4,145 miles through Africa. For many centuries, no one knew where the Nile began. In 460 B.C. the Greek historian Herodotus tried to find the source. The Roman emperor Nero sent troops, but they were blocked by a huge swamp. After the 1600s some thought that the source was Lake Tana in Ethiopia, which is the source of the shorter tributary, the Blue Nile.

British explorers Richard Francis Burton and John Hanning Speke finally found the source of the Nile in 1858. After a long and difficult journey, they found that the White Nile, which contributes 80 percent of the river's water, flows out of Lake Victoria in central Africa.

Why was it difficult to find the source of the Nile?

PUTTING IT TOGETHER

Beginning in the 1850s, European countries began seeking colonies in Asia and Africa. The Dutch were already in Indonesia, the British took control of India, and the French seized present-day Vietnam and Cambodia. This era became known as the Age of Imperialism.

Imperialism could also affect European areas. In the 1840s, there was a terrible crop failure in Ireland. Harsh British rule made the situation worse. Many Irish people left their country to seek a new life in other countries.

Review and Assess

1. Write one sentence for each vocabulary word or term.

   imperialism   sepoy
   nationalism   sphere of influence

2. Why did European countries want colonies?

3. How did colonialism affect the peoples of Africa and Asia?

4. What made imperialism good for European **economies**?

5. What was the **frame of reference** for King Leopold of Belgium?

Activities

Look at the map on page 518. Make a chart. List the name of each African colony and the European country controlling it.

• •

Suppose you were an explorer traveling with Burton and Speke. **Write** a letter to a friend in England. Describe your feelings on finding the source of the river.

519

Reading Political Cartoons

In the 1800s many European countries established colonial empires around the world. There were also people in these countries who disagreed with imperialism. During this time, **political cartoons** began to appear frequently in European newspapers and magazines. A political cartoon is a picture that expresses opinions about government actions, people, events, or newsworthy issues. Political cartoons deal with serious issues, yet often treat them in humorous ways.

Historians study political cartoons because the pictures are valuable historical sources about a time. They also help readers identify the important issues in history.

VOCABULARY

political cartoon
symbol
dialogue

LEARN THE SKILL

Look at the cartoon on this page as you follow these steps.

1. **Identify symbols.**
   Political cartoons often use **symbols**. A symbol is something that stands for something else. You know, for example, that Uncle Sam is a symbol of the United States. A symbol is a way for a cartoonist to refer to a country or a politician.

   The cartoon above is about Great Britain's empire. The head is of John Bull. He is the symbol of Britain, just as Uncle Sam is the symbol of the United States.

Study other symbols in the cartoon. Great Britain is shown as an octopus with many hands grasping British colonies, such as Egypt, Australia, and Canada. Do you think the cartoonist approved of British imperialism?

2. **Look for other clues.**
   Some cartoonists use captions or labels. For instance, in this cartoon some of the lands under Great Britain's control are labeled. Other cartoonists may use **dialogue** (DI uh lahg), or conversation, to help their viewers understand their point of view.

   Neither of the cartoons on pages 520 and 521 have dialogue.

TRY THE SKILL

Look at the cartoon below. It is from a newspaper in 2001.

1. What is this cartoon about? How do you know?

2. What symbols are in the cartoon? What do they stand for?

3. What does the cartoonist want the reader to understand about the event?

4. How does understanding political cartoons of the past help to understand history?

EXTEND THE SKILL

Reading political cartoons can help you learn about the most important issues of today, both in your city or country. Political cartoons give readers something to think about, or sometimes something to laugh about.

Create your own political cartoon. The subject matter can be local, about your school or town, or it can show something happening in another country. Discuss your cartoon ideas with your parents, teachers, or another adult.

- What is the subject matter of your political cartoon?

- Did you use any symbols?

- What feeling is your cartoon expressing?

- How do political cartoons help you understand issues important to you or your community?

The Birth of Modern Japan

Find Out!

How did the Meiji period change Japan?

VOCABULARY

Meiji Restoration
Diet

PEOPLE

Matthew C. Perry
Meiji
Jigoro Kano

READING

Copy this chart. At the top write "Meiji Japan." In the boxes, list changes in Japan during the Meiji Period.

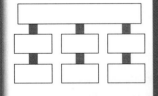

Lesson Outline

• Japan Opens to the World
• The Meiji Restoration
• Japanese Expansion

BUILD BACKGROUND

In 1908, a Japanese scholar named Okuma wrote: "[Japan's] . . . progress . . . has been so sudden and swift that it presents a rare spectacle in the history of the world . . . . [It] is the result of . . . coming into contact with the civilization of Europe and America." In this lesson, you will learn about how and why this contact changed Japan forever.

JAPAN OPENS TO THE WORLD

As you read in Chapter 12, Japan was closed to Europeans in 1635. Only one Western ship was allowed to enter Japan each year, and the Japanese were forbidden to travel outside the country.

Japan Opens Its Doors

By the 1850s, Europeans were demanding that Japan open itself to trade and its markets to western products. The United States also wanted Japan to allow whaling ships and merchant ships to restock in Japanese ports.

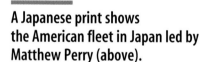

A Japanese print shows the American fleet in Japan led by Matthew Perry (above).

In 1853, President Millard Fillmore sent four ships commanded by Commodore **Matthew C. Perry** to Japan. The President sent a letter saying that the United States wished to have friendly relations with Japan, "But no friendship can long exist unless Japan ceases to act toward Americans as if they were her enemies," the letter warned.

Perry said he would return for the Japanese government's answer in one year. In 1854, Perry returned to Japan with eight warships. Seeing the superior guns on these warships, Japan's leaders realized they had no choice. Two ports were made available to American ships. Britain, France, Russia, and Holland quickly arrived and made their own trade agreements with the Japanese.

READING CHECK How did Japan come into contact with the rest of the world?

THE MEIJI RESTORATION

The Japanese began trading with foreign countries. However, many people in Japan were angry about unfair trade agreements Japanese leaders had signed with foreign countries. Some felt that the shogun had betrayed them. Others struck out against everything Western.

The Emperor Takes Charge

In 1868, several groups of young samurai took over the shogun's palace in Kyoto. They returned control of Japan to the emperor who then took the name **Meiji** (MAY JEE). This event is known as the **Meiji Restoration**. Though the Meiji Restoration was really a revolution, it was called a "restoration" because power was given back to the emperor.

Emperor Meiji began to adopt Western ways of governing. The feudal system was abolished, and governors reported to the central government. Lords turned their lands over to the emperor in exchange for money. The capital was moved to Edo, which was renamed **Tokyo**.

Changes in Japan's Culture

The Meiji government's slogan was "wealthy country and strong arms." One of its first acts was the creation of a modern army in 1871. However, the new government was not democratic. In response to protests, the government created a new constitution and a parliament called the **Diet** (DIE et) by 1889.

Japanese culture changed, too. In 1876, samurai were forbidden to carry the swords that showed their rank. People began to wear Western-style clothing instead of kimonos. They built Western-style buildings, and some began to eat Western foods, such as beef. All children were required to go to school.

Foreign Influences

Japan had been influenced by outside cultures before. China and Korea had been cultural influences for centuries. Now, Japan looked to the West for ideas. The Japanese government sent hundreds of students to the United States and Europe to learn skills such as shipbuilding, navigation, and medicine. Foreigners came to Japan to help the Japanese build telegraph lines, shipyards, and railroads. They also helped the Japanese develop a modern army.

Cultures Exchange

Modern martial arts are one example of how Japan blended cultures. Judo was invented in the late 1800s by a man named **Jigoro Kano**. Kano was a gifted student of Japanese wrestling. He was also an educator who was greatly influenced by German methods of teaching. Kano adapted traditional systems of wrestling into one system so that students could be taught in groups, instead of one at a time. He also invented the familiar training uniform of today, as well as the custom of awarding black belts to advanced students. President Theodore Roosevelt was a judo student while he was in the White House.

 READING CHECK How were Western influences felt in Japan during the Meiji Restoration?

Traditions of clothing and home life (opposite) changed when the Meiji emperor (above) introduced Western-style houses and streets to Japan.

JAPANESE EXPANSION

Japan absorbed Western influences and changed from a feudal society to a modern, industrial nation in a short time. However, cultural influences traveled in both directions. Western artists, such as Vincent van Gogh and Claude Monet, were influenced by colorful Japanese woodblock prints. People in London began to eat Japanese food, and Japanese porcelain and textiles brought high prices in European shops.

A New Asian Power

Between 1883 and 1912, Japanese exports more than doubled world trade. New treaties ensured that Japan could trade fairly with other countries. The Japanese wanted to be equal to the West in all ways.

The islands of Japan have few mineral resources, and the newly industrialized nation needed raw materials for its new industries. In 1894, Japan conquered Korea. In 1895, Japan seized the island of Taiwan from China.

Japanese styles influenced European artists such as Vincent van Gogh.

Musée Rodin, Paris

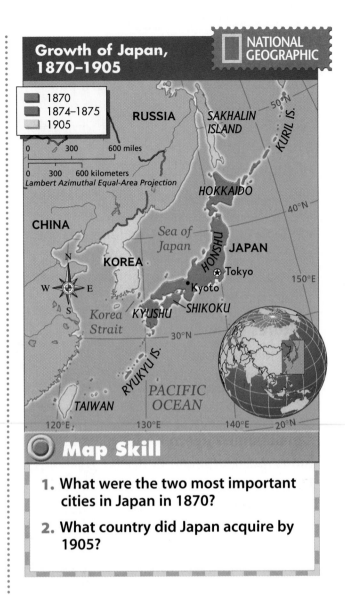

Growth of Japan, 1870–1905

- 1870
- 1874–1875
- 1905

0   300   600 miles
0   300   600 kilometers
Lambert Azimuthal Equal-Area Projection

RUSSIA
SAKHALIN ISLAND
KURIL IS.
CHINA
HOKKAIDO
Sea of Japan
HONSHU
JAPAN
KOREA
Tokyo
Kyoto
Korea Strait
KYUSHU
SHIKOKU
RYUKYU IS.
TAIWAN
PACIFIC OCEAN

Map Skill

1. **What were the two most important cities in Japan in 1870?**

2. **What country did Japan acquire by 1905?**

In 1904, Japan attacked a European power – Russia. The war was short and brutal. To the astonishment of Western governments, Japan won the war. President Theodore Roosevelt won a Nobel Peace Prize for his part in writing the treaty that ended this war.

The Emperor Meiji died in 1912, ending the Meiji era. However, Japan's expansion continued. You will learn more about Japanese imperialism in Chapter 16.

Why did Japan begin to conquer other regions?

PUTTING IT TOGETHER

A fleet of United States warships led by Matthew Perry opened Japan to foreigners in 1854. The Japanese realized they had to modernize quickly to resist European imperialism. A group of samurai overthrew the shogun and the Meiji Restoration began. Japan introduced Western education and a Western style of government. Foreigners were invited to Japan to teach their skills. Within a few

Among American gifts to Japan's emperor was a steam locomotive.

years, Japan had become a modern industrial nation.

Japanese expansion was a result of a need for raw materials and a desire for international respect. Japan seized territory from its neighbors in East Asia. After the defeat of Russia in 1904, Japan was a major world power.

Review and Assess

1. Write one sentence for each vocabulary term.
   Diet
   Meiji Restoration

2. Why did President Fillmore send Matthew Perry to Japan?

3. How did Japan change during the Meiji Restoration?

4. How did the policies of the Meiji Restoration affect the **economy** of Japan?

5. What was the difference in the **frame of reference** of Matthew Perry and the shogun of Japan in 1854?

During the Meiji Restoration the capital was moved to Tokyo. Use a reference source to find interesting facts about Tokyo today. Make a table or chart that lists your facts.

• •

Suppose that you are a Japanese official during Perry's naval visit. **Write** a letter to the Commodore. Explain why you want Japan to remain closed, or to be open to Western ships.

VOCABULARY REVIEW

Each of the following statements contains an underlined vocabulary word or term. Number a sheet of paper from 1 to 5. Beside each number, write T if the statement is true, and F if the statement is false. If the statement is false, rewrite the sentence using the vocabulary word or term correctly.

1. An <u>absolute monarch</u> is a sudden or great change in government.

2. <u>Imperialism</u> is extending one country's power over the government and economy of another country.

3. A <u>mestizo</u> is a person of mixed European ancestry.

4. The <u>middle class</u> is a group of workers who organize to improve working conditions.

5. The <u>Meiji Restoration</u> is a period when Japan began to modernize.

CHAPTER COMPREHENSION

6. How did France change as a result of the French Revolution?

7. How did Napoleon change French law when he was emperor?

8. What happened as a result of Miguel Hidalgo's *The Call of Dolores*?

9. Why is Simón Bolívar known as "The Liberator?"

10. Who was Karl Marx?

11. Which continents were divided into colonies during the Age of Imperialism?

12. Why did Japan open its borders?

13. **Write** a paragraph describing changes caused by the Industrial Revolution.

SKILL REVIEW

14. **Study Skill** What is the subject of the cartoon above? Do you think the cartoonist approves of what the countries represented by their symbols are doing? Explain your opinion.

15. **Study Skill** What is a symbol? What does the cartoonist mean by the symbol of the dragon on the ground?

16. **Reading/Thinking Skill** How can knowing the background of a person in history help you to understand his or her frame of reference?

17. **Reading/Thinking Skill** What was France's Third Estate? What was the point of view of people in the Third Estate regarding King Louis XVI?

18. **Reading/Thinking Skill** What generalization can you make about how nationalism can lead to imperialism?

USING A TIME LINE

1750	1775	1800	1825	1850	1875	1900	1925

c. 1750
The Industrial Revolution begins

1789
French Revolution begins

1796
Toussaint L'Ouverture takes control of Haiti

1821
Bolívar liberates Venezuela; Mexico gains independence

c. 1850
Age of Imperialism begins

1868
Meiji Restoration

1904
Russo-Japanese War begins

1912
Emperor Meiji dies

19. Which event on the time line influenced L'Ouverture's revolution in Haiti? Explain your answer.

20. For about how many years did the Meiji era last?

Activity

***Writing* About Technology** Suppose that you are creating a CD. Your CD will be a virtual museum of technology invented during the Industrial Revolution.

What machines or forms of transportation would you include? What other information or items might you include to explain the Industrial Revolution?

Foldables

Use your Foldable to review what you have learned about Revolutions and Expansion and how they changed the world. Use the sequence of lesson titles on your Foldable to help you tell a sequential story of world events covered in this chapter. If you have difficulty remembering what you read, review your notes under the tabs of your Foldable. Record any questions that you have, and discuss them with classmates, or review the chapter to find answers.

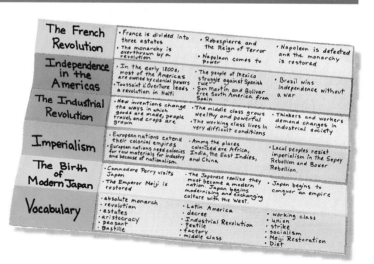

VOCABULARY REVIEW

Number a sheet of paper from 1 to 5. Beside each number write the word from the list below that best completes the sentence.

imperialism   **scientific method**

mestizos   **working class**

Middle Passage

1. The ____ was part of the triangular trade that developed between England, Africa, and North America.

2. Many members of the ____ joined unions to improve factory conditions.

3. Many people in Mexico are ____.

4. The ____ uses inductive reasoning to solve problems.

5. ____ led to the colonization of many countries in Africa and Asia.

TECHNOLOGY

For resources to help you learn more about the people and places you studied in this unit, visit **www.mhschool.com** and follow the links for Grade 6 Unit 4.

SKILL REVIEW

6. **Geography Skill** Suppose you have a historical map and a political map of the same region. How can comparing the two maps help you better understand historical events?

7. **Study Skill** The cartoon above was drawn when children were working in mines. What is the cartoonist's viewpoint on the subject?

8. **Study Skill** What does the cartoonist want readers to think about the people at the top of the cartoon?

9. **Reading/Thinking Skill** What was the frame of reference of the Spanish conquistadors towards the Aztec and the Inca?

10. **Reading/Thinking Skill** How did the frame of reference of Japan's people change during the Meiji era?

1   Galileo spent long hours studying the night sky through the telescope that he designed. His most dramatic discovery was that . . . . Copernicus's heliocentric, or sun-centered, view was correct.

2   [Church leaders] told Galileo that the heliocentric theory went against the teachings of the Church. If Galileo did not stop writing, he . . . . could possibly be put to death.

3   . . . . In 1633, he was arrested and brought to Rome for trial. Galileo was told to take back his heliocentric theory, or face life in prison. Galileo gave up his heliocentric idea, but it was a difficult choice. He knew that his discoveries were correct, but he was a sincerely religious man.

1   This selection's purpose is to—

   A   describe an important decision in Galileo's life
   B   state the writer's opinion about the heliocentric theory
   C   convince readers that Galileo's theory was correct
   D   entertain readers with a story about Galileo

2   What influenced Galileo's decision to give up the heliocentric theory?

   F   He had studied the night sky.
   G   He was a friend of Copernicus.
   H   He was a deeply religious man.
   J   He had designed a new telescope.

WRITING ACTIVITIES

Writing to Persuade   Suppose you had helped Miguel Hidalgo to write *The Call of Dolores. Write* a speech to encourage the people of Mexico to revolt against Spanish rule. In your speech, explain what changes you would make in how Mexico is governed.

Writing to Inform   Suppose that you are writing an anti-slavery article for a newspaper in 1800. In your article, describe the work that enslaved people do and the hardships enslaved people suffer.

Writing to Express   Suppose you went with Captain James Cook to the Pacific. *Write* a journal entry telling how one of the places and people of the Pacific islands are different from those of Europe in 1788.

531

LITERATURE

THE FALL OF THE BERLIN WALL

Selection by Andreas Ramos

Andreas Ramos is a Danish newspaper reporter. In 1989 Ramos, his wife, and two friends decided to go to Berlin to see the destruction of the Berlin Wall that had divided East and West Berlin since 1961. This excerpt comes from his news story about the experience.

At the **checkpoint**, which is a 25-lane place, people milled around. It was nearly 3 A.M. by now. People had climbed up into trees, signs, buildings, everything, to wave and shout. Television teams stood around filming everything. People set up folding tables and were handing out cups of coffee. A Polish

---

checkpoint: (chek' point) a gate or entrance at a national border where travelers must show passports

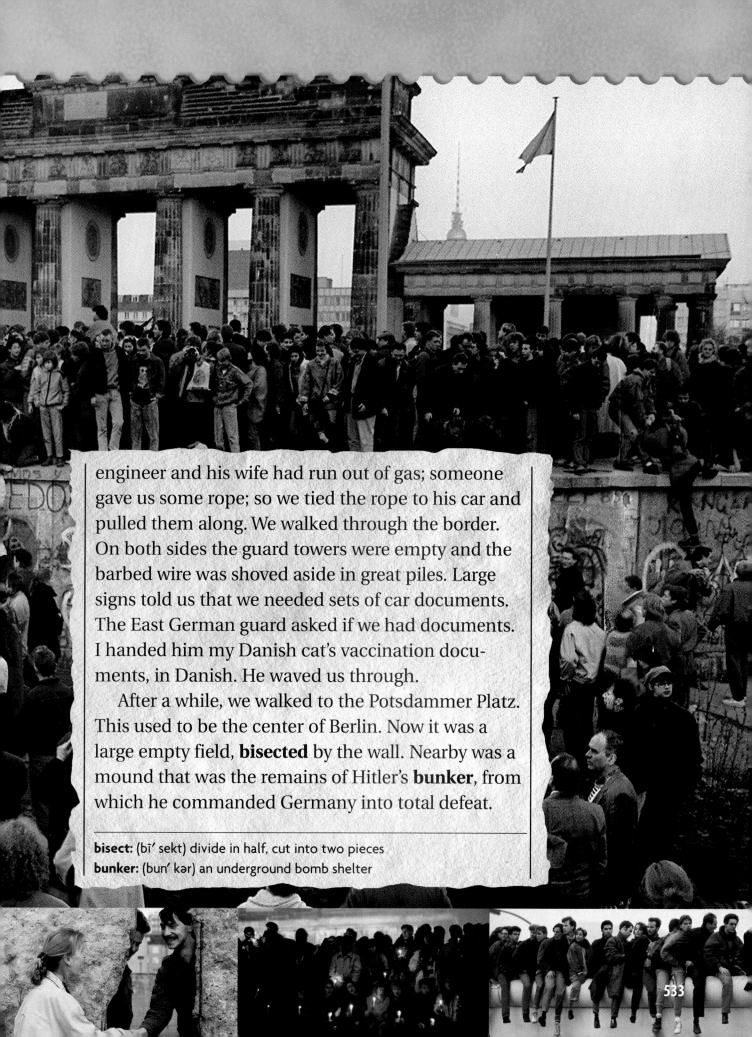

engineer and his wife had run out of gas; someone gave us some rope; so we tied the rope to his car and pulled them along. We walked through the border. On both sides the guard towers were empty and the barbed wire was shoved aside in great piles. Large signs told us that we needed sets of car documents. The East German guard asked if we had documents. I handed him my Danish cat's vaccination documents, in Danish. He waved us through.

After a while, we walked to the Potsdammer Platz. This used to be the center of Berlin. Now it was a large empty field, **bisected** by the wall. Nearby was a mound that was the remains of Hitler's **bunker**, from which he commanded Germany into total defeat.

---

bisect: (bī′ sekt) divide in half, cut into two pieces
bunker: (bun′ kər) an underground bomb shelter

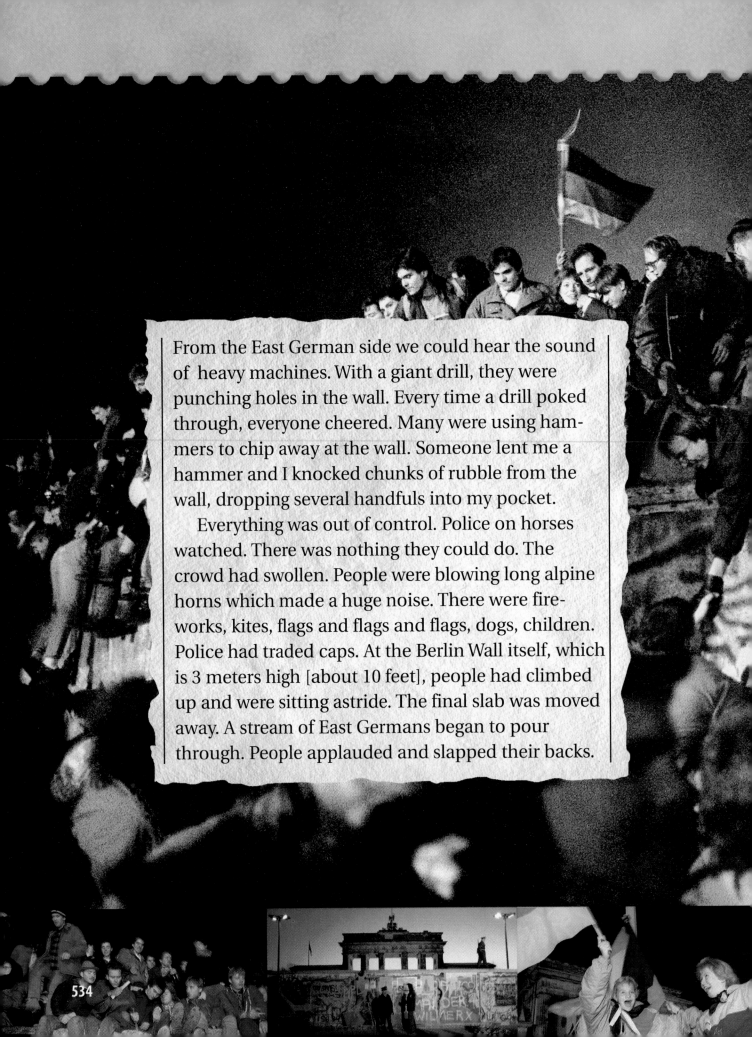

From the East German side we could hear the sound of heavy machines. With a giant drill, they were punching holes in the wall. Every time a drill poked through, everyone cheered. Many were using hammers to chip away at the wall. Someone lent me a hammer and I knocked chunks of rubble from the wall, dropping several handfuls into my pocket.

Everything was out of control. Police on horses watched. There was nothing they could do. The crowd had swollen. People were blowing long alpine horns which made a huge noise. There were fireworks, kites, flags and flags and flags, dogs, children. Police had traded caps. At the Berlin Wall itself, which is 3 meters high [about 10 feet], people had climbed up and were sitting astride. The final slab was moved away. A stream of East Germans began to pour through. People applauded and slapped their backs.

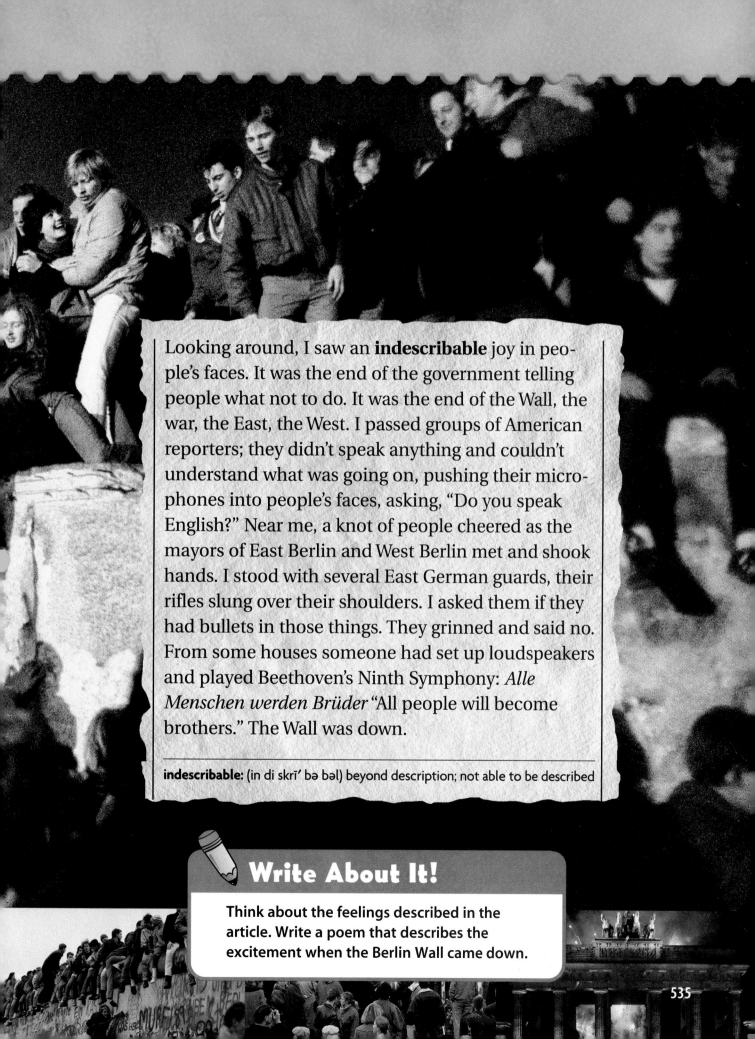

Looking around, I saw an **indescribable** joy in people's faces. It was the end of the government telling people what not to do. It was the end of the Wall, the war, the East, the West. I passed groups of American reporters; they didn't speak anything and couldn't understand what was going on, pushing their microphones into people's faces, asking, "Do you speak English?" Near me, a knot of people cheered as the mayors of East Berlin and West Berlin met and shook hands. I stood with several East German guards, their rifles slung over their shoulders. I asked them if they had bullets in those things. They grinned and said no. From some houses someone had set up loudspeakers and played Beethoven's Ninth Symphony: *Alle Menschen werden Brüder* "All people will become brothers." The Wall was down.

---

indescribable: (in di skrī′ bə bəl) beyond description; not able to be described

Write About It!

Think about the feelings described in the article. Write a poem that describes the excitement when the Berlin Wall came down.

Unit 5

A Stormy Century

TAKE A LOOK

What challenges faced the world in the last 100 years?

During World War II, about 300,000 Allied soldiers were removed from France in one week in 1940. This would be the same as evacuating modern Iceland.

Chapter 16

THE Big IDEAS ABOUT...

Troubled Times

The 1900s were a time of wars and great change. Two world wars caused destruction and many deaths. Governments and empires around the world were overthrown. At the end of World War II, there were two superpowers. For 40 years, these two countries struggled to achieve opposing goals and to influence other nations.

WORLD WAR I

European tensions erupt into war in 1914. The war is long and brutal for the men in the armies and for the people at home.

THE RUSSIAN REVOLUTION

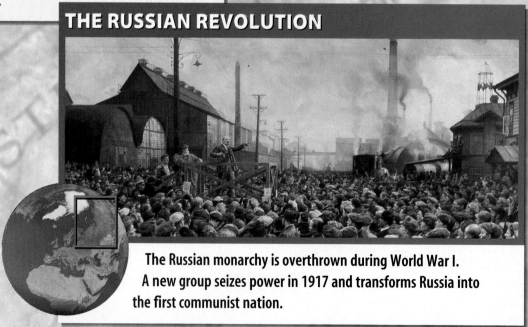

The Russian monarchy is overthrown during World War I. A new group seizes power in 1917 and transforms Russia into the first communist nation.

WORLD WAR II

In 1939, Germany attacks Poland and World War II begins. The United States is attacked by Japan in 1941. In 1945 the war ends.

COMMUNIST CHINA

The Chinese Empire ends in 1911. The new republic struggles through a long civil war with the communists and an invasion by Japan. In 1949, China becomes a communist nation.

THE COLD WAR

The end of World War II is also the beginning of a long period of struggle between communists and the democracies. There are few shooting battles during this war of ideas and words.

Foldables

Make this Foldable study guide and use it to record what you learn about "Troubled Times."

1. Stack three sheets of paper together, leaving a 1" tab between each sheet.

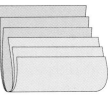

2. Roll the bottom of the three sheets up to make five tabs the same size. Fold and staple.

3. Write the title of the chapter on the large tab, and the five lesson titles on the small equal-sized tabs.

World War I

Find out!

What were the causes and results of World War I?

Lesson Outline
- An Uneasy Peace
- The Great War Begins
- The United States Joins the War

VOCABULARY

alliance
World War I
Central Powers
Allied Powers
front
neutral
armistice
League of Nations
Treaty of Versailles

PEOPLE

Franz Ferdinand
Woodrow Wilson

READING STRATEGY

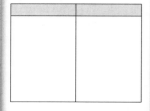

Copy this chart. Write the names of the Central Powers and the Allied Powers in each column.

BUILD BACKGROUND

In the summer of 1914, Sir Edward Grey, Britain's foreign minister, stared gloomily out his window as the streetlamps dimmed across the street. He was deeply worried as Europe slipped toward war. He said to a friend, "The lamps are going out all over Europe. We shall not see them lit again in our lifetime." Europe was at the height of its power and wealth in 1914, and yet it was about to stumble into the worst war in its history.

AN UNEASY PEACE

At the dawn of the 1900s, Europe was wealthy and peaceful. The Industrial Revolution had transformed Europe's cities. Machines in factories turned out the latest products, railroads sped passengers and freight from country to country, and telegraphs and telephones linked the farthest corners of the continent.

Two European Alliances

The countries of Europe had united into two powerful **alliances** (uh LĪ un sez). An alliance is an agreement between countries to act as partners to protect their interests. One alliance connected Germany and a monarchy called Austria-Hungary. The other alliance connected France and Britain to Russia.

These two alliances were deeply suspicious of each other and were convinced that war would occur. The alliances built up large armies and pledged to fight together when war broke out.

Balkan Powder Keg

In many countries of Europe, there was a sense of unity based on shared language and common culture. This new force was called nationalism. Nowhere was nationalism stronger than in the Balkan peninsula in southeastern Europe. Nationalists in Serbia, a Balkan country, were eager to include the Serbians of Austria-Hungary in their new nation.

On June 28, 1914, the heir to the throne of Austria-Hungary, Archduke **Franz Ferdinand**, was visiting Sarajevo, the

World War I (opposite) began with the murder of Franz Ferdinand and his wife Sophie (above) in 1914.

capital of Bosnia, with his wife. Bosnia was a part of Austria-Hungary that nationalists wanted to include in Serbia.

As Franz Ferdinand and his wife rode through Sarajevo, a bomb was thrown at their car. The bomb missed its targets. However, another assassin was waiting. As the car passed a local café, the assassin fired his pistol twice, killing Franz Ferdinand and his wife instantly.

Austria-Hungary blamed Serbia for the tragedy and declared war. Their alliance pulled Germany into the war as well. Russia came to the defense of Serbia. France declared war to support its ally, Russia. On August 3, the German army invaded Belgium. The British, who had promised to defend Belgium, declared war on Germany. The Great War, later called **World War I**, had begun.

How did nationalism lead to the outbreak of war in 1914?

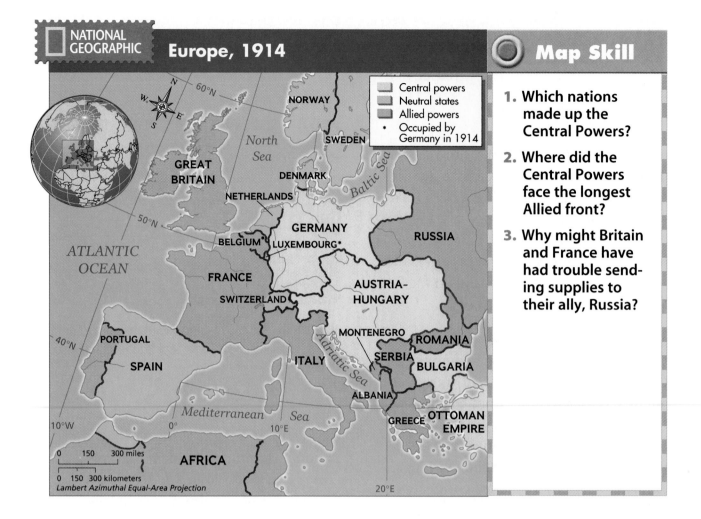

Central powers
Neutral states
Allied powers
• Occupied by Germany in 1914

NORWAY
SWEDEN
North Sea
GREAT BRITAIN
DENMARK
Baltic Sea
NETHERLANDS
GERMANY
RUSSIA
BELGIUM *
LUXEMBOURG *
ATLANTIC OCEAN
FRANCE
SWITZERLAND
AUSTRIA-HUNGARY
PORTUGAL
MONTENEGRO
ROMANIA
SPAIN
ITALY
Adriatic Sea
SERBIA
BULGARIA
ALBANIA
Mediterranean Sea
GREECE
OTTOMAN EMPIRE
AFRICA

0 150 300 miles
0 150 300 kilometers
Lambert Azimuthal Equal-Area Projection

1. Which nations made up the Central Powers?

2. Where did the Central Powers face the longest Allied front?

3. Why might Britain and France have had trouble sending supplies to their ally, Russia?

THE GREAT WAR BEGINS

Because of their location in Europe, Austria-Hungary, Germany, and their allies became known as the **Central Powers**. Russia, France, Britain, Serbia, and others were called the **Allied Powers**. Italy later joined the Allied Powers.

By the autumn of 1914, the Central Powers had forced their way deep into France and Russia, but they were unable to defeat either of these enemies. The Allied Powers had more soldiers and more supplies so they were in a better position to survive a long war.

A New Kind of War

A **front** is the area where enemy armies fight. The war in Europe had two fronts, one in France and one in Russia. Millions of men died as the armies strained to push a few miles east or west.

New technologies had changed warfare in terrible ways. Poison gas killed thousands of soldiers before they realized their danger. Machine guns mowed down attacking armies. In one battle in 1916, more than a million men were killed in a few months.

The fronts seesawed back and forth. Soldiers dug miles of ditches, or trenches, for protection. The worst moments came when the soldiers were ordered "over the top." Scrambling out of their trenches, they advanced through mud, barbed wire, and machine gun fire. Here is how one Allied soldier described the front:

Primary Source:

excerpt from **My Daily Journal,** *written by* **Canadian soldier, Donald Fraser,** **in September 1915**

Tonight we had our introduction to dug-out life. The dug-outs were small, damp and cold and overrun with rats. It is needless to add that once a fighting soldier leaves England he practically sleeps in his clothes till he gets back there again . . . . The rain loosens the earth and the sides cave in. With additional rain the bottom of the trenches becomes liquid mud which defies all efforts at drainage. We shovel, shovel and keep on shoveling but it is of no avail [use], the trench absolutely refuses to clean up. . . . The mud sticks to the shovel and after vigorous efforts to dislodge it, it only comes off to fall into the trench again.

What made life in the trenches difficult?

Women worked in defense factories (right) as men went to war (below).

The Civilian War

World War I was the first "total war." It involved not just the armies at the front, but also the people back at home. In fact, civilians were said to be on the "home front." And they did what they could to help the soldiers win the war.

Factories shifted from automobiles and other consumer goods to making bombs, airplanes, and guns. Women took factory jobs so men could join the army. Woman also became nurses, and drove ambulances.

Governments attempted to save food for the troops. The amount and kind of food that people could buy was controlled. There were "meatless" days to get extra meat for the soldiers. Food prices soared, especially in Germany and eastern European countries. Many people had to eat watery soup made from potato peels.

How did civilians help during World War I?

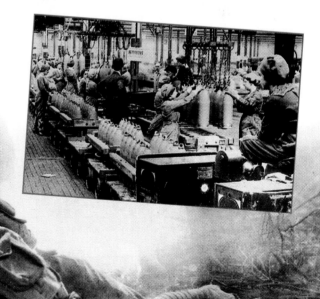

543

THE UNITED STATES JOINS THE WAR

The United States was officially **neutral**; it did not favor either side in the war. However, it sold supplies to the British. The Germans used submarines, called U-boats, to try to stop the supplies from reaching Britain and its allies.

In 1915, a German U-boat sank the *Lusitania*, a British passenger liner carrying war supplies. There were 128 Americans among the dead. American public opinion turned against Germany.

Finally, in April 1917 the United States declared war on Germany and its allies.

A Fokker Triplane

This German plane flew higher and was easier to guide than other warplanes. It was flown by Baron Manfred von Richthofen, the "Red Baron," a famous pilot who died in 1918.

Exploring TECHNOLOGY

The Airplane

Orville Wright flew the first engine-driven airplane in Kitty Hawk, North Carolina, in 1903. Most of the plane was made of canvas and wood, and the flight lasted about 12 seconds.

World War I By 1914 airplanes could fly at least 60 miles per hour. A handful were used in the war to observe enemy troops and positions. Then, in 1915 airplanes were fitted with machine guns. Soon more powerful engines were built and planes became larger and faster. However, most planes were still made of wood.

1920s and 1930s After the war, surplus warplanes were used to carry mail and a few passengers between cities. Airplane technology improved rapidly and by 1939 all-metal airliners could fly 170 miles per hour at 30,000 feet and carry more than 20 passengers.

How did World War I lead to improvements in airplanes?

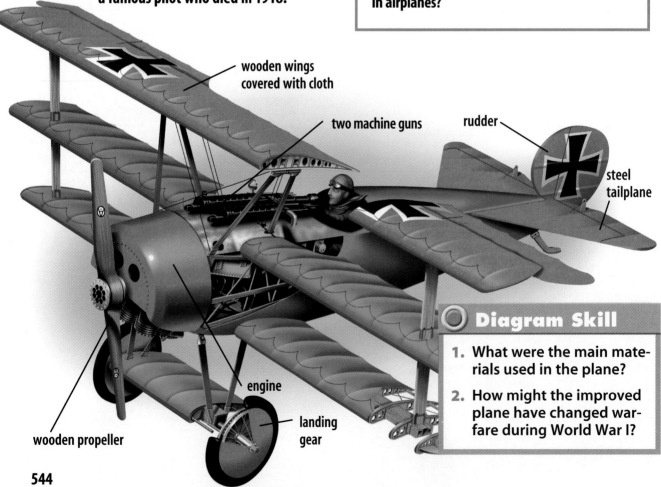

wooden wings covered with cloth

two machine guns

rudder

steel tailplane

engine

wooden propeller

landing gear

Diagram Skill

1. What were the main materials used in the plane?

2. How might the improved plane have changed warfare during World War I?

The War Ends

America's entry helped end the war. At 11:00 P.M. on November 11, 1918, there was an **armistice** (AHR muh stihs), or agreement to stop fighting. The treaty ending the war was signed in 1919 at the palace at Versailles, France. American President **Woodrow Wilson** insisted that the treaty include a **League of Nations**, an international organization dedicated to peace.

The **Treaty of Versailles** blamed Germans for the war and forced them to pay enormous fines. However, Germany was forced to sign it. Even Ferdinand Foch, the Allied commander exclaimed, "This isn't peace! This is an armistice for 20 years!" In 20 years, Europe would be at war again.

Woodrow Wilson

How did U.S. entry help to end World War I?

PUTTING IT TOGETHER

World War I broke out in 1914, and it quickly involved most of the countries of Europe. Once the war began, no one seemed to know how to bring it to an end. No one had expected the war to be as long or as brutal as it became. In 1916, Ireland rebelled against English rule and there was a mutiny in the French army. Both revolts were put down, but the warring powers were exhausted.

After the United States entered the war in 1917, American troops and supplies helped the Allied powers to win. The Treaty of Versailles was signed on June 28, 1919. Although it ended the fighting, it did not end the disputes among the nations. A new war would erupt 20 years later and would drag many more countries into the fighting.

Review and Assess

1. Write one sentence for each vocabulary term.

alliance	League of Nations
armistice	Treaty of Versailles
front	

2. Whose assassination led to the outbreak of World War I?

3. What was the result of the Treaty of Versailles?

4. What effects did World War I have on the **technology** of the airplane?

5. **Make a generalization** about the way World War I was fought.

Use the map on page 542 and a historical map of Europe after World War I to describe changes caused by the war.

• •

Suppose that you are an American keeping a diary in 1918. **Write** a diary entry for the day you heard the news of the armistice.

Lesson 2

The Russian Revolution

How did war and revolution change Russia?

VOCABULARY

tsar
abolish
Duma
Bolshevik
communism
soviet
command
  economy
collective farm
totalitarian

PEOPLE

Nicholas II
Lenin
Josef Stalin

Lesson Outline

• Imperial Russia
• The End of the Tsars
• A New Form of Government
• The Triumph of Communism

BUILD BACKGROUND

"Sire! We workers, our children and wives, the helpless old people who are our parents, we have come to you, Sire, to seek justice and protection."

These were the first words of a letter striking workers tried to present to Russia's ruler in January, 1905. Troops opened fire on the crowd and killed or wounded hundreds of unarmed strikers. It was the beginning of the end for imperial Russia.

READING STRATEGY

Copy this sequence of events chart. Arrange the main events of the Russian Revolution in chronological order.

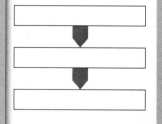

546

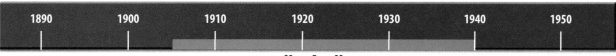
IMPERIAL RUSSIA

The Russian Empire in 1905 stretched thousands of miles across the continents of Europe and Asia. Yet Russians lived much as they had during the Middle Ages.

Nicholas II was the **tsar** (ZAHR), or emperor, and he was convinced that reforms would destroy his empire. Russia had a handful of noble families who controlled enormous wealth and most of Russia's land. At the bottom were millions of poor farmers and industrial workers living in terrible poverty.

Russia's Serfs

Most of Russia's farmers had been serfs. As you read in Chapter 11, serfs were the property of their owners. In 1861, Tsar Alexander II, decided to **abolish**, or end, serfdom. Alexander was worried about a revolution. He said: "It is better to abolish serfdom from above than to wait until the serfs begin to free themselves from below."

Freed serfs were given small plots of land but had to pay heavy taxes. Paying the taxes was difficult, since most families were given too little land to farm successfully. As a result, many farmers gave up their land and moved to Russia's growing cities to find jobs in the new factories that were being built.

READING CHECK How did life change in Russia after the serfs were freed?

Posters like these (opposite) encouraged Russians to support their new government.

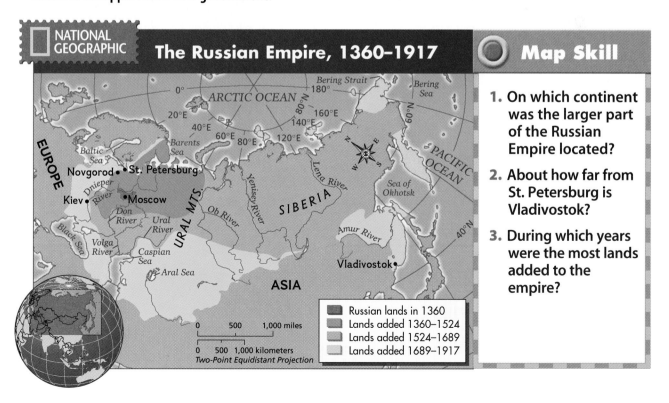

NATIONAL GEOGRAPHIC

The Russian Empire, 1360–1917

Map Skill

ARCTIC OCEAN
Bering Strait
Bering Sea
EUROPE
Baltic Sea
Barents Sea
Novgorod
St. Petersburg
Dnieper River
Kiev
Moscow
Don River
Ural River
URAL MTS.
Ob River
Yenisey River
Lena River
SIBERIA
Sea of Okhotsk
PACIFIC OCEAN
Amur River
Vladivostok
Black Sea
Volga River
Caspian Sea
Aral Sea
ASIA

0   500   1,000 miles
0   500   1,000 kilometers
Two-Point Equidistant Projection

Russian lands in 1360
Lands added 1360–1524
Lands added 1524–1689
Lands added 1689–1917

1. On which continent was the larger part of the Russian Empire located?

2. About how far from St. Petersburg is Vladivostok?

3. During which years were the most lands added to the empire?

THE END OF THE TSARS

By the 1890s factories were springing up in Russia's cities. Their populations increased as many former serfs migrated to cities, especially to the capital, St. Petersburg.

St. Petersburg was a city of palaces, churches, theaters, and universities. However, there were also factories and mills filling the air of poor neighborhoods with smoke and dirt.

The Last Tsar

Conditions for the workers were so bad that they took to the streets, shutting the city down with strikes. Thousands of striking workers marched to the tsar's palace to beg for his help. You have already read how the tsar's soldiers fired into the crowd. So many were killed and injured that the day became known as "Bloody Sunday," and Nicholas II was called "Bloody Nicholas."

The Revolution of 1905

"Bloody Sunday" on January 22, 1905, set off a storm of strikes and revolts. These revolts soon led to revolution. Finally and reluctantly, Nicholas II agreed to allow a parliament, called the **Duma**, to be elected.

The Duma was not trying to change the government completely, but it did try to make Russia more democratic. The tsar was determined to rule alone and refused to allow the changes he had promised. The tsar and the Duma struggled for power for the 12 remaining years of imperial Russia.

Priests led the protests on Bloody Sunday (above), but the tsar and his family (right, above) were not in the capital at the time. The tsar's enormous wealth included his crown of nearly 5,000 diamonds (right).

Russia in World War I

In 1913, the tsar's family, the Romanovs, celebrated 300 years as Russia's ruling dynasty. However, time was running out for the Romanovs. The outbreak of World War I brought imperial Russia's story to a violent conclusion.

World War I was a disaster for Russia. The army suffered defeat after defeat. More than a million Russian troops died. Some soldiers were sent into battle without guns or bullets because Russia's factories could not produce enough to meet wartime demands.

The nation's railroads carried supplies to the front, so only a few trains could bring food and fuel to Russia's cities. Factories and stores often closed because of a lack of goods and materials. More and more people were without work, food, or hope. The failure of the tsar and the government to provide solutions caused Russians to lose confidence in them. Anger grew.

The First Russian Revolution

The situation reached a crisis in March of 1917 when ice and snow prevented farmers from bringing crops to city markets. St. Petersburg's desperate poor lined up for hours in the cold to buy bread, but there was less and less bread to buy.

A mass demonstration was called to protest the terrible conditions. Demonstrators jammed the streets of St. Petersburg. Soon, the calls for "Bread!" gave way to shouts of "Down with the war!" and "Down with the tsar!"

The families of Russian soldiers demonstrate in St. Petersburg.

The demonstrations became riots, frightening the tsar's police. They asked the army to help them maintain order. However, many soldiers joined the rioters and turned against the police. The riots had become a revolution.

Tsar Nicholas was away from the capital, meeting with his generals. He had no idea how serious the situation had become. When he set out by train to reach St. Petersburg, angry railroad workers stopped his train by force. On March 15, 1917, Nicholas II was forced to give up his throne. In June 1918 the tsar and his family were executed.

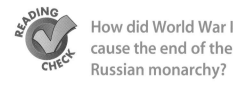

How did World War I cause the end of the Russian monarchy?

Parades (opposite) celebrated the **Bolshevik** victory at the Winter Palace (above). Lenin (right) encouraged workers to seize their factories.

A NEW FORM OF GOVERNMENT

The tsars were gone, but who would rule Russia? After the tsar gave up power in March, the Duma chose new leaders to run the country.

The new leaders meant well, but Russia's problems continued. The war dragged on and Russia continued to lose territory and men. More and more soldiers deserted and made their way back to their homes. Prices rose and food remained scarce. Workers continued to strike because of low wages and bread shortages. Farmers grew tired of waiting for the government to act and seized the land of wealthy landowners.

Radicals Take Over

In these terrible conditions, extreme political groups gained followers. The most successful was a group called the **Bolsheviks**. This group was led by a lawyer named Vladimir Ilyich Ulyanov (VLAD uh meer IHL yitch ool YAH nahf), who called himself **Lenin**. Lenin had

studied the ideas of Karl Marx, whom you read about in Chapter 15. Lenin demanded a second revolution in Russia, one that would change every aspect of Russian life. Lenin and his followers demanded that workers control the government and own all property. Lenin promised Russians "Peace, Land, and Bread." To hungry, war-weary Russians, his promises sounded good.

The Bolshevik Revolution

Lenin and his followers were unable to win a majority in elections for the Duma, so they seized the government by force. With the support of the soldiers in St. Petersburg, Lenin and the Bolsheviks overthrew the Duma in November 1917 and seized power. This marked the beginning of the Bolshevik revolution.

The Bolshevik government soon pulled Russia out of the war by signing a peace treaty with Germany. At the same time, the Bolsheviks encouraged workers to seize their factories and farmers to take the farmland of wealthy nobles. The Bolsheviks also moved the capital of Russia back to Moscow.

Opposition to the Revolution

Many people opposed the Bolshevik takeover. Landowners, factory owners, and nobles saw their wealth and power disappear. Religious groups opposed the Bolsheviks because they closed churches and mosques. Local ethnic groups wanted to break away and form their own countries. Russia was soon engulfed in a terrible civil war between the Bolsheviks and their enemies.

The Russian civil war brought new miseries. Between 1918 and 1920, millions died from disease and starvation, as well as in violent battles that devastated the population.

Why did the Bolshevik takeover lead to civil war?

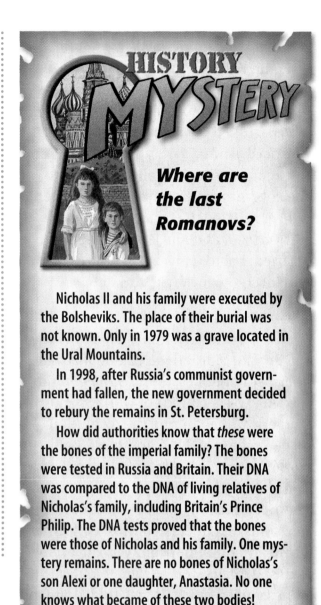

HISTORY MYSTERY

Where are the last Romanovs?

Nicholas II and his family were executed by the Bolsheviks. The place of their burial was not known. Only in 1979 was a grave located in the Ural Mountains.

In 1998, after Russia's communist government had fallen, the new government decided to rebury the remains in St. Petersburg.

How did authorities know that *these* were the bones of the imperial family? The bones were tested in Russia and Britain. Their DNA was compared to the DNA of living relatives of Nicholas's family, including Britain's Prince Philip. The DNA tests proved that the bones were those of Nicholas and his family. One mystery remains. There are no bones of Nicholas's son Alexi or one daughter, Anastasia. No one knows what became of these two bodies!

Why did the new government want to honor the bones?

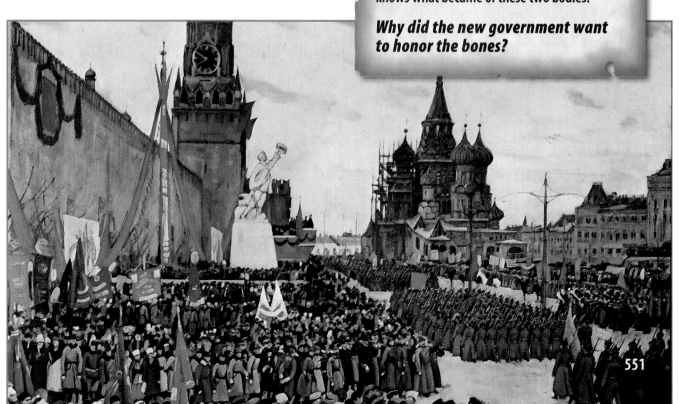

THE TRIUMPH OF COMMUNISM

Lenin believed in **communism**. Communism is a political and economic system in which power, land, and industry are controlled by the government. The Bolsheviks outlawed private property and forced farmers to give all their grain to the government. Communist party members controlled the factories. Churches were closed, and religious leaders were arrested. Lenin replaced religious belief with absolute loyalty to the state.

The New Order Emerges

In 1922, the communists renamed the Russian Empire the Union of Soviet Socialist Republics, or the Soviet Union. A **soviet** was a council of workers and soldiers formed during the revolution.

Lenin died in 1924, and **Josef Stalin** seized power. In 1928, Stalin organized a **command economy**, one in which the central government made most economic decisions. Stalin created huge **collective farms** by combining many small family farms. Workers were assigned to new mines and factories. At first, this command

Exploring ECONOMICS

Russia's Command Economy

Stalin's command economy favored heavy industry, such as steel mills, over industries producing consumer goods. Collective farms produced grain crops for export rather than for the Russian people. Russians stood in line for hours to get scarce and often poor-quality goods.

Central planners also set unrealistic production goals. In addition, corruption was widespread. Russia's command economy was a failure, but it was not apparent for some time. Meanwhile, the Soviet Union became one of the leading industrial nations. It became an important world power in the 1930s.

Plan a classroom mural with central planning. Predict workers, supplies and time needed. Explain your decisions to your classmates.

economy seemed to work and, within ten years, the Soviet Union was transformed into one of the world's most powerful industrial nations.

Stalin (left) forced farmers to join **collective farms** where they worked for the state.

Stalin's Terror

Stalin's Russia was a **totalitarian** (toh tal ih TAIR ee un) nation, a nation where a dictator allows only one political party and controls all aspects of people's lives. Stalin and his Communist Party used terror to control the Soviet Union. People were arrested for receiving letters from foreign countries. Managers were killed because factories or farms did not meet goals. Stalin had more than 15 million people killed or sent to prison camps in Siberia where conditions quickly led to death. Soviet citizens were afraid to speak —even to friends—about Stalin's rule.

READING CHECK How did communism change the way people lived in Russia?

PUTTING IT TOGETHER

The 1900s ushered in a period of great change for Russia. In 1905, Russia's workers rebelled against the rule of Tsar Nicholas II. In 1917, during World War I, the people overthrew the rule of the tsar and replaced it with a more representative form of government. However, the Bolsheviks soon seized power under Lenin and created a communist government. Lenin's successor, Josef Stalin, succeeded in making Russia into an industrial power, but in the process, he formed a totalitarian government that forced the Soviet people to live in terror.

This medal, the Order of Lenin, was established in 1930 and was the highest award of the Soviet Union.

Review and Assess

1. Write one sentence for each vocabulary term.

   collective farm   soviet
   command economy   totalitarian
   communism

2. Why was "Bloody Sunday" an important date in Russian history?

3. How did Russia change between 1914 and the 1930s?

4. How did Stalin change the traditional Russian **economy?**

5. What do you think was the **cause** that led Lenin to sign a peace treaty with Germany and take Russia out of World War I?

Activities

Many Russian cities have changed their names. For example, St. Petersburg has also been called Petrograd and Leningrad. Other Russian cities that have changed their names include Volgograd and Nizhny Novgorod. Research some Russian city name changes. Find out why their names were changed.

Suppose that you work on a collective farm. **Write** a letter to a friend discussing your work and your life on the farm.

553

Lesson 3

World War II

What were the causes and effects of World War II?

VOCABULARY

fascism
Nazi
Axis
Allies
concentration camp
Holocaust

PEOPLE

Winston Churchill
Benito Mussolini
Adolf Hitler
Franklin Roosevelt
Dwight D. Eisenhower
Anne Frank
Raoul Wallenberg

READING STRATEGY

Copy this chart. On it, write the lesson's main idea and supporting details.

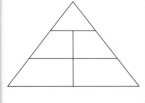

BUILD BACKGROUND

"We shall fight on the beaches, we shall fight on the landing grounds, we shall fight in the fields and in the streets, we shall fight in the hills; we shall never surrender. . . ."

These courageous words from Britain's prime minister, **Winston Churchill**, stirred the British people as Europe plunged into World War II. The war would last for six years and would be fought in Europe, Africa, and Asia, and the islands and waters of the Atlantic and Pacific Oceans.

554

Hitler is shown below. In 1933, he ordered troops to burn books he disapproved of (left). At Dunkirk, (opposite) British troops retreated from France after it was occupied by Germany in 1940.

BAD TIMES AND DICTATORS

During the 1920s, Europe slowly recovered from World War I. In the 1930s, however, an economic depression gripped the world. A depression is a period of economic hardship. As factories closed and people lost their jobs, many Europeans began to look for extreme solutions to their problems.

Two European nations, Italy and Germany, developed a new form of government known as **fascism** (FASH shizm). Fascism is a totalitarian form of government that makes the interests of the nation more important than the interests of the individual. A fascist government was led by a dictator, who was also the head of the only political party allowed.

Benito Mussolini made Italy into the first fascist country in the 1920s. The leader of fascist Germany was **Adolf Hitler**, whose party was known as the **Nazi** (NAH tsee) party. Germany was particularly hard hit by the depression; more than 6 million people were unemployed. Hitler promised to put people back to work. He stirred up hatred of the Jews and wrongfully blamed them for Germany's economic and political problems.

In 1936, a civil war broke out in Spain. Hitler supported a fascist leader named Francisco Franco. Although Franco admired Hitler, he kept out of World War II.

Meanwhile, Hitler threatened the nations surrounding Germany. He demanded that all German-speaking populations become part of Germany. The democracies of Europe seemed unable or unwilling to stop the aggressions of the fascist dictators.

What are the characteristics of a fascist government?

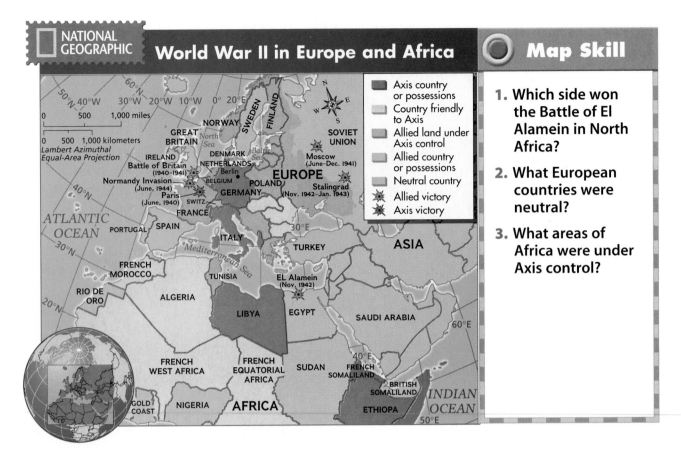

1. Which side won the Battle of El Alamein in North Africa?

2. What European countries were neutral?

3. What areas of Africa were under Axis control?

ANOTHER WORLD WAR

Germany and its allies, Italy and Japan, were called the **Axis** powers. On September 1, 1939, German tanks attacked Poland. The **Allies**, Great Britain and France, declared war on Germany, but they were unable to save Poland. The Soviet Union, which remained a German ally for another two years, seized a chunk of Poland.

In 1940, German forces captured Denmark, the Netherlands, Belgium, and France. Next, Hitler attacked Britain.

The Battle of Britain

The British prime minister, Winston Churchill, told the British people, "I have nothing to offer but blood, toil (work), tears, and sweat." He knew that it would be a long and destructive war.

In the summer of 1940, the Battle of Britain began. Every night for almost a year, waves of German planes bombed British cities. More than 12,000 British people died, but Britain fought on.

The Tide Turns

In June of 1941, Hitler ordered an Axis army of 3 million soldiers to invade the Soviet Union. By November 1941, the Germans had almost reached Moscow. Soviet armies fought fiercely, and they got unexpected help when an early winter set in. The German army ground to a halt, and then retreated leaving 500,000 casualties.

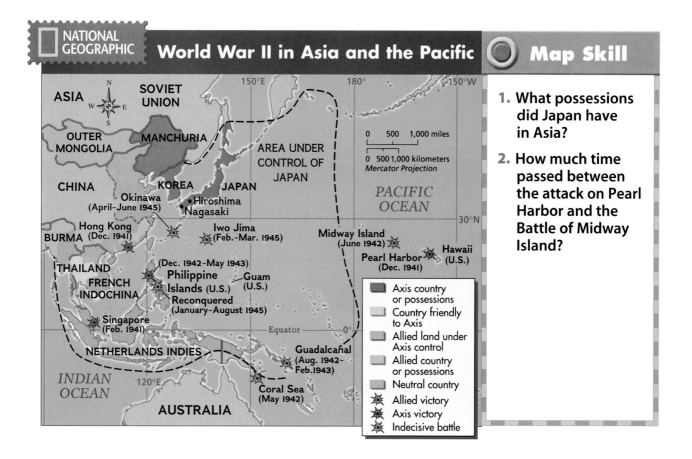

In 1942, Hitler ordered an attack on **Stalingrad**, a city named for Soviet dictator Josef Stalin. German and Soviet troops fought house-by-house until the German army finally surrendered. For the rest of the war, Germany was on the defensive.

America Enters the War

On December 7, 1941, without warning, Japan attacked the U.S. naval base at **Pearl Harbor**, Hawaii. In less than two hours, more than 2,000 people had died, and the American Pacific fleet lay badly damaged. The next day, President **Franklin D. Roosevelt** described December 7 as "a date which will live in infamy [disgrace]," and the United States joined the Allies.

British and American forces fought their way across North Africa and Italy, and the Soviet Union began to push the Germans back to the west. Meanwhile, the Allies were planning a risky and surprise move against the Axis armies in Europe.

D-Day

On June 6, 1944, Allied troops, commanded by a United States general, **Dwight D. Eisenhower**, began "D-Day," the invasion of German-held France. About 2,700 Allied ships carried 200,000 soldiers across the English Channel to the beaches of Normandy following a storm. At the same time, 11,000 Allied planes bombed German defenses.

Allied troops met heavy German fire, but they managed to hold on to the beaches. Once they had established a toehold in Europe, the Allies began to push toward Berlin.

What events led to the defeat of the Nazis in Europe?

Anne Frank (below) died before Nazi **concentration camps** were liberated (above).

THE WAR ENDS IN EUROPE

In less than a year, Allied forces closed in on Germany. Soviet troops from the east and Allied forces from the west raced toward Berlin. On April 30, 1945, Adolf Hitler killed himself in the ruins of Berlin rather than risk capture. A week later, on May 7, Germany surrendered. The war in Europe was over.

The Holocaust

Nazi ideas had been spread by propaganda (prahp uh GAN duh), information or ideas that are spread to try to influence or persuade people to accept a cause or belief. Nazi propaganda was directed against many groups, but it was especially violent toward Jews, Gypsies, and the peoples of eastern Europe.

Only after Allied troops entered German-held territory were the full horrors of Nazi rule revealed. The Nazis had built **concentration camps**, where they had gathered millions of prisoners from all over Europe. Many of these people were murdered in gas chambers. Others were starved and worked to death as slave laborers. This mass slaughter came to be known as the **Holocaust** (HOL uh kawst). The chief victims were 6 million Jewish men, women, and children, about two-thirds of Europe's Jewish population. The Nazis also murdered millions of Gypsies, Poles, Russians and other Slavs, and those who disagreed with their policies in every country they conquered.

Among their victims was a 15-year-old Jewish girl named **Anne Frank**. She and her family spent two years hiding in Amsterdam, the Netherlands. In her diary, Anne wrote:

I hear the ever approaching thunder, which will destroy us too. I can feel the suffering of millions and yet, if I look up into the heavens, I think that it will come [out] right, that this cruelty too will end, and that peace and tranquility will return again.

Anne Frank died in a Nazi camp just before the war ended.

What was the result of the Nazi propaganda?

BIOGRAPHY

Focus On: Courage

Raoul Wallenberg (rah OOL WAHL uhn burg) showed great courage in protecting Hungarian Jews from the Nazis. Wallenberg was a Swedish diplomat who was deeply troubled by Nazi persecution of Jews. The Swedish government sent him to Budapest, Hungary's capital, to try to help.

Wallenberg issued Swedish passes, so Jews could claim the protection of the Swedish government. He boarded trains headed to death camps and issued passports right in front of German soldiers. He also bought buildings and listed them as Swedish government property so that Jews could be sheltered in them. Wallenberg ignored death threats from Nazis and Hungarian fascists to save almost 100,000 Jews.

When Russian troops liberated Budapest from the Nazis in 1945, Wallenberg was taken to a Russian prison and was never heard from again.

Link to Today

Think of someone alive today who has shown great courage. It can be someone you know or someone you have read about. Write a news story that describes the person and how he or she showed courage.

THE LIFE OF RAOUL WALLENBERG	1912 Wallenberg is born in Sweden			1944 Wallenberg goes to Hungary to save Jews	1945 Wallenberg vanishes
	1910	**1920**	**1930**	**1940**	**1950**
LIFE AROUND THE WORLD	1911 Chinese Republic is declared	1929 Stock market crashes in New York	1932 Bolivia and Paraguay war over the Chaco	1945 Mussolini is assassinated	1947 India gains independence

Soldiers raise the American flag at the Pacific Battle of Iwo Jima in 1945.

PEACE IN ASIA

The Nazis were defeated, but the war against Japan continued. The Allies captured one Pacific island at a time, always pushing the Japanese forces back toward their homeland. Air raids flattened Japan's cities and destroyed its war industries, but still Japanese leaders refused to give up.

By August 1945, the Allies were ready to invade Japan, where the Japanese army still had 2 million men ready to defend their homeland.

A New Weapon

Allied leaders wanted to avoid a bloody invasion of Japan that would cost tens of thousands of lives. For some time, Allied scientists had been working on a top-secret project to develop an atomic bomb. On August 6, 1945, the United States dropped the first atomic bomb in history on the city of **Hiroshima** (hihr oh SHEE muh). Most of the city was destroyed in seconds, and at least 80,000 people died.

Japan still did not surrender, so the United States dropped a second bomb three days later on the city of **Nagasaki** (nah guh SAH kee). Japanese leaders surrendered on August 14, 1945.

Why did the United States drop an atomic bomb on Hiroshima?

Exploring TECHNOLOGY

Atomic Power

During World War II scientists working at Los Alamos in New Mexico, Oak Ridge in Tennessee, and other places created the atomic bomb. This weapon used energy created by changing the matter in atoms. Since World War II atomic power, also known as nuclear energy, has had peaceful uses. Nuclear energy is used to produce electricity and in helping to diagnose illnesses. However, some people worry about the radioactive waste produced from such activities because it is harmful to people, animals, and plants.

What are the advantages and disadvantages of nuclear energy?

PUTTING IT TOGETHER

World War II was truly a world war. It was fought in Europe, Asia, Africa, and the islands of the Pacific. By the time the war ended, Europe lay in ruins and more than 50 million people had died. Millions more had been tortured or had had their rights taken away. During this time new weapons caused more destruction than the world had ever before seen.

At the end of the war, the world would change and new causes of conflict would arise between two of the most powerful Allies, the United States and the Soviet Union.

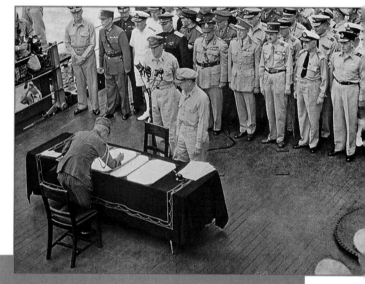

Delighted Londoners (top) celebrate Germany's defeat in May 1945. Japan surrendered aboard the U.S.S. *Missouri* in Tokyo harbor in September 1945 (right).

Review and Assess

1. Write one sentence for each vocabulary term.

   concentration camp   **Holocaust**
   fascism   **Nazi**

2. What is fascism?

3. What were the major causes and effects of World War II?

4. What are some benefits and drawbacks of atomic **technology?**

5. How might the German **frame of reference** have been different if there had been no depression before Hitler came to power?

Activities

Look at the maps on pages 556–557. Make a chart of the Axis countries and the Allied countries during World War II.

• •

 Do some research for a biography of one of the people mentioned in this lesson. **Write** a brief biography that tells why the person is famous.

Recognizing Bias and Propaganda

During World War II, both the Axis and the Allies made use of **propaganda**, persuasive ideas or images that are spread in order to influence people's point of view. Nazi propaganda often contained **bias**, or the favoring of one side over another, to persuade Germans of Nazi beliefs and of constant Nazi victories.

…Twenty thousand [Soviet] soldiers deserted to the German lines after shooting their political [leaders]. 52,000 new deserters were announced today. This is more than a symptom.… Listeners to German radio programs… are executed. The cowardly band of liars in the Kremlin [Soviet government] seems to sense that their fate is near. Moscow newspapers are full of bloodthirsty attacks on those spreading panic and rumors, defeatists and [traitors].…

LEARN THE SKILL

Follow these steps to recognize bias and propaganda.

1. **Identify the topic.**
   The Soviets are cowardly and fearful, brutally suppressing supporters of Germany.

2. **Determine if the source can be believed.**
   The excerpt is from a speech by Nazi propaganda minister Josef Goebbels. He is referring to people the Nazis are fighting. There is a great possibility the speaker is biased.

3. **Look for missing facts or unsupported conclusions.**
   Propaganda makes claims based on unsupported statements. For example, the speech says that 20,000 Soviet soldiers deserted after shooting their leaders. However, it does not say which leaders were shot. Also, the speech tells us that 52,000 "new deserters were announced today," but does not say who announced this fact.

4. **Identify words that indicate bias.**
   Notice such bias words and phrases as *deserters, band of liars, their fate is near, defeatists,* and *bloodthirsty attacks.*

5. **Evaluate the purpose of the message.**
   The speech does not inform about specific battles, political leaders, or executions. It is vague and filled with biased terms. The purpose of the speech is to spread propaganda.

TRY THE SKILL

The excerpt below is from a speech by a Soviet leader in 1941. He is telling the Soviet people about the German invasion of the Soviet Union. Read the excerpt. Follow the steps to identify the use of propaganda in his speech.

> Today at 4 o'clock A.M. . . . without a declaration of war, German troops attacked our country. . . despite the fact that a treaty. . . had been signed between the U.S.S.R. and Germany. . . . Entire responsibility for this predatory [unjustified] attack upon the Soviet Union falls fully and completely upon the German Fascist rulers. . . . Likewise. . . the whole declaration made today by Hitler, who is . . . charging the Soviet Union with failure to observe the Soviet-German pact [treaty]. . . . [is a lie]. The government calls upon you. . . to rally still more closely. . . around our great leader and comrade, Stalin. Ours is a righteous cause. The enemy shall be defeated. Victory will be ours.

1. What is the topic of the speech?

2. Can the speaker be believed? What facts does he use to support his position?

3. Are his facts supported by details?

4. Are words used that indicate bias?

5. How can recognizing propaganda help you to understand what you read?

EXTEND THE SKILL

Propaganda was an important part of World War II. The Axis and the Allies used posters, songs, and speeches to convince people to join their cause.

Find a Web site on the Internet that contains information on a war from the late 20th century. Select a speech or other material to study for bias and propaganda.

- Explain why the item is or is not an example of propaganda.

- How does analyzing sources for facts and opinions help you determine bias and propaganda?

Communist China

How did wars and revolutions change China?

Lesson Outline
- The End of the Empire
- Modern China is Born
- Life in the New China

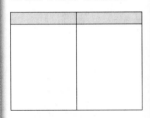
BUILD BACKGROUND

"The present situation is becoming daily more difficult. The various Powers cast upon us looks of tiger-like voracity [hunger], hustling each other to be first to seize our . . . territories."

The last empress of China urged Chinese people to save her power in 1900. However, time was running out for the Chinese Empire. The next century would be a time of vast change. China would first become a republic and then a communist dictatorship.

THE END OF THE EMPIRE

China was deeply respectful of its tradition and history. Moreover, it was isolated from the economic and technological changes of the Industrial Revolution underway in the West. Most Chinese still worked as poor farmers.

Foreigners took advantage of China's weakness. Britain had seized Hong Kong, and Japan had taken the island of Taiwan. As you have read, China was forced to sign humiliating treaties that set up zones within China that were under foreign rule.

The Qing (CHING), or Manchu, dynasty had conquered China in 1644, but later Qing rulers were weak. Many Chinese people hoped for an end to Qing rule. They wanted China to have a democratic government and one that was less influenced by foreign nations.

A New Voice for China

The strongest voice for a more democratic and independent China was that of **Sun Yat-sen** (SUN YAT SEN). Sun wanted a Chinese republic in which foreign nations had no control over China's government. Sun also wanted China to improve its agriculture and industry. Many Chinese agreed with Sun when he said:

> *The real trouble is that China is not an independent country. She is the victim of foreign countries. . . . I set myself the object of the overthrow of the Qing dynasty and the establishment of a Chinese republic in its ruins.*

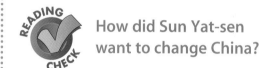

READING CHECK How did Sun Yat-sen want to change China?

Empress Zixi (TSOO SHEE) (right) was the last strong ruler of imperial China. Sun Yat-sen (top, with his wife), helped found a republic in 1912. It lasted until 1949, when communist forces paraded into Beijing (opposite).

565

MODERN CHINA IS BORN

In 1911, the Chinese monarchy was overthrown, and Sun Yat-sen's Nationalist Party formed a new government for China. The Republic of China had problems ruling the country however. Local military leaders, called **warlords**, had seized power in many areas during the struggle to overthrow the Qing dynasty. Nationalist forces, with the help of Chinese and Soviet communists, finally defeated the warlords in 1927.

A New Civil War

Sun Yat-sen had died in 1925. A power struggle immediately broke out, until **Chiang Kai-shek** (CHANG KĪ SHEK), a Nationalist general and the brother-in-law of Sun Yat-sen, took power. Chiang feared the power of the Chinese communists and he attacked them in 1927 at Shanghai and Nanjing. A new civil war soon erupted.

Into the Mountains

In 1934, Chiang's army surrounded the communists in southern China and cut off food and supplies. He hoped to break their power. **Mao Zedong** (MOU DZE DUNG), the communist leader, escaped with 80,000 of his followers. They began a long retreat to the north. This journey is called the **Long March**. Men and women walked almost 6,000 miles in about a year—a distance almost equal to walking across the United States twice!

The marchers had to cross steep mountains in freezing winds. They were poorly clothed and often hungry. The survivors faced more hardships in the rainy marshes of northern China. Finding food and clean water was difficult, and quicksand could swallow the careless.

Only about ten percent of those who began the Long March lived to reach northern China. The survivors gathered at the great bend of the Huang He. Here, at Yan'an, they recovered from their journey and began to spread the ideas of communism among the peasants and farmers in the surrounding area.

China in World War II

In 1937, Japanese forces launched a brutal conquest of China. Communists and Nationalists agreed to cooperate to fight the Japanese invaders. Eight years of terrible suffering followed before Japan surrendered at the end of World War II. Almost immediately, the communists and the Nationalist government renewed their civil war.

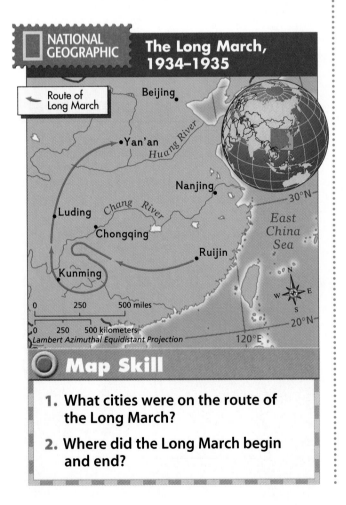

NATIONAL GEOGRAPHIC

The Long March, 1934–1935

Route of Long March

Beijing
Yan'an
Huang River
Nanjing
30°N
Luding
Chang River
Chongqing
East China Sea
Ruijin
Kunming
0   250   500 miles
0   250   500 kilometers
Lambert Azimuthal Equidistant Projection
20°N
120°E

Map Skill

1. **What cities were on the route of the Long March?**

2. **Where did the Long March begin and end?**

Chiang and Mao worked together briefly (right) but Mao soon fled with his followers on the Long March (above).

The Communist Victory

The Nationalists were at a disadvantage. Nationalist troops had done most of the fighting against the Japanese. In addition, inflation was out of control, and the people held the Nationalist government responsible. Chiang also had to fight warlords who had seized power during the war.

Meanwhile, the communists had become very popular in rural areas. They had shown farmers how to produce more crops. While they worked, they also talked with them about communism.

After two years of fighting, the communists drove the Nationalists out of China. Chiang and his followers retreated to the island of Taiwan, where they continued the Republic of China in exile. In 1949, Mao proclaimed the People's Republic of China a communist state.

A New China Emerges

Mao Zedong was the new ruler of China. The warlords and Nationalist leaders were gone. Many Chinese hoped that communism would provide jobs and good government.

The communists provided housing, medical care, and food supplies for city workers. They supported education for all Chinese, as well as equal rights for women. At the same time, they changed China in the same ways communists had changed Russia. Private ownership was ended, and collective farms were formed. They tried to create a modern industrial state from the agricultural society of traditional China.

There was also great suffering. Many people died or disappeared during the first years of communist rule. As many as one million people were killed during the changeover.

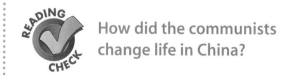

How did the communists change life in China?

LIFE IN THE NEW CHINA

In 1957, Mao proclaimed the "Great Leap Forward." Factories worked day and night to help China industrialize. Families even set up tiny steel-making furnaces in their backyards.

Rural Life

Farmers and their families were forced onto large **communes**, or collective farms. The government decided which crops each commune would produce. Moreover, people in communes were forced to work on bridges, dams, and other government projects. Commune life was a complete change from Chinese traditional life. People worked in teams and families were not allowed to live together. People were told to put loyalty to the government ahead of loyalty to family.

The Great Leap Forward was a disaster. Communes produced less grain than the old family farms. Few Chinese workers knew how to make steel, so much of the steel they made was unusable.

Mao finally gave up on the Great Leap Forward, but as many as 20 million people may have starved to death in the famine that followed.

The Cultural Revolution

In 1966, Mao began a ten-year period called the **Cultural Revolution**. He set out to destroy all noncommunist beliefs. Leaders who opposed him were punished. Mao also encouraged bands of students to break into people's homes to destroy Chinese classics and art. Anyone wearing Western-made clothing or owning Western writings faced attack. Anyone could be accused of working against Mao and forced to confess publicly. Xiao-Yen

Wang describes how as a child she witnessed the Cultural Revolution:

> *I used to sneak to the meetings at my father's institute to see "uncles" and "aunties" from the neighborhood—people I had known since I was two—kneeling head-bowed, wearing big, tall hats and huge signs around their necks saying "I am a traitor." Thousands of people shouted, "Down with the traitor Hong!" "Down with the traitor Zhang!"*

China's "new society" had become a nightmare of fear, chaos, and poverty.

The Cultural Revolution ended with the death of Mao Zedong in 1976. Some of China's new leaders, who had been

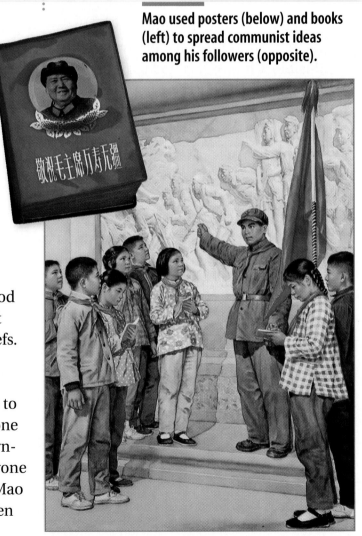

Mao used posters (below) and books (left) to spread communist ideas among his followers (opposite).

568

punished during the Cultural Revolution, returned to power and set off on a new path for their country. In the meantime, China and the United States, which had been suspicious of each other, began to restore their ties after President Richard Nixon made a trip to China. Slowly, China began to recover from its years of chaos and to emerge as a world power.

 How did the Cultural Revolution affect China?

PUTTING IT TOGETHER

China changed drastically in the last 100 years. The overthrow of the Qing dynasty led to two rival armies, the Nationalists and the communists, fighting to control the country. Eventually, the communist army won control of China. The Communist Party modernized China, but also caused great suffering with the Great Leap Forward and the Cultural Revolution.

Review and Assess

1. Write one sentence for each vocabulary term.

   commune   **Long March**
   Cultural Revolution   **warlord**

2. Who led the fight against the Qing dynasty?

 3. How did China change after the fall of the Qing dynasty?

4. Why did the Great Leap Forward fail to improve life in China?

5. What **generalization** can you make about the Great Leap Forward?

Activities

Compare the map on page 566 with a physical map of Asia in the Atlas on page R13. Make a chart or list of the cities on the Long March. Describe the geography surrounding each city.

Write a newspaper article describing the defeat of the Nationalists by the communists in 1949.

The Cold War

How did tensions develop after World War II?

VOCABULARY

iron curtain
Cold War
Berlin Airlift
NATO
Warsaw Pact
arms race
Berlin Wall

PEOPLE

Fidel Castro
John F. Kennedy
Nikita Khrushchev
Mikhail
 Gorbachev
Boris Yeltsin

READING STRATEGY

Copy this main idea chart. Write details in the circles that support the main idea of the lesson.

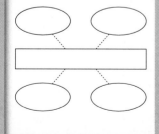

BUILD BACKGROUND

"An iron curtain has descended across the continent [of Europe]. Behind that line lie all the capitals of the ancient states of Central and Eastern Europe. . . . All these famous cities and the populations around them lie in the Soviet sphere. . . ."

With the term "**iron curtain**," Winston Churchill described Europe as being divided between mostly democratic countries in the west and the countries the Soviet Union controlled in the east. For more than 40 years, this iron curtain would divide the world into two rival camps.

THE COLD WAR BEGINS

In February 1945, Franklin D. Roosevelt, Winston Churchill, and Josef Stalin met in the Soviet resort city of Yalta. They discussed plans for what would happen when World War II ended.

They agreed to set up a new organization, called the United Nations, to keep peace in the world. They also agreed to divide postwar Germany into a zone of occupation for each ally.

The Eastern European nations under Soviet control were to have free elections, but Stalin arranged for local communists to seize power. He wanted governments he could control on the borders of the Soviet Union. The United States and Great Britain protested, but Stalin ignored them. The **Cold War** had begun. The Cold War was a struggle of words and ideas between the Soviet Union and the United States and their allies from about 1945 to 1990. During that time no full-scale war broke out.

The Berlin Airlift

The Cold War's first crisis occurred in Berlin, which had also been divided into zones of occupation. However, Soviet-occupied Germany surrounded the entire city. In 1948, the Soviet Union closed the roads into Berlin. Berliners faced starvation without supplies of food and fuel.

For 11 months, American and British planes flew into the city with tons of supplies. This was known as the **Berlin Airlift**. In May 1949, the Soviet Union accepted defeat and lifted its blockade.

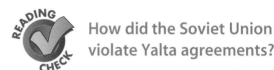 How did the Soviet Union violate Yalta agreements?

The **Berlin Airlift** flew supplies into Berlin (opposite) after the Soviet Union blockaded the city. Churchill, Roosevelt, and Stalin (below) had agreed to divide control of Berlin in 1945.

SEEKING SECURITY

The United States and the Soviet Union feared that a war between them would turn into a nuclear war. As a result, each side took steps to protect itself.

Military Alliances

In 1949, Western European nations, the United States, and Canada formed the North Atlantic Treaty Organization, soon called **NATO** for short. NATO members agreed to defend any member of the alliance if it was attacked.

The Soviet Union formed its own military alliance, known as the **Warsaw Pact**. All the communist nations of Eastern Europe joined the Warsaw Pact.

The Nuclear Arms Race

At the end of World War II, the United States was the only country with atomic weapons. By 1949, the Soviet Union had its own atomic bomb. Later, other nations would develop atomic weapons.

An **arms race** developed between the United States and the Soviet Union as each country raced to have the greatest number of nuclear weapons. This arms race was an important part of the Cold War.

The arms race aroused fears of a nuclear attack. American schoolchildren practiced what to do if a bomb exploded near them. Some families built bomb shelters in their backyards stocked with food and supplies in case of an attack.

Americans worried about communism at home. The government investigated Hollywood leaders and government workers. Both the Soviet Union and the United States arrested people for spying.

NATIONAL GEOGRAPHIC
Europe, 1950

Communist countries
Non-communist countries
— "Iron Curtain"

FINLAND
NORWAY
SWEDEN
North Sea
Baltic Sea
IRELAND
GREAT BRITAIN
DENMARK
50°N
NETHERLANDS
EAST GERMANY
SOVIET UNION
BELGIUM
POLAND
ATLANTIC OCEAN
LUXEMBOURG
WEST GERMANY
CZECHOSLOVAKIA
SWITZERLAND
AUSTRIA
HUNGARY
FRANCE
ITALY
ROMANIA
PORTUGAL
YUGOSLAVIA
BULGARIA
SPAIN
Adriatic Sea
ALBANIA
40°N
Mediterranean Sea
GREECE
0   250   500 miles
AFRICA
Aegean Sea
0   250   500 kilometers
Lambert Azimuthal Equal-Area Projection

● Map Skill

1. **Which country was divided by the Iron Curtain?**

2. **What countries were behind the Iron Curtain?**

The Soviet Union displayed military strength in parades like this one in Moscow's Red Square (left). Cold War conflicts occurred in both Korea and Vietnam (below, left and right).

The Korean War

Korea had been freed from Japanese control after World War II. The Korean peninsula was divided into two nations in 1948: communist North Korea and non-communist South Korea.

In June 1950, North Korean troops invaded South Korea. The United States led armies of the United Nations in the defense of South Korea. The war dragged on with neither side able to claim victory. In 1953, with 5 million dead, both sides agreed to end the fighting, and the pre-war boundary between North Korea and South Korea was restored. The division between the two Koreas remains today.

The War in Vietnam

The United States became involved in a second war in Asia in the early 1960s. Like Korea, Vietnam had been divided into a communist north and a non-communist south. In 1963, it appeared communist forces were planning to seize the entire country. The United States sent supplies and, later, troops to help South Vietnam.

By 1968 there were more than 500,000 United States troops in Vietnam. The war began to divide Americans as more and more soldiers were killed and there was no victory. There were antiwar demonstrations on many college campuses as well as demonstrations in support of the war. In 1973, the United States withdrew from Vietnam. Soon after, North Vietnam seized the rest of Vietnam and included it in its communist state.

READING CHECK Why did the United States become involved in Korea and Vietnam?

HOT SPOTS

The Soviet Union and the United States continued to oppose each other. Trouble in Berlin led to a deepening distrust between the two powers, but Soviet missiles in Cuba nearly led to war.

The Berlin Wall

By 1950, Germany was divided into two countries: democratic West Germany and communist East Germany. Thousands of East Germans tried to flee to West Germany, and the East German government decided to act. One night in August 1961, the East Germans built a concrete wall topped by barbed wire separating East Berlin from West Berlin. Communist guards patrolled the **Berlin Wall**, shooting anyone who tried to cross it.

To the democratic nations of the world, the wall was an ugly symbol of communism until 1989, when it was demolished with the collapse of communism in Europe.

The Cuban Missile Crisis

The next Cold War crisis occurred in Cuba. In 1959, **Fidel Castro** led a rebellion to overthrow Cuba's dictator and set up a new government. Castro was soon receiving economic and military support from the Soviet Union.

In 1961, the United States government supported a group of anti-communist Cubans who attempted to overthrow Castro. The attempt failed.

The Berlin Wall (below) cut through the heart of Berlin, Germany, from 1961 until its destruction (right) in 1989.

It was a beautiful fall evening. . . and I went up into the open air to look and smell it, because I thought it was the last Saturday I would ever see.

A Soviet advisor to Khrushchev echoed the fear that war was coming. He wrote:

I went and telephoned my wife and told her to drop everything and get out of Moscow. I thought [American] bombers were on the way.

At the last minute, Khrushchev ordered the Russian ship to turn back, and the threat of war ended. In 1963, the United States and the Soviet Union signed a treaty banning most kinds of nuclear weapon testing. World leaders hoped that the treaty would reduce the chance that nuclear weapons would ever be used in war.

READING CHECK How did the Cold War affect Berlin and Cuba?

Russian Missiles in Cuba

In October 1962, President **John F. Kennedy** received word that Soviet leader, **Nikita Khrushchev**, had begun to build missile bases in Cuba. Missiles from Cuba could reach the United States quickly, so the threat was very serious.

Kennedy demanded that the Soviets remove the missiles. He also ordered a naval blockade of Cuba to keep the Soviets from delivering additional missiles. He warned the Soviets that the United States would attack Cuba to prevent its use as a missile base.

Tense Moments

For days, the world held its breath as a Soviet vessel loaded with missiles steamed toward Cuba. An advisor to President Kennedy later recalled:

Fidel Castro and Soviet leader Nikita Khrushchev (below) express their country's friendship a year before the Cuban Missile Crisis in 1962 (above).

THE END OF THE COLD WAR

In 1985, a new Soviet leader, **Mikhail Gorbachev** [mih KYL GAWR buh chawf], tried to reform his country. He allowed more freedom for individuals and loosened the Soviet command economy.

The Soviet Union had invaded the neighboring country of Afghanistan (af GAN uh stan) in 1979. This war had proved expensive and bloody. In spite of its powerful military, the Soviet Union could not defeat the Afghan guerillas. Gorbachev withdrew all Soviet troops from Afghanistan in 1989.

Meanwhile, communist Europe was changing. In June of 1989, Poland's opposition party was allowed to have seats in its parliament. Hungary opened its border with the West in October. In November, joyful crowds in Berlin tore down the Berlin Wall. Europe was reunited.

Gorbachev's acceptance of these changes angered some communist leaders in Moscow. **Boris Yeltsin** led the resistance to a communist attempt to overthrow Gorbachev and take control of the government. In the Soviet Union's first free election in 1991, Yeltsin became president of the Russian Republic. The republics that had made up the Soviet Union began to break away. Finally the Soviet Union came to an end after 74 years.

The new Russian state and the United States retained some of their suspicions, especially in discussions of atomic weapons. However, the Cold War had ended. One of Russia's leaders said:

> *The Cold War is over. Our planet, this world, all of Europe are embarking [starting] on a new road. This is going to be a peaceful period.*

READING CHECK What events led to the end of the Cold War?

Soviet leader Mikhail Gorbachev and President Ronald Reagan (left) meet in Geneva, Switzerland. Boris Yeltsin (above) speaks to crowds during a Communist attack on the Soviet government.

Hungarian workers remove a statue of Lenin in 1990 (above). The hammer and sickle (right) was the symbol of communism.

PUTTING IT TOGETHER

The Cold War was a war mostly of words and hostile actions between the Soviet Union and the United States. It began after World War II because Stalin controlled the governments of Eastern Europe and began to spread communism. The United States developed a policy of resisting communist expansion. Although the Soviet Union and the United States did not attack each other during the Cold War, there were real shooting wars in Korea, Vietnam, and Afghanistan. The two nations almost went to war over a Soviet attempt to place nuclear weapons in Cuba. The Cold War ended with the collapse of communism in 1991. In later lessons you will read about the changes that followed the end of the Cold War.

Review and Assess

1. Write a sentence for each vocabulary term.

   arms race   **Cold War**
   Berlin Airlift   **iron curtain**
   Berlin Wall

2. Where did Allied leaders meet to discuss plans for Europe after World War II?

3. What events led to the development of the Cold War?

4. How did **technology** affect the Cold War?

5. How might a Soviet historian's **frame of reference** affect the way he or she writes about the Cold War?

Make a two-column chart of the locations of Cold War conflicts. Write the date and the name of the place where the conflict occurred.

Suppose you are a newspaper reporter in Berlin in 1948. **Write** a news article describing the Berlin Airlift.

VOCABULARY REVIEW

Number a paper from 1–5. Beside each number write the word or term from the list below that best completes the sentence.

Cold War

fascism

totalitarian

Treaty of Versailles

warlords

1. World War I was ended by the ____.

2. ____ rule controls all aspects of people's lives.

3. The power struggle between the United States and the Soviet Union after World War II is the ____.

4. The Nationalist government in China had to defeat local ____.

5. ____ is a totalitarian form of government that puts the interests of the nation above the interests of the people.

CHAPTER COMPREHENSION

6. What event led to World War I?

7. How did the first two rulers of the Soviet Union change the country?

8. What is a command economy?

9. What factors allowed Hitler to gain power in Germany?

10. Why was the battle of Stalingrad a turning point in World War II?

11. What event caused the United States to enter World War II?

12. Which two men struggled for power during China's civil war in the 1930s and after World War II?

13. **Write** a paragraph about the Holocaust.

SKILL REVIEW

14. **Reading/Thinking Skills** What is propaganda? What is bias?

15. **Reading/Thinking Skills** How did the Nazis use bias to gain and to hold on to power?

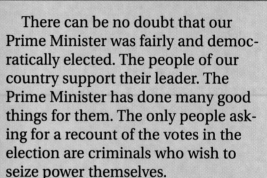

The Examiner

There can be no doubt that our Prime Minister was fairly and democratically elected. The people of our country support their leader. The Prime Minister has done many good things for them. The only people asking for a recount of the votes in the election are criminals who wish to seize power themselves.

16. **Reading/Thinking Skills** How can you tell the paragraph above is propaganda? Make a list of biased words and phrases.

17. **Reading/Thinking Skills** Rewrite the paragraph above as a news article. Do not use biased words.

18. **Reading/Thinking Skills** Summarize the main goals of the Cultural Revolution.

USING A TIME LINE

1910	1920	1930	1940	1950	1960	1970	1980	1990	2000

1914 World War I begins

1917 Russian Revolution

1918 World War I ends

1939 World War II begins

1945 World War II ends; Stalin breaks Yalta promises

1962 Cuban Missile Crisis

1985 Mikhail Gorbachev becomes Soviet leader

1991 Communism ends in Russia

19. For how many years did the Communists control the Russian government?

20. How many years was the world at war during World War I and World War II?

Writing About Technology Suppose that you are a scientist or an engineer working on new technology during World War I or World War II. Do some research and select one new invention from either war. Write a paragraph describing the invention you have chosen. Explain why the technology will help your side in the war.

Use your Foldable to review what you have learned about the period of Troubled Times. Find similarities and differences between wars fought on a battlefield and wars fought through politics and the media. Mentally sequence the events studied in this chapter to form a time line of the first half of the twentieth century. Look at your notes under the tabs of your Foldable to check your memory and responses. Record any questions that you have, and discuss them with classmates, or review the chapter to find answers.

Troubled Times

• Weapons
• The United States helps the Allied Powers win the war.
• The Treaty of Versailles is signed.

World War I
The Russian Revolution
World War II
Communist China
Cold War

THE Big IDEAS ABOUT...

The Spread of Independence

After World War II, countries in Asia, Africa, and the Pacific became independent. Some nations, such as Ghana, achieved independence peacefully. Others, such as Angola, fought long wars to win their freedom. During the next half century, some of these countries would suffer through civil wars and dictatorships.

STRUGGLES IN INDIA

In 1947, British colonial rule ends in India. The former colony becomes two nations—predominantly Hindu India and Muslim Pakistan.

CONFLICT IN THE MIDDLE EAST

In 1948, Israel is born. Palestinians and other Arabs oppose the new state. The next 50 years are a period of wars, violence, and terrorist attacks in the Middle East and elsewhere.

AFRICAN INDEPENDENCE

In 1957, Ghana becomes a nation. Other European colonies in Africa gain independence during the next 30 years.

NATIONS OF SOUTHEAST ASIA TODAY

Although colonial rulers are reluctant to give up Asian colonies, Vietnam, Cambodia, and Indonesia gain independence.

NEW NATIONS IN THE PACIFIC

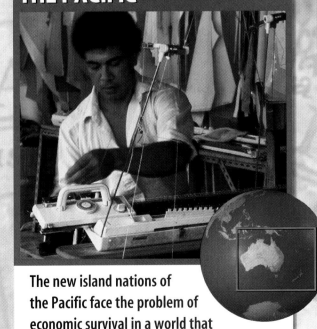

The new island nations of the Pacific face the problem of economic survival in a world that is becoming increasingly industrialized.

Foldables

Make this Foldable study guide and use it to record what you learn about "The Spread of Independence."

1. Fold a sheet of paper in half like a hot dog, but make one side 1" shorter than the other.

2. Make four cuts on the short side to form five tabs.

3. Write the chapter title on the long tab and the lesson titles on the short ones. Draw arrows to connect the five tabs to the chapter title.

4. Collect information under the tabs of your Foldable.

Struggles in India

How did India gain independence?

VOCABULARY

boycott
civil disobedience
Green Revolution

PEOPLE

Mohandas Gandhi
Muhammad Ali Jinnah
Jawaharlal Nehru
Indira Gandhi

READING STRATEGY

Copy this chart. Write "Gandhi Resists British Rule" in the main box. Then list details that support that main idea in the circles.

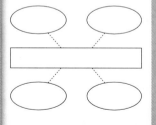

BUILD BACKGROUND

"Brute force is not natural to Indian soil. You will have, therefore, to rely wholly on soul-force. You must not consider that violence is necessary. . . for reaching our goal."

These are the words of **Mohandas Gandhi**, a leader in the Indian struggle for independence. Gandhi showed the world that change does not have to come by force.

BRITISH INDIA

As you read in Chapter 15, India was Britain's richest colony. Although Indians benefitted from British rule, they also resented British control of their country.

British merchants controlled the Indian economy, and politicians in London and in Britain's colonial service controlled the laws and the government. Many British regarded Indians as their social inferiors. Indians were not permitted in British social clubs, and they could not travel in the best railroad seats. India's leaders realized that the situation would not change until their country became independent of Britain.

Gandhi leads his followers on the 240-mile Salt March in 1930 (opposite).

Early Moves for Independence

In 1885, the first Indian National Congress met in Bombay. Many of the 73 delegates had been educated in England. They asked the British to spend less money on the army and to give more Indians positions in India's government. A few Indians also began to talk about independence.

Britain had forced Indians to import cheap British cotton. India's cotton weavers were ruined by this competition. In 1905 Indians began to **boycott** British cloth. A boycott is an organized protest in which people refuse to buy or use something. Indians began wearing homemade cloth as a sign of national pride.

READING CHECK What did Indians dislike about British control of India?

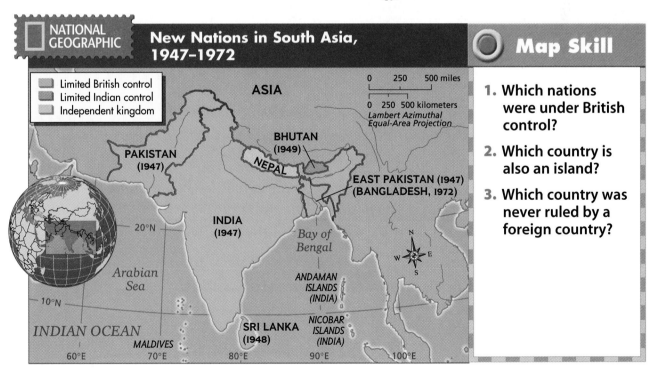

NATIONAL GEOGRAPHIC

New Nations in South Asia, 1947–1972

Limited British control
Limited Indian control
Independent kingdom

ASIA

0   250   500 miles
0   250   500 kilometers
Lambert Azimuthal
Equal-Area Projection

PAKISTAN (1947)
BHUTAN (1949)
NEPAL
EAST PAKISTAN (1947)
(BANGLADESH, 1972)
INDIA (1947)
20°N
Bay of Bengal
Arabian Sea
ANDAMAN ISLANDS (INDIA)
10°N
INDIAN OCEAN
MALDIVES
SRI LANKA (1948)
NICOBAR ISLANDS (INDIA)
60°E   70°E   80°E   90°E   100°E

Map Skill

1. **Which nations were under British control?**

2. **Which country is also an island?**

3. **Which country was never ruled by a foreign country?**

A NON-VIOLENT STRUGGLE

In 1915, a leader emerged who would organize the struggle for independence. His name was Mohandas Gandhi.

Gandhi wanted to end British rule in India. He also hoped for peace between the Muslims and Hindus of India. There were about 350 million Hindus and 100 million Muslims in India at that time. There was constant tension between the two groups. Gandhi also hoped to end discrimination against India's untouchable caste. The untouchables were people outside the Hindu caste system that Hindus considered unclean.

Gandhi lived very simply. He wore only the cloth that he had woven himself. However, he was a lawyer and a very knowledgeable politician. He and his followers used the principle of **civil disobedience** to end British rule. Civil disobedience is a nonviolent protest against a government. A boycott is one form of civil disobedience. So is the refusal to obey laws considered unjust.

In the excerpt below, Gandhi explains nonviolence to his followers.

The Salt March

It was illegal for Indians to make salt themselves. They had to buy salt from British-approved merchants and pay a tax that supported the British colonial government. Gandhi and his followers refused to buy salt from the British dealers. Gandhi led a 240-mile "Salt March" to the sea. There the demonstrators made their own salt from the seawater.

Thousands, including Gandhi himself, were put in jail. This did not stop their protests. In fact, it became a sign of patriotism to be arrested. Soon nearly all of India was following Gandhi's lead.

 **What nonviolent practices did Gandhi use?**

 **Primary Source:** *excerpt from a speech by* **Mohandas Gandhi,** *during the campaign to free India, 1915–1947*

[Nonviolence] must have its root in love. Its object should not be to punish the opponent or to inflict injury upon him. Even when noncooperating with him, we must make him feel that in us he has a friend and we should try to reach his heart. . . .

*It is the **acid test** of nonviolence that . . . there is no **rancor** left behind and, in the end, the enemies are converted into friends. That was my experience with General (Jan Christiaan) Smuts. He started with being my bitterest opponent and critic. Today he is my warmest friend. . . .*

According to Gandhi, what is the acid test of nonviolent conflict?

acid test: something testing the real quality
rancor: hatred

BIOGRAPHY

Focus On: Leadership

Mohandas Gandhi was a special kind of leader. His leadership did not come from winning a war, or from his popularity. Gandhi inspired people with his ideas and with the example of his own life.

Gandhi was born in 1869 in India. It was in South Africa, however, that he began to lead. Gandhi refused to use violence. Instead, he used civil disobedience to shame the government into treating Indian citizens fairly.

Gandhi returned to India in 1915. He realized that British rule would never include Indians, so he began to work for Indian independence.

In 1947, the Indian Republic was born. Independence brought violence between Hindus and Muslims. Gandhi again led by example. He fasted until peace was restored. Sadly, Gandhi was assassinated in 1948 by a Hindu.

Link to Today

Research the civil rights movement in the United States. How did Gandhi's ideas influence Martin Luther King's leadership? Write a paragraph telling about what you learned.

THE LIFE OF MOHANDAS GANDHI	1869 Gandhi is born in India	1907 Gandhi first uses civil disobedience	1930 Gandhi leads the Salt March	1947 India becomes independent	1948 Gandhi is assassinated
	1870 1890	1910	1930	1950	
LIFE AROUND THE WORLD	1869 Suez Canal is opened	1912 China becomes a republic	1929 Great Depression begins	1939 World War II starts	

The new nations were led by Nehru of India (below, left) and Jinnah of Pakistan. Crowds in Calcutta celebrated independence in 1947.

INDEPENDENCE ACHIEVED

After World War II a new government took power in Britain. It was determined to grant Indian independence. Indians were delighted as they worked with British leaders to form a new Indian government. Muslims in India, however, were afraid that a Hindu-led government might treat them unfairly. Muslim Indians began to demand their own country. Gandhi was deeply opposed to dividing India. He believed that Muslims and Hindus could live together. However, the British rulers decided to make two countries, Hindu India and Muslim Pakistan.

In 1947, Britain left India. On August 14, **Pakistan** became an independent Muslim state. It was made up of two widely-separated areas to the east and west of India. **Muhammad Ali Jinnah** (muh HAM ad ah LEE JIHN ah) was chosen as leader of Pakistan. On August 15, India gained independence and made **Jawaharlal Nehru** (juh WAH hur lahl NAY roo) its first prime minister.

Independence did not lead to peace. Almost immediately, violence erupted between Hindus and Muslims. The new leaders of India and Pakistan tried to end the violence. In spite of their efforts, nearly one million people died in violent clashes. About ten million people left their homes and moved across the borders to be with people of their own faith.

Gandhi was deeply saddened by the violence. He announced that he would fast, or not eat, until the violence ended. The people of the two new nations were stunned. The violence did halt as Indians and Pakistanis begged Gandhi to eat. With order restored, Gandhi ended his fast. However, a Hindu fanatic shot him in 1948 because he had tried to protect the rights of Muslims. The writer of the song on page 587 shared Gandhi's great love for all Indians.

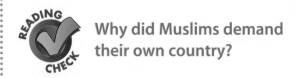 **READING CHECK** Why did Muslims demand their own country?

He Mor Citto

By Rabindranath Tagore

He __ mor ci - ttŏ _____ he mor ci - ttŏ

pu - nnŏ tir - the ja - go re dhi - re _____

E - i bha - rŏ - te - r mŏ - ha - ma - nŏ - ber

sha - gŏ - rŏ - ti - re _____

ja - go re dhi - re _____

Fine

Awake my mind, gently awake
in this holy place of pilgrimage
on the shore of this vast sea
of humanity that is India.

NEW PROBLEMS

Newly independent India faced many problems. Hostility between the Hindu and Muslim populations frequently became violent. India and Pakistan fought wars over the province of Kashmir. A growing population needed food and jobs.

In the 1960s and 1970s, a program called the **"Green Revolution"** helped feed the people of India. It is called a "Green Revolution" because it was a change in crops and agricultural practices. New types of rice and wheat, new fertilizers, and more efficient farming techniques increased India's crops so much that they could even export a surplus.

Changes in India

India wrestled with the status of women and untouchables. Rules against untouchables were made illegal in the Indian Republic in the 1950s, although prejudices against this caste continued. At the same time, Indian women gained the right to vote and own property. In 1966, Jawaharlal Nehru's daughter **Indira Gandhi** (ihn DEE rah GAHN dee), became India's first female prime minister. She continued to work toward transforming India into a growing modern nation.

The **Green Revolution** produced huge crop surpluses in India.

Troubles for Pakistan

Pakistan faced different problems. Pakistan fell under the rule of several military dictators. The economy declined and people had difficulty finding jobs. Meanwhile, East Pakistan felt ignored by the national government in West Pakistan. In 1971, East Pakistan declared its independence and became the nation of **Bangladesh**. Poverty continues to plague both halves of the former Pakistani state.

READING CHECK What happened to the British colony of India after independence?

Indira Gandhi was India's prime minister for 15 years until her murder by two bodyguards in 1984.

PUTTING IT TOGETHER

Britain controlled its Indian colony until 1947. It used India as a source of raw materials and as a market for its products. Indians were treated as second-class citizens. Mohandas Gandhi helped to lead a peaceful struggle for Indian independence. He developed a system of civil disobedience.

Violence broke out between Hindus and Muslims when British rule ended in 1947. Muslims in India moved to Pakistan and Hindus in Pakistan moved to India. In 1971, Pakistan split again and Bangladesh was born. The former "jewel in the crown" of the British Empire became three independent nations: Pakistan, India, and Bangladesh. However tension continued between India and Pakistan, often flaring into violence in places such as Kashmir on the northwest corner of India.

Kashmir continues to be a source of friction between India and Pakistan. Many women (right) work in India's high-tech industries.

Review and Assess

1. Write a sentence for each vocabulary term.
   boycott   **Green Revolution**
   civil disobedience

2. How did Gandhi use civil disobedience in India?

3. How did India become an independent nation?

4. What changes in **technology** made the Green Revolution possible?

5. **Summarize** Gandhi's beliefs about nonviolence.

Look at the map on page 583. Make a chart of the countries of South Asia and the year they became independent.

• •

Suppose that you are an Indian under British rule. **Write** a letter to the British governor telling him why you dislike British rule.

Lesson 2

Conflict in the Middle East

Find Out!

What events led to conflict in the Middle East after 1945?

Lesson Outline
- Independence Movements
- The New State of Israel
- Peace and War
- The Unrest Increases

VOCABULARY

anti-Semitism
Zionism
refugee
intifada
Taliban
terrorism

PEOPLE

Yasir Arafat
Anwar Sadat
Golda Meir
Menachem Begin
Yitzhak Rabin
Saddam Hussein

READING STRATEGY

Copy this chart. Write "Middle East Conflicts" in the center box. In the outer circles, write the names of disputes in the Middle East.

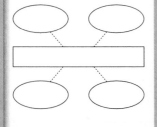

BUILD BACKGROUND

"We . . . hereby proclaim the establishment of the Jewish State in Palestine, to be called Israel. . . . [It] will be open to the immigration of Jews from all countries. . . ."

On May 14, 1948, the founding of the state of Israel changed the history of the Middle East. Conflict broke out almost immediately with Israel's neighbors and has continued for the half century that followed.

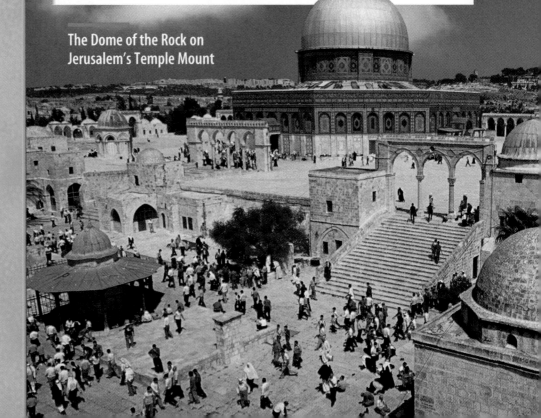

The Dome of the Rock on Jerusalem's Temple Mount

You Are Here
1918 – 2003

INDEPENDENCE MOVEMENTS

The **Middle East** is the land in southwest Asia between the Mediterranean Sea and the Indian subcontinent. When the Ottoman Empire ended after World War I, groups in the Middle East worked to gain independence from the British and French who had taken control of their lands in the former empire.

In 1923, nationalists led by Kemal Atatürk drove foreign troops out and formed the Republic of **Turkey**. **Iraq** and **Saudi Arabia** became independent in 1932. Other nations of the Middle East became independent after World War II.

READING CHECK What happened to the Ottoman Empire after World War I?

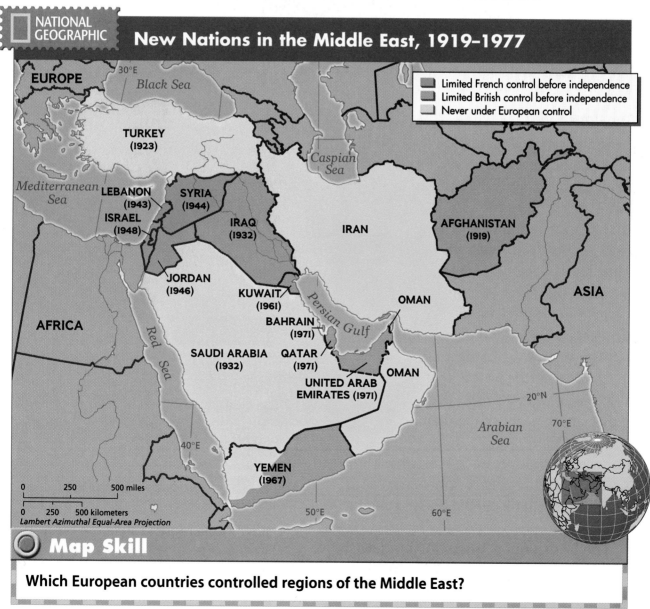

New Nations in the Middle East, 1919–1977

Limited French control before independence
Limited British control before independence
Never under European control

Map Skill

Which European countries controlled regions of the Middle East?

591

THE NEW STATE OF ISRAEL

By the late 1800s, Jews lived throughout the world, from the United States to China. Although they had no country of their own, many Jews kept their own culture, religion, and way of life alive.

Jews were not always welcomed. There was discrimination against Jews in education, jobs, and schools. Discrimination against Jews is called **anti-Semitism**. Because of anti-Semitism in many countries of Europe, many Jews immigrated to the United States in the late 1800s.

A smaller number of Jews went to live in Palestine, which they thought of as their ancient homeland. The Passover holiday phrase, "Next year in Jerusalem" expressed the wish of Jewish people to return to the land where they had once lived.

Tensions Build

Some Jewish leaders were saying that Jews should have a land of their own. This belief is called **Zionism** (Zī uh niz um). Zionism is a movement to establish a Jewish homeland, or nation. The word comes from Mount Zion, a place in Jerusalem. Although Zionism is a movement that began in the late 1800s, the idea of a homeland for the Jews began thousands of years earlier, after the diaspora.

After World War I, Palestine was placed under British rule by the treaties ending World War I. The British had trouble maintaining peace in the region. Most of the Arabs there were Muslims and they opposed a Jewish state in Palestine. Many Arabs in neighboring countries were also opposed to establishing a Jewish state in the region.

The British rulers began to limit Jewish immigration to Palestine. They did this to avoid angering the Arabs and also to stop the increasing violence between the Arabs and the Jews in Palestine.

Jewish immigration continued, however, and increased dramatically after World War II. Many survivors of the Holocaust wanted to leave Europe, and they tried to get into Palestine. By 1947, the Jewish population had reached about 650,000, or about one-third of the population. Most of the remaining two-thirds were Arabs.

The State of Israel Is Established

The United Nations agreed to plan a division of Palestine between Arabs and

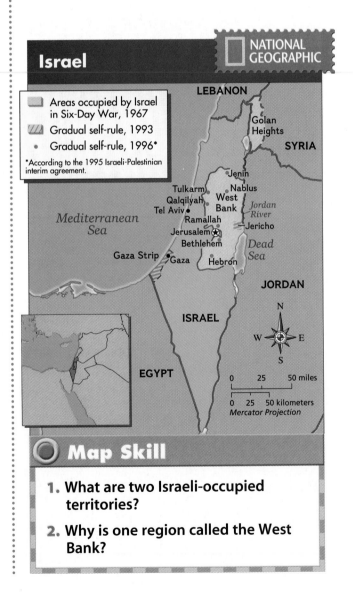

Israel

NATIONAL GEOGRAPHIC

- Areas occupied by Israel in Six-Day War, 1967
- Gradual self-rule, 1993
- Gradual self-rule, 1996*

*According to the 1995 Israeli-Palestinian interim agreement.

LEBANON
Golan Heights
SYRIA
Jenin
Tulkarm · Nablus
Qalqilyah West
Tel Aviv · Bank · Jordan River
Mediterranean Sea
Ramallah
Jerusalem ⊛ · Jericho
Bethlehem
Dead Sea
Gaza Strip · Gaza · Hebron
JORDAN
ISRAEL
EGYPT
N W E S
0   25   50 miles
0   25   50 kilometers
Mercator Projection

● Map Skill

1. **What are two Israeli-occupied territories?**

2. **Why is one region called the West Bank?**

Jews. The Jews in Palestine accepted the United Nations' division. On May 14, 1948, they declared their independence and called their new country **Israel**.

Middle East Wars Begin

The next day, the armies of five Arab countries attacked the new Jewish state. After more than six weeks of fighting, Israel could announce victory. However, this was only the first of several wars between Arab nations and Israel. The conflict continues to this day.

One result of the war of 1948 was that about 750,000 Palestinian Arabs in Israel became **refugees**. Refugees are people who flee their homes for safety. Some refugees chose not to live in the new Jewish state. Others were forced to leave their homes. Many refugees settled in camps in Jordan, Syria, and Lebanon, where they lived in poverty. Another 600,000 Arabs remained in Israel.

A State of War

Armed conflict between the Arabs and Israel continued for years. In 1967, the Israelis began the Six-Day War to prevent an invasion by Arab neighbors. During this war, Israel captured the Golan Heights from Syria and Jordan lost its sections of Jerusalem. Israel's borders moved east to the bank of the Jordan River.

On Yom Kippur, the holiest day in the Jewish religion, in 1973, Israel's Arab neighbors launched another attack. After bitter fighting, and aid supplied by both the Soviet Union and the United States, the war ended with a negotiated peace.

The Palestine Liberation Organization

The Palestinian Liberation Organization (PLO) had been formed in 1964. In

Jewish refugees land in Palestine aboard the refugee ship *Exodus* in 1947.

1967 this group wanted a return of the lands along the West Bank of the Jordan River that they had just lost. They also wanted to establish a Palestinian state in some of the land held by Israel. **Yasir Arafat** was the leader of the PLO and he became the leader of the Palestinians in negotiations with Israel.

Today, the PLO has limited control over parts of the West Bank of the Jordan River. However, Jewish settlements in the area and continued conflict between Jews and Palestinians prevent a permanent peace.

Why is there conflict between Israel and the Arabs of the Middle East?

593

PEACE AND WAR

The Arab-Israeli conflict seemed impossible to settle. Then, in 1977, Egyptian President **Anwar Sadat** made a daring trip to Israel. For the first time a Muslim leader met publicly with Israeli leaders. He and Prime Minister **Golda Meir** began to seek a lasting peace between their two countries. The next year, President Jimmy Carter arranged for President Sadat and Israeli Prime Minister **Menachem Begin** (meh NOK em BAY guhn) to meet at Camp David, a country retreat in Maryland for American Presidents. There the leaders signed an agreement that established peaceful relations between the two nations. Sadat paid for his efforts with his life. In 1981, he was assassinated by Egyptians who opposed the peace agreement.

The Intifada

The Camp David Agreement did not end the struggle between the Palestinians

Golda Meir shakes hands with Anwar Sadat in Israel. Palestinians protest Israeli rule of the West Bank (below left).

and Israel. In 1987, the Palestinians began an **intifada** (ihn te FAH duh), or "uprising." This was a revolt against the Israeli government. Palestinians boycotted Israeli goods and protested in the streets.

In 1993, again with American help, the Israeli government and the PLO agreed to recognize each other and to begin formal negotiations to settle their disagreements. In 1995, Israeli Prime Minister **Yitzhak Rabin** (YIHT zak rah BEEN), one of the leaders of the peace process, was assassinated by a Jewish extremist who opposed the peace agreements.

Israeli leaders and the PLO continued to talk, and peace seemed possible at last. However, the intifada began again in 2000 and quickly led to demonstrations and bloody conflicts between Israeli troops and Palestinian demonstrators.

Revolution in Iran

In 1979, a revolution in Iran overthrew the monarch, Shah Muhammad Reza Pahlevi, who had been westernizing his country. Iran was taken over by Muslim religious leaders. The new Iranian government described itself as an Islamic republic.

Strict rules required women to wear a full-length black body garment in public. Men and women no longer attended the same schools. In 1989, the Iranian government relaxed some of these rules, but Iran continues to be a country strictly controlled by its religious leaders.

Troubles in Afghanistan

As you read in Chapter 16, Soviet troops pulled out of Afghanistan in 1989. Chaos followed the Russian withdrawal. Groups which had fought together against Soviet troops now began to fight each other.

Finally, a group of extremist religious leaders, called the **Taliban**, or "religious students," took power. The Taliban did restore order, but they were harsh rulers. While they were in power, they did not allow women to have jobs, or education. Women had to wear a head-to-toe garment covering them completely. They could not leave their homes without a male family member. Men were beaten if they did not follow strict Islamic laws.

Saudi Arabia

Saudi Arabia follows a strict version of Islamic law. Saudi Arabian women must be completely covered in public. A woman may not drive an automobile and may not go anywhere without a male relative. Thieves in Saudi Arabia can have their hands cut off, and other crimes can be punished by beatings or death by stoning.

 **What are some rules for women in a strict Islamic state?**

Arab women in traditional dress shop in a market in a Palestinian neighborhood.

THE UNREST INCREASES

Over the past 30 years, the Middle East has seen an increase of religious interest, especially among Muslim groups demanding a return to conservative religious practices. Some of these religious groups have turned to violence to achieve their goals.

The United States and the Middle East

The world's largest oil reserves are in countries around the Persian Gulf, such as Saudi Arabia and Kuwait. Control of this oil supply affects the world's economy because most modern countries need oil and gasoline for industry and transportation.

In 1990, **Saddam Hussein** (hoo SANE), the leader of Iraq, invaded the neighboring country of Kuwait. Hussein claimed that Kuwait was a part of Iraq. The rulers of Kuwait appealed to the United Nations for help.

United Nations forces, led by the United States, drove the Iraqis from

American tanks cross the Iraqi desert in 1991.

Kuwait in a few weeks. Saddam Hussein, however, held on in Iraq. The United Nations established a boycott of Iraqi exports, hoping to end Saddam Hussein's rule. At first, UN representatives investigated Iraqi weapons centers, but later the Iraqi dictator refused to cooperate. Saddam Hussein continued to be a threat to peace in the region.

Terrorism

Terrorism, the use of violence for political or other goals, has become an increasing problem. Some terrorist groups are hostile to Western countries, and especially to the United States. These terrorist groups resent foreign, especially non-Islamic, influence in their countries.

In 1983, a building in Lebanon was bombed, and 237 American marines were killed. In 1996, a marine barracks in Saudi Arabia was bombed, killing another 19 Americans. In 1998, two United States embassies in East Africa were bombed, killing 19 Americans and 204 local people. Two years later, an American naval vessel in a harbor in Yemen was bombed, killing 17 U.S. sailors.

On September 11, 2001, terrorists hijacked four passenger jets over the United States. They flew two of these planes into the World Trade Center, twin skyscrapers in New York City. The third jet flew into the Pentagon, near Washington, D.C. The passengers on the fourth plane fought back, causing it to crash into the Pennsylvania woods. About 3,000 people died in these tragedies.

The people who planned the September 11 attacks were believed to be hiding in Afghanistan. President George W. Bush asked the Taliban government to turn the men over for trial. They refused.

The west side of the Pentagon in Washington, D.C., was badly damaged during the attack on September 11, 2001.

The United States began a bombing campaign in October 2001. Within a few weeks, the Taliban lost control of Afghanistan to an alliance of their Afghan opponents.

How did the United States respond to the terrorist attacks of September 11, 2001?

PUTTING IT TOGETHER

The Middle East has been troubled by violence since the end of World War II. In 1948, the nation of Israel was born as a homeland for Jews. Since then, Israel has fought three major wars with its neighbors. More recently, the Middle East has also become the scene of increasing violence by terrorists.

The United States has been involved in the region to protect Israel and in an effort to bring peace to the region. The United States military was used to force Iraqi troops out of Kuwait in 1990. A war in Afghanistan developed after terrorists attacked the World Trade Center and the Pentagon.

A rising threat of terrorism and violence has spread to other regions as the troubles in the Middle East have continued.

Review and Assess

1. Write a sentence for each vocabulary word.

   anti-Semitism   **refugee**
   intifada   **terrorism**

2. What happened on September 11, 2001?

3. What conflicts have troubled the Middle East since 1945?

4. How does the Middle Eastern oil supply affect the world's economy?

5. Find a newspaper article about a current conflict in the Middle East. What is the point of view of the sides involved?

Make a chart of the countries of the Middle East. Include the country and its capital. Research the resources of each country and add the most important ones to your chart.

Write an editorial explaining how people in the Middle East might use non-violent means to solve their differences.

Lesson 3

African Independence

How did African nations gain independence from colonial rulers?

Lesson Outline
• From Gold Coast to Ghana
• Egypt Becomes a Republic
• Independence for Algeria

VOCABULARY

National Liberation Front

PEOPLE

Kwame Nkrumah
Jomo Kenyatta
Gamal Abdel Nasser

READING STRATEGY

Copy this chart. Write the names of African countries in this lesson in one column. Write the name of the country that controlled each one in the next one. Then, write the year the African country became independent.

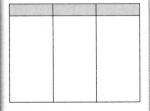

BUILD BACKGROUND

"If we are to remain free, if we are to enjoy the full benefits of Africa's enormous wealth, we must unite to plan for the full [use] of our human and material resources in the interest of all our people."

These were the words of Kwame Nkrumah, the first prime minister of Ghana in 1957. The history of Africa since independence has been troubled. Some of the new nations are still struggling to work in "the interests of all. . . people."

You Are Here
1952 – 1962

FROM GOLD COAST TO GHANA

In 1874, the British established a colony on the west coast of Africa. They called the colony Gold Coast because of its rich sources of gold. These were the same gold sources that had made the West African empires rich.

Over time, the supply of gold dwindled, and the British turned to a new source of wealth. This was cacao, the seed used to make chocolate. By 1920, half the world's supply of cacao came from Gold Coast.

The Rise of African Nationalism

Many Africans in Gold Coast wanted Gold Coast to be an independent country. After World War II, the spirit of independence grew in many African colonies.

The leader in Gold Coast had studied in the United States as a young man. He was **Kwame Nkrumah** (KWAHM ee en KROO muh). To achieve independence, Nkrumah organized boycotts of British goods. Nkrumah also led strikes against British companies in Gold Coast. The British imprisoned him several times, but he continued his fight.

On March 6, 1957, Gold Coast became free. It took the name **Ghana**, from the African kingdom that you read about in Chapter 10. Nkrumah became his new country's leader. He told the people:

> *There is a new Africa in the world, and that new Africa is ready to fight its own battle. . . . It is the only way in which we can show the world we are the masters of our own destiny [fate].*

Kwame Nkrumah (above) waves as Ghana celebrates independence in 1957. Children in Mali (opposite) march in an independence parade in 1960.

Over the next 30 years, leaders in other parts of Africa helped their countries become independent. One of them was **Jomo Kenyatta** (JOH moh ken YAH tuh), who freed **Kenya** in East Africa from British rule. The map on page 601 shows when the African nations became independent.

The end of colonial rule did not always bring democracy or peace. Ethnic rivalries and economic problems made it difficult for some African nations to find stability.

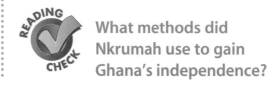

READING CHECK What methods did Nkrumah use to gain Ghana's independence?

599

EGYPT BECOMES A REPUBLIC

The British took control of Egypt in the 1880s. Egypt was important to Great Britain for two reasons. First, Egypt supplied British textile factories with cotton. Second, Egypt's location made it crucial to the British Empire.

The **Suez Canal** cuts across Egypt's Sinai Peninsula from the Mediterranean Sea to the Red Sea. Before the canal was built by British and French investors, ships had to travel around Africa's Cape of Good Hope. The Suez Canal cut 7,000 miles off the journey between Britain and India.

Independence Gained

For Egyptians, British control of the canal was a symbol of their country's weakness. Many Egyptians were angry that their country was controlled by for-

eigners. In 1952, a group of Egyptian army officers seized control of the country. King Farouk of Egypt, who had cooperated with the British, was forced to leave the country. The rebels were led by **Gamal Abdel Nasser** (guh MAHL ahb DEL NAH suhr). Thousands of people celebrated his success in the streets of **Cairo**, the capital. They sang, "Raise up your head, my brother, the days of humiliation have passed."

Two years later, Nasser became president of Egypt. In 1956, he seized the Suez Canal from its British and French owners. He claimed that the canal should belong to the Egyptian people. The British and French, with Israeli help, sent troops to seize the canal. They failed and foreign control of Egypt came to an end.

 READING CHECK **Why was the Suez Canal important to the Egyptians and the British?**

President Nasser addresses the Egyptian people during the Suez Crisis of 1956. Egypt sank ships in the canal (below) to prevent its use.

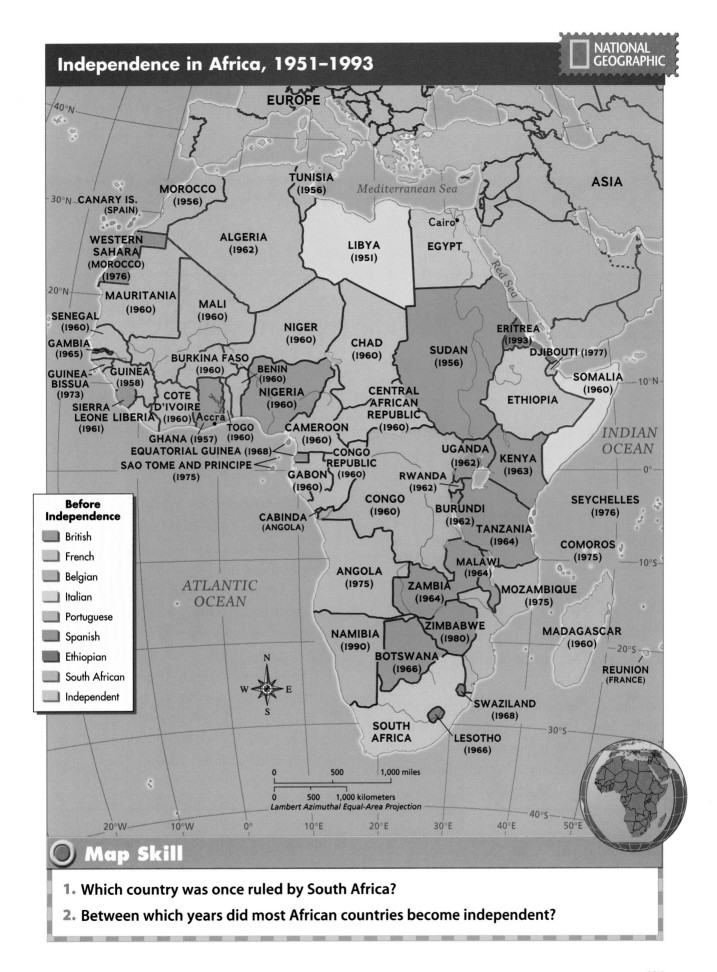

Independence in Africa, 1951–1993

NATIONAL GEOGRAPHIC

EUROPE

ASIA

Mediterranean Sea

40°N

30°N CANARY IS. (SPAIN)

MOROCCO (1956)

TUNISIA (1956)

Cairo

WESTERN SAHARA (MOROCCO) (1976)

ALGERIA (1962)

LIBYA (1951)

EGYPT

20°N MAURITANIA (1960)

MALI (1960)

NIGER (1960)

CHAD (1960)

SUDAN (1956)

ERITREA (1993)

Red Sea

DJIBOUTI (1977)

SENEGAL (1960)

GAMBIA (1965)

BURKINA FASO (1960)

BENIN (1960)

NIGERIA (1960)

CENTRAL AFRICAN REPUBLIC (1960)

SOMALIA (1960)

10°N

GUINEA-BISSUA (1973)

GUINEA (1958)

ETHIOPIA

SIERRA LEONE (1961)

COTE D'IVOIRE (1960)

LIBERIA

Accra

CAMEROON (1960)

INDIAN OCEAN

GHANA (1957)

TOGO (1960)

UGANDA (1962)

KENYA (1963)

EQUATORIAL GUINEA (1968)

CONGO REPUBLIC (1960)

SAO TOME AND PRINCIPE (1975)

GABON (1960)

RWANDA (1962)

0°

SEYCHELLES (1976)

CABINDA (ANGOLA)

CONGO (1960)

BURUNDI (1962)

TANZANIA (1964)

COMOROS (1975)

Before Independence

British
French
Belgian
Italian
Portuguese
Spanish
Ethiopian
South African
Independent

ATLANTIC OCEAN

ANGOLA (1975)

MALAWI (1964)

10°S

ZAMBIA (1964)

MOZAMBIQUE (1975)

NAMIBIA (1990)

ZIMBABWE (1980)

MADAGASCAR (1960)

BOTSWANA (1966)

20°S

REUNION (FRANCE)

N W E S

SWAZILAND (1968)

SOUTH AFRICA

LESOTHO (1966)

30°S

0   500   1,000 miles

0   500   1,000 kilometers
Lambert Azimuthal Equal-Area Projection

40°S

20°W   10°W   0°   10°E   20°E   30°E   40°E   50°E

Map Skill

1. Which country was once ruled by South Africa?

2. Between which years did most African countries become independent?

601

Algerian schoolgirls (left) demonstrated for independence from France, while the Algerian liberation army trained for war.

INDEPENDENCE FOR ALGERIA

There were many French colonies, but **Algeria** was a special colony to the French. Conquered by France in 1830, Algeria was considered a part of the French nation. Moreover, of Algeria's 9 million people, about 1 million were of French background. Many had lived in Algeria for generations. French Algerians could vote in national elections, and they had representatives in the French parliament.

Algerians Demand Equality

The Algerians of French background controlled the economy. They owned most of the land. They were French citizens, while most native Algerians were not. After World War II, native Algerians demanded greater political and economic power.

French settlers refused to yield their hold on the country because they feared they would lose their privileges if the Algerian majority took over. The French government supported the French settlers. In 1954 native Algerians formed the **National Liberation Front** (FLN) to press their demands for freedom.

The French-Algerian War

Late in 1954, the FLN launched a guerrilla war for independence. France sent thousands of soldiers to Algeria. The war dragged on for seven and a half years and was marked by cruelty, torture, and assassinations on both sides. By 1962, the French people had become convinced that they could not win the war.

In 1962 France withdrew its troops from Algeria, and the country became independent. Over 100,000 Algerian and French soldiers had lost their lives in the war, and thousands of civilians were killed as well. Nearly a million French Algerians fled as the new government took control of the country.

In what ways was Algeria different from other French colonies?

PUTTING IT TOGETHER

In the years after World War II, European colonies in Africa began to demand independence. Some, such as Ghana, became independent nations peacefully. Others, such as Algeria, had to fight for their independence. Still others, such as Egypt, simply ended foreign control of their affairs.

At first, independence was greeted with joy as local leaders took control of their governments. However, some of the former colonies had no experience at managing government or their own economies. The Organization for African Unity was created to deal with events on the continent. In Chapter 18, you will read about events in Africa following independence.

Leaders of the Organization for African Unity met in Togo in 2000.

Review and Assess

1. Write a sentence for this vocabulary term.
   National Liberation Front

2. Which country did Kwame Nkrumah lead to independence?

3. How did African countries gain their independence?

4. What were the economic reasons that made European nations want to keep their African colonies?

5. Why did Nasser **make the decision** to seize the Suez Canal?

Activities

Look at the map of Africa on page 601. Choose an African country. Make a chart that shows the country, its capital, population, resources, chief products, and other useful facts. Share your chart with your classmates.

• •

Suppose you are a young African on the day of your nation's independence. **Write** a letter to a friend describing your feelings about independence. You may want to include some details that might accompany independence celebrations.

Recognizing Points of View

After independence, South Africa's white rulers set up a system of discrimination and segregation called apartheid. This system prevented other ethnic groups in South Africa from getting good jobs, housing, and education. Many South Africans, both black and white, worked to end apartheid.

As in South Africa, people around the world often disagree because they have different **points of view**. A point of view is the position from which a person looks at something.

> **VOCABULARY**
>
> point of view

We shall continue to oppose, by all legitimate [legal] means, apartheid. . . . In the African National Congress [an anti-apartheid group], we shall continue to protest most vehemently [forcefully] against discrimination. . . The [white-led government of South Africa] will go down in history, not only as a Government that has made the most tyrannical laws. . . but also [as] a most ruthless Government in dealing with opposition. . . .

– Albert Luthuli

LEARN THE SKILL

Follow these steps to recognize a point of view.

1. **Identify a person's position.**
   How does the speaker quoted in the excerpt feel about the issue? Chief Albert Luthuli, a leader in the fight against apartheid, wrote the above speech in 1953. He believed in ending apartheid by nonviolent means.

2. **Identify which statements in the speech are facts and which statements are opinions.**

There are no facts in the speech, only opinions. Luthuli can pledge to keep fighting against apartheid, but he cannot know how future historians will see South Africa's government. However, his opinions tell a lot about how he feels about the issue.

3. **Identify words or statements that are clues to point of view.**
   Luthuli uses the terms "we shall," "most tyrannical," and "most ruthless." He asks listeners to share his point of view by taking a certain type of action. Other words that are clues to someone's point of view are "in my opinion" and "should."

TRY THE SKILL

Now try identifying the point of view in a letter South African Prime Minister D.F. Malan sent to the African National Congress in 1952 in response to their request to end apartheid.

You [the African National Party] demand that [South Africa] should no longer remain…controlled by Europeans.… [Y]ou apparently wish…that such demands should be regarded as a… gesture of goodwill towards the European community.…Racial harmony cannot be attained [gotten] in this manner…[but will] lead to disaster for all population groups.… The [apartheid] laws are…of a protective nature.…The function of such laws is to protect the interests and the land of the Bantu [native African] Community.…

–D.F. Malan

1. What is the writer's point of view about ending apartheid?

2. Which statements are facts? Which statements are opinions?

3. What words does the writer use to show a point of view?

4. How does recognizing a writer's point of view help you understand past events?

EXTEND THE SKILL

You hear speeches by public figures every day on the television. These speeches reveal a point of view. Choose a public issue today. Write a speech about the issue. Express your point of view in your speech.

● What issue did you choose?

● What is your point of view about the issue?

● How does understanding points of view help you to understand what you hear and read?

Lesson 4

Southeast Asia Today

VOCABULARY

impeach
martial law

PEOPLE

Ho Chi Minh
Ne Win
Suharto
Megawati
  Sukharnoputri
Lee Kwan Yew
Ferdinand
  Marcos
Corazon Aquino

READING STRATEGY

Copy this chart. Write "Country," "Year of Independence," and "Type of Government at Independence" at the top of the columns. Use lesson details to complete the chart.

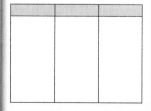

Lesson Outline

• From Colonies to Countries
• Challenges to Democracy
• A Strict Ruler

BUILD BACKGROUND

"We are great believers in the international community. Because the time has passed that we can afford to live isolated. . . . No nation is an island unto itself."

The leader of the campaign for democracy in Myanmar (Burma) stresses the connections of the modern world and the need to work together inside and outside her country.

Street vendors in Hanoi, Vietnam

FROM COLONIES TO COUNTRIES

You have read how most of Southeast Asia became colonies of European countries during the 1800s. In the 1930s and 1940s, Japan conquered much of eastern Asia. After the attack on Pearl Harbor in 1941, the Philippines, which the United States had won in the Spanish-American War of 1898, was also conquered.

After the war ended in 1945, the people of the region wanted independence.

The United States had helped free the Philippines from Japanese rule and had helped to turn the Philippines into a modern nation, but many of its people were tired of foreign rule. In 1946, the Philippines achieved independence from the United States.

Summarize the history of the Philippines between 1898 and 1946.

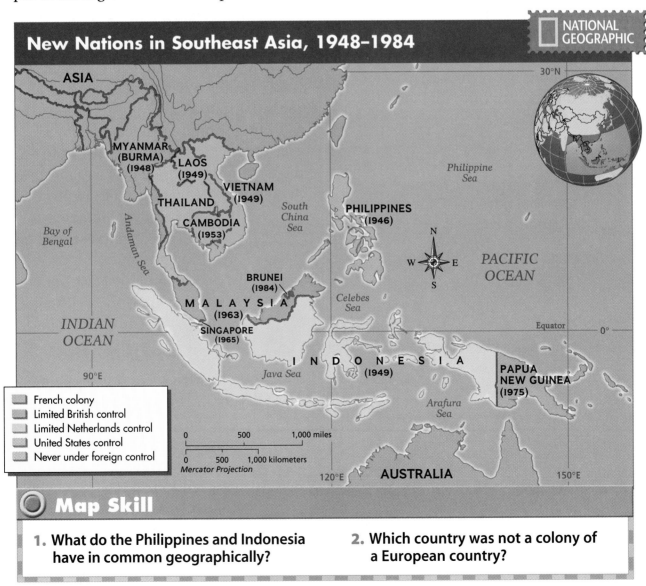

New Nations in Southeast Asia, 1948–1984

NATIONAL GEOGRAPHIC

ASIA

MYANMAR (BURMA) (1948)

LAOS (1949)

VIETNAM (1949)

THAILAND

CAMBODIA (1953)

Philippine Sea

PHILIPPINES (1946)

Bay of Bengal

Andaman Sea

South China Sea

PACIFIC OCEAN

BRUNEI (1984)

Celebes Sea

MALAYSIA (1963)

INDIAN OCEAN

SINGAPORE (1965)

INDONESIA (1949)

Java Sea

Arafura Sea

PAPUA NEW GUINEA (1975)

Equator   0°

30°N

90°E   120°E   150°E

French colony
Limited British control
Limited Netherlands control
United States control
Never under foreign control

0   500   1,000 miles
0   500   1,000 kilometers
Mercator Projection

AUSTRALIA

Map Skill

1. What do the Philippines and Indonesia have in common geographically?

2. Which country was not a colony of a European country?

CHALLENGES TO DEMOCRACY

After World War II, France expected to rule its Asian colonies again. However, a Vietnamese communist, **Ho Chi Minh** (HOH CHEE MIHN), set up a government in northern Vietnam in 1945.

The French battled the communists from 1946 to 1954. Then, at the Battle of **Dien Bien Phu** (dyen byen FOO), the French forces were defeated and had to leave Vietnam.

The United States and Vietnam

The agreement ending the war also recognized the division of Vietnam into two countries; communist North Vietnam and noncommunist South Vietnam. Relations between the two were unfriendly, and war broke out between them in 1958.

Thousands of "boat people" fled Vietnam after the communist victory in 1975.

Ho Chi Minh

As you read in Chapter 16, the United States sent thousands of troops to battle the North Vietnamese communists and their guerrilla allies, the Viet Cong. As it dragged on, some Americans began to think the war could not be won. The United States began to withdraw its troops. In 1973, the last Americans left and in 1975, the North Vietnamese conquered South Vietnam. More than 58,000 Americans and nearly two million Vietnamese had died in the fighting.

The Suffering Continues

Many South Vietnamese feared they would be treated badly by the communists. Many people attempted to leave Vietnam on rafts or small boats. Many of these "boat people" died at sea or were robbed by pirates.

In 1975, Communist leader Pol Pot seized power in Cambodia. He began a reign of terror in which over a million people died. He was forced from power in 1978 by invading Vietnamese troops. The Vietnamese restored order in Cambodia, but they were unpopular. At last, supervised elections in 1993 brought a fragile peace to Cambodia.

Military Rule in Myanmar

Burma was a British colony until 1948, when it became a republic. Poor economic planning, communist unrest, and ethnic minorities caused continuing tension. In 1962, a general named **Ne Win** seized control of the country. He set up a one-party government and took con-

trol of the economy, which did not improve. Ne Win was a harsh ruler. He outlawed opposition and ended the freedoms of the Burmese people.

Ne Win resigned in 1988, but life remained harsh for the people of Burma. A group of generals took power. They changed the name of the country to **Myanmar** (the traditional Burmese name for the country). People in Myanmar continue to live in fear and without freedoms.

Indonesian Independence

Before World War II, an Indonesian leader named Sukarno called for independence from the Netherlands, and Dutch leaders had him arrested. After the war, Sukarno declared Indonesian independence and named himself president. However, the Dutch were not ready to give up their richest colony. Indonesian and Dutch forces struggled until 1949, when the Dutch granted independence to Indonesia.

Opposition to Sukarno's rule developed until 1967, when Sukarno was forced out of office. A military dictator named **Suharto** took over. In 1997 Indonesia seized East Timor, formerly held by Portugal. Demands for independence shook several parts of Indonesia. Even so, the economy improved until 1997, when a world economic downturn caused a crisis in Indonesia. In 1998 Indonesians took to the streets to protest the dictatorship and its corruption. Suharto realized he must resign.

In 1999, Indonesia held its first free election in years. Abdurrahman Wahid (ahb door RAH mahn wah HEED) was elected president and **Megawati Sukharnoputri**, the daughter of Sukarno, was elected vice president.

In 2001, the Indonesian parliament voted to **impeach** Wahid for corruption. Impeach means to charge an official with wrongdoing. To everyone's relief, Wahid agreed to give up power and Vice President Megawati took over.

READING CHECK How is Indonesia's government different from that of Myanmar's?

Myanmar's citizens demand civil rights (bottom) from the military government. Megawati Sukharnoputri became president of Indonesia in 2001 (left).

We Want Democracy in Burma

A STRICT RULER

Singapore is a city and also a country. In 1963, it joined Malaysia, which had gained independence from Britain. Two years later, Singapore declared itself an independent republic.

After independence, Singapore's leader, **Lee Kwan Yew**, focused on building a strong economy. Lee ruled Singapore until he retired in 1990, but his political party continued in power.

Lee Kwan Yew used fear of communism to restrict political freedom and to set up strict laws. However, his policies developed a strong economy and a high standard of living for the people of Singapore.

A History of Independence

Thailand was called Siam until 1938. The kings of Thailand prevented the country from becoming a European colony, but they faced many of the problems of their neighbors in Southeast Asia.

The Vietnam War and a civil war in neighboring Cambodia caused refugees seeking safety to flood into Thailand. Caring for these refugees has become a major concern for the Thai government.

Singapore has many modern skyscrapers. King Bhumipol and Queen Sirikit of Thailand watch the king's 72nd birthday parade.

People Power

In 1965, a young leader named **Ferdinand Marcos** was elected president of the Philippines. During his first term, the economy grew and he was very popular. In time, Marcos became less democratic and the government of the Philippines became more corrupt.

As opposition to him grew, Marcos used propaganda, claiming that anyone who disagreed with him was a communist. He declared **martial law**. Under martial law, the military rules and all freedoms are taken away from the people.

Benigno Aquino, the leader of the opposition to Marcos, fled from the

Philippines. Martial law ended in 1981, and Marcos was reelected. When Aquino returned in 1983, he was murdered at the airport. His death set off demonstrations against Marcos.

Aquino's widow, **Corazon Aquino**, led the opposition, called People Power. In 1986, Marcos resigned and left the country. Corazon Aquino was elected president, and democracy began to return to the Philippines.

How did Corazon Aquino become president of the Philippines?

Corazon Aquino

PUTTING IT TOGETHER

Since the end of World War II, the countries of Southeast Asia have moved from colonies to independence. Some countries, such as Vietnam, had to fight to end colonial rule. Others, such as Singapore, gained independence through peaceful means. In 1999 East Timor voted for and gained their freedom from Indonesian occupation.

After independence, each country went through struggles to become a democracy. In some countries democracy has been achieved. Others, such as Vietnam and Myanmar, still have a long way to go.

Review and Assess

1. Write a sentence for each vocabulary term.

   impeach   martial law

2. Who was the communist leader of North Vietnam?

3. In what ways did Southeast Asian countries become independent?

4. How did the impeachment of President Wahid in Indonesia show the country's respect for its new democracy?

5. How did Ferdinand Marcos use propaganda against his opponents?

Look at the map on page 607. Make a chart of the countries of Southeast Asia. Write the name of the country and the year it became independent. Begin with the country that was never a colony. Then do some research to find each country's capital city and its main products.

. . . .

Suppose you are a reporter in the Philippines during the People Power demonstrations. Write a news article about the events and explain why people are in the streets protesting the rule of Ferdinand Marcos.

New Nations in the Pacific

How did the nations of the Pacific achieve independence?

Lesson Outline
- The Islands Are Settled
- Europeans Arrive
- Australia and New Zealand

VOCABULARY

trusteeship
outback
dominion

READING STRATEGY

Make a chart like this one. Write the main idea "Pacific islands face challenges" in the central box. Write examples that support the main idea in the circles.
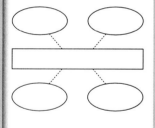

BUILD BACKGROUND

"Talofa! Welcome to Tuvalu Online, a web site dedicated to the South Pacific Polynesian nation of Tuvalu. For the first-time visitors, *'Talofa'* is the Tuvaluan word for hello or welcome. . . ."

Tuvalu is a small island nation in the South Pacific. It is thousands of miles away from the United States, Europe, and South America. However, modern communications and technology have helped Tuvalu to overcome its remote location.

THE ISLANDS ARE SETTLED

The first group of settlers in the Pacific islands were the Melanesians. They sailed from Asia and may be related to the aborigines of Australia. They settled on the islands, such as New Guinea, near Asia.

The Micronesian people settled on the Pacific islands after the Melanesians. They are believed to have come from Southeast Asia. Nations such as Kiribati, and Nauru, are Micronesian cultures.

Historians think the Polynesians kept island-hopping over the centuries. The first Polynesians arrived in the western Pacific islands sometime between 2,000 and 1,000 B.C. By A.D. 400 they had reached Easter Island, near the coast of South America.

Which of the three island groups were the best sailors? Why do you think so?

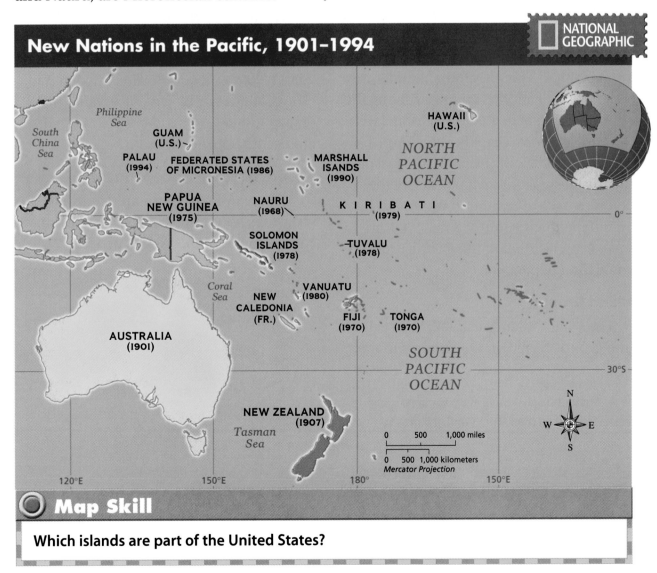

New Nations in the Pacific, 1901–1994

NATIONAL GEOGRAPHIC

Philippine Sea

South China Sea

GUAM (U.S.)

PALAU (1994)

FEDERATED STATES OF MICRONESIA (1986)

MARSHALL ISANDS (1990)

HAWAII (U.S.)

NORTH PACIFIC OCEAN

PAPUA NEW GUINEA (1975)

NAURU (1968)

KIRIBATI (1979)

SOLOMON ISLANDS (1978)

TUVALU (1978)

Coral Sea

VANUATU (1980)

NEW CALEDONIA (FR.)

FIJI (1970)

TONGA (1970)

AUSTRALIA (1901)

SOUTH PACIFIC OCEAN

NEW ZEALAND (1907)

Tasman Sea

0   500   1,000 miles
0   500   1,000 kilometers
Mercator Projection

N
W   E
S

120°E   150°E   180°   150°E

0°

30°S

⊙ **Map Skill**

Which islands are part of the United States?

EUROPEANS ARRIVE

As you read in Chapter 14, the first contact the people of the Pacific had with Europeans was in the Age of Exploration. Between 1850 and 1900, most islands became colonies of European countries. The islands were valuable to their colonizers as refueling stations for coal powered navies. Also, some islands had mineral resources or were near fishing grounds.

Contact with outsiders changed life in the islands. Many people changed or abandoned their traditional customs and took on European and American customs.

From Colonies to Independence

The United Nations (UN) was founded in 1945 as World War II ended. The UN organized the Pacific island colonies into **trusteeships**. This placed them under the supervision of another country. Among the countries that accepted trusteeships were the United States, Great Britain, France, Australia, and New Zealand. The goal of the trusteeships was to help each of the colonies decide whether it wanted to be an independent country. After 1960, an increasing number of the Pacific islands voted for independence.

Island Groups

The Pacific islands can still be divided into groups based on the cultures of their original settlers. The islands of the Polynesian cultures are the most numerous.

Among the Polynesian colonies that voted for independence was Tuvalu. You read about Tuvalu in the opening of the lesson. The nation of Tuvalu was once called the Ellice Islands. They had been grouped with the Gilbert Islands as part of a British Trusteeship.

In 1974, ethnic differences with their neighbors caused the Polynesian people of the Ellice Islands to vote to separate from the Micronesian people of the Gilbert Islands. This new colony was called Tuvalu, and in 1978 it become an independent nation.

Tuvalu is a tiny nation, about one-tenth the size of Washington, D.C. It has only 10,000 people. However, the Tuvaluan Web site keeps Tuvalu connected to the modern world. One of Tuvalu's primary sources of income is selling rights to use its Internet domain.

Nauru Becomes Independent

The people of Nauru are Micronesian. Nauru is about the same size as Tuvalu and also has about 10,000 people.

Students (right) study in a traditional island building on the Pacific island of Vanuatu.

Nauru had rich deposits of phosphate, an ingredient of plant fertilizer. When Nauru was a British colony and later, when it was a trusteeship of Australia, phosphate mines were dug into the island and millions of tons of this valuable mineral were taken away.

Nauru became independent in 1968. It was one of the first Pacific island countries to achieve independence. For the first years of its independence, Nauru was a rich country. Its phosphate earnings were put into investments that paid for many improvements in island life. Recently, the phosphate deposits have begun to run out. At the same time, the investments lost a great deal of money. Nauru will have to find another way to support itself.

Like Tuvalu, Nauru is using modern technology to pay for the costs of government. Nauru has used computers to become a banking center. Billions of dollars are transferred in and out of Nauru's banks each year.

Vanuatu

Compared with Tuvalu and Nauru, Vanuatu, is a large country although it is actually only about the size of the state of Connecticut. Close to 190,000 people live on the island of Vanuatu. That is the population of a medium-size city in the United States.

The people of Vanuatu are Melanesian. Vanuatu was part of a trusteeship run jointly by France and Great Britain until it became independent in 1980. Most people in Vanuatu make a living by farming or fishing. Unlike Tuvalu and Nauru, Vanuatu has not yet discovered a way to use modern technology to help its economy.

READING CHECK How have some Pacific island nations developed modern economies?

Women work in an outdoor market in Vanuatu's capital, Port-Vila. Torches are used for night-fishing.

AUSTRALIA AND NEW ZEALAND

Australia and New Zealand have many things in common. Both are located in the southwestern Pacific and both were once British colonies. They have native populations that were treated unfairly by Europeans, and both have sheep ranching industries. However, each also has its own history and identity.

Australia is a country and a continent. It has a fertile seacoast and the **outback**, a vast desert in the middle of the country. Australia has wildlife not found in other parts of the world. Most famous are marsupials such as kangaroos. A marsupial is an animal that carries its young in a pouch. Another marsupial is the koala.

New Zealand is a country made of two large islands in the Pacific Ocean. The first settlers in New Zealand were the Maori, Polynesians who came to New Zealand more than a thousand years ago.

British settlers arrived in New Zealand in the early 1800s. At first the settlers and Maori lived in peace. However, the discovery of gold led to conflicts in which the Maori were defeated by the British.

Australia and New Zealand Today

In 1901, Australia became a **dominion** of the British Empire. That means it was independent, but it kept some ties to Great Britain. New Zealand became a dominion in 1907. Today Australians and New Zealanders honor Queen Elizabeth II of England as the head of their governments. However, elected officials run the nations' day-to-day affairs.

Both Australia and New Zealand are highly industrialized nations. Modern transportation and technology have helped both nations to overcome their geographical isolation.

The opera house in Sydney, Australia (bottom), has become a symbol of the city. New Zealand (right) is famous for its beautiful fjords and mountains.

Challenges for the Future

The Pacific island nations face problems caused by their location and by limited resources. Some have attracted tourists and others have formed agreements with each other, or with countries such as the United States, to help them survive as independent nations.

The economies of the most industrialized of the Pacific nations, New Zealand and Australia, still depend on sheep herding and farming. In each country, citizens of European descent came to outnumber the original inhabitants. Both Australia and New Zealand continue to struggle with the challenge of granting more rights to the original people of their lands.

What challenges face the Pacific nations?

PUTTING IT TOGETHER

The people of the Pacific island nations are Polynesian, Micronesian, and Melanesian. Their islands became European colonies in the 1800s, but began to gain their independence after World War II. Most of them are very small, and some have used modern technology to join the world economy.

Australia and New Zealand are industrial nations, although New Zealand is less so. Since the 1970s peoples from Southwest Asia and other parts of the world have immigrated to both nations. This has caused their populations to become more diverse.

The kangaroo has become the symbol of Australia. This male kangaroo is about 6 feet tall.

Review and Assess

1. Write one sentence for each vocabulary word.

   dominion   outback

2. Why is Australia's wildlife unique?

3. How did Pacific island nations become independent after World War II?

4. How has **technology** helped the new Pacific island nations to be connected to the rest of the world?

5. **Compare** and **contrast** how Australia and New Zealand became independent with the way Pacific islands became nations.

Choose one of the Pacific islands. Make a brochure for the island to attract interest. Explain the business or tourist advantages of your island.

• •

Suppose you are the leader of one of the Pacific island nations. **Write** a speech to the voters of your island. Your speech should explain how you would improve life on the island. Use persuasive language in your speech.

VOCABULARY REVIEW

Number a paper from 1-5. Beside each number write the term from the list below that best completes the sentence.

anti-Semitism	National Liberation Front
civil disobedience	terrorism
martial law	

1. Under ____, the army rules a nation and ends the legal rights of citizens.

2. ____ is the use of violence for political reasons.

3. Discrimination against Jews is ____.

4. The refusal to obey laws that are considered unjust is ____.

5. The ____ fought to gain the independence of Algeria from France.

CHAPTER COMPREHENSION

6. What were some actions Gandhi took to win independence for India?

7. Why did Pakistan become a separate nation when the British left India?

8. How did Israel become an independent nation?

9. What restrictions are placed on women in Saudi Arabia?

10. What did Nasser do to maintain Egypt's independence?

11. How did the struggle between North and South Vietnam end?

12. How did Indonesia gain its independence from the Netherlands?

13. **Write** a paragraph about the challenges faced by the Maori of New Zealand and Aboriginal people of Australia today.

SKILL REVIEW

14. **Reading/Thinking Skill** What is a point of view?

15. **Reading/Thinking Skill** What was Kwame Nkrumah's point of view about the right way to gain Ghana's independence?

16. **Reading/Thinking Skill** What point of view did Palestinians have when they participated in the *intifada*?

17. **Reading/Thinking Skill** In the photo above, President Mugabe celebrates Zimbabwe's independence. What generalization can you make about why African colonies wanted independence from European rule?

18. **Reading/Thinking Skill** What generalization can you make about the actions of West European nations and the United States in the Middle East since the 1960s?

USING A TIME LINE

1915	1925	1935	1945	1955	1965	1975	1985	1995	2005

1915
Gandhi emerges as a leader in India

1932
Saudi Arabia and Iraq gain independence

1947
India and Pakistan gain independence

1948
Israel becomes a state

1957
Ghana gains independence

1973
U.S. leaves Vietnam

1986
Marcos gives up power in Philippines

1990
Iraq invades Kuwait

2001
Terrorists attack World Trade Center and Pentagon in U.S.

19. What is important about the event that occurred in 1957?

20. What date indicates the first Middle Eastern countries to become independent?

Writing **About History** Suppose that you were writing a report about the Middle East. Write a paragraph about the Camp David Agreement of 1978.

Your report should answer the following questions: Why was this agreement important? What happened in Egypt and Israel after this agreement was signed?

Foldables

Use your Foldable to review what you have learned about the spread of independence. As you look at the countries and regions labeled on the tabs of your Foldable, mentally review the events that led to their independence. Find similarities and differences in the ways in which independence was achieved. Look at your notes under the tabs of your Foldable to check your memory and responses. Record any questions that you have on the back of your Foldable and discuss them with classmates, or review the chapter to find answers.

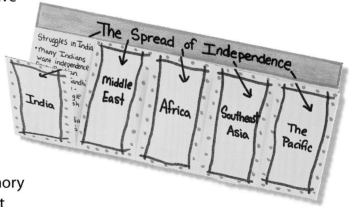

THE Big IDEAS ABOUT...

A Changing World

In the 2000s, nations around the world continue to bring people closer together through technology and world trade. Some of the changes, such as the rules of the European Union, have resulted in economic growth and increased freedoms. Others, such as the increase in terrorism, have shaken the world's confidence. It is a time of great change and many opportunities.

A CHANGING AFRICA

In 1991, South Africa ended white minority rule peacefully, but economic and other challenges remain.

A CHANGING EUROPE

The formerly Communist countries of Europe build more democratic governments and hope to join the European Union.

THE CHANGING AMERICAS

The Americas shake off dictatorships and begin to enter the world economy. However, economic and political challenges continue.

A CHANGING ASIA

China opens to foreign trade, but continues to crack down on protests from its own citizens. Japan and other Asian countries suffer through hard times as economies around the world experience a slowdown.

Foldables

Make this Foldable study guide and use it to record what you learn about "A Changing World."

1. Cut out three large circles of paper. Stack them and fold in half.

2. Staple the circles of paper together along the fold line to form a half-circle book or journal.

3. Open and lay flat, and sketch the globe on the outside. Write the title of the chapter on the front of the journal, and the four lesson titles on the inside pages.

1

A Changing Europe

Find out!

How is Europe changing today?

Lesson Outline

• The European Union
• After Communism
• Challenges Ahead

VOCABULARY

European Union
euro

PEOPLE

Slobodan
 Milosevic

READING STRATEGY

Copy this chart. In the center circle, write "A Changing Europe." Then write changes mentioned in the lesson in the outer circles.

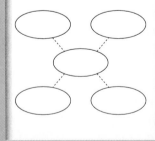

BUILD BACKGROUND

"Europe is a continent, and the European Community is a big country inside this continent. [Within the Community] there are equal countries. . . ."

The speaker is Despina Karanika, a Greek woman who lives in Paris, France. She, like many Europeans, sees Europe as having split into two different groups of countries: those in the EU, and those which are not.

THE EUROPEAN UNION

In 1993, 15 Western European nations signed a treaty forming the **European Union** (EU). The purpose of this organization is to build a common economy among its members. Since then the EU has gotten rid of many barriers to trade and movement among members. For example, cars and trucks in EU countries can travel freely across borders within the EU. A committee meets in Brussels, Belgium, to make rules for the EU.

The Roots of Union

The movement to unite Europe politically and economically began after World War II. Europeans believed that nations that trade freely are less likely to go to war. The European Union is a reorganization of the European Economic Community, also known as the Common Market.

On January 1, 2002, eleven of the EU countries began to use a new common currency, or money, called the **euro**. The euro will make trade inside the EU easier because people will not have to change currencies when trading or traveling within its countries.

Many nations in Europe, especially those that were communist until 1989, would like to become members of the EU. Most Europeans believe that the EU will lead to peace and strong economies.

READING CHECK What is the purpose of the European Union?

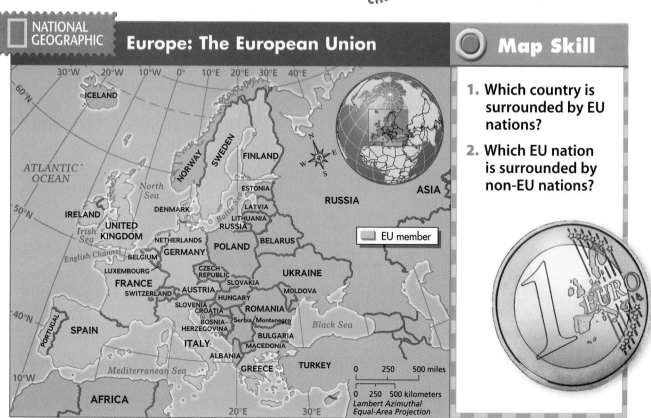

NATIONAL GEOGRAPHIC **Europe: The European Union**

Map Skill

EU member

1. **Which country is surrounded by EU nations?**

2. **Which EU nation is surrounded by non-EU nations?**

0   250   500 miles

0   250   500 kilometers
Lambert Azimuthal Equal-Area Projection

AFTER COMMUNISM

The Cold War ended in 1991 when the Soviet Union collapsed. For most Europeans, however, the destruction of the Berlin Wall in 1989 ended the division of Europe. For over 40 years, Europe had been divided between communist and democratic governments. In 1990, East Germany and West Germany were reunited with great celebrations. It seemed that Europe had at last been put back together.

A New Europe Emerges

After the excitement died down, many people realized that the new Europe would not develop quickly or easily. The economies of many of the formerly communist countries had fallen far behind those of Western Europe.

Hungary and Poland became democracies peacefully. The former Czechoslovakia split into the Czech Republic and Slovakia without conflict. Other East European countries have had a harder time. In Romania, authoritarian rivals and a weak economy have caused continuing unrest. Some nations, such as Bulgaria and Ukraine, struggle with outdated factories and unwanted products as they work to build stronger economies.

The Balkan Wars

In the area called the Balkans, the largest nation was Yugoslavia. It had a stable communist government and several ethnic groups who appeared to live together peacefully. After the end of the Cold War, however, ethnic rivalries swept the nation. With various degrees of violence and tension, four areas of Yugoslavia declared independence: Croatia, Slovenia, Macedonia, and Bosnia and Herzegovina. Yugoslavia was now made up of two republics, Serbia and Montenegro.

The worst of the Balkan conflicts occurred in Bosnia in 1992. A bitter civil war broke out there between Serbs, who are Christians, and Muslims. The fighting was worsened by Yugoslav leader **Slobodan Milosevic**, who aided Bosnia's Serbs.

Countries in the European Union and NATO

Countries in the EU	Countries in NATO
Austria	Belgium
Belgium	Canada
Denmark	Czech Republic
Finland	Denmark
France	France
Germany	Germany
Greece	Greece
Ireland	Hungary
Italy	Iceland
Luxembourg	Italy
Netherlands	Luxembourg
Portugal	Netherlands
Spain	Norway
Sweden	Poland
United Kingdom	Portugal
	Spain
	Turkey
	United States
	United Kingdom

Chart Skill

1. Which non-European countries are in NATO?
2. Why might a European country be in the EU but not in NATO?

NATO forces protect the streets of Bosnia's capital, Sarajevo.

A New Role for NATO

During the struggle for Bosnia, fighting grew especially vicious. Milosevic encouraged his supporters to kill Bosnian civilians and to destroy their villages and homes. The brutal killings shocked the world. Finally in 1995 NATO sent in troops. An agreement to end the fighting soon followed.

After the Bosnian peace treaty was signed, a new crisis developed. Ethnic Albanians, who are Muslim, make up about 90 percent of Kosovo, a province of Serbia. They demanded independence as well. Milosevic ordered his troops to attack Albanians in Kosovo. Once again, civilians were slaughtered and their homes burned. Thousands of Albanians fled the province.

European leaders warned Milosevic to stop the killing, but he ignored them. People in Europe began to demand that their governments take action against Milosevic.

Europe's leaders met to discuss the crisis. NATO forces were ordered to stop the Serbian atrocities and to prevent the Balkan war from spreading. In 1999, NATO air forces began a bombing campaign. Specific targets were Serbian military centers and property that belonged to Milosevic and his party.

The NATO bombing forced Milosevic to end his attacks on the Albanians of Kosovo. NATO troops were then sent into Bosnia and Kosovo to maintain order. Today, the Balkans remain a region of hostile enemies.

In 2001, Slobodan Milosevic was arrested and sent to the Hague in the Netherlands. His trial for crimes against humanity by a United Nations court began in 2002.

How did democratic governments respond to the crisis in the Balkans?

CHALLENGES AHEAD

Many people hoped that the creation of the European Union would bring Europeans closer together. For a brief period, it seemed that Europe would become united after the end of communism. Economic progress has been made, and Europeans are closer today than they have been in many years. However, many challenges remain.

Guest Workers

You have already read about the strong Western European economy. The factories and businesses of Western Europe were so successful during the 1990s that they did not have enough workers to do all the jobs. Workers from poorer countries in Africa, Eastern Europe, and the Middle East moved to Western Europe to find work.

At first, Europeans were happy to have the "guest workers." Over time, some Europeans began to worry about the number of these workers. They thought the immigrants might change national culture and schools, or take away jobs. The presence of

guest workers continues to challenge most Western European governments.

A Graying Population

Another problem facing Europe is the aging of its population. Years of prosperity have improved health and life expectancy. As a result, a large percentage of the population of most Western European countries is older and looking forward to retirement.

Health care and pensions represent an increasing percentage of Europe's national budgets. Many Europeans wonder what will happen when an even larger percentage of their populations depend on governments for their support.

 READING CHECK What are European concerns about the future?

The Turk (on the right) is a guest worker in a German motorcycle factory. Retired Germans enjoy a bicycle tour of eastern Germany (above).

PUTTING IT TOGETHER

For centuries Europe was a continent of many countries. Today, Europe is rapidly changing. The European Union and its 15 member countries are creating an alliance that makes Western Europe's governments and economies closer and more united.

The countries of Eastern Europe and the Balkans want to become members of the EU. After 50 years of living behind the iron curtain, these nations want the benefits of becoming part of Europe again.

Europe faces several challenges. The arrival of large numbers of immigrants, as guest workers, has caused tensions with local workers. An economic slowdown in 1998 increased unemployment and inflation at the same time as a hoof-and-mouth disease outbreak hurt Western Europe's farming industry.

The **European Union** flag flies with the flags of member countries (above). EU passports have replaced national passports in member countries.

Review and Assess

1. Write one sentence for each vocabulary word or term.

   euro
   European Union

2. How has the European Union changed Europe?

3. What are some of the challenges Europeans face today?

4. How has the European Union affected the **economy** of its members?

5. How might a citizen of a non-EU country have a different **point of view** about the European Union than a citizen of an EU country?

Look at the map of Europe on page 623. Make a chart. Write the names of 10 new countries since the end of the Cold War. In another column, write the name of the country they were part of before 1989. In the final column, write the year each became an independent country.

• •

Write an editorial for a Polish, Czech, or Hungarian newspaper. Explain why it would be good for your country to become a member of the EU. Give reasons to support your opinion.

Using Reference Sources And Databases

To learn more about the changes in Europe, you could use a **reference source**, such as an encyclopedia or an atlas. Another way to find information is a **database**. A database contains electronically stored information, such as articles, pictures, maps, or music. Some databases are on **CD-ROM**, a type of computer disk that stores large amounts of information. Other databases are on the Internet, the world-wide computer network. An Internet connection allows you to reach information sources such as libraries, schools, or government offices.

The president of France addresses the European Parliament in Strasbourg, France, in July, 2000.

LEARN THE SKILL

Follow these steps to use reference sources.

1. **Decide what to search for.**
   Suppose you are writing a paper on the European Union. You want to find a map showing which countries are in the Union. What is the best place to find such a map?

2. **Decide which source to use.**
   You could go to your library and find an atlas with maps of Europe. However, additional countries might have joined the Union since the atlas was published. For more recent information, try a CD-ROM or the Internet.

3. **Identify key words or phrases before you begin your search.**
   If you search the Internet using the words "European Union," you will get every possible kind of information from magazine articles to speeches. Narrow your search by using the key words "European Union Members Map."

4. **Select the best site for your purpose.**
   Some Internet sites are unreliable. They may contain opinion or false information. Look for official Web sites for the most reliable information.

TRY THE SKILL

Suppose you want information from the library about major exports of Italy.

1. Which database would you use to search for information on Italy?

2. Where might you find information on Italy's foreign trade?

3. If you want information on a specific Italian export, such as olive oil, what key word or words might you use?

4. How can using reference sources and databases help you to get the information you need to study history?

EXTEND THE SKILL

Using databases can help you to find information quickly. Use the databases in a school or local library and the Internet to search for information on a European country. List the databases you used. Tell which was easiest to use and contained the most useful information.

- How did the databases help you find the information you needed?

- Why is it useful to know how to use a variety of reference sources?

- How can databases help you to learn more about events in history or in the news?

Lesson 2

A Changing Africa

 Find Out!

What are the major challenges facing Africa today?

Lesson Outline
• South Africa's Success
• Civil Wars and Other Challenges
• Africa's Riches

VOCABULARY

apartheid
sanction
genocide
arable
desertification

PEOPLE

Nelson Mandela
Frederik Willem
  de Klerk

READING STRATEGY

Copy this chart. In the middle box write "Africa Faces Challenges." Write some of the challenges in the outer circles.

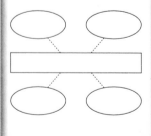

BUILD BACKGROUND

"A man who takes away another man's freedom is a prisoner of hatred, he is locked behind the bars of prejudice and narrow-mindedness. I am not truly free if I am taking away someone else's freedom, just as surely as I am not free when my freedom is taken from me."

The speaker is Nelson Mandela. White minority rulers kept him in prison for 27 years. In 1994, he became the first black president of South Africa.

SOUTH AFRICA'S SUCCESS

South Africa has made a remarkable change to democracy in the last decade. For years the country was divided by **apartheid**, or racial segregation. South Africa's white minority forced the country's black majority to live in neighborhoods called townships. They also had to carry identity cards and were not permitted to vote or protest.

The Movement to End Apartheid

In the 1960s, black South Africans began to demonstrate against apartheid. The leading black African political party was the African National Congress led by Nelson Mandela. The government arrested opponents of apartheid including Mandela. As you read, he spent 27 years in jail.

In the 1980s the United States and other Western democracies set up **sanctions** against South Africa. Sanctions are penalties, such as refusing to buy its products, placed on a nation to make it change its policies.

The sanctions hurt the South African economy. In 1989, the new President of South Africa, **Frederik Willem de Klerk**, decided it was time to change. In 1990, he had Mandela released from prison. In 1991, de Klerk ended apartheid, and three years later set up

free elections. It was the first time blacks were allowed to vote in elections. Nelson Mandela was easily elected president and he served for one term. Since the end of apartheid, black South Africans no longer face legal restrictions, but they continue to suffer from inequality in education and economic opportunities.

South Africa today is working to give all its citizens the same opportunities. It is also building thousands of new houses and schools. You can read the words of South Africa's national anthem on page 633. South Africa's peaceful transition to democracy is a source of pride and provides hope for people across the African continent.

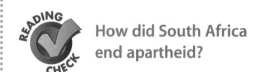

How did South Africa end apartheid?

Black South Africans protest **apartheid** in 1985 (below). They wait in long lines to vote for the first time in 1994 (opposite).

BIOGRAPHY

Focus On: Justice

Nelson Mandela visited the United States for the first time in 1990. On a warm summer night, Yankee Stadium in New York City was packed with a cheering, jubilant crowd. This wasn't a baseball game or a rock concert. The crowd was there to pay tribute to one of the modern heroes of justice.

Mandela had spent 27 years in jail. He was accused of being a terrorist or a communist, but his real "crime" was his belief in justice for all South Africans.

In the years after his release, Mandela was elected president in South Africa's first democratic election. After stepping down as president, Mandela continued his work for justice, traveling across Africa and around the world with a message of justice and cooperation.

Link to Today Nelson Mandela was awarded the Nobel Peace Prize in 1994 for ending apartheid. What leader of today would you nominate for the Nobel Peace Prize because he or she defended justice? Write a paragraph that explains your choice.

THE LIFE OF NELSON MANDELA	1918 Mandela is born in Africa	1962 Apartheid government jails Mandela	1990 Mandela is freed	1994 Mandela becomes South Africa's president

1900   **1930**   **1960**   **1990**   **2020**

LIFE AROUND THE WORLD	1914 World War I begins	1947 India gains independence	1959 Fidel Castro seizes power in Cuba	1997 Hong Kong returns to China

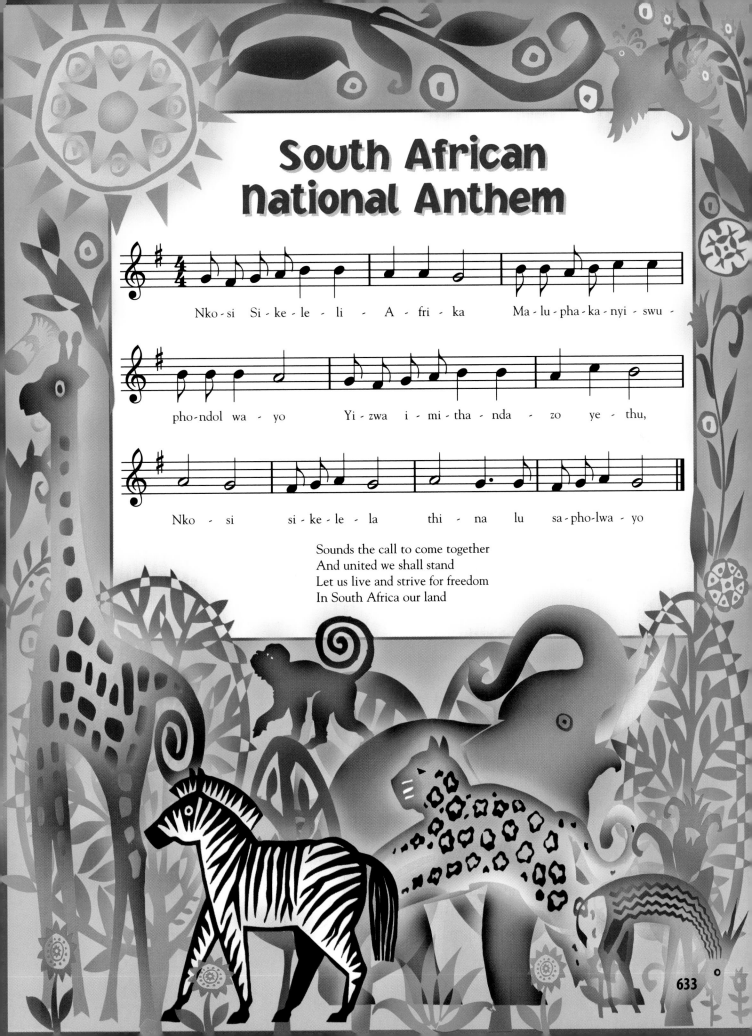

South African national Anthem

Nko - si Si - ke - le - li - A - fri - ka Ma - lu - pha - ka - nyi - swu -

pho - ndol wa - yo Yi - zwa i - mi - tha - nda - zo ye - thu,

Nko - si si - ke - le - la thi - na lu sa - pho - lwa - yo

Sounds the call to come together
And united we shall stand
Let us live and strive for freedom
In South Africa our land

CIVIL WARS AND OTHER CHALLENGES

After independence, many African countries experienced civil wars. They included Rwanda, Angola, Nigeria, Liberia, and Sierra Leone. Many of these wars lasted for years, and some have been extremely brutal. Why have so many African countries suffered from civil war? One reason is Africa's colonial past. When Europeans carved out African colonies in the 1800s, many colonies included more than one ethnic group. Some of these groups had been enemies for hundreds of years. After independence, traditional rivalries led to civil war. Corrupt and dictatorial governments also led to war in some countries.

Rwandan children wait at a refugee camp in the Congo in 1995.

Rwanda

One of the most brutal wars broke out in Rwanda, a Belgian colony that included two main ethnic groups, the Hutu and Tutsi. After independence in 1962, tensions developed between the two groups. In 1993, the president, a Hutu, agreed to share power with the Tutsi.

Shortly afterwards, the president died in a plane crash. His death set off a horrible massacre. Thousands of Hutu soldiers and civilians turned on their Tutsi neighbors and murdered them.

The Hutu planned to murder all Rwandan Tutsi. In this **genocide**, a planned killing of an ethnic group, more than 500,000 people died. In turn, Tutsi rebels attacked the Hutu, and more than

a million Hutu fled to the Democratic Republic of Congo. In 1998 the UN sentenced the Rwandan prime minister during the attacks to life in prison for his part in the genocide. Another 30 leaders of the genocide were awaiting trial.

Angola

Angola, a Portuguese colony, gained independence in 1975, but a 25-year civil war followed. For a time, this war was part of Cold War tensions. The United States backed one side, and the Soviet Union backed the other. Cuban troops went to Angola to support the communist forces.

In 1994, a unity government tried to establish peace but failed, and fighting resumed in 1998. More than 1.5 million Angolans have died in this civil war, and 3.1 million Angolans have become refugees.

The Future

In addition to civil wars, Africa faces other challenges. Some of these threaten Africa's people and others threaten the environment of the continent.

Fighting Disease

Africa's tropical climates and widespread poverty has made it difficult to erase many diseases. The death toll from one disease, AIDS, has been especially high. AIDS is a failure of the human immune system. The virus that causes AIDS has spread around the world, but it is especially challenging in Africa. Millions of Africans have no medical care. As the disease spreads, some communities have become ghost towns. Some families have lost both parents, and the children have no food or shelter.

The disease has no known cure. There are drugs that can slow its progress, but they are very expensive. Few Africans can afford them. The United Nations has tried get these drugs to Africa inexpensively, and African governments have tried to educate their citizens about this deadly disease. Fighting AIDS and other diseases such as the Ebola virus is a challenge for the future.

Advancing Deserts

Africa is also facing an environmental problem. Each year the Sahara desert expands southward. This means that Africa's **arable** land, or land available for crops, is shrinking.

This advance of a desert is called **desertification**. One cause is drought, the lack of rain. However, farmers have also overworked fields or planted damaging crops. Trees and brush have been cut to make more farmland. Without the trees to hold the topsoil, wind and rain have eroded the land. Herders have also overgrazed grasslands. Both the Sahara and the Kalahari deserts are expanding. The United Nations is working with African governments to find ways to halt desertification.

Political Problems

The people of many African countries have had to learn to live together peacefully. As you read, several African nations include rival ethnic groups. Some leaders in the past stirred up trouble among ethnic groups to hold onto power or to gain wealth for themselves.

Coalitions of ethnic groups are working together in many African nations to avoid violence. The search for compromises that balance ethnic interests and rivalries is crucial if countries are to provide opportunity and safety for all citizens.

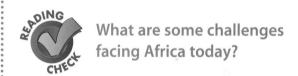

What are some challenges facing Africa today?

A nurse checks a child at a public clinic in Zambia.

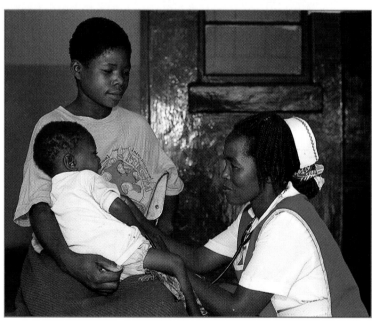

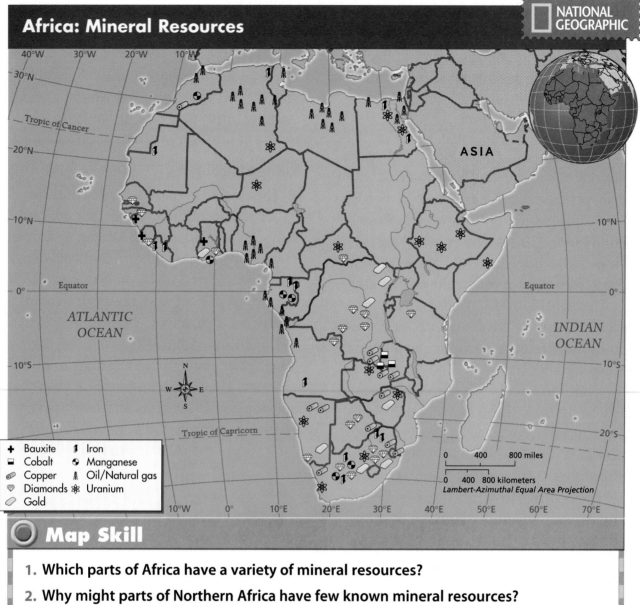

Africa: Mineral Resources

NATIONAL GEOGRAPHIC

ASIA

ATLANTIC OCEAN

INDIAN OCEAN

Tropic of Cancer

Equator

Tropic of Capricorn

Legend:
- + Bauxite
- ▭ Cobalt
- ◉ Copper
- ◈ Diamonds
- ▱ Gold
- ⚑ Iron
- ◔ Manganese
- ⚒ Oil/Natural gas
- ✳ Uranium

0   400   800 miles

0   400   800 kilometers
Lambert-Azimuthal Equal Area Projection

Map Skill

1. Which parts of Africa have a variety of mineral resources?

2. Why might parts of Northern Africa have few known mineral resources?

AFRICA'S RICHES

Africa is rich in natural beauty and in natural resources. It also has many new industries, and its trade with other parts of the world has increased. All of these riches offer Africa hope for the future.

Mineral Resources

Africa is one of the richest continents in terms of natural resources. Nigeria, Algeria, and Libya are leading producers of oil and natural gas. Many of the world's diamonds come from Botswana, the Congo, and South Africa. The Democratic Republic of the Congo is a wealthy land with large deposits of gold, copper, and uranium. Congo also has about 65 percent of the world's cobalt, a valuable mineral used in making steel and other metal products. In addition, Africa has a wide variety of crops and plants for food.

You have read about Africa's two great rivers, the Nile and the Congo. Water-power from the Nile is used to make elec-

Nearly a mile wide, Victoria Falls drops 355 feet on the border of Zambia and Zimbabwe.

PUTTING IT TOGETHER

After they gained independence from their colonial rulers, several African nations plunged into civil war. These wars were especially brutal in Rwanda and Angola. Even so, nations such as South Africa made great strides toward democracy. Apartheid ended in South Africa, and in 1994, Nelson Mandela was elected president in South Africa's first free election for all citizens.

One of Africa's greatest challenges for the future is to erase disease and poverty. Viruses such as the Ebola virus and the one that causes AIDS have caused the deaths of millions of Africans. Desertification, especially to the south of the Sahara, is causing the loss of huge areas of land for farming and grazing.

tricity for Egypt. The Congo has hardly been tapped to make electric power.

Africa's problem and challenge is how to make use of its vast natural wealth to build a better future.

READING CHECK **What natural resources does Africa have?**

1. Write one sentence for each vocabulary word.

   apartheid **genocide**
   arable **sanction**
   desertification

2. What did Frederik Willem de Klerk do?

3. What challenges continue to face African governments?

4. Explain the causes of desertification.

5. Describe a Hutu and a Tutsi's different **points of view** of the 1994 massacre in Rwanda.

Use the map on page 636 to make a chart. Write the names of 10 African countries. In another column, write the natural resources of each country.

• •

Suppose you are Nelson Mandela's biographer. **Write** a brief outline of Mandela's life and explain why he is an important figure in African history.

Being a Good Citizen
Doctors Without Borders

Hawah Kamara is from Liberia, a small nation in West Africa. A civil war erupted in 1989, and Kamara and her family fled to neighboring Sierra Leone.

Kamara received help from Médecins Sans Frontières (MSF), known also by its English name "Doctors Without Borders." For over 30 years, MSF has sent volunteer doctors, nurses, and medical personnel to treat people of all races, religions, and political beliefs for free. For their international relief work, in 1999 MSF received the Nobel Peace Prize.

Kamara and her family returned to Liberia in 1991. A food program run by MSF helped her family to survive in the war-torn capital, Monrovia. Eventually Kamara got a job as a secretary at MSF's Liberia office. "At first, it was just a job for me in a survival time," says Kamara. "It meant a meal before going home and a little money to help my family."

Kamara wondered about MSF volunteers. "Volunteers came to my country from Europe, North America, other parts of Africa, and all over the world. I wondered why these people left behind their warm beds and their comfortable jobs to come here."

In time, Kamara ran the Monrovia office. "In 1997, I was put in charge of. . . Liberia's

"I decided I must do my share."

"It is the satisfaction of knowing you have given someone the chance to live one more day."

feeding centers. . . . At centers I visited, I saw children who had been hiding in the bush [an empty, unsettled area] because of the war and had not eaten. . . . The children not only lived, but got better. . . . After this, I decided I must do my share."

Kamara worked for MSF in Liberia and Sierra Leone. Today she works for the New York office of MSF, recruiting volunteers.

"What people get from working for Doctors Without Borders," she says, "is not something you can buy in a store. It is the satisfaction of knowing you have given someone the chance to live one more day."

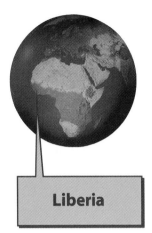

Liberia

Be a Good Citizen

Making Connections

- **What situation might require disaster relief in your community or state?**

- **What volunteer groups provide these services in your community?**

Talk About It!

- **Kamara first learned about MSF as a refugee. How might this have influenced how she feels about the organization?**

- **What do you think Hawah Kamara might say to encourage others to volunteer for MSF?**

Act On It

In the Community

Learn about volunteer groups in your community. Ask representatives to come to your class and talk about their work. Prepare questions to ask them during their visit.

In the Classroom

Make a classroom "news scrapbook." Use the Internet or periodicals to gather information about the activities of Doctors Without Borders around the world. Assemble your findings in a notebook for the classroom library.

The Changing Americas

Find Out!

How are the Americas changing?

Lesson Outline
- The World of the Americas
- North American Neighbors
- South American Neighbors
- Economy of the Americas

VOCABULARY

urbanization
shantytown
duty

PEOPLE
Vicente Fox
Augusto Pinochet
Jean-Bertrand
  Aristide

READING STRATEGY

Copy this Venn diagram. On the left, write some details about Anglo-America. On the right, write some details about Latin America. In the center, write what they have in common.

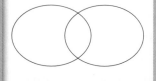

BUILD BACKGROUND

"Let us proceed sensibly and bravely . . . to build a genuine democracy. What is at stake over the next six years is not just the change of a party in power. What is at stake is much more significant and profound: the hopes of millions of Mexicans."

On December 1, 2000, **Vicente Fox** was sworn in as President of Mexico. Since 1929, all presidents have come from the Institutional Revolutionary Party. What made Fox's election important was that he was the first Mexican president elected from another political party.

You Are Here
1970 – 2003

THE WORLD OF THE AMERICAS

The Western Hemisphere includes two cultural regions. The United States and Canada make up Anglo-America. This region was strongly influenced by British culture. The second region, Latin America, includes Mexico, Central America, the Caribbean islands, and South America. It was mostly influenced by Spain, Portugal, and France.

There are some exceptions to these cultural regions. Quebec is a province of Canada, but French is the primary language, and ties to French culture are strong. Some Caribbean islands, like the Netherlands Antilles and the South American country of Suriname, have ties to their Dutch colonizers. Guyana was a British colony, and also has many people whose ancestors came from India. Look at the map. Most South American cities are along the coast. Why might this be true?

READING CHECK What are the two main cultural parts of the Western Hemisphere?

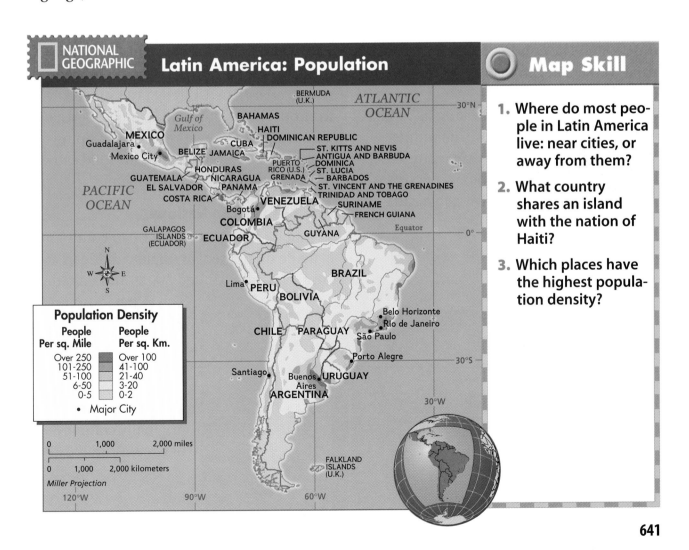

Latin America: Population — Map Skill

1. Where do most people in Latin America live: near cities, or away from them?

2. What country shares an island with the nation of Haiti?

3. Which places have the highest population density?

Population Density

People Per sq. Mile	People Per sq. Km.
Over 250	Over 100
101-250	41-100
51-100	21-40
6-50	3-20
0-5	0-2

• Major City

641

NORTH AMERICAN NEIGHBORS

Mexico is one of the three large countries in North America. Mexico has over 100 million people and its capital, Mexico City, is one of the largest cities in the world.

Mexico began to develop its own industries during World War II. The nation had few large factories at the time. Today, Mexico is a producer of automobiles, oil, electronic appliances, and cotton cloth.

Growth in Mexico

In the 1940s, many of Mexico's people were rural laborers. Although they worked hard, they often could not afford to own any land. When factories were built during World War II, these rural workers came to Mexico City looking for better jobs. Between 1940 and 1970, approximately 3 million people moved to the capital. The continuing arrival of new rural workers began to place a strain on city services.

Mexico continued to develop its industries throughout the 1970s. The profits made a few Mexicans very rich, but they did not always benefit ordinary Mexicans. One Mexican described living in a cardboard box and searching a garbage dump to find food. For many Mexicans, the move to a city had not improved their lives.

Some Mexicans were attracted by higher wages and steady work in the United States. Every year, thousands of Mexicans make the trip north across the border, either legally or illegally. In 1990, 21 percent of the foreign-born people in the United States came from Mexico. Other Mexicans find jobs in *maquiladoras* (mah kee lah DOR ahs), assembly plants set up by American companies just across the Mexican border.

Mexico is a major oil producing nation. Mexico's oil wealth has been a blessing, but it has also caused difficulties. The price of oil was high in the 1970s, so Mexico was able to borrow money for projects such as roads and buildings. The price of oil dropped in the 1980s, and Mexico was unable to repay its loans. By 1995, Mexico was in an economic crisis. The United States agreed to support Mexico's banks, and the crisis eased. Mexico's new president is hoping to put Mexico onto a course of solid economic growth in the years ahead.

Anglo-American Nations

Much of the North American continent is made up of the two Anglo-American countries—the United States and Canada. The two nations are good neighbors and share a long, peaceful history.

The United States and Canada were originally colonies of Great Britain. Not

Workers assemble electronics in an American-owned factory in Mexico.

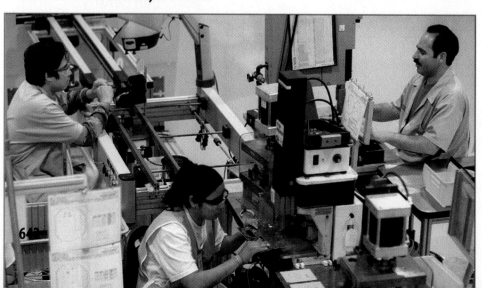

surprisingly, English is the main language of both countries. Much of the culture in both countries comes from Great Britain as well.

Canada and the United States have large groups of Native Americans, and immigrants from Europe have come to both countries throughout their histories. More recently, immigrants from Asia, Africa, and South America have made their way to both countries.

The two nations share many geographical features. Both stretch from the Atlantic Ocean to the Pacific Ocean. They share the Great Lakes, which form part of the boundary between them. They also share the Great Plains and the Rocky Mountains.

Different History

However, there are also differences in the two countries. The United States became independent almost a century before Canada, and Canada has maintained closer ties with Great Britain. In fact, Canadians honor Queen Elizabeth II of Great Britain as the queen of Canada.

The two countries also have important differences in their historical and cultural heritages. One difference is that slavery was always illegal in Canada. In addition, Canada was first settled by French colonists around Quebec. Over the years, Quebec maintained its French language and traditions. Because of this, Canadian law requires that all signs must be in English and in French. However, signs in Quebec are written in French only.

In the United States, there is also a language issue. English is still the primary language. However, a rapidly growing Hispanic population is making Spanish the language spoken by a large percentage of people.

The United States is farther south on the continent, so it has more land suitable for people to live and to farm. Much of Canada's land is too far north and too cold for urban settlements. Today, the population of Canada is 31 million. The United States has more than 275 million people, approximately nine times as many people as Canada.

 How are Canada and the United States both similar and different?

Street signs reflect the French culture of many of Quebec's citizens.

The World's Most Populous Cities

City	Population*
1. Seoul, South Korea	10,231,217
2. São Paulo, Brazil	10,017,821
3. Bombay (Mumbai), India	9,925,891
4. Jakarta, Indonesia	9,112,652
5. Moscow, Russia	8,368,449
6. Istanbul, Turkey	8,274,921
7. Mexico City, Mexico	8,235,744
8. Shanghai, China	8,214,384
9. Tokyo, Japan	7,967,614
10. New York City, U.S.	7,380,906

* population inside the city borders
Source: UN Demographic Yearbook 1997

Chart Skill

1. Which of the world's largest cities are located in the Americas?

2. Why are so many of the world's largest cities also capital cities?

SOUTH AMERICAN NEIGHBORS

Most countries in Latin America share two recent developments: a return to democracy and **urbanization**. Urbanization is the movement of people from the countryside to the cities.

One recent change in Latin America is a movement away from dictatorship. Most of Latin America's countries have elected more democratic governments in recent years. Vicente Fox's election in Mexico is typical of this trend.

Arrest of a Dictator

In Chile, a dictator, General **Augusto Pinochet** ruled the country through the 1970s and 1980s. Pinochet ordered the arrest and imprisonment of many of his opponents. In 1990, a democratically elected government took power in Chile.

In 2000, the ailing former dictator visited Great Britain for medical care. While there, he was arrested for human rights abuses that had occurred while he was ruler of Chile. Pinochet eventually returned to Chile where local judges said he was too ill to stand trial, but the fact that he had been arrested encouraged lovers of democracy and freedom around the world.

Haiti

For years, Haiti was ruled by harsh dictators. In 1990, **Jean-Bertrand Aristide** was elected president in a democratic election. Aristide was overthrown by the military during his term of office, but with the help of U.S. troops, he was restored to power. However, Haiti remains one of the world's poorest countries.

Growing Cities

Many countries in Latin America have become centers of world manufacturing. Thousands of people have left their small farms to live and work in the cities.

Often, there is no place to live when they arrive. Many cities in Latin America have large **shantytowns**, where people erect homes on open land from scrap wood, flattened tin cans, and other waste materials. These communities often do not have clean water, sewers, or electricity.

This growing urbanization is a problem for many countries in Latin America. As you can see from the chart on this page, two of the ten largest cities in the world are in Latin America.

 READING CHECK How has urbanization changed life in Latin America?

644

The Urbanization of Mexico City

Mexico City has had rapid urbanization. At first there was not enough housing for all the people. Later, Mexico City began to solve its urban problems. Look at the charts and graph on this page and answer the questions about Mexico City's growth.

Homes in Mexico City

Year	Number of Homes (thousands)
1970	1,477
1980	2,528
1990	3,041

Source: Ward, Peter M., Mexico City, 1998.

Percentage of Home Ownership in Mexico City

Year	% of Owner Households
1970	42%
1980	54%
1990	69%

Source: Ward, Peter M., Mexico City, 1998.

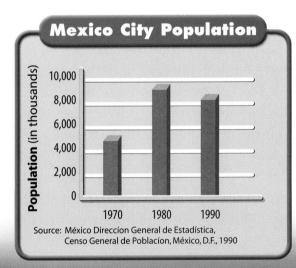

Mexico City Population

Population (in thousands)

Source: México Direccíon General de Estadística, Censo General de Poblacíon, México, D.F., 1990

QUESTIONS:

1. In what year was the population of Mexico City highest?

2. How many new homes were built between 1970 and 1990?

3. What percentage of people owned their homes in 1990? How many people is this?

To learn more, visit our Web site:
www.mhschool.com

ECONOMY OF THE AMERICAS

Trade is one connection among the countries of the Western Hemisphere. In 1992, the United States, Canada, and Mexico agreed to eliminate all trade barriers. The North American Free Trade Agreement, or NAFTA, was a historic agreement. It created a free trade zone in North America. This meant that a car made in the United States, Mexican oil, or Canadian steel could be sold in any of the three countries without **duties**, or import taxes.

In 2001, the leaders of most of the countries in the Western Hemisphere met at Quebec City in Canada. They agreed to extend the free trade agreement to every country in the Western Hemisphere. The plan is to have the agreement in place by 2005. The only requirement for participating is that a country must have a democratically elected government.

Border Challenges

The manufacture and trade of illegal drugs is a difficult problem facing the nations of the Americas. Farmers in Colombia, Peru, and Bolivia receive small profit from the food crops they raise.

However, they can make large profits from raising coca plants that are used to make cocaine, an illegal drug.

Violent criminal gangs make huge profits from the manufacture and sale of these drugs. These gangs have enough money to bribe government officials to avoid arrest. For many years, the United States has joined other nations of Latin America in an effort to stamp out the drug trade.

Immigration and Jobs

Many Latin American nations do not have enough jobs for all of their workers. As a result, many people from these nations come to the United States, one of the world's richest nations, to find work. Some come as legal immigrants, but others cross the border illegally. Mexico and the United States are working together to try to create more job opportunities for Mexicans in their country.

Jobs and the Environment

In Brazil, poor farmers burn the Amazon forest to clear land for crops. Logging and mining operations have also done severe damage to the region. The United States is helping the Brazilian government plan programs to help farmers and to protect the valuable rain forests.

The leaders of 34 NAFTA countries met in Quebec, Canada, in 2001.

The Pan American Games have been held every four years since 1951. Athletes win medals, as at the Olympics.

READING CHECK

How are the nations of the Americas cooperating with each other?

PUTTING IT TOGETHER

There are two culture regions in the Western Hemisphere: Anglo America and Latin America. Two important developments in Latin America are the growth of democracy and urbanization.

The growth of democracy has led to cooperation between nations. The United States, Canada, and Mexico formed the North American Free Trade Agreement. Now the nations of the Western Hemisphere are planning to extend free trade to all countries that have democratic governments. Countries are also cooperating on such problems as the drug trade, illegal immigration, and the destruction of the environment.

The United States and Canada are two close neighbors that share a historical and cultural past. There are also important differences, such as the French culture in Canada and the larger population of the United States.

Review and Assess

1. Write a sentence for each vocabulary word.
   duty   urbanization
   shantytown

2. Why is the election of Vicente Fox important?

Find out! 3. Explain how the Americas are changing today.

4. How has NAFTA affected the **economy** of North America?

5. Describe the different **frames of reference** between a South American and North American.

Use the chart on page 644 to construct a bar graph comparing the population of the largest cities in the Americas. Then locate these cities on a map.

• •

Suppose you are visiting one of the large cities of South America. **Write** a postcard to a friend. Describe what you see in the city.

Using Cartograms

In this chapter, you have read about the countries of the world today. You learned that many differences remain, but that the world is growing closer.

To better understand differences between nations, it is important to be able to measure and compare information about them. One way to do this is with a **cartogram**, a special kind of map that shows economic as well as other categories of information.

VOCABULARY

cartogram

gross domestic product

LEARN THE SKILL

Follow the steps to better understand how to use cartograms like the one on this page.

1. **Identify what is being compared in the cartogram.**
   The title of this cartogram is *The Americas: GDP.* The term GDP stands for **gross domestic product**, which means the total value of all goods and services produced by a country in a certain period, usually one year.

2. **Compare the size of countries in the cartogram.**
   On the political map, Canada is one of the largest countries in the world. You might be surprised to see that Canada is small on the cartogram. This means that the gross domestic product of Canada is small compared to that of Brazil, or of the United States, for example.

3. **Identify the differences between countries.**
   The size of a country on a cartogram has nothing to do with the country's physical size. Compare the size of Bolivia and Venezuela

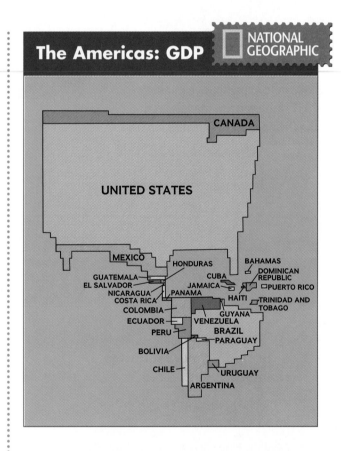

The Americas: GDP   NATIONAL GEOGRAPHIC

CANADA

UNITED STATES

MEXICO

GUATEMALA
EL SALVADOR
NICARAGUA
COSTA RICA
COLOMBIA
ECUADOR
PERU

HONDURAS

JAMAICA
PANAMA

BAHAMAS
DOMINICAN
REPUBLIC
CUBA
PUERTO RICO
HAITI   TRINIDAD AND TOBAGO
GUYANA
VENEZUELA
BRAZIL
PARAGUAY

BOLIVIA

CHILE

URUGUAY

ARGENTINA

on the cartogram. Which country is larger? Now look at the political map. Why is Bolivia smaller on the cartogram than on the political map?

TRY THE SKILL

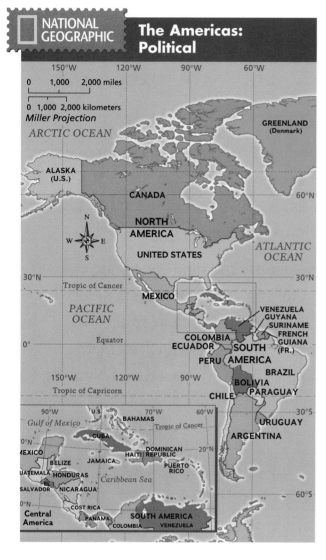

NATIONAL GEOGRAPHIC

The Americas: Political

Use the maps on pages 648 and 649 to help you understand how to use cartograms.

1. How can the political map on this page help you to better understand the cartogram on page 648?

2. Compare the size of the Dominican Republic to the size of Haiti on the political map.

Now compare the size of the two nations on the cartogram. What conclusion can you reach based on this comparison?

3. What did you learn about the nations of the Americas by using this cartogram?

EXTEND THE SKILL

Suppose you want to compare the populations of the countries in the Americas. Go to a reference source to find this information. Then think how a cartogram with these facts might help you.

● Would a cartogram be a useful way to find this information?

● What other types of information might you show on a cartogram?

● Why might a cartogram be easier to use than a table? Why might you also need a table to gather information?

● How can a cartogram help you to understand current events and events in history?

A Changing Asia

Lesson Outline
• China and the World
• The Asian Boom
• Tyranny in Asia
• Asian Challenges

VOCABULARY

World Trade
  Organization
Pacific Rim

PEOPLE

Deng Xiaoping
Kim Il Sung
Aung San Suu Ky
Dalai Lama

READING STRATEGY

Copy this chart. On the right, write some good changes in Asia. On the left, write some changes that have been harmful.

BUILD BACKGROUND

"I hope the whole nation works hard along with residents of the capital city to stage successful 2008 Olympic Games. I also welcome our friends around the world to visit Beijing in 2008."

This is how the leader of China welcomed the choice of Beijing for the 2008 Olympics. Chinese people danced in the streets of the capital, but there were others who were less pleased by the choice. The Olympics debate focused on several of Asia's coming challenges.

CHINA AND THE WORLD

Mao Zedong died in 1976. The next leader of China, **Deng Xiaoping** (DUNG SHOW PING), moved China away from Mao's strict communism.

Farmers were given more control over their time, and they were allowed to sell surplus crops for profit. Deng allowed bright Chinese students to study abroad. He also encouraged foreign companies to do business in China. The Chinese economy expanded.

A Movement for Democracy

By the spring of 1989, many Chinese hoped that the collapse of communism in Europe might spread to China. In May 1989, a crowd of more than one million students gathered in Beijing, the capital city of China to demand democratic reforms. The site of the protest was the center of the city, **Tiananmen Square**.

Deng Xiaoping decided to use China's army to end the protest. Dozens of tanks rumbled into the square and soldiers fired at the unarmed students. Hundreds of protestors were killed.

China and the West

Deng Xiaoping died in 1997. After his death, China allowed more private businesses in China and loosened the government's control over many businesses.

In the 1990s, China applied for membership in the **World Trade Organization** (WTO), an international organization that establishes rules for manufacturers in all member countries. In 1999, China was voted into the World Trade Organization. In the year 2000 the United States and China signed a trade agreement.

Hong Kong

Hong Kong was a prosperous manufacturing and trading city. However, it was a British colony. In 1997, Hong Kong was returned to Chinese control. The Chinese had promised not to interfere with business and political traditions there. For the most part life in Hong Kong continued as it had before.

How did China change after the death of Mao Zedong?

A lone student faces the tanks sent to Tiananmen Square in 1989. University students celebrate the selection of Beijing for the 2008 Olympics (opposite).

651

THE ASIAN BOOM

For hundreds of years, much of the European and American trade had centered on the Atlantic Ocean. After World War II, the countries of the **Pacific Rim**, around the Pacific Ocean, became centers of global trade.

Postwar Growth

After World War II, Japan's cities lay in ruins. China's economy was wrecked by years of war and the communist takeover. The other nations of Asia were largely agricultural lands with traditional economies.

By 1980, Japan had grown into the second largest economic power in the world after the United States. In Japan, the government and business leaders had worked together to avoid competition and waste. Japanese workers were well-educated and well-trained. Government protection made it possible for Japanese companies to grow.

Asian Tigers

Other Asian countries had begun to expand their economies by this time. Business experts called South Korea, Taiwan, Singapore, and Malaysia the "Asian Tigers" because they had become so important economically.

Japan and other Asian countries built economies based on exports. Japan, Singapore, Malaysia, and Taiwan often imported unfinished products for clothing, cameras, VCRs, stereo equipment, computers, and cars. They exported the finished products.

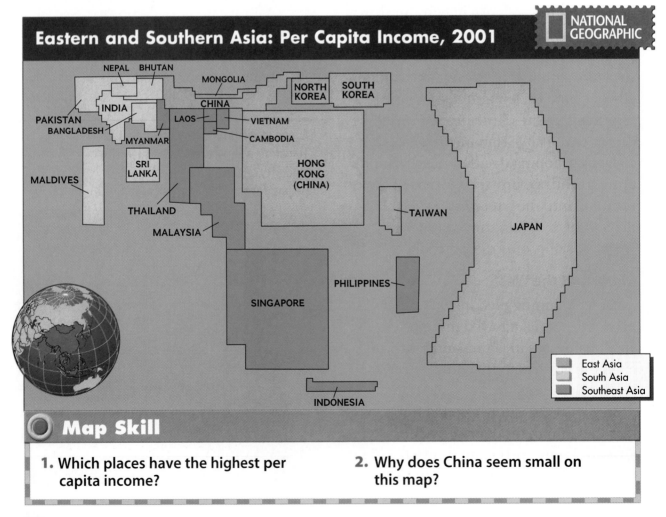

Eastern and Southern Asia: Per Capita Income, 2001

NATIONAL GEOGRAPHIC

NEPAL BHUTAN
MONGOLIA
NORTH KOREA SOUTH KOREA
INDIA
CHINA
PAKISTAN
BANGLADESH
LAOS VIETNAM
MYANMAR CAMBODIA
SRI LANKA
HONG KONG (CHINA)
MALDIVES
TAIWAN
JAPAN
THAILAND
MALAYSIA
PHILIPPINES
SINGAPORE
INDONESIA

East Asia
South Asia
Southeast Asia

Map Skill

1. Which places have the highest per capita income?

2. Why does China seem small on this map?

652

Japanese money dealers (far right) trade yen, Japanese money, for foreign currency.

Boom and Bust

In the 1970s, the Japanese economy soared and the American economy slowed. Many people felt that American manufacturers should study Japanese production methods.

For example, Japanese cars had fewer problems and lasted longer than American-made cars. Business experts said that the Japanese had superior manufacturing techniques. They understood the importance of quality, or making products that had fewer mistakes or defects. The words "Made in Japan" were a statement of quality.

Hard Times for Japan

By the mid-1980s, the United States economy had recovered and was growing rapidly. By the 1990s, the Japanese economy was slowing down.

There were several reasons for the Japanese slump. The first was competition. Japan had been a world leader in quality manufacturing. By the 1990s, the United States and other countries were able to compete successfully.

Government trade policies once protected businesses and helped the Japanese economy grow, but now they forced businesses to compete on their own. The following excerpt explains what happened to workers when many businesses stopped growing.

How did Japan's economy get into trouble?

Primary Source:

excerpt from **"Japanese Can't Count on Lifetime Jobs"**
— *The Labor Educator, 1999*

For decades . . . when a Japanese worker was hired by a company, he could expect to work there until he retired. . . . in return, companies would receive loyalty and hard work from their employees . . .

With the country suffering from seven years of economic recession, all that has changed . . . Almost twice as many people are looking for jobs as there are job openings. . . . workers at age 45 and over have been particularly hard hit by the mass layoffs.

Even more than the loss of income, they feel the shame and humiliation of being forced into the ranks of the jobless, a fate that would have seemed impossible just a few years ago.

Why were Japanese workers especially unprepared for job layoffs?

Police in Myanmar block the entrance to the home of government critic Aung San Suu Kyi.

TYRANNY IN ASIA

Some Asian countries are successful democracies with strong economies. However, communist and military governments still rule other Asian nations.

Vietnam

After the country was united in 1975, Vietnam began to recover from decades of war. From the mid-1980s to the 1990s, the Vietnamese economy grew rapidly. In the late 1990s, however, Vietnam suffered from a financial crisis.

In November of 2000, President Bill Clinton traveled to Vietnam. He was the first United States President to visit Vietnam since 1966. Clinton's visit marked a new period in relations between the two countries.

North Korea

North Korea has had a communist government since 1945. Until his death in 1994, the leader was **Kim Il Sung**. He isolated North Korea from the rest of the world. Kim was called the "Great Leader," but he was a harsh dictator.

Kim's son, Kim Jong-il, took over when his father died. Today, North Korea's economy is in ruins, and the country cannot raise enough food to feed its own people. Thousands have died of starvation.

North Korea has also tried to make nuclear weapons. In 1994, the United States reached an agreement with North Korea that ended the country's production of nuclear weapons. However, the United States has continued to watch North Korea closely.

Myanmar

In Chapter 17, you read about the military dictatorship in Myanmar, or Burma. In 1988, students and workers protested against military rule. The army responded quickly, and thousands of protesters were killed. Thousands more were arrested.

Worldwide criticism forced Myanmar's generals to hold elections in 1999. The country's pro-democracy leaders defeated the military's candidates. The generals arrested the democratic candidates, and closed universities. They also established tight control over the nation in order to prevent protests.

READING CHECK Which Asian countries are still communist dictatorships?

BIOGRAPHY

Focus On: Loyalty

Aung San Suu Kyi (OUNG SAHN SOO CHEE) is a fighter for democracy in Myanmar. When she was two years old, her father, a military leader who fought for Burma's independence from Great Britain, was assassinated. Loyalty to her father's memory inspired her to fight to free her country from military dictatorship. She tried to use the nonviolent policies of Gandhi, the Indian leader.

Suu Kyi spoke at hundreds of rallies. Often, soldiers pointed rifles at her while she addressed the crowds. They never actually fired at her, but they killed and tortured hundreds of her supporters. In 1989, the military dictators of Myanmar imprisoned Suu Kyi for six years. While in prison, she was awarded the Nobel Peace Prize in 1991.

Suu Kyi summarized her fight in these words: "The struggle for democracy and human rights in Burma is a struggle for life and dignity. . . . The people of my country want two freedoms that spell security: freedom from want and freedom from fear."

Link to Today Think of another leader who has remained loyal to a cause or an idea. It can be someone famous, or someone in your community. Write a paragraph comparing this leader to Aung San Suu Kyi.

THE LIFE OF AUNG SAN SUU KYI	1945 Suu Kyi is born in Burma (now Myanmar)	1988 Suu Kyi cofounds the National League for Democracy	1991 Suu Kyi is awarded the Nobel Peace Prize	1995 Suu Kyi is released from prison
1940 — **1985** — **1990** — **1995** — **2000**				
LIFE AROUND THE WORLD	1959 Castro makes Cuba into a communist state	1989 Chinese protestors are attacked in Tiananmen Square, Beijing, China	1991 Iraq is defeated in the Persian Gulf War	1994 South Africa holds first free election

655

ASIAN CHALLENGES

When the communists took over China in 1949, the Nationalist government fled to Taiwan, an island located off the east coast of China. There they set up the Republic of China. Taiwan prospered and became one of the Asian Tigers, quickly developing an export economy.

China and Taiwan have been separate countries for more than 50 years. However, both the Taiwanese and the Chinese say that Taiwan and China are one country. Both governments claim to be the only real government of both Taiwan and mainland China.

The United States has supported Taiwan in its battles with communist China. However, it does not recognize Taiwan's government as the government of China. The United States hopes that China will settle the Taiwan issue peacefully, but people on Taiwan do not want to be part of communist China.

Tibet presents a different kind of challenge to China's leaders. Tibet is an ancient Buddhist country high in the Himalaya Mountains. At various times in history, Tibet was part of the Chinese Empire. However, Tibetans did not want to be part of China and revere their ruler, the **Dalai Lama**, as the spiritual leader of Tibet.

In 1950, China invaded and conquered Tibet. Chinese authorities persecuted Buddhist monks and made it difficult for Tibetans to follow traditional customs. The Dalai Lama escaped to India in 1959. From his exile, the Dalai Lama has continued to work to free Tibet from Chinese rule.

China's government had dealt harshly with other ethnic minorities, such as those who live on the northern steppes.

The Dalai Lama, Tibet's religious leader, campaigns for greater freedom for his people.

International human rights groups are hoping that these abuses will lessen as China becomes increasingly involved in the world community.

Economic Crisis

After the economic growth in the 1970s and 1980s, the Asian Pacific Rim countries went into shock in the 1990s when their economies suddenly worsened. Banks failed and the value of their currencies dropped. Inflation, unemployment, and unrest followed. In Indonesia, the nation that was hardest hit, about one in every five people lost their jobs. The unrest was so severe the government fell.

Among the main reasons for the economic crisis were poor economic policies and a world recession. It is hoped that economic and other reforms will turn the economies around in the 2000s.

What are the major challenges facing Asia?

PUTTING IT TOGETHER

The countries of the Pacific Rim enjoyed great economic growth in the 1970s and 1980s. Led by Japan, the Asian Tigers developed an export economy that reached customers all over the world.

In China, Deng Xiaoping relaxed the rules of Communism allowing great growth in China. But in 1989, he ordered tanks into Tiananmen Square to crush a student protest for more democracy. Western democracies have granted China membership in the World Trade Organization. And China has won the right to host the Olympic games.

Japan was an economic leader in the 1970 and 1980s. Japanese companies worked closely with the government. They developed innovative products and manufacturing methods. But in the 1990s, Japan fell on hard times caused by economic troubles at home and abroad.

Asia has countries that are far from becoming democracies. Vietnam and North Korea have communist governments. Myanmar is a military dictatorship.

Among the challenges facing Asia are peaceful solutions to China's problems with Taiwan and Tibet, and a return to economic health for the entire Pacific Rim.

A worker in Singapore packages compact discs. Americans purchase about 25 percent of Singapore's exports.

Review and Assess

1. Write a sentence for each vocabulary term.

   Pacific Rim   World Trade Organization

2. What country in Asia has a military dictatorship that canceled elections?

3. How did Asia's Pacific Rim change in the late twentieth century?

4. How is Taiwan a problem for China?

5. How do you think the changes in employment practices that occurred in the 1980s and 1990s changed the frame of reference of some Japanese?

Use the map of Asia on page R12 to make a chart. Identify which Asian countries are located on islands or peninsulas. Indicate which are on the main landmass. How do you think Asia's geography affects trade?

Suppose you are a spectator at the Olympic Games in Beijing in 2008. Write a brief report on how you think hosting the Olympics might change China.

VOCABULARY REVIEW

Each of the following statements contains an underlined vocabulary word. Number a sheet of paper from 1 to 5. Beside each number write **T** if the statement is true and **F** if the statement is false. If the statement is false, rewrite the statement using the vocabulary word correctly.

1. The <u>euro</u> is a unit of currency used by the European Union.

2. <u>Genocide</u> is the system of laws that once separated races in South Africa.

3. <u>The Pacific Rim</u> is an organization that oversees the islands of the Pacific Ocean.

4. The movement of the population from urban areas to rural areas is called <u>urbanization</u>.

5. <u>Sanctions</u> are trade agreements made between friendly nations.

CHAPTER COMPREHENSION

6. Why was the European Union created?

7. What are guest workers? What role do they play in Europe's economy?

8. How did South Africa change in the early 1990s?

9. Why have Africa's rich resources not always benefited the people of Africa?

10. How has China become part of global organizations? Why is China sometimes criticized by other countries?

11. What happened to the economy of Japan in the 1990s? Why did these changes take place?

12. What is NAFTA? Why was it formed?

13. **Write** a paragraph to describe how technology can change a culture. Describe the benefits and drawbacks of the changes.

SKILL REVIEW

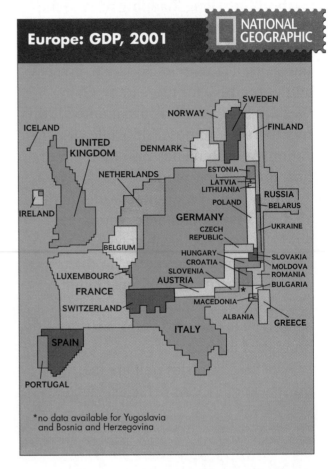

Europe: GDP, 2001 NATIONAL GEOGRAPHIC

*no data available for Yugoslavia and Bosnia and Herzegovina

14. **Geography Skill** In this cartogram, what do the sizes of the countries represent?

15. **Geography Skill** Which country has the highest GDP in Europe? Which country has the lowest GDP?

16. **Study Skill** What is a database? What are some examples of information you might find on a database?

17. **Reading/Thinking Skill** Which ethnic group in Rwanda had a bias against the Tutsi in the 1990s?

18. **Reading/Thinking Skill** Suppose an unemployed American says that free trade is not a good idea. How might being unemployed influence this person's point of view?

USING A TIME LINE

1970	1975	1980	1985	1990	1995	2000	2005	2010

c. 1975 Japan's economic boom begins

1989 Protest in Tiananmen Square

1992 NAFTA agreement

1993 European Union formed

1995 World Trade Organization formed

1997 Hong Kong returned to China

2008 Olympic Games in Beijing

19. Which events on the time line mark economic agreements between countries?

20. How many years are there between the Tiananmen Square protest and the Olympic Games that will be held in Beijing?

Activity

Writing About Economics How has increased world trade affected your life? Make a list of products from other countries that you use. Write the name of the manufacturing country next to each product. Research and list some of the things the United States exports to other countries.

Foldables

Use your Foldable to review what you have learned about our changing world. As you look at the globe sketched on the front of your Foldable, mentally review what world changes have occurred in your lifetime. Why do world changes have a greater impact on the average citizen of the world today than they did a hundred years ago? Look at your notes on the inside of your Foldable to review what you learned. Record any questions that you have, and discuss them with classmates, or review the chapter to find answers.

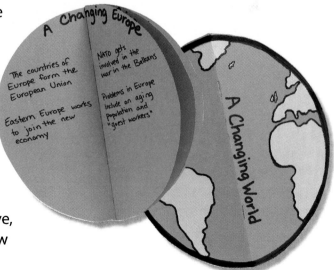

VOCABULARY REVIEW

Number a sheet of paper from 1 to 5. Beside each number write the word or term from the list below that matches the description.

alliance   **euro**

anti-Semitism   **sanction**

civil disobedience

1. Penalty placed on a nation
2. Non-violent methods of protest
3. An agreement between countries to act as partners for their mutual benefit
4. Discrimination against Jewish people
5. A unit of currency in Europe

TECHNOLOGY

For resources to help you learn more about the people and places in this unit, visit **www.mhschool.com** and follow the links for Grade 6, Unit 5.

SKILL REVIEW

6. **Reading/Thinking Skill** What is propaganda? What kind of propaganda might Mao Zedong and the Chinese communists have spread throughout China during the Cultural Revolution?

7. **Reading/Thinking Skill** How does understanding different points of view help you to understand events in history?

8. **Study Skill** How are a reference source and a database similar and different?

9. **Geography Skill** What does the cartogram on this page show? How can you compare data on the cartogram to find information?

10. **Geography Skill** Which country has the greatest population? Which country has a larger population, India or Mexico?

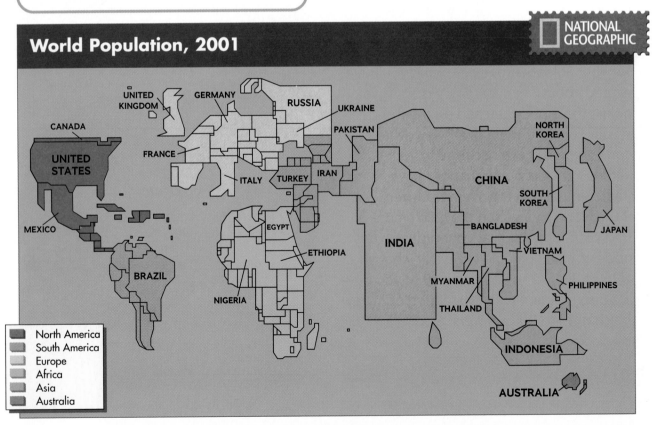

NATIONAL GEOGRAPHIC

World Population, 2001

Legend:
- North America
- South America
- Europe
- Africa
- Asia
- Australia

1   In 1915, a leader of India emerged . . . . His name was Mohandas Gandhi.

2   Ghandi lived very simply. . . . However, he was a lawyer and a very knowledgeable politician. He and his followers used the principle of civil disobedience to end British rule. Civil disobedience is a nonviolent protest against a government. A boycott is one form of civil disobedience. So is the refusal to obey laws considered unjust. Gandhi wrote:

[Nonviolence] must have its root in love. . . . Even when noncooperating with him, (the British) we must make him feel that in us he has a friend and we should try to reach his heart. . . .

1 In this selection, the word *civil* means—

A polite or courteous

B cultured and elegant

C citizen or community

D laws that relate to individual rights

2 With which of these sayings might Gandhi have been most likely to agree?

F Things are easier said than done.

G Leave well enough alone.

H Might makes right.

J Love your enemy.

WRITING ACTIVITIES

Writing to Express *Write* a journal entry for an Allied soldier who fought at the front during World War I.

Writing to Inform *Write* a paragraph that explains what happened in the formerly communist countries of Europe after the Cold War ended.

Writing to Persuade Suppose you believe in the ideas of Mohandas Gandhi. *Write* a newspaper editorial explaining why his techniques are the best way to gain independence or peace. Include some examples in your editorial.

661

CONCLUSION

Geography

"There is nothing permanent except change."—Heraclitus

ADAPTING

How did early people use their environment? How are people changing their environment today? How might people change their environment in the future?

People live in a variety of environments in the world today. Cultures have adapted to survive in their geographical region, but geography changes. Volcanoes erupt, rivers change course, harbors fill with silt. People adapt to life in the changed conditions. Around the world people have been adapting to their geography since the dawn of time. We continue to do what humans have always done.

To read about the spread of deserts, read page 635.

To read about urbanization, read page 645.

about 12,000 B.C.
Humans cross the land bridge from Asia to Alaska.

about 600 B.C.
Nok people of Africa begin to mine iron.

A.D. 79
Pompeii is buried when Mt. Vesuvius erupts.

| 12000 B.C. | 1000 B.C. | 800 B.C. | 600 B.C. | 400 B.C. | 200 B.C. | A.D. 1 | A.D. 200 | A.D. 400 |

about 1000 B.C.
Farmers along the Huang He build levees.

To read about changing environments for human needs, see page 147.

Activity Some day, people will live in new environments such as outer space, or under the oceans. How would they adapt to these environments? Research some techniques that scientists are studying to make life possible in new environments.

To read about people's adaptation to their environments, see page 423.

about A.D. 900
The Anasazi build adobe houses.

about A.D. 1400
Inca farm on terraces in the Andes.

A.D. 1914
Panama Canal opens.

A.D. 600   A.D. 800   A.D. 1000   A.D. 1200   A.D. 1400   A.D. 1600   A.D. 1800   A.D. 2000

A.D. 1100
Europeans begin deforestation for farming.

about A.D. 1960
The Sahara Desert begins to expand to the south.

History and Culture

"History is a ship carrying living memories to the future."
—Stephen Spender

BELONGING

What are some features of a culture? What makes a culture change throughout history? What changes might take place in cultures in the 2000s?

History is something that happens every day. Of course, it doesn't look like history when you are living in it. The ancient Greeks did not know that the government they developed would influence people for thousands of years. It takes time to understand important events and their effect on cultures and lives. History is also the story of lives, the lives of the famous and of ordinary people. As Abraham Lincoln once said, "Fellow citizens, we cannot escape history!"

To learn more about how cultures celebrate, see page 128.

To read about how cultures combine old and new ideas, see page 524.

3500 B.C.
The Sumerians develop cuneiform.

A.D. 500
Kingdom of Ghana begins to rule West Africa.

3500 B.C.	400 B.C.	200 B.C.	A.D. 1	A.D. 200	A.D. 400	A.D. 600

300 B.C.
Kingdom of Kush becomes a center of trade and the arts.

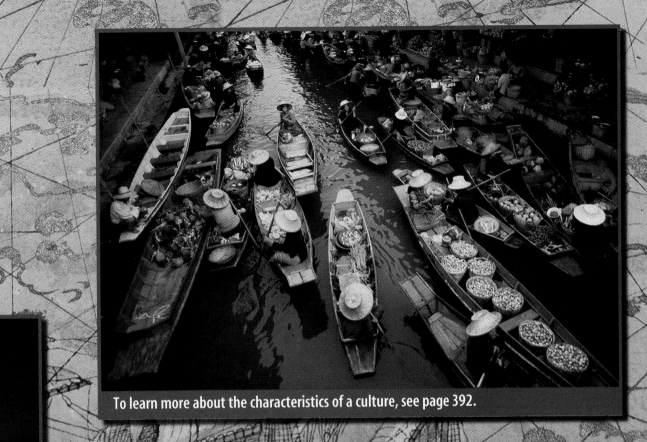

To learn more about the characteristics of a culture, see page 392.

Activity Research some part of the culture you live in: its sports, education, or traditions. Then prepare a presentation for your class.

To find out how cultural features are passed on, read page 48.

A.D. 800
Baghdad becomes capital
of Muslim Caliphate.

about A.D. 1700
Age of Enlightenment
begins.

A.D. 800	A.D. 1000	A.D. 1200	A.D. 1400	A.D. 1600	A.D. 1800	A.D. 2000

about A.D. 1500
Great Wall of China is
completed by Ming rulers.

A.D. 1914
World War I begins a
century of conflict.

Government and Citizenship

"The government is us: we are the government, you and I."
—Theodore Roosevelt

PARTICIPATING

In what ways can a citizen take part in government? What responsibilities does a citizen have? How can being a good citizen help government serve people well?

People have had governments since they first began living in groups. Not surprisingly, there have been many kinds of governments. Some have benefited only the rulers. Others have given power to ordinary people. Today, this kind of democratic government is found on every continent.

Read about citizens who have recently won the right to vote on page 631.

To learn about forms of government, see page 223.

about 1800 B.C.
Hammurabi puts his laws in writing.

508 B.C.
Democracy begins in ancient Athens.

| 1800 B.C. | 1000 B.C. | 900 B.C. | 800 B.C. | 700 B.C. | 600 B.C. | 500 B.C. | 400 B.C. | 300 B.C. | 200 B.C. | 100 B.C. |

To read how governments can help people, read page 626.

Activity Suppose that a committee from a foreign country wants to form a democratic government for their nation. They ask you to help them design their new government. Describe some basic principles or ideas that you think such a government should follow.

See how you can take part in government every day on pages 583–584.

A.D. 1215
King John of England signs the Magna Carta.

A.D. 1787
U.S. Constitution is written.

A.D. 1789
French Revolution begins.

A.D. 1991
Apartheid ends in South Africa.

A.D. 1200   A.D. 1300   A.D. 1400   A.D. 1500   A.D. 1600   A.D. 1700   A.D. 1800   A.D. 1900   A.D. 2000

A.D. 1822
Latin America becomes independent.

A.D. 1867
Meiji Restoration begins in Japan.

Economics and Technology

"The digital future is more important than ever."—Bill Gates

CONNECTING

Why do some things cost more than others? Why are some products made in other countries? How will computers change the way we live, work, and play? How does technology create and solve problems?

From the cities of Sumer to your local shopping mall, economics and technology have shaped people's lives. The world today is more interdependent than ever before. The Internet makes it possible for people on opposite sides of the planet to communicate and do business instantly. Science and medicine help people live longer and healthier lives.

Technology is designed to save labor, time, and solve problems. It can also create new opportunities. The key to success in the future is being able to use the newest technologies.

For more about world trade, see page 652.

To read more about a new currency, read page 623.

6000 B.C.
Agriculture begins at Catal Huyuk.

A.D. 80
Rome's Colosseum is completed.

A.D. 400
Chinese manufacture steel.

6000 B.C.	3000 B.C.	200 B.C.	A.D. 1	A.D. 200	A.D. 400	A.D. 600

3000 B.C.
Bronze work begins in Mesopotamia.

200 B.C.
Chinese weights and measures are standardized.

A.D. 300
Gold-salt trade develops in West Africa.

Read about the development of trade on page 48.

You can read about changes technology is making in life today on page 628.

Activity Research the price of different items in various stores in your town or neighborhood. Which ones are made in other countries? Why are some products expensive and others cheap?

A.D. 970
Chinese invent
paper money.

A.D. 1448
Guttenberg invents
the printing press.

A.D. 1915
Henry Ford invents
the assembly line.

A.D. 2005
International Space Station
is scheduled for completion.

A.D. 800   A.D. 1000   A.D. 1200   A.D. 1400   A.D. 1600   A.D. 1800   A.D. 2000   A.D. 2200

A.D. 1200
Modern banking
emerges in Europe.

A.D. 1700
Industrial Revolution
begins in Britain.

A.D. 1969
Internet
begins.

A.D. 2002
The euro is
introduced.

Reference Section

The Reference Section has many parts, each with a different type of information. Use this section to look up people, places, and events as you study.

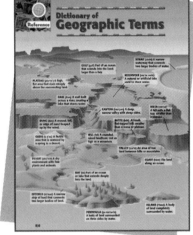

Taj Mahal

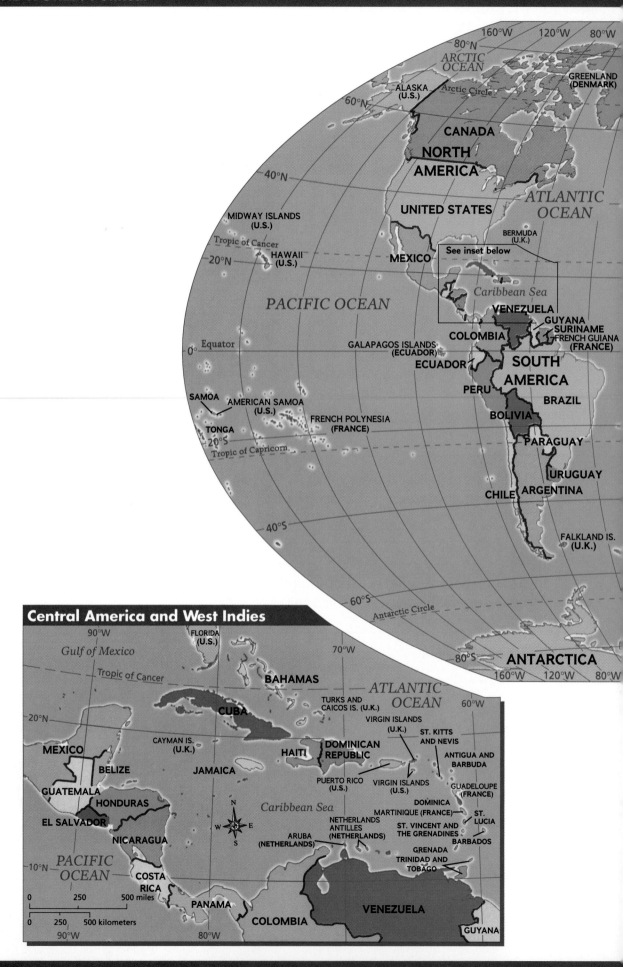

160°W   120°W   80°W

80°N
ARCTIC
OCEAN

ALASKA
(U.S.)   Arctic Circle   GREENLAND
(DENMARK)

60°N

CANADA

NORTH
AMERICA

ATLANTIC
OCEAN

40°N

UNITED STATES

BERMUDA
(U.K.)

MIDWAY ISLANDS
(U.S.)

See inset below

Tropic of Cancer

20°N   HAWAII
(U.S.)   MEXICO   Caribbean Sea

VENEZUELA

PACIFIC OCEAN   GUYANA
SURINAME
FRENCH GUIANA
(FRANCE)

COLOMBIA

0°   Equator   GALAPAGOS ISLANDS
(ECUADOR)   SOUTH
AMERICA

ECUADOR

PERU   BRAZIL

SAMOA   AMERICAN SAMOA
(U.S.)   BOLIVIA

FRENCH POLYNESIA
(FRANCE)

TONGA   PARAGUAY

20°S   URUGUAY
Tropic of Capricorn

CHILE   ARGENTINA

40°S

FALKLAND IS.
(U.K.)

60°S   Antarctic Circle   ANTARCTICA

80°S

160°W   120°W   80°W

Central America and West Indies

90°W   FLORIDA
(U.S.)   70°W

Gulf of Mexico   ATLANTIC
OCEAN

Tropic of Cancer   BAHAMAS   60°W

20°N   TURKS AND
CAICOS IS. (U.K.)

CUBA   VIRGIN ISLANDS
(U.K.)   ST. KITTS
AND NEVIS

CAYMAN IS.
(U.K.)   ANTIGUA AND
BARBUDA

MEXICO   HAITI   DOMINICAN
REPUBLIC

JAMAICA   GUADELOUPE
(FRANCE)

BELIZE   PUERTO RICO
(U.S.)   VIRGIN ISLANDS
(U.S.)

GUATEMALA   DOMINICA
MARTINIQUE (FRANCE)   ST.
LUCIA

HONDURAS   Caribbean Sea

EL SALVADOR   ST. VINCENT AND
THE GRENADINES

NICARAGUA   NETHERLANDS
ANTILLES
(NETHERLANDS)   BARBADOS

N
W   E
S   ARUBA
(NETHERLANDS)   GRENADA

10°N   PACIFIC
OCEAN   TRINIDAD AND
TOBAGO

COSTA
RICA

0   250   500 miles

PANAMA   VENEZUELA

0   250   500 kilometers

COLOMBIA   GUYANA

90°W   80°W

R4

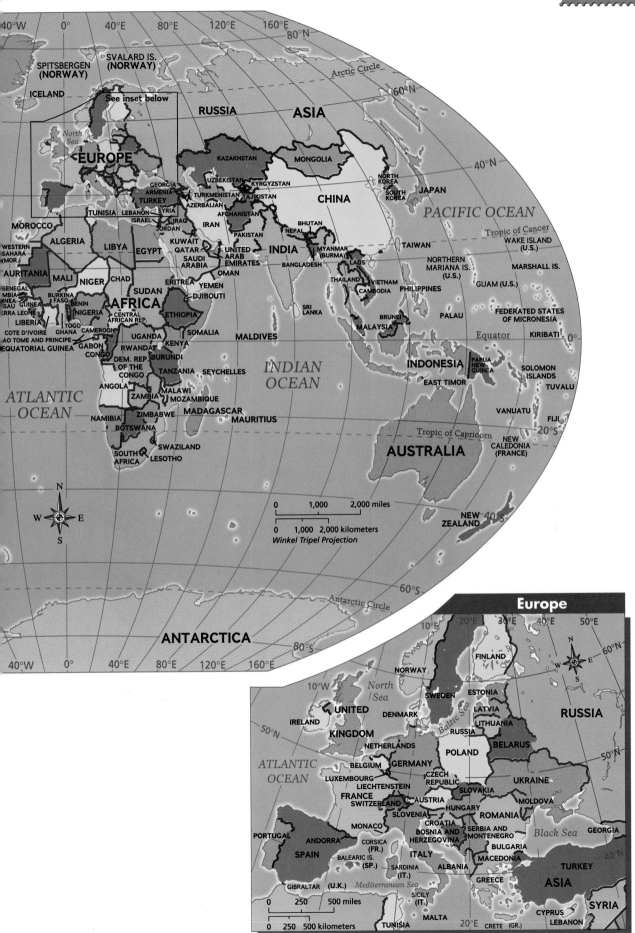

40°W 0° 40°E 80°E 120°E 160°E

80°N

SPITSBERGEN
(NORWAY)

SVALARD IS.
(NORWAY)

Arctic Circle

ICELAND

See inset below

North
Sea

60°N

RUSSIA   ASIA

EUROPE

KAZAKHSTAN   MONGOLIA

40°N

GEORGIA   UZBEKISTAN KYRGYZSTAN   NORTH
ARMENIA   KOREA
TURKEY   TURKMENISTAN TAJIKISTAN CHINA   JAPAN
                AZERBAIJAN
TUNISIA LEBANON SYRIA   AFGHANISTAN   SOUTH   PACIFIC OCEAN
         ISRAEL IRAQ   KOREA
MOROCCO   JORDAN   IRAN   PAKISTAN

                KUWAIT   BHUTAN   TAIWAN   Tropic of Cancer   WAKE ISLAND
WESTERN ALGERIA LIBYA EGYPT QATAR   UNITED INDIA NEPAL   (U.S.)
SAHARA   SAUDI   ARAB   MYANMAR   NORTHERN
(MOR.)   ARABIA EMIRATES   (BURMA)   MARIANA IS.   MARSHALL IS.
AURITANIA MALI NIGER CHAD   OMAN   BANGLADESH LAOS   (U.S.)
SENEGAL   ERITREA YEMEN   THAILAND VIETNAM   GUAM (U.S.)
MBIA   BURKINA   DJIBOUTI   CAMBODIA   PHILIPPINES
SAU GUINEA FASO BENIN SUDAN   SRI   FEDERATED STATES
ERRA LEONE   NIGERIA AFRICA ETHIOPIA   LANKA   OF MICRONESIA
LIBERIA   CENTRAL   BRUNEI   PALAU
COTE D'IVOIRE AFRICAN REP.   MALDIVES   MALAYSIA   Equator   KIRIBATI   0°
AO TOME AND PRINCIPE CAMEROON UGANDA KENYA
EQUATORIAL GUINEA GABON   PAPUA
         CONGO RWANDA BURUNDI   INDONESIA NEW   SOLOMON
                DEM. REP.   INDIAN   GUINEA ISLANDS
                OF THE   TANZANIA SEYCHELLES   OCEAN   EAST TIMOR   TUVALU
                CONGO
         ANGOLA   MALAWI   VANUATU
ATLANTIC   ZAMBIA MOZAMBIQUE   FIJI
OCEAN   MADAGASCAR   NEW   20°S
         NAMIBIA ZIMBABWE MAURITIUS   Tropic of Capricorn   CALEDONIA
           BOTSWANA   (FRANCE)
              SWAZILAND   AUSTRALIA
           SOUTH   LESOTHO
           AFRICA

N
W   E
S

0   1,000   2,000 miles

0 1,000 2,000 kilometers
Winkel Tripel Projection   NEW   40°S
                                            ZEALAND

60°S

Antarctic Circle

ANTARCTICA   80°S

40°W 0° 40°E 80°E 120°E 160°E

10°E 20°E 30°E 40°E 50°E

N
W   E   60°N
S

FINLAND

NORWAY

North   SWEDEN ESTONIA
Sea   RUSSIA
                Baltic Sea   LATVIA
UNITED   DENMARK   LITHUANIA
IRELAND   50°N
KINGDOM   RUSSIA   BELARUS
50°N   NETHERLANDS   POLAND
         BELGIUM GERMANY   UKRAINE
ATLANTIC LUXEMBOURG CZECH
OCEAN   LIECHTENSTEIN REPUBLIC SLOVAKIA
         FRANCE   AUSTRIA   MOLDOVA
         SWITZERLAND   HUNGARY   ROMANIA
                    SLOVENIA CROATIA
              MONACO   BOSNIA AND SERBIA AND Black Sea   GEORGIA
PORTUGAL ANDORRA   HERZEGOVINA MONTENEGRO
              CORSICA   BULGARIA
         SPAIN (FR.)   ITALY   MACEDONIA   TURKEY
              BALEARIC IS. SARDINIA ALBANIA   ASIA
              (SP.) (IT.)   GREECE
GIBRALTAR (U.K.) Mediterranean Sea
                         SICILY   SYRIA
                         (IT.)   MALTA   CYPRUS LEBANON
0   250   500 miles

0   250   500 kilometers   TUNISIA   CRETE (GR.)   20°E

R5

ARCTIC OCEAN

0°   30°E   60°E   90°E   120°E   150°E   180°

Arctic Circle

60°N

URAL MTS.

Ob River

Volga River

ASIA

EUROPE

GOBI

ALPS

Mont Blanc
(4,807 m)

Mt. Elbrus
18,510 ft. (5,642 m)

HINDU KUSH

30°N

SYRIAN
DESERT

SAHARA

Nile River

HIMALAYA

Mt. Everest
29,035 ft. (8,850 m)

Chang River

Tropic of Cancer

AFRICA

DECCAN
PLATEAU

Ganges River

PACIFIC OCEAN

Mt. Kilimanjaro
19,340 ft.
(5,895 m)

INDIAN OCEAN

Equator

0°

ATLANTIC
OCEAN

NAMIB DESERT

KALAHARI
DESERT

GREAT
SANDY
DESERT

Tropic of Capricorn

Cape of
Good Hope

AUSTRALIA

E

30°S

Mt. Kosciusko
7,310 ft.
(2,228 m)

0   1,000   2,000 miles

0   1,000   2,000 kilometers
Winkel Tripel Projection

60°S

ANTARCTICA

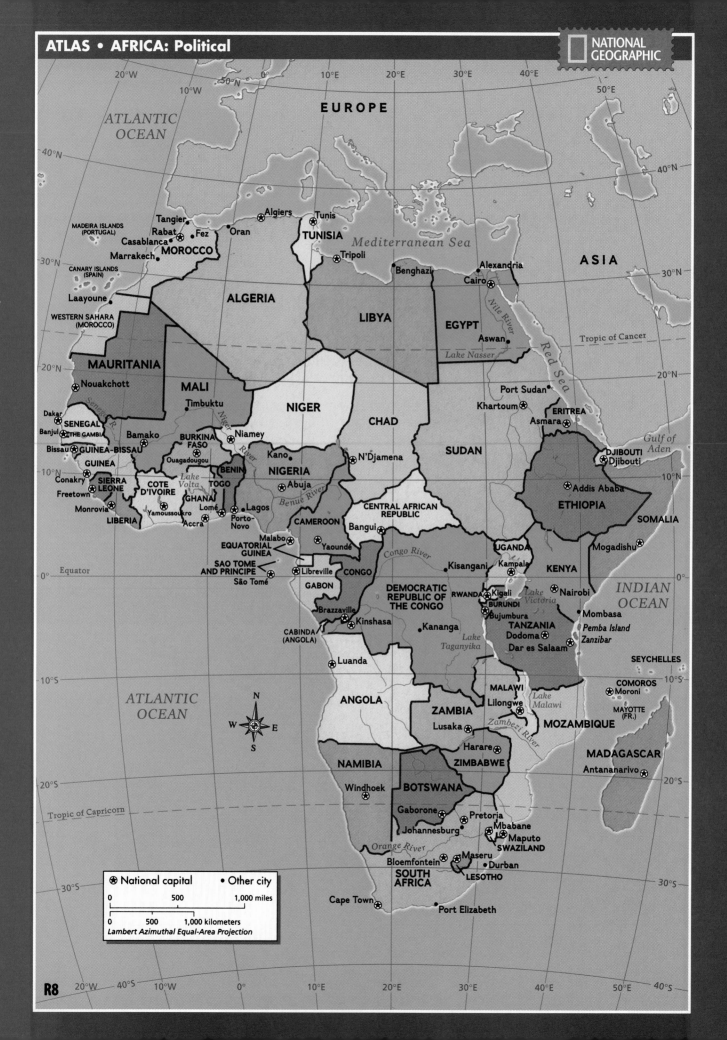

EUROPE

ATLANTIC OCEAN

ASIA

Mediterranean Sea

MADEIRA ISLANDS (PORTUGAL)

Tangier
Algiers
Tunis

Rabat • Fez
Oran
TUNISIA

Casablanca
MOROCCO
Tripoli

Marrakech

Benghazi
Alexandria
Cairo

CANARY ISLANDS (SPAIN)

ALGERIA
LIBYA
EGYPT

Laayoune

Nile River

WESTERN SAHARA (MOROCCO)

Aswan
Lake Nasser
Tropic of Cancer

MAURITANIA
Nouakchott

MALI
Timbuktu
NIGER
CHAD
SUDAN
Port Sudan
Khartoum
ERITREA
Asmara

Senegal R.

Dakar
SENEGAL
Bamako
BURKINA FASO
Niamey
Niger River
Kano
N'Djamena
Gulf of Aden

Banjul
THE GAMBIA
DJIBOUTI
Djibouti

Bissau
GUINEA-BISSAU
Ouagadougou
BENIN
NIGERIA

GUINEA
Lake Volta
TOGO
Abuja
CENTRAL AFRICAN REPUBLIC
Addis Ababa
ETHIOPIA

Conakry
SIERRA LEONE
COTE D'IVOIRE
GHANA
Lomé
Lagos
Benue River
Bangui
SOMALIA

Freetown
Yamoussoukro
Accra
Porto-Novo
CAMEROON
UGANDA
Mogadishu

Monrovia
LIBERIA
Malabo
EQUATORIAL GUINEA
Yaoundé
Congo River
Kisangani
Kampala
KENYA

SAO TOME AND PRINCIPE
Libreville
CONGO
DEMOCRATIC REPUBLIC OF THE CONGO
RWANDA
Kigali
Lake Victoria
Nairobi
INDIAN OCEAN

São Tomé
GABON
Equator

Brazzaville
Kinshasa
BURUNDI
Bujumbura
Mombasa

CABINDA (ANGOLA)
Kananga
TANZANIA
Dodoma
Pemba Island
Zanzibar

Luanda
Lake Tanganyika
Dar es Salaam
SEYCHELLES

ATLANTIC OCEAN
ANGOLA
MALAWI
Lilongwe
Lake Malawi
COMOROS
Moroni

ZAMBIA
MOZAMBIQUE
MAYOTTE (FR.)

Lusaka
Zambezi River
MADAGASCAR

N
W E
S

Harare
ZIMBABWE
Antananarivo

NAMIBIA
BOTSWANA

Windhoek
Gaborone
Pretoria
Mbabane
Maputo
SWAZILAND

Tropic of Capricorn

Johannesburg
Maseru
Durban
LESOTHO

Bloemfontein
SOUTH AFRICA
Port Elizabeth

Cape Town

⊛ National capital   • Other city

0   500   1,000 miles

0   500   1,000 kilometers
Lambert Azimuthal Equal-Area Projection

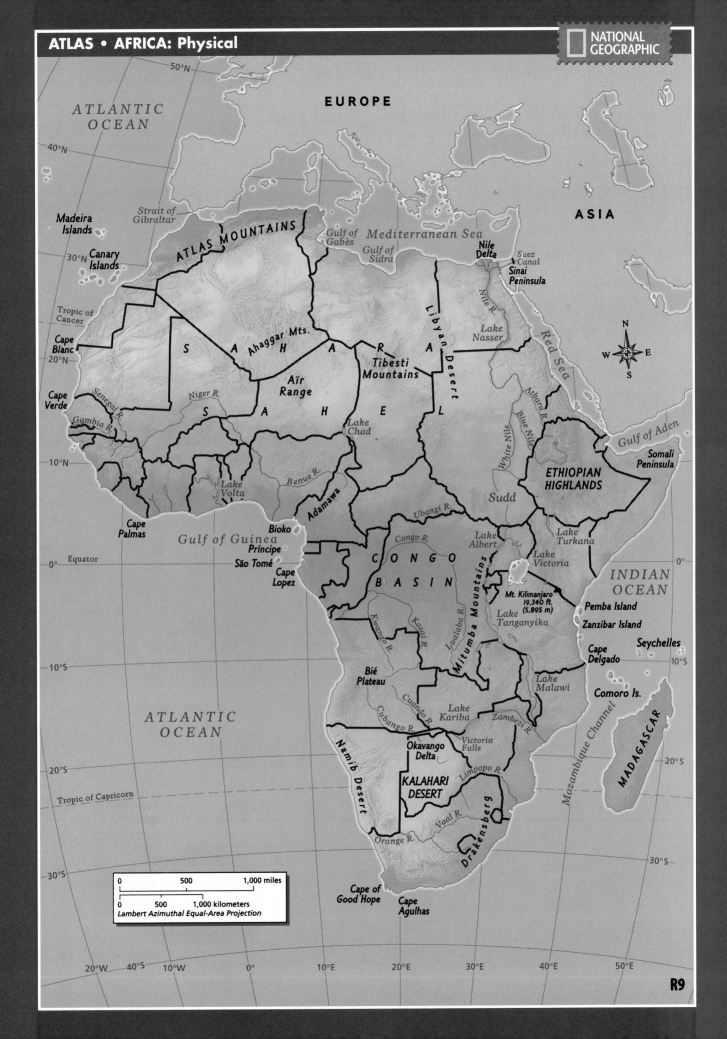

NATIONAL GEOGRAPHIC

EUROPE

ASIA

ATLANTIC OCEAN

Madeira Islands

Strait of Gibraltar

Canary Islands

Tropic of Cancer

Cape Blanc

Cape Verde

Gambia R.

Senegal R.

Niger R.

S A H A R A

ATLAS MOUNTAINS

Ahaggar Mts.

Aïr Range

S A H E L

Gulf of Gabès

Mediterranean Sea

Gulf of Sidra

Tibesti Mountains

Libyan Desert

Nile Delta

Suez Canal

Sinai Peninsula

Nile R.

Lake Nasser

Red Sea

Gulf of Aden

Somali Peninsula

Lake Chad

Benue R.

Lake Volta

Cape Palmas

Gulf of Guinea

Bioko

Príncipe

São Tomé

Cape Lopez

Adamawa

Equator

Congo R.

C O N G O B A S I N

Ubangi R.

Kwango R.

Kasai R.

Lualaba R.

Mitumba Mountains

Sudd

Lake Albert

Lake Turkana

ETHIOPIAN HIGHLANDS

Lake Victoria

White Nile

Blue Nile

Atbara R.

INDIAN OCEAN

Mt. Kilimanjaro 19,340 ft. (5,895 m)

Lake Tanganyika

Pemba Island

Zanzibar Island

Cape Delgado

Seychelles

Comoro Is.

Bié Plateau

Cuando R.

Cubango R.

Lake Kariba

Zambezi R.

Lake Malawi

Victoria Falls

Okavango Delta

Namib Desert

KALAHARI DESERT

Limpopo R.

Mozambique Channel

MADAGASCAR

ATLANTIC OCEAN

Tropic of Capricorn

Vaal R.

Orange R.

Drakensberg

Cape of Good Hope

Cape Agulhas

N W E S

50°N

40°N

30°N

20°N

10°N

0° Equator

10°S

20°S

30°S

0°

10°S

10°S

20°S

30°S

40°S

20°W

10°W

0°

10°E

20°E

30°E

40°E

50°E

0   500   1,000 miles
0   500   1,000 kilometers
Lambert Azimuthal Equal-Area Projection

R9

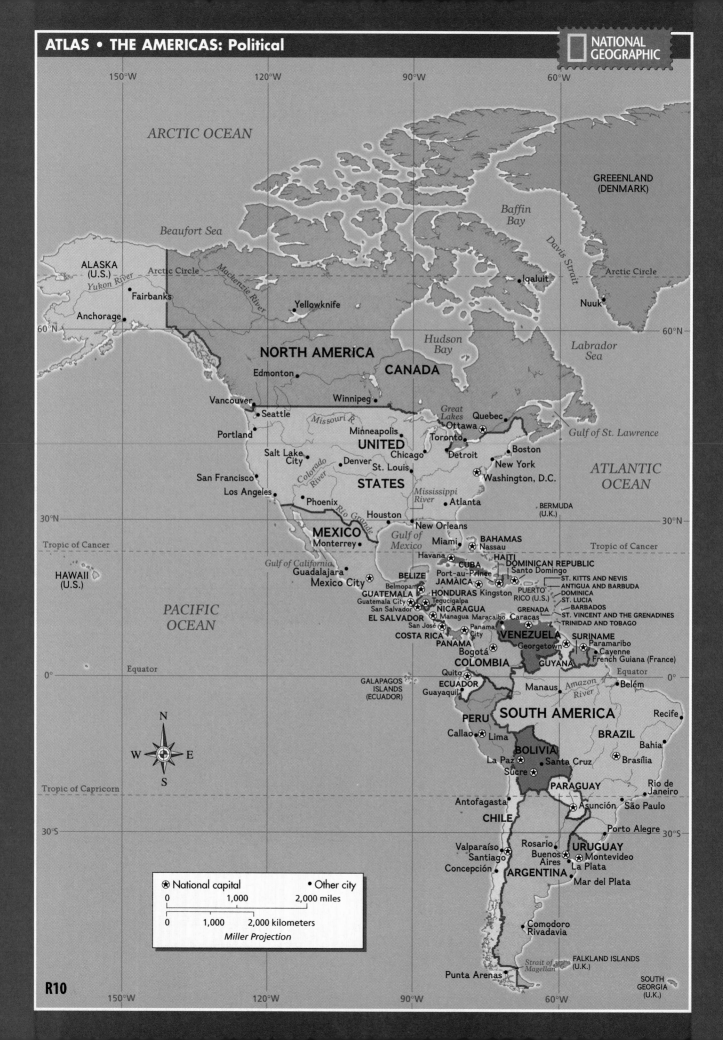

ARCTIC OCEAN

ALASKA (U.S.)

Arctic Circle
Yukon River
Mackenzie River

Beaufort Sea

Fairbanks

Anchorage

60°N

Baffin Bay

Davis Strait

Iqaluit

Arctic Circle

Nuuk

GREEENLAND (DENMARK)

NORTH AMERICA

CANADA

Hudson Bay

Labrador Sea

60°N

Edmonton

Vancouver
Seattle
Winnipeg
Missouri R.
Great Lakes
Quebec
Ottawa
Toronto
Gulf of St. Lawrence

Portland
Minneapolis
UNITED
Boston
Detroit
New York
ATLANTIC OCEAN

Salt Lake City
Denver
Chicago
St. Louis
Washington, D.C.

San Francisco
Colorado River
STATES

Los Angeles
Phoenix
Mississippi River
Atlanta
BERMUDA (U.K.)

30°N
Rio Grande
Houston
30°N

Tropic of Cancer
MEXICO
New Orleans
Tropic of Cancer
Monterrey
Gulf of Mexico
Miami
BAHAMAS
Nassau

Gulf of California
Havana
HAITI
DOMINICAN REPUBLIC

HAWAII (U.S.)
Guadalajara
CUBA
Port-au-Prince
Santo Domingo
ST. KITTS AND NEVIS

Mexico City
BELIZE
JAMAICA
PUERTO RICO (U.S.)
ANTIGUA AND BARBUDA

PACIFIC OCEAN
Belmopan
Kingston
DOMINICA

GUATEMALA
HONDURAS
ST. LUCIA

Guatemala City
Tegucigalpa
BARBADOS

San Salvador
NICARAGUA
GRENADA
ST. VINCENT AND THE GRENADINES

EL SALVADOR
Managua
Maracaibo
Caracas
TRINIDAD AND TOBAGO

San José
Panama City
VENEZUELA
SURINAME
Paramaribo

COSTA RICA
Georgetown
Cayenne

PANAMA
French Guiana (France)

Bogotá
GUYANA

COLOMBIA

Equator
Quito
Equator

GALAPAGOS ISLANDS (ECUADOR)
ECUADOR
Manaus
Amazon River
Belém

Guayaquil

PERU
SOUTH AMERICA
Recife

Callao
Lima
BRAZIL
Bahia

BOLIVIA
Brasília

N
La Paz
Santa Cruz

W   E
Sucre
Rio de Janeiro

S
PARAGUAY

Tropic of Capricorn
Antofagasta
Asunción
São Paulo

CHILE
Porto Alegre
30°S

30°S
Valparaíso
Rosario
URUGUAY

Santiago
Buenos Aires
Montevideo

Concepción
La Plata

ARGENTINA
Mar del Plata

National capital   • Other city

0   1,000   2,000 miles

0   1,000   2,000 kilometers
Miller Projection

Comodoro Rivadavia

FALKLAND ISLANDS (U.K.)

Strait of Magellan

R10
Punta Arenas
SOUTH GEORGIA (U.K.)

150°W   120°W   90°W   60°W

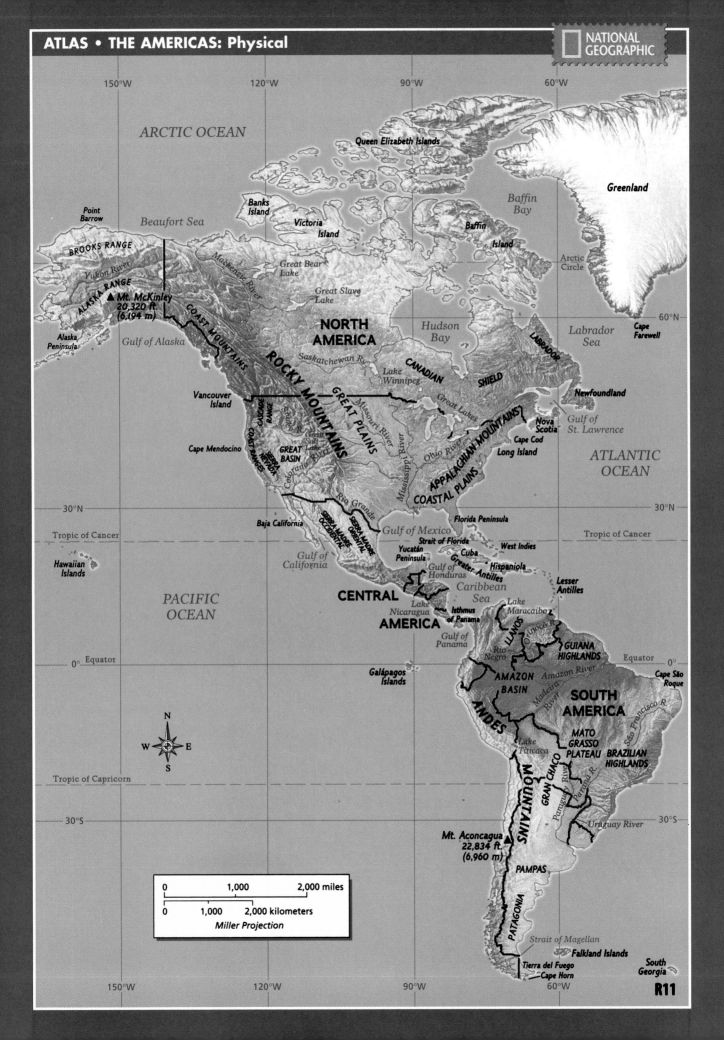

ARCTIC OCEAN

Queen Elizabeth Islands

Greenland

Banks Island

Victoria Island

Baffin Bay

Baffin Island

Point Barrow

Beaufort Sea

BROOKS RANGE

Yukon River

Mackenzie River

ALASKA RANGE

▲ Mt. McKinley 20,320 ft. (6,194 m)

Alaska Peninsula

Gulf of Alaska

Great Bear Lake

Great Slave Lake

NORTH AMERICA

Hudson Bay

Arctic Circle

60°N

Labrador Sea

Cape Farewell

COAST MOUNTAINS

Saskatchewan R.

CANADIAN

SHIELD

LABRADOR

Newfoundland

Vancouver Island

ROCKY MOUNTAINS

Lake Winnipeg

Great Lakes

Gulf of St. Lawrence

Nova Scotia

CASCADE RANGE

Snake R.

GREAT PLAINS

Missouri River

Cape Cod

Long Island

ATLANTIC OCEAN

Cape Mendocino

COAST RANGES

SIERRA NEVADA

GREAT BASIN

Great Salt Lake

Colorado River

Ohio River

APPALACHIAN MOUNTAINS

Mississippi River

COASTAL PLAINS

30°N

30°N

Tropic of Cancer

SIERRA MADRE OCCIDENTAL

SIERRA MADRE ORIENTAL

Rio Grande

Gulf of Mexico

Florida Peninsula

Tropic of Cancer

Baja California

Gulf of California

Yucatán Peninsula

Strait of Florida

West Indies

Cuba

Greater Antilles

Hispaniola

Hawaiian Islands

PACIFIC OCEAN

Gulf of Honduras

Caribbean Sea

Lesser Antilles

CENTRAL

Lake Nicaragua

Isthmus of Panama

Lake Maracaibo

AMERICA

Gulf of Panama

ILLANOS

Orinoco R.

GUIANA HIGHLANDS

Galápagos Islands

0° Equator

Rio Negro

AMAZON BASIN

Amazon River

Equator 0°

Cape São Roque

Madeira River

SOUTH AMERICA

ANDES

Lake Titicaca

MATO GRASSO PLATEAU

São Francisco R.

BRAZILIAN HIGHLANDS

GRAN CHACO

Paraná R.

N
W E
S

Paraguay River

Uruguay River

Tropic of Capricorn

30°S

30°S

Mt. Aconcagua 22,834 ft. (6,960 m)

MOUNTAINS

PAMPAS

0   1,000   2,000 miles
0   1,000   2,000 kilometers
Miller Projection

PATAGONIA

Strait of Magellan

Falkland Islands

Tierra del Fuego
Cape Horn

South Georgia

150°W

120°W

90°W

60°W

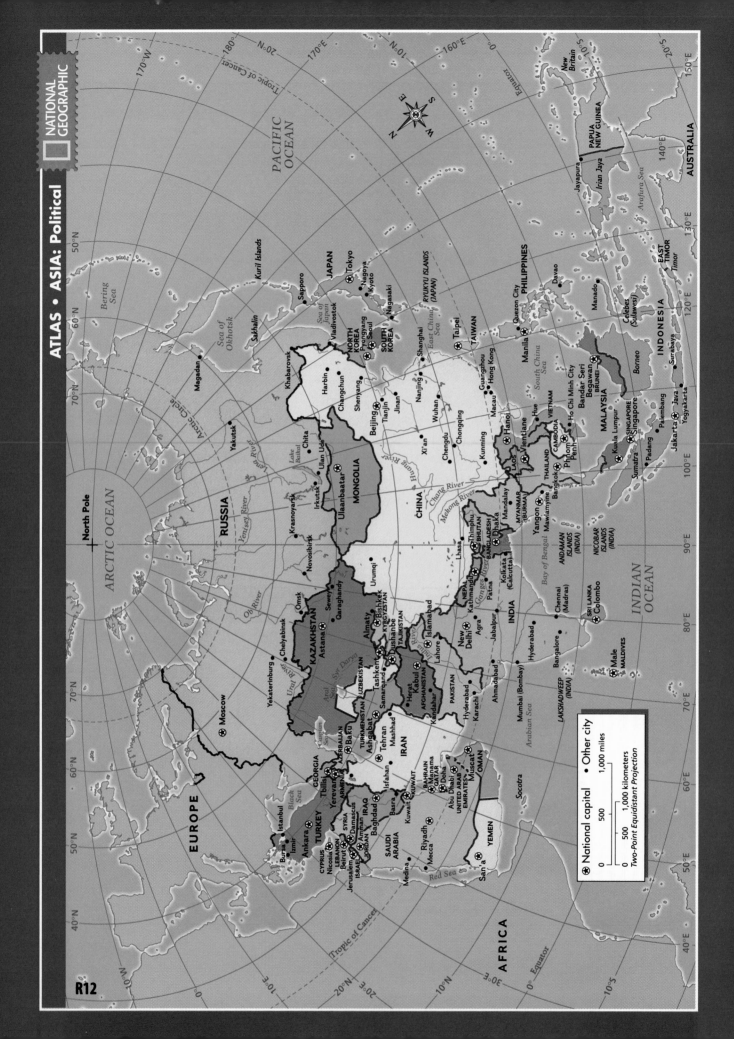

NATIONAL
GEOGRAPHIC

PACIFIC
OCEAN

ARCTIC OCEAN

North Pole

EUROPE

AFRICA

Tropic of Cancer

Equator

Arctic Circle

RUSSIA

Moscow

Yekaterinburg

Chelyabinsk

Omsk

Novosibirsk

Krasnoyarsk

Irkutsk

Chita

Ulan Ude

Yakutsk

Magadan

Khabarovsk

Vladivostok

Sakhalin

Kuril Islands

Bering
Sea

Sea of
Okhotsk

Sea of
Japan

JAPAN

Tokyo
Nagoya
Kyoto
Sapporo
Nagasaki

Ob River

Ural River

Yenisey River

Lena River

Lake
Baikal

MONGOLIA

Ulaanbaatar

Harbin

Changchun

Shenyang

NORTH
KOREA

Pyongyang

SOUTH
KOREA

Seoul

Beijing

Tianjin

Jinan

Shanghai

Nanjing

CHINA

Xi'an

Chengdu

Wuhan

Chongqing

Kunming

Guangzhou

Hong Kong

Macau

Taipei

TAIWAN

RYUKYU ISLANDS
(JAPAN)

East China
Sea

South China
Sea

PHILIPPINES

Quezon City

Manila

Davao

Manado

Chang River

Hwang River

Mekong River

Lhasa

Thimphu

BHUTAN

NEPAL

Kathmandu

Dhaka

BANGLADESH

Kolkata
(Calcutta)

Patna

New
Delhi

Agra

Jabalpur

INDIA

Hyderabad

Bangalore

Chennai
(Madras)

Mumbai (Bombay)

Ahmadabad

Karachi

Hyderabad

PAKISTAN

Lahore

Islamabad

Kabul

AFGHANISTAN

Kandahar

Herat

Mashhad

Tehran

IRAN

Isfahan

Mandalay

Yangon

MYANMAR
(BURMA)

Mawlamyine

Naypyidaw

Hanoi

Vientiane

LAOS

THAILAND

Bangkok

Phnom
Penh

CAMBODIA

VIETNAM

Ho Chi Minh City

Hue

Bandar Seri
Begawan

BRUNEI

MALAYSIA

Kuala Lumpur

SINGAPORE
Singapore

Sumatra

Padang

Palembang

Jakarta

INDONESIA

Borneo

Celebes
(Sulawesi)

Surabaya

Yogyakarta

Java

EAST
TIMOR

Timor

New
Britain

PAPUA
NEW GUINEA

Jayapura

Irian Jaya

AUSTRALIA

Arafura Sea

Bay of Bengal

ANDAMAN
ISLANDS
(INDIA)

NICOBAR
ISLANDS
(INDIA)

SRI LANKA

Colombo

Male
MALDIVES

LAKSHADWEEP
(INDIA)

INDIAN
OCEAN

Arabian Sea

Socotra

YEMEN

San'a

Red Sea

Mecca

Medina

SAUDI
ARABIA

Riyadh

Kuwait

KUWAIT

BAHRAIN
Manama

QATAR
Doha

Abu Dhabi

UNITED ARAB
EMIRATES

Muscat

OMAN

Basra

Baghdad

IRAQ

SYRIA

Damascus

Amman

JORDAN

ISRAEL

Jerusalem

LEBANON

Beirut

CYPRUS

Nicosia

TURKEY

Ankara

Istanbul

Izmir

Bursa

Black Sea

GEORGIA

Tbilisi

ARMENIA

Yerevan

AZERBAIJAN

Baku

Caspian
Sea

TURKMENISTAN

Ashgabat

Tashkent

UZBEKISTAN

Samarqand

Aral
Sea

Syr Darya

KAZAKHSTAN

Astana

Sewey

Qaraghandy

Almaty

Bishkek

KYRGYZSTAN

Dushanbe

TAJIKISTAN

Indus River

Ganges River

Urumqi

Kaesong

Ordos

Kuala Lumpur

Tigris River

KAZAKHSTAN

Omsk

Xi'an

Brahmaputra

Map legend:
⊛ National capital   • Other city

0   500   1,000 miles
0   500   1,000 kilometers
Two-Point Equidistant Projection

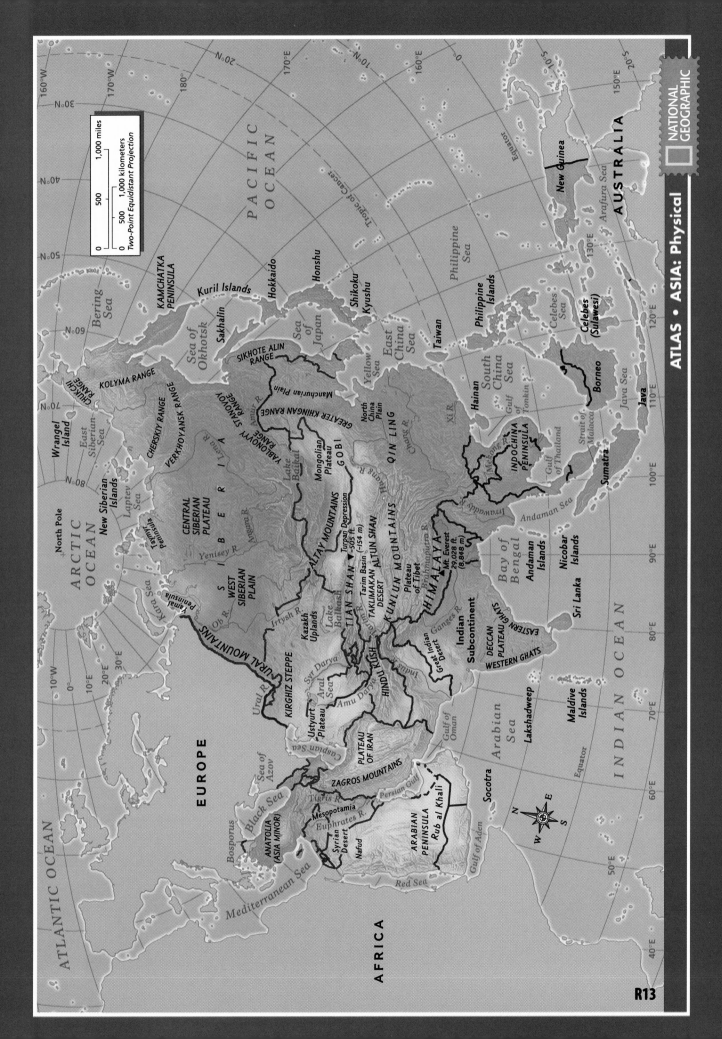

NATIONAL GEOGRAPHIC

1,000 miles
500
1,000 kilometers
500
Two-Point Equidistant Projection

ARCTIC OCEAN

North Pole

ATLANTIC OCEAN

EUROPE

AFRICA

PACIFIC OCEAN

AUSTRALIA

INDIAN OCEAN

Bering Sea
KAMCHATKA PENINSULA
Kuril Islands
Hokkaido
Honshu
Shikoku
Kyushu
Sea of Japan
Sea of Okhotsk
Sakhalin
CHUKCHI RANGE
KOLYMA RANGE
Wrangel Island
East Siberian Sea
CHERSKIY RANGE
VERKHOYANSK RANGE
New Siberian Islands
Laptev Sea
SIBERIA
Lena R.
YABLONOVYY RANGE
STANOVOY RANGE
SIKHOTE ALIN RANGE
Amur R.
GREATER KHINGAN RANGE
Manchurian Plain
Lake Baikal
Mongolian Plateau
GOBI
North China Plain
Yellow Sea
East China Sea
Taiwan
South China Sea
Hainan
Philippine Islands
Philippine Sea
Celebes Sea
Celebes (Sulawesi)
Borneo
Java Sea
Java
Sumatra
Strait of Malacca
Gulf of Thailand
INDOCHINA PENINSULA
Gulf of Tonkin
Mekong R.
Xi R.
Chang R.
QIN LING
Huang R.
CENTRAL SIBERIAN PLATEAU
Yenisey R.
Angara R.
ALTAY MOUNTAINS
Turpan Depression
-505 ft. (-154 m)
TIAN SHAN
Tarim Basin
TAKLIMAKAN DESERT
ALTUN SHAN
KUNLUN MOUNTAINS
Plateau of Tibet
HIMALAYA
Mt. Everest
29,028 ft. (8,848 m)
Brahmaputra R.
Irrawaddy R.
Andaman Sea
Bay of Bengal
Andaman Islands
Nicobar Islands
Sri Lanka
WEST SIBERIAN PLAIN
Ob R.
Irtysh R.
Lake Balkhash
Kazakh Uplands
Ganges R.
Indus R.
Indian Subcontinent
Great Indian Desert
DECCAN PLATEAU
EASTERN GHATS
WESTERN GHATS
URAL MOUNTAINS
Ural R.
KIRGHIZ STEPPE
Syr Darya
Aral Sea
Amu Darya
HINDU KUSH
Ustyurt Plateau
Caspian Sea
PLATEAU OF IRAN
Maldive Islands
Lakshadweep
Yamal Peninsula
Kara Sea
Taymyr Peninsula
Sea of Azov
Black Sea
Bosporus
ANATOLIA (ASIA MINOR)
Tigris R.
Mesopotamia
Euphrates R.
Syrian Desert
Nafud
ZAGROS MOUNTAINS
Persian Gulf
ARABIAN PENINSULA
Rub al Khali
Gulf of Oman
Arabian Sea
Socotra
Gulf of Aden
Red Sea
Mediterranean Sea
Equator
Tropic of Cancer
New Guinea
Arafura Sea

N
E
S
W

160°W 170°W 180° 170°E 160°E 150°E 130°E 120°E 110°E 100°E 90°E 80°E 70°E 60°E 50°E 40°E
30°N 40°N 50°N 60°N 70°N 80°N
20°E 10°E 0° 10°W 20°W 30°E
20°N 10°N 0° 10°S 20°S

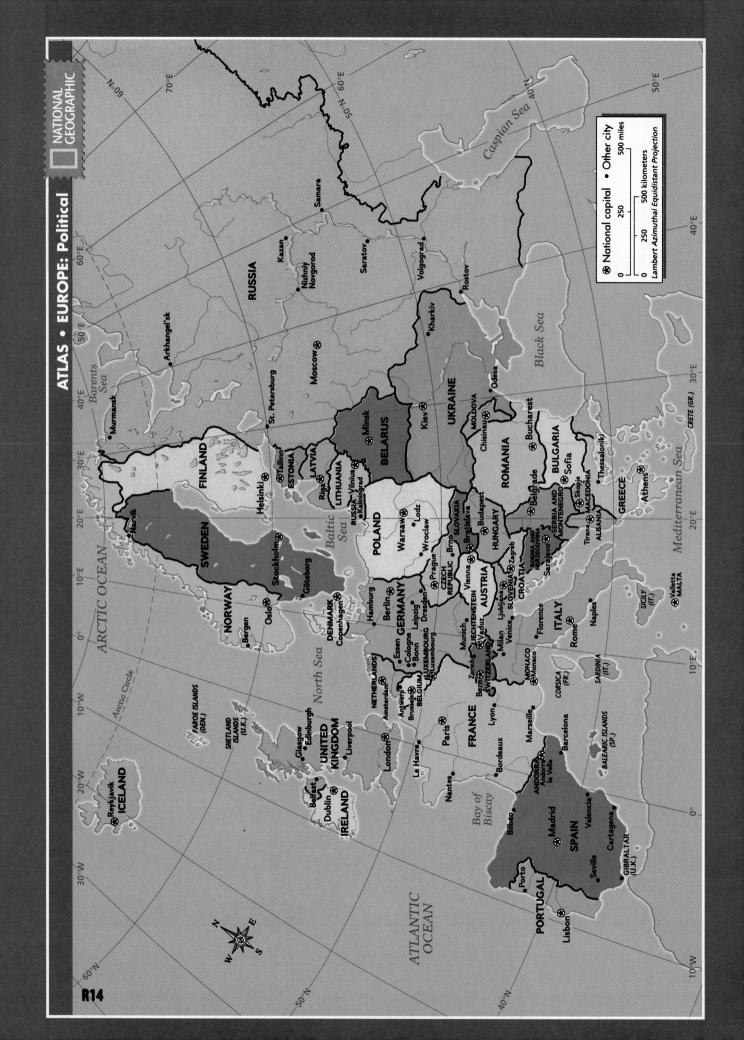

NATIONAL
GEOGRAPHIC

National capital • **Other city**

0   250   500 miles
0   250   500 kilometers
Lambert Azimuthal Equidistant Projection

RUSSIA

Arkhangel'sk

Murmansk

Barents Sea

Samara

Kazan

Nizhniy Novgorod

Saratov

Volgograd

Moscow

St. Petersburg

Rostov

Kharkiv

Caspian Sea

FINLAND

Helsinki

Tallinn

ESTONIA

LATVIA

Riga

Minsk

BELARUS

Kiev

UKRAINE

Odesa

Black Sea

MOLDOVA

Chisinau

Bucharest

ROMANIA

BULGARIA

Sofia

Belgrade

SERBIA AND MONTENEGRO

Skopje

MACEDONIA

Thessaloníki

GREECE

Athens

Vilnius

LITHUANIA

Kaliningrad

RUSSIA

SWEDEN

Narvik

Stockholm

Göteborg

Oslo

NORWAY

Bergen

DENMARK

Copenhagen

Baltic Sea

POLAND

Warsaw

Lodz

Wroclaw

Brno

Prague

CZECH REPUBLIC

SLOVAKIA

Bratislava

Budapest

HUNGARY

Zagreb

CROATIA

SLOVENIA

Ljubljana

BOSNIA AND HERZEGOVINA

Sarajevo

Tirana

ALBANIA

Hamburg

Berlin

Leipzig

Dresden

GERMANY

Essen

Cologne

Bonn

LUXEMBOURG

Luxembourg

NETHERLANDS

Amsterdam

Antwerp

Brussels

BELGIUM

Munich

LIECHTENSTEIN

Vaduz

Zurich

SWITZERLAND

Bern

AUSTRIA

Vienna

Milan

Venice

MONACO

Monaco

Florence

Rome

ITALY

Naples

Valletta

MALTA

SICILY (IT.)

SARDINIA (IT.)

CORSICA (FR.)

Mediterranean Sea

CRETE (GR.)

FRANCE

Paris

Le Havre

Nantes

Bordeaux

Lyon

Marseille

Bay of Biscay

Barcelona

BALEARIC ISLANDS (SP.)

ANDORRA

Andorra la Vella

Bilbao

Madrid

SPAIN

Valencia

Cartagena

Seville

GIBRALTAR (U.K.)

Porto

PORTUGAL

Lisbon

Glasgow

Edinburgh

UNITED KINGDOM

Liverpool

London

Belfast

Dublin

IRELAND

SHETLAND ISLANDS (U.K.)

FAROE ISLANDS (DEN.)

Reykjavik

ICELAND

ARCTIC OCEAN

Arctic Circle

North Sea

ATLANTIC OCEAN

N
W   E
S

R14

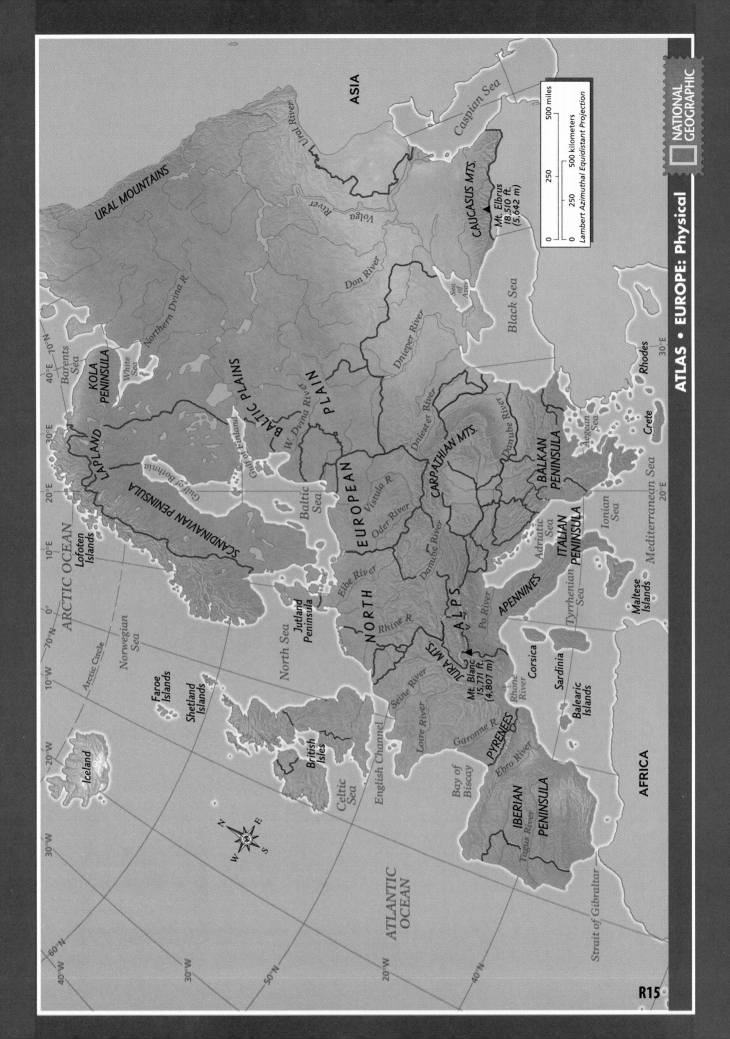

ASIA

URAL MOUNTAINS

Ural River

Volga River

Caspian Sea

CAUCASUS MTS.

Mt. Elbrus
18,510 ft.
(5,642 m)

Black Sea

Don River

Sea of Azov

Dnieper River

500 miles

250

500 kilometers

250

250

0

Lambert Azimuthal Equidistant Projection

Barents Sea

40°E

70°N

KOLA PENINSULA

White Sea

Northern Dvina R.

BALTIC PLAINS

PLAIN

30°E

LAPLAND

Gulf of Finland

W. Dvina River

EUROPEAN

Dniester River

CARPATHIAN MTS.

Danube River

BALKAN PENINSULA

Rhodes

30°E

SCANDINAVIAN PENINSULA

20°E

Baltic Sea

Vistula R.

Oder River

Danube River

ALPS

Aegean Sea

Crete

ARCTIC OCEAN

Lofoten Islands

10°E

NORTH

Elbe River

Rhine R.

Po River

APENNINES

ITALIAN PENINSULA

Ionian Sea

Mediterranean Sea

20°E

Norwegian Sea

0°

Jutland Peninsula

North Sea

Adriatic Sea

Tyrrhenian Sea

Maltese Islands

70°N

Arctic Circle

10°W

Faroe Islands

Shetland Islands

JURA MTS.

Mt. Blanc
15,771 ft.
(4,807 m)

Seine River

Loire River

Corsica

Sardinia

Balearic Islands

20°W

British Isles

Celtic Sea

English Channel

Bay of Biscay

PYRENEES

Garonne R.

Rhône River

Iceland

30°W

ATLANTIC OCEAN

Ebro River

IBERIAN PENINSULA

Tagus River

Strait of Gibraltar

AFRICA

40°W

30°W

50°W

20°W

40°N

60°N

N E S W

R15

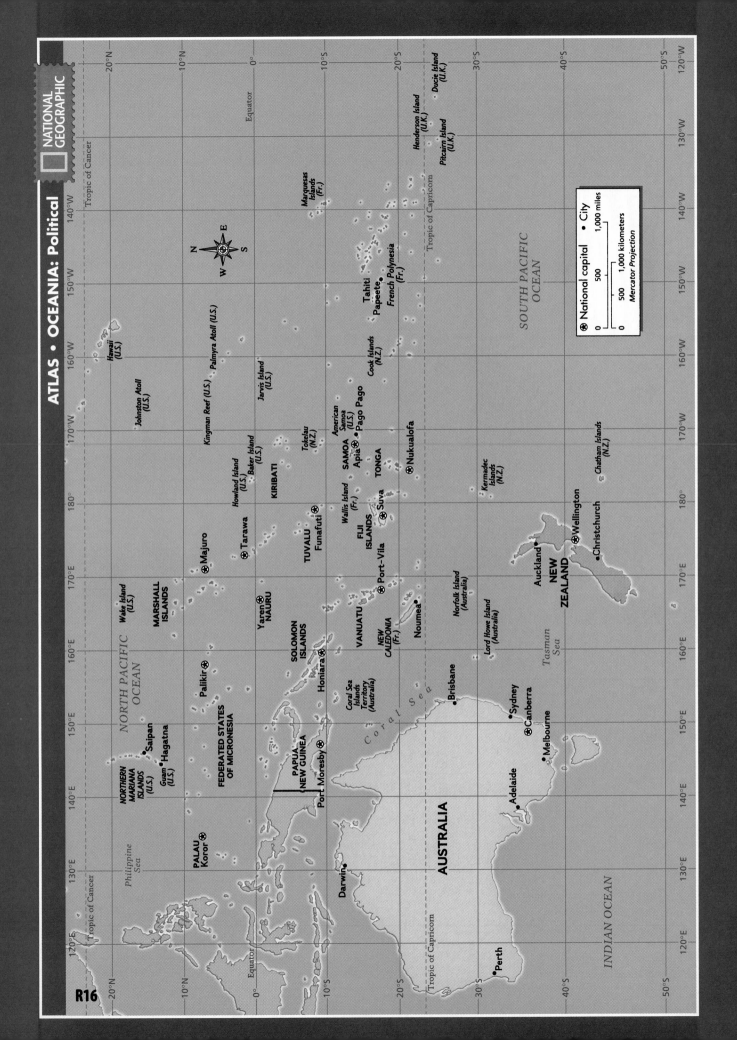

NATIONAL GEOGRAPHIC

Scale legend:
⊕ National capital
• City

0   500   1,000 miles
0   500   1,000 kilometers
Mercator Projection

20°N
10°N
0°
10°S
20°S
30°S
40°S
50°S

120°E
130°E
140°E
150°E
160°E
170°E
180°
170°W
160°W
150°W
140°W
130°W
120°W
110°W

Tropic of Cancer
Equator
Tropic of Capricorn

Hawaii (U.S.)
Johnston Atoll (U.S.)
Kingman Reef (U.S.)
Palmyra Atoll (U.S.)
Jarvis Island (U.S.)
Howland Island (U.S.)
Baker Island (U.S.)
KIRIBATI
Tarawa ⊕
Majuro ⊕
MARSHALL ISLANDS
Wake Island (U.S.)
Yaren ⊕ NAURU
TUVALU
Funafuti ⊕
Tokelau (N.Z.)
American Samoa (U.S.)
Pago Pago
SAMOA
Apia ⊕
Wallis Island (Fr.)
FIJI ISLANDS
Suva ⊕
TONGA
Nukualofa ⊕
Marquesas Islands (Fr.)
Tahiti
Papeete
French Polynesia (Fr.)
Cook Islands (N.Z.)
Henderson Island (U.K.)
Ducie Island (U.K.)
Pitcairn Island (U.K.)

NORTH PACIFIC OCEAN
SOUTH PACIFIC OCEAN
Philippine Sea

NORTHERN MARIANA ISLANDS (U.S.)
Saipan
Guam (U.S.)
Hagatna
PALAU
Koror ⊕
FEDERATED STATES OF MICRONESIA
Palikir ⊕
SOLOMON ISLANDS
Honiara ⊕
PAPUA NEW GUINEA
Port Moresby ⊕
VANUATU
Port-Vila ⊕
NEW CALEDONIA (Fr.)
Noumea
Norfolk Island (Australia)
Kermadec Islands (N.Z.)
Lord Howe Island (Australia)
Coral Sea Islands Territory (Australia)
Coral Sea
Darwin
AUSTRALIA
Brisbane
Perth
Adelaide
Sydney
Canberra ⊕
Melbourne
Tasman Sea
NEW ZEALAND
Auckland
Wellington ⊕
Christchurch
Chatham Islands (N.Z.)
INDIAN OCEAN

R16

South China Sea

20°N

Tropic of Cancer

10°N

Borneo

Philippine Islands

Philippine Sea

Palau

Equator

Sulawesi (Celebes)

East Timor

Timor

Arafura Sea

INDIAN OCEAN

AUSTRALIA

GREAT VICTORIA DESERT

Kimberley Plateau

Macdonnell Ranges

GREAT DIVIDING RANGE

Mt. Kosciuszko 7,310 ft. (2,228 m)

Murray River

Darling River

Tasmania

Gulf of Carpentaria

Torres Strait

New Guinea

Coral Sea

Solomon Islands

M E L A N E S I A

Santa Cruz Island

Vanuatu

New Caledonia

Lord Howe Island

Tasman Sea

NEW ZEALAND

North Island

Mt. Cook 12,349 ft. (3,764 m)

South Island

Stewart Island

Norfolk Island

Kermadec Islands

Chatham Islands

C a r o l i n e   I s l a n d s

Yap Islands

Guam

Northern Mariana Islands

Tropic of Cancer

NORTH PACIFIC OCEAN

M I C R O N E S I A

Wake Island

Bikini Atoll

Marshall Islands

Ratak Chain

Ralik Chain

Nauru

Gilbert Islands

Tuvalu

Fiji Islands

Howland Island

Baker Island

Phoenix Islands

Tokelau

Samoa Islands

Tonga Islands

Johnston Atoll

Kingman Reef

Palmyra Atoll

Jarvis Island

P O L Y N E S I A

Line Islands

Cook Islands

Society Islands

Austral Islands

French Polynesia

Tuamotu Archipelago

Tropic of Capricorn

SOUTH PACIFIC OCEAN

Hawaiian Islands

Marquesas Islands

Pitcairn Island

Henderson Island

Ducie Island

Equator

N
W   E
S

120°E 130°E 140°E 150°E 160°E 170°E 180° 170°W 160°W 150°W 140°W 130°W 120°W

20°N 10°N 0° 10°S 20°S 30°S 40°S 50°S

0   500   1,000 miles

0   500   1,000 kilometers

Mercator Projection

Reference

Countries of the World

AFGHANISTAN

CAPITAL ★ Kabul

POPULATION: 25.8 million

MAJOR LANGUAGES: Pashtu and Afghan Persian

AREA: 250,000 sq mi; 647,500 sq km

LOCATION: Asia

ALBANIA

CAPITAL ★ Tirana

POPULATION: 3.5 million

MAJOR LANGUAGES: Albanian and Greek

AREA: 11,100 sq mi; 28,748 sq km

LOCATION: Europe

ALGERIA

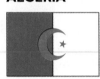

CAPITAL ★ Algiers

POPULATION: 31.2 million

MAJOR LANGUAGES: Arabic, French, and Berber

AREA: 919,595 sq mi; 2,381,751 sq km

LOCATION: Africa

ANDORRA

CAPITAL ★ Andorra la Vella

POPULATION: 67,600

MAJOR LANGUAGES: Catalan, French, and Castilian Spanish

AREA: 181 sq mi; 468 sq km

LOCATION: Europe

ANGOLA

CAPITAL ★ Luanda

POPULATION: 10.4 million

MAJOR LANGUAGES: Portuguese and Bantu

AREA: 481,350 sq mi; 1,246,700 sq km

LOCATION: Africa

ANTIGUA AND BARBUDA

CAPITAL ★ St. John's

POPULATION: 67,000

MAJOR LANGUAGE: English

AREA: 171 sq mi; 442 sq km

LOCATION: Caribbean Sea

ARGENTINA

CAPITAL ★ Buenos Aires

POPULATION: 37.4 million

MAJOR LANGUAGES: Spanish, English, and Italian

AREA: 1,072,067 sq mi; 2,736,690 sq km

LOCATION: South America

ARMENIA

CAPITAL ★ Yerevan

POPULATION: 3.3 million

MAJOR LANGUAGE: Armenian

AREA: 11,500 sq mi; 29,800 sq km

LOCATION: Asia

AUSTRALIA

CAPITAL ★ Canberra

POPULATION: 19.2 million

MAJOR LANGUAGES: English and aboriginal languages

AREA: 2,966,150 sq mi; 7,686,500 sq km

LOCATION: Pacific Ocean

AUSTRIA

CAPITAL ★ Vienna

POPULATION: 8.1 million

MAJOR LANGUAGE: German

AREA: 32,375 sq mi; 83,851 sq km

LOCATION: Europe

AZERBAIJAN

CAPITAL ★ Baku

POPULATION: 7.7 million

MAJOR LANGUAGES: Azeri, Russian, and Armenian

AREA: 33,430 sq mi; 86,600 sq km

LOCATION: Asia

THE BAHAMAS

CAPITAL ★ Nassau

POPULATION: 0.3 million

MAJOR LANGUAGES: English and Creole

AREA: 5,380 sq mi; 13,940 sq km

LOCATION: Caribbean Sea

BAHRAIN

CAPITAL ★ Manama

POPULATION: 0.6 million

MAJOR LANGUAGES: Arabic, English, Farsi, and Urdu

AREA: 240 sq mi; 620 sq km

LOCATION: Asia

BANGLADESH

CAPITAL ★ Dhaka

POPULATION: 131.3 million

MAJOR LANGUAGES: Bangla and English

AREA: 55,598 sq mi; 143,998 sq km

LOCATION: Asia

BARBADOS

CAPITAL ★ Bridgetown

POPULATION: 0.3 million

MAJOR LANGUAGE: English

AREA: 166 sq mi; 430 sq km

LOCATION: Caribbean Sea

BELARUS

CAPITAL ★ Minsk

POPULATION: 10.4 million

MAJOR LANGUAGES: Byelorussian and Russian

AREA: 80,200 sq mi; 207,600 sq km

LOCATION: Europe

BELGIUM

CAPITAL ★ Brussels

POPULATION: 10.3 million

MAJOR LANGUAGES: Dutch (Flemish) and French

AREA: 11,781 sq mi; 30,518 sq km

LOCATION: Europe

BELIZE

CAPITAL ★ Belmopan

POPULATION: 0.3 million

MAJOR LANGUAGES: English, Creole, and Spanish

AREA: 8,867 sq mi; 22,965 sq km

LOCATION: North America

BENIN

CAPITAL ★ Porto-Novo

POPULATION: 6.4 million

MAJOR LANGUAGES: French and Fon

AREA: 43,483 sq mi; 112,620 sq km

LOCATION: Africa

BHUTAN

CAPITAL ★ Thimphu

POPULATION: 2.0 million

MAJOR LANGUAGES: Dzongkha and Nepali

AREA: 18,147 sq mi; 47,000 sq km

LOCATION: Asia

BOLIVIA

CAPITALS ★ Sucre (judicial) and La Paz (administrative)

POPULATION: 8.3 million

MAJOR LANGUAGES: Spanish, Quechua, and Aymará

AREA: 424,162 sq mi; 1,098,580 sq km

LOCATION: South America

BOSNIA AND HERZEGOVINA

CAPITAL ★ Sarajevo

POPULATION: 3.9 million

MAJOR LANGUAGES: Serbian, Croatian, Bosnian

AREA: 19,741 sq mi; 51,129 sq km

LOCATION: Europe

BOTSWANA

CAPITAL ★ Gaborone

POPULATION: 1.6 million

MAJOR LANGUAGES: English and Setswana

AREA: 231,800 sq mi; 600,360 sq km

LOCATION: Africa

BRAZIL

CAPITAL ★ Brasília

POPULATION: 162.7 million

MAJOR LANGUAGES: Portuguese, Spanish, French, and English

AREA: 3,286,470 sq mi; 8,511,957 sq km

LOCATION: South America

BRUNEI

CAPITAL ★ Bandar Seri Begawan

POPULATION: 0.3 million

MAJOR LANGUAGES: Malay, English, and Chinese

AREA: 2,228 sq mi; 5,770 sq km

LOCATION: Asia

BULGARIA

CAPITAL ★ Sofia

POPULATION: 8.6 million

MAJOR LANGUAGE: Bulgarian

AREA: 42,822 sq mi; 110,910 sq km

LOCATION: Europe

BURKINA FASO

CAPITAL ★ Ouagadougou

POPULATION: 12.3 million

MAJOR LANGUAGES: French and Sudanic languages

AREA: 105,870 sq mi; 274,200 sq km

LOCATION: Africa

BURUNDI

CAPITAL ★ Bujumbura

POPULATION: 6.2 million

MAJOR LANGUAGES: Kirundi, French, and Swahili

AREA: 10,745 sq mi; 27,830 sq km

LOCATION: Africa

CAMBODIA

CAPITAL ★ Phnom Penh

POPULATION: 12.5 million

MAJOR LANGUAGES: Khmer and French

AREA: 69,900 sq mi; 181,040 sq km

LOCATION: Asia

CAMEROON

CAPITAL ★ Yaoundé

POPULATION: 15.8 million

MAJOR LANGUAGES: English and French

AREA: 183,567 sq mi; 475,440 sq km

LOCATION: Africa

CANADA

CAPITAL ★ Ottawa

POPULATION: 31.6 million

MAJOR LANGUAGES: English and French

AREA: 3,851,788 sq mi; 9,976,148 sq km

LOCATION: North America

Countings of the World

CAPE VERDE

CAPITAL ★ Praia
POPULATION: 0.4 million
MAJOR LANGUAGES: Portuguese and Crioulo
AREA: 1,557 sq mi; 4,033 sq km
LOCATION: Africa

CENTRAL AFRICAN REPUBLIC

CAPITAL ★ Bangui
POPULATION: 3.6 million
MAJOR LANGUAGES: French and Sango
AREA: 240,534 sq mi; 622,984 sq km
LOCATION: Africa

CHAD

CAPITAL ★ N'Djamena
POPULATION: 8.7 million
MAJOR LANGUAGES: French and Arabic
AREA: 495,752 sq mi; 1,284,000 sq km
LOCATION: Africa

CHILE

CAPITAL ★ Santiago
POPULATION: 15.3 million
MAJOR LANGUAGE: Spanish
AREA: 292,258 sq mi; 756,950 sq km
LOCATION: South America

CHINA

CAPITAL ★ Beijing
POPULATION: 1.273 billion
MAJOR LANGUAGES: Mandarin and local Chinese dialects
AREA: 3,705,386 sq mi; 9,596,960 sq km
LOCATION: Asia

COLOMBIA

CAPITAL ★ Bogotá
POPULATION: 40.4 million
MAJOR LANGUAGE: Spanish
AREA: 439,735 sq mi; 1,138,910 sq km
LOCATION: South America

COMOROS

CAPITAL ★ Moroni
POPULATION: 0.6 million
MAJOR LANGUAGES: French, Arabic, and Comoran
AREA: 838 sq mi; 2,170 sq km
LOCATION: Indian Ocean

CONGO

CAPITAL ★ Brazzaville
POPULATION: 2.9 million
MAJOR LANGUAGES: French, Kikongo, Lingala, and other African languages
AREA: 132,046 sq mi; 342,000 sq km
LOCATION: Africa

DEMOCRATIC REPUBLIC OF CONGO

CAPITAL ★ Kinshasa
POPULATION: 53.6 million
MAJOR LANGUAGES: French, Swahili, Lingala, Kikongo and other Bantu dialects
AREA: 905,365 sq mi; 2,344,885 sq km
LOCATION: Africa

COSTA RICA

CAPITAL ★ San José
POPULATION: 3.5 million
MAJOR LANGUAGES: Spanish and English
AREA: 19,652 sq mi; 50,898 sq km
LOCATION: North America

CÔTE D'IVOIRE (Ivory Coast)

CAPITAL ★ Yamoussoukro
POPULATION: 14.8 million
MAJOR LANGUAGES: French and many African languages
AREA: 124,502 sq mi; 322,462 sq km
LOCATION: Africa

CROATIA

CAPITAL ★ Zagreb
POPULATION: 4.3 million
MAJOR LANGUAGE: Serbo-Croatian
AREA: 21,829 sq mi; 56,537 sq km
LOCATION: Europe

CUBA

CAPITAL ★ Havana
POPULATION: 11.2 million
MAJOR LANGUAGE: Spanish
AREA: 44,218 sq mi; 114,524 sq km
LOCATION: Caribbean Sea

CYPRUS

CAPITAL ★ Nicosia
POPULATION: 0.8 million
MAJOR LANGUAGES: Greek, Turkish, and English
AREA: 3,572 sq mi; 9,251 sq km
LOCATION: Mediterranean Sea

CZECH REPUBLIC

CAPITAL ★ Prague
POPULATION: 10.3 million
MAJOR LANGUAGES: Czech and Slovak
AREA: 30,464 sq mi; 78,902 sq km
LOCATION: Europe

DENMARK

CAPITAL ★ Copenhagen
POPULATION: 5.4 million
MAJOR LANGUAGES: Danish and Faeroese
AREA: 16,631 sq mi; 43,075 sq mi
LOCATION: Europe

DJIBOUTI

CAPITAL ★ Djibouti
POPULATION: 0.5 million
LANGUAGES: Arabic, French
AREA: 8,490 sq mi; 22,000 sq km
LOCATION: Africa

DOMINICA

CAPITAL ★ Roseau
POPULATION: 0.1 million
LANGUAGES: English, Creole
AREA: 290 sq mi; 751 sq km
LOCATION: Caribbean Sea

DOMINICAN REPUBLIC

CAPITAL ★ Santo Domingo
POPULATION: 8.6 million
MAJOR LANGUAGES: Spanish
AREA: 18,704 sq mi; 48,442 sq km
LOCATION: Caribbean Sea

EAST TIMOR

CAPITAL ★ Dili
POPULATION: 749,298
LANGUAGES: Tetun, Mambae, Makasae, other local languages
AREA: 5,763 sq mi; 14,874 sq km
LOCATION: Asia

ECUADOR

CAPITAL ★ Quito
POPULATION: 13.2 million
LANGUAGES: Spanish, Quechua
AREA: 106,822 sq mi; 276,670 sq km
LOCATION: South America

EGYPT

CAPITAL ★ Cairo
POPULATION: 69.5 million
MAJOR LANGUAGES: Arabic, English, and French
AREA: 386,900 sq mi; 1,002,000 sq km
LOCATION: Africa

EL SALVADOR

CAPITAL ★ San Salvador
POPULATION: 6.2 million
LANGUAGES: Spanish, Nahua
AREA: 8,260 sq mi; 21,393 sq km
LOCATION: North America

EQUATORIAL GUINEA
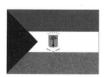
CAPITAL ★ Malabo
POPULATION: 0.5 million
MAJOR LANGUAGES: Spanish, Fang, and Bubi
AREA: 10,830 sq mi; 28,051 sq km
LOCATION: Africa

ERITREA

CAPITAL ★ Asmara
POPULATION: 4.3 million
LANGUAGES: Tigrinya, Arabic
AREA: 45,754 sq mi; 121,300 sq km
LOCATION: Africa

ESTONIA

CAPITAL ★ Tallinn
POPULATION: 1.5 million
MAJOR LANGUAGES: Estonian, Latvian, Lithuanian, and Russian
AREA: 18,370 sq mi; 47,549 sq km
LOCATION: Europe

ETHIOPIA

CAPITAL ★ Addis Ababa
POPULATION: 65.9 million
MAJOR LANGUAGES: Amharic, English, and local languages
AREA: 446,952 sq mi; 1,157,585 sq km
LOCATION: Africa

FIJI

CAPITAL ★ Suva
POPULATION: 0.8 million
MAJOR LANGUAGES: Fijian, Hindi, and English
AREA: 7,078 sq mi; 18,333 sq km
LOCATION: Pacific Ocean

FINLAND

CAPITAL ★ Helsinki
POPULATION: 5.1 million
MAJOR LANGUAGES: Finnish and Swedish
AREA: 130,558 sq mi; 338,145 sq km
LOCATION: Europe

FRANCE

CAPITAL ★ Paris
POPULATION: 59.6 million
MAJOR LANGUAGE: French
AREA: 211,208 sq mi; 547,030 sq km
LOCATION: Europe

GABON

CAPITAL ★ Libreville
POPULATION: 1.2 million
MAJOR LANGUAGES: French, Fang, and Bantu dialects
AREA: 103,346 sq mi; 267,667 sq km
LOCATION: Africa

THE GAMBIA

CAPITAL ★ Banjul
POPULATION: 1.4 million
MAJOR LANGUAGES: English and Mandinka
AREA: 4,093 sq mi; 10,600 sq km
LOCATION: Africa

GEORGIA

CAPITAL ★ Tbilisi
POPULATION: 5.0 million
MAJOR LANGUAGES: Georgian and Russian
AREA: 26,900 sq mi; 69,700 sq km
LOCATION: Asia and Europe

Countries of the World
Germany • Iraq

GERMANY

CAPITAL ★ Berlin
POPULATION: 83.0 million
MAJOR LANGUAGE: German
AREA: 137,826 sq mi; 356,970 sq km
LOCATION: Europe

GHANA

CAPITAL ★ Accra
POPULATION: 19.9 million
MAJOR LANGUAGES: English and African languages
AREA: 92,100 sq mi; 238,537 sq km
LOCATION: Africa

GREECE

CAPITAL ★ Athens
POPULATION: 10.6 million
MAJOR LANGUAGES: Greek, English, and French
AREA: 50,961 sq mi; 131,990 sq km
LOCATION: Europe

GRENADA

CAPITAL ★ St. George's
POPULATION: 0.1 million
MAJOR LANGUAGES: English
AREA: 133 sq mi; 344 sq km
LOCATION: Caribbean Sea

GUATEMALA

CAPITAL ★ Guatemala City
POPULATION: 13.0 million
MAJOR LANGUAGES: Spanish and Indian languages
AREA: 42,042 sq mi; 108,889 sq km
LOCATION: North America

GUINEA

CAPITAL ★ Conakry
POPULATION: 7.6 million
MAJOR LANGUAGES: French, Soussou, and Manika
AREA: 94,925 sq mi; 245,857 sq km
LOCATION: Africa

GUINEA-BISSAU

CAPITAL ★ Bissau
POPULATION: 1.3 million
MAJOR LANGUAGES: Portuguese and Crioulo
AREA: 13,948 sq mi; 36,125 sq km
LOCATION: Africa

GUYANA

CAPITAL ★ Georgetown
POPULATION: 0.7 million
MAJOR LANGUAGES: English and Amerindian dialects
AREA: 83,000 sq mi; 214,969 sq km
LOCATION: South America

HAITI

CAPITAL ★ Port-au-Prince
POPULATION: 7.0 million
MAJOR LANGUAGES: French and French Creole
AREA: 10,714 sq mi; 27,750 sq km
LOCATION: Caribbean Sea

HONDURAS

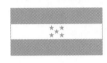

CAPITAL ★ Tegucigalpa
POPULATION: 6.4 million
MAJOR LANGUAGE: Spanish
AREA: 43,872 sq mi; 112,492 sq km
LOCATION: North America

HUNGARY

CAPITAL ★ Budapest
POPULATION: 10.1 million
MAJOR LANGUAGE: Hungarian
AREA: 35,919 sq mi; 93,030 sq km
LOCATION: Europe

ICELAND

CAPITAL ★ Reykjavik
POPULATION: 0.3 million
MAJOR LANGUAGE: Icelandic
AREA: 39,709 sq mi; 102,846 sq km
LOCATION: Europe

INDIA

CAPITAL ★ New Delhi
POPULATION: 1 billion
MAJOR LANGUAGES: Hindi, English, and 14 other official languages
AREA: 1,229,737 sq mi; 3,185,019 sq km
LOCATION: Asia

INDONESIA

CAPITAL ★ Jakarta
POPULATION: 228.4 million
MAJOR LANGUAGES: Bahasa Indonesian, English, Dutch, and Javanese
AREA: 735,268 sq mi; 1,904,344 sq km
LOCATION: Asia

IRAN

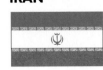

CAPITAL ★ Tehran
POPULATION: 66.1 million
MAJOR LANGUAGES: Farsi, Turkic, and Kurdish
AREA: 636,293 sq mi; 1,648,000 sq km
LOCATION: Asia

IRAQ

CAPITAL ★ Baghdad
POPULATION: 23.3 million
MAJOR LANGUAGES: Arabic and Kurdish
AREA: 168,920 sq mi; 434,913 sq km
LOCATION: Asia

IRELAND

CAPITAL ★ Dublin
POPULATION: 3.8 million
MAJOR LANGUAGES: English and Irish Gaelic
AREA: 27,136 sq mi; 70,282 sq km
LOCATION: Europe

ISRAEL

CAPITAL ★ Jerusalem
POPULATION: 5.9 million
MAJOR LANGUAGES: Hebrew, Arabic, and English
AREA: 8,020 sq mi; 20,772 sq km*
LOCATION: Asia
*does not include the 2,402 sq mi of the Gaza Strip and the West Bank

ITALY

CAPITAL ★ Rome
POPULATION: 57.7 million
MAJOR LANGUAGE: Italian
AREA: 116,500 sq mi; 301,278 sq km
LOCATION: Europe

JAMAICA

CAPITAL ★ Kingston
POPULATION: 2.7 million
MAJOR LANGUAGES: English and Jamaican Creole
AREA: 4,411 sq mi; 11,424 sq km
LOCATION: Caribbean Sea

JAPAN

CAPITAL ★ Tokyo
POPULATION: 126.8 million
MAJOR LANGUAGE: Japanese
AREA: 145,874 sq mi; 377,815 sq km
LOCATION: Asia

JORDAN

CAPITAL ★ Amman
POPULATION: 5.2 million
MAJOR LANGUAGE: Arabic
AREA: 34,573 sq mi; 89,544 sq km
LOCATION: Asia

KAZAKHSTAN

CAPITAL ★ Astana
POPULATION: 16.7 million
MAJOR LANGUAGES: Kazakh and Russian
AREA: 1,049,000 sq mi; 2,717,300 sq km
LOCATION: Asia

KENYA

CAPITAL ★ Nairobi
POPULATION: 30.8 million
MAJOR LANGUAGES: English and Swahili
AREA: 224,960 sq mi; 582,646 sq km
LOCATION: Africa

KIRIBATI

CAPITAL ★ Tarawa
POPULATION: 94,000
MAJOR LANGUAGES: Gilbertese and English
AREA: 280 sq mi; 726 sq km
LOCATION: Pacific Ocean

KOREA, NORTH

CAPITAL ★ Pyongyang
POPULATION: 22.0 million
MAJOR LANGUAGE: Korean
AREA: 46,768 sq mi; 121,129 sq km
LOCATION: Asia

KOREA, SOUTH

CAPITAL ★ Seoul
POPULATION: 48.0 million
MAJOR LANGUAGE: Korean
AREA: 38,031 sq mi; 98,392 sq km
LOCATION: Asia

KUWAIT

CAPITAL ★ Kuwait
POPULATION: 2.0 million
MAJOR LANGUAGE: Arabic
AREA: 6,880 sq mi; 17,820 sq km
LOCATION: Asia

KYRGYZSTAN

CAPITAL ★ Bishkek
POPULATION: 4.7 million
MAJOR LANGUAGES: Kyrgyz and Russian
AREA: 76,000 sq mi; 198,500 sq km
LOCATION: Asia

LAOS

CAPITAL ★ Vientiane
POPULATION: 5.6 million
MAJOR LANGUAGES: Lao, French, and English
AREA: 91,429 sq mi; 236,800 sq km
LOCATION: Asia

LATVIA

CAPITAL ★ Riga
POPULATION: 2.4 million
MAJOR LANGUAGES: Latvian and Russian
AREA: 25,400 sq mi; 65,786 sq km
LOCATION: Europe

LEBANON

CAPITAL ★ Beirut
POPULATION: 3.6 million
MAJOR LANGUAGES: Arabic and French
AREA: 4,015 sq mi; 10,400 sq km
LOCATION: Asia

Countries of the World
Lesotho • Mauritius

LESOTHO

CAPITAL ★ Maseru
POPULATION: 2.2 million
MAJOR LANGUAGES: Sesotho and English
AREA: 11,720 sq mi; 30,355 sq km
LOCATION: Africa

LIBERIA

CAPITAL ★ Monrovia
POPULATION: 3.2 million
MAJOR LANGUAGES: English and ethnic languages
AREA: 43,000 sq mi; 111,370 sq km
LOCATION: Africa

LIBYA

CAPITAL ★ Tripoli
POPULATION: 5.2 million
MAJOR LANGUAGES: Arabic, Italian, and English
AREA: 679,536 sq mi; 1,759,998 sq km
LOCATION: Africa

LIECHTENSTEIN

CAPITAL ★ Vaduz
POPULATION: 33,000
MAJOR LANGUAGE: German
AREA: 61 sq mi; 157 sq km
LOCATION: Europe

LITHUANIA

CAPITAL ★ Vilnius
POPULATION: 3.6 million
MAJOR LANGUAGES: Lithuanian, Russian, and Polish
AREA: 25,212 sq mi; 65,300 sq km
LOCATION: Europe

LUXEMBOURG

CAPITAL ★ Luxembourg
POPULATION: 0.4 million
MAJOR LANGUAGES: Luxembourgisch, German, French, and English
AREA: 999 sq mi; 2,586 sq km
LOCATION: Europe

MACEDONIA

CAPITAL ★ Skopje
POPULATION: 2.0 million
MAJOR LANGUAGES: Macedonian and Albanian
AREA: 9,928 sq mi; 25,713 sq km
LOCATION: Europe

MADAGASCAR

CAPITAL ★ Antananarivo
POPULATION: 16.0 million
MAJOR LANGUAGES: French and Malagasy
AREA: 226,660 sq mi; 587,050 sq km
LOCATION: Indian Ocean

MALAWI

CAPITAL ★ Lilongwe
POPULATION: 10.5 million
MAJOR LANGUAGES: English and Chichewa
AREA: 45,747 sq mi; 118,484 sq km
LOCATION: Africa

MALAYSIA

CAPITAL ★ Kuala Lumpur
POPULATION: 22.2 million
MAJOR LANGUAGES: Malay, English, and Chinese dialects
AREA: 128,328 sq mi; 332,370 sq km
LOCATION: Asia

MALDIVES

CAPITAL ★ Malé
POPULATION: 0.3 million
MAJOR LANGUAGE: Divehi
AREA: 115 sq mi; 298 sq km
LOCATION: Indian Ocean

MALI

CAPITAL ★ Bamako
POPULATION: 11.0 million
MAJOR LANGUAGES: Bambara and French
AREA: 478,819 sq mi; 1,240,142 sq km
LOCATION: Africa

MALTA

CAPITAL ★ Valletta
POPULATION: 0.4 million
MAJOR LANGUAGES: Maltese and English
AREA: 122 sq mi; 316 sq km
LOCATION: Mediterranean Sea

MARSHALL ISLANDS

CAPITAL ★ Majuro
POPULATION: 71,000
MAJOR LANGUAGES: English, Marshallese dialects, and Japanese
AREA: 70 sq mi; 181 sq km
LOCATION: Pacific Ocean

MAURITANIA

CAPITAL ★ Nouakchott
POPULATION: 2.7 million
MAJOR LANGUAGES: Arabic and French
AREA: 397,953 sq mi; 1,030,700 sq km
LOCATION: Africa

MAURITIUS
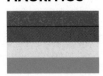
CAPITAL ★ Port Louis
POPULATION: 1.2 million
MAJOR LANGUAGES: English, Creole, and French
AREA: 787 sq mi; 2,040 sq km
LOCATION: Africa

MEXICO

CAPITAL ★ Mexico City
POPULATION: 101.9 million
MAJOR LANGUAGE: Spanish
AREA: 761,600 sq mi;
1,972,547 sq km
LOCATION: North America

MICRONESIA

CAPITAL ★ Palikir
POPULATION: 135,000
MAJOR LANGUAGES: English,
Trukese, Yapese, and Kosrean
AREA: 271 sq mi; 703 sq km
LOCATION: Pacific Ocean

MOLDOVA

CAPITAL ★ Chisinau
POPULATION: 4.4 million
MAJOR LANGUAGES: Moldovan,
Russian, and Gagauz
AREA: 13,000 sq mi; 33,700 sq km
LOCATION: Europe

MONACO

CAPITAL ★ Monaco
POPULATION: 32,000
MAJOR LANGUAGES: French,
Italian, Monégasque, and English
AREA: 0.7 sq mi; 1.9 sq km
LOCATION: Europe

MONGOLIA

CAPITAL ★ Ulan Bator
POPULATION: 2.7 million
MAJOR LANGUAGES: Khalkha
Mongolian, Turkic, Russian, and
Chinese
AREA: 604,250 sq mi;
1,565,000 sq km
LOCATION: Asia

MOROCCO

CAPITAL ★ Rabat
POPULATION: 30.6 million
MAJOR LANGUAGES: Arabic,
Berber, and French
AREA: 172,413 sq mi; 446,550 sq km
LOCATION: Africa

MOZAMBIQUE

CAPITAL ★ Maputo
POPULATION: 19.4 million
MAJOR LANGUAGES: Portuguese
and African languages
AREA: 303,073 sq mi; 799,380 sq km
LOCATION: Africa

MYANMAR
(Burma)

CAPITAL ★ Yangon
POPULATION: 42.0 million
MAJOR LANGUAGE: Burmese
AREA: 261,220 sq mi; 678,560 sq km
LOCATION: Asia

NAMIBIA

CAPITAL ★ Windhoek
POPULATION: 1.8 million
MAJOR LANGUAGES: English,
Afrikaans, and German
AREA: 318,261 sq mi; 824,296 sq km
LOCATION: Africa

NAURU

CAPITAL ★ Yaren
POPULATION: 12,000
MAJOR LANGUAGES: Nauruan and
English
AREA: 8 sq mi; 21 sq km
LOCATION: Pacific Ocean

NEPAL

CAPITAL ★ Kathmandu
POPULATION: 25.3 million
MAJOR LANGUAGE: Nepali
AREA: 54,463 sq mi; 141,059 sq km
LOCATION: Asia

THE
NETHERLANDS

CAPITAL ★ Amsterdam
POPULATION: 16.0 million
MAJOR LANGUAGE: Dutch
AREA: 16,033 sq mi; 41,526 sq km
LOCATION: Europe

NEW
ZEALAND

CAPITAL ★ Wellington
POPULATION: 3.5 million
MAJOR LANGUAGES: English and
Maori
AREA: 103,884 sq mi; 270,534 sq km
LOCATION: Pacific Ocean

NICARAGUA

CAPITAL ★ Managua
POPULATION: 4.9 million
MAJOR LANGUAGE: Spanish
AREA: 50,180 sq mi; 130,000 sq km
LOCATION: North America

NIGER

CAPITAL ★ Niamey
POPULATION: 10.4 million
MAJOR LANGUAGES: French,
Hausa, and Djerma
AREA: 489,206 sq mi;
1,267,044 sq km
LOCATION: Africa

NIGERIA

CAPITAL ★ Abuja
POPULATION: 126.6 million
MAJOR LANGUAGES: English,
Hausa, Yoruba, Ibo, and Fulani
AREA: 356,700 sq mi;
923,853 sq km
LOCATION: Africa

Countries of the World
Norway • St. Kitts and Nevis

NORWAY

CAPITAL ★ Oslo
POPULATION: 4.5 million
MAJOR LANGUAGE: Norwegian
AREA: 125,049 sq mi; 323,877 sq km
LOCATION: Europe

OMAN

CAPITAL ★ Muscat
POPULATION: 2.6 million
MAJOR LANGUAGE: Arabic
AREA: 82,030 sq mi; 212,458 sq km
LOCATION: Asia

PAKISTAN

CAPITAL ★ Islamabad
POPULATION: 144.6 million
MAJOR LANGUAGES: Urdu, Punjabi, Sindhi, and English
AREA: 310,400 sq mi; 803,936 sq km
LOCATION: Asia

PALAU

CAPITAL ★ Koror
POPULATION: 18,902
MAJOR LANGUAGES: Palauan and English
AREA: 196 sq mi; 508 sq km
LOCATION: Pacific Ocean

PANAMA

CAPITAL ★ Panama City
POPULATION: 2.8 million
MAJOR LANGUAGES: Spanish and English
AREA: 29,761 sq mi; 77,082 sq km
LOCATION: North America

PAPUA NEW GUINEA

CAPITAL ★ Port Moresby
POPULATION: 5.0 million
MAJOR LANGUAGES: Pidgin English, English, and Motu
AREA: 178,704 sq mi; 462,840 sq km
LOCATION: Pacific Ocean

PARAGUAY

CAPITAL ★ Asunción
POPULATION: 5.7 million
MAJOR LANGUAGES: Spanish and Guarani
AREA: 157,047 sq mi; 406,752 sq km
LOCATION: South America

PERU

CAPITAL ★ Lima
POPULATION: 27.5 million
MAJOR LANGUAGES: Spanish, Quechua, and Aymará
AREA: 496,222 sq mi; 1,285,216 sq km
LOCATION: South America

PHILIPPINES

CAPITAL ★ Manila
POPULATION: 82.8 million
MAJOR LANGUAGES: Filipino and English
AREA: 115,830 sq mi; 300,000 sq km
LOCATION: Pacific Ocean

POLAND

CAPITAL ★ Warsaw
POPULATION: 38.6 million
MAJOR LANGUAGE: Polish
AREA: 120,727 sq mi; 312,683 sq km
LOCATION: Europe

PORTUGAL

CAPITAL ★ Lisbon
POPULATION: 10.1 million
MAJOR LANGUAGE: Portuguese
AREA: 35,550 sq mi; 92,075 sq km
LOCATION: Europe

QATAR

CAPITAL ★ Doha
POPULATION: 0.8 million
MAJOR LANGUAGES: Arabic and English
AREA: 4,000 sq mi; 11,437 sq km
LOCATION: Asia

ROMANIA

CAPITAL ★ Bucharest
POPULATION: 22.4 million
MAJOR LANGUAGES: Romanian, Hungarian, and German
AREA: 91,700 sq mi; 237,500 sq km
LOCATION: Europe

RUSSIA

CAPITAL ★ Moscow
POPULATION: 145.5 million
MAJOR LANGUAGE: Russian
AREA: 6,592,800 sq mi; 17,075,400 sq km
LOCATION: Europe and Asia

RWANDA

CAPITAL ★ Kigali
POPULATION: 7.3 million
MAJOR LANGUAGES: Kinyarwanda, French, and English
AREA: 10,169 sq mi; 26,338 sq km
LOCATION: Africa

ST. KITTS AND NEVIS

CAPITAL ★ Basseterre
POPULATION: 38,800
MAJOR LANGUAGE: English
AREA: 65 sq mi; 169 sq km
LOCATION: Caribbean Sea

ST. LUCIA

CAPITAL ★ Castries
POPULATION: 158,000
MAJOR LANGUAGES: English and French patois
AREA: 238 sq mi; 616 sq km
LOCATION: Caribbean Sea

ST. VINCENT AND THE GRENADINES

CAPITAL ★ Kingstown
POPULATION: 116,000
MAJOR LANGUAGE: English
AREA: 150 sq mi; 389 sq km
LOCATION: Caribbean Sea

SAMOA

CAPITAL ★ Apia
POPULATION: 179,100
MAJOR LANGUAGES: Samoan and English
AREA: 1,093 sq mi; 2,831 sq km
LOCATION: Pacific Ocean

SAN MARINO

CAPITAL ★ San Marino
POPULATION: 25,000
MAJOR LANGUAGE: Italian
AREA: 23 sq mi; 62 sq km
LOCATION: Europe

SÃO TOMÉ AND PRÍNCIPE

CAPITAL ★ São Tomé
POPULATION: 165,000
MAJOR LANGUAGE: Portuguese
AREA: 370 sq mi; 958 sq km
LOCATION: Gulf of Guinea, Africa

SAUDI ARABIA

CAPITAL ★ Riyadh
POPULATION: 22.8 million
MAJOR LANGUAGE: Arabic
AREA: 865,000 sq mi; 2,250,070 sq km
LOCATION: Asia

SENEGAL

CAPITAL ★ Dakar
POPULATION: 10.3 million
MAJOR LANGUAGES: French and Wolof
AREA: 75,954 sq mi; 196,722 sq km
LOCATION: Africa

SERBIA AND MONTENEGRO

CAPITAL ★ Belgrade
POPULATION: 10.7 million
MAJOR LANGUAGES: Serbian, Croatian and Bosnian
AREA: 39,449 sq mi; 102,169 sq km
LOCATION: Europe

SEYCHELLES

CAPITAL ★ Victoria
POPULATION: 79,000
MAJOR LANGUAGES: English, French, and Creole
AREA: 175 sq mi; 453 sq km
LOCATION: Indian Ocean

SIERRA LEONE

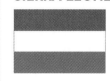

CAPITAL ★ Freetown
POPULATION: 5.4 million
MAJOR LANGUAGES: English, Mende, Temne, and Krio
AREA: 27,925 sq mi; 73,326 sq km
LOCATION: Africa

SINGAPORE

CAPITAL ★ Singapore
POPULATION: 4.3 million
MAJOR LANGUAGES: Chinese, English, Malay, and Tamil
AREA: 247 sq mi; 639 sq km
LOCATION: Asia

SLOVAKIA

CAPITAL ★ Bratislava
POPULATION: 5.4 million
MAJOR LANGUAGES: Slovak and Hungarian
AREA: 18,917 sq mi; 48,995 sq km
LOCATION: Europe

SLOVENIA

CAPITAL ★ Ljubljana
POPULATION: 2.0 million
MAJOR LANGUAGE: Slovenian
AREA: 7,819 sq mi; 20,251 sq km
LOCATION: Europe

SOLOMON ISLANDS

CAPITAL ★ Honiara
POPULATION: 0.5 million
MAJOR LANGUAGES: English, Pidgin English, and Melanesian languages
AREA: 11,500 sq mi; 29,785 sq km
LOCATION: Pacific Ocean

SOMALIA

CAPITAL ★ Mogadishu
POPULATION: 7.5 million
MAJOR LANGUAGES: Somali, Arabic, Italian, English
AREA: 246,199 sq mi; 637,655 sq km
LOCATION: Africa

SOUTH AFRICA

CAPITALS ★ Pretoria, Cape Town, and Bloemfontein
POPULATION: 43.6 million
MAJOR LANGUAGES: Afrikaans, English, Zulu, and other African languages
AREA: 471,440 sq mi; 1,221,030 sq km
LOCATION: Africa

Countries of the World
Spain • Tunisia

SPAIN

CAPITAL ★ Madrid
POPULATION: 40.0 million
MAJOR LANGUAGES: Spanish, Catalan, Galician, and Basque
AREA: 199,365 sq mi; 505,992 sq km
LOCATION: Europe

SRI LANKA

CAPITAL ★ Colombo
POPULATION: 19.4 million
MAJOR LANGUAGES: Sinhala, Tamil, and English
AREA: 25,332 sq mi; 65,610 sq km
LOCATION: Indian Ocean

SUDAN

CAPITAL ★ Khartoum
POPULATION: 36.1 million
MAJOR LANGUAGES: Arabic, Nubian, and Sudanic languages
AREA: 967,491 sq mi; 2,505,802 sq km
LOCATION: Africa

SURINAME

CAPITAL ★ Paramaribo
POPULATION: 0.4 million
MAJOR LANGUAGES: Dutch, Surinamese, and English
AREA: 63,251 sq mi; 163,820 sq km
LOCATION: South America

SWAZILAND

CAPITAL ★ Mbabane
POPULATION: 1.1 million
MAJOR LANGUAGES: Swazi and English
AREA: 6,704 sq mi; 17,363 sq km
LOCATION: Africa

SWEDEN
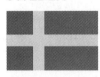
CAPITAL ★ Stockholm
POPULATION: 8.9 million
MAJOR LANGUAGE: Swedish
AREA: 173,800 sq mi; 449,964 sq km
LOCATION: Europe

SWITZERLAND

CAPITAL ★ Bern
POPULATION: 7.3 million
MAJOR LANGUAGES: German, French, Italian, and Romansch
AREA: 15,941 sq mi; 41,288 sq km
LOCATION: Europe

SYRIA

CAPITAL ★ Damascus
POPULATION: 16.7 million
MAJOR LANGUAGES: Arabic, French, and English
AREA: 71,498 sq mi; 185,180 sq km
LOCATION: Asia

TAIWAN

CAPITAL ★ Taipei
POPULATION: 22.4 million
MAJOR LANGUAGES: Mandarin
AREA: 13,895 sq mi; 35,988 sq km
LOCATION: Asia

TAJIKISTAN

CAPITAL ★ Dushanbe
POPULATION: 6.6 million
MAJOR LANGUAGES: Tajik and Russian
AREA: 55,300 sq mi; 143,100 sq km
LOCATION: Asia

TANZANIA

CAPITAL ★ Dar es Salaam
POPULATION: 36.2 million
MAJOR LANGUAGES: Swahili and English
AREA: 364,879 sq mi; 945,037 sq km
LOCATION: Africa

THAILAND

CAPITAL ★ Bangkok
POPULATION: 61.8 million
MAJOR LANGUAGES: Thai, Chinese, and English
AREA: 198,455 sq mi; 514,000 sq km
LOCATION: Asia

TOGO

CAPITAL ★ Lomé
POPULATION: 5.1 million
MAJOR LANGUAGES: French, Kabye, Ewe, Mina, and Dagomba
AREA: 21,925 sq mi; 56,785 sq km
LOCATION: Africa

TONGA

CAPITAL ★ Nuku'alofa
POPULATION: 104,000
MAJOR LANGUAGES: Tongan and English
AREA: 290 sq mi; 751 sq km
LOCATION: Pacific Ocean

TRINIDAD AND TOBAGO

CAPITAL ★ Port-of-Spain
POPULATION: 1.2 million
MAJOR LANGUAGES: English, Hindi, French, and Spanish
AREA: 1,980 sq mi; 5,128 sq km
LOCATION: Caribbean Sea

TUNISIA

CAPITAL ★ Tunis
POPULATION: 9.7 million
MAJOR LANGUAGES: Arabic and French
AREA: 63,170 sq mi; 163,610 sq km
LOCATION: Africa

TURKEY

CAPITAL ★ Ankara

POPULATION: 66.5 million

MAJOR LANGUAGES: Turkish, Kurdish, and Arabic

AREA: 300,947 sq mi; 779,452 sq km

LOCATION: Asia and Europe

TURKMENISTAN

CAPITAL ★ Ashgabat

POPULATION: 4.6 million

MAJOR LANGUAGES: Turkmen, Russian, and Uzbek

AREA: 188,500 sq mi; 488,100 sq km

LOCATION: Asia

TUVALU

CAPITAL ★ Funafuti

POPULATION: 11,000

MAJOR LANGUAGES: Tuvaluan and English

AREA: 10 sq mi; 26 sq km

LOCATION: Pacific Ocean

UGANDA

CAPITAL ★ Kampala

POPULATION: 24.0 million

MAJOR LANGUAGES: English, Luganda, Swahili, and Bantu languages

AREA: 91,459 sq mi; 236,880 sq km

LOCATION: Africa

UKRAINE

CAPITAL ★ Kiev

POPULATION: 48.8 million

MAJOR LANGUAGES: Ukrainian, Russian, Romanian, and Polish

AREA: 233,000 sq mi; 603,700 sq km

LOCATION: Europe

UNITED ARAB EMIRATES

CAPITAL ★ Abu Dhabi

POPULATION: 2.4 million

MAJOR LANGUAGES: Arabic, Persian, English, Hindi, and Urdu

AREA: 32,000 sq mi; 82,880 sq km

LOCATION: Asia

UNITED KINGDOM

CAPITAL ★ London

POPULATION: 59.6 million

MAJOR LANGUAGES: English, Welsh, and Scottish Gaelic

AREA: 94,247 sq mi; 244,100 sq km

LOCATION: Europe

UNITED STATES

CAPITAL ★ Washington, D.C.

POPULATION: 281.4 million

MAJOR LANGUAGES: English and Spanish

AREA: 3,536,341 sq mi; 9,159,123 sq km

LOCATION: North America

SOURCES: *Time Almanac 2002* and *CIA World Factbook*

URUGUAY

CAPITAL ★ Montevideo

POPULATION: 3.4 million

MAJOR LANGUAGES: Spanish and Brazilero

AREA: 68,040 sq mi; 176,224 sq km

LOCATION: South America

UZBEKISTAN

CAPITAL ★ Tashkent

POPULATION: 25.2 million

MAJOR LANGUAGES: Uzbek, Russian, and Tajik

AREA: 172,700 sq mi; 447,400 sq km

LOCATION: Asia

VANUATU

CAPITAL ★ Port-Vila

POPULATION: 193,000

MAJOR LANGUAGES: Bislama, English, and French

AREA: 5,700 sq mi; 14,763 sq km

LOCATION: Pacific Ocean

VATICAN CITY (The Holy See)

CAPITAL ★ Vatican City

POPULATION: 880

MAJOR LANGUAGES: Italian and Latin

AREA: 0.17 sq mi; 0.44 sq km

LOCATION: Europe

VENEZUELA

CAPITAL ★ Caracas

POPULATION: 23.9 million

MAJOR LANGUAGES: Spanish and Indian dialects

AREA: 352,143 sq mi; 912,050 sq km

LOCATION: South America

VIETNAM

CAPITAL ★ Hanoi

POPULATION: 79.9 million

MAJOR LANGUAGES: Vietnamese, French, Chinese, English, and Khmer

AREA: 127,246 sq mi; 329,566 sq km

LOCATION: Asia

YEMEN

CAPITAL ★ San'a

POPULATION: 18.1 million

MAJOR LANGUAGE: Arabic

AREA: 203,850 sq mi; 527,970 sq km

LOCATION: Asia

ZAMBIA

CAPITAL ★ Lusaka

POPULATION: 9.8 million

MAJOR LANGUAGES: English and Bantu dialects

AREA: 290,586 sq mi; 752,618 sq km

LOCATION: Africa

ZIMBABWE

CAPITAL ★ Harare

POPULATION: 11.4 million

MAJOR LANGUAGES: English, Shona, and Ndebele

AREA: 150,698 sq mi; 390,308 sq km

LOCATION: Africa

Reference

Dictionary of Geographic Terms

STRAIT (strāt) A narrow waterway that connects two larger bodies of water.

GULF (gulf) Part of an ocean that extends into the land; larger than a bay.

RESERVOIR (rez′ər vwär) A natural or artificial lake used to store water.

PLATEAU (pla tō′) A high, flat area that rises steeply above the surrounding land.

DAM (dam) A wall built across a river, creating a lake that stores water.

MESA (mā′sə) A hill with a flat top; smaller than a plateau.

CANYON (kan′yən) A deep, narrow valley with steep sides.

DUNE (dün) A mound, hill, or ridge of sand heaped up by the wind.

BUTTE (būt) A small, flat-topped hill; smaller than a mesa or plateau.

OASIS (ō ā′sis) A fertile area that is watered by a spring in a desert.

HILL (hil) A rounded, raised landform; not as high as a mountain.

VALLEY (val′ē) An area of low land between hills or mountains.

DESERT (dez′ərt) A dry environment with few plants and animals.

COAST (kōst) The land along an ocean.

BAY (bā) Part of an ocean or lake that extends deeply into the land.

ISTHMUS (is′məs) A narrow strip of land that connects two larger bodies of land.

ISLAND (ī′lənd) A body of land completely surrounded by water.

PENINSULA (pə nin′sə lə) A body of land surrounded on three sides by water.

VOLCANO (vol kā'nō) An opening in Earth's surface through which hot rock and ash are forced out.

MOUNTAIN (moun'tən) A high landform with steep sides; higher than a hill.

HARBOR (här'bər) A sheltered place along a coast where boats dock safely.

PEAK (pēk) The top of a mountain.

GLACIER (glā'shər) A huge sheet of ice that moves slowly across the land.

CANAL (kə nal') A channel built to carry water for irrigation or transportation.

LAKE (lāk) Body of water completely surrounded by land.

TRIBUTARY (trib'yə ter ē) A smaller river that flows into a larger river.

SOURCE (sôrs) The starting point of a river.

PORT (pôrt) A place where ships load and unload their goods.

TIMBERLINE (tim'bər līn) A line above which trees do not grow.

WATERFALL (wô'tər fôl) A flow of water falling vertically.

PLAIN (plān) A large area of nearly flat land.

RIVER BASIN (riv'ər bā'sin) All the land that is drained by a river and its tributaries.

MOUNTAIN RANGE (moun'tən rānj) A row or chain of mountains.

RIVER (riv'ər) A stream of water that flows across the land and empties into another body of water.

BASIN (bā'sin) A bowl-shaped landform surrounded by higher land.

DELTA (del'tə) Land made of soil left behind as a river drains into a larger body of water.

MOUTH (mouth) The place where a river empties into a larger body of water.

MOUNTAIN PASS (moun'tən pas) A narrow gap through a mountain range.

OCEAN (ō'shən) A large body of salt water; oceans cover much of Earth's surface.

Gazetteer

This Gazetteer is a geographical dictionary that will help you to pronounce and locate the places discussed in this book. Latitude and longitude are given for cities and some other places. The page numbers tell you where each place appears on a map or in the text.

A

Aachen (ä′khən) Capital of Charlemagne's empire, c. 800; a city in present-day Germany; 51°N, 6°E. (m. 341, t. 342)

Adula (ə′dü lə) The chief port city of Aksum, a powerful African kingdom, about 350–900. (m. 317, t. 317)

Africa (af′ri kə) The world's second largest continent, lying south of Europe between the Atlantic and Indian oceans. (m. 313, t. 312)

Agra (ä′grə) A city in north-central India; capital of the Mughal Empire around 1564–1658; 27°N, 78°E. (m. 395, t. 397)

Aksum (äk′süm) A powerful African kingdom and trading center, about 350–900, located in what is today Ethiopia. (m. 317, t. 316)

Alexandria (al ig zan′drē ə) A city in Egypt founded c. 332 B.C. by Alexander the Great; 31°N, 30°E. (m. 209, t. 210)

Algeria (al jêr′ ē ə) A country in western North Africa; 30°N, 2°E. (m. 601, t. 602)

Alps (alps) Europe's highest mountains, extending in an arc from the Mediterranean coast to the Balkan Peninsula. (m. 219, t. 219)

Amazon River (am′ə zon riv′ər) The longest river in South America, flowing from the Andes Mountains to the Atlantic Ocean. (m. 417, t. 419)

Anatolia (an ə tō′lē ə) Asia Minor; a peninsula in western Asia. Today the country is Turkey. (m. 382, t. 381)

Andes Mountains (an′dēz moun′tənz) The world's longest mountain chain, stretching along the west coast of South America. (m. 417, t. 418)

Angkor (ang′kôr) Ruined city in Cambodia; capital of the Khmer around 850–1430; 14°N, 104°E. (m. 409, t. 410)

Ankgor Wat (ang′kôr wat) A Hindu temple built by the Khmer king Suryavarman II in the early 1100s. (t. 408)

Antarctica (ant ärk′ti kə) An ice-covered continent surrounding the South Pole. (m. R4)

Anyang (än′yäng) The ancient Chinese capital of the Shang dynasty; 36°N, 114°E. (m. 151, t. 151)

Arabia (ə rā′bē ə) A large peninsula in southwestern Asia. (m. 283, t. 282)

Arabian Sea (ə rā′bē ən sē) A body of water that lies between Arabia and India; the northwestern part of the Indian Ocean. (m. 283, t. 283)

Arctic Ocean (ärk′tik ō′shən) The body of water north of the Arctic Circle and surrounding the North Pole. (m. R4)

Asia (ā′zhə) The largest continent, bounded on the west by Europe and Africa, on the south by the Indian Ocean, and on the east by the Pacific Ocean. (m. 377, t. 376)

Assyria (ə sîr′ē ə) An ancient country along the Tigris River in present-day Iraq. The country centered around the city of Ashur in the 2200s B.C. (m. 67, t. 66)

Athens (ath′ənz) For many years the most powerful of all ancient Greek city-states; capital of present-day Greece; 38°N, 23°E. (m. 189, t. 192)

Atlantic Ocean (at lan′tik ō′shən) The body of water separating Europe and Africa from North and South America. (m. R4, t. 337)

Attica (at′i kə) A peninsula in east-central Greece on the Aegean Sea on which Athens was built. (m. 185, t. 185)

Australia (ôs trāl′yə) The world's smallest continent, bounded by the Indian and Pacific oceans; also a country. (m. 481, t. 481)

pronunciation key

a	at	ī	ice	u	up	th	thin
ā	ape	îr	pierce	ū	use	th	this
ä	far	o	hot	ü	rule	zh	measure
âr	care	ō	old	ù	pull	ə	about, taken,
e	end	ô	fork	ûr	turn		pencil, lemon,
ē	me	oi	oil	hw	white		circus
i	it	ou	out	ng	song		

Austria-Hungary (ô'strē ə hung'gə rē) A monarchy from 1867 to 1918 that included present-day Austria, Hungary, Bosnia and Herzegovina, the Czech Republic, Slovakia, and parts of Italy, Slovenia, Croatia, Poland, and Romania. (m. 542, t. 541)

Babylon (bab' ə lōn) An ancient Mesopotamian empire that extended throughout the eastern portion of the Fertile Crescent in the 1700s B.C. (m. 67, t. 67)

Baghdad (bag'dad) Capital and cultural center of the Muslim caliphate from A.D. 762 to 1100; present-day capital of Iraq; 33°N, 44°E. (m. 294, t. 295)

Baltic Sea (bal'tik sē) A sea in northen Europe bounded by Sweden, Finland, Russia, Estonia, Latvia, Lithuania, Poland, Germany, and Denmark. (m. R14, t. 337)

Bangladesh (bän glə desh') A nation established in 1971 on the Indian subcontinent, and mostly surrounded by India; from 1947 to 1971 known as East Pakistan. (m. 583, t. 588)

Beijing (bā'jing') The capital of the People's Republic of China; first became China's capital during the reign of Kublai Khan in the 1200s; 40°N, 116°E. (m. 389, t. 389)

Bering Strait (ber'ing strāt) A narrow stretch of water separating Alaska from Siberia. (m. 259, t. 259)

Berlin (bər lin') The capital of Germany, divided from 1945 to 1990 into West Berlin and East Berlin; 53°N, 13°E. (m. R14, t. 571)

Blombos Cave (blom bōz kāv) An archaeological site in South Africa where humans lived about 70,000 years ago; 34°S, 30°E. (m. 32, t. 32)

Border Cave (bôr'dər kāv) A major archaeological site in Zululand, South Africa and home of Old Stone Age hunters and gatherers; 27°S, 32°E. (m. 32, t. 32)

Brazil (brə zil') The largest nation in South America, on the northeastern part of the continent. (m. 649, t. 502)

Burma, See *Myanmar*

Byzantine Empire (bi'zən tēn em'pīr) The name by which the eastern half of the Roman Empire became known some time after A.D. 400. (m. 248, t. 250)

Cairo (kī'rō) The capital of modern Egypt and the largest city in Africa; 30°N, 31°E. (m. 601, t.600)

Cambodia (kam bō'dē ə) A nation in Southeast Asia. (m. 607, t. 408)

Canaan (kā' nən) Present-day Israel and Palestine in what was the southwestern portion of the Fertile Crescent, west of the Jordan River. (m. 73, t. 73)

Canada (kan'ə də) A country in North America bordering the northern part of the United States. (m. R10, t. 643)

Canadian Shield (kə nā'dē ən shēld) A large rocky plain in northern Canada that was formed by glaciers during the Ice Age. (m. 259, t. 260)

Caribbean Sea (kar ə bē'ən sē) A sea bounded on the north and east by the West Indies, by Central America on the west, and South America on the south. (m. 497, t. 497)

Carthage (kär'thij) An ancient city on the north coast of Africa; 37°N, 10°E. (m. 226, t. 226)

Catal Huyuk (cha'tal hū'yūk) The first known city, existed more than 8,500 years ago in present-day Turkey; 38°N, 34°E. (m. 46, t. 46)

Chang Jiang (chäng je'ang) The longest river in China, flowing from Tibet into the East China Sea. It is also known as the Yangtze River. (m. 147, t. 148)

Chartres (shärt) A city in northwestern France, noted for its cathedral; 48°N, 1°E. (m. 352, t. 353)

China (chī'nə) A nation in East Asia, and the most populous country in the world. (m. 147, t. 651)

Colosseum (kä lə sē'əm) A large stadium in ancient Rome where athletic events took place. (t. 235)

Congo River (kon'gō riv'ər) A major river in Africa's central plateau that flows west from Zaire to the Atlantic Ocean. (m. 313, t. 314)

Constantinople (kon stan tə nō'pəl) A city established as the new capital of the Roman Empire by the emperor Constantine in A.D. 330, now called Istanbul; 41°N, 29°E. (m. 248, t. 248)

Copán (kō pän') An ancient city of Middle America, in what is now Honduras, that was a center of classic Maya culture; 15°N, 89°W. (m. 266, t. 266)

Cordoba (kor'də bə) City in southern Spain that after its capture by the Muslims in 710 became an important cultural center, and during the tenth century, the capital of the Caliphate; 35°N, 5°W. (m. 294, t. 294)

Crete (krēt) A Greek island in the Mediterranean Sea, southeast of Greece; it was home of the ancient Minoan culture about 5,000 years ago. (m. 185, t. 185)

Cuzco (küs'kō) A city in southern Peru; capital of the Inca Empire from the 1200s to the 1500s; 14°S, 72°W. (m. 431, t. 431)

Delhi (del' ē) India's second largest city; was the country's capital from 1912 until 1931; 29°N, 76°E. (m. 393, t. 395)

Dolores (də lôr'əs) A city in central Mexico where Miguel Hidalgo began Mexico's independence movement in 1810; 29°N, 108°W. (m. 497, t. 498)

Dominican Republic (də min'i kən ri pub'lik) A Caribbean nation, on the eastern part of Hispaniola, that gained independence from Spain in 1844. (m. 649)

E

Edo (ed′ō) The former name of Tokyo, Japan; became capital under the rule of the Tokugawa shoguns in the 1600s; 36°N, 140°E. (m. 401, t. 524) See *Tokyo*

England (ing′ glənd) Part of the United Kingdom, on the island of Britain. (m. 348, t. 342)

Egypt (ē′jipt) A country in northeast Africa; birthplace of ancient Egyptian civilization. (m. 589, t. 82)

Ethiopia (ē thē ō′pē ə) A country in eastern Africa. (m. R8, t. 317)

Euphrates River (ū frā′tēz riv′ər) A river in southwestern Asia that flows through the southern part of the Fertile Crescent. (m. 55, t. 54)

Eurasia (yu̇ rā′zhə) A large land mass that includes the continents of Europe and Asia. (t. 337)

Europe (yu̇r′əp) The continent north of Africa between Asia and the Atlantic Ocean. (m. R14, t. 336)

F

Fatehpur Sikri (fa′tē′ pu̇r sik′rē) Briefly capital city of the Mughal Empire until its source of water dried up; capital was moved to Agra in 1586. (t. 397)

Fertile Crescent (fûrt′əl kres′ənt) A fertile region in southwestern Asia that includes Mesopotamia and the eastern Mediterranean. (m. 55, t. 54)

Florence (flôr′əns) A city in present-day Italy; one of the great centers of Renaissance art; 44°N, 11°E. (m. 357, t. 357)

Forbidden City (fər bid′ən sit′ē) A walled area in Beijing built 1417–1420, during the Ming dynasty, that contained the palaces of the emperors. (t. 390)

France (frans) A country in western Europe; part of the ancient Frankish Empire. (m. R14, t. 342)

G

Gaul (gôl) An ancient region and Roman province that included most of present-day France. (m. 235, t. 233)

Germany (jûr′ mə nē) A country in central Europe; part of the ancient Frankish Empire. (m. R14, t. 341)

Ghana (gä′nə) An empire, from about 400 to 1235, located at the southwestern edge of the Sahara Desert; a present-day country in western Africa on the Gulf of Guinea. (m. 601, t. 599)

Gobi Desert (gō′bē dez′ərt) A large desert in east-central Asia. (m. 377, t. 378)

Great Rift Valley (grāt rift val′ē) A series of cliffs and valleys caused by powerful prehistoric earthquakes that extends from Mozambique in southeastern Africa north to the Red Sea. (m. 313, t. 31)

Great Wall of China (grāt wôl əv chī′nə) A long defensive wall extending 1,500 miles (2,415 km) through northern China; built between 1300 and 1600. (t. 162)

Great Zimbabwe (grāt zim bäb′wē) A city in southern Africa that rose to power in the 1300s through gold mining and trading; 20°S, 30°E. (m. 329, t. 329)

Greece (grēs) A country on the Balkan Peninsula in southeast Europe, including many islands in the Mediterranean, Ionian, and Aegean seas; home of ancient Greek civilization. (m. 185, t. 184)

Guangzhou (gwäng′jō) A major port city in southeastern China; also known as Canton. 23°N, 114°E. (m. 389, t. 388)

Guatemala (gwä tə mä′ lə) A country in the northern part of Middle America; included in the ancient Maya civilization. (m. 497, t. 266)

H

Haiti (hā′tē) A Caribbean nation, on the western part of Hispaniola, that gained independence from France in 1804. (m. 497, t. 497)

Harappa (hə ra′pə) A city of the ancient Harappan civilization, c. 2500–1600 B.C., located in the Indus Valley of South Asia; 31°N, 73°E. (m. 119, t. 119)

Hawaii (hə wī′ ē) A U.S. state made up of many islands in the Pacific Ocean; 20°N, 158°W (m. 481, t. 479)

Himalaya (him ə lā′ə) The world's highest mountain range, forming the northern border of the Indian subcontinent. (m. 377, t. 377)

Hindu Kush (hin′ dü küsh) Mountain range in central Asia that creates the northwestern border of the Indian subcontinent. (m. 119, t. 122)

Hiroshima (hir ə shē′ mə) A port in southwestern Japan on the island of Honshu; city where the first atomic bomb was dropped in 1945; 34°N, 132°E. (m. 557, t. 560)

Hispaniola (his pən yō′lə) A Caribbean island settled by Spaniards in 1493; a present-day island that is divided into the Dominican Republic and Haiti. (m. 465, t. 465)

Hong Kong (häng käng) A large city and center of international trade in mainland China; it was a British colony from 1842 to 1997. 22°N, 114°E. (m. R12, t. 651)

Huang He (hwäng hu̇) [Yellow River] A river that flows from the Tibetan Plateau, across northern China, and into the Yellow Sea. (m. 147, t. 147)

I

India (in′dē ə) The largest nation of the Indian subcontinent; became independent from British rule in 1947. (m. 583, t. 582)

Indian Ocean (in′dē ən ō′shən) The body of water south of Asia, between Africa and Australia. (m. R4)

Indochina (in dō chī′ nə) A peninsula in Southeast Asia; includes Myanmar (Burma), Cambodia, Laos, Malaysia, Singapore, Thailand, and Vietnam. (m. 518, t. 516)

Indus River (in'dəs riv'ər) A river that flows from Tibet, through the Himalaya and across present-day Pakistan into the Arabian Sea. (m. 113, t. 112)

Iran (ĭ' rän) A country in southwestern Asia; 30°N, 55°E (m. 591, t. 592)

Iraq (i rak') A nation of western Asia that became independent in 1932. (m. 591, t. 591)

Israel (iz'rē əl) A country in western Asia, created in 1948 as a home for the Jews; ancient kingdom of Israelites. (m. 589, t. 76)

Istanbul (is tan bül') Largest city in present-day Turkey; formerly the ancient city of Constantinople and later the capital of the Ottoman Empire; 41°N, 29°E. (m. 382, t. 382)

Italy (i'tə lē) A country in southern Europe made up of the Italian Peninsula and various islands in the Mediterranean Sea; birthplace of ancient Roman and Etruscan civilizations. (m. 219, t. 218)

Japan (jə pan') An island nation off the eastern Asian mainland. (m. 401, t. 400)

Jerusalem (jə rü'sə ləm) An ancient city in western Asia; capital of present-day Israel; 31°N, 35°E. (m. 73, t. 76)

Judea (jü dē'ə) The land in the eastern Mediterranean region populated by Jews at the time of the Roman Empire. (m. 241, t. 241)

Kenya (ken' yə) A country in East Africa; 0°N, 39°E. (m. 601, t. 599)

Kerma (kâr' mə) The ancient capital of the kingdom of Kush in Upper Nubia. (m. 103, t. 104)

Kumbi Saleh (küm'bē sa'lē) The capital of the ancient empire of Ghana. (m. 321, t. 320)

Kush (Kůsh) An ancient kingdom in northeastern Africa, conquered by Egypt. It later regained independence and flourished through trade between c. 500 B.C. and A.D. 150. (m. 98, t. 98)

Kyoto (kyō'tō) A city in Japan; formerly the emperor's capital during the rule of the shoguns; 35°N, 136°E. (m. 404, t. 404)

La Venta (lə vent'ə) An ancient island town of Middle America on the east coast of what is now Mexico; center of Olmec culture in 1000 B.C.; 18°N, 94°W. (m. 265, t. 265)

Lake Tanganyika (lāk' tang' ə nē kə) Second deepest lake in the world, located in east-central Africa; 5° S, 30° E. (m. 313, t. 314)

Lake Texcoco (lāk tā skō'kō) A lake in what is now central Mexico on which the Aztec built Tenochtitlán, their capital. (m. 423, t. 423)

Lake Titicaca (lāk tit i kä' kə) The largest lake in South America and the highest navigable lake in the world. It is located in the Andes on the border between Peru and Bolivia; 16 °S, 71°W. (m. 431, t. 431)

Lake Victoria (lāk vik tôr' ē ə) The largest lake in Africa, located in the east-central part of the continent. (m. 313, t. 314)

Laos (lä'ōs) A nation in Southeast Asia, between northern Thailand and northern Vietnam. (m. 607, t. 134)

Lima (lē'mə) The capital of Peru, founded by Francisco Pizarro in 1535; 12°S, 77°W. (m. 465, t. 467)

Lower Egypt (lō'ər ē'jipt) The northern part of ancient Egypt. (m. 83, t. 83)

Macedonia (mas i dō'nē ə) An ancient kingdom that under the rule of Alexander the Great conquered Greece and the Persian Empire in the 300s B.C. (m. 202, t. 204)

Machu Picchu (mäch'ü pēk'chü) The site of a ruined Inca city on a peak in the Andes northwest of Cuzco, Peru; 13°S, 72°W. (m. 431, t. 435)

Mali (mä'lē) African empire that flourished between the 1200s and 1400s; a present-day country in West Africa. (m. 321, t. 324)

Mecca (mek'ə) An Arabian oasis city believed to be the birthplace of Muhammad; 21°N, 40°E. (m. 287, t. 287)

Medina (mə dē'nə) An Arabian oasis town to which, according to Muslim writings, Muhammad migrated in A.D. 622; 24°N, 40°E. (m. 287, t. 288)

Mediterranean Sea (med i tə rā'nē ən sē) A large, almost landlocked arm of the Atlantic Ocean touching Europe, Asia, and Africa. (m. 189, t. 188)

Mekong River (mā'kong' riv'ər) A river in Southeast Asia that flows from Tibet to the South China Sea. (m. 409, t. 409)

Memphis (mem'fis) Capital of Egypt's Old Kingdom, located on the Nile near present-day Cairo; 29°N, 31°E. (m. 90, t. 90)

Meroë (mer' ə wē) The ancient capital of the kingdom of Kush from 300 B.C. to A.D. 300 (m. 103, t. 106)

Mesa Verde (mā' sə vâr' dē) Ancient Anasazi cliff dwelling in what is present-day Colorado; 35°N, 108°W. (m. 275, t. 274)

Mesopotamia (mes ə pə tā'mē ə) The region between the Tigris and Euphrates rivers; birthplace of the Sumerian and Babylonian civilizations. (m. 55, t. 55)

Mexico (mek'si kō) A nation in North America, south of the United States. (m. 497, t. 498)

Mexico City (mek′si kō sit′ē) The capital and largest city of Mexico; formerly Tenochtitlán, it became the capital of New Spain after the Spanish conquered the Aztec in the 1500s; 19°N, 99°W. (m. 465, t. 467)

Middle America (mid′əl ə mer′i kə) An ancient region of North America that included southern Mexico and much of Central America. It was the birthplace of the ancient Olmec and Maya civilizations. (m. 263, t. 259)

Middle East (mid′əl ēst) A region of southwestern Asia that stretches from Turkey to Afghanistan. (m. 591, t. 590)

Minoa (mə′ nō ə) Powerful civilization of ancient Crete, named after King Minos, from 2000-1400 B.C.; 35° N, 25° E. (m. 189, t. 189)

Mogadishu (mōg ə dish′ü) A coastal city that dominated African gold trade between about 1000 and 1300; the present-day capital of Somalia; 2°N, 45°E. (m. 330, t. 331)

Mohenjo-Daro (mō hen′jō där′ō) A city of the ancient Harappan civilization, located in the Indus Valley; 27°N, 68°E. (m. 119, t. 119)

Mombasa (mom bä′sä) An important Swahili city-state and trading center between 1100 and 1500; the main port of Kenya on the Indian Ocean; 4°N, 40°E. (m. 330, t. 331)

Moscow (mäs′kou) The capital and largest city of Russia; 56°N, 38°E. (m. R14, t. 575)

Mount Everest (mount ev′ər əst) The tallest mountain in the world, located in the Himalaya on the border between Nepal and Tibet; 28°N, 87°E. (m. 377, t. 377)

Mount Kilimanjaro (mount kil ə mən jär′ō) The tallest mountain in Africa, located in northeastern Tanzania; 3°S, 37°E. (m. 313, t. 314)

Mount Olympus (mount ə lim′pəs) The highest mountain in Greece, where the ancient Greeks believed many of their gods and goddesses lived; 40°N, 22°E. (m. 191, t. 194)

Mount Sinai (mount sī′ nī) Mountain where, according to the Bible, the Ten Commandments were given to Moses; thought to be in the Gebel Musa on the Sinai Peninsula. (m. 73, t. 75)

Myanmar (mī ən mär) A nation in Southeast Asia on the Bay of Bengal also called Burma. (m. 607, t. 606)

Mycenae (mī sē′ nē) Ancient city on the Peloponnesus Peninsula of Greece, 1450–1100 B.C.; 40°N, 20°E. (m. 189, t. 189)

N

Nagasaki (nä gə sä′ kē) A city in Japan on the western coast of the island of Kyushu. It was the second city struck by an atomic bomb in 1945; 33°N, 130°E. (m. 557, t. 560)

New South Wales (nü south wālz) English colony founded on the east coast of Australia in 1788; currently a state of Australia. (m. 481, t. 481)

New Spain (nü spān) Spanish colony in North America including Mexico, Central America, the southwest United States, and many of the Caribbean islands from the 1500s to the 1800s. (m. 465, t. 467)

Niger River (nī′jər riv′ər) A river flowing from western Africa into the Gulf of Guinea. (m. 313, t. 314)

Nile River (nīl riv′ər) The world's longest river, which flows over 4,000 miles northward through East Africa into the Mediterranean Sea. (m. 83, t. 82)

Nineveh (nin′ ə vəh) An ancient city on the Tigris River and the capital of Assyria from 704 B.C. to 612 B.C. (m. 67, t. 67)

Normandy (nôr′mən dē) A region in northwestern France on the English Channel. (m. 556, t. 343)

North America (nôrth ə mâr′i kə) The third largest continent, located in the Western Hemisphere. (m. 259, t. 258)

North China Plain (nôrth chī′nə plān) A large, lowland region of eastern China that is watered by the Huang He; birthplace of Chinese civilization. (m. 147, t. 147)

North European Plain (nôrth yür ə pē′ən plān) A large, fertile area that extends from the Atlantic Ocean to the Ural Mountains. (m. 337, t. 339)

North Sea (nôrth sē) A large arm of the Atlantic Ocean, between Great Britain and continental Europe. (m. 337, t. 337)

Nubia (nü′bē ə) An ancient kingdom south of Egypt. (m. 98, t. 97)

P

Pacific Ocean (pə sif′ik ō′shən) The world's largest body of water, bounded by the Americas on the east and Asia and Australia on the west. (m. R4, t. 479)

Pacific Rim (pə sif′ik rim) The countries bordering on or located in the Pacific Ocean—especially the rapidly developing Asian countries on the Pacific. (m. R4, t. 652)

Pakistan (pak′i stan) One of two independent nations formed on the Indian subcontinent in 1947. (m. 583, t. 586)

Palestine (pal′ə stīn) Ancient region in southwestern Asia that became the home of the Jews; the ancient Roman name for Judea; in recent times, the British protectorate that became Israel in 1947. (m. 591, t. 591)

Pantheon (pan′thē on) A large, domed temple built in ancient Rome to honor many gods and goddesses. (t. 237)

Paris (par′is) Capital and largest city of France; 49°N, 2°E. (m. R10, t. 490)

Parthenon (pär′thə non) A temple to the goddess Athena, built 447–432 B.C. on the Acropolis in Athens. (t. 199)

Pearl Harbor (pûrl här′bər) A United States naval base in Hawaii that was bombed by the Japanese in 1941, causing the United States to enter World War II; 21°N, 158°W. (m. 557, t. 557)

Peloponnesus (pel ə pə nē′səs) A mountainous peninsula in southern Greece, between the Ionian and Aegean seas. (m. 185, t. 185)

Persian Gulf (pûr′zhən gulf) A body of water east of the Arabian Peninsula that separates Arabia from Iran. (m. 283, t. 283)

Peru (pə rü′) A colony in South America held by Spain from the 1500s to the 1800s; present-day country in western South America. (m. 465, t. 467)

Petra (pē′trə) The ancient Arabian capital of Nabataea, in what is today Jordan; 30°N, 35°E. (t. 284)

Phnom Penh (pə nom′ pen) The capital of Cambodia; first became capital during the Khmer rule in the 1400s; 12°N, 105°E. (m. 409, t. 411)

Phoenicia (fə nē′shə) An ancient seafaring civilization located on the eastern shore of the Mediterranean Sea. (m. 185, t. 186)

Pompeii (pom pā′) An ancient city in southwestern Italy that was buried by the eruption of Mount Vesuvius in A.D. 79; 41°N, 14°E. (m. 235, t. 236)

Portugal (pōr′ chə gəl) A country on the Iberian Peninsula in southwestern Europe. (m. R14, t. 456)

Pyrenees (pîr′ ə nēz) Mountain range that separates France from Spain. (m. 337, t. 339)

Q

Qin (chin) An ancient kingdom in northern China that rose to power under Emperor Shihuangdi in 221 B.C. (m. 161, t. 160)

Qinling Mountains (chin′ling′ moun′tənz) A mountain range in north-central China. (m. 161, t. 161)

R

Red Sea (red sē) A narrow sea between Arabia and northeastern Africa. (m. 283, t. 283)

Rocky Mountains (rok′ē moun′tənz) A mountain range in North America that stretches from Alaska into Mexico. (m. 259, t. 260)

Rome (rōm) The capital of ancient Rome and the name of an empire that included the lands around the Mediterranean and that stretched north through Europe into southern Britain; capital of present-day Italy; 42°N, 12°E. (m. 226, t. 222)

Russia (rush′ə) A country in eastern Europe and northern Asia; the largest country in the world; a republic of the Soviet Union from 1922 to 1991. (m. 547, t. 546)

S

Sahara (sə har′ə) The largest desert in the world, covering most of northern Africa. (m. 313, t. 313)

Sahel (sə həl′) The dry, grassy region south of the Sahara Desert, extending from Senegal to the Sudan. (m. 313, t. 313)

Saudi Arabia (sä′ ŭ dē ə rā′bē ə) A country in southwestern Asia occupying most of the Arabian Peninsula; 20°N, 45°E. (m. 591, t. 591)

Seine River (sān riv′ər) A river that flows from eastern France northward into the English Channel. (m. 337, t. 338)

Serbia (sûr′bē ə) Formerly part of Yugoslavia in eastern Europe, now the nation of Serbia and Montenegro; it includes the region of Kosovo. (m. 623, t. 624)

Sicily (sis′ə lē) An island in the Mediterranean Sea off the southwest tip of the Italian peninsula. (m. 219, t. 219)

Silk Road (silk rōd) An ancient network of overland trade routes that stretched from China to what is present-day Iran. (t. 389)

Singapore (sing′ə pōr) A city and independent republic in Southeast Asia; 1°N, 104°E. (m. 607, t. 610)

Songhai (sông′hī) The most powerful empire in West Africa from about 1490 to 1590. (m. 321, t. 326)

South America (south ə mâr′i kə) The fourth largest continent, located in the Western Hemisphere. (m. R10, t. 499)

Southeast Asia (south ēst′ ā′zhə) A region of southern Asia bounded by the Indian and Pacific oceans. (m. 607, t. 606)

South Korea (south kə rē′ə) A country in East Asia on the southern part of the Korean Peninsula; also a Pacific Rim nation. (m. R12, t. 573)

Soviet Union (sō′vē et ūn′yən) The name commonly used for the Union of Soviet Socialist Republics, which was a country in eastern Europe and northern Asia; the largest country in the world from 1922 to 1991. (m. 556, t. 552)

Spain (spān) A country in the Iberian Peninsula in southwestern Europe. (m. R14, t. 294)

Sparta (spär′tə) The largest ancient Greek city-state, located on the southern Peloponnesus; 37°N, 22°E. (m. 189, t. 192)

St. Petersburg (sānt pē′tərz bûrg) A Russian port city on the Baltic Sea; formerly the capital of Russia, it was called Leningrad when Russia was part of the Soviet Union; 60°N, 30°E. (m. 547, t. 550)

Stalingrad (stä′lən′ grad) A city in southern Russia on the Volga River that was attacked by German troops in 1942; the city is now known as Volgograd; 49°N, 44°E. (m. 556, t. 557)

Strait of Magellan (strāt əv mə jel'ən) A narrow waterway at the southern tip of South America, linking the Atlantic and Pacific oceans. (m. 459, t. 459)

Suez Canal (sü ez' kə nal') A canal in northeastern Egypt connecting the Mediterranean and Red seas. (t. 600)

Sumer (sü'mər) A group of ancient city-states in southern Mesopotamia; the earliest civilization in Mesopotamia. (m. 60, t. 58)

T

Taj Mahal (täzh mə häl') A grand tomb in Agra, India, built by Mughal emperor Shah Jahan to honor his wife, Mumtaz Mahal. (t. 398)

Tanzania (tan zä nē' ə) Republic in East Africa formed in 1964 by union of Tanganyika and Zanzibar; 5°S, 35°E. (m. R8, t. 31)

Tenochtitlán (te noch tēt län') The capital of the Aztec Empire, founded around 1325 on the site of present-day Mexico City; 19°N, 99°W. (m. 423, t. 422)

Thailand (tī'land) A nation in Southeast Asia, formerly called Siam. (m. 607, t. 607)

Thames River (temz riv'ər) A navigable river in Great Britain that flows east through London to the North Sea. (m. 337, t. 338)

Thebes (thēbz) An ancient city in Upper Egypt that became the capital of the New Kingdom; 26°N, 33°E. (m. 90, t. 95)

Tiananmen Square (tyen'än men skwâr) A square in Beijing, China, where government troops killed hundreds of people who were demonstrating for democratic reform in 1989. (t. 651)

Tiber River (tī'bər riv'ər) A river flowing southward from north-central Italy across the Latium plain, and into the Tyrrhenian Sea. (m. 219, t. 219)

Tibetan Plateau (ti bet'ən pla tō') A high mountain plateau in Asia. (m. 147, t. 147)

Tigris River (tī'gris riv'ər) A river in southwestern Asia that flows through the eastern part of the Fertile Crescent. (m. 55, t. 54)

Timbuktu (tim buk tü') A trade and cultural center of the Songhai Empire in the 1400s; a present-day town in the West African country of Mali; 16°N, 3°W. (m. 321, t. 324)

Tokyo (tō'kyō) The capital and largest city in Japan; formerly called Edo; 36°N, 140°W. (m. 526, t. 524) See also *Edo*.

Tonle Sap (tän lä' sap) A lake in western Cambodia. (m. 409, t. 409)

Turkey (tùr'kē) A nation established in 1923 in western Asia and southeastern Europe. (m. 591, t. 592)

U

United States (ū nī'tid stāts) A nation mainly in North America consisting of fifty states, the District of Columbia, several territories, and the Commonwealth of Puerto Rico. (m. R16, t. 651)

Upper Egypt (up'ər ē'jipt) The southern part of ancient Egypt. (m. 83, t. 83)

V

Valley of Mexico (val'ē əv mek'si kō) A fertile valley between two mountain chains in central Mexico. (t. 423)

Venezuela (ven ə zwā'lə) A country in northern South America on the Caribbean Sea. (m. R10, t. 500)

Versailles (vâr sī') A historic city in north-central France that contains the grand palace of Louis XIV; 49°N, 2°E. (t. 490)

Vietnam (vē et näm') A nation in Southeast Asia that was divided from 1954 until 1975 into North Vietnam and South Vietnam. (m. 607, t. 516)

Victoria Falls (vik tôr' ē ə fälz) A 350-foot waterfall on the Zambezi River between Zambia and Zimbabwe in southern Africa; 16°S, 29°E. (m. 313, t. 314)

W

Wales (wāls) Part of the United Kingdom, on the southwest coast of the island of Britain. (m. 349)

West Bank (west bangk) An area in western Asia west of the Jordan River; controlled by Israel from 1967 to 1995, after which Palestinians gained partial control. (m. 592, t. 593)

X

Xianyang (shē än'yang) Capital city of the Qin dynasty during the rule of the emperor Shihuangdi; 34°N, 109°E. (m. 161, t. 161)

Y

Yucatán (yü' kə tan) A peninsula in present-day Mexico, ruled by several ancient empires; 20°N, 90 °W. (m. 266, t. 266)

Yugoslavia (yü gō slä' vē ə) A nation that included the republics of Bosnia and Herzegovina, Croatia, Macedonia, and Slovenia until 1991; became the nation of Serbia and Montenegro in 2002. (m. 623, t. 624)

Z

Zambezi River (zam bē'zē riv'ər) A river in southern Africa, flowing east through Zimbabwe and Mozambique into the Indian Ocean. (m. 313, t. 314)

Zanzibar (zan'zə bär) An important Swahili city-state and trading center between 1100 and 1500; an island port in Tanzania in the Indian Ocean; 6°S, 39°E. (m. 330, t. 331)

Biographical Dictionary

The Biographical Dictionary tells you about the people you have learned about in this book. The Pronunciation Key tells you how to say their names. The page numbers tell you where each person first appears in the text.

A

Abraham (ā′brə ham), 1700s B.C. Founder of Judaism; led his family from Ur to Canaan. (p. 73)

Ahmose I (äm′ōs), d. 1546 B.C. New Kingdom pharaoh who drove out the Hyksos and reunited Egypt. (p. 97)

Akbar (ak′bär), A.D. 1542–1605 Ruler of the Mughal Empire in India from A.D. 1556 to 1605. (p. 395)

Akhenaton (äk ə nät′ on), 1380–1362 B.C. Pharaoh who instituted monotheism. (p. 100)

Alexander the Great (al ig zan′dər), 356–323 B.C. King of Macedonia; his conquests spread Greek culture throughout parts of three continents. (p. 208)

Amenhotep I (äm′ən hō′tep), 1514–1493 B.C. Pharoah who defended and expanded Egyptian territory. (p. 98)

Aquino, Corazon (ə kə′no kôr ə zōn′), A.D. 1933–President of the Philippines, 1986–1992. (p. 611)

Arafat, Yasir (ar′ə fat), A.D. 1929– Leader of the Palestine Liberation Organization. (p. 593)

Aristide, Jean Bertrand (är′is tēd), A.D. 1953– First elected president of Haiti in 1990. (p. 644)

Aristotle (ar′ə stot əl), 384–322 B.C. Greek philosopher; private teacher of Alexander the Great. (p. 209)

Askia Muhammad (a′skē ah), A.D. 1430–1538 King of the Songhai Empire in West Africa. (p. 326)

Atahualpa (ä tə wäl′pə), A.D. 1502?–1533 Last Inca emperor, killed by Francisco Pizarro. (p. 466)

Augustus (ô gus′təs), 63 B.C.–A.D. 14 First Roman emperor; established the Pax Romana. (p. 234)

Aung San Suu Kyi (əwn sən sü kē), A.D. 1945– Burmese political leader; Nobel Peace Prize winner. (p. 655)

Avicenna (av ə sen′ə), A.D. 980–1037 Persian philosopher and physician. (p. 296)

B

Babur (bäb′ər), A.D. 1483–1530 Founder of the Mughal dynasty in India. (p. 395)

Begin, Menachem (bā′gin mə näk′ əm), A.D. 1913–1992 Israeli Prime Minister, 1977–1983; Nobel Peace Prize recipient. (p. 594)

Benedict (ben′i dikt), A.D. 480?–547 Italian monk; founder of the Benedictine order. (p. 351)

Bolívar, Simón (bō lē′vär, sē mōn′), A.D. 1783–1830 Leader of the struggle for independence in South America. (p. 496)

C

Cabral, Pedro (kə bräl′), A.D. 1467?–1520? Portuguese navigator; claimed Brazil for Portugal. (p. 465)

Caesar, Julius (sē′zər, jül′yəs), 100–44 B.C. Roman general who became the republic's dictator in 45 B.C. (p. 233)

Cartier, Jacques (kər tyä′), A.D. 1491–1557 First French explorer to reach Canada. (p. 460)

Castro, Fidel (kas′trō fē del′), A.D. 1926– Cuban revolutionary leader; premier of Cuba since 1959. (p. 574)

Cervantes, Miguel de (sər van′ təz), A.D. 1547–1616 Spanish writer; author of *Don Quixote*. (p. 361)

pronunciation key

a	at	ī	ice	u	up	th	thin	
ā	ape	îr	pierce	ū	use	th	this	
ä	far	o	hot	ü	rule	zh	measure	
âr	care	ō	old	ù	pull	ə	about, taken,
e	end	ô	fork	ûr	turn		pencil, lemon,
ē	me	oi	oil	hw	white		circus
i	it	ou	out	ng	song		

Champollion, Jean (shäm pōl yän′), A.D. 1790–1832 Translator of the Rosetta Stone. (p. 94)

Charlemagne (shär′lə män), A.D. 742–814 Frankish king and emperor from 800 to 814. (p. 341)

Chiang Kai-shek (chang′kī shek′), A.D. 1887–1975 Chinese Nationalist leader. (p. 566)

Churchill, Winston (chûr′chil), A.D. 1874–1965 British prime minister from 1940 to 1945; 1951 to 1955. (p. 554)

Cleopatra (klē ə pa′trə), 69–30 B.C. Egyptian queen who supported Julius Caesar in the civil war in Rome. (p. 233)

Columbus, Christopher (kə lum′ bəs), A.D. 1451?–1506 Italian explorer in the service of Spain who arrived in the Americas in 1492. (p. 458)

Confucius (kən fū′shəs), 551–479 B.C. Chinese philosopher who stressed the need to respect tradition. (p. 155)

Constantine (kon′stən tēn), A.D. 280–337 Roman emperor; chose Constantinople as new Roman capital; encouraged Christianity. (p. 244)

Cook, James (kúk), A.D. 1728–1779 Explorer who claimed Australia for England. (p. 478)

Copernicus, Nicolaus (kə pûr′ni kəs), A.D. 1473–1543 Polish astronomer; established theory of heliocentrism. (p. 449)

Cortés, Hernando (kôr tes′, er nän′dō), A.D. 1485–1547 Spanish conquistador who defeated the Aztec. (p. 466)

 D

Da Gama, Vasco (də gä′mə, väs′cō), A.D. 1460?–1524 Portuguese navigator who in 1498 sailed from Europe around Africa to Asia. (p. 457)

Da Vinci, Leonardo (də vin′chē, lē ə när′dō), A.D. 1452–1519 Italian Renaissance artist, inventor, and scientist. (p. 358)

David (dā′vəd), c. 1085–973 B.C. King of Israel who made Jerusalem his capital. (p. 76)

De Klerk, F.W. (də klerk′), A.D. 1936– South African president from 1989 to 1994; worked for a peaceful transition to majority rule. (p. 631)

Deere, John (di′ər), A.D. 1804–1886 Inventor of the cast-steel plow. (p. 507)

Deng Xiaoping (dung′ shou′ping′), A.D. 1904–1997 Chairman of the Chinese Communist Party and premier of the People's Republic of China. (p. 651)

Dias, Bartolomeu (dē′ash, bâr tù lù mä′ù), A.D. 1450?–1500 Portuguese ship captain; sailed around the southern tip of Africa in 1487. (p. 457)

Diocletian (dī ə klē′shən), A.D. 245–313 Roman emperor who divided the empire in two. (p. 248)

 E

Eisenhower, Dwight D. (īz′en ha′ù ər), A.D. 1890–1969 U.S. World War II commander and president, 1953–1961. (p. 557)

Eleanor of Aquitaine (el′ə nər uv ak′ wə tān), A.D. 1122–1204 Queen of France and later of England; encouraged development of medieval art, poetry, and culture. (p. 345)

Elizabeth I (i liz′ə bəth), A.D. 1533–1603 Queen of England from 1558 to 1603. (p. 369)

Enheduana (en hed wän′ ə), c. 2300–2225 B.C. Sumerian priestess, poet, and daughter of Sargon. (p. 61)

Equiano, Olaudah (i kwē ä′nō, ōl′ə dä), A.D. 1750–1797 African American who wrote about life in slavery. (p. 472)

Ezana (eh′zan a), c. A.D. 300 King of Aksum who introduced Christianity to his kingdom. (p. 317)

pronunciation key

a	at	ī	ice	u	up	th	thin
ā	ape	îr	pierce	ū	use	th	this
ä	far	o	hot	ü	rule	zh	measure
âr	care	ō	old	ù	pull	ə	about, taken,
e	end	ô	fork	ûr	turn		pencil, lemon,
ē	me	oi	oil	hw	white		circus
i	it	ou	out	ng	song		

F

Frank, Anne (frangk), A.D. 1929–1945 German-Jewish girl who, with other Jews, was hidden from the Nazis from 1942 to 1944; she was found and sent to a concentration camp where she died. (p. 558)

Franz Ferdinand (franz fur′də nand), A.D. 1863–1914 Archduke of Austria whose assassination led to the outbreak of World War I. (p. 541)

Fu Hao (fü′hou′), 1100s B.C. Chinese noble woman. Her tomb contained records of her times. (p. 152)

Fulton, Robert (fült′en), A.D. 1765–1815 Inventor of the first practical steamboat. (p. 506)

G

Gao Zu (gəw zə), 259–195 B.C. Founder of the Han dynasty of China. (p. 166)

Galilei, Galileo (gal ə lā′ē, gal ə lā′ō), A.D. 1564–1642 Italian astronomer, mathematician, and physicist. (p. 449)

Gandhi, Indira (gän′dē), A.D. 1917–1984 Prime minister of India from 1966 to 1977; 1980 to 1984. (p. 588)

Gandhi, Mohandas (gän′dē), A.D. 1869–1948 Indian political and religious leader; he supported the use of nonviolent methods to bring independence. (p. 582)

Genghis Khan (geng′gəs kän′), A.D. 1162?–1227 Mongol conqueror of China, and parts of Asia and Europe. (p. 389)

Gilgamesh (gil′gəməsh), c. 2600 B.C. Legendary Mesopotamian king and hero. (p. 62)

Gorbachev, Mikhail (gôr′bə chəf), A.D. 1931– Soviet general secretary of the Communist Party from 1985 to 1990, and last president of the Soviet Union, 1990–1991. (p. 576)

H

Hammurabi (hä mu̇ rä′bē), 1800?–1750? B.C. King of the Babylonian Empire; creator of one of the world's oldest known codes of law. (p. 67)

Hannibal (han′ə bəl), 247?–183? B.C. Carthaginian general in the Second Punic War. (p. 226)

Hatshepsut (hat shep′süt), 1520?–1482 B.C. Female Egyptian pharaoh. (p. 98)

Henry VIII (hen′rē), A.D. 1491–1547 King of England from 1509 to 1547 and founder of the Church of England. (p. 368)

Henry, Prince (hen′rē), A.D. 1394–1460 Portuguese prince who directed the search for a sea route to the gold mines of western Africa. (p. 457)

Hidalgo, Miguel (ē däl′gō), A.D. 1753–1811 Mexican priest and revolutionary who led a revolt that started the Mexican war of independence. (p. 498)

Hildegard of Bingen (hil′ də gärd), A.D. 1098–1179 Medieval female writer and religious leader. (p. 351)

Hitler, Adolf (hit′lər), A.D. 1889–1945 German dictator; founded the National Socialist (Nazi) Party, which led Germany during World War II. (p. 555)

Ho Chi Minh (hō′chē′min′), A.D. 1890–1969 Communist independence leader in Vietnam. (p. 608)

Homer (hō′mûr), c. 700s B.C. Ancient Greek poet. (p. 194)

Hsing Yü (zhing yü), c. 200 B.C. Chinese general who fought against the Qin. (p. 164)

Hussein, Saddam (hü sän′), A.D. 1937–Dictator of Iraq; defeated in the 1991 Gulf War. (p. 596)

I

Ignatius of Loyola (ig nä′shəs), A.D. 1494–1556 Founder of the Jesuit order of Roman Catholic priests. (p. 370)

Iturbide, Agustin de (ē tür bē′dä), A.D. 1783–1824 Mexican soldier and leader; he won Mexican independence from Spain; ruler of Mexico. (p. 498)

---

pronunciation key

a	**a**t	ī	**i**ce	u	**u**p	th	**th**in
ā	**a**pe	îr	p**ier**ce	ū	**u**se	<u>th</u>	**th**is
ä	f**a**r	o	h**o**t	ü	r**u**le	zh	mea**s**ure
âr	c**a**re	ō	**o**ld	u̇	p**u**ll	ə	**a**bout, tak**e**n,
e	**e**nd	ô	f**o**rk	ûr	t**ur**n		p**e**ncil, lem**o**n,
ē	m**e**	oi	**oi**l	hw	**wh**ite		circ**u**s
i	**i**t	ou	**ou**t	ng	so**ng**		

Biographical Dictionary

J

Jayavarman II (jä yä vär'män), A.D. 800s One of the first Khmer kings of Cambodia. (p. 409)

Jesus (jē'zəs), 4? B.C.–A.D. 29? Jewish religious leader whose teachings became the foundation of Christianity. (p. 241)

Jinnah, Mohammad Ali (jin'ə), A.D. 1876–1948 First president of Pakistan from 1947 to 1948. (p. 586)

John I (jon), A.D. 1167?–1216 King of England from A.D. 1199 to 1216; in 1215 he signed the Magna Carta. (p. 346)

K

Kennedy, John F. (ken'i dē), A.D. 1917–1963 35th President of the United States from 1961 to 1963. (p. 575)

Kenyatta, Jomo (ken'yät ä), A.D. 1893–1978 African political leader and Kenya's first president. (p. 599)

Khadija (kä dē'jä), d. A.D. 619 A wealthy merchant who became the first wife of Muhammad. (p. 287)

Khrushchev, Nikita (krüsh'chef), A.D. 1894–1971 General secretary of the Soviet Communist Party from 1958 to 1964. (p. 575)

Khufu (kü fü'), 2650?–2600? B.C. Egyptian pharaoh who built the Great Pyramid. (p. 92)

Kim Il Sung (kim'il'süng'), A.D. 1912–1994 North Korean dictator. (p. 654)

Kublai Khan (kü'blə kän'), A.D. 1215–1294 Grandson of Genghis Khan, founder of China's Yüan dynasty. (p. 389)

L

Lalibela (lä'lē be lä), born A.D. 1100s King who ruled Ethiopia from about A.D. 1185 to 1225. (p. 319)

Lao Zi (laŭ' dzə), 606–530 B.C. Chinese philosopher and founder of Taoism. (p. 155)

Las Casas, Bartolomé de (läs käs'äs), A.D. 1475–1566 Spanish priest who wrote and spoke out against unjust treatment of Native Americans. (p. 473)

Lee Kwan Yew (lē kwôn yū), A.D. 1923– First prime minister of Singapore. (p. 610)

Lenin, Vladimir Ilyich (len'in), A.D. 1870–1924 Bolshevik leader and founder of the Soviet Union. (p. 550)

Leo X (lē'ō), A.D. 1475–1521 Pope when the Reformation began. (p. 367)

Liliuokalani (li lē'ü wō kə län'ē), A.D. 1838–1917 Last queen of Hawaii. (p. 479)

Liu Ping (lē ü pâng), ruled 206–195 B.C. Founder of China's Han dynasty. (p. 164)

Locke, John (läk'), A.D. 1632–1704 Enlightenment political thinker who said that the right to rule comes from the governed. (p. 454)

Louis XVI (lü'ē), A.D. 1754–1793 King of France; executed during the French Revolution. (p. 489)

Luther, Martin (lüth'ər), A.D. 1483–1546 German monk and leader of the Protestant Reformation. (p. 366)

M

Machiavelli, Niccolo (mäk'ē ə vel ē), A.D. 1469–1527 Italian Renaissance political thinker. (p. 358)

Magellan, Ferdinand (mə jel'ən), A.D. 1480?–1521 Portuguese explorer in the service of Spain; set out to find an all-water route to Asia. (p. 459)

Mandela, Nelson (man del'ə), A.D. 1918– South African civil rights leader who became president of South Africa in 1994. (p. 631)

Mansa Musa (män'sä mü'sä), A.D. 1297?–1337? Emperor of Mali from 1312 to 1337, when the kingdom was at its peak of wealth and power. (p. 324)

pronunciation key

a	at	ī	ice	u	up	th	thin
ā	ape	îr	pierce	ū	use	<u>th</u>	this
ä	far	o	hot	ü	rule	zh	measure
âr	care	ō	old	ù	pull	ə	about, taken,
e	end	ô	fork	ûr	turn		pencil, lemon,
ē	me	oi	oil	hw	white		circus
i	it	ou	out	ng	song		

Mao Zedong (mou′dze′dung′), A.D. 1893–1976 Chinese communist leader. (p. 566)

Marcos, Ferdinand (mär′kōs), A.D. 1917–1989 President, later dictator of the Philippines, 1965–1986. (p. 610)

Marie Antoinette (mə rē′ an twə net′), A.D. 1755–1793 Queen of France from 1774 to 1793; executed during the French Revolution. (p. 491)

Marx, Karl (märks), A.D. 1818–1883 German philosopher, economist, socialist. (p. 510)

McCormick, Cyrus (mə kôr′ mik), A.D. 1809–1884 Inventor of the mechanical reaper. (p. 507)

Medici, Lorenzo (med′i chē), A.D. 1449–1492 Renaissance ruler of Florence and patron of art. (p. 357)

Meiji (mā′jē′), A.D. 1852–1912 Japanese emperor from 1867 to 1912, during Japan's modernization. (p. 524)

Meir, Golda (me īr′), A.D. 1898–1978. Israeli prime minister; made peace with Egypt. (p. 594)

Menes (mē′nēz), 3100? B.C. King of Upper Egypt who united Upper and Lower Egypt. (p. 89)

Michelangelo (mī kəl an′jə lō), A.D. 1475–1564 Italian Renaissance sculptor, painter, architect, and poet. (p. 359)

Minamoto Yoritomo (yōr ē tō′mō), A.D. 1147–1199 Japanese shogun, or military commander. (p. 402)

Milosevic, Slobodan (məl ō′səv ich) A.D. 1941– Serbian leader; tried for war crimes in 2002. (p. 624)

Moctezuma (mäk tə zü′mə), A.D. 1468?–1520 Aztec emperor defeated by the Spanish. (p. 466)

Morelos, José María (mō re′lōs), A.D. 1765–1815 Mexican priest and revolutionary. (p. 498)

Moses (mō′ziz), c. 1200s B.C. Prophet who led the Israelites out of slavery in Egypt. (p. 74)

Muhammad (mü ham′əd), A.D. 570?–632? Founder of Islam. (p. 287)

Murasaki Shikibu (mür ä säk′ē shē kē′bü), A.D. 978?–1026? Japanese author who wrote *The Tale of Genji*, thought to be the world's first novel. (p. 404)

Mussolini, Benito (mü sə lē′nē), A.D. 1883–1945 Italian fascist leader. (p. 555)

N

Napoleon Bonaparte (nə pō′lē ən bō′nə pärt), A.D. 1769–1821 French revolutionary general who became Emperor Napoleon I of France in 1804. (p. 491)

Nasser, Gamal Abdel (nas′ər), A.D. 1918–1970 First president of Egypt from 1956 to 1970. (p. 600)

Nehru, Jawaharlal (nā′rü), A.D. 1889–1964 Prime minister of India from 1947 to 1964. (p. 586)

Newton, Isaac (nü′tən), A.D. 1642–1727 English scientist who studied gravity and was one of the inventors of calculus. (p. 448)

Nicholas II (nik′ə ləs), A.D. 1868–1918 Last Russian tsar from 1894 to 1917. (p. 547)

O

Osman (äs män′), A.D. 1258–1326? Founder of the Ottoman dynasty. (p. 381)

P

Paul (pôl), A.D. 11?–67? Follower of Jesus who helped spread Christianity throughout the Roman world. (p. 243)

Pericles (per′i klēz), 495?–429 B.C. Athenian leader who made sure all citizens could take part in government. (p. 200)

Perry, Matthew (per′ē), A.D. 1794–1858 U.S. naval officer who sailed to Japan in 1853 with a demand that Japanese ports be opened to U.S. trade. (p. 523)

pronunciation key

a	at	ī	ice	u	up	th	thin
ā	ape	îr	pierce	ū	use	th	this
ä	far	o	hot	ü	rule	zh	measure
âr	care	ō	old	u̇	pull	ə	about, taken,
e	end	ô	fork	ûr	turn		pencil, lemon,
ē	me	oi	oil	hw	white		circus
i	it	ou	out	ng	song		

Peter (pē'tər), A.D. 5?–67? One of the 12 apostles of Jesus. (p. 242)

Petrarch (pe'trärk), A.D. 1304–1374 Italian Renaissance poet and humanist. (p. 358)

Philip II (fil'əp), 382–336 B.C. King of Macedonia, father of Alexander the Great. (p. 204)

Pisan, Christine de (pē'sän), A.D. 1363–1430 French poet and writer. (p. 358)

Pizarro, Francisco (pē sär'rō), A.D. 1471?–1541 Spanish conquistador who defeated the Inca. (p. 466)

Plato (plā'tō), 428?–347? B.C. Greek philosopher and student of Socrates. (p. 201)

Polo, Marco (pō'lō), A.D. 1254–1324 Italian merchant who traveled to China. (p. 389)

Pompey (päm'pā), 106–48 B.C. Roman politician and general; enemy of Julius Caesar. (p. 233)

Rabin, Yitzhak (rä bēn'), A.D. 1922–1995 Prime minister of Israel; negotiated a peace plan with Palestinians. (p. 594)

Ramses II (ram'sēz), 1304–1237 B.C. Pharaoh who defeated the Hittites. (p. 100)

Rhazes (rä'zēs), A.D. 864–930 Medieval Muslim doctor. (p. 296)

Robespierre, Maximilien (rōbz'pē âr), A.D. 1758–1794 French revolutionary leader during the Reign of Terror. (p. 491)

Roosevelt, Franklin Delano (rō'zə velt), A.D. 1882–1945 The 32nd President of the United States; led the nation against the Axis powers in World War II. (p. 557)

S

Sadat, Anwar (sə dät'), A.D. 1918–1981 Egyptian president who established peaceful relations with Israel in 1978. (p. 594)

San Martín, José de (sän mär tēn'), A.D. 1778–1850 Argentine soldier who freed Argentina and Chile from Spanish rule. (p. 499)

Sargon (sär'gon), died 2279? B.C. King who united the city-states of Sumer to create an empire. (p. 61)

Scipio Africanus (sip'ē ō), 234?–183? B.C. Roman general who defeated Hannibal. (p. 227)

Shah Jahan (shä jə hän'), A.D. 1592–1666 Mughal emperor of India; built the Taj Mahal. (p. 397)

Shakespeare, William (shāk'spēr), A.D. 1564–1616 English dramatist and poet. (p. 360)

Shihuangdi (shē'hwäng dē), 259?–210 B.C. Chinese emperor who unified China and founded the Qin dynasty. (p. 161)

Siddhartha Gautama (sid där'tə gȯ'tə mə), 563?–483? B.C. Ancient Indian religious leader, known as the Buddha, who founded Buddhism. (p. 130)

Sinan (sē nän'), A.D. 1489–1588 Ottoman architect; he designed more than 300 buildings. (p. 383)

Socrates (sok'rə tēz), 470?–399 B.C. Greek philosopher who discussed laws, customs, values, and religion with students. (p. 201)

Solomon (säl'ə mən), c. 988–930 B.C. Son of David and king of Israel; built the temple at Jerusalem. (p. 76)

Stalin, Josef (stä'lin), A.D. 1879–1953 Soviet revolutionary and dictator who ruled the Soviet Union from 1924 to 1953. (p. 557)

Sukarnoputri, Megawati (sə kärn'o püt rē), A.D. 1947– became president of Indonesia, in 1999. (p. 609)

pronunciation key

a	at	ī	ice	u	up	th	thin
ā	ape	îr	pierce	ū	use	th	this
ä	far	o	hot	ü	rule	zh	measure
âr	care	ō	old	u̇	pull	ə	about, taken,
e	end	ô	fork	ûr	turn		pencil, lemon,
ē	me	oi	oil	hw	white		circus
i	it	ou	out	ng	song		

Suleyman (sü'lā män), A.D. 1495?–1566 Sultan of the Ottoman Empire from 1520 to 1566. (p. 382)

Sun Yat-sen (sùn' yät' sen'), A.D. 1866–1925 Founder of the Republic of China in 1912. (p. 565)

Sunjata (sän jä'tä), died. A.D. 1255 King of Mali who conquered all of Ghana. (p. 324)

Suryavarman II (sur yə vär'mən), A.D. 1100s Khmer king. (p. 410)

 T

Theodora (thə äd'ö ra), A.D. c. 500–548 Byzantine empress; wife of Justinian. (p. 251)

Tokugawa Ieyasu (tō kü gä'wä ē yä'sü), A.D. 1543–1616 Founder of the Tokugawa Shogunate. (p. 403)

Toussaint L'Ouverture (tü sän' lü vər tyür'), A.D. 1743?–1803 revolutionary Haitian leader. (p. 497)

Tutankhamun (tü täng kä'mən), 1371?–1352 B.C. Egyptian pharaoh; his tomb was discovered in 1922. (p. 96)

 U

Urban II (ər'bən), A.D. 1042–1099 Medieval pope who called for the First Crusade in 1095. (p. 352)

 V

Veale, Elizabeth (vēl, i liz' ə bəth), A.D. 1767–1850 Helped establish the production of wool as an important Australian industry. (p. 486)

Vespucci, Amerigo (ä mer ē' gō ves pü' chē), A.D. 1454–1512 Italian navigator who explored the coast of South America for Spain. (p. 458)

 W

Wallenberg, Raoul (wäl'ən bərg), A.D. 1912–1947? Swedish diplomat who saved thousands of Jews during World War II; disappeared in Soviet-occupied Europe. (p. 559)

Wang Mang (wäng mäng), 45 B.C.–A.D. 23 Usurper who took over China's throne, founding his own dynasty from A.D. 9–25. (p. 170)

Watt, James (wot), A.D. 1736–1819 Scottish engineer who developed an early steam engine. (p. 505)

William the Conqueror (wil'yəm), A.D. 1027–1087 Duke of Normandy; in 1066 he became the first Norman king of England. (p. 343)

Wilson, Woodrow (wil'sən), A.D. 1856–1924 28th President of the United States during World War I; he helped establish the League of Nations. (p. 545)

Wudi (wü'dē'), 100s B.C. Han emperor who ruled China from 140 B.C. to 87 B.C.; he set up a system of schools that prepared students for government jobs. (p. 167)

Wu Hou (wü hōw), A.D. 625–705 Empress of China during the Tang Dynasty. (p. 387)

Wuwang (wü wəng), c. 1134–1115 B.C. Founder of the Zhou dynasty of China. (p. 153)

 Y

Yeltsin, Boris (yel'tsin), A.D. 1931– First president of post-Soviet Russia. (p. 576)

 Z

Zheng He (chəng hö), 1371–1435 A.D. Chinese explorer and diplomat. (p. 390)

Zhou, Duke of (jō), c. 1000 B.C. Ancient Chinese leader; praised by Confucius. (p. 153)

Glossary

This Glossary will help you to pronounce and understand the meanings of the vocabulary in this book. The page number at the end of the definition tells where the word first appears.

A

abolish (ə bol′ ish) To end, stop. (p. 547)

aboriginal people (ab ə rij′ ə nəl pē′ pəl) The group of people who first inhabited Australia. (p. 482)

absolute location (ab sō lüt′ lō kā′ shən) The longitude and latitude of a place. (p. H11)

absolute monarch (ab′sə lüt mon′ərk) A ruler, or monarch, with unlimited power. (p. 489)

acropolis (ə krop′ə lis) A large hill in ancient Greece where city residents sought shelter and safety in times of war and met to discuss community affairs. (p. 190)

adobe (ə dō′ bē) A type of clay and straw brick used for building by Native Americans and Spanish colonists in the Southwest. (p. 274)

aerial photograph (ar ē əl fō tō graf) A photograph taken from the air. (p. H11)

agora (ag′ər ə) A central area in Greek cities used both as a marketplace and as a meeting place. (p. 190)

agriculture (ag′ri kul chər) The raising of crops and animals for human use. (p. 45)

algebra (al′je brə) A type of mathematics to which Muslims made great contributions. (p. 297)

alliance (ə lī′əns) An agreement between countries to work together in war or trade. (p. 541)

Allied Powers (al′īd pou′ərz) In World War I, the nations who worked together against the Central Powers; included Serbia, Russia, France, Britain, and the United States. (p. 542)

Allies (al′īz) In World War II, the nations allied against the Axis powers, including Britain, China, France, the Soviet Union, and the United States. (p. 556)

alternative (ôl tûr′ nə tiv) Another way of doing something. (p. 86)

Anglican Church (ān′ gli kən chûrch) The Church of England started by Henry VIII. (p. 368)

anthropologist (an thrə pä′ lə jist) A person who studies human beings and their beliefs and ways of life. (p. 613)

anti-Semitism (an tē sem′i tiz əm) Discrimination against and hatred of Jews. (p. 592)

apartheid (ə pär′tīd) The government policy of strict and unequal segregation of the races as practiced in South Africa from 1948 to the early 1990s. (p. 631)

apostle (ə pos′əl) One of the 12 closest followers of Jesus, chosen by him to help him teach. (p. 242)

aqueduct (ak′wə dukt) A raised, arched structure built to carry water over long distances. (p. 70)

arabesque (ar ə besk′) Arab design marked by flowing, lacy ornaments often including leafy forms and vines. (p. 298)

arable (ar′ə bəl) Land fit for or used for the growing of crops. (p. 635)

archaeologist (är kē ol′ə jist) A person who studies the remains of past cultures. (p. 15)

archipelago (är kə pel′ə gō) A large group of islands. (p. 377)

architecture (är′ki tek chər) The art and science of planning and constructing buildings. (p. 138)

aristocracy (ar ə stok′rə sē) The class of a society made up of members of noble families, usually the most powerful group. (p. 489)

armistice (är′mə stis) An agreement to stop fighting; a truce. (p. 545)

pronunciation key

a	at	ī	ice	u	up	th	thin
ā	ape	îr	pierce	ū	use	th	this
ä	far	o	hot	ü	rule	zh	measure
âr	care	ō	old	ů	pull	ə	about, taken,
e	end	ô	fork	ûr	turn		pencil, lemon,
ē	me	oi	oil	hw	white		circus
i	it	ou	out	ng	song		

arms race (ärmz rās) A race to build the most powerful weapons. (p. 572)

artifact (är′tə fakt) An object made by someone in the past. (p. 14)

assembly (ə sem′blē) A lawmaking body of government made up of a group of citizens. (p. 200)

astrolabe (as′trə lāb) An instrument invented by Muslims that is used to determine direction by figuring out the position of the stars. (p. 297)

Axis (ak′sis) In World War II, the nations who fought the Allies, including Japan, Germany, and Italy. (p. 556)

ban (ban) to prohibit especially by legal means. (p. 451)

barter (bär′ tər) To trade things for other things without using money. (p. 69)

basin (bā′ sin) A low, bowl-shaped landform surrounded by higher land. (p. 314)

Bastille (bas tēl) A prison fortress in Paris that was attacked and destroyed on July 14, 1789, at the start of the French Revoloution. (p. 490)

Berlin Airlift (bər lin′ ar′ lift) Delivery of food and supplies to Berlin during Stalin's blockade of the city from 1948 to 1949. (p. 571)

Berlin Wall (bər lin′ wôl) A wall that separated communist East Berlin and democratic West Berlin. It was torn down in 1998 as part of a democratic revolution. (p. 574)

bias (bī′ əs) A strong feeling for or against a person or thing that prevents fairness. (p. 562)

bishop (bish′ əp) A church official who leads a large group of Christians in a particular region. (p. 243)

Bolshevik (bōl shə′ vik) A member of the Russian Social Democratic party that seized power in Russia in November 1917. (p. 550)

Boxer (bäk′ sər) A member of a group that tried to drive foreigners out of China in 1900. (p. 517)

boycott (boi′kot) A form of protest in which people join together to refuse to buy goods. (p. 583)

Buddhism (büd′iz əm) A religion founded in India by Siddhartha Gautama which teaches that the most important thing in life is to reach peace by ending suffering. (p. 134)

bureaucracy (byū rok′rə sē) The large organization that runs the daily business of government. (p. 167)

C

caliph (kā′lif) A Muslim leader who had both political and religious authority. (p. 293)

caliphate (kā′ lə fāt) Lands ruled by the Islamic caliphs. (p. 293)

calligraphy (kə lig′ rə fē) Arabic handwriting designed in an artistic style. (p. 298)

caravan (kar′ə van) A group of people and animals traveling together for safety, especially through a desert. (p. 284)

caravel (kar′ə vel) A sailing ship developed in Portugal in the 1400s that had greater directional control than earlier ships and could sail great distances more safely. (p. 457)

cardinal directions (kärd′ən əl di rek′shənz) The directions north, south, east, and west. (p. H13)

cartogram (kär′tə gram) A special kind of map that distorts the shapes and sizes of countries or other political regions to present economic or other kinds of data for comparison. (p. 648)

caste system (kast sis′təm) The social system in Hindu society in which a person's place is determined by the rank of the family into which he or she is born. (p. 126)

cataract (ka′ tə rakt) A steep rapid in a river. (p. 103)

cathedral (kə thē′drəl) A large Christian church that is the official church of the bishop, an important member of the clergy. (p. 353)

CD-ROM (sē′ dē′ räm′) A type of reference source similar to a compact disc that is "read" by a computer. It combines text, sound, and even short films. See **reference source**. (p. 628)

census (sen′səs) A periodic count of all the people living in a country, city, or other region. (p. 235)

Central Powers (sen′trəl pou′ərz) In World War I, the nations who fought against the Allied Powers, including Austria-Hungary and Germany. (p. 542)

century (sent′ chə rē) A period of one hundred years. (p. 64)

chinampas (chin äm′paz) One of the floating islands made by the Aztec around Tenochtitlán for growing crops. (p. 423)

chivalry (shi′ vəl rē) The qualities of the ideal knight, including politeness, bravery, honor, and protecting the weak. (p. 345)

Christianity (kris chē an′i tē) A religion based on the teachings of Jesus, as recorded in the New Testament. (p. 241)

citadel (sit′ə dəl) A walled fort that protects a city. (p. 119)

citizen (sit′ə zən) A person with certain rights and responsibilities in his or her country or community. (p. 191)

Glossary

city-state (sit'ē stāt) A self-governing city, often with surrounding lands and villages. (p. 60)

civil disobedience (siv'əl dis ə bē'dē əns) A means of protest by refusing to obey a law that is considered to be unjust. (p. 584)

civil war (siv'əl wōr) An armed conflict between groups within one country. (p. 233)

civilization (siv ə lə zā'shən) A culture that has developed systems of specialization, religion, learning, and government. (p. 47)

Classic Period (klas'ik pēr'ē əd) A time of great cultural achievement for a civilization. (p. 266)

climate (klī' mit) The weather pattern of an area over a long period of time. (p. 5)

code of law (kōd uv lô) A written set of laws that apply to everyone under a government. (p. 68)

codex (kō'deks) A manuscript page such as the kind used by the Aztec to record historical, religious, governmental, and scientific knowledge. (p. 426)

Cold War (kōld wôr) A term used for the battle of words and ideas that developed between the democratic nations of the West and the Soviet Union and Eastern Europe from about 1945 to 1990. (p. 571)

collective farm (kə lek' tiv färm) A large farm made up of many small family farms. (p. 552)

colony (kol' ə nē) A territory or community that is under the control of another country. (p. 201)

command economy (kə mand' ē kä' nə mē) An economy completely controlled by a central government. (p. 552)

commodity (kə ma' də tē) Something that can be bought and sold. (p. 190)

commune (kom'ūn) A community in which resources, work, and living space are shared by all members of the group. (p. 568)

communism (kom'yə niz əm) A political and economic system in which the government controls all land and industry. (p. 552)

complex (käm' pleks) A group of buildings. (p. 410)

concentration camp (kon sən trā'shən kamp) A place where people are imprisoned because of their heritage, religious beliefs, or political views. (p. 558)

conclusion (kən klü'zhən) A final statement or opinion reached by putting together information about a subject. (p. 428)

Confucianism (kən fū'shə niz əm) In China, a system of beliefs and behavior based on the teachings of Confucius, who said that people should lead good lives by studying ancient traditions and stressed the importance of respecting one's family and ancestors. (p. 167)

conquistador (kon kēs'tə dôr) A Spanish conqueror who came to the Americas to search for gold and land. (p. 466)

consequence (kän' sə kwens) A result of an action. (p. 42)

consul (kon'səl) One of two elected officials of the Roman Republic who commanded the army and was a supreme judge. (p. 225)

cotton gin (kot'ən jin) A machine that separates seeds from cotton fibers, invented by Eli Whitney in 1793. (p. 476)

covenant (kəv' ə nənt) A special agreement. (p. 73)

Creole (krē' ōl) A person of Spanish descent who is born in the Americas. (p. 468)

crucifixion (krü sə fik' shən) Execution on a cross. (p. 242)

Crusade (krü sād') Any of the journeys and battles undertaken by European Christians between 1095 and 1270, to win control of the Holy Land (Palestine) from the Muslims. (p. 352)

Cultural Revolution (kul'chər əl rev ə lü'shən) A campaign in China, 1966–1976, in which the Communist Party, under Mao Zedong, called for the destruction of all noncommunist beliefs. (p. 568)

culture (kul' chər) The way of life of a group of people at a particular time, including their daily habits, beliefs, and arts. (p. 6)

cuneiform (kū nē' ə fōrm) A system of writing that used wedge-shaped symbols to represent sounds, ideas, and objects; developed in ancient Sumer. (p. 59)

custom (kus'təm) A way of living that people of the same culture practice regularly over time. (p. 9)

---

daimyo (dī' mē yō) A Japanese feudal baron. (p. 402)

database (dā' təbās) A reference source that contains information, such as articles, pictures, maps, and music that has been stored electronically. (p. 628)

decision (di sizh'ən) A choice made from a number of alternatives. See **conclusion**. (p. 86)

decision making (dis izh'ən māk'ing) Choosing from a number of alternatives to achieve a goal. (p. 86)

Declaration of the Rights of Man (dek lə rā'shən) A statement issued by the French National Assembly in August 1789 proclaiming that all men were "born and remain free and equal in rights." (p. 490)

decree (di krē') An order usually having the force of law. (p. 502)

deforestation (dē for ə stā'shən) The process of clearing the land of forests, often to make space for farms and cities. (p. 338)

degree (di grē′) In geography, a unit of measurement that indicates the distance between lines of latitude and longitude; a unit of measurement for temperature. (p. 116)

delta (del′tə) The flat, fan-shaped land made of silt deposited at the mouth of a river. (p. 83)

demand (di mand′) In economics, people's desire for a particular item and their ability and willingness to pay for it. See **supply**. (p. 323)

democracy (di mok′rə sē) A system of government in which citizens vote to make governmental decisions. (p. 193)

depression (di presh′ən) A severe slowdown in business characterized by high unemployment and falling prices. (p. 555)

desertification (di zər ti fi kā′ shən) The process of becoming a desert from land mismanagement or climate change. (p. 635)

dharma (där′mə) In Hinduism, the laws and duties that guide the behavior of each caste member. (p. 126)

Diaspora (dī as′pər ə) The scattering of Jews to many parts of the world. (p. 76)

dictator (dik′tā tər) A ruler who has absolute power. (p. 233)

distortion (di stôr′shən) In cartography, or mapmaking, the unavoidable inaccuracy caused by stretching or cutting parts of the globe to fit them onto a flat map. (p. 36)

distribution map (dis trə bū′shən map) A special purpose map that shows how a particular feature such as population density is spread over an area. (p. H18, 158)

domesticate (də mes′ti kāt) To train plants or animals to be useful to people. (p. 45)

dominion (də min′ yən) A self-governing nation other than the United Kingdom in the British Commonwealth of Nations that acknowledges the British monarch as chief of state. (p. 616)

drought (drout) A long period of dry weather. (p. 55)

dry farming (drī fär′ ming) A technique for growing crops in an area with limited rainfall. (p. 274)

Duma (dūma) The legislative assembly of Russia. (p. 548)

duty (dū′ tē) Import tax. (p. 646)

dynasty (dī′nə stē) A line of rulers who belong to the same family. (p. 150)

E

Eastern Orthodox Christianity (ēs′tərn ôr′thə doks kris chē an′i tē) A branch of Christianity that developed in the Byzantine Empire and that does not recognize the pope as its supreme leader. (p. 251)

economy (i kon′ə mē) The way a country manages money and resources for the production of goods and services. (p. 94)

Eightfold Path (āt′fōld path) In Buddhism, the basic rules of behavior and belief leading to an end of suffering. See **Four Noble Truths**. (p. 133)

elevation (el ə vā′shən) Height above sea level. (p. 228)

elevation map (el ə vā′shən map) A map that shows the height of land above sea level. (p. H17)

El Niño (el nē′ nyō) An irregularly recurring flow of unusually warm surface waters in the Pacific Ocean that disrupts typical regional and global weather patterns (p. 420)

embargo (em bär′ gō) A restriction that a government puts on the buying and selling of certain goods, especially on the importing or exporting of certain goods. (p. 575)

empire (em′pīr) A group of lands and peoples ruled by one government. (p. 61)

Enlightenment (en lī′ tən mənt) A European movement of the eighteenth century marked by a rejection of many traditional social, religious, and political ideas and with an emphasis on rationalism. (p. 454)

epic (e′ pik) A long poem that tells the story of heroes in legend or history. (p. 194)

equal-area projection (ē′kwəl är′ē ə prə jek′shən) A map that is useful for comparing sizes of land masses, on which shapes at the center are fairly accurate but are very distorted at the edges of the map. (p. 36)

erosion (i rō′zhən) The gradual wearing away of soil and rock by wind, glaciers, or water. (p. 56)

estates (e stāts′) The three social classes into which France was divided before the French Revolution and which include the clergy, the aristocracy, and the common people. (p. 489)

euro (yür′ ō) The currency of most countries of the European Union. (p. 623)

European Union (EU) (yür ə pē′ən ün′yən) A group of European nations working to build a common economy and create cultural ties throughout Europe. (p. 623)

---

pronunciation key

a **a**t; ā **a**pe; ä **fa**r; âr **ca**re; e **e**nd; ē **me**; i **i**t; ī **i**ce; îr **pie**rce; o **ho**t; ō **o**ld; ô **fo**rk; oi **oi**l; ou **ou**t; u **u**p; ū **u**se; ü **ru**le; u̇ **pu**ll; ûr **tu**rn; hw **wh**ite; ng **so**ng; th **th**in; <u>th</u> **th**is; zh mea**s**ure; ə **a**bout, tak**e**n, penc**i**l, lem**o**n, circ**u**s

evaluate (i val′ū āt) To judge. (p. 43)

excavate (eks′ kə vātə) To dig or to scoop out earth. (p. 15)

expedition (ek spi dish′ən) A group of people who go on a trip for a specific reason. (p. 97)

export (ek′ sport) To send goods to other countries for sale or use. (p. 642)

factory (fak′tə rē) A building in which machines used to manufacture goods are located. (p. 505)

famine (fam′in) A widespread lack of food resulting in hunger and starvation. (p. 147)

fascism (fash′iz əm) A totalitarian government that promotes a form of nationalism in which the goals of the nation are more important than those of the individual. (p. 555)

feudalism (fū′də liz əm) Starting in Europe around A.D. 800, a system for organizing and governing society, based on land and service. See **fief**, **vassal**. (p. 344)

fief (fēf) In the Middle Ages, a property given to a vassal in exchange for loyalty. (p. 344)

Five Pillars (fīv pil′ərz) The five basic duties of all Muslims. (p. 289)

fjord (fyôrd) A long, narrow inlet of the sea between high cliffs. (p. 338)

flaking (flā′ king) A process of shaping stone by chipping pieces off the edges. (p. 39)

Four Noble Truths (fôr nō′bəl trüthz) In Buddhism, the principles that rule life and promise an end to suffering. See **Eightfold Path**. (p. 133)

frame of reference (frām əv ref′ rəns) The basis, including experience, education, and nationality, that a person uses when forming a point of view. (p. 494)

front (frunt) An area where enemy armies fight. (p. 542)

gaucho (gaü′ chō) South American cowhand. (p. 419)

gene (jēn) One of the tiny units of a cell of an animal or plant that determines the characteristics that an offspring inherits from its parent or parents. (p. 18)

generalization (jen ər ə lə zā′shən) A broad statement that points out a common feature shared by different kinds of examples. (p. 230)

genocide (jen′ ə sīd) The deliberate and systematic destruction of a racial, political, or cultural group. (p. 634)

geocentric (jē ō sen′trik) The idea that Earth is the center of the universe and that the sun, stars, and planets revolve around Earth. (p. 449)

geography (jē og′rə fē) The study of Earth's environment and how it shapes people's lives and how Earth is shaped in turn by people's activities. (p. 4)

gladiator (glad′ē ā tər) A Roman athlete, usually a slave, criminal, or prisoner of war, who was forced to fight for the entertainment of the public. (p. 235)

global grid (glō′bəl grid) Pattern formed on a map or globe by the crossing of parallels and meridians. This pattern makes it possible to pinpoint exact locations. (p. 117)

globe (glōb) A round model with a map of the world on it. (p. H11)

glyph (glif) A writing symbol, often carved into stone, that stands for an object or a sound. See **stela**. (p. 268)

gorge (gôrj) Mountain pass with steep rocky sides. (p. 148)

Gothic (gä′ thik) A style of architecture developed in Europe between 1100 and 1500, characterized by pointed arches, rib vaulting, and flying buttresses. (p. 353)

granary (grā′ nə rē) A storehouse for grain. (p. 329)

Grand Canal (grand kə nal′) A waterway in China connecting Beijing with cities to the south. (p. 387)

grand mufti (grand muf′tē) A religious leader of the Ottoman Empire responsible for interpreting the laws of Islam. (p. 382)

Grand School (grand skül) A school begun by Confucian scholars in China that trained students for government jobs. (p. 167)

gravity (grav′i tē) The force that pulls objects toward Earth and that draws planets into orbits around the sun. (p. 452)

Green Revolution (grēn rev ə lü′shən) A campaign by the government of India in the 1950s to increase agricultural productivity. (p. 588)

grid (grid) A pattern of intersecting lines that divides a map or chart into small squares. (p. 116)

griot (grē′ō) An oral historian and musician who became important in western Africa in the 1500s and still carries on oral traditions today. (p. 326)

gross domestic product (grōs də mes′tik prod′ukt) The total value of goods and services produced by a country during a year. (p. 648)

hacienda (hä sē en′də) A large agricultural estate owned by Spaniards or the Roman Catholic Church in Spain's American colonies. (p. 468)

harbor (här′bər) A sheltered place along a coast used to protect boats and ships. (p. 185)

heliocentric (hē lē ō sen′trik) Copernicus's idea that Earth and the other planets revolve around the sun. (p. 449)

Hellenism (he lə ni′ zəm) A culture that was a blend of Greek ideas and the traditions of Africa and Asia in ancient times. (p. 212)

hieroglyphics (hī ər ə glif′iks) The ancient Egyptian system of writing that used symbols to stand for objects, ideas, or sounds. (p. 92)

hijra (hij′rə) The migration of Muhammad from Mecca to Medina in A.D. 622, marking the founding of Islam. (p. 288)

Hinduism (hin′dü iz əm) The religion of India that grew out of the beliefs of the ancient Aryan peoples; it stresses that one main force connects all of life. (p. 124)

historical map (hi stôr′i kəl map) A map that shows information about the past. (p. H17, 196)

Holocaust (hol′ə kôst) The deliberate killing of six million men, women, and children by the Nazis during World War II solely because they were Jewish. (p. 558)

humanism (hū′mə niz əm) An idea important to the Renaissance that focused on human values and what people can achieve in this world. (p. 357)

hunter-gatherer (hun′tər gath′ər ər) A person who meets needs by hunting animals and gathering plants. (p. 33)

hydroelectric power (hī drō i lek′ trik pou′ ər) Electricity created by generators run by rapidly flowing water. (p. 315)

icon (ī′ kän) A symbol that stands for something else. (p. 406)

impeach (im pēch′) To charge a government official with wrongdoing. (p. 609)

imperialism (im pir′ē ə liz əm) The extension of a nation's power over other lands by military, political, or economic means. (p. 515)

indulgence (in dul′jəns) In the Roman Catholic Church, a pardon from punishment for a sin in exchange for an offering. (p. 367)

Industrial Revolution (in dus′ trē əl rev ə lü′ shən) A time when great technological advances changed the way goods were made and the ways people lived; it began in England in the 1700s and then spread throughout Europe and the United States. (p. 505)

intermediate directions (in tər mē′dē it di rek′shənz) The directions halfway between the cardinal directions; northeast, southeast, southwest, and northwest. (p. H13)

intifada (in tə fä′də) The Palestinian uprising against Israeli rule that began in 1987. (p. 594)

iron curtain (ī′ ərn kər′ tin) The imaginary border dividing Europe into communist and noncommunist countries from 1948 to 1991. (p. 570)

irrigation (ir i gā′shən) The watering of dry land by means of canals or pipes. (p. 55)

Islam (is läm′) The religion of Muslims based on the teachings of the prophet Muhammad in the A.D. 600s. (p. 287)

isthmus (is′məs) A narrow strip of land that connects two larger land masses. (p. 417)

Jesuit (jezh′ ü it) A member of the Society of Jesus, a Roman Catholic religious order for men founded by Ignatius of Loyola in 1540. (p. 370)

Judaism (jü′dē iz əm) The religion of the Jewish people. (p. 72)

jury (jùr′ē) A group of citizens chosen to hear evidence and make a decision in a court of law. (p. 200)

Justinian Code (ju stin′ ē ən kōd) A code of law that standardized laws in the Byzantine Empire and dealt with marriage, property rights, slavery, crime, and women's rights. (p. 251)

Kaaba (kä′bə) A sacred Muslim shrine in Mecca. (p. 287)

karma (kär′mə) In Hinduism and Buddhism, the end result of all of a person's good and bad acts, which determines his or her rebirth. (p. 132)

kiva (kē′ və) A pit structure used by the Anasazi for religious ceremonies. (p. 274)

land bridge (land brij) A bridge between two larger pieces of land formed by a small strip of land and is often temporary. (p. 259)

large-scale map (lärj skāl map) A map that provides many details about a small area by measuring lesser distances in small units. (p. 348)

---

pronunciation key

a **a**t; ā **a**pe; ä f**a**r; âr c**a**re; e **e**nd; ē m**e**; i **i**t; ī **i**ce; îr p**i**erce; o h**o**t; ō **o**ld; ô f**o**rk; oi **oi**l; ou **ou**t; u **u**p; ū **u**se; ü r**u**le; ù p**u**ll; ûr t**u**rn; hw **wh**ite; ng so**ng**; th **th**in; th **th**is; zh mea**s**ure; ə **a**bout, tak**e**n, penc**i**l, lem**o**n, circ**u**s

Latin America (lat'in ə mer'i kə) The cultural region including Mexico, Central America, the Caribbean, and South America that has been strongly influenced by Spain and Portugal. (p. 497)

latitude (lat'i tüd) Distance north or south of the equator, measured by a set of imaginary lines, or parallels, that run east and west around Earth. See **parallel**. (p. H11, 116)

League of Nations (lēg əv nā'shənz) An international organization created in 1929 by the Allied Powers to try to prevent future wars. (p. 545)

legalism (lē' gəl izm) A philosophy of strict government in China in the 200s B.C. in which citizens were encouraged to serve the needs of the state. (p. 162)

legend (lə jind') A guide that shows what each symbol on a map stands for. (p. H15)

levee (lev'ē) A wall built along a riverbank to prevent flooding. (p. 55)

Line of Demarcation (līn əv dē mär kā'shən) An imaginary line drawn through North and South America in 1494 to divide the claims of Spain and Portugal. (p. 465)

locator (lō'kāt ər) A small map that shows where the subject area of a main map is located. (p. H15)

loess (les) A fine, yellow soil that is easily carried by wind and rain, found in China. (p. 147)

longitude (lon'ji tüd) Distance east or west of the prime meridian measured by a set of imaginary lines, or meridians, that run north and south from Earth's poles. See **meridian**. (p. H11, 116)

Long March (long march) The escape of Mao Zedong and his followers from southern China to the north after enemy troops surrounded them in 1934. (p. 566)

M

Magna Carta (mag'nə kär'tə) A legal document written by English lords in 1215 that stated certain rights of the barons, merchants, and clergy, which limited the power of the king. (p. 346)

maize (māz) Corn; a crop first grown in Middle America about 5000 B.C. (p. 267)

Mandate of Heaven (man'dāt uv hev'ən) The belief that the Chinese emperor's right to rule came from the gods. (p. 153)

manor (man'ər) In the Middle Ages, a large self-sufficient estate granted to a lord and worked by serfs. (p. 344)

map (map) A drawing that shows the surface features of an area. (p. H11)

map key (map kē) A list of map symbols that tells what each symbol stands for. (p. H15, 196)

map symbol (map sim' bol) Something that stands for something else on a map. (p. H15)

martial law (mär' shel lä) Military rule or authority over a civilian population. (p. 610)

medium of exchange (mē' dē əm əv iks chānj') usually a metal with a value people will accept, such as gold. (p. 69)

Meiji Restoration (mā' jē' res tə rā' shən) The overthrow of Japan's shogun in 1868 and restoration of power to the emperor Meiji. (p. 524)

menu (men' ū) A list of operations to choose from on a computer. (p. 406)

mercator projection (mər kä'tər prə jek'shən) A map that shows accurate shapes of land masses and correct straight-line directions, but which is distorted for areas near the poles. (p. 37)

meridian (mə rid'ē ən) Any line of longitude east or west of Earth's prime meridian. See **parallel**. (p. H11, 117)

Messiah (mə sī'ə) A special leader the Jewish people believe will be sent by God to guide them and set up God's rule on Earth. Christians believe Jesus to be the Messiah. (p. 241)

mestizo (me stē'zō) A person of mixed Native American and Spanish ancestry. (p. 468)

Middle Ages (mid'əl āj'əz) A period in European history between A.D. 500 and about the 1400s. (p. 340)

middle class (mid'əl klas) A class of society that includes professionals and businesspeople that began to grow during the Industrial Revolution. (p. 508)

Middle Passage (mid'əl pas'ij) The difficult voyage made by enslaved Africans across the Atlantic Ocean to the West Indies where they were sold. (p. 474)

Middle Way (mid'əl wā) In Buddhism, a way of life, neither too strict nor too easy that results from following the Eightfold Path. (p. 133)

migrate (mī'gr āt) To move from one place to another to live, especially a large group of people. (p. 44)

minaret (mi nə ret') A tall, slender tower attached to a mosque from which prayer calls are made. (p. 298)

missionary (mish'ə ner ē) A person who teaches his or her religion to people with different beliefs. (p. 469)

monarchy (mon'ər kē) A government ruled by a king or queen. (p. 191)

monastery (mon'ə ster ē) A community in which monks lead lives devoted to religion. (p. 351)

monk (mungk) A man who devotes his life to a religious group, often giving up all he owns. See **monastery**. (p. 131)

monotheism (mon'ə thē iz əm) A belief in one God. See **polytheism**. (p. 75)

monsoon (mon sün') A seasonal wind that blows across South Asia bringing dry weather in the winter and heavy rains in the summer. (p. 378)

mosque (mosk) A Muslim place of worship. (p. 288)

mummification (mu mi fi kā′ shən) The process of preserving a dead body through embalming and drying. (p. 91)

Muslim (muz′ ləm) A person who follows the practices of Islam, the religion founded by Muhammad. (p. 287)

Napoleonic Code (nə pō lē ä′ nik kōd) A set of laws that emphasized order over individual rights, established by Napoleon I of France. (p. 492)

National Liberation Front (nash′ə nəl lib ər ā shən frunt) An organization formed in 1954 in Algeria to fight France for independence. (p. 602)

nationalism (nash′ə nə liz əm) A strong loyalty to one's own country and culture. (p. 515)

NATO (nā′tō) The North Atlantic Treaty Organization, a military alliance formed in 1949 by nations in western Europe and North America. (p. 572)

navigable (nav′i gə bəl) Able to be traveled by boats or ships. (p. 338)

Nazi (nä′ tsē) A member of the political party that controlled Germany under the leadership of Adolf Hitler from 1933 to 1945. (p. 555)

Neolithic Era (nē ō lith′ik îr ′ə) The last period of the Stone Age when human beings began to develop agriculture, and use tools and weapons made from shaped and polished stone. See **New Stone Age** (p. 45)

neutral (nü′ trəl) Not taking sides in a war or conflict. (p. 544)

New Stone Age (nü stōn āj) The period of human prehistory that lasted from 12,000 years ago to about 6,000 years ago, during which people still depended mainly on stone tools and began experimenting with agriculture. (p. 45)

New Testament (nü tes′tə mənt) The second part of the Christian Bible, containing descriptions of the life and teachings of Jesus and of his early followers. (p. 241)

95 Theses (thē ′sēz) Martin Luther's arguments for reform of the Roman Catholic Church. (p. 366)

Northwest Passage (nôrth′west′ pas′ij) A water route that explorers searched for from the 1500s to the 1700s; believed to flow through North America to connect the Atlantic and Pacific oceans. (pp. 460–461)

nun (nun) A woman who devotes her life to religion, often living in a convent. (p. 351)

oasis (ō ā′sis) A well-watered area in a desert. (p. 283)

Old Kingdom (ōld king′dum) Egypt from about 2700 B.C. to about 2200 B.C. when early pharaohs united Upper Egypt and Lower Egypt. (p. 89)

Old Stone Age (ōld stōn āj) The period of human prehistory that lasted until about 12,000 years ago, during which stone tools were the most common technology used by humans. See **Paleolithic Era**. (p. 31)

oligarchy (ol′i gär kē) A type of government in which a small group of citizens control decision-making. (p. 191)

oracle bones (ôr′ə kəl bōnz) In ancient China, a cattle or sheep bone used to predict the future. (p. 152)

oral history (ôr′ əl his′ tə rē) Spoken records, including stories, that have been passed from one generation to the next. (p. 14)

orator (ôr′ ə tər) A person who is a skilled public speaker. (p. 204)

outback (out′ bak) The wild or largely undeveloped rural part of Australia. (p. 616)

outline (out′ līn) A plan for organizing written information about a subject. (p. 12)

Pacific Rim (pə sif′ik rim) The ring of countries surrounding the Pacific Ocean. (p. 652)

Paleolithic Era (pā lē ō lith′ik e′rə) The earliest part of the Stone Age characterized by tools made of crudely chipped stone and by cave art. (p. 31)

pampas (pam′ pəz) A treeless plain in the southern part of South America extending from the Atlantic Ocean to the Andes Mountains. (p. 419)

papyrus (pə pī′rəs) A kind of paper made from papyrus, a reed plant growing along the Nile, that the ancient Egyptians used for writing. (p. 93)

parable (par′ə bəl) A simple story that contains a message or truth. (p. 242)

parallel (par′ə lel) In geography, any line of latitude north or south of the equator; parallels never cross or meet. See **meridian**. (p. H11, 116)

patriarch (pā′ trē ärk) The leader of Christians of Aksum; a leader of Eastern Orthodox Christians. (p. 317)

patrician (pə trish′ən) A member of the noble families who controlled all power in the early years of the Roman Republic. (p. 223)

Glossary

patron (pā′trən) A supporter of the arts. (p. 357)

patroon (pətrün′) Under Dutch colonial rule in the area that is now New York and New Jersey, a person who owned a large amount of land and was given certain rights and privileges. (p. 470)

Pax Romana (paks rō mä′nə) A period of peace for the Roman Empire that began with the rule of Augustus in about 27 B.C. and lasted around 200 years. (p. 234)

peasant (pez′sənt) A small farm owner or farm worker. (p. 489)

Peloponnesian War (pel ə pə nē′zhən wôr) A war fought between Athens and Sparta in the 400s B.C., ending in a victory for Sparta. (p. 202)

penal colony (pē′ nəl kä′ lə nē) A colony where prisoners are sent as punishment. (p. 482)

peninsula (pə nin′sə lə) An area of land almost entirely surrounded by water. (p. 185)

persecution (pûr si kyū′ shən) A policy of arresting, injuring, or killing members of a religious or ethnic group. (p. 248)

perspective (pûr spek′ tiv) A technique used by artists during the Renaissance that seemed to create three dimensions on the flat surface of a painting. (p. 358)

phalanx (fā′ langks) A Macedonian battle formation of infantry standing in close ranks with their shields and long spears overlapping each other. (p. 204)

pharaoh (fâr′ō) The title used by the rulers of ancient Egypt. (p. 89)

philosophy (fə los′ə fē) The study of or search for truth, wisdom, and the right way to live. (p. 201)

physical map (fiz′i kəl map) A map that primarily shows natural features of Earth, such as lakes, rivers, mountains, and deserts. (p. H17)

physical region (fiz′ i kəl rē′ jən) An area with physical features that set it apart from neighboring areas. (p. 5)

pilgrimage (pil′grə mij) A journey for religious purposes. (p. 289)

pit house (pit haus) A structure dug 2 to 3 feet into the ground where the ancient Hohokam lived. (p. 273)

plague (plāg) A terrible disease that spreads quickly and kills many people. (p. 353)

plebeian (pli bē′ən) A common farmer, trader, or craft-worker in ancient Rome. (p. 223)

point of view (point əv vū) The position of someone toward the world or a subject, shaped by his or her social position, profession, attitudes, and feelings. (p. 604)

polar projection (pō′lər prə jek′shən) A map projection that shows the area around the North or South Pole. (p. 37)

polis (pō′lis) A city-state in ancient Greece. (p. 190)

political cartoon (pə lit′i kəl kär tün′) A drawing that states an opinion about a political matter. (p. 520)

political map (pə lit′i kəl map) A map mainly showing political divisions, such as national or state boundaries, cities, and capitals. (p. H16)

polytheism (pol′ē thē iz əm) The belief in many gods and goddesses. See **monotheism**. (p. 61)

pope (pōp) The bishop, or church leader, of Rome and head of the Roman Catholic Church. (p. 243)

population density (pop yə lā′shən den′si tē) The number of people living per a given unit of area. (p. 158)

porcelain (pōr′ sə lən) A type of ceramic material that is hard and white. (p. 388)

prime meridian (prīm mə rid′ē ən) The line of longitude marked 0° on the world map, from which longitudes east and west are measured. (p. H11, 117)

primary source (prī′mer ē sôrs) A first-hand account of an event or an artifact created during the period of history being studied. See **secondary source**. (p. 14)

problem (prä′ bləm) A question, situation, or condition that is difficult, confusing, or not resolved. (p. 42)

projection (prə jek′shən) A way of placing parts of Earth onto a flat map. (p. 36)

propaganda (prop ə gan′də) The spreading of persuasive ideas or attitudes that are often exaggerated or falsified in order to help or hurt a particular cause or group. (p. 562)

prophet (prä′ fit) A person who is believed to speak for God. (p. 74)

Protestant (prä′ təs tənt) A Christian who belongs to one of the churches that split from the Roman Catholic Church during or after the Reformation. (p. 368)

province (prov′ ins) A division of land within an empire or country. (p. 161)

pueblo (pweb′ lō) A Spanish word meaning "village" used to refer to the apartment-style homes of the Native Americans of the Southwest or to the people living in them. (p. 274)

Punic War (pū′nik wôr) A conflict between Rome and Carthage in the 200s B.C., ending in a victory for Rome. (p. 226)

pyramid (pir′ ə mid) A massive structure built of stone, usually having a square base and four triangular sides that slope upward. (p. 91)

Q

Quechua (ke′ chə wə) The language of the Inca, now spoken mainly in Peru and Ecuador. (p. 431)

quipu (kē′pū) Knotted cords used for record-keeping by the Inca. (p. 434)

Quran (kủ rän') The most holy book of Islam, believed to contain the teachings of Allah, or God, to Muhammad. (p. 289)

R
---

rain forest (rān fōr'ist) A warm, wet forest that receives more than 80 inches of rain per year. (p. 261)

Reconquista (rē kōn kēs' tə) A war fought from 718 to 1492 by Christians to recapture Spain from Muslims. (p. 352)

reference source (re' fər ənts sôrs) A book or other source that has facts about many different subjects. (p. 628)

Reformation (ref ər mā'shən) A movement beginning in Europe in the 1500s, to bring reform to the Roman Catholic Church, and leading to Protestantism. (p. 367)

refugee (ref yū jē') A person who flees his or her country for safety. (p. 593)

region (rē'jən) An area with common features that set it apart from other areas. (p. 5)

reincarnation (rē in kär nā'shən) A Hindu belief that people move in a constant cycle of life, death, and rebirth. (p. 126)

relative location (re' lə tiv lō kā' shən) The location of a place in relation to another place: *the United States is south of Canada.* (p. H13)

relief (ri lēf') The use of shading on a map to show changes in elevation. (p. H17)

Renaissance (ren ə säns') A period of great cultural and artistic change that began in Italy around 1350 and spread throughout Europe. (p. 356)

representative (rep ri zen'tə tiv) A person who is elected by citizens to speak or act for them. See **republic**. (p. 224)

republic (ri pub'lik) A form of government in which citizens elect representatives to speak or act for them. (p. 223)

revolution (rev ə lü'shən) The overthrow of an existing government and its replacement with another; any sudden or very great change. (p. 489)

S
---

sacrifice (sak' rə fīs) A gift or offering made to a god, usually an animal or a human. (p. 424)

Sahel (sä' hil) Dry grasslands south of the Sahara. (p. 313)

saint (sānt) A woman or man considered by a religious group to be especially holy. (p. 351)

samurai (sam'ū rī) A class of soldiers in feudal Japan who were loyal only to their lords. (p. 402)

sanction (sangk'shən) A penalty placed against a nation to make it change its behavior, such as a refusal to buy its goods or sell it products. (p. 631)

savanna (sə van'ə) A broad, grassy, plain with few trees, found especially in large parts of Africa. (p. 314)

scale (skāl) A unit of measure on a map, such as an inch, that is used to represent a distance on Earth. (p. H14)

scientific method (sī ən tif'ik meth'əd) A way of studying things through questioning and thorough testing. (p. 454)

scribe (skrīb) A professional writer who kept records and copied letters and official documents. (p. 59)

secondary source (sek'ən der ē sôrs) A record of the past, based on information from primary sources. (p. 14)

seismograph (sīz'mə graf) A scientific instrument that could detect earthquakes hundreds of miles away, invented during the Han dynasty. (p. 168)

Senate (sen'it) The lawmaking body and most powerful branch of government in ancient Rome's republic. (p. 224)

sepoy (sē' poi) A member of a group of Indian soldiers who staged a rebellion against British rule in 1857. (p. 517)

serf (sûrf) In the Middle Ages, a person who was bound to work on a noble's manor. (p. 344)

shah (shä) Persian for "emperor." (p. 397)

shantytown (shan' tē toun) A community where homes are flimsy and built from scrap wood or metal; they often do not have clean water, sewers, or electricity. (p. 644)

Shinto (shin'tō) A Japanese religion marked by the belief in the spirits of nature. (p. 401)

shogun (shō'gən) The ruler of feudal Japan from the 1100s to the 1800s who, although appointed by the emperor, ruled the country as a military dictator. (p. 402)

Silk Road (silk rōd) An ancient network of overland trade routes that streched from China to what is now Iran. (p. 389)

silt (silt) A mixture of tiny bits of soil and rock carried and deposited by a river. (p. 55)

---

pronunciation key
a **a**t; ā **a**pe; ä **fa**r; âr **ca**re; e **e**nd; ē **me**; i **i**t; ī **i**ce; îr **pie**rce; o **ho**t; ō **o**ld; ô **fo**rk; oi **oi**l; ou **ou**t; u **u**p; ū **u**se; ü **ru**le; ů **pu**ll; ûr **tu**rn; hw **wh**ite; ng **so**ng; th **thi**n; th **thi**s; zh mea**s**ure; ə **a**bout, tak**e**n, penc**i**l, lem**o**n, circ**u**s

slash and burn (slash and bûrn) A farming method involving the cutting of trees, then burning them to provide ash-enriched soil for the planting of crops. (p. 265)

small-scale map (smôl skāl map) A map that shows a big area in less detail by measuring its distance in large units. (p. 348)

social pyramid (sō´shəl pir´ə mid) A diagram illustrating the social order divisions within a culture; usually showing the most powerful person or group at the peak and the least powerful groups at the bottom. (p. 106)

socialism (sō´shə liz əm) An economic and political system based on collective or government ownership and control of all resources and industry; also a political philosophy based on the writings of Karl Marx. (p. 510)

software (soft´ wâr´) Written or printed programs and information used in a computer. (p. 406)

source (sôrs) Anything that provides information or evidence. (p. 14)

soviet (sō´ vē´ et) A council of workers and soldiers formed during the Russian Revolution. (p. 552)

specialize (spesh´ ə līz) To spend most of one's time doing one kind of job. (p. 47)

sphere of influence (sfēr əv in´flü əns) Regions of other countries that European countries controlled during the 1800s. (p. 517)

stela (stē´lə) A tall, flat stone, often carved with writing, used to mark an important historical event. (p. 268)

steppe (step) A dry, grassy, treeless plain found in Asia and eastern Europe. (p. 148)

strait (strāt) A narrow channel, or body of water, connecting two larger bodies of water. (p. 459)

strike (strīk) A refusal to work as a protest against unfair treatment. (p. 510)

subcontinent (sub kon´tə nənt) A large landmass that is connected to a continent. (p. 113)

sultan (sult´tən) Supreme ruler of the Ottoman Empire. (p. 382)

summary (sum´ə rē) A brief statement of main ideas. (p. 270)

supernova (sü´ pə nō´ və) The explosion of a star in which the center of the star collapses under gravity, increasing the star's brightness. (p. 275)

supply (sə plī´) In economics, the quantity of a good, product, or resource that producers are able and willing to produce. See **demand**. (p. 323)

surplus (sûr´plus) An extra supply of something, such as crops, that is not needed immediately. (p. 46)

symbol (sim´bəl) Anything that stands for something else. (p. 520)

Taliban (tal´ i ban) A group of strict Islamic religious leaders that controlled most of Afganistan from 1992 to 2001. (p. 595)

technology (tek nol´ə jē) The use of skills and tools to meet practical human needs. (p. 39)

telescope (tel´ə skōp) An optical instrument for making distant objects, such as planets and stars, appear nearer and larger. (p. 450)

temperate (tem´pər it) Mild; moderate. (p. 337)

Ten Commandments (ten kə mand´mənts) According to the Hebrew Bible, the laws God gave to Moses on Mount Sinai. (p. 75)

terrace (ter´is) A level platform of earth built into a hillside, usually used for farming. (p. 434)

terrorism (ter´ ər i zəm) The use of fear and violence to gain political goals. (p. 596)

textile (teks´tīl) A cloth fabric that is either woven or knitted. (p. 505)

timberline (tim´bər līn) An imaginary line on high mountains or in the arctic; above or beyond it trees cannot grow. (p. 418)

theory (thē´ ə rē) An idea that has not yet been proved. (p. 275)

time line (tīm līn) A diagram that shows when events took place during a given period of time. (p. 64)

Torah (tôr´ə) The first five books of the Hebrew Bible containing the laws and teachings of Judaism. See **Judaism**. (p. 75)

totalitarian (tō tal i târ´ē ən) Relating to totalitarianism, meaning a system of government in which a dictator or a small group of leaders control all aspects of people's lives. (p. 553)

Treaty of Versailles (trē´tē əv vâr sī´) The treaty that the Allied Powers forced Germany to sign at the end of World War I. (p. 545)

triangular trade (trī ang´gyə lər trād) From the 1500s to the mid-1800s, the trade routes between the Americas, England, and Africa, which formed a triangle and involved the buying and selling of captive Africans as well as guns, sugar, and iron goods. (p. 475)

tribune (trib´ūn) An elected leader of ancient Rome who represented the interests of the plebeians. (p. 224)

tribute (trib´ūt) A tax, often in the form of crops, paid by one ruler to another, usually to ensure peace or protection. (p. 138)

tropical (trop´i kəl) Of or relating to the area of Earth between the Tropic of Cancer (23.5°N) and the Tropic of Capricorn (23.5°S). (p. 261)

trusteeship (trus tē′ ship) The administrative authority over a trust territory given to a country by the United Nations. (p. 614)

tsar (zär) The title of Russia's emperor before 1917. (p. 547)

Twelve Tables (twelv tā′belz) The earliest written collection of Roman laws, drawn up by patricians about 450 B.C., that became the foundation of Roman law. (p. 225)

unification (ū nə fi kā′shən) The joining of separate parts, such as kingdoms, into one. (p. 89)

union (yün′ yən) A group of workers who join together to improve wages or working conditions. (p. 510)

United Nations (ū nī′tid nā′shənz) An organization founded in 1945 whose members include most of the world's nations. It works to preserve world peace, settle disputes, and aid international cooperation. (p. A10)

urbanization (ur bən ə zā′shən) The spread of cities. (p. 644)

values (val′ūz) Ideals or beliefs that guide the way people live. (p. 8)

vassal (vas′əl) In the Middle Ages, a noble who usually was given a fief by his lord in exchange for loyalty. (p. 344)

Vedas (vā′dəz) In Hinduism, the ancient books of sacred songs on which much of its religious beliefs are based. (p. 125)

volcano (väl kā′ nō) An opening in the surface of the earth through which molten rock, gases, and rock fragments are forced out. (p. 220)

warlord (wôr′lôrd) A strong local military leader who takes advantage of political unrest to seize power in the area. (p. 566)

Warring States Period (war′ing stāts pir′ ē əd) The period between 475 B.C. and 221 B.C. after the Zhou Empire in China ended and local rulers went to war with each other. (p. 155)

Warsaw Pact (wôr′sô pakt) A military alliance formed in 1955 by the Soviet Union and seven East European nations. (p. 572)

working class (wûrk′ing klas) People who work for wages, such as factory workers and manual laborers. (p. 508)

World Trade Organization (world trād ôr gə nə zā′ shən) An international organization that establishes rules for manufacturing in all member countries. (p. 651)

ziggurat (zig′ù rat) A large pyramid with several stories built by the ancient Sumerians, Assyrians, and Babylonians. (p. 60)

Zionism (zī′ə niz əm) A movement to create a national homeland for the Jewish people. (p. 592)

pronunciation key
a at; ā ape; ä far; âr care; e end; ē me; i it; ī ice; îr pierce; o hot; ō old; ô fork; oi oil; ou out; u up; ū use; ü rule; ù pull; ûr turn; hw white; ng song; th thin; th this; zh measure; ə about, taken, pencil, lemon, circus

Reference

Index

This index lists many topics that appear in the book, along with the pages on which they are found. Page numbers after a *c* refer you to a chart, after an *m* refer you to a map. Page numbers after a *p* indicate photographs or artwork.

Index

Credits

Cover Design: The Mazer Corporation

Maps: National Geographic

Charts: Doug Horne

Chapter Opener map: Leah Palmer Preiss

Illustrations: Bernard Adnet: R30–R31; Nick Backes: 169; Bill Cigliano: 362; Domenick D'Andrea: 258; Daniel Del Valle: 21, 87, 349, 463; David Diaz: 633; John Edens: 71, 205, 343, 519, 551; S. Saelig Gallagher: 440-443; Patrick Gnan: 47, 59, 152, 190, 505, 506; Doug Horne: 106; Michael Jaroszko: 120, 176-179, 250, 353; Tim Lee: 180; Joe Lemonnier: 231; Jerry Lofaro: 91; Albert Lorenz: 70; Jeff Mangiat: 40, 48, 56, 84, 89, 92-93, 168, 201, 378, 544; Tom Pansini: 21, 175, 303, 412, 439, 531, 661; Tony Randazzo: 164; Robert Schuster: 34; Walter Stuart: 262, 429, 629; Robert Van Nutt: 86, 304-307; Raul Vitale: 224, 344-345; 101, 304-307; Phil Wilson: 199, 210-211, 202-203; Paul Wright: 22-25; Heidi Younger: 587.

Photography: All photographs are by Macmillan/McGraw-Hill (MMH) except as noted below.

Cover/A17, t: Keren Su/Corbis; b. David Muir/Masterfile.

Front Matter: A1: tl. © Michael Krasowitz/FPG International; tm. © Jerry Tobias/Corbis; tr. © Simon Wilkinson/The Image bank; ml1. © LWA-Dann Tardif/Corbis Stock Market; mr.1 © Elyse Lewin Studio Inc./The Image Bank; ml.2 © Vicky Kasala/The Image Bank; m. © Elyse Lewin Studio Inc./The Image Bank; mr.2. © LWA-Dann Tardif/Corbis Stock Market; mr.3 © Ghislain & Marie David de Lossy/The Image Bank; b.l © Vicky Kasala/The Image Bank; bm. © Ross Whitaker/The Image Bank; br. © AJA Productions/The Image Bank; border © PhotoLink/Photo Disc; A2: br. © Joseph Sohm/Corbis; tr. Hulton Archive/Getty; A3: tr. © Joseph Sohm; Visions of America/Corbis; bl. © National Archives; A4: tr. © Joseph Sohm/Corbis; b. © Ken Karp/MMSD; Poster Prop: ml. © Jeff Maloney/PhotoDisc/PictureQuest; Poster Prop: bl. © Ron Chapple/Thinkstock/PictureQuest; Poster Prop: br. © Corbis; Poster Prop: tl. © Tyler Stableford/Brand X Pictures/PictureQuest; Poster Prop: mr. Corbis Image/PictureQuest; Poster Prop: mml. © Stockbyte/PictureQuest; Poster Prop: bmr. © Corbis; Poster Prop: bml. © Corbis; Poster Prop: tr. © Tyler Stableford/Brand X Pictures/PictureQuest; Poster Prop : tm © BananaStock/BananaStock, Ltd./PictureQuest; Poster Prop: mmr. Alvis Upitis/Brand X Pictures/PictureQuest; A5: tr. © Joseph Sohm; Visions of America/Corbis; b. © Ken Karp/MMSD; Poster Prop: tml. © Corbis; Poster Prop: tr. © Bettmann/Corbis; Poster Prop; m. © Corbis; Poster Prop: tmr. © Corbis Images/PictureQuest; Poster Prop: tl. © Cindy Lewis Photography; Poster Prop: b. © Corbis; A6; b. © Ken Karp/MMSD; tr. © National Archives; A7; bkgd. © Jim Cummins/FPG; br. © Ken Karp/MMSD; A8 bkgd. © Associated Press, AP; bl. © Bettmann/Corbis; A9: bkgd. © Louise Gubb/SABA; bl. © Associated Press/Pool Photo; A10: tr. © Vanessa Vick/Photo Researchers; b. Courtesy of United Nations International Research and Training Institute for the Advancement of Women; A11: bm. © AP Photo/Sayyid Azim; tr. WFP/Rein Skullerud; tm. © AP Photo/Donald Stampfli; A12: bkgd. © Stuart Westmorland/Corbis; tr. © K. Dannemiller/Saba; mr. © C. Seghers 2/Photo Researchers, Inc.; br. © Tom Wagner/Saba; A13: mr. © Reuters NewMedia Inc./Corbis; br. Alberto Garcia/SABA; bkgd. Bluey Thompson/Associated Press; tr. Obed Zilwa/Associated Press; A14: bkgd. © Luis Romero/AP; tr. © AFP/Corbis; A15: bkgd. Rusty Kennedy/Associated Press; tr. © 1995 Jerry Wachter/Photo Reseachers; mr. © Duomo/Corbis; A16: bkgd. NASA/Science Photo Library/Photo Researchers; bl. © AFP/Corbis.

H5: Bob Krist/Corbis; H9: m. Novastock/Stock Connection/PictureQuest; ml. PhotoDisc; bl. Yann Layma/Getty Images; br. Francois Gohier/Photo Researchers; H10: tl. Ric Ergenbright/Corbis; tr. James L. Stanfield; mr. PhotoDisc; bl. James L. Stanfield; H12: Francois Gohier/Photo Researchers, Inc.

2-3: © I.T.P./International Stock Photography; 4: b. © Dean Conger/Corbis; 4-5: t. © Craig Lovell/The Viesti Collection, Inc.; 4-5: bkgd. © Maresa Pryor/Animals Animals/Earth Scenes; 5: b. © Roberto Arakaki/International Stock; t. © Fred Bruemmer/Peter Arnold Inc.; 6: t. © Paul Thimpson/International Stock; mr. © Tibor Bognar/Corbis Stock Market; b. © A. Ramey/Stock Boston; 8: br. © Wolfgang Kaehler; t. © Jeremy Hartley/Panos Pictures; 8-9: bkgd. Scala/Art Resource; 9: b. © Tony Freeman/PhotoEdit; t. © Peter Menzel/Stock Boston; 10-11: background (Granger Collection); © 1963 Erich Hartmann/Magnum Photos Inc.; t. © Georgina Bowater/Corbis Stock Market; 11: b. © Panoramic Images, photo by B. Gardel; t. © Tony Freeman/PhotoEdit; 14: t. © The Bridgeman Art Library; b. © Marc and Evelyne Bernheim/Woodfin Camp; m. Réunion des Musees Nationaux/Art Resource, NY; 14-15: bkgd. John Mead/Science Photo Library/Photo Researchers Inc; 15: b. © McDonald Institute for Archaeological Research; t. © Alexander Tsiaras/Science Source/Photo Researchers, Inc. ; 16: t. © Roger Wood/Corbis; 16-17: bkgd. Kenneth Garrett; 17: b. © George Hamiliton/Photo Researchers, Inc.; t. © Patrick Ward/Corbis; 18: b. © Rob Levine/The Stock Market; t. Reunion des Musees Nationaux/Art Resource, N.Y.; 19: t. Michael Stephens/Associated Press, PA; b. © Michael Freeman/Phototake/Picturequest; bkgd. Leonard Lessin/Peter Arnold Inc.; ml. © AFP/Corbis; 26-27: © O. Louis Mazzatenta/National Geographic Image Collection; 28: b. © Gaillarde Fra/Gamma; 29: t. © Erich Lessing/Art Resource; 30: © Gaillarde Fra/Gamma; 31: tr. © Kenneth Garrett; 32-33: t. © Ira Block; 33: mr. George Holton/Photo Researchers; bl. © Stephen J. Krasemann/Photo Researchers; tm. © Kenneth Garrett; 34: bl. © George Holton/Photo Researchers; tr. © Snowdon/Hoyer/Woodfin Camp & Associates; 37: tl. © David L. Thompson/Ancient Art & Architecture Collection LTD; br. © The Bridgeman Art Library; 35: tr. © The Bridgeman Art Library; m. © Ira Block; 38-39: © Pierre Boulat/Woodfin Camp & Associates; 39: bl. © David Brill; tr. © P. Boulat/Woodfin Camp & Associates; mr. © Steve Elmore/The Stock Market; 40: bl. Courtesy of the Australian Museum; tl. © Brian Wilson/Ancient Art & Architecture Collection; br. © Steve Elmore/The Stock Market; tr. © Kenneth Garrett/National Geographic Society; 41: Ancient Art & Architecture; 42: © Gaillarde Fra/Gamma; 43: b. © Tim Hauf Photography/Visuals Unlimited; 44: © H. Tom Hall/National Geographic Image Collection; 45: tr. © Dr. James Meelaart; br. © Dr. James Meelaart; 49: l. © James Meelaart; r. © James Meelaart; 52: br. © R. Sheridan/Ancient Art & Architecture Collection; bl. © University Museum/University of Pennsylvania; 53: b. © Folio, Inc.; t. © Bettmann/Corbis/Colorized by Walter Stuart; 54: full. © Nik Wheeler/Corbis; 57: l. © Erich Lessing/Art Resource; r. © R. Sheridan/Ancient Art & Architecture Collection; 58-59: b. © The British Museum; 60: bl. © Bolton Picture Library; 60-61: br. © Georg Gerster/Photo Researchers, Inc.; 61: tr. Iraq Museum Baghdad/Art Resource; 62: © Georg Gerster/The Image Works; 63: Giraudon; 65: © Erich Lessing/Art Resource; 66: full © The Bridgeman Art Library; 68: © Musee de Louvre, Paris; 69: © Erich Lessing/Art Resource; 71: © Baghdad Museum/Hirner Fotoarchive/Art Resource; 72: . © David Lees/Corbis; 74: t. © NYC Christie's Images, Ltd.; b. © Richard T. Nowitz; 75: The Jewish Museum, NYC; 76: Milton Feinberg/Stock Boston; 77: © Joe Atlas/Brand X Pictures/PictureQuest; 78: © Erich Lessing/Art Resource; 80: Giraudon; 81: tl. © Scala/Art Resource, NY; tr. Lee Boltin; b. © Archivo Iconografico, S.A./Corbis; 82: © Marcel & Eva Malherbe/The Image Works; 85: © The British Museum; 88: © Werner Forman Archive/Art Resource; 91: © Michael Halford/British Museum; 93: mr. © Kenneth Garrett/National Geographic Society; tr. © Wolfgang Kaehler; 94: bl. © The British Museum; 94-95: t. © Boltin Picture Library; 96: © Lee Boltin; 97: © Kenneth Garrett/National Geographic Society; 98: © The Bridgeman Art Library; 99: © Brian Brake/Photo Researchers, Inc.; 100: © Eric Lessing/Art Resource; 101: © Gianni Dagli Orti/Corbis; 102: Courtesy of the Museum of Fine Arts Boston; 104: m. © The Bridgeman Art Library; tr. © The Bridgeman Art Library; 104-105: b. © Enrico Ferorelli/Mira; 105: tr. © Robert Caputo/Aurora; 107: tr. © Archivo Iconografico, S.A./Corbis; m. © Erich Lessing/Art Resource; 108: © The British Museum; 110: l. © Michael K. Nichols/National Geographic; r. © Randy Olsen/National Geographic ; 111: tl. © The Bridgeman Art Library; tr. © Dinodia; bl. © Allan Eaton/Ancient Art & Architecture Collection; 112-113: b. © Susan McCartney; 114: bl. © Keren Su/Corbis; 114-115: t. © Jonathan S. Blair/National Geographic; 115: m. © Randy Olsen/National Geographic; 118: © Delip Mehta/Woodfin Camp and Associates; 121: br. Jehangir Gazdar/Woodfin Camp: tl. Contact Press Images; 123: © Ric Ergenbright/Corbis; 124: © 2000 Dennis Cox/D.E. Cox Photo Library; 125: © Historical Picture Archive/Corbis; 126: tr. © Dinodia Picture Agency; tl. © Erica Lanser/Black Star Publishing/PictureQuest; 127: © Robert Frerck/Odyssey Productions; 128: bl. © Dinodia Picture Agency, Bombay, India/The Bridgeman Art Library; tr. © Historical Picture Archive/Corbis; 129: © Lindsay Hebberd/Woodfin Camp & Associates; 130: © Christie's Images, London/Bridgeman Art Library, London/Superstock; 131: © The Granger Collection; 132: bl. © Hilarie Kavanagh/Tony Stone Worldwide/Getty; tr. © Dennis Cox/ChinaStock; 133: bl. © Ric Ergenbright Photography; br. © Ric Ergenbright; 134-135: t. © Lindsay Hebberd/Woodfin Camp & Associates; 135: ml. © J.R. Naylor/Ancient Art & Architecture Collection LTD; m. Reunion des Musees Nationaux/Art Resource, NY; 136: b. © Superstock; ml. © Superstock; 138: © SEF/Art Resource, NY; 139: tl. © Michael W. Meister; 139: m. © Burstein Collection/Corbis; 140: t. Courtesy of STEP; b. Courtesy of STEP; 144: bl. © Eye Ubiquitous/Corbis; br. © China Span; 145: t. © 1995 Dennis Cox/ChinaStock; bl. © Erich Lessing/Art Resource; 146-147: © ChinaStock; 148-149: t. © Tom Sobolik/Black Star Publishing/PictureQuest; 149: m. © 1995 Dennis Cox; 150-151: © Laurie Platt Winfrey, Inc.; 152: m: British Library/Werner Forman Archive/Art Resource, Inc.; 153: © Courtesy of the Arthur M. Sackler Gallery, Smithsonian Institution, Washington, D.C.; 154: © Reunion des Musees Nationaux/Art Resource, NY; 155: br © ChinaStock; bl. © Giraudon/Art Resource; 156: © ChinaStock; 157: © Seth Joel/Woodfin Camp & Associates; 160: © Dallas and John Heaton/Corbis; 163: © ChinaStock; 164: tr. © O. Louis Mazzatenta/National Geographic; 165: © ChinaStock; 166: © Burstein Collection/Corbis; 167: © Eric Lessing/Art Resource; 168: r. Michael Holford; 170: tr. © Wang Lu/China Stock; 170: b. © Bibliotheque Municipale, Poitiers; 171: © Rietberg Museum, Zurich; 180-181: © Frank Chmura/Panoramic Images; 182: t. Thouvenin/Explorer/Photo Researchers Inc.; b. Erich Lessing/Art Resource; 183: t. © The Bridgeman Art Library; 183: b. © Mike Andrews/Ancient Art & Architecture Collection Ltd.; 184: © 2001 Mauritius, Plessner/Black Star; 185: Scala, Art Resource; 186: b. © Noboru Komine/Photo Researchers, Inc.; tr. © John Elk III/Bruce Coleman Inc.; 187: tl. © 2001 Shapiro, Irving/Black Star; tr. R Sheridan/Ancient Art Architecture Collection; 188: © Edmund Nagele/International Stock; 190: © David Lees; 191: Acropolis Museum, Athens, Greece/Spiros Tselentis/Super Stock; 192: t. © Eric Lessing/Art Resource; b. © Edmund Nagele/International Stock; 193: t. The Granger Collection; tr. © C.M. Dixon; 194: t. © Araldo de Luca/Corbis; bl. The Art Archive/Bibliotheque des Arts Decoratifs Paris/Dagli Orti; 195: mr. © FPG International; tr. Réunion Des Musees Nationaux/Art Resource N Y; 197: © Noboru Komine/Photo Researchers Inc; 198: © Guido Cozzi/Bruce Coleman Inc.; 200: br. Art Resource; tr. © Noboru Komine/Photo Researchers Inc; 201: © Ron Chapple/FPG International; 204: © Photography by Eric Lessing; Museo Archeologico Nazionale, Naples, Italy/Art Resource,NY; 206: tl. Courtesy of Nadia Lokma; br. Courtesy of Ruth Jacoby; 207: Courtesy of Mohammad Rafique Mugal; 208: Art Resource; 210: © Boltin Picture Library; 212: bl. Christie's Images; br. Scala/Art Resource, NY; 213: tr. Christie's Images; mr. © Erich Lessing/Art Resource; 216: t. © Ric Ergenbright Photography; 217: tl. Prenestino Museum, Rome, Italy/ET Archive. London/SuperStock; tr. © Ronald Sheridan/Ancient Art & Architecture Collection; bl. © Miwako Ikeda/International Stock; 218-219: © Paul Stephan/Photo Researchers; 220: Christie's Images/SuperStock; 221: © Michael S. Yamashita/Corbis; 222: © R Sheridan/Ancient Art & Architecture Collection Ltd.; 223: © Amanda Merullo/Stock Boston; 225: Scala/Art Resource, NY; 227: tl. © R Sheridan/Ancient Art & Architecture Collection Ltd.; b. © The Bridgeman Art Library; 228: tr. © The Bridgeman Art Library; b. Scala/Art Resource; 229: mr. Ronald Sheridan/Ancient Art & Architecture Collection Ltd; tr. Ronald Sheridan /Ancient Art & Architecture Collection Ltd; 230: Réunion des Musees Nationaux/Art Resource, NY; 231: © The Bridgeman Art Library; 232: Erich Lessing/Art Resource; 233: b. Art Resource; mr. © Ronald Sheridan/Ancient Art & Architecture Historical Museum of Vienna; 234: © Nimatallah/Art Resource, NY; 236: tl. Ric Ergenbright Photography; tr. Alinari/Giraudon; 237: Scala/Art Resource, NY; 238: Stockman/International Stock; 239: © Hal Beral/Visuals Unlimited; 240: Kurrt Scholz/Superstock; 242: The Granger Collection; 244: bl. The Pierpont Morgan Library/Art Resource, NY; 244-245: t. Ken Cavanagh/Photo Researchers, Inc.; 245: ml. © Alan Oddie/Photoedit; 246: © Adam Woolfitt/Corbis; 249: b. © The Art Archive; t. © Roberto Arakaki/International Stock; 250: Super Stock; 251: R Sheridan /Ancient Art & Architecture Collection; 252: R Sheridan /Ancient Art & Architecture Collection; 253: tl. Cameraphoto/Art Resource, NY; m. Ronald Sheridan/Ancient Art & Architecture Collection, Ltd.; 254: © Giuseppe Valeriani/Wood River Gallery/PictureQuest; 256: © Michael P. Gadomski/Photo Researchers, Inc.; 257: t. © Robert Frerck/Panoramic Images; bl. Richard A. Cooke, III; 260: bl. © Raymond Gehman/Corbis; br. © Tom & Pat Leeson/Photo Researchers, Inc.; tl. © D. Robert Franz/Bruce Coleman Inc.; tr. © Tom Bean/Corbis; 261: bl. © Superstock; tr. © John R. Foster/Photo Researchers, Inc.; tl. © Michael P. Gadomski/Photo Researchers, Inc.; br. © Bruce Coleman, Inc.; 264: © Nathaniel Tarn/Photo Researchers, Inc.; 265: © Kenneth Garrett/National Geographic Society; 268: © Vautier/Woodfin Camp, Inc.; 269: ml. © The Lowe Art Museum, The University of Miami/Superstock; tl. © Will & Deni McIntyre/Photo Researchers, Inc.; 270: © Kal Muller/Woodfin Camp & Associates; 271: © Oleg Cajko/Panoramic Images; 272: © David L. Brown H/Panoramic Images; 273: © Richard A. Cooke/Corbis; 274: © Superstock; 276: mr. Ohio Historical Society; tr. © Superstock; 277: Werner Forman Archive Peabody Museum, Harvard University, Cambridge, MA/Art Resource, NY; 278: © Mark Burnett/Photo Researchers, Inc.; 280: © Christie's Images/Superstock; t. © Christie's Images; bl. © Angelo Hornak/Corbis; 282: © Ray Ellis/Photo Researchers, Inc.; bl. © Steve Kaufman; 283: © McDonald Wildlife Photography/Animals Animals; 284: b. © Tom Hollyman/Photo Researchers, Inc.; tr. © Noburu Komine/Photo Researchers, Inc.; 285: © Superstock; 286: © Noburu Komine/Photo Researchers, Inc.; 288: br. © Nabeel Turner/Tony Stone Images; bl. © John Moss/Photo Researchers, Inc.; 289: © The Bridgeman Art Library; 290: tr. © Robert Azzi/Woodfin Camp & Associates; b. © John Schlden/Visuals Unlimited, Inc.; 291: tl. © Nicholas Devore/Tony Stone Images; mr. The Lowe Art Museum, The University of Miami/Superstock; 292: © Superstock; 293: © SEF/Art Resource, NY; 295: tl. © Littaye Alain/Gamma; br. © Bibliotheque Nationale, Paris/A.K.G., Berlin/Superstock; 296: tl. © Giraudon/Cairo National Library; ml. © The Granger Collection ; 297: b. © The Granger Collection; mr. © Giraudon; 298: m. © Hermitage Museum, St. Petersburg, Russia/Leonid Bogdanov/Superstock; br. © The Bridgeman Art Library; 298-299: t. © Paul Almasy/Corbis; 299: m. © Christie's Images; 308-309: © Brian A. Vikander; 310: t. © Balfour, D. ABPL/Animals Animals; b. Super Stock; 311: t. © Charles & Josette Lenars/Corbis; bl. © H. Von Meiss-Teuffen/Photo Researchers; 312: © Frans Lanting/Minden Pictures; 314: tr. © Harvey LLoyd/The Stock Market; 314-315: b. © Fred Hoogervorst/Panos Pictures; 315: m. © Mitsuaki Iwago/Minden Pictures; tr. © UNEP/Peter Arnold, Inc.; 316: © Neil Cooper/Panos Pictures; 318: bl. © Professor David W. Phillipson; tr. © Professor David W. Phillipson; br. © Kal Muller/Woodfin Camp & Associates; 319: r. Copyright Trustees of the British Museum; m. Copyright Trustees of the British Museum; 320: James Alan Brown/Visuals Unlimited; 322: b. Volkmar K. Wentzel/National Geographic Society Image Collection; tl. Aldo Titino/Art Resource, Inc.; 323: The Granger Collection; 324: © The Granger Collection; 326: bl. R Sheridan/Ancient Art & Architecture Collection; l. © Jack Vartugian; 327: © Jeffrey Ploskonka/National Museum of African Art; 328: © Groenendyk/Photo Researchers; 329: © Bertram G. Murray Jr./Earth Scenes; 330: © Werner Forman Archive; 331: m. © David Keith Jones/Images of Africa Photobank; tr. © Delmar Lipp/Lee Williams; 334: t. Panoramic Images; b. Eric Lessing /Art Resource; bl. A. K. G. Berlin/SuperStock; 335: tl. © Andre Hote/International Stock; tr. Monumenti Musei E Gallerie Pontificie; 336: © Chris Warren/International Stock; 338: tl. © Hilary Wilkes/International Stock; b. © Premium Stock/Corbis; 339: tl. © Steve Vidler/Superstock; m. © Owen Franken/Corbis; 340: By Courtesy of the Board of Trustees of the Victoria and Albert Museum, London/Bridgeman Art Library, London/Superstock; 341: Germanisches National Museum, Nuremberg Germany/Lauros-Giraudon, Paris/Super Stock; 342: br. © National Portrait Gallery, London; 342-343: t. © Giraudon; 346: © The Art Archive/Guildhall Library/Eileen Tweedy; 347: © Pascal Lebrun/Gamma Liason; 348: © Paul Thompson/International Stock Photo; 350: © Andre Jenny/International Stock; 351: The Granger Collection; 353: © Massimo Listri/Corbis; 354: © Bettmann/Corbis; 355: © The Art Archive/Musee Conde Chantilly/Dagli Orti; 356: Phyllis Greenberg /Earth Scenes; 358: Artist Unknown/Stock Montage/Superstock/colorized by Walter Stuart; 359: tr. © The Bridgeman Art Library; b. © The Art Archive/Musee du Louvre Paris/Dagli Orti; 360: ml. © Metropolitan Museum of Art/H.O. Havemeyer Collection, bequest of Mrs. H.O. Havemeyer; tl. © Photography by Eric Lessing; National Gallery, London, Great Britain/Art Resource, NY; tr. © Archivo Iconografico, S.A./Corbis; 361: The Louvre, Paris; 363: tr. Courtesy of Performing Arts Library; mr. © The Granger Collection; 364: tl. Courtesy of Yoshitaka Arai; br. Courtesy of Maxine Lipson; 365: Courtesy of Taniuska Haslam; 366: A. K. G. Berlin/SuperStock; 367: tr. © Art Resource; br. © The Bridgeman Art Library; 368: br. Bibliotheque Nationale/Jean Loop Chainet Photo; tl. Scala/Art Resource; 369: Woburn Abbey, by kind permission of the Marguess of Tavistock and the Trustees of the Bedford Estates; 370: Scala /Art Resource; 371: m. The Pierpont Morgan Library/Art Resource, NY; tl. © The Art Archive/Chiesa del Gesu Rome/Dagli Orti (A); 374: t. © Ric Ergenbright; bl. © 96 Harvey Lloyd/The Stock Market; br. © Oldrich Karasek/Peter Arnold Inc.; 375: tl. © Wolfgang Kaehler; tr. © Superstock; bl. © Gavin Bellier/The Stock Market; 376-377: © Michael Andrews/Earth Scenes; 378: tr. © 2000 Hardie Truesdale; 379: © M.P. Kahl/Photo Researchers, Inc.; 380: Bibliotheque Nationale in Paris; 381: © Erich Lessing/Art Resource; 383: tl. © Topkapi Palace Museum, Istanbul, Turkey/The Bridgeman Art Library; br. © 1994 J. Sapinsky/The Stock Market; 384: b. © Steve Vidler/Superstock; t. © Michael Thompson/Earth Scenes; 385: © 2000 Palace Arts Foundation, Inc. Photograph by Haidye Cangökçe; 386: Christie's Images; 387: Christie's Images; 388: bl. Giraudon/Art Resource NY; br. © Will & Deni McIntyre/Photo Researchers, Inc.; 389: © Ancient Art and Architecture Collection; 390: Wolfgang Kaehler; 391: tl. © George Holton/Photo Researchers, Inc.; t. © Liu Liqun/Corbis; 392: bl. © Christie's Images; br. © Asia Society, New York: Mr. and Mrs. John D. Rockefeller 3rd Collection; 393: © Wang Lu/China Stock; 394: © George Hunter/Superstock; 396: mr. © B. D. Rupani/Dinodia Picture Agency; t. © Christina Dameyer/Photo 20-20; 397: m. Reunion Des Musees Nationaux/Art Resource N Y; br. © B. D. Rupani/Dinodia Picture Agency; 398: tl. © Air India Library; tr. © British Library, London, UK/The Bridgeman Art Library; b. © Ronald Sheridan

Acknowledgments (continued from page ii)

From **An Anthropological Report on the History of the Miamis, Weas and Eel River Indians** by Glen Black Laboratory of Archaeology. Copyright 1996 by Glen Black Laboratory of Archaeology and the Trustees of Indiana University. http://www.gbl.Indiana.edu

From **Bolshevism: The Road to Revolution** by Alan Woods. Copyright © 1999 by Alan Woods. Reprinted by permission of Wellred Publications, London, U.K.

From **Chandogya Upanishad** translated by HinduNet. Copyright © 1994 HinduNet. http://www.hindunet.org/upanishads/chandogya/

From **The Cold War** by Martin Walker. Copyright © 1993 by Walker and Watson Ltd. A John Macrae Book, Henry Holt and Company, NY.

From **Corpus of Early Arabic Sources for West African History**, translated by J.F.P. Hopkins, edited and annotated by N. Levtzion & J.F.P. Hopkins. Copyright 1981 by University of Ghana, International Academic Union, Cambridge University Press. Reprinted with the permission of Cambridge University Press.

From **Daily Journal of Private Fraser, 1915-1916** edited by Reginald H. Roy, Canadian Expeditionary Force. Copyright © 1985 by Sono Nis Press, Victoria, B.C.

From **The Diary of a Young Girl: The Definitive Edition** by Anne Frank. Otto H. Frank & Miriam Pressler, editors, translated by Susan Massotty. Translation copyright © 1995 by Doubleday, a division of Bantam Doubleday Dell Publishing Group, Inc. Used by permission of Doubleday, a division of Bantam Doubleday Dell Publishing Group, Inc.

Excerpt "The First Flute" from **The Enchanted Orchard and Other Folktales of Central America** by Dorothy Sharp Carter. Copyright © 1973 by Dorothy Sharp Carter. Reprinted by permission of Harcourt Brace & Company.

From **He Mor Citto** by Rabindranath Tagore. Copyright © 1961 by Sangent Natak Akadem First Edition.

From **Hoe Ana** transcribed by Kathy B. Sorenson. Copyright © 1991 by Kathy B. Sorenson.

From "Japanese Can't Count on Lifetime Jobs," from **The Labor Educator.** Copyright © 1999 by The Labor Educator. http://.www.laboreducator.org

Excerpt "Losing A Topknot" from **Karate-Do: My Way of Life** by Gichin Funakoshi. Copyright © 1975 by Gichin Funakoshi. Reprinted by permission of HarperCollins.

From **Lost City of the Incas** by Hiram Bingham and New World News. Copyright © 2001 by Labyrinthina. http://www.labyrinthina.com/bingham.htm

From **The Mind of Mahatma Gandhi** edited by R.K. Prabhu and U.R. Rao. Copyright © 1988 by R.K. Prabhu and U.R. Rao. Reprinted by permission of GreenLeaf Books, Baltimore, MD.

From **Mme. Sun Yat-sen** by Jung Chang with Jon Halliday. Copyright © 1986 by Jung Chang and Jon Halliday. Penguin Books.

From **The Monkey Kid: About Cultural Revolution.** Copyright © 1998 by the Beijing-San Francisco Film Group. http://www.bsffilmgroup.com/CulturalRevolution-link.html

From **A Personal Account of the Fall of the Berlin Wall: The 11th and 12th of November, 1989**, by Andreas Ramos. Copyright © 1995 by Andreas Ramos. http://www.andreas.com/berlin.html

From **Secrets of the Ice Man** by Dorothy Hinshaw Patent. Copyright © 1999 by Dorothy Hinshaw Patent. Reprinted by permission of Benchmark Books, Marshall Cavendish Corporation.

From **Sunjata** retold by Nick Bartel. Copyright © 2001 by Nick Bartel. http://nisus.sfusd.k12.ca.us/schwww/sch618/sundjata/sundjata.html

From **The Travels of Marco Polo**, a modern translation by Teresa Waugh from the Italian by Maria Bellonci. Translation copyright 1984 by Sadgwick and Jackson Limited. Facts on File Publications, N.Y.

Excerpt from **The World in 2002.** Copyright © 2001 by The Economists Newspaper Limited. http://www.theworldin.com/arts/sci/5.html